D0501985

THE BITTER TASTE
OF VICTORY

A Nosegay: A Literary Journey from the Fragrant to the Fetid (ed.)

Modernism on Sea: Art and Culture at the British Seaside (ed. with Alexandra Harris)

Literature, Cinema, Politics 1930–1945: Reading between the Frames

New Selected Journals of Stephen Spender (ed. with John Sutherland)

The Love-charm of Bombs: Restless Lives in the Second World War

THE BITTER TASTE OF VICTORY

Life, Love, and Art
in the Ruins of the Reich

Lara Feigel

BLOOMSBURY PRESS

NEW YORK · LONDON · OXFORD · NEW DELHI · SYDNEY

Bloomsbury Press
An imprint of Bloomsbury Publishing Plc

1385 Broadway
New York
NY 10018
USA

50 Bedford Square
London
WC1B 3DP
UK

www.bloomsbury.com

BLOOMSBURY and the Diana logo are trademarks of Bloomsbury Publishing Plc

First published in Great Britain 2016
First U.S. edition 2016

© Lara Feigel, 2016

ISBN: HB: 978-1-63286-551-9
ePub: 978-1-63286-553-3

Library of Congress Cataloging-in-Publication Data has been applied for.

2 4 6 8 10 9 7 5 3 1

Typeset by Newgen Knowledge Works (P) Ltd., Chennai, India
Printed and bound in the U.S.A. by Berryville Graphics Inc., Berryville, Virginia

To find out more about our authors and books visit www.bloomsbury.com.
Here you will find extracts, author interviews, details of forthcoming
events, and the option to sign up for our newsletters.

Bloomsbury books may be purchased for business or promotional use. For
information on bulk purchases please contact Macmillan Corporate and
Premium Sales Department at specialmarkets@macmillan.com.

For John

Contents

Preface   ix

Maps   xiii

Introduction   1

PART I: The Battle for Germany, 1944–45

1 'Setting out for a country that didn't really exist'   13
   Crossing the Siegfried line: November–December 1944
2 'Nazi Germany is doomed'   28
   Advance into Germany: January–April 1945
3 'We were blind and unbelieving and slow'   43
   Victory: April–May 1945

PART II: Ruin and Reconstruction, May–December 1945

4 'Complete Chaos Guaranteed'   71
   Occupation: May–August 1945
5 'Berlin is boiling in sweltering summer heat'   99
   Berlin: July–October 1945
6 'A pain that hurts too much'   120
   German Winter: September–December 1945

PART III: Judgement and Hunger, 1945–46

7 'You'll hang them anyhow'   143
   Nuremberg: November 1945–March 1946
8 'Let Germany Live!'   168
   Fighting the Peace: March–May 1946

9 'Let this trial never finish'   187
   Boredom: May–August 1946
10 'The law tries to keep up with life'   198
   Judgement: September–October 1946

PART IV: Tension and Revival, 1946–48

11 'Their suffering, and often their bravery,
   make one love them'   221
   Cold War: October 1946–October 1947
12 'I've been the Devil's General on earth too long'   251
   Artistic enlightenment: November 1947–January 1948
13 'In Hell too there are these luxuriant gardens'   275
   Germany in California: January–June 1948

PART V: Divided Germany, 1948–49

14 'If this is a war who is our enemy?'   305
   The Berlin Airlift: June 1948–May 1949
15 'Perhaps our deaths will shock you into attention'   335
   Division: May–October 1949

Coda: 'Closing time in the gardens of the West'   357

Notes   371
Bibliography   409
Acknowledgements   421
Index   425

Preface

When I tell people that I am writing a book about postwar Germany, they often ask if 'Feigel' is a German name. In fact as far as I know its origins are Polish; when my father's stepfather moved to Belgium in the 1920s he must have altered the spelling to fit in. Or perhaps it was just before the war that he changed his name from sounding Jewish to sounding German. At that stage he was married to my grandmother's sister, and I now realise that I don't know my actual grandfather's name. What I do know is that the Germans were not popular either with my father's Jewish family, who spent the war in concentration camps, or with my mother's Dutch family, who spent the war eating tulip bulbs in occupied Amsterdam. My Dutch grandmother still freezes every time she hears German spoken and is alarmed when I go to Germany.

And yet I have been drawn repeatedly to Berlin, a city I love, whose stacked up layers of history I find endlessly compelling. My German is better than either my (nonexistent) Dutch or Yiddish. Am I erasing family history as I cycle happily down Unter den Linden or past the Reichstag, carelessly oblivious of the buildings where Hitler plotted the events that destroyed the lives of my grandparents? Or am I confronting something that neither side of my family is able to confront, forcing us into the pan-European future that so many people (but not, I think, my grandparents) hoped to bring about in 1945? If I am then it took me some time to reach this point, and it now seems inevitable that I should have arrived in Germany in the safe company of 1940s British writers.

My interest in the Second World War began in London and not in Europe. This was a war where the tragedy played out on a manageable scale: a war where people had parties and love affairs amid the bombing and, most crucially, a war that could be talked about and written about. Often it is only in retrospect that we see why we write the books we do.

In India a year after it was published, I was asked by a journalist how I'd come to write *The Love-charm of Bombs*, my chronicle of the lives of five writers in wartime London. Had my own family been based in London? I answered that in fact I thought this exuberant celebration of Englishness (albeit in the company of one exiled Austrian writer, Hilde Spiel) was a retreat from my family, where the war was unmentionable, both for the Dutch and the Jews. You do not ask any of my grandparents casually what they were doing in the war, and as a result I know of their experiences only in pieced-together fragments, too shocking to be referred to again.

It is both strange and inevitable that this revelation should occur so far from home. Now it seems obvious that *The Love-charm of Bombs* came out of a lifelong desire to make myself as English as possible, chiefly through immersing myself in English literature past and present. For all those years of studying English literature, of reading delightedly about redoubtable English eccentrics from a lost age, I was creating an alternative ancestry for myself. And then in identifying myself with Elizabeth Bowen as she paced along the blacked-out streets, in imagining myself sheltering from the bombs with Graham Greene, I was claiming the war in London as my own heritage.

But it turned out to be more complicated. Not all British writers stayed put in London; some went to Germany and Austria. They visited the remains of the concentration camps where my father's family had been imprisoned; they saw Hitler's emaciated victims. While editing Stephen Spender's journals, I travelled to Germany with him in 1945, reading his astonishing account of the German ruins. While writing *The Love-charm of Bombs*, I followed Graham Greene and Elizabeth Bowen to Austria and Peter de Mendelssohn to Germany. It turned out that dozens of British and American literary and artistic figures had been sent to Germany in 1945 to witness the destruction, or begin to help reconstruct the country their governments had destroyed. Alongside Spender, there were other British figures I had written about previously: W. H. Auden, Humphrey Jennings, Rebecca West. Perhaps even more interesting were the Americans: Martha Gellhorn, Ernest Hemingway, Lee Miller. And then there were the Germans and

Austrians, sent to Germany in the uniform of the conquerors: Klaus and Erika Mann, Carl Zuckmayer, Billy Wilder.

Fascinated by these unexpected stories of Anglo-German collisions, I found that I could not stay away from the war in Europe forever. I found that the world of literary London and the world of my family were not as easily separable as I had made them. I had already come to love Berlin, where I had discovered a life of cycling, swimming and cafés that was conducive to writing. Now I became more concerned with peeling back its layers of history and seeing what remained of the Nazi era, curiously overlaid with the legacy of the Occupation that had ended up dividing the city in two.

I've now spent more time in Germany than anyone else on either side of my family. I also know more about the war in Europe than I initially wanted to know. Whether 1945 was a moment of hope or a moment of despair is explored in the pages that follow. What is certain is that it was a time that put any neat cataloguing of nationality in doubt. Indeed, for people like Stephen Spender this disruption of straightforward boundaries between nations was a positive effect of a war that had the potential to reconfigure Europe as a transnational entity united by its common culture. Perhaps one day another journalist will ask me if the book reflects my own wartime heritage and no doubt I will be surprised by my answer. Perhaps that will be the moment when I make sense of my English accent and preoccupations, my eastern European and Dutch ancestry and my German name.

Germany 1945: Zones of Occupation

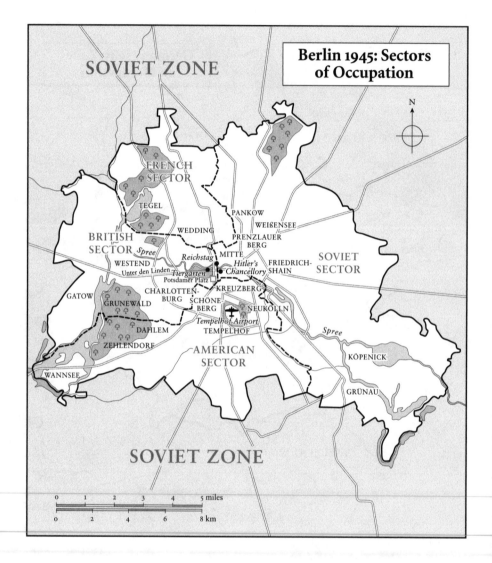

Berlin 1945: Sectors of Occupation

SOVIET ZONE

N

FRENCH SECTOR

TEGEL

PANKOW

WEDDING

WEIßENSEE

PRENZLAUER BERG

BRITISH SECTOR

Spree

MITTE

WESTEND

Reichstag

Hitler's Chancellory

FRIEDRICH-SHAIN

SOVIET SECTOR

Unter den Linden

Tiergarten

Potsdamer Platz

GATOW

CHARLOTTEN-BURG

KREUZBERG

GRUNEWALD

SCHÖNE-BERG

NEUKÖLLN

Spree

DAHLEM

Tempelhof Airport

TEMPELHOF

KÖPENICK

ZEHLENDORF

AMERICAN SECTOR

WANNSEE

GRÜNAU

SOVIET ZONE

0   1   2   3   4   5 miles

0   2   4   6   8 km

Introduction

To arrive in Germany in the final months of the Second World War was to confront an apocalypse. Berlin, Munich, Cologne, Frankfurt, Hamburg, Dresden – the old names had nothing to do with the rubble that now spread for mile after mile, scattered with corpses. In Berlin, the streets were not flattened altogether. Instead, only the façades remained; thin strips of mortar and plaster whose blown-out windows exposed emptiness where homes had crumbled behind them.

Almost all the cities in Germany had been badly bombed. By the end of the war a fifth of the country's buildings were in ruins.[1] Most of Germany had been plunged into darkness as one power station after another was bombed out of action; there was no city where gas, water and electricity were functioning at the same time. The streets in the city centres were eerily empty. Those people who remained had burrowed underground into cellars, basements or bomb craters, emerging to scavenge for food or water in the debris. The rows of flattened or hollowed houses were populated chiefly by *Trümmerfrauen* or 'rubble women', wiry figures employed by the Allies to clear away the mountains of pulverised buildings by hand.[2]

Between cities, the smashed Autobahnen were crowded with refugees. Much of the nation was on the move, with no particular destination. In September 1944 there had been 7.5 million foreigners in

Germany and they were all now attempting to return home or to reach one of the Allied DP (Displaced Persons) camps. In addition there were millions of Germans rendered homeless by the bombing and there would soon be nearly 13 million Germans expelled from Czechoslovakia, Poland, Yugoslavia, Hungary and Romania, once their borders were redrawn to include former parts of Germany.[3] The roads thronged with families, trailing handcarts with children or elderly relatives perched on top of furniture; with former Wehrmacht soldiers, recognisable, according to one observer, by their filthy grey uniforms hanging from gaunt limbs, their feet bound in bandages and their 'countenance of defeat'.[4]

These were the scenes that confronted Ernest Hemingway and his soon-to-be ex-wife Martha Gellhorn when they arrived in the spring of 1945, competing to be among the first to witness the effects of the bombing. Relatively well fed on army rations and well dressed in American army uniforms, they stood out among the tattered Germans who rushed towards them, audaciously claiming them as liberators. They found that maps made no sense. North and south, left and right lost all meaning when there were no crossroads or corners to differentiate one pile of debris from another. Entering Cologne in March 1945, Gellhorn wondered if what she saw was too nightmarish to be real. This seemed not so much a city as 'one of the great morgues of the world'. But she did not grieve for the devastation because she was too appalled by the spectacle of 'a whole nation passing the buck': no one was prepared to admit to being a Nazi. This was a view shared by the photographer Lee Miller, who found the inhabitants of Cologne 'repugnant in their servility, hypocrisy and amiability'.[5]

Other Allied reporters were able to be more sympathetic. The British writer George Orwell followed Gellhorn to Cologne later in March and was distressed that a whole city could be reduced to 'a chaos of jagged walls, overturned trams, shattered statues and enormous towers of rubble out of which iron girders thrust themselves like sticks of rhubarb'. But when the concentration camps were liberated in April 1945, and journalists confronted the piled up corpses and skeletal survivors, it became even harder to pity the defeated Germans. Now

Miller, Gellhorn and others asked themselves where this evil had come from and to what extent all Germans were responsible, or at least complicit in the horror.[6]

Hemingway, Gellhorn, Miller and Orwell were among the first British and American cultural figures to arrive in Germany. They were sponsored by governments who had made provision for journalists as part of the war effort, wanting them to report on the strength of their forces and the brutality of the enemy. The US government had also sent in actors and singers to entertain the troops, so Hemingway's old friend Marlene Dietrich arrived in Germany shortly after he did, as a USO (United Services Overseas) entertainer, proud to be serving her new government though shocked to see her homeland in tatters. She was too loyal to the US and too angry with her former compatriots to feel much sympathy. 'I guess Germany deserves everything that's coming to her,' she told a reporter.[7]

In May 1945, Germany surrendered and Britain, the US, the Soviet Union and France divided the defeated country into four zones, each sending in additional forces of occupation to administer their area. Berlin was also partitioned into four sectors, though it lay in the Soviet zone. At Potsdam in July, the occupiers took responsibility for reconstructing the country economically, politically and, more surprisingly, culturally. As a result, a new cohort of British and American writers and artists arrived in Germany to help rebuild the country their armed forces had just spent five years destroying.

German speakers were needed for this task. Several of the figures who might be termed 'cultural ambassadors' were writers who had spent time in Germany before the war. Among them were two British poets, W. H. Auden, sent by the American government to report on civilian responses to bomb damage, and his friend Stephen Spender, posted by the British government to assess the state of German universities. Auden and Spender had been drawn to Germany in the 1920s, attracted by its atmosphere of sexual promiscuity and its artistic avant-garde. Now looking expectantly for the seedy Berlin bars and snug Munich coffee houses where they had once watched cabaret and discussed philosophy, they encountered only wreckage; the playground of their youth had been razed to the ground. Wandering around the destroyed city of Darmstadt, Auden found himself constantly in tears, reporting that 'the people . . . are sad beyond belief'.[8]

The Allies also made use of the exiled Germans now living in Britain and the US. The Austrian film-maker Billy Wilder was sent by the American government to act as a film officer in their zone, returning to Berlin, where he had made his home until 1933 when Hitler had made it too dangerous for him as a Jew. Surrounded by former friends, he might have been expected to feel pity for the humiliated Germans, but he was spending his time watching hour after hour of concentration camp footage and he could not distinguish between the gaunt inhabitants of the bombed city and the perpetrators of the death camps. 'They burned most of my family in their damned ovens!' Wilder said. 'I hope they burn in hell!'[9]

Sent to be in charge of newspapers in the British zone of Berlin, the exiled German novelist Peter de Mendelssohn had come to see the Germans as a 'band of thieves and murderers and abject criminals', but was more troubled than Wilder by the sight of the ruined cities of his youth. He found that not only maps but language itself had become inadequate. 'We used to have a vocabulary with which to describe bombed cities,' he said, but now words like 'damaged, blasted, burnt-out, shattered, broken' and terms like 'debris, collapsed wall, bricks, masonry, bent girders, fallen beams' had become redundant. There was no 'damage' because the damaged thing itself had disappeared. Instead one needed 'new eyes to see, and totally new words to describe' what he could only evoke metaphorically as a 'white sea of rubble, faceless and featureless in the bright sunlight, acres and acres of white, bleached bones, the sprawling skeleton of a giant animal'.[10]

This book tells the story of Germany between 1944 and 1949 through the eyes of twenty writers, film-makers, painters, actors and musicians who arrived in Germany from Britain and the US and struggled to make sense of the postwar world. In addition to those already introduced, other important figures include Thomas Mann and his children Klaus and Erika Mann, all in Germany as Americans; the German-

American playwright Carl Zuckmayer; the British film-maker Humphrey Jennings; novelist Rebecca West; painter Laura Knight; and publisher Victor Gollancz. Jean-Paul Sartre and Simone de Beauvoir (visiting the French zone), Bertolt Brecht (visiting the Soviet zone), the German composer Paul Hindemith, the American novelist John Dos Passos and the British novelist Evelyn Waugh all make brief appearances as well. The focus is on the better-known figures to visit Germany for the obvious reason that their reports had more impact in the US and in Britain. All of them were influential, affecting public opinion about postwar Germany in their home countries, shaping Allied reconstruction policy in Germany or producing important works of art in response to their encounters with the defeated nation.

Individually, these figures often had diverse, personal reasons for volunteering to be in Germany, driven by curiosity or by a desire to help or punish, or by a more simple need to find former friends or family members. Collectively, they were dispatched by governments who placed journalism and, more controversially, the arts, at the centre of their plans for reconstructing Germany.

From 1942, when postwar planning for Germany became more a likelihood than an aspiration, diplomats and economists in Britain and the US had been asking themselves what kind of future there could be for this country once it had been defeated. How was the nation to be both punished and reconstructed and what constituted punishment and reconstruction? How would the Allies impose a settlement on Germany that would ensure the country could never again devastate Europe? How were the architects of the fighting, bombing, and genocide in the concentration camps to be held to account?

In 1945 official estimates for the expected duration of the Allied Occupation varied from ten to fifty years. The most urgent task for the Allies as they began to rule this divided country was to feed their new subjects and to attempt to restore electricity, gas, water and transport to their zones. But from the start, it was clear that this was not only to be a question of rebuilding the houses, streets, and in some cases whole towns that had been destroyed by the Allied bombing, nor of financial help. Postwar Germany had become Britain and America's dilemma. It was essential to create a peaceful and stable nation if future wars were to be avoided, and it was for this reason that culture came to play a crucial role in the reconstruction programme.

At Potsdam the Allies authored an agreement to prepare the Germans 'for the eventual reconstruction of their life on a democratic and peaceful basis'. This was to be achieved through denazification, disarmament, demilitarisation, democratisation and re-education. Denazification involved both the straightforward task of removing Nazis from positions of power and the more complex but also more fundamental task of reconfiguring German society to be less militaristic. The arts would be vital in introducing the Germans to alternative philosophies and modes of interaction. For the Americans, democracy was not just the American political system but the American way of life, and that included everything from behaviour on public transport to dance styles, and was demonstrable through art, music, books and especially films.[11]

Germany was to be reborn; its citizens as well as its cities were to be reconstructed. This was a campaign for the minds of the Germans – a 're-education' in the ideas of peace and civilisation.[12] So, suddenly, a generation of British and American writers, film-makers, artists, musicians and actors found themselves the vanguard of the campaign to remake a country. The immediate postwar period was a time when culture mattered, when writers and artists were seen as fundamental in securing a peaceful postwar settlement not just in Germany but in Europe as a whole. When UNESCO – the United Nations Educational, Cultural and Scientific Organisation – was founded in November 1945 to prevent war, it guided itself by the credo that 'since wars begin in the minds of men, it is in the minds of men that the defences of peace must be constructed'. This was accepted by politicians and sponsors in Britain, the US and other founding countries as a manifesto for cultural transformation. Often the cultural figures entering Germany in 1945 were hoping to forge not just a new denazified Germany but a new pacifist Europe. [13]

The story told here falls into two distinct periods. The first is the phase between 1944 and 1946, which was a period of urgent reconstruction and cultural idealism; a time when the Allies planned fundamentally to denazify Germany and tried to use culture as a means to do so. This period culminated in the trial of twenty-two Nazi leaders at Nuremberg between November 1945 and October 1946 – an epic court case that was observed by writers including Rebecca West, John Dos Passos and Erika Mann. After the trial ended in the autumn of 1946, the Germans were transformed from prisoners to subjects. At the same time, the differences between the Soviet and the western zones of Germany became more marked and the co-operation of the Allies in ruling Berlin broke down. The onset of the Cold War and the change in enemies it entailed left the British and the American authorities keen to co-operate with the Germans in the struggle against the Russians, leaving denazification anachronistic and unnecessary. This impacted directly on artists visiting Germany from Britain or the US because after 1947 they were part of the Allied armoury of the Cold War.

Ultimately this is a story of individuals whose aims did not always or indeed often coincide with those of their governments. Even in 1945, several of the visiting writers and artists found the Allied aims absurd. The British and Americans in Germany were all officially 'occupying forces', segregated from the Germans in cafés and shops and forbidden from socialising with them. The booklet British soldiers and civil servants were issued with before leaving for Germany informed them that there could be no good Germans: 'The Germans are not divided into good and bad Germans . . . There are only good and bad elements in the German character, the latter of which generally predominate.' But for writers such as Spender and Auden, who had admired Germany and many of its inhabitants before the war, this seemed ridiculous, as did the possibility of transforming the German nation through British and American culture. Had not the Germans had a far superior *Kultur* of their own, which had dominated the artistic landscape of Europe for several centuries? This led to a second question. If German literature, music and film had not prevented the German people from following Hitler (if indeed the concentration camp at Buchenwald had been within walking distance of Goethe's former house in Weimar, the symbolic capital of the *Kulturnation*), how was British and American culture going to do it?[14]

By 1947 the views of most of the protagonists had diverged from those of their governments and those, such as Klaus Mann, who still visited Germany became isolated individuals, bemoaning a moment when the opportunity to forge both a new Germany and a new Europe had been lost. In the end, most of the figures explored here had less effect on Germany than Germany had on them. As a result this is not so much a history of Germany in the years after the war as the story of a group of writers and artists who found that the encounter with ruined Germany necessitated a period of personal reconstruction. Broken by their own helplessness in the face of wreckage on a scale they had never believed possible in 1945, then disappointed by the failure of the Allies to use culture in winning the peace, they cast around hopelessly for possible modes of redemption.[15]

Some of them sought to counteract hatred and bitterness with love, defying the stench of death by committing themselves to living. But as the intense suspended present of war gave way to postwar, this became more difficult. A more durable promise for redemption was offered by art itself. In 1945, both Spender and Klaus Mann committed themselves to a vision of a new united Europe, underpinned by a shared artistic heritage that would allow nationalism to be replaced by a common consciousness of collective humanity. Most of the artists, however, sought a more personal form of reconstruction through artistic creation. They oscillated between seeing Germany as a real place, with bureaucratic, practical problems, and a dream setting, in which every object was symbolic. As they confronted the dilemma of German reconstruction, they created a genre of art that explored questions of guilt, atonement and redemption against a background of apocalyptic ruin.

This is a genre in which we could include works as diverse as Martha Gellhorn's novel *Point of No Return*, Stephen Spender's account of his time in Germany, *European Witness*, W. H. Auden's allegorical poem 'Memorial for the City', Billy Wilder's triumphantly comic film *A Foreign Affair*, Humphrey Jennings's documentary *A Defeated People*,

Laura Knight's paintings of the Nuremberg trial, Lee Miller's obliquely surrealist German photographs, Rebecca West's strangely personal account of her time in Nuremberg 'Greenhouse with Cyclamens' and Klaus Mann's unfinished novel *The Last Day*.[16] All of these works used the concrete landscape of the bombed cities, the concentration camps or the fallen pomp of the Third Reich to explore more metaphysical questions of guilt. Surveying Germany from the perspective of an outsider, these artists saw in Germany's tragedy the larger tragedy of the human condition.

In the late 1940s the artistic landscape of Germany was dominated by a genre that came to be known as *Trümmerliteratur* (rubble literature) or *Trümmerfilm* (rubble film): art set in the ruins of the bombed cities, imbuing the 'zero hour' after the war with physical form and exploring the relationship between architectural and psychological destruction.[17] Perhaps the genre of works set in Germany by British and American visitors could be called 'outsider rubble literature', or even *Fremdentrümmerliteratur*. This is a genre that asked, ultimately, what right the Allies had to judge Germany from outside when they were guilty too. Surely they shared the responsibility for Germany's crimes because they had allowed them to happen? The Allies had condoned Hitler's initial aggression and then, during the war, had fought to win rather than to prevent inhumanity, failing to free Jews in the territories they liberated or to exploit their knowledge of what was happening to the Jews to influence world opinion about the Nazis. 'The victors who seat us on the defendants' bench must sit next to us. There is room,' the German writer Erich Kästner observed in his diary on 8 May 1945.[18]

This genre of 'outsider rubble literature' includes Thomas Mann's great postwar novel *Doctor Faustus*, a book written by a man who had not seen the ruins he described, but who had heard about them from his friends and children who visited Germany and now imaginatively recreated them from his study in California in frightening detail. It is a novel that takes on new resonance and becomes more movingly confessional when read alongside *Point of No Return* or *A Foreign Affair* because Mann's troubled distance from the scenes he describes becomes the central emotion of his book.

All these works are acts of reckoning that at the same time enabled a kind of tolerance in the face of bitter disappointment. Collectively, they demonstrate the slow, ambivalent reconstruction of the human spirit; for their creators, they formed part of a process of attempting to learn to live again. For the participants of this book, the experience first of the bombed cities and the concentration camps, then of the cool Realpolitik of the Allies was too distressing to be forgotten. The Occupation and the *Wirtschaftswunder*, or economic miracle, of 1950s West Germany may have counted as a success story for the Allies but in the midst of the occupation forces' frantic efforts at reconstruction, a series of individual tragedies played out, set against a background of ruined buildings and scattered bones.

This book is in part an attempt to reconcile or at least to disentangle these two stories. The four years after the war are the bridge between two worlds we know well: the devastation and horror of the Second World War and the powerful and peaceful Western Europe of today, dominated by a prosperous, liberal Germany. In between these is another world that might have been; one that the cast of this book hoped to bring into being, but in the end were defeated from creating, first by German intransigence and then by the all-consuming pragmatism of Cold War politics. This is the story of a group of artists who fought to bring a new order into existence and then, when the fight became hopeless, mourned all that they had lost.

PART I

The Battle for Germany

1944-45

I

'Setting out for a country that didn't really exist'

Crossing the Siegfried line:
November–December 1944

During the autumn of 1944 Ernest Hemingway and Martha Gellhorn raced each other to the front line. For five years of war Gellhorn had taunted her husband for his apparent weakness; while she covered the conflict in Europe as a war correspondent, Hemingway preferred to remain safely in Cuba, attempting to sink German submarines from his fishing boat. As far as he was concerned, he had been heroic enough in the First World War and Spanish Civil War, when his relationship with Gellhorn had begun. At forty-four he wished to remain at home writing his novels with Gellhorn by his side. 'ARE YOU A WAR CORRE-SPONDENT OR WIFE IN MY BED?' he asked her in a cable. Gellhorn saw it differently. It was Hemingway who had made her a war correspondent; Hemingway who had taken a promising young novelist with honey blonde hair and improbably long legs and exposed her to the sight of civilian slaughter in the Spanish Civil War, browbeating her into writing about it. She had fallen in love with him as a comrade in reckless bravery and was frustrated to find herself married to a compla-cent coward who had lost interest in the fate of his world.[1]

When Gellhorn returned from Europe to see her husband in March 1944, Hemingway woke her in the night to 'bully, snarl, mock' her for seeking excitement and danger in Europe. 'My crime was to have been at war when he had not.' Eventually, Hemingway decided to take up Gellhorn's gauntlet. But, unlike in Spain, they were to be competitors rather than collaborators. Hemingway's previous two wives had accepted that there was only room for one great writer in the house. Gellhorn's attempts at independence seemed to demonstrate a waning love and he wanted to wound her in return. He therefore used his superior reputation to attach himself to *Collier's*, Gellhorn's own magazine. Each publication could only officially employ one war correspondent so this left Gellhorn unauthorised. What was more, Hemingway procured a seat on one of the few aeroplanes flying to London and pretended to his wife that women were barred from the aircraft. Gellhorn made the crossing on a vulnerable and rat-infested cargo ship and was furious when she discovered that she could have been on the plane after all.[2]

By the time the couple were reunited in London in May, Hemingway had found an alternative, more compliant lover, the journalist Mary Welsh, while Gellhorn was determined to have as little as possible to do with her dishonest, competitive and too frequently drunken husband. They made their separate ways to Europe, with Gellhorn getting far closer to the D-Day landings than Hemingway, despite the official order barring women from the battlefields. Hemingway beat Gellhorn to liberated Paris where he loitered with Mary Welsh at the end of August, departing briefly to Rambouillet where he contravened the regulations for war correspondents by stacking his room with hand grenades, Sten guns, carbines and revolvers and unofficially directing intelligence operations.[3]

The focus of the European war effort had turned to Germany. Now that Paris and Rome had been liberated, the world was waiting for the conquest of Berlin. The end of the war in Europe had become contingent on Germany's surrender and this was to be brought about by destroying the country by air and leaving helpless the army on the ground. In the East, the Russians began an enormous offensive called Operation Bagration on 22 June, co-ordinating air, artillery, tanks and infantry in an effort to recapture Belorussia and push west into Poland and Germany. Within five weeks, the Red Army had broken through the German line, expelling Germans from Belorussia; simultaneously they launched an attack on Poland that brought them within sight of Warsaw by the end of July. On the western front, the war effort was focused on penetrating the German defensive Siegfried Line and crossing the Rhine. For the British at least this was partly an attempt to beat the Russian advance into Germany and stop them setting up a communist regime.[4]

As Allied generals such as Bernard Montgomery, Dwight Eisenhower, George Patton and Omar Bradley debated how best to manoeuvre their troops into Germany, war correspondents such as Hemingway and Gellhorn tried to attach themselves to army units likely to be sent towards the Rhine. For five years, Germany had seemed unreal and distant; the word 'Germany' conjured a place of mythical evil. Now it was about to become real again and everyone involved in the war wanted to be the first to see it. The New York-based Anglo-Irish writer James Stern, describing his motives for visiting Germany, wrote that he 'thought of the prospect of returning with a mixture of horror and fascination. I felt that it would be like setting out for a country that didn't really exist.'[5]

Throughout the autumn of 1944, war correspondents and entertainers convened in Paris between trips to the front and contrived to join the troops entering the growing sliver of Germany occupied by the Allies. Hemingway, Gellhorn, the American photographer and war correspondent Lee Miller and the German-born movie star Marlene Dietrich were among the British and American literati to wander restlessly through Parisian boulevards, drink in the cafés of the Left Bank and visit the liberated French intelligentsia, in a bizarre, shabby imitation of life in 1920s Paris.

The city had gone mad, Lee Miller announced in an article for *Vogue* describing the early weeks after the liberation. Pretty girls lined the streets, screaming and cheering; the air was filled with perfume that the French had been saving for this moment. For Miller, as for Hemingway and Gellhorn, this was a return home. The former lover and collaborator of Man Ray and the muse of the surrealists (she was currently engaged in an affair with the British surrealist painter Roland Penrose), Miller had lived in Montparnasse in the 1930s and she was now revisiting former haunts. All of these visitors tried to find the city they had once loved beneath the wounds of Nazism while they celebrated this small victory in the midst of an apparently endless war.[6]

By September 1944, the Western Allies were racing ahead of the Russians in the competition to enter German territory and Hemingway triumphed in his contest with Gellhorn. On 1 September he received a telegram from his current hero, Buck Lanham, commander of the Fourth Infantry Division's 22nd Regiment. 'Go hang yourself, brave Hemingstein,' Lanham jeered, 'we have fought at Landrecies and you were not there.' The next morning Hemingway began making his way to Landrecies, on the Franco-Belgian border; he was with Lanham when the 22nd Regiment began its assault on the Siegfried Line on 7 September. Two days later Hemingway was camping with the regiment in the forest on the Belgian-German border near Hemmeres, sleeping on a pine-needle floor. It was freezing and wet and he came down with a cold, but he wrote contented, loving letters to Mary Welsh declaring that he was now 'committed as an armored column in a narrow defile'.[7]

This was a happiness occasioned both by the reciprocity of his love for Mary Welsh and by the war. Though in Cuba Hemingway had resisted Gellhorn's call to arms, he was as temperamentally restless as she was. He too was calmed by the intense immediacy of battle and now told his son Patrick that he had never been more satisfied nor more useful. While in the forest he met Bill Walton, a suave *Time* reporter colleague of Welsh's whom Hemingway had befriended that summer in London and Paris. Like Hemingway, Walton was a journalist determined to prove his own heroism; he had parachuted with the US troops into Normandy on D-Day. Now Hemingway had the satisfaction of saving his friend's life. Recognising the sound of an incoming German plane, he ordered Walton to jump out of a jeep moments before it was strafed.

Hemingway entered Germany with the first American tanks on 12 September and moved into a farmhouse near Bleialf which he and his army companions nicknamed 'Schloss Hemingstein'. Here he shared a double bed with Walton and was glad to reprise the heroic role he had already played in two wars. When a shell landed outside the house, breaking windows and eradicating lights, Hemingway calmly continued eating in the darkness while the officers around him hid under the table.

Two months later Hemingway's triumphant report of the battle would appear in *Collier's*. 'A lot of people will tell you how it was to be first into Germany and how it was to break the Siegfried Line and a lot of people will be wrong.' It was the infantry who had cracked the line, not the air force; the infantry who had made their way through grim, forested country until they reached a hill and 'all the rolling hills and forests that you saw ahead of you were Germany'. They had passed the pillboxes that some 'unfortunate' people believed constituted the Siegfried Line, made it past the concrete fortified strong-points and then, in a freezing gale, penetrated the West Wall that many Germans considered impenetrable. Even at the time, Hemingway wrote, it was a battle that felt more cinematic than real; it would be easy to turn it into a movie: 'The only thing that will probably be hard to get properly in the picture is the German SS troops, their faces black from the concussion, bleeding from the nose and mouth, kneeling in the road, grabbing their stomachs, hardly able to get out of the way of the tanks.' Patriotically, he concluded that these scenes made him feel that 'it really would have been better for Germany not to have started this war in the first place'.[8]

The Allies' incursion into Germany continued with a three-week battle for Aachen, which was the first German city to surrender on 21 October. Immediately, Allied war correspondents arrived to witness the destruction wrought by their armies and airforces and to interview the defeated Germans. As participants in the Allied war effort, they were intended to produce reports indicting German brutality but instead they often ended up describing the astonishing devastation of the city. Aachen had been heavily bombed in 1943 and shelled throughout the three weeks of battle. Now 85 per cent of the town was in ruins and only 14,000 of the prewar population of 160,000 remained.[9] In parts of the city there was row after row of plaster-decorated façades still presenting a semblance of ordinary architecture while in fact there were no houses behind them; elsewhere there was mile after mile of rubble. Only the cathedral stood tall, towering eerily over a sea of ruins. When the inhabitants remained they were living in basements, frightened both of the Americans and of their German rulers, who hurled abuse at them on the radio, accusing them of cowardice for surrendering. The streets were lined with the skeletal remains of their bombed inhabitants and the whole city seemed to exude the smell of rotting flesh.[10]

Among the first Allied visitors to Aachen was Erika Mann. Once a bohemian German actor, car racer and cabaret writer, Mann was now an American war correspondent, defiantly proud of her army uniform and Anglo-American accent. She was also the daughter of the German writer Thomas Mann, a US citizen and the most prestigious spokesman for German literature in exile. For several months she had been driving around Europe in a battered Citroën bestowed on her by a friend in the French resistance shortly before he died.

Mann had spent the early years of the war broadcasting for the BBC in London and had seen the destruction created by the London Blitz. As an American war correspondent, she had then come close to the battlefields of France, Belgium and Holland. However, nothing had prepared her for the flattened German cities. Like many returning Germans, Mann found it hard to take in the transformation of her former homeland or to believe that this 'phantastically ruined' waste-land had really been a city.[11] But she had little sympathy either for the vanished buildings or for their demoralised inhabitants. She was determined not to reveal her own German identity and kept up an American persona to stop herself striking out and hitting the unrepentant Germans she now encountered. Meeting a group of German police-men currently being 're-educated' by the Americans, Mann was shocked by the 'complete lack of feeling of their collective guilt' displayed by the men, who asked her naively what plans were being laid in Washington for German reconstruction. How did the Americans intend to strengthen the German economy? As a war correspondent had Mann come across any interesting stamps? Perhaps she could help fill the gaps in their collections?[12]

Staggered that the Germans could be so oblivious to her own outrage, Mann asked them questions in return. As Military Government policemen, did they expect to run into trouble among Germans still wanting to display the Nazi flag? Immediately, three or four policemen assured her that the Germans were ready to abandon Nazism. Their failure to do so was explained by a familiar mantra: 'Terror!' 'Dictatorship!' 'The Gestapo!' It seemed to Mann that this was becoming a childish song, intoned everywhere. 'In one breath as it were, these Germans would tell you that a) Nazism was kept alive in Germany by a mere handful of hated fanatics, while b) every German was watched over by two Nazis.' She believed that Nazism had finally become objectionable but thought that it had lost popularity not because of its moral depravity but because of its military weakness. 'Germany's leading criminals stand accused today not of being criminals but of being failures.'[13]

Writing to her brother Klaus in the English language she had determinedly made her own, Erika said that it was 'phantastic' to be back in the 'Hunland' and that she was convinced more than ever of the hopelessness of the Germans. 'In their hearts, self-deception and dishonesty, arrogance and docility, shrewdness and stupidity are repulsively mingled and combined.' She was now certain that neither she nor her brother would be able to live again anywhere in Europe, which was in as bad a state morally as it was physically. This was a 'bitter pill' to swallow, even though she had already been loyally committed to Uncle Sam.[14]

Erika Mann had very little patience with anyone who claimed to have been duped by the Nazis. She herself had openly mocked and resisted them even before they came to power, though in the very early days it was Klaus who was the politically orientated Mann sibling, warning the world about the dangers of fascism in 1927. Erika's own political stance began spontaneously and passionately five years later when she recited a pacifist poem by Victor Hugo at an anti-war meeting. A group of Brownshirts broke up the gathering and threw chairs at her, denouncing her as a 'Jewish traitress' and 'international agitator'. Fired from her acting role after the Nazis threatened to boycott the theatre unless she was dismissed, she felt called upon to make a stand. She was successful in suing both the theatre and a Nazi newspaper who had described her as a 'flatfooted peace hyena' with 'no human physiognomy'. After examining several photographs of Erika, the judge declared that her face was in fact legally human. Galvanised into politicial activism, Erika opened the Pepper Mill revue in Munich on 1 January 1933, collaborating with her lover the actor Therese Giehse and a troupe of players to perform anti-Nazi satirical cabaret until the Nazis drove them out of Germany two months later.[15]

Having retained her uncompromising stance throughout twelve years of exile, Erika was certainly not prepared to mellow now. She was exhausted by her year of press camp cots and army rations; aware that her thirty-eight-year-old body was taking the same battering as the car given to her by her dead friend. She missed her parents (at home in the plush comfort of Los Angeles) and her brother Klaus (stationed in Italy reporting for the US army). But she was propelled by hatred of the Germans who had driven her family from their homes and killed many of her friends. The people who confronted her daily exhorting sympathy for the destruction of their cities or demanding additions to their stamp collections were the same Germans who had thrown chairs at her in Munich and burned thousands of the books she loved. She was determined to play whatever part she could in witnessing their humiliation and convincing them of their guilt.

———

In early October, Ernest Hemingway was forced abruptly to return from Germany to France because he had been court-martialled for joining in the combat at Rambouillet. If he wished to free himself, he now had to forsake his own heroism and pretend that he had not borne arms. His anger was compounded by an encounter in Paris with Martha Gellhorn, who suggested dinner only to spend the evening demanding a divorce. Hemingway was reluctant; he preferred leaving to being left and had not quite lined up his next wife. None the less, he found solace in the arms of Mary Welsh, and the company of his old friend Marlene Dietrich who took to sitting on Hemingway's bathtub at the Ritz and singing to him while he shaved. This was the first time Hemingway and Dietrich had met in a war zone and it suited them well. Both were in love with courage and were foolhardily determined to emerge as heroes.

Dietrich had come to Europe from America in April as a USO entertainer. She would later look back on her time with the army as one of the happiest periods in her life. Night after night she shivered stoically in sequined dresses as she sung to US troops of love and home and reminded them of the softer and more romantic world they were fighting to regain. She was in her forties with a grown-up daughter but here once again she could be a youthful sweetheart. According to one colonel, Dietrich seemed to look each soldier straight in the eye and say: 'You mean something to me. I hope somehow I get through to you that I want to be here with you.' These were her boys; she was beloved by all and especially by the generals, whom she flattered and adored. She had spent September in the protection of the swashbuckling General 'Old Blood and Guts' Patton, enjoying taking on the role of First Lady to a war hero. Early on Patton asked her if she was afraid of performing so close to the fighting. She assured him that she was brave; she had no fear of dying. But as a German by birth who was reviled by the Nazis for taking US citizenship, she was aware that she would have enormous propaganda value as a prisoner of war: 'They'll shave off my hair, stone me, and have horses drag me through the streets. If they force me to talk on the radio, General, under no circumstances believe anything I say.' Patton handed her a revolver and instructed her to use it swiftly if captured.[16]

While Hemingway and his 'Kraut' were swapping war stories, Gellhorn returned to London, 'to eat and sleep'. She was feeling frighteningly lonely as she took stock of the end of her marriage. The relationship with Hemingway had lasted seven years and Gellhorn had admired him for some time before that. In 1931 she had told a childhood sweetheart that she took her code from Hemingway's *A Farewell to Arms*, where the hero tells his lover 'You're brave. Nothing ever happens to the brave.' This was enough for her: 'A whole philosophy – a banner – a song – and a love.' Meeting Hemingway in 1936 and accompanying him to Spain the following year brought just the shared bravery, the love and the song that she had longed for. But their hopes in Spain for a better world had been shattered and their years in Cuba had blunted the passion. Hemingway's competitive anger and jealousy had exhausted her; marriage itself seemed fundamentally incompatible with spontaneous happiness.[17]

'I can resign myself to anything on earth except dullness, and I do not want to be good,' Gellhorn had told her friend Hortense Flexner in 1941; 'Good is my idea of what very measly people are, since they cannot be anything better. I wish to be hell on wheels, or dead. And the only serious complaint I have about matrimony is that it brings out the faint goodness in me, and has a tendency to soften and quiet the hell on wheels aspect, and finally I become bored with myself. Only a fool would prefer to be actively achingly dangerously unhappy, rather than bored: and I am that class of fool.'

Gellhorn had always felt compelled to run away from the people she loved, restlessly seeking out new people and places or disappearing alone to write. In the same letter she told Flexner that she wanted 'a life with people that is almost explosive in its excitement, fierce and hard and laughing and loud and gay as all hell let loose' and the rest of the time she wanted to be alone to work and think 'and let them kindly not come to call'. Marriage was not conducive to this kind of balance; she was now on her way to freeing herself from its snare.[18]

But if she was pleased to escape marriage, Gellhorn could still mourn those early, heady days of love, which she had looked back on nostalgically in a letter to Hemingway the previous June. Longing to be young and irresponsible together again, she begged her husband to give up the prestige and the possessions and return to Milan, with Hemingway brash in his motorcycle sidecar and Gellhorn 'badly dressed, fierce, loving'. This was when they were intense, reckless and noisy, before marriage had polished off the edges and left their voices low and quiet. It was too late to return to Milan; both their love and the city itself had been smashed up by war. All that remained was for Gellhorn to regain her freedom and to seek out reckless intensity alone. And there was a danger that too much freedom would lead to a desolate rootlessness.

'I am so free that the atom cannot be freer,' she wrote to her friend Allen Grover; 'I am free like nothing quite bearable, like sound waves and light.'[19]

In London, Gellhorn wrote a report of the battles she had witnessed in Italy. Published in *Collier's* in October, it undermined the heroic accounts in Hemingway's articles, suggesting that war, even when victorious, was too chaotic to be strategic and too costly to be triumphant: 'A battle is a jigsaw puzzle of fighting men, bewildered, terrified civilians, noise, smells, jokes, pain, fear, unfinished conversations and high explosive.' Gellhorn mocked later historians who would neatly catalogue the campaign, noting that in 365 days of fighting the Allied armies advanced 315 miles. They would be able to explain without sadness what it meant to break through three fortified lines, they would describe impassively how Italy had become a giant mine, but they would fail to capture the essence of the battle. She ended the piece on a caustic note. 'The weather is lovely and no one wants to think of what men must still die and what men must still be wounded in the fighting before peace comes.'[20]

London had provided Gellhorn with the food and rest she sought but she was soon anxious to return to the jigsaw of fighting men and to follow Hemingway into Germany. The relative ordinariness of London life made her aware of her own homelessness. She told her mother that she wanted to return home but aged thirty-six she still had no home to go to. 'Home is something you make yourself and I have not made one.' Still lonely, Gellhorn made her way back to France where she informed readers of *Collier's* that the wounds of Paris (prisons, torture chambers, unmarked graves) would never heal. Published in the same issue as an article by Hemingway extolling the friendliness of the American GIs, Gellhorn's piece describes the red-hot hooks in the prison at Romainville and the cemetery where Germans brought in the bodies of dead prisoners in trucks. 'It is impossible to write properly of such monstrous and incredible and bestial cruelty: you will find it impossible to believe such things exist.' Before the war started Gellhorn had told a friend that she felt her role in life was to 'make an angry sound against injustice', paying back for her own good luck by defending the unlucky. The unlucky were now proliferating and Gellhorn's anger was becoming uncontainable.[21]

She left Paris and wandered to the Ardennes, installing herself in a farmhouse in Sissonne where part of the US army was based, training and regrouping between attacks. One day a group of soldiers came across her and demanded to see her papers. Finding that she was not officially accredited to be in a war zone, they led her to the tent of General James M. Gavin, who was the leader of the elite 82nd Airborne Division.

At thirty-seven, Gavin was the youngest divisional commander in the US army. He was tall, boyish and charming, with the looks of a Hollywood hero. He carried a rifle instead of a pistol, wanting to shoot accurately and far, and was renowned for always fighting on the front line beside his men. He also exuded the confidence of swift youthful success. At the start of the war the 82nd had been under Bradley's command and Gavin (then a colonel) was assigned as the commanding officer of its new Parachute Infantry Regiment, as part of a general move towards airborne warfare. He was so successful in aiding the Allied encroachment into Sicily that he was entrusted with three airborne regiments for the Normandy landings. In August, Gavin had been promoted to general and put in charge of the entire 82nd Airborne Division, who were chosen to capture two bridges in Holland in September to enable Allied troops to cross the Lower Rhine and encircle German forces defending the frontier.

Now, Gavin and his division were waiting for their next instructions in the relative safety of Sissonne. He was inclined to behave leniently toward this beautiful intruder. He told Gellhorn that he would let her go unnoticed and asked her for the name of her hotel in Paris, planning to look her up when next on leave. Shortly afterwards, he tracked her down at the Hôtel Lincoln. More used to commanding troops than seducing women, Gavin was peremptory. Gellhorn disliked being summoned 'like a package and pushed into bed', but she succumbed none the less and the results were electrifying. Afterwards she wrote that he had taught her 'what I had guessed, read about, been told about; but did not believe; that bodies are something terrific'.

This was the first sexually satisfying relationship of her life. She later described sex with Hemingway as 'wham bam thank you maam' without the 'thank you'.[22]

Gavin, like Gellhorn, was married, with a wife and child waiting for him in America, but he too was determined to live riskily and intensely in the continuous present of war. Later in November he was posted to the liberated area of Holland, instructed to retain order in the towns he had helped to destroy, and he invited Gellhorn to accompany him. The consequence was a triumphant paean to the 82nd Airborne Division, published in *Collier's* in December. Regular readers may have wondered what had changed since Gellhorn's report on the Italian front a month earlier; war was no longer quite as miserable as it had looked then. The article begins with Gellhorn informing her readers that the troops of the 82nd 'look like tough boys and they are'. They are good at their trade and they walk as if they know it and it is a pleasure to watch them: 'You are always happy with fine combat troops because in a way no people are as intensely alive as they are . . . You do not think much about what war costs because you are too busy being alive for the day, too busy laughing and listening and looking.'[23]

Gellhorn and Gavin quickly began to fight about the methods of war. She could not forget the costs of conflict for long and she complained in *Collier's* later in December about the death of the Dutch town of Nijmegen, ravaged in part by Gavin's division. Although she announced dutifully at the start of the article that the moral of the story was that 'it would be a fine thing if the Germans did not make war', she described the destruction in too much detail for the reader to remain oblivious of the perpetrators of this particular carnage. The piece ends with a portrait of a little girl of four, her arms both broken by shell fragments and her head gashed: 'All you could see was a tiny soft face, with enormous dark eyes, utterly silent eyes looking at you.'[24]

By December 1944 Gellhorn was back in Paris, where she once again crossed paths with Hemingway, who returned from his second sojourn in Germany on 5 December. For three weeks he had been reporting on the experiences of Lanham's division in the savage battle of Hürtgen Forest. This campaign in the dense conifer woodland between Bonn and Aachen had begun in mid-September and was initially expected to last a few weeks. The Allies intended to clear a wide pathway through fifty square miles of forest to provide entry into Germany. However, the terrain was ferociously inhospitable; the Germans had prepared the forest with mines and barbed wire which were now hidden by the mud and snow. The battle was already two months in by the time Hemingway arrived on 15 November and showed no sign of coming to a close. In three days in mid-November, Lanham's 22nd Infantry Regiment incurred more than 300 casualties, including all three battalion commanders and about half the company commanders. By the time that this stage of the battle ended in mid-December, 24,000 Americans had been killed, wounded, captured or were missing.

This was a much bleaker experience than Hemingway's summer campaigns. He was in Germany once again but without the excitement of being the first to break through the Siegfried Line. His overwhelming experience was of mud, rain and shells. The consolations were the camaraderie of army life – Hemingway entertained Lanham in the evenings with impressions of the mating antics of African lions – and the possibilities for hunting. He might now be forbidden to bear arms against the Germans but it did not stop him shooting deer and cows.

Hemingway returned to Paris with pneumonia, but after a couple of weeks in bed he followed Lanham's division to Rodenbourg (ten miles north-east of Luxembourg City) where they invited Gellhorn to spend Christmas with them. Her visit was a disaster. Lanham instantly disliked Hemingway's wife, finding her distant and ungrateful. Gellhorn felt embarrassed and powerless surrounded by her husband's war cronies, though she fared better at dinner with General Bradley, who was 'much smitten' with this enticing war correspondent whom his aide described in his diary that night as 'a reddish blonde woman with a cover girl figure, a bouncing manner and a brilliant studied wit where each comment seems to come out perfectly tailored and smartly cut to fit the occasion, yet losing none of the spontaneity that makes it good'.

Meeting Gellhorn for the first time at a party on New Year's Eve, Hemingway's friend Bill Walton was impressed by 'her elegant hair, the tawny-gold colour' and by her bearing – 'like that of a fine race horse' – and was horrified by Hemingway's rudeness to her. Chided by his friend for his boorish behaviour, Hemingway retorted that 'you can't hunt an elephant with a bow and arrow'.[25]

For both Gellhorn and Hemingway, this trip signified the end of the marriage. 'I wasn't meant for every day consumption,' Gellhorn had told a lover twelve years earlier, 'you'll have to think of me as oysters – you wouldn't want oysters everyday for breakfast?' Hemingway was not meant for daily consumption either; shared everyday life had become impossible for them. Afterwards he told his son that they were going to divorce and he was planning to take Mary Welsh home to Cuba: 'We want some straight work, not be alone and not have to go to war to see one's wife . . . Going to get me somebody who wants to stick around with me and let me be the writer of the family.' Ernest Hemingway wanted no more part in the war and had lost interest in following the army into Germany; he would leave Martha Gellhorn to see the ruined cities without him.[26]

2

'Nazi Germany is doomed'

Advance into Germany: January–April 1945

Nineteen forty-five began depressingly for the Allies. The European war, which had looked as if it might be coming to an end the previous summer, threatened to drag on for several months. On 16 December 1944 the Germans had launched a counterattack in the Ardennes that was initially surprisingly successful. Two days into the battle General James Gavin's 82nd Airborne Division was summoned to help stop the German advance to the River Meuse. By Christmas the 82nd was on the attack, but many of the surrounding troops were still fighting defensively and it took until 25 January to force the Germans back to their starting point.

Throughout Europe, German casualties were multiplying staggeringly. In the East, the Soviet army had launched the greatest offensive of the war in Poland, gaining the ground from the Vistula to the Oder in only a couple of weeks. By the end of the month they were forty miles from Berlin. During the course of January, 450,000 German soldiers were killed; this was more than the total number of British or American soldiers killed in all theatres during the entire war. At this stage, about 250,000 Germans from East Prussia fled the advancing Red Army, beginning to trek toward the Oder and into central Germany. But none of this deterred Hitler, who insisted that the country continue to commit itself to the fight, sending in seventeen-year-old recruits with barely any training.[1]

General Omar Bradley now prepared to continue the American counter-offensive launched in January by forcing an entry into the Eifel across the German border and summoned Marlene Dietrich (currently stationed with his troops) to his trailer in the Belgian part of the forest. He told her that his army group would enter Germany the next day and that the unit she was travelling with would be one of the first in. He thought that she would be in danger of capture and wanted her to stay behind. However, Dietrich was determined to accompany him. 'He seemed distant, thoroughly uninterested in how much I cared to go in with the first troops,' she reported to her ex-husband Rudi Sieber, with whom she retained a loyal though occasionally exploitative friendship. She decided optimistically that it was because Bradley was unbearably lonely and that all generals must be as lonely as he was. 'GIs go into the bushes with the local girls, but Generals can't do such things.' They were guarded too stringently to 'kiss and tumble' in the hay and were desperately in need of female company.[2]

Bradley was certainly not the most licentious of generals but he seems to have been grateful for Dietrich's concern. One way or another, she convinced him to take her with him. She was assigned two bodyguards who accompanied her to Stolberg and then to Aachen. This was her first sight of the ruins of her former homeland and she was as shocked as Erika Mann had been four months earlier. The streets were still lined with corpses and hardly any rubble had been cleared.

Billeted in a house where the bombing of the front wall had left a bathtub suspended in mid-air, Dietrich's troupe took over the local cinema where they performed in freezing conditions with no fuel. At one stage the German caretaker produced a thermos and poured Dietrich a cup of coffee. Other members of her troupe were worried that it might be poisoned. She insisted that it was safe and asked the caretaker why he was wasting his precious coffee on an American citizen. 'Yes, yes, but The Blue Angel,' he said, wistfully recalling her most famous German film (*Der blaue Engel*). 'Ah! I can forget what you are, but The Blue Angel? Never!' Aside from her duties entertaining the troops, Dietrich was often instructed to shout in German into the loudspeaker in the main square, telling people to go home and close their shutters instead of congregating in the street where they obstructed the tanks. She was infested with lice, she had to sleep with a wet towel on her face to deter the rats, but she was enjoying playing the part of soldier and had no sympathy for the inhabitants of the ruins, though elsewhere in Germany her mother and elder sister Liesel were among them.[3]

By February 1945, the Allies were hopeful that no further German counterattacks would be attempted and that a German defeat was imminent. They now had to decide how best to govern Germany when it fell into their hands. On 4 February the US, British and Russian leaders Franklin D. Roosevelt, Winston Churchill and Joseph Stalin met for a week's conference in Yalta, partly to plan the defeat and reconstruction of Germany.

The conference was dominated by internal tensions. Churchill was distrustful of Stalin and concerned about the Soviet takeover of Poland; Roosevelt was more trusting of Stalin but was interested primarily in the formation of the United Nations Organisation, which was to be his legacy; Stalin was determined to increase the Soviet power base in Eastern Europe. Since the leaders had met at Teheran a year earlier, the Soviet military position had improved enormously. Now that the Red Army was a mere forty miles from Berlin, Stalin felt able to dictate terms. However, there was broad concurrence when it came to the question of Germany. The three men agreed that Germany and Berlin would be split into four occupation zones (with France to be given a share of the British and US portions of the country) and that Germany would pay reparations and would undergo a process of demilitarisation and denazification.[4] The Allies were explicit that it was not their purpose to destroy the people of Germany, but that 'only when Nazism and militarism have been extirpated, will there be hope for decent life for Germans, and a place for them in the comity of nations'.[5]

This was an odd conversation to have in the context of a continued war. But then the situation itself was odd; the Allies were continuing to destroy a country they already partially ruled. 'I dislike making detailed plans for a country which we do not yet occupy,' Roosevelt had complained in October 1944, but this was just what he was doing. The future peace and prosperity of the US as well as Britain, France and the Soviet Union seemed to depend on creating a peace-loving and obliging Germany and on forging a world in which co-operation was more enticing than war. On the ground in Germany, Hemingway, Gellhorn and Dietrich certainly did not concern themselves with the fate of the Germans; Erika Mann asked only that they should all publicly repent and declare their collective guilt. But at home in Britain and the US, politicians, civil servants and academics were engaging in more specific conversations about the future of Germany and Europe and the more moderate among them saw culture and cultural figures as potentially crucial to denazification.[6]

Despite the conciliatory tone of the report from the Yalta Conference, there were influential voices in both countries calling for the harshest treatment of Germany possible. In 1941 the chief diplomatic adviser to the British government, Robert Vansittart, had published a small book stating that there was no such thing as a 'good German': 'the better a German is the *more* likely he is to join in war'. For Vansittart, the Second World War had been largely perpetrated by the Prussians who had also brought about the First World War; the Germans were a 'race of hooligans' and 'a breed which from the dawn of history has been predatory and bellicose'. Vansittart's was not a lone voice. In September 1943 Churchill informed the House of Commons that the Germans combined 'in the most deadly manner' the qualities of the warrior and the slave. They hated the spectacle of freedom in others and their militarism had to be 'absolutely rooted out' if Europe was to be spared a third 'more frightful conflict'.[7]

By September 1944 the US treasury secretary Henry Morgenthau had gained wide support in the British Cabinet for his 'Program to Prevent Germany from Starting a World War III', asking for a decentralised, demilitarised and deindustrialised Germany. Essentially this plan, if implemented, would turn Germany into a giant farm. Roosevelt echoed Morgenthau's views in a memorandum complaining that too many Anglo-Americans believed the German populace was not responsible for events in Germany: 'That unfortunately is not based on fact.

The German people as a whole must have it driven home to them that the whole nation has been engaged in a lawless conspiracy against the decencies of modern civilisation.'[8]

These hard-line views were contested at every stage by more moderate figures. In 1942 the campaigning writer and publisher Victor Gollancz challenged Vansittart for his blinkeredness. As far as Gollancz was concerned, the war was caused more by monopoly capitalism than by German militarism. 'If we concentrate our minds on the special German responsibilities and the special German problem, we are failing to see the wood for the trees.' Given that numerous British politicans and journalists had supported Hitler in the 1930s, they shared some responsibility for the war: 'I confess that self-righteous indignation about the cowardice of the German people, in the situation in which they find themselves, makes me feel a little sick. It comes particularly ill from those who hobnobbed with Hitler while in the next street Germans were being tortured for their bravery and independence by Hitler's Gestapo.'[9]

Many of the actual government policy papers produced in both Britain and the US fell between the views of Morgenthau and Gollancz. It was generally agreed that the Germans would need to undergo a thorough process of 'denazification' and that this would entail a fundamental shift in the German attitude. In January 1944 a joint paper on 'German Re-Occupation' produced by the British Political Warfare Executive and the BBC suggested that the central aim of the media in Germany after the war would be the 'control and remoulding of the German mind', arresting the 'development of a purely decadent trend as followed the last war and led to the rise of the Nazi type'. Although this paper echoed Vansittart in seeing the German people as universally flawed, it also offered more chance for change or 'remoulding' than he generally allowed, and offered the Germans the possibility of eventually living in a civilised denazified society rather than in the kind of giant farm proposed by Morgenthau.[10]

Both the British and the US government actively sought views about the future of Germany from independent intellectuals. In April 1944 a conference investigating 'Germany after the war' was organised at the College of Physicians and Surgeons at Columbia University by the Joint Committee on Post-war Planning. It was attended by a range of academics, psychiatrists and psychologists hoping to understand the effects of German culture on German character and to explore possibilities for modifying the national psychological make-up. A resumé of the conference was provided in Britain by Henry Dicks, a psychiatrist who was advising British military intelligence on German morale. According to Dicks, the main assumption of the delegates was that enduring peace with Germany would require a change in the Germans themselves. Nazism was one 'grotesque and naked' expression of ideals that had long prevailed in Germany and the behaviour of the Germans resulted from their national character. The following February Dicks would advise that in order to bring about a change of this kind, rations in Germany should be kept well below those of the Allies.[11]

One of the organisers of the conference was the American psychiatrist Richard Brickner, who claimed that the Germans as a race were paranoid and that for peace to endure the United Nations needed to create infrastructures that would make non-paranoia emotionally attractive. Brickner was influenced by the work of the anthropologist Margaret Mead, who had argued in a 1942 book that the American 'democratic character structure' could be a model for German re-education and global citizenship. In Mead's view, 'democracy' characterised the generic American mentality and was evident in everything from their selection of governmental candidates to their behaviour in street cars. Although the democratic assumption was to say that all societies were equal, Mead believed that some societies (such as Germany's) were incompatible with living on a world scale. Americans – 'freedom's own children' – were poised as anthropologists to enlighten the world.[12]

Mead's work was influential for the cultural programmes developed in Washington in the lead up to the Occupation, which were intended to serve the aims articulated at Yalta, offering the Germans a 'decent life' and a place in 'the comity of nations' once they submitted to a process of denazification and demilitarisation. If the Allies were going to transform the whole German psyche, then literature, film and the media would prove one way to do it. Semantically, the word 'culture' refers both to works of art and to the broader way of life of a community.[13] It was therefore well placed to be at the centre of an initiative that sought to combine social anthropology with artistic propaganda. The Allied cultural programme elided these two meanings of culture so that it incorporated everything from questions of public manners to high art.[14]

In September 1943, the chief of the Allied Forces Information and Censorship Section General Robert McClure had proposed the establishment of a Publicity and Psychological Warfare section for the Anglo-American Supreme Headquarters, Allied Expeditionary Forces (SHAEF). The following spring, as SHAEF's Supreme Commander, General Dwight Eisenhower put McClure in charge of this division. At this stage he was entrusted with the task of convincing the German soldiers that the Allies were certain to win the war. It was agreed that later he would be responsible for converting (or 're-educating') German civilians towards peace and democracy.

Already there was some discussion of cultural media that could be enlisted for this purpose. In Britain, the Political Warfare Executive issued a draft German armistice in February 1944, stipulating that the victors would seize control of German press, publications, film, broadcasting and theatre and explaining that this was necessary both on negative and positive grounds. Negatively, the Allies would need to 'prevent the dissemination' of news, rumours or opinions likely to endanger the occupying forces or foster resentment of the Allies; positively, they needed to appropriate the media in order to influence German opinion in directions calculated to minimise resistance, convince the German people 'that the terms imposed upon them are the just and inevitable consequence of their aggressive war' and 'eradicate Nazism and Militarism and encourage democratic initiative and ideas'.[15]

In the US the Office of War Information declared in July that motion pictures would be instrumental in 'reorienting and re-educating the German mind out of its enslavement to Nazi and militarist doctrine'. The selection of films was 'an act of political warfare – warfare against an idea'. Simultaneously the US government was issuing books to enemy prisoners of war and liberated civilians, urged by Archibald MacLeish (poet and Librarian of Congress) to 'recognise the power of books as truly as the Nazi mob which dumped them on fire'. Books by Hemingway, Thomas Mann, Carl Zuckmayer, John Dos Passos and others were distributed liberally around the world, in part by Mann's own publisher Gottfried Bermann-Fischer, now in exile in New York. American officials were keen to continue this translation programme in Germany, believing that books exerted a 'greater influence' in Germany than in the US and were more likely to 'mold public opinion' than newspapers and periodicals. They wanted to use the translation programme both to inculcate a more tolerant world view and to persuade the Germans to treat American culture with more respect than they did at present. This is a vision of cultural policy in which culture (the arts) is able to showcase a nation's culture (its way of life) in order to reorient the minds and therefore the general culture (way of life) of another nation. It was somewhat naïve, given that most of these authors had been both available and popular in Germany in the early 1930s and had neither instilled tolerance nor prevented the Germans from voting in the National Socialists. But it was a vision that would guide Allied policy in Germany in subsequent months.[16]

At Yalta it was clear that for the Allies to be able to effect the kinds of changes they intended to bring about in Germany, they needed an unconditional surrender. 'Nazi Germany is doomed,' the three leaders stated in the declaration following Yalta. 'The German people will only make the cost of their defeat heavier to themselves by attempting to continue a hopeless resistance.' The controversial two-day bombing campaign in Dresden that started on 13 February 1945 was intended to enable the advance of the Red Army and to prevent the German redeploying forces from the West to the East. It also had the effect of frightening the Germans with a terrifying display of power.[17]

Some 796 bombers visited Dresden that night, creating a firestorm that eliminated much of the city. The former academic Victor Klemperer was one of many refugees to evacuate his home during the night. As one of the few surviving Jews in Dresden, he had just been issued with a deportation order by authorities still madly devoted to implementing racial policies even in the midst of apocalyptic chaos. Now he stripped off his yellow star and joined the crowds leaving the devastated city: 'Fires were still burning in many of the buildings on the road above. At times, small and no more than a bundle of clothes, the dead were scattered across our path. The skull of one had been torn away, the top of the head was a dark red bowl. Once an arm lay there with a pale, quite fine hand, like a model made of wax such as one sees in barbers' shop windows . . . Crowds streamed unceasingly between these islands, past these corpses and the smashed vehicles, up and down the Elbe, a silent, agitated procession.'

There were over 25,000 dead in Dresden. The bodies were collected in large pyres and burned swiftly to avoid a health crisis. Of the city's 220,000 homes, 75,000 were completely destroyed and 18,500 severely damaged; there were 18 million cubic metres of rubble. The Allies seemed determined to ensure that the country they inherited was even more helpless than it necessarily was. Yet still the German leaders demanded that the struggle continue. In a set of instructions issued for the impending battle of Berlin, the leadership insisted that it mattered less that the soldiers defending the city were equipped with weapons than that 'every fighter is inspired and permeated by the fanatical will TO WANT TO FIGHT'. Surrender had proved disastrous in 1918. Now Hitler had resolved to grind down the invader into a state of collapse or to end in heroic and apocalyptic flames.[18]

The war was becoming almost as demoralising for the onlookers as for the defeated victims. It certainly did not feel as if victory was within sight. At the start of February 1945 Collier's published a private letter written late at night by Martha Gellhorn, asking her editors for a rest. The magazine's editors claimed that they had printed this personal missive because it revealed the war-weary state of mind. Gellhorn was furious, ostensibly because she felt the truth of war was unprintable, but perhaps more because she did not want her own vulnerability broadcast to a nation that included her husband and lover. 'Today,' she had written in the letter, 'I saw pictures of two bodies, dug up from some boneyard in Toulouse. They were bodies of what had once been two Frenchmen aged 32 and 29, but they had been tortured by the Gestapo until they died. I look at anything, you see, because I do not admit that one can turn away; one has no right to spare oneself. But I never saw faces (decayed in death, of course, anyhow) with gouged-out eyes. I thought I'd seen it all but evidently not.'[19]

While Gellhorn was reeling from the sights of war, Gavin was in the Hürtgen Forest, where he was sent to prepare a mission to cross the turbulent Rur river. He found, as Lanham's regiment had before him, that the forest was too muddy to be traversed by jeep so he wandered on foot, trying to avoid the barbed wire and pillbox fortifications, crossing a mountain stream six feet wide. He was relieved when the division was posted back to Sissonne on 17 February, before the mission could be accomplished. In Sissonne he received a visit from another blonde American beauty, though this one had been German until she had taken US citizenship in 1939. Earlier in the year, Gavin's press officer, Buck Dawson, had called on Marlene Dietrich in Paris and begged her to come and visit the 82nd. Dietrich now appeared asking for Dawson, entertained the troops with songs, magic acts and autographs and fell swiftly in love with their general. Here was another hero to impress with her courage; another lonely American to remind of the comforts of home.

Gavin was captivated by Dietrich but he did not summon her to bed. Instead she returned to Paris, to her lover the actor Jean Gabin, for whose sake she had come to Europe in the first place. Gavin, meanwhile, continued to write letters of love and longing to Gellhorn: 'I have always thought that love like this was something that imaginative people wrote about in books, but something that never really happened,' he told her. Gellhorn herself carried on flitting frenetically from place to place, not often enough in Gavin's direction.

In March she finally made it to Germany, in a British aircraft on a dangerous night mission. Hemingway may have been the first to reach Germany by land, but Gellhorn now saw it flattened below her, 'and a blacker, less inviting piece of land I never saw. It was covered with snow. There were mountains; there was no light and no sign of human life, but the land itself looked actively hostile.' According to the *Collier's* headline she was the 'first girl correspondent' to go on a combat mission over Germany. Her nose ran; her oxygen mask slipped off; she felt as though an enormous weight was crushing her. But she impressed the pilot with her bravery and she had achieved a minor victory in the competition with her soon-to-be ex-husband.[20]

As Gellhorn watched new ruins being created from the skies, Lee Miller finally travelled to Germany from Paris, where she had been based since the previous summer, photographing and reporting on fashion shows, paintings and torture chambers. She had visited the Siegfried Line at Luxembourg and the front line at Jebsheim in France, where she saw her first war dead and, writing in *Vogue*, wondered why she had been cosseted as a child when it had prepared her so badly for the sights she was now witnessing. At home, the dead were decently arranged and distantly peaceful; now they were discarded in the streets. 'Why should I have been put to bed for ten hours sleep . . . We should have been exposed to night clubs and sleep-snatching and alarms and excursions to prepare us for this, our life. Why meals at regular hours, with calories and vitamins and bulk considered? We should have been made to scrounge like street arabs, survive on a crust and beg our way.'[21]

Arriving in Germany, Miller was even more shocked by the scenes she encountered. 'Germany is a beautiful landscape dotted with jewel-like villages, blotched with ruined cities, and inhabited by schizophrenics,' she wrote in her report. She was repelled by the immaculate villages where birches and willows still flanked the streams and little girls in white dresses promenaded after their first communion. Mothers sewed and swept and baked; farmers ploughed and harrowed; they all seemed like ordinary people, but Miller reminded herself and her readers that they were the enemy and needed to remain figures of hate.[22]

When she visited Cologne soon after it was captured in March 1945, Miller confronted a city where 100,000 people were apparently living in vaulted basements beneath the ruins. She found the few who did emerge from the ground repellent in their obsequiousness. They invited her to dine, begged rides in military vehicles and tried to cadge cigarettes and chewing gum. 'How dared they?' she asked; 'What kind of idiocy and stupidity blinds them to my feelings? What kind of detachment are they able to find, from what kind of escape zones in the unventilated alleys of their brains are they able to conjure up the idea that they are liberated instead of conquered people?'

Cologne had been bombed in a staggering 262 separate air raids since 1940 and had been chosen for the RAF's first thousand-bomber raid in 1942. Now only 20,000 people remained out of a population of 700,000 and there was 24 million cubic metres of debris in need of clearing. The city's three bridges were buried in the river and most of its public buildings were reduced to jagged chaos. As in Aachen, the cathedral remained eerily undamaged, towering above a flattened wasteland, apparently ready to crumble down onto the tiny figures trading in the black market below. On one side of the sooty building there was a gash that seemed to one observer to be a fresh red wound that bled at twilight.[23]

This was the city that greeted George Orwell when he arrived towards the end of March as a war correspondent for the *Observer*. Like Miller, Orwell had come from Paris, where he had been pleased to find himself drinking with Hemingway at the Ritz. After the relatively picturesque ruins of London and Paris, he was startled by the complete destruction of Cologne, lamenting the loss of the Romanesque churches and museums.

Orwell was less straightforward in his German-hating than Miller. That January he had mocked the simplicity of the British anti-German fervour in two of his regular columns in the socialist magazine *Tribune*. Reading a copy of the *Quarterly Review* from the Napoleonic Wars, he had been impressed to find French books respectfully reviewed at a time when Britain was fighting for its existence in a bloody and exhausting war. He complained that no such reviews of German literature could appear in the press now, although the situation was very similar. In fact, as Orwell well knew, the situation was very different; any works of literature to come out of Nazi Germany would be endorsed by the fascists. The Allies were fighting partly in the name of all the German cultural figures who had been persecuted by the Nazis. But Orwell's complaints the following week were more convincing. Visiting a London exhibition of waxworks illustrating German atrocities, he was sickened by captions inviting people to 'Come inside and see real Nazi tortures, flogging, crucifixion, gas chambers' and advertising a children's amusement section at no extra charge. Nazi-hating was being used to justify sadist pornographic voyeurism: 'If it were announced that the leading war criminals were to be eaten by lions or trampled to death by elephants in the Wembley Stadium, I fancy the spectacle would be quite well attended.'[24]

None the less Orwell's irritation with the venomous German-hating of his compatriots did not lead him to sympathise with them now. When he caught the eyes of the defeated Germans he saw only a kind of beaten defiance. Like Erika Mann and Lee Miller, he thought that these Germans were more ashamed of losing the war than of the atrocities committed in their name. Most of the people he met claimed to have been forced to join the Nazi Party (NSDAP) against their will.

He was more sympathetic to the somewhat callously named 'Displaced Persons' who now thronged the streets of Germany wheeling carts filled with their few tatty possessions. In theory, the foreign workers whom the Nazis had deported from all over Europe were now free. However, in the absence of anywhere to live, they were attempting to find shelter in the 'DP' camps or beginning their desultory journey home, wandering through a hostile country where they were still under threat from shells and bombs. The Allied authorities had already made plans to shelter and repatriate these people but had not expected numbers to increase so quickly.

Already by 16 March 1945, the US Military Government had estimated that there were 58,000 DPs under its control; by the end of March this figure had grown to 250,000 and by 14 April it was over a million. A month later there would be 2 million DPs in Germany. Orwell was distressed to see that the DPs who initially welcomed the British and Americans as liberators quickly became disillusioned when they realised that their hunger was not a priority to an army still intent on winning the war.[25]

Orwell's despondency about Germany was suddenly compounded by personal despair. A week into his trip he became very ill with a chest infection and was worried enough about his health to draw up notes for his literary executor. In fact, he began to recover but he now discovered that two days earlier his wife Eileen Blair had died in England. He had known that she was going to hospital for a minor operation but had not realised it could have potentially fatal consequences. By the time he reached home he was too late to attend her funeral. Aged forty-one, he was left a widower with responsibility for their newly adopted son Richard. Unable fully to comprehend this personal bereavement, Orwell focused on returning to Europe, possibly preferring to think about loss on a bigger and therefore more manageable scale. 'I want to go back and do some more reporting,' he told a friend on 4 April, 'and perhaps after a few weeks of bumping about in jeeps etc I shall feel better.'[26]

It was apparent to everyone that the war was now in its final phase. Most of the Anglo-Americans who toured Germany in April reflected on the problems of reconstruction. In London, waiting to return to Europe, Orwell wrote an article for the *Observer* insisting that a rural slum of the kind envisaged by Morgenthau would not help Europe. Germany was Europe's problem and the rest of Europe had to realise that the impoverishment of one country would impact unfavourably on the world as a whole. He thought it was absurd to debate the ethics of bombing – 'war itself is inhumane' – and the important question concerned the ethics of reparations versus reconstruction.[27]

Germany was becoming more of a rural slum by the day, but still the high command failed to surrender. On 16 April a Soviet force comprising 2.5 million troops, 6,250 tanks and 42,000 artillery pieces and mortars began the assault on the remaining Wehrmacht defending the path to Berlin. It could only be a matter of weeks before the capital fell and in an article published on 22 April, Orwell, now back in Germany, observed that it was an understatement to say that the Germans knew they were beaten. Most regarded the war as a past event and its continuation as a lunacy in which they had no part and for which they need feel no responsibility. Some German civilians had even applied to the Military Government to provide them with anti-aircraft guns to keep the German planes away.[28]

The German resistance on the west bank of the Rhine had now been eliminated and in the area around Cologne, Gavin's 82nd Airborne Division occupied one village and town after another. Generally the

Germans welcomed the Americans as liberators, grateful that they were not under the control of the Russians who were heard to be serial-raping women in the areas they conquered. 'A girl's been turned into a woman/ A woman turned into a corpse,' wrote the novelist Alexander Solzhenitsyn, who had been one of the Russian soldiers to conquer Königsberg in January, describing the dead body of a small violated girl on a mattress.[29]

Gellhorn managed to catch up with Gavin's division in the middle of April. After she left, the general wrote to say he was pining for her far more than he had expected and that he was beginning to lose interest in the war: 'I have a feeling all day that for the first time in two years they can take the war and stuff it.' He had come to realise that he had been treating the excitement of battle like a drug that he needed in periodic doses. Now, for once, he was content to sit and wait. 'Today I feel like saying to hell with the war, what good is it anyway. I want to be with my Martha.' She was, he informed her, the most wonderful and remarkable person ever to come into his life and he wished he could do something about it other than punching his typewriter.

In her absence he was busy trying to set up baby clinics, schools and shoe repair shops, beginning to reconstruct the country they were still bombing. After four years of seeing the German civilians as targets, Gavin and his fellow generals were now required to see them as needing help and nourishment. Once McClure's Publicity and Psychological Warfare section had arrived, they would even be required to entertain the conquered nation with a view to demonstrating the superiority of the American way of life. Yet meanwhile the battle continued and Gavin was not alone in feeling at a loss. For most soldiers on the ground the sense of anti-climax was palpable. The war was ending piecemeal around them in one minor confrontation after another. There would be no great crash of victory, just more and more destruction until there was too much damage to continue.[30]

3

'We were blind and unbelieving and slow'

Victory: April–May 1945

During the spring of 1945 a series of German concentration camps was liberated by the Western Allies. US troops entered Ohrdruf, Nordhausen and Buchenwald between 4 and 11 April and the British liberated Bergen-Belsen four days later. Visiting Ohrdruf, General George Patton looked down into a pit where arms, legs and ripped torsos stuck out of a pool of dank green water and had to rush behind a shed to vomit. At Buchenwald, American soldiers were shocked to find 700 emaciated children among the remaining 21,000 prisoners while at Bergen-Belsen the 60,000 inmates were even closer to death than anywhere else because the food distribution and medical services had ceased to function some days earlier. Here it was hard to distinguish some of the living prisoners from the corpses that surrounded them. Over 34,000 of the camp's inmates had died since February and there were no facilities for burial, so rotting corpses were piled up around the camp. On 19 April, BBC journalist Richard Dimbleby broadcast a report describing his day in Belsen as the most horrible of his life: 'I picked my way over corpse after corpse in the gloom . . . Some of the poor starved creatures . . . looked so utterly unreal and inhuman that I could have imagined that they had never lived at all.'[1]

The existence of the concentration camps had been known about since the 1930s and revelations about the Nazi atrocities had been circulated after the Red Army liberated the extermination camps at Majdanek in July 1944 and Auschwitz-Birkenau in January 1945. But it was only now that the full scale of organised mass murder became widely known to the British and American public.[2] The liberating troops toured the mass death chambers and crematoria with sickened awe and then set about reporting the horrors both to the press at home, and to the Germans who had lived beside these death factories for years apparently oblivious to what they contained. Patton forced the citizens of Weimar to tour the camp at Buchenwald, determined that they should recognise their complicity in crimes committed only metres from their homes.

On 29 April 1945 the 42nd and 45th Infantry Divisions entered the notorious camp at Dachau, liberating 32,000 inmates. Even before entering the camp, the soldiers were confronted with the stench of death. Hurrying to evacuate prisoners from Buchenwald as the Americans arrived, the SS (*Schutzstaffel* or elite Protection Squadron) had shipped a trainload of 2,000 to Dachau. Almost all had died of starvation on the way and the train of corpses now stood outside the gate. Opened in 1933, Dachau had originally housed political prisoners and the emphasis had been on forced labour rather than mass death, unlike the extermination camps such as Auschwitz-Birkenau and Treblinka.[3] However, since 1940 Dachau had been overcrowded with prisoners from Eastern Europe, many of them Jews, and in the final months of the war food and water supplies had broken down after thousands of prisoners had been moved to Dachau from concentration camps nearer to the Allied lines. Where Buchenwald had one block in which fifty to a hundred people died each day, Dachau had six of these blocks. There were 1,500 emaciated corpses still piled up in the crematorium, which had run out of fuel some days earlier.[4]

For many of the liberators of Dachau, this would be the most scarring experience of the war. The US army newspaper *Stars and Stripes* reported that American soldiers and journalists had been 'mobbed, kissed, thrown into the air and carried on shoulders through a sea of weeping, cheering, laughing prisoners' in heart-rending scenes of emancipation. But the screams emanating from the prisoners were not necessarily screams of joy as the reporter suggested. Within eighteen hours of the liberation of the camp, 135 former captives died as a result of illness and starvation. Some of the rescued inmates emerged from the middle of piles of rotting corpses and there was even one prisoner still alive on the death-train outside the camp. The shrieking was quickly followed by violence. An American soldier lent his bayonet to a prisoner to behead a guard; other guards were beaten to death with spades or shot.[5]

Lee Miller arrived the day after the troops. She was accompanied by Dave Scherman, who had long been her professional collaborator and had now become her lover and emotional crux in Roland Penrose's absence. As they drove through the town of Dachau, the sun was shining and white sheets were hanging from the windows of sumptuous villas alongside the railway line that led to the camp. Before entering, they inspected the train of corpses, now surrounded by flies. Miller photographed the train from the siding, furiously and bemusedly documenting what she saw. Inside the camp they found survivors loading the dead onto cars for disposal or lying weakly in their bunks. In the few minutes it took Miller to take her photographs, two men were found dead and the corpses were dragged out and thrown on the heap outside the block. 'Nobody seemed to mind except me,' Miller observed in her article. She was disturbed to find that the Angora rabbits in the prison farm and the horses in the stables were well fed.[6]

Miller wrote to her editor at *Vogue* that Dachau contained all she would ever hear or close her ears to about a concentration camp. Even the empty dusty yards seemed to conjure visions of the thousands of condemned feet that had crossed them; 'feet which ached and shuffled and stamped away the cold and shifted to relieve the pain and finally became useless except to walk them to the death chamber'. She fell on her knees in the middle of the miles of gravelled earth and felt the fierce pain of a tiny sharp stone on her kneecap, reflecting that hundreds of inmates had fallen like that every day and every night. If they could get up again they lived. If they were too weak they were left to join the piles of corpses in the crematorium.[7]

On 1 May, Hitler's death was announced. According to the official German statement, he had died fighting Soviet troops. The German government was now in the hands of Grand Admiral Karl Dönitz, who had been the commander-in-chief of the German navy since 1943. Lee Miller heard the news while at Hitler's private apartment at 16 Prinz-regentenplatz in Munich, ten miles from Dachau, where she and Scherman had set up home with some American troops a few hours after leaving Dachau. Though spacious, the apartment was ordinary, lacking grace, charm, or intimacy. There was an out-of-tune Bechstein piano, an excellent radio, and linen and silver marked with the initials 'AH'. Miller found that Hitler became 'less fabulous and therefore more terrible' now that he could be envisaged in a domestic setting. She made the most of the visual possibilities created by the combination of fascism and domesticity, photographing Scherman seated at Hitler's desk and a GI reading *Mein Kampf* on Hitler's bed. She also posed for what would soon be a famous photograph of her soaping herself in Hitler's bath.[8]

Neither Miller nor Scherman had bathed for weeks and they appreciated the sudden luxury. But for Miller this was more than an act of cleansing. Composing the *mise en scene* for the photograph, she placed her army boots at the foot of the bath, rubbing the mud of Dachau into the white bathmat. Within the tableau, she was surveyed both by a photograph of Hitler, whose triumphant stance suggested he had just conquered the bathroom from behind the taps, and by a nude classical statuette, whose bent arm echoed Miller's own more tentative pose.

There is no simple message in Miller's picture but by juxtaposing the clumsy brutality of her muddy boots with the pomp of the military leadership and the classical beauty both of the sculpture and of her own, huddled and fragile naked figure, she was asking how these incongruous elements could have come together. The Nazi leadership had been famous for finding a place for art within the torture chamber and the battlefield. Already, there were frequent tales of the concentration camp commandants who went home from a day of gassing Jews to listen to Beethoven. 'He shouts stab deeper in earth you there you others you sing and you play,' the poet Paul Celan memorably observed in his poem '*Todesfuge*' ('Death Fugue'); 'he writes when the night falls to Germany your golden hair Margarete.' By bringing the statue into the frame with Hitler, Miller was undermining the notion that art could be redemptive simply through its purity or detachment.[9] She was also investigating the way that she, like the Nazi high command, could cross easily in a single day from the mud of the death camp to the neat cleanliness of a bathroom, continuing with the trivial routines of everyday life.

Over the course of the next year one journalist after another would be troubled by the ordinariness of the Nazi leaders; they did not seem that different from anyone else. It was this in part that Miller was demonstrating with her photograph, revealing a world in which it had become possible to leave the most unimaginably horrible of scenes to bathe in an innocuous bathroom. In the process she was asking if the mud that she had trampled into Hitler's bathmat was mud that now besmirched the whole world; if she, an 'Aryan'-looking young woman, whose eyes carefully avoided the gaze of the camera, was implicated in the responsibility for the skeletal figures she had left behind at Dachau.

Shortly after hearing the news of Hitler's death, Miller and Scherman visited the square stucco villa of the Führer's lover, Eva Braun, and Miller napped on Eva's bed, finding it comfortable but macabre to doze on the pillow of a dead couple and be glad of their demise. Here again Miller was exploring the sensual experience of being Hitler. Having lain naked in his bath, she was now experiencing the smell of his pillow against her face, the lumps of his mattress beneath her body. In his bath and his bed there was physical proof of Hitler's banal ordinariness; Miller knew as few others could that the apparent embodiment of evil had also taken corporeal form. This was difficult and dangerous knowledge and Miller observed herself grinding her teeth and snarling, filled with hate and despair. It took greater effort to write about than to photograph the scenes she was witnessing. She struggled with writing even in easy circumstances and now Scherman had to provide her with reassurance, sex and cognac as she sat up late into the night agonising over her articles.

The war in Europe was effectively over but the Allies were still waiting for the Germans to surrender. By 3 May, Berlin had fallen to the Russians. The previous day the German forces in Italy had capitulated and James Gavin had received the surrender of the entire German 21st Army (some 150,000 men) at Ludwigslust, Germany.[10] Occupying Ludwigslust, Gavin ordered all the town's inhabitants over the age of ten to view the repulsive remains of the nearby camp at Wöbellin. He then made the grander residents of Ludwigslust rebury the dead from the camp in a park in front of the main palace, observed by the town's entire populace.

Gavin's actions here were typical. Now that the behaviour of the Germans in the concentration camps had been revealed, it seemed absurd to be setting up schools and clinics for them. Were the Germans really entitled to reconstruction, even once they were denazified? And could you change the mentality of a population capable of carrying out deeds like these with such apparently calm functionality? Too busy, exhausted and appalled to answer these questions, Allied generals could only demand that the Germans should come to share their confusion by confronting their own misdeeds.

From Ludwigslust, Gavin wrote to Gellhorn, still longing for her and wondering when they were next going to meet. He had received a wire from her a few days earlier from Paris but had just heard that she was in Germany. Gavin was hoping that she was coming to find him, but in fact she was on her way to Dachau where she arrived on 3 May.

In a single day at Dachau, Gellhorn lost her new-found enthusiasm for life. 'I did not know, realise, find out, care, understand what was happening,' she wrote in disbelief. Years later she said that she had lost her youth at Dachau and was never able to hope again. 'It is as if I walked into Dachau and there fell over a cliff and suffered a lifelong concussion, without recognising it.' She was frightened by the surviving inhabitants: skeletons sitting in the sun, searching themselves for lice, who seemed to have no age or recognisable face. 'No expression shows itself on a face that is only yellowish stubbly skin stretched across bone.' Talking to a Polish doctor who had been a prisoner in Dachau for five years, she learnt about the experiments conducted within the prison. The camp scientists had killed 600 people testing to see how long pilots could survive when shot down over water, leaving the victims for several hours in great vats of sea water eight degrees below zero. In an article published in June, Gellhorn told the readers of *Collier's* that they bore some guilt for the scenes she had witnessed; it had taken the Americans twelve years to open the gates of Dachau. 'We were blind and unbelieving and slow, and that we can never be again.'[11]

Gellhorn did not go to find Gavin in Ludwigslust. She was not ready for ordinary happiness. Instead she went to Bergen-Belsen, where she watched bulldozers burying the heaped corpses, and then flew to Paris from Regensburg, travelling in a C-47 aircraft carrying American POWs. Waiting for the plane, the passengers sat in the shade under the wings. When they were invited to board they ran onto the aircraft as though escaping from a fire. Gellhorn did not look out of the windows as they flew away from a country that at that moment she wished to leave behind for ever.

On 7 May the Germans surrendered at last in a schoolhouse in Reims. Symbolically, the Allied victory was undermined by the continued absence of Hitler's body. The newspapers announced that an initial search in Berlin had failed to locate his corpse so the Russians were still hunting the capital for his remains. It was just about possible that the German leader had escaped and was waiting to attempt to resurrect the Fatherland. In fact the Russians had found and identified the body on 5 May but were keeping the discovery of his suicide secret, partly to fuel the rumour that Hitler was hiding in Bavaria (US-occupied territory) and partly to promote Stalin's propaganda that the West secretly wanted to do a deal with the Nazis.[12]

Initially, the occupied towns had been administered by the troops who had conquered them. Several makeshift governments had been established, usually led by the Bürgermeister, or head of the local government, unless he was a known Nazi. Curfews were imposed by the Allies and radios, weapons and cameras confiscated. Because at this stage the Occupation was so arbitrary, the nature of the occupying regime varied radically from town to town. In general, the Russians and the French (who had gone beyond their remit in seizing towns throughout the territory of Baden) were more punitive than the British and the Americans, having suffered more on their own soil.[13] Now the four

Allies began to assign more formal occupation governments, though the official zones had not yet been finally allocated.

The eighth of May was VE Day, celebrating Victory in Europe. Gellhorn spent it in her Paris hotel crying in the arms of a French acquaintance and talking about Dachau. In Germany the next day, Marlene Dietrich made her first trip to a concentration camp. She had heard rumours during the war that her sister Liesel was in Belsen, although she was neither Jewish nor an obvious enemy of the Nazis. Now General Bradley arranged for Dietrich to travel to Belsen in his army plane, but she did not make it into the camp. Talking to British army captain Arnold Horwell (assistant commandant of the liberated camp), Dietrich learnt that her sister and her husband Georg Willi had in fact simply lived in the town of Belsen and had worked closely with the Nazis in charge of the concentration camp. Georg Willi had even run the cinema at Belsen for the SS. Horwell reported to his wife that he had given Dietrich enough details about the camp 'to make her almost sick'. Liesel had spent her childhood following around her adored younger sister, so terrified of displeasing her that she frequently made mistakes just through trying too hard. Now she had directed her efforts into pleasing the wrong superiors and Dietrich would never forgive her. She ensured that Horwell did his best to save Liesel and her husband from jail but after that she disappeared from Liesel's life. In the future, she would deny that she had ever had a sister.[14]

Dietrich was unusual among early Allied visitors to the liberated camps in apportioning guilt solely to the Germans. For Gellhorn and Miller, being on the 'right side' was not enough. If Germany was Europe and America's dilemma then since the opening of the concentration camps it had also become a personal dilemma for them as well. The question facing them now was how to redeem the horrors they had witnessed. Would trying and punishing the Nazis be enough or would the whole world remain guilty in some way? There was also the question of what to do with all their hatred. Neither could acclimatise to watching Allied commanders such as Gavin helping the unrepentant Germans. They sought refuge in writing their reports, with Miller insisting to the readers of *Vogue* that Dachau was close enough to the town that there could be no doubt that the inhabitants knew what was happening. 'The railway siding into the camp runs past quite a few swell villas and the last train of dead and semi-dead deportees was long enough to extend past them.'[15]

At the end of April 1945, George Orwell had reported in the *Observer* that as he drove through the cherry-fringed winding roads of the German countryside he was asking himself one question over and over again: 'It is to what extent can the so obviously simple and gentle peasants who troop to church on Sunday mornings in decent black be responsible for the horrors of the Nazis?' For Orwell the question had two possible answers: the ordinary Germans might or might not be guilty. For Martha Gellhorn there could be no doubt of their collective guilt. Now on the west bank of the Rhine with Gavin, she complained scornfully to readers of *Collier's* that no one in Germany admitted to being a Nazi. There may have been some in the next village; that town a dozen miles away had been a 'veritable hotbed' of Nazism; round here everyone had been busy hiding Jews. Unwittingly echoing Erika Mann, Gellhorn suggested that it should be set to music, so that the Germans could sing a 'We were never Nazis!' refrain.[16]

Gellhorn was not impressed by the spectacle of a whole nation passing the buck and she was especially unimpressed by the day–night divide. By day the Americans were the answer to the German prayer; by night the Germans took pot shots at Americans and burned down the houses of Germans who had accepted posts in the Military Government. A few months earlier, Gellhorn had been angry about the scale of destruction wrought by the Allies. But she had been hardened by her experience at Dachau and so was dismissive of Germans who complained about their own suffering under the bombs. 'Our soldiers say, "They asked for it,"' when they surveyed the ruined cities. This was now Gellhorn's answer as well.[17]

Fuelled by rage, Gellhorn saw all the Germans as a single homogeneous mass. She made no distinctions of class or politics, forgetting or ignoring the fact that there had even been some surviving Jews cowering from the bombs alongside their persecutors. She also saw the Germans' humility before their conquerors as more conniving than it might have been. For many of the Germans, what manifested itself as sycophancy was driven by fear. During the war they had been informed by Nazi propaganda that the British or Americans would castrate all Germans once defeated and would waste no time in implementing the Morgenthau Plan, turning Germany into a giant farm. Distrustful and anxious as well as hungry and often ill, the inhabitants of the bombed cities could not do much more than assert their compliance and beg for compassion from their occupiers.

In a radio broadcast made to the Germans from the US on 10 May, Thomas Mann reiterated the message of collective guilt propounded by Miller and Gellhorn. Though Mann's tone was more sorrowful than angry – he was not snarling with hate like Miller – he had no doubt that all his former countrymen were implicated in Germany's guilt. Like Miller and Gellhorn, Mann took the dilemma of Germany personally; all the more personally in his case because, unlike Dietrich, he did not separate himself from the Germans. Beginning a discussion that would culminate in *Doctor Faustus*, Mann lamented that as the bells of victory boomed and glasses clinked, he and his compatriots had to lower their heads in shame. He was ashamed that Germany had failed to free itself from National Socialism: to bring about its liberation with the sound of bells and the music of Beethoven, rather than waiting to be liberated from outside.

As Mann's first proclamation after the end of the war, this speech carried great significance. The exiled philosopher Ludwig Marcuse later described Mann as the 'Kaiser of all the German emigrants, and in particular the overlord of the tribe of writers', stating that 'everything was expected of him, he was credited with everything, he was made responsible for everything'. A Nobel-prize winner whose erudite novels carried great weight among both German and American intellectuals, Mann was now the foremost German man of letters in the US and an honoured guest at the White House. [18]

During the war Mann had made broadcasts to the German public, urging them to turn away from Nazism. Now he was talking more specifically to the German writers and artists who had stayed. There was a tendency for German artists to describe themselves using the term 'inner emigrant', implying that it was possible to remain physically present in Germany but to distance themselves mentally from the world around them, absenting themselves ideologically. Mann was aware that the months that followed would be dominated by a dialogue between the 'outer' and the 'inner' emigrants in which both made a claim to have suffered more and sinned less than the other. He wanted to forestall this by emphasising the inevitable grey areas when it came to questions of guilt and blame and acknowledging that although he may now be an American citizen, he shared the guilty burden of his former countrymen.[19]

Mann was right to include himself among the guilty. He had disappointed his brother, the novelist Heinrich Mann, with his own militarism in the First World War (at one point he celebrated the sinking of the 1,200 civilian passengers on board the British *Lusitania*) and had disappointed his most politicised children Erika and Klaus with his failure publicly to condemn the National Socialists in their early years of power. Although he had censured them when they came second in the 1930 German election and had resigned from the executive committee of the German Writers' League in 1933, he had been reluctant to make the decisive breach that would lead to the banning of his work in Germany.

In 1933 Thomas Mann and his wife Katia followed Erika and Klaus into exile, frightened that their lives were endangered by Katia's Jewishness and the radicalism of their elder children. Soon they would be joined by their remaining four children. But Mann's ability to equivocate about even the most simple matters was part of his greatness, as was his determination to admit his most unpleasant feelings to himself. He observed in his diary in April 1933 that he was beginning to suspect that 'in spite of everything this process is one of those that has two sides to them'. He was wondering if in fact 'something deeply significant and revolutionary' was taking place in Germany and thought that after all it was 'no calamity' that the domination of the legal system by the Jews had ended. This moment of anti-Semitism was not characteristic for Mann, who had never been troubled by his wife's Jewishness. But he was prepared to consider the matter from multiple points of view.[20]

By May 1933 Mann had made up his mind enough to inform Albert Einstein that he was convinced that the 'German Revolution' was 'completely wrong and evil', but despite this new conviction, he hesitated, refusing to leave his German publishing house and even speaking out publicly against his son Klaus's anti-Nazi émigré journal *Die Sammlung*. This was partly because he believed that as a great writer his foremost loyalty was to literature. After the Nazi putsch known as 'The Night of the Long Knives' in 1934, Mann wrote in his diary that he wished his heart could be colder, enabling him to be less disturbed by these events. 'What does the history of the world matter to me, I probably ought to think, if only it lets me go on living and working?'[21]

When Mann did finally make a political statement, it was not on behalf of the anti-fascist exiles but in defence of his Jewish publisher, who was attacked by an émigré newspaper as a Jewish protégé of Goebbels. It was Erika who forced a more decisive breach, insisting that the history of the world mattered. She found her father's protest unacceptable and informed him that it was now going to be difficult for her to look him in the eye. Certain that the Jewish publisher had indeed compromised problematically with the regime, Erika told her father that it was time to choose between his daughter and his editor: 'This friendly time is predestined to separate people – in how many cases has it happened already. Your relation to Dr Bermann and his publishing house is indestructible – you seem to be ready to sacrifice everything for it. In that case if it is a sacrifice for you that I, slowly but surely, will be lost for you – then just never mind. For me it is sad, and terrible. I am your child.'

Thomas asked Erika for patience, but she had none left. Katia intervened, drafting an open letter to the newspapers that she demanded her husband should complete. Finally, in February 1936, Thomas Mann spoke out in an open letter to the anti-Semitic journalist Eduard Korrodi stating that German anti-Semitism was not just directed against the Jews but was directed 'against Europe and against that higher Germanism itself' and against the 'classical foundations of Western morality'. National Socialism was creating 'a ruinous alienation between Goethe's country and the rest of the world'.[22]

Now, after his years of broadcasting to the Germans as a patriotic American, Mann had earned the right to berate his former countrymen for their foolishness. He was worried that they would continue to believe in their military superiority and urged them to see that this was a myth. In a delicate balancing act, Mann reprimanded his former countrymen while not removing himself from blame. The Germans (and he included himself in the first person plural) needed to 'enhance our modesty' by recognising the superior military skill of the Allies. The impossible task now confronting Mann was to join the conquerors from his adopted country in convincing his former compatriots of their guilt, without shirking his responsibility as a German writer.[23]

Mann's sons Golo and Klaus were enlisted in the Allied army whose military skill he was commending, though admittedly as reporters rather than as combatants. Since the start of the war, both men had been committed to helping defeat the Nazis physically as well as intellectually. In May 1940, Golo Mann had put on hold his career as an academic historian to volunteer with the Red Cross in France. He was almost immediately imprisoned in a French concentration camp, though he was released after three months with American help and escaped across the Pyrenees to Lisbon and then to America, accompanied by his uncle Heinrich.[24] A year later, once the US had entered the war, Klaus Mann attempted to enlist in the army. After being repeatedly rejected by military authorities who were doubtful about his health and his sexual orientation, Klaus feigned some heterosexual lust, pointing out the desirability of the bosom of a girl outside the window, and was accepted as an American soldier in 1942.

Following years as an outsider, he was delighted to be defending his new homeland. 'We German refugees . . . were eager to contribute our bit to the fight against the Brown Plague,' he said later; 'I was happy and proud therefore, to join the army of my new country, the United States of America.' In 1943 Golo was able to enlist as well, working for the Office of Strategic Services (OSS) in Washington and then making radio commentaries for the German language division of the American

Broadcasting Station in London and then Luxembourg, informing the Germans about the bombing of their cities from across the border.[25]

Klaus Mann's unit had been in Europe since the spring of 1943 and he was currently stationed in Italy working for the Psychological Warfare section. His task was to report on the war for *Stars and Stripes* and to give speeches on loudspeakers urging the German troops in Italy to surrender. 'Do you want to die for a lost cause?' he had asked them in January. 'Why do you still lie in the dirt out here risking your lives?' There was coffee and buttered bread waiting for them in the American POW camp. But although he dissociated himself from the foolishness of the German soldiers, Klaus like his father had returned mentally to his former homeland during the months of its protracted defeat. While in Italy, he had received intermittent letters from Erika describing her adventures in Aachen and he was now eagerly trying to persuade his superiors that it was time for him to go back to Germany as well.[26]

For Klaus Mann the desire to return to Germany was bound up with his feelings of ambivalent closeness towards his father and elder sister. He minded deeply that Erika was seeing the ruins of their homeland without him. 'It's an eternal pity that we can't explore German cities together,' he complained. Now he wanted to return to the country where they had grown up, both to make sense of his own past and to regain the bond with his sister that he worried he was in the process of losing.[27]

Since childhood, the two eldest Mann siblings had been so close that they were frequently mistaken for twins or lovers. In fact Erika was a year older than the brother she affectionately knew as 'Eissi' and both were more often attracted to their own sex. None the less, their relationship had the quality of a marriage. As children, they remained apart from their four younger siblings and their schoolmates, embedded in an endlessly proliferating make-believe world. Outsiders were struck by the exclusivity of their uncompromising intelligence and by their androgyny. Erika was a tomboy with dark messy hair; Klaus was girlishly lovely with shoulder-length blond curls.

When it seemed time to leave bourgeois Munich for bohemian Berlin, they went together, Klaus aged seventeen and Erika aged eighteen. What was more, they fell in love together, creating an incestuous quartet held together primarily by the siblings' own tight bond. Aged eighteen, Klaus proposed to Pamela Wedekind (daughter of Frank Wedekind, a well-known and scandalous playwright) who was Erika's lover at the time.[28] Klaus's 1924 play *Anja and Esther* was written for his sister and his fiancée and explored the relationships of 'a neurotic quartet of four boys and girls' who are 'madly in love with each other, in the most tragic and mixed up fashion'. Two years later the rising star Gustaf Gründgens invited Klaus to stage the play in Hamburg, suggesting that he and Klaus take on the roles of the two boys. [29]

Gründgens was handsome, shabby and ambitious. He was as impressed by Klaus's elevated background as Klaus was by his new friend's self-confident charm. The two men fell in love, with Gründgens publicly pronouncing Klaus as the poet of the younger generation and proposing marriage to Erika. Pamela did not attend her lover's wedding and Erika and her husband honeymooned at a hotel where Erika and Pamela had holidayed one month earlier with Pamela passing herself off as a man. Gründgens was supportive of Erika's acting career but his relationship with Klaus was becoming more rivalrous than loving; Klaus's parentage became problematic when it eclipsed Gründgens' own stardom. When *Anja and Esther* opened in Hamburg, Germany's most popular magazine, *Die Berliner Illustrierte Zeitung*, ran a feature on the quartet that focused chiefly on the illustrious parentage of the Manns and Wedekind and cropped Gründgens out of the photograph featured on the cover. It was unsurprising that both the love affair and the marriage were over within three years, although Klaus remained irritably obsessed with Gründgens and would use his estranged lover as the model for his portrayal of a self-serving actor who sells his soul to the fascist Devil in his 1936 novel *Mephisto*.[30]

The Mann siblings' commitment to bohemianism was partly a reaction against their parents, whom they believed had both failed to fulfill their early radical promise. In 1901 aged twenty-six, Thomas Mann had shocked his family with his damning portrayal of his bourgeois childhood world in *Buddenbrooks*. In 1903, Katia Pringsheim had been the first female student to enroll in the University of Munich. Meeting

Thomas shortly after this, she initially attracted him with her haughty refusal to produce her ticket on a tram. But in Klaus and Erika's view, their parents had succumbed to respectability in marrying each other. Katia abandoned her studies to become the quiet wife of a great man and Thomas remained sexually only partially fulfilled, knowing that he was primarily homosexual. Erika and Klaus were determined to avoid the unhappy compromises of their parents, although both would always feel compelled to seek their father's approval.

Neither Klaus nor Erika felt obliged to marry each other's lovers again but in 1935 when Erika needed to marry an Englishman to gain a British passport, it was to a homosexual man that she turned. She met the British poet W. H. Auden through his collaborator the novelist Christopher Isherwood, who had become a friend in Amsterdam. Worried that her German citizenship would soon be revoked, she asked Isherwood to marry her. Squeamish about marriage and anxious about the safety of his own German male lover, Isherwood cabled to London to ask Auden to do it instead. Erika Mann and Wystan Auden married in June 1935, with Erika sporting a man's tailored suit and jacket as her second bridal costume.

Erika made it clear with her attire that she like Klaus remained part of a bohemian world of outsiders that excluded her parents and their respectable literary circle. However the bond between the siblings was loosening and this was painful for them both. Erika found her brother's dependence on drugs increasingly estranging as it became evident that his chemical experiments of the 1920s had developed into an addiction to a revolving combination of morphine, cocaine and heroin. 'Don't take any more "tuna" [heroin],' Erika commanded Klaus in a letter in 1937; 'It is unhealthy! It is expensive! It is dangerous! Don't you recognise that?' In the same letter she acknowledged the growing distance between them, saying that 'we are too far removed from one another and it gnaws at my marrow'.[31]

Erika and Klaus none the less continued to lecture together in the late 1930s and co-authored two books about Germany and the Germans. In *The Other Germany* (1940) they analysed Nazism as a German disease, suggesting that it had 'deep roots in the character and psyche of the stricken nation', at the same time as they pleaded for the recognition of an Other Germany, the enlightened land that had produced great music, philosophy and literature. But the gulf between the siblings increased as they pursued their separate wars. Erika left for London in the summer of 1940 as a correspondent for the BBC, convinced of the need to 'leave behind my beautiful, cosy American lifestyle' and enter a war zone. Klaus, missing his sister desperately, chose not to follow her but to found another literary journal, *Decision,* which launched in 1941 with an editorial where Klaus defended his right to start a literary magazine at such a perilous time. The Nazis had put culture itself in danger. What was needed to combat them was 'a new forum for the creative spirit – *now,* at precisely this moment of fatal decisions'.[32]

For Klaus it seemed essential that his magazine should be published in the US. That land that Erika had seen as irresponsibly beautiful and cosy was for Klaus 'the last haven of free thought and free expression'. This was an old debate. These were the battle lines that had separated Martha Gellhorn and Ernest Hemingway, that now divided the British artists who had moved to America – Klaus's brother-in-law W. H. Auden, Christopher Isherwood, Benjamin Britten – from the friends they had left behind in London.[33]

Klaus quickly abandoned his own position. Unlike Auden and Isherwood he was not a pacifist. He had told Isherwood early in the war that although he could not conceive of killing anyone himself, he was convinced that if you allowed the Nazis to continue unrestricted you would let civilisation itself be destroyed. In 1941 he had argued with Auden on the radio, pleading for activism among artists where Auden maintained that poets and writers should avoid taking a political stance. By joining the US army, he went one step further than his sister in committing to the war effort. Now he was embedded even more deeply in the war than she was, but still the rift between them grew as their war experiences diverged and letters went missing or remained unwritten.[34]

The distance between the siblings was reflected by Erika's choice of lovers. Since emigrating to the US in 1936, she had become chiefly heterosexual and kept her male lovers apart from Klaus. In 1941 she had fallen in love with the sixty-five-year-old German composer Bruno Walter, who resembled her father more than her brother in his old-world German dignity; indeed, Erika had known him since her childhood as a friend of her father's and the father of her friend Lotte. This was the first time that she had been properly in love with a man and it was serious, on her side if not on his, although the intensity was tempered when she began a simultaneous affair with the American war correspondent Betty Knox.

As well as seeking a paternal lover, Erika was strengthening her ties with her father. Her years of rebellion were over and she was prepared to be the loyal favourite daughter Thomas Mann needed. Soon after she moved to the US, Erika had stopped mocking the Nazis through cabaret and started criticising them in lectures instead. Her father commended her decision, writing that she was 'speaking in my stead as my daughter and as my intellectual disciple'. This was an honour that Erika increasingly coveted. After returning home to Los Angeles from Germany in January 1945, she longed to go back to Europe but stayed out of duty to her father whose health was weak and whose seventieth birthday she wished to celebrate with him in June.[35]

Partly because of her divided loyalties, Erika was not writing to Klaus as frequently as he would wish. Relations between them became more strained as he took offence at her silence and she bridled at his willingness to find it estranging. 'You should be aware of the fact that I am physically incapable of resenting anything you do or say,' Erika told her brother in February, pained that he could deem it possible she would punish him by not writing. Addressing him as 'little old spouse', she insisted that if it were not for her loyalty to their father she would return to Europe and to her brother as quickly as possible. 'Needless to say my heart aches and itches even now, wanting to be where "once mighty" surrenders and "once arrogant" (the German people) remain just as arrogant as ever,' she told Klaus on VE Day, as he finally made his way to Munich to revisit their former family home.[36]

Klaus had persuaded his superiors to send him to Germany to report on conditions in the US zone. Now, as his father's speech was broadcast across the nation, Klaus wandered through the ruins of the city to the house in Poschinger Strasse where he, Erika and their siblings had grown up. In a radio broadcast entitled 'An American Soldier Revisiting his Former Homeland', Klaus Mann later described the strangeness of walking through once-familiar streets, now reduced to ruin and rubble. Lacking the old landmarks, he found it almost impossible to make his way from the city centre to their house. Munich had been badly bombed in the final year of the war, with three-quarters of the old city centre destroyed. Ninety-two of the city's cultural and religious buildings had been obliterated by the bombing; a further 182 were damaged, including the cathedral, the old town hall and the National Theatre.[37]

The Manns' house was an empty shell, with the inside burned out, the roof destroyed and the staircase in pieces. But surprisingly there was a girl standing on the balcony in front of Klaus's bedroom. Taking on the role of conqueror, he asked her in German with an American accent what she was doing. She replied that she had taken refuge there after being bombed out and invited him up using a makeshift ladder. It turned out that during the war the SS had taken over the house and established a *Lebensborn*, a place where 'racially superior' young men and women had sex to propagate the German race. 'They didn't do it for the fun of it,' the girl assured Klaus earnestly. 'Many fine babies were begotten and born in this house . . .'[38]

Throughout the war, Klaus Mann had believed that 'when the Dictator has vanished – and only then, will it again be possible . . . to live in Germany, without fear and without shame'. He was now sad to find that this was not the case. In an article in *Stars and Stripes* he complained that the shock of defeat had failed to enlighten the Germans: 'the German people show no trace of a sense of responsibility, much less a sense of guilt'. He visited some German artists, his former friend the actor Emil Jannings (who had starred alongside Marlene Dietrich in Josef von Sternberg's immensely popular 1930 film *The Blue Angel*, which was scripted by Carl Zuckmayer from a novel by Heinrich Mann) and the composer Richard Strauss, and came away sure that both were unrepentant Nazis. Strauss complained only about Hitler's deplorably one-sided musical taste: 'Hardly ever did he go to hear any of my operas.'[39]

Like his father, Klaus was convinced that the war had been conducted by the German people as a whole. And in some moments he too included himself among the guilty. Witnessing his young American lover Thomas Quinn Curtiss ('Tomski') departing for training in National Guard Uniform during the war, Klaus had felt that as a German he was responsible for the loss of youthful lives. 'I don't want to excuse myself – quite the contrary, I want to stress my own share of guilt and responsibility,' he wrote in a draft letter to Tomski at the time. Now his disappointment with the German nation came together with his sadness at returning to Germany without his sister. On 16 May 1945 he sent a lengthy report of the trip home to his father, intending it also for Erika. He told his 'Magician-Dad' that it would be a grave mistake on his part to return to Germany and play any kind of political role there: 'Conditions here are too sad. All your efforts to improve them would be hopelessly wasted. In the end you would be blamed for the country's well-deserved, inevitable misery. More likely than not, you would be assassinated.' Evidently it would take decades to reconstruct the German cities and the spiritual rehabilitation of the 'morally mutilated, crippled' nation would take even longer.[40]

Two weeks later Thomas Mann gave a speech at the US Library of Congress on 'Germany and the Germans'. Here he followed his son's lead in emphasising his new American citizenship, stating that he was addressing his audience as an American and that as an American he was a citizen of the world. He shared the world's concern about Germany and found that 'Germany's horrible fate . . . compels our interest, even if this interest is devoid of sympathy'. At the same time he was more explicit than he had been in his radio broadcast to the Germans in stating that he remained a German in spite of his new passport and that he could not separate himself from the fate of his nation. It would be dishonest to commend himself as 'the good Germany' in contrast to the wicked, guilty Germany over there with which he had nothing in common. He had been nurtured in the provincial cosmopolitanism of the old German world; he had felt in himself the potential for religious fanaticism that this entailed.

Here Mann developed the arguments propounded in Klaus and Erika Mann's *The Other Germany* in seeing Nazism as a peculiarly German psychosis. He even suggested that there was a secret union of the German spirit with the demonic. Both Goethe's Faust and the Devil who seduced him could be seen as fundamentally German figures; in this reading Goethe, like Mann, was diagnosing the demonic in the German soul. Now Germany had made a Faustian pact with the Devil. The German urge for liberty was always tantamount to inner enslavement because it entailed an attack upon the liberty of others.

In Mann's somewhat selective narrative, the inwardness of German Romanticism, with its tenderness, passion and reverie, had resulted both in the Pan-Germanism of Bismarck and the death-driven megalomania of Hitler.[41] Goethe's Werther, knocking 'with cold, unflinching hand' at the 'brazen portals of Death', Wagner's Tristan and Isolde, dreaming together of a *'sehnend verlangter Liebestod'* (yearned for, longed for death-in-love) and craving death as an 'endless realm of ecstatic dreams', were the antecedants of the warrior heroes called into being by Hitler.[42] So too, the German Romantics had shared Hitler's vision of a *völkish* German identity grounded in folk blood and soil. As far as Mann was concerned there were not 'two Germanys, a good one and a bad one, but only one, whose best turned into evil through devilish cunning'. Wicked Germany was good Germany in guilt and ruin.[43]

Mann was unwittingly echoing the American psychologists at the 1944 conference. In Henry Dicks's conference report, the delegates viewed Nazism as one expression of ideals that had long prevailed in Germany. But Mann was interested specficially in German artists and the Germany he described was a country whose writers and artists were even more culpable than the rest of its citizens because they had placed themselves and their art above politics and had been encouraged to do so by the rest of the nation, effectively being granted political immunity.

In *The Other Germany*, Klaus and Erika Mann explained to their American readers that the Germans loved to stress the difference between their concept of *Kultur* and the more superficial western concept of *Zivilisation*. Though they did not discuss it here, both the tardiness of their father's own confrontation with the Nazis and his more problematic nationalist leanings were a product of this divide. In his *Reflections of a Nonpolitical Man*, published a year into the First World War, Thomas Mann had patriotically pledged his allegiance to the German war effort on the grounds that the war represented a conflict between German *Kultur* and the *Zivilisation* of the rest of Europe. He wanted Europe to be reorganised around German *Kultur*, which he saw as representing the spirit of 'progress, revolution, modernity, youth and originality'. In 1919 he regretfully saw the British and US victory as completing the 'civilising, rationalising, pragmatising of the West which is the fate of every aging culture'.[44]

In Mann's case these were not purely nationalist sentiments. He hoped that German *Kultur* could be used to bring about a more unified Europe. But it is easy to see how this argument could be used for nationalist ends by others. It is also easy to see how the German elevation of *Kultur* created a society in which artists were able to distance themselves from politics and therefore to avoid speaking out against the regime. In the eighteenth and early nineteenth centuries this was partly because Germany was fundamentally a *Kulturnation* rather than a political state: a collection of separate political entities that shared a common language and culture. But even after the unification of Germany in 1871, Germany needed its artists to provide its national identity and those artists often distanced themselves from politics, partly because writers who dared to question the censors ended up jailed or exiled.[45] This changed during the Weimar Republic, when the new atmosphere of political freedom brought on a new left-wing political engagement among German artists, especially in Berlin where it coincided with a moment of sexual and artistic experimentation. By the time that Hitler came to power, *Kultur* and *Zivilisation* were inextricably entwined, though it took a great number of German intellectuals some years to realise this.

When Mann pleaded for the supremacy of German culture in the First World War, he was pleading for culture and politics to remain separate. By the time that he spoke out against the Nazis in 1936, he was aware that this had proved impossible. Even during the Weimar Republic, Mann had come to see the necessity that German artists needed to do all they could to support democracy in Germany.[46] Under National Socialism, the German notion of culture as high art had become untenable when Hitler appropriated art for his mass rallies.[47] Hitler and Goebbels's *Kunstpolitik* made art serve politics and politics serve art. When Hitler attended Wagner's *Parsifal* before going into battle, he was suggesting that war was a continuation of art by other means. If it had taken Mann some years to admit this publicly, it took many of his contemporaries a lot longer. Over the next four years the personal dilemma faced by both Thomas and Klaus Mann was going to be whether they could separate their fates from those of their wicked countrymen; whether redemption for Germany was possible and what role they as writers could play in bringing it about; whether remodelling themselves as Americans was enough to escape guilt and despair.

Mann's new government shared his view that there was only one Germany, although governmental officials tended to be more prosaic in the qualities they ascribed to it. The twenty-first of May 1945 saw the publication of the 'Directive to the Commander in Chief of the US Occupation Forces' (known as JCS 1067), which was to form the basis for policy in the US zone. This document condemned the 'fanatical' and 'ruthless' German megalomania, stating in terms reminiscent of Mann's that the Germans could not 'escape responsibility for what they have brought upon themselves'. As a result, Germany was not being occupied for the purpose of liberation but as 'a defeated enemy nation'. The troops were forbidden to fraternise with Germans and were to concentrate on denazifying and demilitarising Germany. Political activities of all kinds were banned and all existing schools were to be closed. Freedom of speech, press and religious worship was permitted, though any newspapers had to be licensed by the Allies.[48]

It was clear in the instructions issued to both British and US Control Commission employees that they were being sent in as enemy occupiers rather than liberators. A March 1945 broadcast to American soldiers on the Armed Forces Radio Service informed them that after 'a good clean fight' you could shake hands with the opponent but that this had not been a good clean fight. They should not be misled into thinking 'Oh, well, the Germans are human' because the murderer and the cannibal were human too, but it did not make them humane. A month later an American training film entitled *Your Job in Germany* instructed recruits that although they would come across some 'mighty pretty scenery', they were in 'enemy country': 'You are not being sent into Germany as educators. You are soldiers on guard . . . Every German is a potential source of trouble . . . The German people are not our friends . . . They're not sorry they caused the war, just sorry they lost it.'

The British arriving in Germany were issued with the booklet on 'The German Character' that took Thomas Mann's line in challenging the distinction between 'good' and 'bad' Germans: 'There are only good and bad elements in the German character, the latter of which generally predominate.' The Germans exalted death rather than life and were maudlin, suicidal and sadistic. The booklet ended with a list of dos and don'ts: do give orders, be firm, keep the Germans in their place and display cold, correct aloofness; don't try to be kind ('it will be regarded as a weakness'), show any aversion to another war (the British must be prepared to go to war again, if Germany fails to learn her lesson) or even show hatred ('the Germans will be flattered').[49]

The enemy status of the Germans was formalised by the non-fraternisation rule enforced by both the British and US governments. Since first entering Germany, Allied troops had been forbidden from socialising with the Germans. When the Americans arrived in Frankfurt they were even prevented from speaking to the 106 remaining Jews. This policy was widely criticised both by the Germans and by Allied observers and seemed to contradict the desire to re-educate the Germans out of their allegedly maudlin, suicidal and sadistic tendencies. An unsigned article in the British *New Statesman* in April 1945 complained that it was impossible to re-educate a people without first establishing common ground. 'Defeat and occupation give them their physical lesson. Now the spiritual lesson must follow.' In May the Psychological Warfare Division representative at SHAEF, Richard Crossman, complained that the non-fraternisation orders prevented the British from organising anything. The Germans were disappointed that the Allies seemed to have no interest in exposing them to the influence of the outside world for which many of them had hungered for years.[50]

There was no mention of culture in JCS 1067 and this accorded with the non-fraternisation orders. On 3 May, *The New York Times* had reported a directive from Washington for Germany to be re-educated with a 'very austere programme', wholly lacking in entertainment for at least six months after its resistance ended. 'We are not going to try to make life pleasant for the Germans,' the Director of European Operations for the Office of War Information had announced. Although several departments had talked about using cinema as a means of re-education, film, theatre and literature were deliberately omitted from JCS 1067 and it was left up to individual departments to work out a cultural policy.[51]

As far as occupation directive JCS 1067 was concerned, the reconstruction of Germany was a practical, albeit partly intellectual, act. Could the Germans learn to give up arms and stop terrorising the world? As far as Thomas Mann was concerned, it was a more metaphysical one, involving the purging of the German soul. Could the Germans learn to give up the dangerous pleasures of the sublime? For many of the Anglo-American intellectuals who were determined to get to Germany in the summer of 1945, the answer to the German dilemma lay in managing to make the spirit of Mann compatible with the spirit of JCS 1067. Mann might be right that the good and the bad German elements were inextricable from each other but in practical terms it was crucial to separate the Nazis from their victims. This was going to involve a lot of form-filling and red tape.

PART II

Ruin and Reconstruction

May–December 1945

4

'Complete Chaos Guaranteed'

Occupation: May–August 1945

Where Gellhorn, Hemingway, Miller and Dietrich had spent the autumn of 1944 determined to get to Germany chiefly as spectators, wanting to be at the fulcrum of the war and to see the land from which the Nazi evil was emanating, writers and film-makers including Stephen Spender, W. H. Auden, Billy Wilder, Humphrey Jennings and Goronwy Rees went to Germany in the summer of 1945 aiming to help rehabilitate the country in one way or another. Summoned before the Joint Selection Board of the Control Commission in London the previous winter, Spender had suggested that as a British poet who had spent time in Germany in the 1930s he might be useful in helping locate and direct any new literary and cultural movement that would emerge at the end of the war. 'Do you think that after the Nazis there can really be such a development?' the incredulous interviewer asked. Spender was sure that there could be and that enabling it was as crucial as the rest of the Allied reconstruction programme. Initially, Spender was rejected by the board, but he spent the spring of 1945 trying to persuade them to send him to Germany, convinced that it would take people like him with an understanding of the German language and culture to make a difference in transforming the troubled German psyche described by Thomas Mann.[1]

In June, Spender's friend John Lehmann would publish an editorial in his magazine *Daylight*, stating that if Britain had a 'political mission of reconciliation and restoration' in ruined Europe, she also had 'a cultural mission no less important'. In his view, Europe was to be saved by 'an *evolutionary* humanism', developed from centuries of civilising culture, and Britain could be 'the guide and inspiration of such a humanism'. This was a view that Spender broadly shared, but in his opinion the evolutionary humanism was also already present in German culture. He saw the task of the British poet in Germany as being to remind both the British and the Germans of their shared cultural roots. It was with this in mind that he had written articles about Hölderlin and Goethe during the war, defying the lines of antagonism Orwell had described in his *Tribune* column by suggesting that the British were capable of contemplating the literary greatness of the nation they were fighting. Unlike Mann, Spender still believed in the possibility of the 'good' German and he now wished to make contact with the German writers he respected, to remind them of their shared humanist heritage and encourage them to write again. He would then persuade the Allied authorities to publish their books, thus encouraging a new spirit of tolerance and individualism among the Germans.[2]

Spender's vision of the transformative power of art and of the artist as cultural ambassador was idealistic. But his broader belief that British and American intellectuals should go into Germany and talk to people was widely shared. On 20 May the German theatre critic Curt Riess published an article in *The New York Times* that acted as a call to arms for American intellectuals with an interest in Germany. Like his friend Klaus Mann, Riess had emigrated to the US in the 1930s and had spent the war as a war correspondent in the American army. On VE Day he was in Berchtesgaden, the site of Hitler's southern headquarters, and he then went on to explore Munich with Klaus Mann. Riess was as frustrated by the German hypocrisy as Gellhorn, Miller and the Manns were, describing ironically in his article how after three weeks in Germany he had come to feel 'the highest respect for Hitler, who evidently ran this country for thirteen years against the furious opposition, or at least the silent disapproval, of all its seventy-odd million inhabitants'. He was irritated with the arrogance of German businessmen who told him that the world had to do something for Germany, implying that a world without Germany would not be worth living in. In his view, the Americans were faced with a long-drawn-out battle for re-education.[3]

Riess questioned the US directive for cultural austerity by suggesting that re-education could only be achieved by rehabilitating cultural channels and convincing the Germans that newspapers, literature and theatre were not merely vehicles for propaganda as they had been in Nazi times. The Allied governments needed to send intellectuals with an understanding of the Germans to do this and needed to allow them to talk to the natives. In fact, Riess's government, if not Spender's, somewhat inadvertently already had the matter in hand. But rather than being sent in as cultural experts, many of the first intellectuals to be posted to Germany by the US government were part of the US Strategic Bombing Survey, which sent over a thousand military and civilian experts (known as 'Ussbusters') to examine the impact of bombing campaigns in Germany and Japan.

Early in 1945, W. H. Auden had offered his services to the US government in helping to rehabilitate Germany. He, like Spender, had loved Germany before the Nazis came to power. Indeed, it was Auden who had introduced Spender to Germany. As an Oxford undergraduate, Auden had appointed himself leader of a coterie of brilliant, homosexual young writers. Spender – tall, shambling, red-faced, innocent – was assigned the role of disciple, lolloping behind the more self-assured poet. It was natural that after failing to take his degree at Oxford Spender should follow Auden to Germany, joining his friend in learning about psychoanalysis and sexology and making the most of Berlin's atmosphere of promiscuity, falling in love with mercenary, pretty German boys.

Since then Spender had partially freed himself from Auden's influence. He had at least publicly abandoned pretty boys for respectable young women, marrying the writer Inez Pearn and then the pianist Natasha Litvin. After Auden's departure to America, Spender had consolidated his independent position on the London literary scene, co-publishing Cyril Connolly's influential wartime journal *Horizon*. It was typical, though, that Auden should once again make it to Germany before Spender, although he set about trying to get there some months later. His Ussbuster papers came through remarkably quickly and he left the US at the end of April, pausing in London to show off his American uniform and American accent: 'my dear, I'm the first major poet to fly the Atlantic,' he announced to Spender.[4]

Auden flew into Frankfurt just before the war ended. As the plane landed, passengers could see into the rows of burned-out houses, peering through the shells at the smashed shards of furniture.[5] He proceeded amid the ruins with his usual sense of entitlement. He commandeered the personal services of a young blond chef called Hans and adapted his uniform, removing the helmet liner and donning carpet slippers instead of shoes. Having unearthed a supply of Rhine wine, he took at least one full bottle to bed with him each night. Auden's unit began in Darmstadt, in the Rhine-Main area, and by 29 May they were touring Bavaria, interviewing civilians along the way. Typically, Auden designated himself as the team's leader and dubbed himself 'Research Chief'. In Kempten he met Lincoln Kirstein, the American ballet impresario, who was a friend from New York and was now in Germany with the Monuments, Fine Arts and Archives section, attempting to find and protect great works of art. Kirstein was impressed when he looked inside Auden's jeep and found that he had acquired a cooking pot, mattress, box of books, standard lamp, phonograph with records, crate of wine and plaque of Wagner's profile.

Unlike Spender, Auden does not seem to have had a definite vision of what he wanted to do in Germany. Although he was wondering about writing a book of his experiences, he did not see himself as a poet talking to poets or as being responsible for the redemption of the German soul. Like his brother-in-law Klaus Mann, Auden was appalled by the self-serving pomposity of the more prosperous Germans. However, Auden was more troubled than Mann, Gellhorn or Miller by the devastation of the German cities. His chief sympathy was with the survivors of concentration camps whom he found whispered like gnomes; he cabled home for money to help a woman who had been in Dachau. But this did not preclude pity for so-called Aryan Germans. Over the course of the war Auden had gradually committed to pacifism. His decision to move to America was in part a decision to stay away from politics because his left-wing political activism of the 1930s had given way to religion. Although he helped his German exiled friends to produce material aimed at persuading the US to enter the war, he was never convinced that fighting back was the answer. 'Of course it matters whether the Chinese win or the Japanese,' he wrote in his notebook, pondering the Sino-Japanese war in the summer of 1939, 'but even if the Chinese lose, or the oppressed are suppressed, it does not mean the end of progress, only that its rate of development is slower . . . if war could have been avoided it would be better still.'[6]

Auden had been depressed about the bombing of the German cities when he read about it during the war. He was all the more distressed to see the effects of the bombing now. In Darmstadt he was billeted in a house belonging to a Nazi couple who had left their children with their grandparents. Here he found himself responsible for telling the couple that their parents had killed themselves and taken it upon themselves to kill their children as well. According to the Ussbuster reports, Darmstadt itself had been 92 per cent destroyed in a fifty-one minute bombing raid in September 1944. Auden's friend and colleague James Stern described this pink city, built of the local red sandstone, as now looking like a high sea: 'a tempestuous ocean of pink rubble with jagged, perforated walls sticking up between the great waves'. The locals talked about the September raid as 'The Nightmare'; a moment they could never forget but could also never describe.[7]

As analysts for the 'Morale Division', Auden and James Stern's task was to interview the civilian population about their experiences of bombing and its aftermath. Stern shared Auden's view that the Germans should be treated with compassion. He could understand their fear of their occupiers. One of his interviewees told him that he had expected that the Americans would send all the Germans back to the US as slaves after the war. 'We heard that we wouldn't be allowed out on the streets, that we women would be raped by Negroes, that we'd be separated from our husbands and our children deported,' another informed him. This fear had only been confirmed by some aspects of the Occupation: the non-fraternisation rule had made it impossible for the occupiers to demonstrate their reasonableness. So he could see that they were frightened as well as sycophantic when they expressed gratitude to their occupiers and denied any residual allegiance to the Nazis.[8]

And he could see, too, that the Germans' apparent lack of guilt was also a manifestation of bemusement. Watching a group looking at the vast posters where shots of dead children and babies lying on their backs on the ground were captioned with the question 'Who is guilty?', Stern tried to imagine what they were thinking as they turned away with 'dumb, expressionless faces'. He decided that they were still stunned by bombardment, fear and defeat; still ignorant after years of lies and propaganda; that the feeling of guilt was 'so colossal they simply cannot face it, much less give it expression'. And as a result he was able to sympathise with them and began to feel a degree of guilt for his own role in exacerbating their grief with his probing questions. 'What do you say, you damned Gallup-poller you,' Stern asked himself, when across the table there was simply a 'forlorn life with nothing to live for, and not the courage to take it because as long as the heart goes on beating life is dear'?[9]

Both Stern and Auden were careful to differentiate between different groups of Germans. They were better able to perceive the complex range of German reactions to defeat than Gellhorn and Miller, or even Erika and Klaus Mann. They could see that it might be reasonable to expect the intellectuals to have resisted Hitler in the early 1930s but that this had been more difficult for the working-class Germans who had emerged out of a decade of poverty, hyper-inflation and hunger resulting from the punitive terms of the Treaty of Versailles. Thomas Mann may have been right that there were German characteristics that made them unusually susceptible to Hitler (Stern found a large number of his interviewees displayed a mixture of self-pity and sentimentality that he had learned to identify with cruelty), but there was also no doubt that there were living conditions that made Hitler's rise to power far more possible than it would have been at other times.[10]

Though Erika Mann felt justified in retrospectively expecting more resistance to Hitler from her compatriots in the early 1930s, there was a limit to what could be expected in the 1940s. Not everyone could go into exile, which became anyway less and less practical a possibility. And once the war had started, even so small an act of resistance as hiding a Jewish friend was ridden with danger. By 1944 it was common to see Germans as well as captured enemy troops hanging from lamp posts in streets: the possibility of effectively resisting Hitler had become untenable. And yet some people did continue to resist, despite the dangers. In an attempt to convince the Allied authorities that not all Germans were undeserving Nazis, Auden and Stern obtained statements from students involved in a large anti-Nazi uprising in Munich in January 1943 and also from the German philosophical economist Alfred Weber and liberal politician Emil Henk who had played a part in the events leading up to the attempt on Hitler's life in July 1944.[11]

Auden wrote to Stern's German wife Tania that although their work was interesting, he had spent much of his time in tears. 'The people . . . are sad beyond belief.' He told another friend that he found the word 'morale' in the title of the 'Morale Division' embarrassing: 'It is illiterate and absurd. How can one learn anything about morals, when one's actions are beyond any kind of morality? *Morale* with an "e" at the end is psycho-sociological nonsense. What they want to say, but don't say, is how many people we killed and how many buildings we destroyed by that wicked bombing.' In an unpublished interview for *Time* magazine Auden described scornfully how they had asked people if they minded being bombed. 'We went into a city which lay in ruins and asked if it had been hit. We got no answers that we didn't expect.'[12]

On 5 June 1945 the four military governors of Germany – Eisenhower, Montgomery, Georgy Zhukov and Jean de Lattre de Tassigny – signed the 'Declaration of Defeat and Assumption of Sovereignty' in Berlin. Now that the Germans had officially ceded their sovereignty, the zones drawn up at Yalta came into play. The British zone in the north-west of Germany included the largely empty farmlands of Schleswig-Holstein, the industrial and farming areas of Lower Saxony and the industrial area of the Rhineland and the Ruhr. It was the most bomb-damaged of the four zones, with 22 per cent of its dwelling houses destroyed and 35 per cent damaged. The US zone encompassed 41,000 square miles of south-east and central Germany including all of Bavaria. The main cities (Munich, Frankfurt, Nuremberg, Stuttgart, Mannheim and Karlsruhe) were all badly bombed but the countryside was relatively undamaged. The Russian zone covered the north-east of Germany, with Berlin in its centre, while the French would be given a small corner in the south-west, carved out of the original British and US portions, at the end of July.[13]

The unconditional surrender was unprecedented; that day Germany ceded powers that were not allowed for in international law, handing over sovereignty to the Allies in what constituted a kind of annexation. Germany was now effectively a colony jointly ruled by Britain, the US, France and the Soviet Union. The British in particular were used to colonial rule and from the start the London officials planning the Occupation saw it in distinctly colonial terms. The Control Commission for Germany (CCG) informed its staff that Germany was to be re-educated through democracy and that British democracy was 'the most robust in the world: It is on British soil that it flourishes best, but we do export it, and, tended carefully, it grows and flourishes in diverse lands.'[14]

The colonial aspect of the Occupation seemed especially evident in the non-fraternisation rule, which was becoming increasingly comical. On 7 June, *Stars and Stripes* reported that there were now prophylactic stations established in the US zone, although it was not regarded as any relaxation of the non-fraternisation rules. The official medical spokesman issued a somewhat confusing message: 'The Army strongly advises continence, knowing that some soldiers will by law of averages engage in promiscuous relations with women. Inside Germany the Army orders non-fraternisation. But that law of averages is still at work: Hence, pro stations.' And the absurdity of the non-fraternisation rules became even more apparent when the famous Hamburg Circus reopened on 12 June. The circus was being revived for the benefit of the British army and Germans were barred from the shows. The entertainers were generally Displaced Persons from Russia, Czechoslovakia and

Poland. Although the organisers were keen to employ some of the former German circus stars, the current regulations forbade British soldiers from applauding Germans. After some discussion German animals were, however, deemed acceptable; performing horses, brown bears and lions which had been hungry for years were now being properly fed.[15]

British troops in Hamburg wanting to be entertained by a more highbrow art form could also go to the theatre, where there was no danger of Anglo-German contamination. At the end of May, Sybil Thorndike, Laurence Olivier, Ralph Richardson and sixty-two other members of the Old Vic theatre company had arrived from London, under the auspices of ENSA (Entertainments National Services Association). They performed *Peer Gynt, Arms and the Man* and *Richard III* in Hamburg and Lubeck and at Bergen-Belsen concentration camp to packed and enthusiastic audiences. They were all given the honorary rank of lieutenant and had to wear uniform when offstage.

The actors experienced the usual ambivalence of Anglo-American onlookers confronting the German ruins. On their way into Germany the pilot banked down over Essen to show them the damage and Sybil Thorndike began to cry. She had read about the bombing of Essen and Hamburg in the newspaper during the war but it was shocking to see the realities of the air campaign now. The centre of Hamburg had been flattened in an eight-day bombing raid in 1943 whose codename 'Operation Gomorrah' had proved horribly apposite. During the night of 27/28 July alone, twelve square miles were reduced to rubble and 18,474 people killed in a firestorm created by the combined might of 729 heavy bombers. By the end of the war 43,000 had been killed, 900,000 evacuated and 61 per cent of houses and flats destroyed. Much of the city was now a desolate wasteland. Walking around the centre, Thorndike wondered where people lived. 'I'm just bowled over with it,' she told her husband; 'I think English people should see it – and the senselessness and waste of war and the hatred engendered.' One day they escaped into the German countryside, accompanied by an army officer. Watching as a farmer went by on a cart drawn by two horses and piled with hay, Thorndike said: 'It's so beautiful, this is what we fought the war for, a free and a decent and an open life like this. . . we must preserve it.' Later she was distressed to receive a visit from a security officer who told her it was improper to be heard speaking about the enemy in such favourable terms.[16]

Thorndike spoke good German and was frustrated not to be able to talk to any of the people she saw. After a few days she decided to risk being sent back to England for breaking the non-fraternisation rule and started chatting to shopkeepers, room maids and farm workers. 'I feel this in some way is a sign of friendliness,' she wrote, 'or rather a desire for peace.' But her friendliness was curbed when they visited Bergen-Belsen concentration camp, where the head of the Red Cross medical team had asked if they would stage a matinee for the staff. The camp still had 40,000 inmates and there were 10,000 corpses rotting in the sun. Thorndike was taken around the children's hospital where she was appalled by the skeletal figures. She talked to a woman who had witnessed her husband and daughter being shot and was now watching her remaining daughter dying – 'a poor little girl like a ghost with a shaven head'. Afterwards the actors were unable to eat their lunch but they managed to perform *Arms and the Man* in the vast cinema where Marlene Dietrich's sister and her husband had made their living entertaining the camp commandants during the war. 'I was in a haze, a nasty evil-smelling haze,' Thorndike wrote. 'I'll never forget this all my life. Oh, war turns people into monsters – though some heroism comes sometimes, doesn't it? I'll never get over today – never.'[17]

Back in Hamburg the company was joined by the writer and artist Mervyn Peake, who was in Germany as a war artist accompanied by the journalist Tom Pocock. Like Thorndike, Peake was horrified by the plight of the German civilians and then sickened by a visit to Belsen, where he sketched the skeletal figures dying before his eyes and wrote a poem about a consumptive woman he saw in the hospital. In the poem Peake asks how, watching the woman in the 'hour before her last', he could want to paint her, 'her limbs like pipes, her head a china skull'. If his schooled eyes can see the ghost of a great painting in the body of a dying woman then where is mercy? The poet is appalled by his own emotional vacancy and vows to remember the moment in all its horror:

> Her agony slides through me: I am glass
> That grief can find no grip
> Save for a moment when the quivering lip
> And the coughing weaker than the broken wing
> That, fluttering, shakes the life from a small bird
> Caught me as in a nightmare? . . .
> Those coughs were her last words. They had no weight
> Save that through them was made articulate
> Earth's desolation on the alien bed.
> Though I be glass, it shall not be betrayed,
> That last weak cough of her small trembling head.[18]

More than most of the writers and artists in Germany that summer, Peake had come with a clear sense of mission; he had felt that he could somehow lessen human antagonism by illustrating the images of war. In his view, this was the role of the writer or artist in a time of crisis. Writing to his wife from Paris on the way to Germany, he told her that he would not forget 'the reasons which prompted me to try and go to where people suffer. I will miss you desperately, but I will be proud to do something which we both believe in.' Once there, he found in the sights of ruined Germany a version of his own grotesque style; here were the shapes of his imagination given architectural and human form. However, he was no longer sure that sketching them was going to do much to save humanity and it was a relief to join the Old Vic troupe in Hamburg and relax into the more familiar world of the theatre. Peake drew Olivier in his costume with a false nose as Richard III and joined in the theatrical parties. None the less his wife reflected that he seemed to have changed dramatically when he returned from Germany in July. 'He was quieter, more inward-looking, as if he had lost, during that month in Germany, his confidence in life itself.'[19]

These visits to Bergen-Belsen went some way to convincing Thorn-dike and Peake of the validity of the non-fraternisation policy. If most Germans had been complicit in the concentration camps – if it was culpable simply not to protest – then they could not be treated as friends. But the problem remained that the Germans could not continue as the enemy indefinitely and that re-education was only going to occur through interaction. On 12 June the law was changed so that British and US troops were allowed to speak to and play with children. The Americans were now less committed than the British to the non-fraternisation rule and it seemed likely that it would be overturned within the next few months. But if they were no longer going to behave antagonistically to the Germans, then how were they going to convince them of their guilt? This was the question that confronted the film-maker Billy Wilder when he arrived in Germany in June, sent by the US to be partially responsible for film in the American zone.

An Austrian-Polish Jew, Wilder had been a successful film-maker in Berlin before emigrating to the US after the Nazis came to power in 1933. Arriving in New York aged twenty-eight, Wilder spoke no English but he had always been impertinently resourceful so he managed to persuade friends to give him work in the film industry. As in Berlin, his rise to success was rapid and by 1945 he was an obvious candidate for the govern-ment to send to help reconstruct the German film industry and determine how to use film as a vehicle for democratic propaganda. Wilder was furi-ous with both the Austrians and the Germans, whose anti-Semitism he had always recognised, and wanted little to do with any of them, but he was keen to find the whereabouts of his mother and grandmother, whom he suspected may have died in concentration camps. In May he travelled to London as the production chief for the film, theatre and music control section of the Psychological Warfare Division (PWD). His role was initially to advise on the kind of films to be produced in Britain for German consumption during the postwar years.

At this point a documentary of concentration camp footage was being prepared in London, intended to record the German atrocities

and to convince the Germans of their guilt. In February, Sidney Bernstein, chief of PWD's Film Section, Liberated Areas, had told General
McClure that the Soviet authorities were preparing to make a film
using concentration camp footage and that he thought the Western
Allies should do the same. McClure was reluctant, believing that films
exhibited in Germany should demonstrate 'the way of living in democratic countries' rather than showing war footage. Bernstein began to
watch footage produced by the Americans liberating the first concentration camps and then visited Bergen-Belsen on 22 April to record
sound interviews with British officials and the German SS, wanting to
produce definitive proof of the German atrocities. He now persuaded
McClure to let him make a full-length documentary as a combined
Anglo-American production, aiming to convince the Germans to
forsake National Socialism and, 'by reminding the German people of
their past acquiescence in the perpetuation of such crimes, to make
them aware that they cannot escape responsibility for them, and thus
to promote German acceptance of the justice of Allied occupation
measures'.[20]

When Wilder arrived in London the film was already in production.
Alfred Hitchcock was advising on the final cuts with editors Stewart
McAllister and Peter Tanner. Wilder's task was to watch hour after hour
of concentration camp footage, helping select scenes for the film. As he
sat through sickening shots of crematoria, ash piles and lampshades
made of human skin, he waited anxiously to see whether he would
recognise his mother or grandmother in the piles of skeletal corpses.
Asked years later about the footage, Wilder remembered one scene in
particular: 'There was an entire field, a whole landscape of corpses. And
next to one of the corpses sat a dying man. He is the only one moving
in this totality of death and he glances apathetically into the camera.
Then he turns, tries to stand up, and falls over, dead. Hundreds of
bodies, and the look of this dying man. Shattering.'[21]

In the middle of June 1945, Wilder was sent to Germany via Paris.
Initially he was based at Bad Homburg, the spa town near Frankfurt
where McClure's PWD had its HQ. Sections of both the British and
the US occupation forces were headquartered in spa towns that formed

odd havens of undamaged, self-satisfied German *Gemütlichkeit* amid the ruins. The headquarters at Bad Homburg were more military than the equivalent British HQ at Bad Oeynhausen in Westphalia. The PWD had set themselves up in a barbed-wire enclosed compound that had previously been a training facility for German railway workers. It included twenty-five houses, a large auditorium, a mess with a bar and a kitchen. Wilder was reporting to McClure and working closely with his deputy, an American colonel called William Paley who was in charge of operations. He became friends with both Paley and his assistant, Davidson Taylor, who was responsible for the Film, Theatre and Music Control Section. Wilder and Paley managed to concoct elaborate dinners in Paley's kitchen, using a broken toaster as a barbecue and eating food that Wilder bartered for cigarettes in the German country-side. Wilder especially enjoyed the straightforwardness of this male companionship because it followed a period of unusually complicated womanising in LA, where his marriage was in jeopardy because he was having simultaneous affairs with two actors, the twenty-one-year-old Doris Dowling and the twenty-two-year-old Audrey Young.

Paley and Taylor now became so frustrated by the slowness of Bernstein's film in London that they decided to make their own concentration camp documentary in Bad Homburg. The Russian film-maker Sergei Nalbandov had already been trying to assemble some of the footage; now Taylor suggested that Wilder should take over and prepare the script. The film would then be assembled in Germany under Wilder's supervision. Wilder began some work on this project but in the meantime McClure decided to test screen a two-reel preview of the atrocity documentary from London entitled *KZ* (*Konzentrationslager*). Cinemas were officially closed to German audiences until July, but the army opened a selection of cinemas advertising a series of films including the innocuous-sounding *Welt im Film no 2*, which was the *KZ* documentary masquerading as a newsreel.

Wilder and Taylor attended one of these screenings at the Licht-spiele in Erlangen on 25 June. The other films advertised included *Duke Ellington and Orchestra* and *Cowboy*. They reported that when the title *KZ* appeared on the screen there was a gasp throughout the audience. Expressions of shock and horror were audible through-out the screening; whether because the audience resented being hoodwinked into watching the footage or because the atrocities came as a revelation is unclear. Their report went on: 'When the title "Buchenwald" came on the screen, the audience spoke the word almost as one man. The atmosphere was electric throughout the film, and a palpable feeling of incredulity ran through the audience when the narrator said that the wife of the commandant at Buchenwald had made lamp shades from tattooed human skin. We have footage showing this collection of tattoos and why it was not used I cannot say.'[22]

After the documentary was finished three women left, looking ill, but the rest of the audience waited for the cowboy film that had been advertised and were disappointed to learn that the programme was in fact over. Wilder and Taylor seem to have been surprised that anyone should want to see a film about cowboys after being exposed to lamp-shades made of human skin. But this was the first cinema screening the Germans had attended since the Reich Minister for Public Enlighten-ment and Propaganda Joseph Goebbels shut the cinemas in 1944. They had been overwhelmed already by shots from the concentration camps on posters and noticeboards erected by the Allies. And they were hungry, homeless and worn down by years of war and months of occu-pation. The previous summer James Stern had suggested that the German guilt was 'so colossal they simply cannot face it, much less give it expression'. What Wilder saw as callousness may simply have been bemused horror; a helpless sense of guilt that brought with it a desper-ate desire for escapism.[23]

The scepticism of the audience about some of the footage in the documentary convinced Taylor of the urgent need for a longer and more verifiable film so he continued to try to persuade his superiors that Wilder should make one. Wilder was keen to do this. As far as he was concerned, his role as a film-maker in Germany was to convince the German people of their guilt. He was too angry to be interested in enabling the kind of mutual tolerance demanded by Spender or Auden. But it was not at all clear that he would be granted permission, though it seemed absurd both to Taylor and Wilder that the Americans had sent one of their most successful film-makers to Germany without forming a clear idea of what he should do there. McClure did not seem especially convinced that Wilder should be film-making at all.

This indecisiveness and inefficiency was typical of both the American and the British bureaucracies. The difficulties were partly the result of a lack of clarity about responsibility at home. In the US, both the Department of State and the War Department felt they had the right to determine matters in Germany. In Britain responsibility for the Occupation had been passed from the War Office to the Foreign Office, and then back again. Both bureaucracies were excessive and the British in particular had far too many employees who were unclear about their exact tasks. The British CCG (Control Commission Germany) had already earned the nicknames 'Charlie Chaplin's Grenadiers' and 'Complete Chaos Guaranteed' from an admittedly biased army. Returning from Germany in June, Richard Crossman complained that the British Military Government officials were trying to implement countless detailed regulations without a picture of the overall policy: 'Not one of the dozens with whom I talked has the vaguest idea what the end result of it all is meant to be. Is Germany to be dismembered? Is there to be a Central German Government? Or is Military Government to take its place? What forces in Germany should replace Nazism and Militarism? Will there be co-ordination between the four occupying Powers and if so, in what form?' [24]

Part of the problem, for the divisions responsible for the arts at least, was that the exact policy of the Western Allies on culture remained unclear. There was still a widespread sense that it would be wrong to put time or money into entertaining a country with whom they remained at war. The British Control Commission was restrained by a government anxious not to irritate a war-weary populace by seeming to treat the Germans anything but stringently. On 5 July, Churchill's Conservative government was replaced by Clement Attlee's Labour party in a landslide victory won with Attlee's pledges for a welfare state.

Having promised the British free schools and healthcare and an improved standard of living, it was going to be hard to justify deflecting British food to Germany, let alone supporting the revival of German culture.

In this respect the Soviet zone was far ahead of the British and US zones, liberated culturally by the very different Soviet attitude towards denazification. For the Russian occupiers, denazification was not a question of the mentality of individuals but of the structure of society. They believed that once capitalism had been replaced by communism, the threat of German fascism would be eliminated. Therefore they could be more lenient towards individual Germans than their western counterparts, who were set on a course of individual rehabilitation that necessitated a period of German guilt.

As head of the Political Department of the Soviet Military Administration, Major General Sergei Tulpanov was in charge of both culture and politics in the Soviet zone and was convinced that the two were inextricable. Through culture the Russians could persuade the world that the country of Pushkin and Tolstoy was a civilised one (and that the excesses of the Russian soldiers were mere accidents of war) and could convert the Germans to the communist cause. Tulpanov's assistant, the art historian Major Alexander Dymschitz, was open-minded and liberal and knew far more about German history and literature than most Anglo-American officials.[25]

From the start of the Occupation, the Russians decided that culture in Germany would be very different from culture in the Soviet Union. Recently the German communist politician Anton Ackermann had issued a manifesto suggesting that German culture needed to be organised on broad, anti-fascist democratic principles rather than along the stricter lines of communist culture in Moscow, where he was living in exile. Bourgeois art could be encouraged and satire could be tolerated. Later Tulpanov said that Germany was given its comparative cultural freedom because at this point it was in a state that resembled the *Sturm und Drang* period of the Soviet Union in the 1920s; the Germans were not yet ready for Stalinist culture.[26] The Russians therefore gave the Germans a relatively free hand in resurrecting the film studios and printing presses in their zone and set about reviving the musical and theatrical scene. It would be a while before the Western Allies caught up.

———

While Wilder waited to find out exactly what was required of him, Auden was posted to Bad Homburg as well. The bombing survey was almost completed and he was being dispatched home earlier than expected. Predictably his debriefing took several weeks longer than it needed to, but his stay at Bad Homburg was enlivened by the arrival of another expatriate Ussbuster, the composer Nicolas Nabokov. An aristocratic Russian by birth (and the cousin of the writer Vladimir Nabokov), Nabokov had left Russia after the Revolution and had lived a happily cultured expatriate life in 1920s Berlin and Paris before emigrating to the US after Hitler's rise to power. Now an American citizen, Nabokov combined old-world European charm with new-world ease and means. He was destined to be a success in postwar Germany, although his months as an Ussbuster had been dispiriting.

Nabokov's first impressions of Bad Homburg were inauspicious. Arriving on a cold summer night at 3 a.m., he surveyed the dining hall and found that it was strewn with debris. There were empty beer cans, gin and whiskey bottles, broken glasses and filthy paper napkins scattered across the floor. Unable to find any coffee or gin, Nabokov spread his sleeping bag on the bar and fell asleep. He woke up to find a face leaning over him saying: 'Why, for God's sake! What are *you* doing here in this place?'

Clean-shaven and washed, Auden was ready for his breakfast and was irritated to find that the dining room was still dirty and occupied by sleeping Ussbusters. He was pleased, however, to see his friend. Nabokov and Auden spent the next couple of weeks walking in the pine woods and drinking on the terrace where they talked about Stravinsky, Goethe and Kierkegaard. Both were keen to avoid their Ussbustian colleagues.

'Most of them are crashing bores, my dear,' Auden complained to Nabokov on his first day. 'They have *no* or *wrong* ideas about everything and belong to the world that neither you nor I can possibly like or condone.' Auden was impatient with the debriefing sessions they were forced to sit through, which he saw as comprised chiefly of bogus socio-political jargon. 'All of this is *waste*, my dear. But it better remain that way. It is none of *our* concern.'

Despite his insouciance, Auden remained troubled by the destruction he had witnessed in the German cities, unable to see how devastation on that scale could be condoned: 'Are we justified in replying to *their* mass murder by *our* mass murder? It seems terrifying to me, don't you agree?'[27]

By the time that Auden's stay came to a close in August, summer seemed to be over and the compound was enveloped in a continual grey mist. The night before Auden left, he and Nabokov sat in an empty room next to the bar with private supplies of gin and whiskey from their rooms. Auden asked Nabokov if he planned to stay in Germany and Nabokov sought his friend's advice. Nabokov himself had escaped communist Russia for the US and he was now worried that the Americans underestimated the brutality of conditions in the Soviet Union. He was rightly anxious about the fate of the Russian Displaced Persons imported by the Nazis to Germany who were being sent back to the Soviet Union. Visiting DP camps in Hanover and Hamburg, he had been besieged by outstretched hands reaching out to him with bits of crumpled paper announcing in Cyrillic script that the bearer had a friend in Chicago or New York. He was now wondering about staying in Germany as an anti-Stalinist and offering his services to the PWD.

Auden said he could not answer his friend that late in the evening and suggested they had coffee at 6.30 the next morning before he left. Nabokov arrived in the breakfast room shortly after the appointed time and was reprimanded for being eight minutes late. They sat in silence sipping their institutional coffee while Auden returned grumpily to the crossword puzzle he was engaged in solving. Eventually Auden looked at his watch and complained that he was meant to be leaving in six minutes but could not see the bus.

'Now about your question, Nicky,' Auden said impersonally. 'My answer to it is neither yes or no, or rather neither stay nor go – it is *entirely* your own business. I'm sorry, Nicky, you've got to make up your own mind. No one can, or should, make it up for you. It would be improper and wrong.' He paused to smile at his friend. 'But if you do go to Berlin, I may perhaps come and see you there. May I?'[28]

The bus arrived; Auden stood up to leave and gave Nabokov one final homily: 'As for the substance of your question, it is indeed horrid and monstrous! It is barbarous to send people back to hell without even asking them for their consent! But then, what humans do to each other is usually messy . . . and a *sin* against God's laws. Nicky, whatever you do, keep well . . . and drop me a line.'[29]

Auden did not visit Nabokov in Berlin after returning to the US. Neither did he write the book he had wondered about writing about Germany. Since moving across the Atlantic, Auden had lost interest in pontificating as a public intellectual, so he was not going to pen any essays on the state of Germany or Europe. And it took four years before he could find in the German ruins material for poetry.

In 1949 Auden returned imaginatively to the barbed wire and battered buildings, attempting to find a personal mode of redemption. His poem 'Memorial for the City' opens from the perspective of 'the eyes of the crow and the eye of the camera' with which Auden and his strategic bombing unit had been required to survey the bomb damage in Germany. Now these lying eyes range across the cities of the world, from Homer's time to the present, settling briefly on a place across the square between burnt-out lawcourts and police headquarters, where barbed wire runs past the cathedral 'far too damaged to repair', around the Grand Hotel 'patched up to hold reporters', near the 'huts of some Emergency Committee', traversing 'the abolished City'. This is the familiar world of Frankfurt or Darmstadt, evoked in all its specificity. But it is also the world of poetic nightmare because:

> Across our sleep
> The barbed wire also runs: It trips us so we fall[. . .]
> It keeps on growing from the witch's head.

Auden used the wartime bombsites to ask why we build cities when we then annihilate them, bending our creative ingenuity to making instruments of destruction. But he was writing with a detachment enabled by time and distance; with a detachment that seems to have been necessary for him before he could write about the ruins at all. Therefore he juxtaposed this recent history with the history of Christendom, seeking redemption through the Christian faith that he had embraced ten years earlier:

> As we bury our dead
> We know without knowing there is reason for what we bear,
> That our hurt is not a desertion, that we are to pity
> Neither ourselves nor our city;
> Whoever the searchlights catch, whatever the loudspeakers blare,
> We are not to despair.[30]

―――

Shortly before Auden left Bad Homburg for London, Spender arrived at the British headquarters in Bad Oeynhausen. He was two months behind his friend but he had made it at last and he was determined to be as useful as possible, although he was sad to leave behind his new son Matthew who had been born in March. His mission was to investigate the intellectual climate of German universities in the Rhineland. This was a task that suited him well, enabling him to meet some of the Germans he had known before the war, though his superiors made it clear that he had been sent as a German-speaking intellectual rather than a poet. His remit was education rather than literature.

In the report of his trip later published as *European Witness*, Spender described Bad Oeynhausen as 'a large sprawling nineteenth-century health resort, full of ugly villas'. The architects had surrounded each villa with a skirt and bodice of billowing trees, so that today they flaunted their last-century modesty like middle-aged over-dressed women. The villas were absurdly accoutred with ornate towers and domes. This smugly comfortable spa town had now been filled with army signs and with British soldiers hurrying around in heavy boots. Their mess tins and red tape struck an anti-romantic note against a background that should be filled with shepherds.[31]

Spender was briefed on his tasks by a former Oxford don who was now an army brigadier. His chief assignment was to interview German intellectuals. This meant that he was exempt from the non-fraternisation rules, which had anyway been relaxed once again so that the Allies could now fraternise with Germans in public places. He was anxious to start immediately but was forced to wait in Bad Oeynhausen while transport could be found for him. While there he bumped into Goronwy Rees, a London writer and celebrated cad with whom Spender had once collaborated in translating Büchner's play *Danton's Tod* (*Danton's Death*). Rees found Bad Oeynhausen even more sinister than Spender did. He thought that the smug and stuffy atmosphere suggested that the oppressive mood of Bismarck's Germany remained unscathed. And he felt that the unreality of the spa town was harmful for the occupiers. 'It was rather as if the Germans, having conquered Britain, had decided to govern it from Llandrindod Wells.' But as the senior intelligence officer for William Strang, the political adviser to the commander-in-chief, Rees was now based at a separate headquarters in Lübeck, where he took Spender for the night.[32]

Rees told Spender about the destruction he had seen in the Ruhr, where broken arches and girders projected crazily into the sky, and the dead cities failed to provide food, water, shelter or heating – able to support the life only of rats. Over the next few days Spender made his way slowly to Cologne, driving past bombsites and destroyed bridges in a car that repeatedly broke down along the way. Arriving in Cologne on 11 July, Spender saw the jagged rubbish confronted earlier in the spring by Miller and Orwell and realised for the first time what total destruction meant. His initial impression was that there was not a single house left standing. The walls were merely insubstantial masks in front of the hollow and putrid emptiness of gutted interiors.[33]

Ten years earlier Spender had been to Cologne when it was the hub of the Rhineland, with a large shopping centre and streets full of bustling restaurants, theatres and cinemas. It took a great effort of the imagination to juxtapose the Cologne he remembered with the putrescent corpse-city of today; he could not believe that the thousands of people trudging through the blackened streets were the same crowds that had been window shopping or hailing taxis a few years earlier. It was only the cathedral that reminded the onlooker that this had been a great city. Spender was sure that the devastation was too great ever to be healed. Where in London the surrounding life of the people filled up the gaps and wounds left by the bombing, here the inhabitants became parasites sucking at a dead carcass as they dug among the rubbish for food.

In the published account of his visit to Cologne, Spender described the destruction and reflected that it was serious in several senses:

> It is a climax of deliberate effort, an achievement of our civilisation, the most striking result of co-operation between nations in the twentieth century. It is the shape created by our century as the Gothic cathedral is the shape created by the Middle Ages. Everything has stopped here, that fusion of the past within the present, integrated into architecture . . . that long, gigantic life of a city has been killed . . . The destruction of the city itself, with all its past as well as its present, is like a reproach to the people who go on living there. The sermons in the stones of Germany preach nihilism.

All the visitors to defeated Germany had to confront the apparent meaninglessness of absolute ruin. Gellhorn and Miller had taken refuge in anger; Auden had been silenced by despair. Here Spender performed the dexterous feat of locating meaning specifically in meaninglessness. This nonsensical rubble was fitting as the architectural achievement of his times.[34]

Having observed the wreckage, Spender's next task was to interview the inhabitants and to see if any kind of redemption could be found from the nihilism that surrounded them. As well as seeking out intellectuals, he interviewed people he met along the way. Early on he talked to six DPs whom he found sitting on a bench gazing dully out over the Rhine. At first he thought they were German POWs returning home. They were angry to be mistaken for 'German swine' and announced that they were Poles, who had lost all their relatives when the Germans burned their towns, hanging people on trees. They were dismissive of the sensitivity with which the British were now treating the Germans: 'you calculate the rations they should have, as though they were being cared for in a hospital'. Spender felt frightened by their apathy and frightened, too, that there seemed to be a menacing quality in their despair. The fires which had burned the cities of Europe were still smouldering in the minds of men.[35]

The first German Spender actively sought out was his former teacher and mentor, the literary critic Ernst Robert Curtius. When Klaus Mann had interviewed Curtius a couple of weeks earlier, he had found him ominously 'unchanged' and arrogantly contemptuous of the 'barbaric Americans' occupying Germany. Spender was more disposed to be sympathetic toward the older man, having spent much of the war worrying about his safety; indeed it was partly with Curtius in mind that Spender had first thought of coming to Germany. In his 1939 'September Journal', Spender had recalled his first talk with Curtius at a Bierhalle in Baden. Here Spender had behaved with the same good-natured clumsiness with Curtius as he had with Auden, talking constantly and indiscreetly about his life in Hamburg. Curtius laughed, apparently at as well as with the younger man, leading Spender to reflect that 'because he saw so far beyond me and at the same time loved me, I owe more to him than to any other person'. The pair walked in the Black Forest, swam, discussed literature and drank beer in the evenings.[36]

The friendship was erotically charged. They read carnal poems in a Greek anthology together and Curtius asked Spender for pornographic details of his encounters with boys in Hamburg. But it was primarily an intellectual exchange. When Spender had left Oxford without a degree, he was frustrated that his tutors seemed to have little to teach him. Now at last he had met someone who seemed never to lose sight of the direct connection between literature and living, making Spender feel that he could grasp hold of the literature they read and use it to live better. Through Curtius, Spender made contact with the Germany of Goethe, Hölderlin and Schiller; a country he described in Nietzschean terms as 'an Apollonian Germany, a Germany of the sun, not the Germany of Hitler who rouses himself from a torpid dullness into a frenzy of words and actions'. He also learnt from Curtius an understanding of a connected and continuous tradition of European literature that stretched from the Greeks and Romans through to the Middle Ages and on to the present and made it impossible to separate one nation culturally from another.[37]

It was partly with Curtius in mind that Spender had written his articles about Hölderlin and Goethe during the war. Now both Spender and Curtius were married (Curtius to a former student) and both had endured five years of brutal war. Spender was relieved to find that although half of Bonn was destroyed, Curtius's ground-floor flat was in an almost untouched part of the city. Curtius was moved to see Spender and took him into his library, a bare empty room with no carpets and few books, where his wife Ilse supplied a meal of cabbage and potatoes.

Curtius was one of the few German intellectuals Spender respected who had stayed in Germany throughout Hitler's regime. Spender now tried to work out what this meant. Since 1933 he had wondered why his mentor did not leave Germany and had decided that it was because Curtius felt too rooted in the Germany of Goethe to imagine life elsewhere. Initially Curtius's flat had provided a hub for people to come to upbraid the Nazi regime, usually from a Catholic point of view. The Nazis made his life difficult and Spender assumed that he had eventually compromised in one way or another to avoid being imprisoned. He was disappointed to find that Curtius shared the general tendency to dismiss the Germans collectively without including himself in their shame. Curtius was not a Thomas Mann, seeing in his own German Romantic past the seeds of Nazism. Instead, he told Spender blithely that there was almost no intellectual life left in the whole of Germany and that it would have been impossible for German intellectuals to put up a collective resistance against Hitler: 'You seemed to expect us to stand up or go out into the street and say that we opposed the war and the Party. But what effect could that have had except our own destruction? It certainly would not have stopped the war. It was not we in Germany but you, the democracies, the English, the French and the Americans, who could have stopped the war at the time of the Occupation of the Rhineland. What were we to think when you let Hitler march in?'[38]

There was considerable truth in this. Certainly, there was an element of hypocrisy in the Allied outrage at the concentration camps, given that when Britain and then the US did wage war against Germany it was in response to German imperialist aggression rather than to the Nazis' blatant disregard of human rights. Even now many of the Allied leaders placed more emphasis on the Prussian militarism of the Germans than on their persecution of the Jews, and were not doing as much as they could have done for Hitler's Jewish victims.[39] And Curtius was correct that even when it came to imperialist aggression, the Allies had allowed a generous degree of leeway. He was probably also right that, for most intellectuals, active resistance would have resulted in clear consciences but dead bodies. However, Spender was not so much disappointed that intellectuals such as Curtius had failed to resist as disturbed that they did not seem more conflicted now. He was saddened, too, by the indiscriminate criticism of the Occupation made by the Curtiuses and other intellectuals.

People in Bonn complained that the Americans had been too slow in liberating the Rhineland and especially Bonn, dismissing the German offensive in the Battle of the Bulge as a few shots made by frightened SS men. 'We can understand that American civilisation is unwarlike and that the Americans do not want to practise military virtues,' one professor said patronisingly, 'but you have no idea how difficult it is being conquered by a people who can't fight. Everything happens so slowly.'[40]

––––––––

Gradually, Spender became exhausted by the scale of ignorance on both sides. Even the German-educated elite seemed unwilling to admit their culpability, while many of the British officers he spoke to seemed ignorant of Nazism and its evils. Several officers told him that they sympathised with the Nazis because they were fellows who stood up for their country, whereas the refugees were rats who had let their country down.

Already it was clear that the process of denazification was absurdly unfair. Millions of Germans had been presented with *Fragebogen* (questionnaires) asking 133 questions over the course of twelve pages, described by the visiting Swedish novelist Stig Dagerman as 'a kind of ideological equivalent of tax returns'. These were designed to ascertain the interviewees' relation to Nazism and militarism but asked along the way whether the bombing had affected their health and about their sewage, electricity and drainage.[41] Many Germans were rightly outraged to be presented with these forms. The names of the interviewees were drawn at random and there was an element of absurdity in the selection. There were questionnaires assigned to some Germans who had been imprisoned in concentration camps and to some former high-ranking Nazis including Hermann Göring's wife Emmy Sonnemann, who filled in the form in Straubing prison while her husband awaited trial. And to many Allied officials the results of the *Fragebogen* seemed almost irrelevant. Americans granting newspaper licenses ignored the forms and elected instead to get potential applicants drunk, believing that inebriated conversation was more revealing than sober box-ticking.[42]

Attempting to make sense of the tragic-comic chaos surrounding him, Spender became overcome by a sensation of nausea that was as physical as mental. This began with a feeling of violent homesickness. He lay on his bed reading French books which consoled him because they had been written in a world where plans, thoughts and relationships could grow. In Germany, Spender felt that it was impossible to create a free atmosphere in which good could take root and develop. The Germans had deprived themselves and the rest of Europe of freedom and in the process had turned Germany into a ruined prison where the Allies served as unwilling jailers.

Retreating back to Paris in August, Spender analysed his nausea and decided that the people of Europe were faced with a choice. They were now familiar with a kind of destruction that they had never previously contemplated. It was quite possible to imagine any town in Europe pulverised into a desert of rubble. The idea of destruction had become oddly fascinating and people had to decide collectively whether to embrace or resist it. For Spender, it was essential that a new pattern of world society designed to secure peace should come into being. It would be modelled according to the necessities of future world-unity and not according to existing interests. The ruins of Germany testified to the need for a united Europe: 'behind London, Paris, Prague, Athens, are those shadows, those ghosts, the destroyed towns of Germany which are also the part of the soul of Europe which has collapsed visibly into chaos and disintegration. Their ruin is not just their ruin, it is also pestilence, the epidemic of despair spreading over and already deep-rooted within Europe, the black foreshadowing of the gulf which already exists in us – the gulf which we can still refuse.'[43]

Thwarted by both the British and the Germans, Spender was no longer so optimistic that it was possible to reconcile the spirit of JCS 1067 with the spirit of Thomas Mann. Like Auden and Wilder, he was giving up on the possibility of having any impact on Germany. Instead, he sought a higher ideal in a vision of European unity. This was in part inspired by the prewar ideals of Curtius, though he had lost some faith in the man himself.[44] From now on Spender would be less concerned with reviving culture in Germany than in attempting to bring about a shared cultural vision for Europe.

5

'Berlin is boiling in sweltering summer heat'

Berlin: July–October 1945

On 2 July 1945 Berlin was officially opened to the Western Allies. Since the city had fallen to the Russians in May, very few British or American soldiers had been allowed in. An American reconnaissance party of 500 men had been turned away on 17 June on the grounds that the Western Allies had still not retreated to the demarcation lines agreed at Yalta. The handful of western journalists who managed to reach Berlin reported on the strangeness of seeing the German capital strewn with Russian signs and Slavic faces; even the clocks were aligned to Moscow time. They were also struck by the unusually vertical quality of the ruins. In parts of the city centre there was street after street of ghostly façades, defying gravity in their refusal to topple.

Now advance units of occupation forces arrived to set up communication facilities and prepare for the troops. Billets were in short supply so they camped in the Grunewald, the forest to the south-west of Berlin. The next day a train of sixty jeeps brought the first British, US and French troops and foreign correspondents into the city that for six years of war and two months of occupation they had been waiting to claim as their own. On 12 July four-power rule officially began in Berlin. Each commandant was to take a fifteen-day turn ruling the city and the Western Allies were now responsible for importing food across the Soviet zone to feed people in their sectors of Berlin.

Partly because the city had been closed for so long, the entry to Berlin now took on the excitement that crossing the Siegfried Line into Germany held during the latter stages of the war. Amid the persistent cosiness of their headquarters in German spa towns, or amid the crumbling opulence of The Ritz in Paris, British and American soldiers, officials and journalists waited impatiently to be sent into the former capital of the Reich. And they were not disappointed by what they found. Corpses still lined the streets, the ruins stank, but one by one the nightclubs and bars reopened; even in tatters Berlin retained the excitement and edge of its hedonistic past. For its conquerors, Berlin became the site of a summer-long cocktail party taking place against the backdrop of an overheated morgue.

Erika Mann was on one of the jeeps entering Berlin on 3 July. She had returned to Germany in June, going straight to Munich where she registered a claim on the family house. Unlike Klaus, Erika remained determinedly unsentimental while visiting the lost city of her childhood, staying clear of the remains of Poschinger Strasse. This was more difficult in Berlin, which she described in an article as 'one of the most unreal places imaginable'. Here was ruin on an even greater scale than she had seen in Aachen or Munich. The city centre seemed 'a kind of lunar landscape – a sea of devastation, shoreless and infinite'. And the resourcefulness of the inhabitants made the landscape all the more unreal. Well-dressed men with dispatch cases climbed piles of debris looking for goods to sell on the black market; German girls on bicycles smiled and flirted with Amerian GIs; in a large tenement building she found someone playing a Prussian marching tune on a miraculously intact piano. Erika was angered once again by the lack of obvious guilt. Moving swiftly and talking loudly, these people seemed to have no idea that they had deprived her of her home.[1]

Erika Mann's arrival was closely followed by the appearance of the German novelist Peter de Mendelssohn, who was now a British citizen garbed in army uniform and assigned to be in charge of newspapers for the Western Allies. Initially, he was employed by the Americans; his task was to investigate the journalists remaining in Berlin and license a newspaper in their zone. On 15 July de Mendelssohn wrote to his wife, the Austrian novelist Hilde Spiel (who was waiting at home with their children in Wimbledon), describing his first impressions of the city where he had once lived: 'Berlin is boiling in sweltering summer heat, and the stench and odour that rises from the canals and river arms of the inner city, still packed with thousands of rotting human bodies, make one really sick . . . In a few days this town is going to be a cesspool. Again, as with most other things in Berlin, one can only say: there has never been anything like this anywhere before.'[2]

De Mendelssohn and Spiel had spent the war in London saving pennies and dodging bombs. Successful writers in Berlin and Vienna in the 1930s, they had found themselves starting again in a new language and a new country, struggling to forge a new reputation in exile. Initially, de Mendelssohn had been reluctant to return to Germany, unwilling to undertake the task of going to reform that 'band of thieves and murderers and abject criminals' who remained. But now he was revelling in the unfamiliar luxury and power. Both de Mendelssohn and Erika Mann were stationed with other British and American officials in the south-west suburb of Zehlendorf, which was relatively untouched by the bombing. Here the air was clean and birch trees swayed gently in the summer breeze. There were French windows open onto the terrace and drinks on the coffee table and it was hard to believe that they were only minutes away from some of the worst destruction the world had ever known.[3]

De Mendelssohn was making the most of the culture that had started reviving within days of the fall of Berlin. In the 1920s, Berlin had been one of the creative capitals of Europe; a city where new intellectual and artistic ideas could flourish and new art forms like the cabaret and the cinema could take flight. This was the home of German Expressionism (created in part by immigrants from Russia who brought Soviet art and theatre to the city) and of the International Modern Style. It was natural that Billy Wilder had gravitated to Berlin from Austria; that Klaus and Erika Mann had made their way there from Munich, seeking the city that Klaus referred to as 'Sodom and Gomorrah in a Prussian tempo'; that W. H. Auden, Christopher Isherwood and Stephen Spender had moved there from London, allured by the city's atmosphere of artistic innovation and sexual freedom. If there was going to be a postwar German cultural revival to combat the years of Nazi repression then it seemed inevitable that it would take place in Berlin.[4]

On 12 May the ban on film and theatre that Goebbels had imposed on Germany had been lifted and a few days later the German bass baritone Michael Bohnen had found himself in front of the remains of what had once been the Theater des Westens in Charlottenberg. The outer walls were still standing but there was no sign of a roof; the stage was burned out and the orchestra reduced to a mass of rubble; corpses littered the balconies. Bohnen wandered up and down in front of the ruins, shaking his head. A couple of hours later he realised that he was no longer alone. There were two former stagehands and a chorus girl beside him. Then three musicians appeared, announcing that they had heard a rumour that the theatre was going to be reopened.

At this stage there was no press or mail in the city but none the less singers, painters, stage hands, prompters and ballet masters quickly learned that the theatre was opening again. They found their way to the shell of the theatre and began sweeping away debris with their hands, burying corpses and building a makeshift roof. Once the renovations were underway, Bohnen sat in the corner auditioning singers and musicians and examining sketches by scene painters. He began to hire people, though he had no money to pay them and the denazification orders meant that he had to turn away seventy-five good singers and musicians who had been members of the NSDAP. Seats were brought in from other destroyed theatres; a curtain was patched together from scraps of old material. On 15 June, only a month after the repairs had begun, the theatre reopened with the new name of the Städtische Oper (Municipal Opera House). From the start every performance sold out, attended both by Germans and Russians. Here at least there were none of the anxieties about fraternisation that beset the British when they reopened the circus in Hamburg.

This was the first of many theatres to reopen in Berlin in the early months after the war. Every day the Soviet-licensed newspaper, the *Berliner Zeitung*, listed performances and auditions occurring throughout the city. To put so much energy into reviving theatres when people were dying of starvation all around them seemed somewhat mad, or at least it would have done anywhere else. But it made sense here, if only because this was the spirit of old Berlin. For the performers and theatre enthusiasts starving in the ruins, the theatre offered a means of keeping going in a city it would be easy otherwise to give up as dead.

On 13 July, Peter de Mendelssohn saw Schiller's *Der Parasit* (*The Parasite*) in what he thought an excellent production at the Deutsches Theater in the Soviet sector. This was the opening night and it was a special performance with all seats reserved for the 'victims of fascism'.[5] He told his wife that the theatre stood in a completely bomb-shattered neighbourhood just off the Friedrichstrasse but was itself remarkably unharmed: 'To the left and right there is just ruins. The theatre has not a scratch, inside there isn't a spot on the deep red velvet and plush of the seats, not a spot on the white and gilded ceiling, not a glass bead of the lovely old chandeliers has fallen or broken. It was a memorable evening.'[6]

Unfortunately, *Der Parasit* was withdrawn after two weeks. The play ended with the words 'Justice! You only see that on the stage!' Hearing this, the disillusioned Berliners tended to applaud over-enthusiastically, disgruntled at the injustice of the Occupation. The outraged authorities closed down the play. But for every production that closed there were another five waiting in the wings to take its place as the strange cultural frenzy continued.[7]

De Mendelssohn found that it was easy to succumb to the creative energy igniting the city and wondered if he was wrong to do so. He was appreciative of the Germans' attempts at cultural renewal but like Spender he was sceptical about the intellectuals' assumption that they remained unscathed by Nazism and could therefore continue as normal. Meeting a group of Berlin intelligentsia at a party, he was astonished by the way they all asked naturally after German exiled writers such as Carl Zuckmayer and Thomas Mann, assuming that the continuity of life which had somehow been preserved for them had also been preserved by these writers in exile. Was it vanity, he wondered, or illusion, or incomprehension of what these years had meant to the rest of the world? But he could see that there was little point disapproving of the Germans for their ignorance. As the party wore on he began to feel that the Russians, Americans and Germans shared an instinctive belief that it may be better just to leave things as they were: 'not go any further into the whole argument of guilt, innocence and responsibility, knowledge and ignorance at any rate on this level of educated civilised people . . . there might be an advantage in having a tacit agreement to leave this whole complex alone, not to wake the sleeping lion'. [8]

They had succumbed to the charms of the Berliners and of their strange ruined city. The Allies may have defeated the Germans in war but the Germans looked set to challenge the Allies in peace.

———

The US sector of Berlin was initially administered by Floyd Lavinius Parks's 1st Airborne Army, but on 5 August 1945, James Gavin's 82nd Airborne Division was assigned to replace them. Gavin arrived on 25 July, after an enjoyable few days of leave with Gellhorn in the US, and spent his time reconnoitering the city. Returning to Europe, he had found it 'wonderful to be back into things again', reporting proudly to Gellhorn that he was 'boiling along at top speed'. But it was more fun when she was there to speed along with and on 1 August he begged her to join him: 'Darling everything I do and everywhere I go I think of how it will look when you are here and how it will look to you.' He was anxious about her fidelity; neither of them was especially monogamous by nature but he was determined that their relationship should not be on a 'ships-that-pass-in-the-ETO[European Theater of Operations]-basis'.[9]

Four days later the 82nd took over the US sector and Gavin assumed his seat on the Allied Kommandatura. The tasks facing him were enormous. Of the 245,000 buildings in the city, 28,000 had been destroyed and 20,000 were so badly damaged that they could not be rebuilt. It was the only city in Germany where you could walk for two miles without finding a single habitable house. There were Berliners living with five or six people to one room in basements. The Russians had arrived with typhus and venereal disease, which meant that 10 per cent of the 110,000 women raped in Berlin had been infected with syphilis and gonorrhoea that they were now trying to treat without antibiotics. Erika Mann may have convinced herself that the swift-moving and loud-talking Berliners were unfairly prosperous but throughout June there were a hundred Berliners a day dying of typhus and paratyphus carried by human lice. In a sermon in Dahlem in July the anti-Nazi theologian Otto Dibelius had complained that the mortality figures in Berlin were rising rapidly. Before the war, 200 people a day had died in the city; during the war this had risen to 250; now it was around 1,000, even though the population had shrunk. The Russians had made efforts to feed the Berliners, delivering 188,000 tons of food in three months, but there were still chronic shortages. Children were dying for lack of milk so it was disastrous when the Russians rounded up the remaining ninety cows in a farm in Dahlem and sent them back to the Soviet Union at the end of June.[10]

'Well the town is ours, what is left of it,' Gavin told Gellhorn. He had been drinking Armagnac with her friend the photographer Robert Capa, rationing his mentions of her name for the sake of discretion. He was now preparing to work with the Russians, unimpressed by their extensive looting of the US sector: 'Even the telephones were ripped out and shipped back to Russia, but a funny thing, they shipped all of the telephone directories back with them. Like children. I believe they really figured the directories would work in Russia. Probably spend most of their time dialing the chancellery and asking for Adolph Hitler.'

The Russians were not alone in extracting reparations from Germany, but they were certainly less discriminating in their looting. They felt entitled to be callous at the end of a war that had resulted in the deaths of between 23 and 26 million Soviet citizens. This was one person in eight of the population and dwarfed the 405,399 American dead. Unlike the Americans, the Russians had experienced the brutal invasion of their homeland, fleeing from the invading Germans in the summer of 1941; they were now determined to exact revenge.[11]

One of the first acts Gavin performed in his new role was to set up a telephone conversation between Marlene Dietrich and her mother,

Josephine von Losch. Dietrich had received no news of her mother during the war and had worried that she was being persecuted on account of her daughter's defection from Germany or hit by the Allied bombs. Generals Patton and Bradley had both sent in emissaries to locate Josephine early in July and discovered that she had in fact survived. Now Gavin arranged for a phone conversation, recorded for posterity. Speaking in English because of the censors, Marlene assured her mother that both she and Liesel were well:

> 'Mami, you suffered for my sake. Forgive me.'
> 'Yes, my love.'
> 'Mami, take care of yourself.'
> 'Yes. Goodbye.'
> 'Goodbye, Mami.'
> 'Goodbye, my heart. Goodbye.'

Gavin then set about arranging a travel permit for Dietrich to come to Berlin and visited Josephine himself. 'PLEASANT VISIT WITH YOUR MOTHER SHE IS FINE THE 82ND IS LOOKING FORWARD TO SEEING YOU SOON GENERAL GAVIN,' he reported by telegram.[12]

Gavin was expected to fine-tune his policies in Berlin on the basis of the results of another two-week conference between the Allies, which had been made public on 3 August. This time the British, Russians and Americans (now represented by Harry Truman, who had taken over as President following Roosevelt's death in April) had met at Potsdam, to the south-west of Berlin, to discuss once again how to take measures to ensure that 'Germany never again will threaten her neighbours or the peace of the world'. The resulting document insisted that it was not the intention of the Allies to destroy or enslave the German people: 'It is the intention of the Allies that the German people be given the opportunity to prepare for the eventual reconstruction of their life on a democratic and peaceful basis. If their own efforts are steadily directed to this end, it will be possible for them in due course to take their place among the free and peaceful peoples of the world.'

The chief purposes of the Occupation were described as disarmament, demilitarisation, denazification (which also involved convincing the Germans that 'they cannot escape responsibility for what they have brought upon themselves' and bringing the war criminals to judgement), democratisation (preparing the way for renewed democracy in Germany) and re-education. No specific mention was made of culture but the agreement opened the way for denazification, democratisation and re-education to be pursued partially through cultural means. The victors also agreed to establish a 'Council of Foreign Ministers' from Britain, the US, the Soviet Union, France and China who would meet periodically to negotiate the terms of peace treaties with the Axis powers.[13]

The Allied-licensed newspapers in Germany responded respectfully to the results of the Potsdam Conference. 'The German people are granted the possibility of reconstructing their lives on a democratic and peaceful basis,' the *Berliner Zeitung* proclaimed. But the Germans were generally too preoccupied with questions of day-to-day survival to be interested in these cogitations. When Bertolt Brecht's 1928 play *The Threepenny Opera* (*Die Dreigroschenoper*) opened at the Hebbel Theater in the American sector a week later, the audience applauded riotously at Brecht's famous words 'first comes food, then morality' ('*Erst kommt das Fressen, dann kommt die Moral*'), hoping that their occupiers could learn this lesson. The Berliners were more concerned with actions than words and were reassured to see that their city was gradually being reconstructed. By 14 August mail had resumed and there were over 300 Berlin postmen back at work; 10,000 telephones were now in service again. Gradually, the trams began to run, with eighty-three trams traversing a distance of twenty-two miles.[14]

On 6 and 9 August 1945 the world's first atomic bombs were dropped on Hiroshima and Nagasaki. It was immediately apparent that the world would never be the same again. This was the moment when the US lost its sheen as a guarantor of freedom both for many of the German exiles who had proudly taken American citizenship and for many of its native citizens. Klaus Mann complained that his adopted country was not going to 'stop fooling around with devastating gadgets before they'll have blown up our whole little universe . . . Not that I think it would be a major loss if our earth went to pieces!' It was in response to the atomic bomb that George Orwell coined the phrase 'cold war' in a *Tribune* article entitled 'You and the Atomic Bomb', where he stated that the world was heading 'not for general breakdown but for an epoch as horribly stable as the slave empires of antiquity'. Presciently, Orwell suggested that the atomic bomb would paralyse the world by making its strongest nations 'at once *unconquerable* and in a permanent state of "cold war"' with their neighbours.[15]

Possessing the atomic bomb gave the Americans new confidence in their position in Germany. Now the Germans knew that the US had this new weapon at its disposal, surely they would not be so foolish as to risk another war? And if Germany was no longer capable of waging war, perhaps it was less necessary laboriously to change every aspect of German life. Perhaps they could just be left to their own devices and pathologies. On 7 August, Eisenhower and Montgomery had issued statements to the Germans assuring them that they were there to help rebuild their life on a democratic basis. Montgomery promised that soon they would have the freedom to determine their own mode of living, subject only to the provisions of military security. Drew Middleton reported in *The New York Times* that the political rehabilitation of Germany was expected to progress at a faster rate than previously planned. The US would start reducing the army in its zone and attempt to restore a central German government.

On 15 August, Europe celebrated Victory in Japan (VJ) Day and James Gavin took stock of the end of the war. He admitted to Martha Gellhorn that although he abhorred the brutality of war he would miss 'the excitement of it, the companionship with fine men that it has given me and the deep appreciation of simple things'. Back in the US, he had the tedium of a failing marriage and life in an army base to return to. He was unlikely to seduce a woman like Gellhorn again. Brought up in an orphanage and then adopted by coal miners, his own origins were humble; his first jobs had been in a newsagents and a barbers' shop. He was aware that if they had met in the US he would not have been in Gellhorn's league and that returning home he would be defined by class instead of rank once more.[16]

But although the war was over, Gavin's tasks were more difficult than ever. With his troops gradually diminishing, he attempted to embark on the impossible task of reconstructing Berlin. He told Gellhorn that he had never worked so hard with so little sense of accomplishment. 'I feel like a small boy trying to hold the dam but the dam has about a hundred holes in it.' He was aware that the situation would become more difficult as winter set in. There was no coal allocated to the Berlin civilians so he was sure that people would starve and freeze. The railroads and bridges had still not been repaired, which made it very difficult to transport food to Berlin through the Russian zone. 'When a train leaves the US zone and enters Russia on the way to the US sector of Berlin it may as well have gone off Cape Cod into the Atlantic.' Sometimes trains took five hours and sometimes five days. Against this background, he felt Gellhorn's absence more than ever. She was due to arrive in London in September and he was determined to find a way to bring her to Berlin as a correspondent.[17]

While he waited for Gellhorn, Gavin was pleased to entertain Billy Wilder, who arrived in the city in early August, instructed to investigate the film studios in the US zone and to begin reviving the German film industry. Wilder was billeted with the 82nd Airborne Division and he set about getting to know the soldiers and exploring the town. For Wilder, this was a homecoming in a way that his arrival in Germany had not been. Twenty years ago he had fallen in love with Berlin, discovering a way of life exactly suited to his own frantically speedy personality. Now he found that 'it looked like the end of the world'.[18]

He asked his driver to take him to the cemetery where his father lay buried, in the Soviet sector. The Jewish burial ground had become a battlefield in the final days of the war and it was now scattered with blasted headstones, burnt trees and tank tracks. They were met by an emaciated rabbi and a one-legged gravedigger who informed Wilder that it would be difficult to locate his father's grave. Wilder's helpless rage for the plight of the Jews was exacerbated when he heard the terrible story of the rabbi, who had survived the war in Berlin by remaining in hiding for years. When the Soviet soldiers appeared in April, he and his wife had rushed out to greet them, delighted to be liberated at last, but the rabbi was forced to watch as the conquerors raped and killed his wife.

Wilder felt sorry for his city but he had no sympathy for its Aryan inhabitants. When a German shouted '*arschloch*' at him and his driver while they were speeding down the Kurfürstendamm, he stopped and reprimanded him, telling him to wait while he summoned the authorities. He was delighted to find that his assailant was still standing there hours later when he drove past again.[19]

Between forays to the haunts of his youth and drinking sessions with Gavin's troops, Wilder visited the film studios as instructed. He reported that UFA's Babelsberg studios in the US sector were in good condition but absurdly, the Tempelhof studios were cut in half by the demarcation line between the US and Soviet sectors: 'The gentlemen who thought out this demarcation line certainly qualify for a new vaudeville act: sawing a live studio in half.' The word 'live' was inappropriate because the heart and the lungs had been removed; the Russians had taken all the usable equipment back to the Soviet Union. However, Wilder was no longer a dedicated employee of the PWD. What he now wanted to do most of all was to make a film for Paramount, his own production company, set in the Berlin ruins.[20]

'I found the town mad, depraved, starving, fascinating as a background for a movie,' he wrote in a report to his superiors on 16 August. He was impressed by the speed with which the Americans were opening up the cinemas and exhibiting their documentaries and by the newsreels that carried with them a lesson, a reminder and a warning. 'A good job has been done, no doubt.' But once the novelty wore off it would be increasingly difficult to deliver the lesson. The Germans would not come week after week to act the guilty pupil. They would be happy to watch glamorous Hollywood films, of course, but these could play very little part in their re-education: 'Now *if* there was an entertainment film with Rita Hayworth or Ingrid Bergman or Gary Cooper, in Technicolor if you wish, and with a love story – only with a very special love story, cleverly devised to help us sell a few ideological items – such a film would provide us with a superior piece of propaganda: they would stand in long lines to buy it and once they bought it, it would stick. Unfortunately, no such film exists yet. It must be made. I want to make it.'²¹

The film he was proposing was the simple story of an American GI and a German Frau, whose husband had been killed in action. At the start the German woman would have nothing to live for; by the end she would have recovered a little hope. Cannily, Wilder quoted Eisenhower to support this message: 'let us give them a little hope to redeem themselves in the eyes of the world.' The GI was not going to be a flag-waving hero: 'I want him not to be too sure of what the hell this was all about.' The film would touch on fraternisation, on homesickness and on the black market. In the end the boy would not get the girl; he would go back home with his division while the girl left behind would see the light. Wilder had spent time in Berlin, had talked to Gavin and his troops, and had fraternised with Germans from bombed-out university professors to 'three cigarette-chippies' in the nightclubs. He had almost sold his wristwatch at the black market under the Reichstag and he had secured the copyright to songs by Friedrich Holländer, the composer of the songs in *The Blue Angel*. He was ready to go home and write the script.²²

It seems astonishing that within two months Wilder had come so far from sitting watching reel after reel of concentration camp footage, recoiling helplessly from the scenes he was witnessing. If PWD had been more appreciative of him, he might still have been making the atrocity film. But he was foremost a film-maker and he remained a Berliner. He was not going to stay and fight his way stickily through red tape. He was going to go home and make a comedy set in that 'mad, depraved, starving, fascinating' town. What was more, he already knew who he wanted to play the Frau. He was going to attempt to persuade Marlene Dietrich to take on the role of a Nazi whore.

———

Although Wilder's time in Berlin had not been especially successful for the PWD, employees of the newly rebranded Information Control

Division (ICD) continued their attempts to revive the film industry without him.[23] In the three months since the end of the war, the US occupation authorities had abandoned their plans for a 'very austere program' of reconstruction, increasingly aware that they needed to compete with the Russians for popularity and influence. Both the British and the Americans were now committed to using culture as part of their re-education initiative, though there was still no clear policy on how this was to be done and limited dialogue between ICD and its British equivalent (the British Information Services Control Branch) and the departments responsible for education or denazification.[24]

The first cinemas to reopen in Berlin had been in the Soviet sector but there were now twenty functioning cinemas in the US sector as well. The Germans were also starting to attend plays and concerts in all the sectors. The Americans had considerable work to do if they were going to catch up with the Soviet cultural programme in Germany. In Berlin in particular the Russians had made the most of their head start to race ahead in commandeering the city's cultural institutions. Within days after the end of the war they had taken over the Nazi Reichskulturkammer (Reich Chamber of Culture) in Charlottenberg and instituted a committee to verify the status and politics of Berlin's artists and intellectuals using the Nazi files still housed in the building. Leading writers, poets and actors were classified for Class II rations, placing their dietary needs in the same category as *Trümmerfrauen,* only just below those of 'heavy labourers and workers in hazardous trades'. Presided over by the actor-director Paul Wegener, the building was renamed the Kammer der Kunstschaffenden (Cultural Workers Chamber) and endowed with departments related to music, literature, theatre and cinema. On 3 July the Russians had appointed the German communist writer Johannes Becher to run a new 'Kulturbund zur demokratischen Erneuerung Deutschlands' (Cultural Alliance for the Democratic Renewal of Germany). Becher had recently returned to Berlin in June after twelve years of exile in the Soviet Union. A successful writer in Germany before Hitler came to power, he was delighted to have a chance to help direct the postwar cultural scene.[25]

Ostensibly, both the Kammer and the Kulturbund were vehicles for cross-zonal co-operation. The Kulturbund was not officially a communist initiative and had the potential to create a consensus between liberal and communist intellectuals, especially given that the Russians were prepared for the artistic scene in their zone of Germany to be freer and more controversial than that in the Soviet Union. In this respect, Becher was an ideal choice to run the Kulturbund, which he wanted to be an organisation for the intelligentsia in all four sectors, enabling them to provide a model for the renewal of the German people on a new and progressive basis. The Kulturbund was now housed alongside the Kammer in its building on Schlüterstrasse, with its home in the British sector giving it the potential to cross boundaries in this way.

As a reasonably liberal socialist and a German writer who went against Thomas Mann in celebrating a 'good' German tradition embodied in the Enlightenment humanism of Goethe, Schiller and Lessing, Becher endowed bourgeois German artists who had compromised with Nazism with the moral respectability of communist affiliation at the same time as he granted the communists artistic integrity by affiliating the party with Germany's greatest artists and intellectuals.[26] He had widespread support among the intelligentsia in all zones, especially when he established a club in Berlin for cultural figures called Die Möwe ('The Seagull'), which provided literary Berliners with unrationed food and warmth and then founded the Aufbau Verlag in August, publishing books that had been banned during the war years or written in exile. He quickly became the cultural gatekeeper for émigrés to approach when hoping to return to Germany from the US, Britain or the Soviet Union.

But Becher's popularity among the German intelligentsia was treated ambivalently by the Russians. His commitment to reviving Germany through the 'true German cultural values' represented by Enlightenment humanism and given form by the writings of Goethe, Schiller and Lessing went against communist orthodoxy. Tulpanov worried that Becher was catering to what the intelligentsia wanted rather than leading them and was therefore reluctant to give him free reign. And the

British and Americans, too, were becoming suspicious of Becher and of both the Kammer and the Kulturbund, which they saw as too similar to the Nazi cultural organisations and too allied to Soviet ideals of culture. It seemed anomalous that these Soviet-sponsored bodies were operating in the western sectors of the city.[27]

There were signs that the existing East-West co-operation in the cultural sphere was going to be difficult to maintain. Because the Russians had been so hasty in reviving culture across the city and because theatres and other cultural venues were unfairly distributed between the sectors, all four of the Allies were now organising and supporting cultural ventures in each other's territory, which created the need for complicated negotiations. At the same time they were ultimately responsible for all that occurred within their own sectors. This would have been difficult enough if they had all been disposed towards compromise but in fact the political agendas in Washington and Moscow tied the hands of even the most conciliatory cultural officials.

At the start of August the Russians closed a production of the American playwright Thornton Wilder's *Our Town* at the Deutches Theater after only two days. The play had been put on by a collective of former members of the Deutsches Theater, who had been naïve in thinking that an American play was going to be acceptable in the Soviet sector. A few days later the theatre critic Paul Rilla explained in the *Berliner Zeitung* that the play had demonstrated excessive formal experimentation and concern with 'private emotions': 'why not instead a new, robust dramatic form and up-to-date content?' Nicolas Nabokov, now appointed to Berlin to be in charge of music for the Americans, struggled with the intransigence of both the US and Soviet governments. Going to see *Madame Butterfly* in the Soviet sector with an American general, he found himself required to explain the plot of the opera. When he learnt that it involved an American officer impregnating a Japanese girl and then returning home to marry someone else, the general was furious. 'You knew that *they* were going to permit the Krauts to put on American uniforms and go through that . . . insulting . . . that slanderous rigmarole! And you didn't *do* anything about it! You didn't protest?'[28]

Nabokov was discovering that the problems of quadripartite government were magnified in Berlin: 'Berlin was only *more* corrupt, *more*
decadent, *more* degenerate than the rest of Germany, and its ostenta-
tious morbidity was more apparent because it was the seat of the most
emasculated government in the world: ineffectual, cumbersome and
absurd.' He was frustrated because he was caught between the practical
impossibility of housing and feeding orchestras (did trombonists really
need more calories than string players?) and the political impossibility
of mediating between East and West. His role in Germany was to
'establish good psychological and cultural weapons with which to
destroy Nazism and promote a genuine desire for a democratic
Germany'. One of his tasks was to track down the Soviet administra-
tors in charge of the press, radio, film, theatre and music in their sector
and to persuade them to establish a Quadripartite Directorate of Information Control so that there could be clear cultural policy across the
sectors. He had expected establishing a directorate of this kind to be
difficult but he had not expected it to be so hard just to find the Russians
concerned. For two months he ate caviar with charming and taciturn
Soviet officials who were unable or unwilling to tell him about any of
their colleagues' job titles or responsibilities. It was all the more difficult
because the Russians kept trying to convince him that he was one of
them – 'we need composers in Russia,' Tulpanov urged him – because
he was a Russian by birth, even though he was there specifically as an
anti-communist.[29]

East-West co-operation was even more difficult when it came to
governing the city more generally. At the start of September, Gavin
took his turn as the head of the entire Kommandatura, which he
reported to Gellhorn made him responsible for '887,000 very hungry
but rather docile Krauts'. Their food consumption was 600 tons daily,
which was a 'hell of a lot of potatoes' and involved vast numbers of
trains. The fuel situation was looking disastrous for the coming winter.
He found that the Kommandatura was proving increasingly unwork-
able as a means of solving these problems.[30]

The Kommandatura was built on an inherent contradiction. Because
each representative of the four occupying powers had the power of

veto and the French and Russians in particular were determined to use it, there was no real necessity to work together. In the case of nonagreement their own national policies would prevail. But however ineffectual it was, by its very existence the Kommandatura embroiled the Allies in hours of pointless discussion. Gavin wasted a whole morning debating the relative merits of dry and fresh milk with the British, French and Russians.[31]

Battling with the intransigent Russians and the hungry Germans, Gavin wondered how to restore order in a city that often seemed unruleable. Like Wilder he was caught up in the crazy energy of the ruined town but it was rather less fun if you were meant to be in charge of it. None the less he was sure that all of his difficulties would diffuse if only his lover would appear. 'Darling, all of this doesn't mean a damn thing if I know that you are going to be here,' he told his 'darling Marty'. 'So please, hurry.'[32]

Gellhorn was too slow. On 19 September, Marlene Dietrich arrived in Berlin using travel orders arranged by Gavin. She had been wanting to see her general again for months. After they last met she had told her daughter Maria that they had not slept together because her feelings for him were more a 'fan-type crush' than sexual passion and, perhaps more decisively, because he had not asked her. This time Gavin succumbed more easily. 'I have decided that there will never be any more between us than there is constancy in our hearts and if it is not there there is nothing,' he had written to Gellhorn in July. But he had not seen her for almost three months and the image of the absent woman was swiftly displaced by the presence of one of the world's most seductive movie stars. Here was Marlene Dietrich in army uniform, low-voiced, funny and adoring. The two quickly began an affair.[33]

Dietrich herself was losing patience with Jean Gabin, her film-star lover with whom she was living in Paris. He was jealous and temperamental and they were quarrelling. She was grateful to escape to Berlin, the city where she had been born and where she had begun her career, singing cabaret in nightclubs and seducing cinema audiences as the matter-of-fact showgirl in *The Blue Angel.*

Dietrich was distressed both by the scale of the destruction and by the continual noise created by the American authorities, who were using dynamite to level the ruins. Her former house in Schöneberg had been reduced to a façade, with a balcony still hanging precariously from the wall. When it was first bombed her mother had spent her days searching the rubble for her possessions and had found a bronze mask of Marlene's face still intact. But Dietrich was happy to hear the Berlin dialect again and pleased still to be popular among the locals. 'The Berliners love me,' she told her ex-husband Rudi proudly, 'bring me everything from photos to their ration of herring.' She had been to the theatre and met up with old friends and had even wondered about reviving her pre-war lesbian singing act.[34]

Within days of arriving, Dietrich began performing two shows a day for the army, as popular with the troops as she had always been. When she first had a day off between shows, she sped to Czechoslovakia to look for Rudi's parents. After a nightmarish journey she was told that they had left the Displaced Persons camp they had been assigned to. She returned to Berlin dispirited but found that they had walked all the way to her mother's house from Czechoslovakia. They were shaking with fright because they had been told they were not entitled to ration cards and would have to go to another camp. This was Gavin's rule – a harsh but apparently necessary measure to prevent Berlin overcrowding and starving in the winter – but by the next day Gavin had found heavy-labour ration cards for Rudi's parents so that they would be able to stay.

On 2 October, Dietrich flew back to Paris. Later that day Martha Gellhorn arrived in Berlin. Between the departure and the arrival of his two lovers, Gavin wrote a letter to Dietrich celebrating their ten days together. 'I love you and think you should be on a pedestal. I want you there, that is part of loving you.' He missed her already, complaining that there was now a void in his existence that no one and nothing could fill. 'Until I am in your arms again I will be completely at a loss.' He now had nothing to look forward to at noon, in the evening, at night, any time.[35]

In fact Gavin had the arms of another beautiful woman to look forward to. When Gellhorn appeared later that day she was allocated a room close to his, in the staff quarters of the 82nd Airborne Division, on the grounds that she was writing about the unit's exploits for the *Saturday Evening Post*. The couple resumed where they had left off in June, with Gavin showing Gellhorn around Berlin, and reminding her that bodies were 'something terrific'. The next day he took her with him to supervise the digging of corpses out of the flooded subway. 'I've given up deads since Dachau,' she wrote in her diary; 'the desolation – women working in the rubble. The women with dyed yellow hair and that grey thick German skin . . . Hospital – 30 hunger cases out of 960 patients. Germany should be a colony – will never be a democracy. Forecast Russo-American war . . . Danced 9 hours.'[36]

This was the life that Gellhorn led best. She may have been upset by the corpses and the starving patients, she may have been furious with the undemocratic and sycophantic Germans, but she was able to dance for nine hours with her lover in the continued suspended present of war. They lived intensely together for an ecstatic week, fired with the feverish energy of the city. 'What shall I do when this easy comradely life goes to pieces?' Gellhorn asked in her diary on 10 October. 'Am really unsuited for anything else.' She departed to London the following day and Gavin wrote to Dietrich in Paris, explaining his silence on the grounds that he had been waiting for a visitor who could deliver a letter personally rather than trusting the postal system. He was listening happily to the records she had given him of her singing. He now regretted that they had seen so little of each other before Berlin; he had waited too long to find her. 'You are a wonderful person Marlene, beautiful, lovely, most unselfish.'[37] Gavin was courting Dietrich in the language of her own songs. 'I am made for love from head to toe,' Marlene sang to her Jimmie from the army gramophone with the same Berlin accent that he heard every day on the street. When she sang this song in *The Blue Angel*, she was seducing a stuffy professor who quickly proved unable to resist her charms. Gavin did not see why he should withstand them either.

At one point in the Berlin film Billy Wilder had gone home to write, the James Gavin-inspired soldier-hero explains (in the third person) why he is too busy cavorting with his German temptress to slow down and wave the American flag:

> During the war he couldn't go fast enough for you. Get on that beach-head, get through those tank traps, and *step on it, step on it. Faster* – a hundred miles an hour, twenty-four hours a day, through burning towns and down smashed *Autobahnen.* Then one day the war is over. And you expect him to jam on those brakes and stop like that? Well, everybody can't stop like that. Sometimes you skid quite a piece. Sometimes you go into a spin and smash into a wall or a tree and bash your fenders.

James Gavin himself was finding it hard to slow down. Burdened by the responsibility for keeping a whole city alive and depressed by the prospect of returning home, he was determined to take what excitement the war still had to offer, able only to continue 'boiling along at top speed'. It was possible that he was going too fast; that even he could not sustain simultaneous affairs with two women with quick wits, famous legs and luxuriant blonde hair who had become the darlings of the American army. But he was certainly not going to jam on the brakes and stop.

6

'A pain that hurts too much'

German Winter: September–December 1945

After leaving Berlin, Martha Gellhorn wrote to James Gavin telling him that she did not think they had a future together. 'Dearest Love, dearest Jimmy and darling,' she began, 'I have thought of nothing but you all these days.' She mistrusted herself and she feared the evolution of their love. He would fall more in love with her; she would fall more in love with him; she would create an alluring story about him in her mind, turning him into several people he was not. She would rely on her story, while he would simply rely on her, or on the version of her that existed in his mind. Love was a conjuring trick – 'done with the most beautiful mirrors in the world' – but it was convincing enough that soon they would strive for permanence. Marriage would come next, destroying the illusion as it had with Hemingway, and Gellhorn was sure that she could not marry Gavin: 'I simply could not be a good army wife. I'd be dreadfully bad at it, I know: it is sickening to realise that two people alone are not a world nor even a life; we live in a fixed specific world (I, on the other hand, am only happy if living in every available world and obeying the rules of none), and we live with count-less people.'

She was too old and spoiled to make polite conversation with other army wives and he would grow impatient with her before long. It was important to realise this now, while they were happy together; while she loved him so much that the days seemed 'fuzzy dreams' and she was living suspended in time, waiting to see him again. She was depressed by the prospect of a future without him and she worried that she was doomed to live alone because she seemed to belong nowhere. 'My feet are cold every night without you, and presently I suppose I will be cold throughout.'[1]

Gavin's own feet were cooling rapidly under his American army blankets. Autumn set in early in 1945 and by September it was clear that the winter would be as bad as the pessimists had feared. Already on 23 August, Peter de Mendelssohn had observed to his wife that autumn was beginning and Berlin had ceased to smell; he was anxious that the winter was going to be unendurable and that the Germans were not doing enough to prepare for it. The health and food situation in the ruined German cities was deteriorating quickly. Water was polluted because of breaks in pipes and 80 per cent of sewage in the British zone was not reaching the sewage works. The tuberculosis rate for Germany as a whole was now triple the rate that had prevailed before Germany's defeat. All but one of the forty-four hospitals in the British sector were badly damaged and on 15 October *The New York Times* reported a frightening shortage of medicine throughout Berlin.[2]

The next day there was a ration cut in the US zone, taking the daily calorie count (for those fortunate enough to acquire their full rations) to a debilitating 1,345. In the British zone the daily rate was even lower. During the summer the British had been importing 70,000 tons of wheat and 50,000 tons of potatoes a month from Britain; this was unsustainable and it was becoming almost impossible to feed the Ruhr area, which had previously imported its food from eastern Germany. The 1945 harvest was extremely poor, with rye now 44 per cent and potatoes 45 per cent below the 1943 produce. As a result of the official shortages, people relied more and more on the black market where prices inflated rapidly as demand escalated. There was more food to be gained scouring the ruins for cigarette ends than finding a job clearing those ruins. 'How can I afford to look for work? I have a family to feed,' went a line in a popular joke. That winter 60,000 Berliners died, with 167 committing suicide. For those fighting to keep the population alive it seemed increasingly absurd to think in terms of guilt.[3]

As the days darkened, there were shortages of electricity throughout Germany. In Berlin there was only a current for a few hours a day and people never knew exactly when it would come on. Candles were only available on the black market; light bulbs were a rarity. In theory, each Berlin family was allocated a tree for firewood but it was hard to police this and by the end of 1945 the whole Tiergarten (the large park running through the centre of the city) had been hacked down to stumps. Onlookers were struck by the absurdity of the pompous statues of dead German heroes standing nakedly in a wilderness of mud.[4]

Berlin, which had seemed so alluringly vibrant that summer, now felt unrelentingly depressing for the British and American occupiers, even though they were living in relative luxury compared to the natives they were there to help. Peter de Mendelssohn was determined to winter in London and return the following spring. Curt Riess now found that he could not stay in Berlin longer than a week at a time without becoming depressed. He escaped to the more hopeful atmosphere of Paris or Switzerland every ten days. Visiting the city in November, as part of a larger trip to report on the Nuremberg trials, the American novelist John Dos Passos observed that Berlin was bleaker than the other beaten-up towns: 'There, that point in a ruined people's misery had been reached where the victims were degraded beneath the reach of human sympathy.' He was disheartened to find that the Berliners were too miserable to incite his sympathy. It seemed that sympathy depended on a process of empathetic identification that ceased to function when the gulf between the onlooker and the victim was too great. Dos Passos wondered if this had also been the case for the Germans who had complacently watched the suffering of their Jewish neighbours.[5]

Now stationed in Berlin, Goronwy Rees was also finding the city depressing. He was especially distressed by his own house in the Grunewald, where the German wife and daughter of the former owner had been installed in the basement to attend to his needs. Both were prematurely aged, with dirty white hair and a 'crazed look' in their eyes. And both were devoting their time to trying to keep alive the daughter's baby, who lay day after day in a cot in the shade of the trees in the garden, 'perfectly still, perfectly silent, never uttering a cry either of pain or of pleasure'.[6]

Rees gave the baby his rations and watched as the women fed him milk and smeared chocolate on his lips, waiting for a sign that he was still human. But gradually the whites of his eyes took on the sickly yellow of his face; his stomach became distended and enlarged; he could neither eat nor digest. The baby was starting to resemble a motionless tiny effigy of the kind found on family tombs in country churches. He lay still and unsmiling while the women brushed away the flies that settled on his face. Rees's dreams became haunted by the sight of the two women bent anxiously over the dying baby's cot, watching intently as if they knew that any moment might be his last. And he found that 'it seemed futile and ironical beyond all measure that for me five years of war should end with that scene in the garden where the two bomb-crazy women and their baby presented so perfect an image of what victory really means'.[7]

That dying baby was one of thousands of Berliners who were unlikely to survive the winter. In the British sector the death rate of children under a year old in December 1945 was one in four, bringing new and devastating loss to families already torn apart by the war. As food supplies and healthcare deteriorated, the very young and the very old were especially at risk. On 3 November, Marlene Dietrich's mother, Josephine von Losch, died of a heart attack in her furnished room in Friedenau. She had survived almost six years of war but was too frail to endure the Occupation, despite living more luxuriously than most Berliners. Dietrich was in Paris and asked James Gavin to arrange for her mother's burial. He was worried that he was too visible a figure to oversee the digging of a German's grave so he delegated the task to his PR officer, Barney Oldfield, who conducted four paratroopers to Berlin's Schöneberg cemetery.[8]

Oldfield later recalled the graveyard itself as resembling a Dracula film: there were graves blown apart and coffins on their ends with partial remains spilling out. The whole place stank of death. They waited until it was dark to dig the grave and then at two in the morning they went to Josephine's room where they lifted her body into a casket made from old German school desks, which they transported to the cemetery in an army truck. Later in the morning Dietrich arrived, accompanied by Bill Walton (now the *Time* bureau chief in Berlin, he had made friends with Dietrich in Paris) and by three professional mourners. Dietrich dropped a handful of earth onto the lid and was then led away by Walton. Oldfield waited until it was dark again before fully covering the grave. It was not a ceremonious funeral, but it was far more than any other German received that year.[9]

Dietrich had flown to Berlin from Paris on the same plane as Martha Gellhorn, who was still researching her article on the 82nd Airborne Division. The two women do not seem to have become well enough acquainted on their journey to compare notes on their shared lover. But once they had arrived in Berlin, it was difficult for Gavin to keep his two conquests happy and apart. Dietrich had expected the return to Berlin to involve a reunion with her new uniformed hero. 'Oi yoi yoi is my life messed up,' she had told Rudi from Paris in October; 'I wish I could stay with the Army – There everything is clear and easy.' It was clearer and easier when you had your general to yourself, and she was disconcerted to find that Gellhorn was promptly established as his official mistress. Gellhorn herself had heard rumours about her lover and Dietrich but assumed that it was a minor flirtation, and that Dietrich was one of the many women to be impressed by the general's film-star glamour. This was true, but this time the love-struck fan was a film-star herself. And there were people determined to divide Gavin and Gellhorn.[10]

During this trip to Berlin, Gellhorn was spending considerable time with Charles Collingwood, a radio journalist who was funnier and worldlier than Gavin. Dietrich informed Gavin that his lover was more enamoured with Collingwood than she was with him and Gavin started a jealous scene with Gellhorn. Angry and confused, he told her that he was going out for a walk and then stayed out all night. Bill Walton, himself half in love with Gellhorn and pleased to rupture the relationship with the general, reported to Gellhorn that Gavin had gone straight to Dietrich and that they had been having an affair since the summer. Gellhorn decamped to Paris where the general assailed her with explanatory missives and she replied with a tirade of astonished fury.

'Poor James,' she began, 'the first time I read your letter I was so angry I could hardly breathe.' She had spent the week in anguish – 'like someone who has swallowed a bayonet' – and was now amazed that he had the audacity to blame Walton for the crash. Gavin had held Gellhorn's presence in the staff house responsible for their problems; this was absurd when they had been so happy there in October. And he had provided a resumé of his movements that she considered mere bad manners when the essential facts of his infidelity were unchanged. What was most humiliating was that he was the one initially to demand monogamy: 'I may tell you that you can sleep with everyone you like including sing-song girls and goats, only you can't launch me into a career of absolute fierce faithfulness and expect me to enjoy being made a fool of.'[11]

This is partly the outrage of wounded pride. It was humiliating to be the last one to know about her lover's infidelity. But the brisk anger masked a more bewildered grief. Gellhorn may not have believed that their relationship had any future, but it was still serious on her side. She had entrusted part of herself into Gavin's keeping and expected him to treat it with care. If all that time half of his mind had been with Dietrich, he had been slighting the moment that he and Gellhorn were creating together. And if they did not have that moment then what did they have, in a world of broken marriages, ruined buildings and warring nations? She betrayed her misery alongside her anger. She had believed in Gavin like God – 'you were not only my lover but by golly my hero' – so there had been no need to lie to her when he could have told her any truth he liked. There had been snow in Berlin the night he left her. She had looked out of the window on to the white streets below and seen the beginning of winter and death. 'I stayed in that room weeping as I really did not believe I ever could or would again, for two hours; and every night since it has come back to me the same way, like a pain that hurts too much.' Luckily, she observed curtly, none of it mattered. They were only two, not especially important people and they had a lot of work to do. She was 'furiously angry' about a campaign that had been instituted to save German children while children in Holland, Poland and Greece were starving. She was determined to register protest against whatever forms of 'crookedness' she saw.[12]

Gellhorn's hatred of the Germans had begun during a time of anger with Hemingway and was now swelling during a period of rage with Gavin. There is a lack of proportion here; it is one thing to be moved by the plight of the children in Holland, but quite another to be 'furiously angry' about a campaign to stop another set of children from starving. Even the most militaristic of onlookers tended to admit that German children could not be held responsible for the war. If anyone was crooked, it was Gavin, and Gellhorn's protest was directed against the two-facedness of men who extorted trust and vulnerability only to betray it.

She went to the French countryside to write the report on the 82nd Airborne Division she still owed the *Saturday Evening Post*, describing their heroism through fiercely clenched teeth. The resulting piece is admiring of Gavin and his troops but refuses to take them too seriously. Gellhorn points out wherever she can how much pleasure the division has acquired from the war. In Sicily the wine was copious and the girls pretty; they swam and ate well. In England they indulged in a lot of brawls in pubs. Gavin himself is given his own paragraph of muted praise, seen through the eyes of his men to whom he is known as 'Slim Jim' or 'General Jim.' They love him because he is one of them; he is brave and cheerful in combat, always jumping out of the lead plane first; he wears his hat cockily and has a 'charming Irish face'. He is also, she writes somewhat bitterly, extremely lucky.[13]

The article ends on a note of desolation that reflects Gellhorn's own: 'Now that there is time to think and remember, the feeling of loneliness begins. So many dead, and so many who started straight and young and will not have whole bodies again. Any man who went through part of those 371 days of combat will never be the same; he may forget what changed him, but the change is there.'

Gellhorn does not quite excuse Gavin here, but she is more thoughtfully aware of him as a man shaped by war than she was in the angry letter from Paris. 'Slim Jim' with his hat cocked and his continual good fortune is the kind of happy-go-lucky buccaneer who might fall into the arms of a film-star siren without quite noticing his own hypocrisy. A general who has spent 371 days watching his straight, young soldiers being killed and maimed is too lonely a man to sleep alone by choice.[14]

Wilder's hero asks how he can be expected to jam on the brakes and stop. Sometimes you skid or spin and smash into a wall or a tree and bash your fenders. The real-life general had done just that; his fenders were bruised and he was reeling from the crash. He tracked Gellhorn down in Paris and they had sex once more. She said later that it was 'more exciting physically' than it had ever been but that part of her had already withdrawn. Her relationship with Gavin no longer felt real to her. She had hardened her heart and become worldly in the process; she was now more at home with urbane and ironic men like Collingwood or Walton.[15]

Either on that visit or, more gallantly, once Gellhorn had departed for London, Gavin visited Dietrich in Paris as well. They had dinner and listened to gypsy violin music, indulging in the kind of maudlin, romantic scene that Dietrich loved best. Arriving back to the US in time for Christmas, Gavin sent Dietrich a telegram to say that he was pining for her and wrote to Gellhorn to say that she was part of him and everything he did. He felt ill when he thought about how much he had hurt her in Berlin and he would never do it again. No one had made him feel this intensely in love before; he did not know what he would do without her.

That winter in Germany, the bleakness of the postwar world was becoming apparent. During the war, speeding between the terror of conflict and the halcyon perfection of interludes of peace, it had been easy to fall in love. Gellhorn, Gavin and Dietrich may all have known that love was an illusion, but if the conjuror's mirrors were beautiful enough then it did not seem to matter. In the spring and summer of 1945, driving in jeeps amid the ruins they had conquered, partying in the rubble of Berlin, the headiness of wartime could continue. But there was the stench of the corpses in the bombed cities; there were the sickening scenes in the camps. What kind of love could be idealistic and confident enough to continue in the face of that? Certainly none of them was equipped with sufficient capacity for hope. For all three, love was a means of fighting loneliness and it was a hard battle to win. What they were left with were staged romantic moments that left increasingly little emotional residue behind. This was very different from the kind of love in which even the most ordinary moment is ecstatically charged and in which every experience is half perceived through the eyes of the other. 'Darling everything I do and everywhere I go I think of how it will look when you are here and how it will look to you,' Gavin had written to Gellhorn in August. This was no longer true.[16]

Each of the participants in this glittering but tarnished love triangle left Germany behind that Christmas: Dietrich for Paris and then the US, Gavin for the US, Gellhorn for Java and then for London. And for all three of them, the departure from Germany was an act of defeat. Germany had become a personal dilemma for each of them; Gavin and Dietrich at least were in a position to influence the course of the nation's fate. But their hopefulness about Germany had become entwined with their hopefulness about love. And so the contradictions and ruin of the defeated nation now seemed too difficult to overcome. Victory had proved lonelier and less hopeful than war.

———

Departing from Germany, Gellhorn placed her faith in literature rather than love. She began to write an autobiographical novel responding to her experiences in Germany, attempting a slow and painful process of personal reconstruction. She was one of several of the writers and artists in Germany that winter who sought artistic redemption in the face of suffering that seemed to become more hopeless by the day. In December, an article in the *British Zone Review* proclaimed that efforts were to be made 'to effect a radical and lasting change of heart in the hard-working, efficient, inflammable, ruthless and war-loving German people', asserting that the spiritual regeneration of the German people would be 'the greatest and most durable guarantee of the peace of Europe that we could hope to attain'. There was no doubting the truth at least of the second part of the statement, but most of the cultural emissaries sent from Britain and the US were beginning to doubt whether they could play an active part in it or more fundamentally whether culture could be used to alter the mentality of a nation. Instead their role seemed to be to attempt to describe the indescribable, not necessarily, as Mervyn Peake had initially hoped, in order to lessen human antagonism by illustrating the images of war, but simply to find some kind of order in the chaos and confusion that surrounded them.[17]

When Peter de Mendelssohn had complained that summer that they no longer had 'a vocabulary with which to describe bombed cities', he was in part challenging writers to find a new way to write about total destruction. This was a task that several German writers had already begun; de Mendelssohn himself would soon translate into English the 'inner emigrant' writer Hermann Kasack's *The City beyond the River* (*Die Stadt hinter dem Strom*), one of the first examples of *Trümmerliteratur*, or rubble literature. Now many of the British and American writers and film-makers in Germany began to undertake this task as well, creating works of 'outsider rubble literature' and film in which the German ruins are seen partially or wholly from the position of the occupiers and therefore inflected with questions of guilt and blame. If there were positive effects of sending in artists to Germany amid the conquerors then they took the form of these books and films, rather than of any obvious immediate developments in German culture or changes in the German psyche.[18]

Three British artists were engaged in the task of literary or cinematic creation in the winter of 1945. Stephen Spender had returned to Germany for two months in September, this time inspecting the German libraries that had been closed down in May, and wrote the book that would be published as *European Witness* describing both his trips. The writer Alan Ross was stationed on the Wilhelmshaven naval base that autumn (having joined the Royal Navy in 1941) and wrote his first volume of poems, *The Derelict Day*, as a response to his experiences in Germany. The film-maker Humphrey Jennings had been sent to Germany for two months in September 1945, making a film called *A Defeated People* for the Ministry of Information, aiming to convince the British of the need for the Allied Occupation and of its successes so far.

As they attempted to create art out of the wreckage of a starving and freezing nation, Spender, Ross and Jennings were all searching for symbols of ruin and redemption. For Goronwy Rees, the dying baby in his house in the Grunewald had come to represent a devastated country where very little hope was possible and the notion of 'victory' was absurdly misplaced. That winter, Spender, Ross and Jennings tested one symbol after another, wanting to capture the simultaneous misery of the Germans and their occupiers and of the DPs who still wandered down the *Autobahnen* in rags or lived in constrained poverty in the DP camps.

Ross's German poems depict landscapes that briefly offer the conso-lation of symbolising a nation's hope and despair but then end up simply as debris in all its tedium. 'German gun site' opens with a July sun that 'conveys a meaning into death'. But what that meaning is remains unclear. The poem is essentially a list of bleak images drawn from the gunsite: broken trains, shells 'discarded like cigarettes', damaged bridges, photos of naked girls pinned on the mud walls. Simi-larly in 'Occupation' the poet finds that 'the flat unchanging/ Scene becomes a snare' for the onlooker who seeks to imbue it with meaning. The poet's own failure to find significance in the images becomes symp-tomatic of the occupiers' failure to find meaning in the country they are governing. More bleakly, 'Occupation troops' describes men who have become so used to the familiar aspect of death that they 'no longer notice/ the decaying air' in which they live. Only sometimes at night, walking blindly with girls under cold stars, they are touched with compassion and feel a 'common sense of futility'.[19]

Visiting Berlin towards the end of his German trip, walking through the ruins of the city he had once loved, Stephen Spender found in the remains of the Reichstag and the Chancellery mysteries to be solved, metonyms in need of decoding. The Chancellery in particular seemed 'still full of clues, and almost of footmarks'. There were rooms full of papers; there were the chairs remaining in Hitler's main reception room with the stuffing ripped out of them; there was Hitler's desk with its massive marble top in the garden where it had been flung;

there were the books on architecture above Hitler's bed. Spender wondered if it was these books that would yield the most meaning. The Führer had spent the last months of his life resuming his architectural studies. Perhaps the clue to Nazism lay in Hitler's failure to pass the examination to study architecture in Vienna. 'The architect who failed to build had turned the foundations of every city in Germany to sand.'[20]

People as well as objects were potential symbols; especially people who no longer seemed human. That summer Spender had visited a DP camp and observed that collectively the DPs looked like human animals who had been crammed into a foreign zoo. Now Ross watched the DPs swarming through the streets of Hamburg, picking among the rubbish for scraps and pushing their hand carts and prams through the wreckage and found, like Dos Passos in Berlin, that there was a level of suffering that was dehumanising in its extremity. In Ross's poem 'Displaced Persons', the scavenging homeless search like animals for food. Outcasts in a postwar no-man's land, they are the 'inhabitants of a dead terrain': '*We are, most of all, a nuisance to ourselves.*'[21]

Ross's vision of Germany was unredeemed. Given these poems, it is unsurprising that he was relieved when he was sent home to London at the end of the year. But if his was one of the bleakest and most hopeless accounts of postwar Germany by a British writer, this was partly the result of his medium. Poetry does not require the poet to be practical. As a fellow poet, Spender also thought in imagistic terms and could be similarly despairing. But he was in Germany to be useful and his book was partly a work of journalism that was more hopeful when more pragmatic. Writing his book on his return to London, he found that he was able to find cause for optimism among the German ruins. 'If we can find ten good Germans, we can save the spiritual life of Germany,' he advised. If the Allies could locate ten Germans respected both by their compatriots and the outside world then these model citizens could lead Germany into Europe. It was in this spirit that Spender turned the rubble into a figure of collective destruction that he saw as making an eloquent plea for a comparably effortful collective act of creation that would take the form of forging a European community.[22]

Humphrey Jennings too was determinedly optimistic. His role in Germany was a propagandist one. He was there to make a film convincing the British that the sacrifices they made on behalf of the Occupation were worthwhile. In this respect Jennings had been an obvious person to choose for the task. Working for the Crown Film Unit in wartime London, he had made films reminding the British what they were fighting for – the windy beaches, vulnerably clad in barbed wire, the lunchtime concerts in the National Gallery – using avant-garde montages of sounds and images. He was loyally British and temperamentally sanguine. Despite this, his hopefulness faltered during his early weeks in Germany, when it seemed to him that almost every characteristic that the British strived to cultivate had been lost by the Germans: 'exiled, thrown into gas chambers, frightened, until you have a nation of near zombies with all the parts of human beings but really no soul'.

This vision of the Germans is present in Jennings's film, where we are told that the British will stay in Germany until they are shown definite signs that the next generation will grow up sane and Christian again. However, partly because he was making a propaganda film, partly because of his own idealism, Jennings was searching for a symbol of redemption. He found it in the figure of the German child.[23]

All the visitors to Germany that winter struggled with the question of German children. If they were too young to have perpetrated the evils of the camps, were they innocent enough to provide Germany with hope? Or had they already been sufficiently indoctrinated for re-education to be necessary? Were these years of humiliated defeat going to leave them thirsting for revenge as Hitler had after the First World War? There were few people who thought, like Gellhorn at her most pessimistic, that excessive effort should not be made to feed the German children given that they were tainted by the general German disease. Most people tended to respond more ambivalently. In a poem entitled 'Hamburg: Day and Night', Ross described the bare-footed children walking along Hamburg's Steindamm, dawdling and displaying 'like tickets, their dirty and disfigured limbs'. This image is too depressing to be hopeful but is also too pitiful to be condemnatory.[24]

Like Gellhorn, Jennings was initially sceptical about the innocence of the German children. In Aachen early in his visit he saw a mass of white-Sunday-frocked school children standing tightly together in military fashion and singing 'Lili Marlene' at the tops of their voices as they rushed through the empty streets. These children were too regimented to initiate a new way of life; they had inherited the orderliness of their elders. However, as Jennings spent more time in Germany he saw more cheerful and individualistic youths playing in the street and became hopeful that German children were not as different from British children as he had feared. His film ends with an image of German children dancing joyfully in a circle. This is doubly promising because it echoes a sequence in Jennings's wartime film *Listen to Britain* where the circling children are a symbol of the sustaining nature of British lightheartedness in a time of war. In *A Defeated People* the dancing children become a sign of the playfulness latent in Germany; it is the duty of the British army to stay and cultivate this potential amid the debris. For Jennings art had provided a mode of redemption both for himself and for Germany. Identifying the figure of the German child had enabled him to become less despairing about the postwar world. It had also allowed him to believe in the transformative potential of his own art; to believe in himself as a cultural emissary. This film was going to enable the British to make the Germans less 'hard-working, efficient, inflammable, ruthless and war-loving', as instructed in the *British Zone Review*.[25]

Bumping into Jennings in Düsseldorf in September, Stephen Spender was irritated by Jennings's optimism. He saw him as over-confident in his ebullience and was maddened by 'his Adam's apple, his flapping ears, his pin-head face, and his bumptious expression, which looks odd in a man who now has white hair'. As far as Spender was concerned, the last thing the British needed was a film documenting the activities of the Military Government in Germany. Meeting Jennings again in Hamburg, Spender was dismissive of the film-maker's assertion that the military was doing a tremendous job. According to Jennings, accounts of the looting, raping and shooting perpetrated by the Russians in Berlin were 'grossly exaggerated' and reconstruction was working wonderfully: telephones were working; traffic was flowing in an orderly manner. 'I cannot carry on this kind of argument,' Spender reflected in *European Witness*, where Jennings is half-heartedly disguised with the patronising name 'Boyman'. 'Perhaps I exaggerate, but the homelessness of thousands of people, the ruins, the refugees, the distress, the hunger, haunt me, and since I have no statistical picture in my mind I do not even know whether I exaggerate.'

On the authority of the Oberbürgermeister in Berlin, Jennings said that he did not think thousands would starve to death in Berlin that winter. He admitted that a few thousand might indeed die in the DP camps but did not seem to think this was a relevant factor. 'If he were a German,' Spender complained sardonically, 'for the same statistical reasons, presumably he would not think Belsen a relevant factor.'[26]

Spender's competitiveness with Jennings was unnecessarily puerile. Jennings too had been moved by the suffering he had witnessed though he had chosen not to show this to Spender. If there was a contest for powers of sympathy, the choice between the two men would be close. But for Spender the larger question remained one of postwar humanity's relationship with destruction, where Jennings's concerns were narrower and more immediate. After all, Spender himself had been seduced by Weimar Germany; he had found in the German poets a vision that seemed more cosmic and more profound than anything he could find in England. As a result he, like Thomas Mann, was prepared to see the German dilemma as one that involved the individual and his country wrestling with the Devil in their souls rather than one involving the British supplying the Germans with telephone wires and traffic signs.

Spender's dual vision of Germany as both a political and a spiritual dilemma is evident in *European Witness*, which emerged out of Spender's 'Rhineland Journal', published shortly after his trips in *Horizon*. Here Spender's practical concern as a journalist was to argue for the need for a united Europe and urgently to explain the dangerousness and seriousness of destruction on this scale. But the passage where he described the destruction as 'serious in more senses than one' demonstrated the poet's vision as well as the public intellectual's; attempting to decode the metonyms of the Chancellery or the Reichstag, he was a poet in search of an image. Like Auden, Spender the poet had been rendered silent by the German ruins, though he had found in the London bombsites rich material for poetry during the war. But *European Witness* is none the less as much the work of a poet as a journalist; a poet too frightened by the dead cities to turn them into poems – frightened by the way that the landscapes around him can metamorphose into nightmares.[27]

At the end of *European Witness*, Spender describes the way that the Nazis preoccupied not only his waking thoughts but his dreams for many years. 'And in my dreams, I did not simply hate them and put them from me. I argued with them, I wrestled with their spirits, and the scene in which I knew them was one in which my own blood and tears flowed. The cities and soil of Germany where they were sacrificed were not just places of material destruction. They were altars on which a solemn sacrifice had been performed according to a ritual in which inevitably all the nations took part. The whole world had seemed to be darkened with their darkness, and when they left the world, the threat of a still greater darkness, a total and everlasting one, rose up from their ashes.' For Spender, despite his hope for a new Europe, the darkness remained. It was latent in the faces of the apathetic DPs wandering through Germany and of the embittered Germans who still regretted merely losing the war. It was latent, too, in the nations that had reduced Germany to rubble. The nightmare waited to engulf the Germans and their occupiers alike.[28]

That autumn, the differences between Jennings and Spender were being echoed in the press in a debate between German writers who had remained in Germany and the exiled Thomas Mann. In August, the ageing author Walter von Molo had published an open letter to Mann in various American-licensed newspapers in Germany and in newspapers in the US and England, begging Mann to come back and help reconstruct his homeland and insisting that writers like von Molo himself had stayed simply because they had nowhere else to go. Von Molo characterised wartime Germany as a 'huge concentration camp', suggesting that all Germans were victims and that exile was a privilege. He assured Mann that the *Kulturnation* remained distinct from the *Staatsnation*, representing the real Germany: 'In its innermost core, your people, which has now been starving and suffering for a third of a century, has nothing in common with the misdeeds and crimes, the shameful horrors and lies, the fearsome aberrations of the diseased, who, for this very reason trumpeted so much about their health and perception.'

Mann was unsurprisingly furious. Von Molo claimed to admire Mann but it seemed as though he had failed to read the texts of Mann's postwar broadcasts and speeches before writing to him. This was exactly the kind of easy shedding of blame that Mann deplored. If Mann as an exile was prepared to accept some responsibility for the Nazi crimes then how could von Molo believe that the people who had compromised with Hitler were blameless?[29]

Mann wrote a reply to von Molo headed 'Why I am not returning to Germany', which he sent to the New York magazine *Aufbau* (*Reconstruction*) and to newspapers in Germany. He began by saying that he should be glad that Germany wanted him to return, but that he could not imagine that an old man with his heart weakened by exile could do much to help the prostrated German citizens. It was impossible to wipe out twelve years of exile; to forget the years of wandering from country to country, worrying about passports, while his ears rang with tales of shameful barbarism in his lost, estranged homeland.

Mann reminded von Molo, as Spender had reminded Curtius, that if all the intellectuals had risen up collectively against the regime then the course of events might have been different. As it was, the Germans had not freed themselves. Mann was proud to be a US citizen with English-speaking grandchildren growing up around him in America. He repeated his previous arguments: that there could be no good German and that Mann himself felt identified with 'a Germany that finally succumbed to its temptation and made a pact with the Devil'. Now, as someone tainted with German evil, he was afraid of German ruins: 'the ruins of stone and the human ruins'. But he did believe in Germany's future and hoped that she would find a new way of life in tune with the innermost tendencies and needs of the nation. Behind Germany's isolation had always been her need for love. 'Let Germany renounce her vainglory, hatred and egoism, let her find again her love, and she will be loved.' Meanwhile, he dreamt of feeling the soil of the old continent under his feet and one day, 'if God wills', he would see it again.[30]

Before Mann's reply was published, von Molo's letter was followed by a statement from the novelist Frank Thiess who endorsed von Molo's views and said that 'inner emigration' was more honest and patriotic than physical emigration. In a piece of disturbingly fascist rhetoric, Thiess claimed that German writers needed 'German space, German earth, and the echo of the German people' and then went on to explain his own failure to emigrate as a desire for spiritual growth. During the Third Reich he had assured himself that,

> if I were to succeed in surviving . . . this horrible epoch, I would have won so much for my spiritual and human development that I would emerge richer in knowledge and experience than if I had observed the German tragedy from the balcony and orchestra seats of foreign countries. It makes a difference whether I experience the burning of my home myself or watch it in the weekly newsreel, whether I am hungry myself or simply read about starvation in newspapers . . . I believe it was more difficult to keep one's personality here than to send messages to the German people from over there . . . We do not expect any reward for not having deserted Germany.

Thiess's statement was not endorsed by many other writers. Becher informed him furiously that his letter was 'inappropriate in its timing, its content, and its tone'. But Mann, in his orchestra seat in California, felt helpless in the face of ignorance and blindness on this scale. He complained in his journal on 18 September that Thiess's declaration was 'distorted and provocative' and that the Germans were manifestly '*une race maudite*' (an accursed race).[31]

Mann was saddened to find himself divided from the 'inner emigrants'. He had not always seen 'inner emigration' as cowardly or problematic, as Klaus and Erika did. Indeed, he had been one of the first people to use the term, privately, when he described himself as an 'inner emigrant' in his diary in 1933. Ten years later he had used the term publicly in a speech in Washington where he declared that his own suffering as an exile was comparable to the alienation faced by those anti-Nazi Germans who had remained in Germany: 'Believe me, for many there Germany has become just as foreign as it is for us; an "inner emigration" with numbers in the millions there is waiting for the end, just as we are waiting.'

For Mann, although there could not be a 'good' Germany, distinct from the bad Germany, there could be a *Kulturnation*; Goethe's Germany could survive political strife. And the *Kulturnation* could be kept alive both by inner and outer emigrants. This chimed with the point that both von Molo and Thiess were making now. But like Spender, Mann thought that the 'inner emigrants' should be less self-righteous in proclaiming their own suffering and more sympathetic to the suffering of exiles. For Thiess to be the loyal defender of the *Kultur-nation* and Mann the disloyal deserter was absurd.[32]

Mann's answer to von Molo was published in Germany on 10 October 1945. The Germans remained unconvinced by his arguments and many of the responses to his article echoed Thiess. On 23 October, Edwin Redslob wrote an article in the Berlin *Tagesspiegel* (a newspaper set up in the US sector by Peter de Mendelssohn) comparing German suffering during and after the war to the suffering of Christ on the cross. In December the novelist Otto Flake claimed in the *Badener Tageblatt* that Germany had in fact performed a heroic and altruistic task, demonstrating the dangers of nihilism to the rest of the world.[33]

Mann's rejoinder to these remarks was surprisingly mild. He gave a broadcast insisting that he could help Germany best from California. There he could write articles convincing the many fascists remaining in Germany to renounce their megalomania and persuading the Americans not to let the German children starve. This did little to ameliorate the situation. 'We can achieve reconciliation with the entire world, but not with Thomas Mann,' the Hamburg journalist Herbert Lestiboudois announced in January. Mann-hating had now become a strangely enjoyable pursuit. Mann's son Golo was currently living in Germany, running a radio station for the Americans called 'Radio Frankfurt', and he reported home to America that the Germans were 'profoundly happy' about his father's correspondence with von Molo: 'To have a pretended reason for bitterness, for disappointment, a chance to attack, to lament over fallen moral grandeur – Oh what fun they got out of that!'[34]

Spender, Jennings, Mann and von Molo were all looking, in their very different fashions, for a way to redeem Germany and therefore to redeem the world. This was the mission of their governments as well and as far as they were concerned, one way to do this was to put the Nazis on trial. Those figures who had haunted Spender's dreams throughout the war, sacrificing his own blood and tears, needed to be judged and hanged as public expiation for the nation's sin. That September, the British put the commanders of Bergen-Belsen on trial in the sleepy little town of Lüneberg, forty miles north-east of Belsen. According to Jennings, this was the only town in Germany to lack a filthy smell and be almost untouched by the bombing. For the next two months, German journalists reported dutifully on the horrors revealed in the dock, grateful to have a focus for blame and to see the guilt as individual rather than collective. Watching the trial in October, Alan Ross wrote a poem where he described the defendants as already in the process of dying. 'The faces no longer/ Display emotion, but a sense of failure.' The case had meaning but no valid spirit; 'The world's crime is absolved in unimportant/ Deaths.'[35]

Meanwhile the occupying powers prepared for a much bigger trial. In November the leading Nazis would be placed in the dock at Nuremberg. Excitedly, the German papers listed the senior Nazis about to be judged and found wanting. Prominent space was given to lists of the defendants, each accompanied by a photograph. There is a disturbing element of nostalgia in these accounts of those same men whose images had dominated the German newspapers only six months earlier. If Germany had made a pact with the Devil then she had gained a period of carefree freedom in exchange. It now seemed to both Mann and Spender that the Germans failed to understand that those years of freedom had come to an end. The Devil simply demanded a few more victims be sacrificed along the way.

PART III

Judgement and Hunger

1945–46

7

'You'll hang them anyhow'

Nuremberg: November 1945–March 1946

In November 1945 lawyers, judges and journalists from across the world converged in Nuremberg. A decade earlier this had been the scene of the Nazi rallies triumphantly filmed by Leni Riefenstahl. Then the neat medieval Bavarian city had been swathed with swastikas. Tens of thousands of adoring Germans screamed and swooned as Adolf Hitler, Joseph Goebbels, Hermann Göring and Julius Streicher ushered in a new world. Now Hitler and Goebbels were dead, while Göring and Streicher were confined in thirteen-foot cells in the city jail, furnished only with an iron bedstead, a straw mattress and a wooden table and chair. The city had been bombed and shelled to fragments, leaving its inhabitants living underground in freezing cellars.

That August, Göring and Streicher had been transferred to the Nuremberg jail from a prison in Mondorf-les-Bains, a small town in Luxembourg where fifty-two high-ranking Nazis were held by the Americans. Just before they were moved, the prisoners had received a visit from Erika Mann, the only woman permitted to enter the jail they had constructed out of the former Grand Hotel. This, she wrote in an article for *Liberty* magazine, was an adventure she had anticipated for over twelve years. For a decade these men had wielded power over her family, banning them from publication and listing their names in their black books. Now they were a sad and bedraggled group of delusional prisoners, denied ties and shoelaces, although Göring was occasionally granted a top hat at meal times. The regime here was spartan: pillows were only allowed to prisoners who became ill and food was limited to 1,550 calories a day. None the less, the authorities were determined to keep their more famous Nazis alive. Erika was informed that when a thunderstorm had frightened Göring into a minor heart attack, the creator of the Blitzkrieg had been provided with a mattress for his campbed and breakfast in bed.

Erika Mann was shown around the cells and encouraged to peer at the inmates in their living room, but was not introduced by name. Hermann Göring, former field marshal and commander-in-chief of the German Luftwaffe, was in bed when she entered his cell and she was shocked by the fifty-two-year-old's physical diminution. The prison regime had cured him both of his drug addiction (to paracodeine) and his corpulence. He had lost thirty pounds and his tanned skin now seemed to hang off his face and body. Afterwards she was told that Göring regretted not knowing the identity of his visitor as he would have liked to explain himself to her. If he had been in charge of the Mann case, he would have handled it differently, he claimed. 'Surely a German of the stature of Thomas Mann could have been adapted to the Third Reich.' The others were less conciliatory. '*Du lieber Gott!*' Streicher exclaimed, 'and that woman has been to my room.'[1]

At the end of August, a convoy of ambulances drove the 300 miles from Mondorf-les-Bains to Nuremberg, transporting the most important prisoners to the jail where they would await their trial. The windows were blackened to hide their identity from retributive victims or admiring fans. Erika Mann followed at the start of November, excited by the prospect of witnessing the final humiliation of these men. Since visiting the prisoners in August, Erika had become progressively weaker. She had been constantly moving for five months, never remaining at a single address for more than a few days, catching lifts on army vehicles or driving her own increasingly decrepit car. The nervous and self-righteous energy that propelled her criss-crossing journey across the country was running out.

In August she had told her mother that she no longer had the strength
to write letters. She hardly had enough strength to travel, either, but
she managed to reach Rome in September, to see Klaus for the first
time in three years. Her visit was not a success. Aware that his days as a
reporter were numbered, Klaus was busy trying to make himself indispensable to the film-maker Roberto Rossellini, so there were members
of the crew for the film that would become *Rome, Open City* constantly
present. On their final night they at last had dinner alone and Klaus
spent the evening berating Erika for abandoning him in 1940. 'It might
be that the moment was not altogether well chosen (on your part, I
mean),' she wrote to him afterwards; 'Perhaps it was, though, and I
deserve nothing but reproaches.'[2]

By the end of October, Erika had lost her voice and had to cancel a
well-paid American lecture tour. Determined to write even if she could
not speak, she remained in Europe as a journalist. By the time she reached
Nuremberg, her voice had returned but she was finding the privations of
army life increasingly onerous. Journalists in Nuremberg were billetted in
a tastelessly ornate but barely heated palace, formerly owned by the Faber
pencil family and nicknamed 'Schloss Schrecklich', where they lived in
very basic conditions. Drink was plentiful but the food was largely from
tins; sleeping in makeshift twelve-bedded dormitories, the journalists
woke each other up clambering into bed after late-night drinking sessions.
This set-up was hardly conducive to recovery.

The trial was scheduled to begin on 20 November. The day before it
started Erika Mann met John Dos Passos who had arrived from Berlin.
Dos Passos was an old though somewhat estranged friend of Hemingway's, schooled in the same reportage tradition and determined to
witness history. Having already seen the carcasses of several other
destroyed German cities (in Frankfurt he had found that his surroundings resembled a town 'as much as a pile of bones and a smashed skull
on the prairies resembles a prize Hereford steer'), his first act on arriving in Nuremberg was to seek out the ruins of the 'old city of toymakers
and Meistersingers'.[3]

He found that the view was dominated by the isolated arches of
smashed churches, towering hazardously over the rubble. It was a

bright, cold day so the taller remains were outlined crisply against the sky. In an open space in the rubbish, Dos Passos encountered German women wrapped thickly in coats and sweaters boiling potatoes on a stove improvised from a sheet of galvanised roofing. He asked them where they lived and was directed to the concrete entrance of an air-raid shelter. These people seemed more hostile to their occupiers than the natives Dos Passos had met elsewhere in Germany. He had to duck to avoid a shower of stones flung at him; there was a swastika freshly chalked on the wall. The citizens of Nuremberg were resentful that their town had once again become the setting for a symbolic rallying of power. Ultimately, they stood to gain no more from the trials than they had from Hitler's rallies.

Dos Passos visited the Palace of Justice where the tribunal would commence the next day. It was a dark pink sandstone building half a mile from the old town, pockmarked with bullets and shell holes. Inside, there were German POWs high up on stepladders applying fresh paint to the walls. German scrubwomen garbed in heavy knitted stockings and big boots were scouring the marble floors. The corridors thronged with efficient Allied visitors: American secretaries whose heels clacked cheerfully as they passed; French women with high-piled Paris turbans.

Touring the palace, Dos Passos caught a sudden glimpse of the Nazi prisoners taking their daily exercise. The jail where the twenty-one senior Nazis were now held was connected to the courthouse by a wooden covered walkway and its exercise yard was visible from the windows. Dos Passos was not close enough to perceive their faces and saw only a group of prisoners in American fieldjackets walking briskly apart at equal distance from each other. 'Funny to think those guys may hang in a couple of months,' a voice said behind him; 'they look just like anybody.'[4]

Several of the defendants were household names in Britain and the US. Chief among them was Göring. Then there was Joachim von Ribbentrop, Hitler's foreign minister; Streicher, the publicist of the Nazi Party; Albert Speer, Hitler's architect and Minister for Armaments and War Production; and Rudolf Hess, who had been deputy leader of

'Are you a war correspondent or wife in my bed?' Hemingway and Gellhorn holidaying in Waikiki, Hawaii, 1941.

'You're brave. Nothing ever happens to the brave.' Gellhorn with Indian soldiers of the British Army at Cassino, Italy, 1944.

'Ships that pass in the E.T.O.': Martha Gellhorn (*above*), General James Gavin, Marlene Dietrich (*left*).

Cologne, March 1945. According to Gellhorn, this was not so much a city as 'one of the great morgues of the world'.

The general and the movie star. Dietrich seemed to look each soldier straight in the eye and say: 'You mean something to me. I hope somehow I get through to you that I want to be here with you.'

'Nobody seemed to mind except me.' Lee Miller in Hitler's apartment at 16 Prinzregentenplatz, photographed by David Scherman.

Mervyn Peake, 'Condemned Cell at Belsen with Nazi War Criminal'.

'Madly in love with each other, in the most tragic and mixed up fashion'. Klaus (*left*) and Erika Mann (pictured here in 1930) were often mistaken for twins or lovers.

'An American Soldier Revisiting his Former Homeland'. Klaus Mann in the Manns' house in Poschingerstrasse, May 1945.

Stephen Spender (*left*) – tall, shambling, red-faced, innocent – was assigned the role of disciple, lolloping behind the more self-assured poet, W. H. Auden (*right*), 1945.

Ussbusters: W. H. Auden and James Stern (*right*) in Germany, May 1945.

'A kind of lunar landscape – a sea of devastation, shoreless and infinite': Berlin, 1945.

the NSDAP before he defected by parachuting into Scotland in 1941 and who was now arguably unfit for trial because of his apparently comprehensive amnesia and mental imbalance. Others such as Hans Frank, the governor-general of Poland, and Alfred Jodl, the chief of the operations staff, were less well known. Some had been selected more as representatives of an element of Nazi aggression than for their own criminality.

—

The choice as to which Nazis to try had been a slow and difficult one for the four Allied powers, as indeed had been the decision as to whether to try them at all. Until remarkably late in the day, Winston Churchill and many others in Britain had argued that the Nazi leaders should be shot without trial in a political rather than a judicial act. For Churchill and his supporters (who included the Archbishop of York), a trial would be too dangerous because it would involve making up new laws which the defence could easily undermine. It was the Americans and, somewhat surprisingly, the Russians, who insisted on a full trial; the Americans because a trial would be consistent with the American Bill of Rights and the Russians because they were practised at staging show trials and had no doubt as to what the outcome would be. It was not until the beginning of May 1945 that the British agreed to co-operate in an international tribunal, aware that they would be left in an embarrassing position if the others proceeded without them.

In the months leading up to the tribunal, the Allies had debated how many Nazis to put in the dock. When he planned to shoot the Nazi leaders, Churchill had fifty to a hundred candidates in mind, but it was evident that only a smaller number could be tried formally. By June 1945 the Allies were agreed that some of the defendants would serve symbolic roles: Julius Streicher would represent anti-Semitism and Ernst Kaltenbrunner, head of the Reich Main Security Office, would represent the system of state terror. They also debated how exactly the trial would proceed. The main architect of the charter formulating the principles of the tribunal was the American chief prosecutor, Robert Jackson, a crusader for the rule of law who was determined to set a precedent for a new international judicial standard, while also drawing on the 1928 Kellogg-Briand Pact outlawing war and the 1929 Geneva Convention. Jackson's task was an extremely difficult one. He had to reconcile the Anglo-American common law tradition with the very different civil law traditions of France and the Soviet Union and to devise a list of charges that the British, French and Soviet legal teams would all ratify. In the end the tribunal was founded primarily on American notions of justice; as in the common law tradition, the defendants would be able to defend themselves against clearly formulated charges.

In drawing up the charges, Jackson and his team had to find a way to indict individuals simultaneously for particular acts of terror and for creating the system that produced them. He could use as a basis a list of war crimes drawn up in 1919, but this needed adapting so that the long-planned German aggression would be more criminal than the arguably defensive acts of brutal warfare committed by the Allies.[5] Jackson solved this problem by inventing the charge of conspiracy. The German crimes were worse than the Allied crimes because since 1933 they had engaged in a concerted conspiracy to subjugate Europe. By July, Jackson had divided the charges into four counts: participation in a common plan or conspiracy for the accomplishment of a crime against peace; planning, initiating and waging wars of aggression and other crimes against peace; war crimes; crimes against humanity. The charges were outlined in the indictment published on 18 October 1945 and issued to the defendants the following day.

Most radical of the charges was 'crimes against humanity'. If Nuremberg was to serve as a mode of redemption – to make the world a better, more peaceful and humane place – then it was chiefly through this charge. For the first time, a government was responsible to an international court for its actions not against other nations but against its own people. Specifically, here the German leaders were on trial for authorising torture and genocide against their own subjects, in particular political opponents and Jews, although the mention of the Jews was added as something of an afterthought. According to Article 6c of the charter, they were charged with 'murder, extermination, enslavement, deportation, and other inhumane acts committed against any civilian population, before or during the war, or persecutions on political, racial or religious grounds in execution of or in connection with any crime'.[6]

Everyone involved in setting up the tribunal was convinced that it would have a crucial significance for the Occupation as a whole. Potentially the trial could persuade ordinary Germans of their guilt and provide them with tools for redemption or at least re-education. By officially condemning the senior Nazis, the Allies would make clear what in particular about their actions they saw as criminal. The Germans could then be educated to avoid these crimes in the future. And not just Germans but other warmongering nations would be deterred by the new costs of aggression. In June, Jackson had informed Truman that the tribunal would demonstrate that a war of aggression was a crime and that modern international law no longer accepted that those who incited war were engaged in legitimate business. 'Thus may the forces of the law be mobilised on the side of peace.'[7]

Now, Jackson and the three other chief prosecutors were in Nuremberg. Sir Hartley Shawcross led the British team while Roman Andreyevich Rudenko and François de Menthon headed the Russian and French teams. The judges were the American Francis Biddle (who had replaced Robert Jackson as attorney-general during the war, only to be dismissed once Truman came into office), the British Sir Geoffrey Lawrence (Lord Justice of Appeal at home), the French Henri Donnedieu de Vabres and the Russian General Iona Nikitchenko (vice-chairman of the Soviet Supreme Court and a former lecturer in criminal law).

All of these men were already finding life in Nuremberg claustrophobic. Biddle, who was an East Coast aristocrat and former friend of Roosevelt's, was disturbed to find himself sharing a villa with his alternate, or assistant, complaining in letters home to his wife that he had been returned to 'fraternity life'. He was also distressed that much of the basic furniture had arrived after they did, fresh eggs and milk were unobtainable and there were no lightbulbs bright enough for him to read in the evenings. Frustratingly, the army was unsympathetic to his plight, impatient with a trial that involved bringing over 600 men to kill a mere twenty-one Nazis and with senior officials who seemed unaware that resources were so overstretched that there were GIs living nearby in tents. Luckily Biddle had made friends very quickly with the British alternate, Norman Birkett, a tall angular man who was known in London as one of the great trial lawyers of his day and was generally seen to possess one of the most astute legal minds in Nuremberg. Biddle and Birkett shared a love of literature and the arts, though Biddle's cultural credentials were worn more ostentatiously.[8]

On 20 November 1945 the tribunal began. It was an icy, grey day and Dos Passos found that the courthouse felt warm and luxurious in contrast to the cold outside. Certainly, it would have seemed that way to the town's starving inhabitants if they had been allowed in to witness the events apparently staged partly for their benefit. The courtroom was a dark, wood-panelled room with thick bottle-green curtains and marble surrounds to the walls that smelt of the fresh paint applied the previous day. Because the tribunal was being filmed, the curtains were permanently drawn to exclude daylight and the artificial lighting quickly made the room oppressively hot and bright. The prisoners were already seated when Dos Passos entered, installed on two benches guarded by the white-helmeted American Military Police who were known as 'Snowdrops' on account of their hats. The guards seemed to Dos Passos to have the look of a high-school basketball team, their eager innocence highlighted by the contrast with the worn and crumpled faces of the defendants.

Dos Passos entered the press area, which was on the far side of the room from the prisoners, behind the prosecutors' tables and in front of the gallery for general spectators. This was the most comfortable part of the courtroom; the generously upholstered seats were spaced unusually widely apart. Here he was joined by reporters including Erika Mann, Peter de Mendelssohn, Janet Flanner and William Shirer. Leading journalists and writers from all the Allied nations had come to Europe out of both curiosity and duty. Shortly before the trial began, Erika Mann had encouraged her American readers to attend to the events in

Nuremberg on the grounds that: 'It is incredibly important for the future of mankind to state in front of the eyes of the whole world that there are certain laws and rights for all peoples of the earth and that everyone who transgresses these norms will be held responsible.' Mann and many of her fellow journalists believed that it was crucial that the tribunal receive widespread international attention if they were to succeed in providing a template for the re-education of Germany and a deterrent against future persecution and war. [9]

The opening session on 20 November was preceded by half an hour of frantic whirring as the press photographers snapped the defendants. Once the trial was in progress, filming would be restricted to the cameras installed in sound-proof booths. The onlookers spent the morning staring at the prisoners, whom many of them had seen only on film. Most journalists were surprised by the ordinariness of these men who for years had seemed to personify evil. Deprived of the heroic camera angles and podiums of Riefenstahl's films and of their extravagant uniforms, they looked elderly, sallow and small. Dos Passos found that Göring had the 'leaky-balloon' look of a fat man who had lost a great deal of weight; Hess's 'putty face' had fallen away leaving him with a pinched nose and hollow eyes; Ribbentrop, in dark glasses, had the 'uneasy trapped expression of a defaulting bank cashier'; Streicher looked like a horrible cartoon of a 'foxy grandpa'. He went on to observe the lawyers, struck by Biddle's 'long sanctimonious face' with its tall forehead and thin nose and by the 'indescribable Hogarthian look' of the British. Like so many aspects of the trial, the judges' costumes had proved impossible to standardise. All except the Russians were attired in gowns (though without judicial wigs) where the Soviet judges were dressed in military uniforms that seemed to place an inappropriate emphasis on their dual role as assessors and victors.[10]

At last the tribunal began, but the first day was dominated by the reading of the lengthy and tediously repetitive indictment. Dos Passos found that the separate charges began to merge. 'Shooting, starvation and torture . . . tortured and killed . . . Shooting, beating and hanging . . . shooting, starvation and torture'. His attention shifted back to the prisoners, listening to the accounts of their misdeeds. He thought that

Göring had the 'spoiled, genial, outgoing, shrewdly self-satisfied' face of an actor, which sometimes bore the 'naughty-boy expression of a repentant drunkard'. As the morning progressed, Göring acquired a kind of grandeur, taking on the aspect of a 'master of ceremonies'. He was chastened by some of the revelations in the indictment, hiding his face during the passages describing the concentration camps, but he gazed round the room expectantly demanding a laugh when the prosecutors mentioned the 87 million bottles of champagne he had plundered from France. Hess spent his time reading, except when Hitler's name was first mentioned and he sat up and smiled manically. In the afternoon Ribbentrop collapsed and had to be taken out and sedated.[11]

The second day opened with the defendants' pleas. Called upon to speak first, Göring started reading from a typewritten speech. 'Before I answer the question of the Tribunal whether or not I am guilty,' he began, but was immediately cut off by Lawrence who informed him that he must simply plead guilty or not guilty. 'I declare myself in the sense of the indictment not guilty,' Göring replied. Most of the responses were uniform, though Jodl added that 'for what I have done or had to do I have a pure conscience before God, before History and my people' and Hess shouted simply 'Nein', in keeping with his role as resident madman.[12]

The pleas were followed by Robert Jackson's speech opening the prosecution for the Americans. Each of the Allies had taken one set of charges as the focus for their work and the Americans were responsible for the charge of conspiracy. Jackson interpreted this liberally, irritating the British by ranging across the entire case on the grounds that the original conspiracy had developed into the crime of aggressive war. Quoting from the plethora of German documents uncovered by the Allies, Jackson described the history of the Nazi Party, the persecution of the Jews and the early experiments in aggression. He went on to outline the treatment of POWs and occupied civilians, the establishment of the concentration camps and the planning of genocide. 'The privilege of being the first trial in history for crimes against the peace of the World imposes a grave responsibility,' he stated. 'The wrongs which we seek to condemn and punish have been so calculated, so malignant and so devastating that civilisation cannot survive their being repeated.'[13]

Jackson touched on the charge of 'crimes against humanity', describing the conspiracy of the Nazi leaders to annihilate the Jewish race: 'The most savage and numerous crimes planned and committed by the Nazis were those against the Jews . . . It is my purpose to show a plan and design, to which all Nazis were fanatically committed, to annihilate all Jewish people . . . The avowed purpose was the destruction of the Jewish people as a whole . . . The conspiracy or common plan to exterminate the Jews was . . . methodically and thoroughly pursued . . . History does not record a crime ever perpetrated against so many victims or one ever carried out with such calculated cruelty.'

According to Jackson, the common sense of mankind demanded that the law should not stop with punishing 'little people' for acts of this kind. It had to reach men who possessed themselves of great power and used it to set evils in motion. This was another of the radical innovations of the trial's charter: to make it possible to punish leaders who did not stain their own hands with blood but were tainted by it none the less. Jackson's was a notion of conspiratorial rather than collective guilt. The German world too, he said, had 'accounts to settle with these defendants'; they had tricked and subdued their own citizens.[14]

The courtroom was impressed both by Jackson's calmness and rhetorical fervour and by the extent of the evidence amassed. 'The Nazi defendants are going to be convicted by their own words, their own records, their own foul deeds,' the American journalist William Shirer observed. 'The idiots wrote everything down.' Shirer was not especially captivated by Jackson's oration; he thought he was too slow and dismissed him as 'no Cicero'. Dos Passos was much more enamoured: 'I doubt if there is a man or woman in the courtroom who does not feel that great and courageous words have been spoken,' he recorded in his diary; 'We Americans get a little proudly to our feet because it was a countryman of ours who spoke them.' He wrote home to his wife that Jackson had represented America as he liked to see it represented: 'reasonable, practical and full of a homey kind of dignity'. Again, he had spent the day observing the accused and this time he thought that they appeared more uneasy. 'When the prosecutor reaches the crimes against the Jews, they freeze into an agony of attention.' They seemed to cringe and shudder as they heard their own words quoted out of secret diaries; Göring's steps faltered as he left the room.[15]

Dos Passos departed from Nuremberg two days later, leaving journalists including Mann and de Mendelssohn to observe the case for the prosecution becoming increasingly tedious. The focus was now on the hierarchy of the Nazi Party and their control over state machinery. Some correspondents began skipping sessions but de Mendelssohn was determined to be there for everything. 'I'm possessed by the feeling that I shall never see anything like this again in my life,' he told his wife. 'This is absolutely historic . . . one just cannot afford to miss a single moment of it.'[16]

Both de Mendelssohn and Mann were present on 26 November when the pace of the drama suddenly quickened. The court was shown a Soviet documentary of extermination camp footage. As in the film that Billy Wilder had been editing in the summer, there were rivers of bodies scattered manically by giant bulldozers, lampshades made of human skin and piles of bones heaped up outside crematoria. The journalists watched the reactions of the defendants. Göring looked on with studied calm throughout but could not help frantically wiping his sweaty palms at the end; Ribbentrop tried to cover his face with his hands but kept peering through his fingers at the screen; Wilhelm Keitel wiped his reddened eyes with his handkerchief.

At the end of the film the judges filed out. One journalist asked: 'Why can't we shoot the swine now?' The defendants remained on their bench, where Hess started to say 'I don't believe it', but was silenced by Göring. In his cell that night Göring complained to the Allied psychiatrist that the film had shifted the sympathies of the audience just when many onlookers had been on his side. Most of the other prisoners denied that they had known the details of the camps. Hess, still claiming amnesia (though a few days later he would admit that his memory loss had been simulated), congratulated the Allies on improving the drama in the courtroom. 'Here at last is something interesting. Up to now I have been bored to distraction. I am no longer allowed to take a book into court. Today there was something to see!'[17]

Erika Mann interviewed the defence lawyers and ridiculed the cowardliness of their arguments. It had turned out, she wrote scathingly, that all of the accused were merely middle men: 'Like the rest of their countrymen they have done, seen and known nothing. They all say "horrible, horrible, horrible!", but as far as they are concerned the responsible parties are not in the courtroom.'

These lawyers were in a difficult position; they were German lawyers who had been appointed late in the day and were uneasily aware that the guilt of their clients extended to most of their compatriots. They had begun by questioning the legality of the court and the possible neutrality of the conqueror judges, but these arguments were becoming less tenable as more and more hard evidence was produced. That afternoon Erika Mann heard one lawyer declare 'the sooner my client is hanged, the better'. Ribbentrop's counsel seemed to her paler than he had looked before. 'I feel more and more like a deputy defendant,' he complained, 'sitting shield-like in front of these men. But as a German I, too, have to pay, even if ten days ago I did not know yet how dear was the price.'[18]

As December began and Nuremberg became covered with snow, both the Anglo-American and German publics became less interested in the proceedings at the trial. The London *Evening Standard* enlivened its coverage by sending the in-house cartoonist David Low to observe the courtroom. For Low this was primarily a visual spectacle: Frick was dirty brown and Funk light green. Like Dos Passos, Low found the defendants oddly ordinary and oddly small. He was captivated by Göring, who flapped his hands, stroked his mouth and patted his hair in a manner that seemed calculated to convey expression without words. Low enjoyed conveying this on paper although he was interrupted from his work when Göring turned his gaze to hook the cartoonist's eye: 'After about 20 seconds of mutual glaring it dawned on me that he was trying to stare me down. The childish vanity of it! How silly! (I won, by the way).'[19]

LOW'S NUEREMBERG SKETCHBOOK — № 1

The Allied-sponsored newspapers continued dutifully to provide news of the tribunal but most of their readers were focused on questions of survival. '*Deutschland, Deutschland ohne alles*,' began a parody of the national anthem going about at this time, '*ohne Butter, ohne Fett*' (without butter, without fat). Hunger levels were now dangerously high throughout Germany. Partly as a result of this, Peter de Mendelssohn found that the attitude of the Germans he met towards the trial was one of 'contemptuous indifference'. They were unable to see why the victors did not just hang the twenty men immediately, as Hitler would have done. 'The trial?' one man said to William Shirer, who had gone out into the snowy ruins to interview the cave-dwellers beneath; '*Ja* – propaganda! You'll hang them anyhow. So you make a trial for propaganda. Why should we pay any attention? We're cold. We're hungry.' One man who had once been a distinguished engineer complained that Göring had been quite right to build up his air force and that if he had only done a better job of it Nuremberg would not be in ruins.[20]

On 19 December, Erika Mann went on the radio to inform the German people about the importance of the proceedings. She insisted that although the trial was not sensational, it was all the more effective in its understated carefulness:

> It is not intended for the excitement or entertainment of the present but rather for the edification of the future, enabling later generations to learn from history. And there is an educational value in the pedantic way in which an enormous number of facts is presented in a very quiet and undramatic manner. I think this has a great advantage in terms of history.

But she did not have much impact on her listeners, who continued to complain that this was both a show trial and an unnecessary expense. And the trial's critics were amused that the proceedings were not only tedious but frequently shambolic. The American prosecutors had not put sufficient effort into pruning their speeches or deciding precisely on the relevance of their evidence. At one stage Captain Sam Harris began a speech on the Germanisation of occupied territories with the announcement that 'my knees haven't knocked so much since I asked my wonderful little wife to marry me'. Francis Biddle wrote 'Jesus' in his notebook, irritated that an American lawyer had embarrassed the profession in front of the British.[21]

Surveying the court from the judges' platform, both Biddle and Lawrence interrupted the prosecutors frequently and tersely with demands for clarity and relevance. Increasingly the proceedings were marked by a palpable tension between Biddle and Jackson. For years in the US, Biddle had been subservient to Jackson, serving as solicitor-general after Jackson was promoted from solicitor-general to attorney-general in 1940, and then filling Jackson's vacated post once again as attorney-general. Now as judge, Biddle was in the senior position and enjoyed making this apparent. He also believed himself to be superior to the other judges, even though Lawrence was technically in charge. 'Lawrence depends on me for everything and I'll run the show,' he had written in his notebook after grudgingly nominating Lawrence as chair. The British were characteristically suspicious of non-self-deprecating arrogance and were dismissive of Biddle in private, as were many of the journalists. Erika Mann announced proudly to her father that she had gained approbation in the press camp for coining the phrase 'too biddle and too late'.[22]

These personal rivalries and tensions were exacerbated by the homesick loneliness of almost everyone at Nuremberg. The judges in particular were isolated, cut off both from their compatriots and from the locals by the high security of their armoured cars. They felt that it would be inappropriate to socialise with the prosecutors and so remained secluded in their villas, busy entertaining the VIP visitors sent from home whose reactions to the drama in the courtroom were predictable. The monotony was occasionally interrupted by an invitation to a Russian party. After one of these, the Soviet alternate Alexander Volchkov drove Biddle back to his villa where Biddle was surprised to find the Russian embracing him like an 'affectionate bear cub' before springing back into his car and bursting into song.[23]

Unlike the judges, the journalists and lower-level officials could assuage their loneliness at the Grand Hotel, which provided a beacon of light in a city blacked out at night. Once this had been the hotel where foreign VIPs were housed during Nazi rallies; now it was filled with the Allied conquerors, drinking amid the red plush furnishings and artificial marble of the reception hall and jitterbugging in the Marble Room. Here underfed singers, dancers, acrobats and midgets came in tarnished finery to entertain the imprisoned victors.

On 20 December the court adjourned. Erika Mann spent Christmas in Zurich with an incestuous ensemble composed of her brother Klaus, her lover Betty Knox and her former lover Therese Giehse. It was a happy reunion for both lovers and siblings but Erika's health continued to deteriorate. On New Year's Day she checked into hospital, succumbing at last to the illness she had been postponing all winter. This seems to have been not so much a particular virus as a general physical collapse. She claimed rather improbably in a letter to Lotte Walter that she had come down with an array of diseases that included mumps, toxic poisoning, foot-and-mouth disease and an unusually strong cough. She recovered in a spa in Arosa, where she felt cut off from life in California and especially from Bruno Walter, whom she yearned for despite the presence of Betty Knox. In the letter to Lotte, Erika commanded Lotte and her father to feel embraced and begged them both to write swiftly. 'I want to know everything – what you do and what you don't do, conduct, think, read, talk and mean,' she demanded, adding that she would like reassurance that they also thought of her with affection. It was difficult writing to a lover via his daughter; the colourful list of her physical afflictions had to serve as her statement of need.[24]

Francis Biddle had a relatively healthy Christmas in England at the house of Norman Birkett, where the two men spent their evenings reading poetry and listening to gramophone records. At the start of January the court reconvened and the next few weeks were spent hearing the case for the British prosecution, which focused on the arguments against the individual defendants. There were now Germans alongside the Allies in the spectators' gallery. One of the defence lawyers had complained after the Christmas break that his family thought of the trial as something 'taking place on the moon' and suggested that seats should be allocated to Germans, although not many took up the offer.[25]

Most Germans continued to feel distant from the tribunal, although it was broadcast twice a day on the radio. The US authorities estimated that 19 per cent of newspaper columns in their zone were devoted to coverage of the proceedings, but there was only one newspaper for five inhabitants in both the US and the British zone and after twelve years of inaccurate news coverage the Germans had little faith in the news reports anyway. Aware of the limited immediate impact of the trial, the Allies continued to seek other ways to confront the Germans with their culpability. Near the end of January the US concentration camp documentary was finally ready to screen in their zone. Released under the title *Die Todesmühlen* (*Death Mills*), this was a twenty-two minute version of the film that did not incorporate the editing done by Billy Wilder.

As well as exhibiting the appalling conditions of the camps, the film reminded its audiences of how difficult it had been for ordinary Germans not to know of their existence. They had lived within walking distance, heard the cries of the victims and smelt the stench of their corpses; they had eaten produce fertilised by human bone and worn

wigs made from human hair. The film emphasised the distasteful efficiency of the camps – the assembly-line operation of death – and
showed surviving men, women and children transformed by years of
humiliating imprisonment into 'animal-like creatures'. The final
sequence superimposed shots of mass graves onto images from Riefenstahl's footage of the Nuremberg rallies. An imaginary German
spectator commented: 'Yes, I remember – at the Nuremberg party
assembly I yelled "Heil!", then when the Gestapo took my neighbour I
thought "What do I care?"'

Attendance at a screening of *Death Mills* was compulsory in some
parts of Bavaria for anyone who wanted to obtain their food ration
cards, although the Information Control Division was sceptical about
this enforced viewing. But after it had been screened for a month only
12 per cent of Bavarians responding to a survey had seen the film, which
is not that surprising as only 35 per cent of Bavarians went to the cinema
at all. It was clear that there was no easy way to convince a starving
nation of its crimes, though the lawyers at Nuremberg continued in
their attempts. On 17 January 1946 the French case for the prosecution
opened with a speech from the chief prosecutor, François de Menthon.
This comprised an admirably calm description of the German Occupation of France and an analysis of German guilt. Now that Jackson and
Shawcross had detailed the particular crimes committed by the Nazis,
de Menthon proposed to explain how they had happened. Specifically,
he wanted to describe how all the 'organised and vast criminality' sprang
from what he termed 'a crime against the spirit': 'This sin against the
spirit is the original sin of National Socialism from which all crimes
spring.'[26]

Up to this point, there had been no suggestion in the courtroom that
the entire German nation was guilty. Jackson had been careful in his
speech to imply that ordinary Germans themselves could be victims of
the Nazi conspiracy. Now de Menthon suggested that the German
nation as a whole had been 'intoxicated' by Nazism for years: 'certain
of their eternal and deep seated aspirations, under this regime, have
found a monstrous expression; their entire responsibility is involved,
not only by their general acceptance but by the effective participation

of a great number of them in the crimes committed.' The Germans had sinned primarily through their emphasis on racial origin, believing that 'man, of himself, has no value except when he is of service to the German race'. This was the principle behind all the Nazi crimes.[27]

Like Erika Mann, de Menthon saw the trial as the first step to German re-education. The condemnation of Nazi Germany by the tribunal would constitute a first lesson to the German people, enabling the process of spiritual denazification to begin. Like Thomas Mann, de Menthon suggested that Germany had strayed into the realm not merely of villainy but of hell. Nazism's 'original sin' had been to exploit 'one of the most profound and most tragic aspects of the German soul'; having seduced the Germans into devilishness the Nazis had utilised the inventions of contemporary science to attempt to plunge the world 'into a diabolical barbarism'. That spring Mann had complained that Germany's best had turned into evil through 'devilish cunning'. Now the French prosecutor was suggesting that the tribunal at Nuremberg had the power to judge the corruption of the German soul.[28]

De Menthon's speech was lauded by the judges and more surprisingly by the prisoners. Biddle thought this the most interesting and most moving of the prosecutors' speeches, though he was hardly unbiased when it came to comparing it with Jackson's. In his autobiography Biddle later praised de Menthon for seeking to distinguish and understand 'the German soul within the dark cloud of German action', and for speaking about the Germans 'as members of a group to which all human beings belonged'. On the day of the speech itself, Hans Frank, the former governor-general of Poland and the only defendant publicly to repent, lauded de Menthon for delivering a stimulating speech. 'That is more like the European mentality. It will be a pleasure to argue with that man.'[29]

Perhaps Frank was pleased that de Menthon had avoided the term 'crimes against humanity' in his speech, focusing instead on 'crimes against peace'. He had made no reference to the deportation or murder of the Jews, referring only to the damage to 'their personal rights and to their human dignity'. This reflected a widespread tendency among the Allies to forget the racial specificity of Hitler's victims. At Nuremberg,

Jackson's opening remarks about the annihilation of the Jews had been followed by a case for the prosecution chiefly focused on the Nazi war crimes rather than the Jewish genocide. Similarly, *Death Mills* made no mention of the 6 million Jewish dead. The victims of the camps were described as being of 'all the religious faiths, all political beliefs, condemned by Hitler because they were anti-Nazi'. The newsreels about Bergen-Belsen in British cinemas did not generally refer to the skeletal figures as Jews. It would be another ten years before the people of Europe confronted their Jewish dead.[30]

The French prosecutor's speech provoked renewed speculation about who exactly was on trial in Nuremberg. Birkett suggested in a letter three days later that there were now two trials going on simultaneously: 'the trial of the defendants in the dock and the greater trial of a whole nation and its way of thought'. The tribunal had become a locus for the debate about collective guilt that had been playing out in the German press since the end of the war. When Erika Mann complained about the 'complete lack of feeling of their collective guilt' displayed by the German policemen, and when Ernst Robert Curtius told Stephen Spender that the Germans were all guilty and could achieve nothing without wholesale repentance, they were representative of a wider school of thought.[31]

The reasons why collective guilt applied more to the Germans than to the citizens of other totalitarian regimes were obvious. Hitler had always insisted that he represented the will of the people; it was evident that the concentration camp system had required the co-operation of hundreds of thousands of Germans; there had been no wide-scale protest from either the intellectuals or the masses. It was easier for exiles than 'inner emigrants' to maintain this position without also holding themselves accountable and many Germans inside and outside Germany followed Thomas Mann's line that no one could escape judgement, urging full-scale repentance. 'We are being made responsible, but we do not want to be made responsible,' complained Pastor Niemöller, an influential priest who had been interned in Dachau. 'And by refusing to be made responsible we are depriving ourselves of the possibility of becoming free again.'[32]

Two of the most thoughtful accounts of collective guilt came from the exiled philosopher Hannah Arendt (now based in the US) and her former teacher Karl Jaspers, who had remained in Germany throughout the Third Reich although, unlike Curtius, he had been barred from his teaching position on account of his problematic views and his Jewish wife. As a Jew, Arendt had left Germany hurriedly for Paris in 1933. She had lost her German citizenship in 1937 and been interned in a concentration camp in France in 1940 as an 'enemy alien'. In 1941 she managed to escape the camp and emigrate to the US with her mother and husband, the German Marxist philosopher and poet Heinrich Blücher. She had quickly gained status in the US as a philosopher and public intellectual and in 1944 she became the director of research for the Commission of European Jewish Cultural Reconstruction. As the war came to an end, Arendt took it upon herself to pronounce judgement on the question of German guilt. She felt betrayed by her former countrymen and especially by her former teacher and lover, Martin Heidegger, who at least until 1934 had been openly enthusiastic about Nazism and who had remained a member of the Nazi Party until its demise. 'I can't but regard Heidegger as a potential murderer,' Arendt would say sadly the following year.[33]

In an essay entitled 'Organised Guilt and Universal Responsibility', which was published in the US in January 1945 and in Germany in 1946, Arendt reminded her readers that a central thesis of Nazism was that there was no difference between Nazis and Germans. This had been made manifest by the general order subordinating all soldiers to the party and by the allocation of duties of mass murder in the concentration camps to members of the Wehrmacht. The Nazis had allowed this to be public knowledge because they wanted the Allies to abandon the distinction between Germans and Nazis so that in the event of defeat the victorious powers would be unable to distinguish between them. For Arendt the lines between so-called good and bad Germans had become so blurred that 'the only way we can identify an anti-Nazi is when the Nazis have hanged him'. The totalitarian policy had made the existence of each individual in Germany dependent upon committing or being complicit in crimes.[34]

This was primarily a political analysis, but Arendt went further in suggesting that philosophically not only all Germans but all of their contemporaries were implicated in Nazi evil. Anyone who still distinguished between 'good' and 'bad' Germans did not apprehend the magnitude of the catastrophe. The challenge was not to disentangle the good from the bad but to decide how the world outside Germany was to conduct itself when confronting a people for whom the boundaries between the guilty and the innocent had been effaced. She believed that the most honest reaction was to recoil in shame; not shame at being German, but shame at being human, when humans were capable of these deeds: 'For the idea of humanity, when purged of all sentimentality, has the very serious consequence that in one form or another men must assume responsibility for all crimes committed by men and that all nations share the onus of evil committed by all others. Shame at being a human being is the purely individual and still non-political expression of this insight.' The survivors were left needing to develop a personal sense of shame as an expression of their repulsion at evil. They needed as well to forge a politics that fostered collective awareness of man's capacity for evil.[35]

When she wrote this essay, Arendt had had almost no contact with anyone in Germany for years. After the war came to an end, she began to rekindle lost friendships, especially with Karl Jaspers, to whom she now sent regular food parcels. Writing to thank her, Jaspers observed that his task was to rebuild order out of chaos. He pronounced himself 'optimistic, provided world history does not just roll over and destroy us', although it was impossible to do much thinking in the midst of all the day to day chores.[36]

In Germany, Jaspers was engaged in thinking about the same questions as Arendt. Near the end of the war he had declared in his diary that 'whoever survives must decide upon a task to which he will dedicate the remainder of his life'. His task was to rebuild intellectual life in Germany and for this he needed to establish how to wrest hope from guilty defeat. In August 1945 he displayed the kind of shame described by Arendt in a lecture celebrating the reopening of the medical school of Heidelberg University where he was once again employed:

> We survivors did not seek death. We did not go out on the streets when our Jewish friends were led away, nor did we cry out until they destroyed us as well. We preferred to stay alive on the weak, if justified grounds that our death would not have helped anyway. That we live is our guilt. We know before God, what deeply humiliates us.

Unlike Curtius, Jaspers was determined to include himself among the guilty Germans, though it was inevitably difficult to strike a balance between self-recrimination and analysis. And his views had won him the respect of the occupiers. His former student Golo Mann had arrived in Heidelberg earlier in the month, pleased to make contact with his teacher, whom he found had become 'very white, thin and old'. Mann told a friend that Jaspers was one of the few people in Germany who had not become 'strange and unattractive foreigners' to him and reported that the American officers frequently called on the philosophy professor, asking him to explain Germany to them.[37]

Jaspers was moved by Arendt's essay, when he read it in December, and told her that it had made him feel he was 'breathing the air I so yearn for: openness and justice and a hidden love that scarcely allows itself expression in language'. He persuaded the editor of *Die Wandlung* (a new journal Jaspers had founded with three colleagues) to translate the essay into German and publish it in April 1946. Arendt's piece in part prompted the thinking that led to a series of lectures in the winter of 1945/46 which he would publish as *Die Schuldfrage* ('The Question of German Guilt') in 1946. Here he distinguished between criminal, political, moral and metaphysical guilt, suggesting that political guilt was collective (this was the kind of guilt on trial in Nuremberg) while metaphysical guilt was universal (leading to the shame described by Arendt).[38]

Arendt was sceptical about Jaspers's views. She complained to him in August 1946 that his definition of Nazi policy as a crime ('criminal guilt') seemed inadequate. 'The Nazi crimes, it seems to me, explode the limits of the law; and that is precisely what constitutes their monstrousness. For these crimes, no punishment is severe enough.'

For Jaspers, Arendt's response had the danger of elevating Nazi guilt beyond the criminal and therefore endowing it with 'greatness' and losing sight of its banality. He had more time than Arendt did for the Nuremberg trials. She had stated specifically in the January 1945 essay that 'we will not be aided either by a definition of those responsible, nor by the punishment of "war criminals"'. Evil was to be fought by people 'filled with a genuine fear of the inescapable guilt of the human race'. She complained to Jaspers in the August 1946 letter that if the Allies were to hang Göring it would be completely inadequate. The guilt of the Nazi leaders overstepped and shattered all legal systems, hence their smugness in the dock.[39]

Whether guilt was seen as afflicting the Germans or humanity as a whole, it did not provide much of a practical template for life. It is therefore not surprising that those politically concerned with the actualities of postwar Germany tended to reject the idea of collective guilt and to allow for the possibility of the good German, needing some people to be left to govern Germany. None the less, they still insisted on the need for a general acknowledgement of responsibility, if only as a first step towards re-education.

The contradictions in these simultaneous positions were demonstrated by the rhetoric of both the Western and the Eastern Allies. As a communist newly arrived from the Soviet Union, Johannes Becher to some extent followed the Soviet position that the Germans were Hitler's first victims (a view also publicly propounded by Bertolt Brecht) and that the Germans were more in need of societal than individual reform. In the first issue of his magazine *Aufbau* in January 1946, Becher lauded the court at Nuremberg for putting the senior Nazis on trial, stating: 'We bear witness to the monstrous crimes committed by the Nazi war criminals against us, the German people.' Becher claimed here not only that all the soldiers who had been killed were victims of the political deception of the Nazis but that 'what was done to the Jews was done to *us*', though he did add that Nuremberg needed to be 'accompanied by an *inner* judgement that every German must carry out upon himself' and that they would probably find that nobody was free from blame. Talking to foreign visitors, however,

Becher was more dismissive of his compatriots. Interviewed by William Shirer, Becher complained about the lack of guilt among the survivors, claiming that the 'deadness of the German soul' was far worse than the physical ruins of the bombed cities. He had been shocked to find that many Germans regretted 'the loss of their little flats and their ugly furniture' more than they regretted the loss of human life. In his opinion the need for warmth and shelter did not allow the German people to have 'dead souls and nitwit minds and not the slightest desire to make good their awful crimes'.[40]

These contradictions were also present in the rhetoric and policy of the occupation forces. In theory, the Allies all allowed for the possibility of the good German. Even Morgenthau and Vansittart saw Germans as communally displaying the vice of rabid militarism rather than as collectively guilty in a more metaphysical sense. But as the Allied forces liberated one camp after another and examined the systematic horrors wrought by the Germans, they developed a rhetoric that implied collective guilt. '*Diese Schandtaten – Eure Schuld!*' ('These atrocities – your fault') proclaimed the posters laying the sights of the camps before the locals of the towns they adjoined. In the final edit of *Death Mills* the word 'Nazi' had been replaced with 'German' in the commentary to underline the responsibility and guilt of all Germans. It is not surprising that at least one of the prosecutors at Nuremberg should put the entire German nation on trial along with their leaders.

8

'Let Germany Live!'

Fighting the Peace: March–May 1946

The case for the prosecution at Nuremberg finally came to a close on 7 March 1946, after seventy-three days. Following five long months of winter, the weather was starting to thaw but the majority of Germans were weak from cold and hunger and the food situation showed no signs of improving. By the end of March rations had dropped to 1,275 calories in the US zone and 1,043 in the British zone. The writer Ernst Jünger complained that they were now half what they had been the previous year. 'This is a death sentence for many who up to now have only been able to keep their heads above water with the greatest effort, above all children, old people and refugees.'¹

The government and public in Britain and the US were becoming frightened by the continuing desperate conditions in Germany. At the start of January, John Dos Passos had published an article in *Life* magazine headed 'Americans are Losing the Victory in Europe', reporting the 'sobering experience' of being glared at accusingly by Europeans who felt that the Americans may have helped sweep away Hitlerism but had inflicted a cure that was worse than the disease. They were disappointed by the American handling of DPs and black markets and by their 'fumbling timidity' with the Russians. Later that month, the former prime minister Winston Churchill had warned the House of Commons that Britain could not afford to let chaos and misery continue indefinitely in their zone of Germany: 'The idea of keeping scores of millions of people hanging about in a subhuman state between earth and hell, until they are worn down to a slave condition or embrace communism, will only breed at least a moral pestilence and probably an actual war . . . Let Germany live!'[2]

Churchill had the situation in Germany in mind when he gave a speech in Fulton, Missouri on 5 March announcing that 'from Stettin in the Baltic to Trieste in the Adriatic an iron curtain has descended across the Continent'. He condemned not only the creation of totalitarian governments in Eastern Europe and the Soviet Union but the 'enormous and wrongful inroads upon Germany' made by the Russian-dominated Polish government. 'This is certainly not the liberated Europe we fought to build up,' he complained; 'nor is it one which contains the essentials of permanent peace.'[3]

In Nuremberg, the defendants were delighted to read reports of Churchill's speech just as the case for the prosecution was reaching its end. They were immediately hopeful that the rift between the Western Allies and the Soviet Union would widen and that the British and Americans would recognise the former Nazi leaders as their comrades. Albert Speer later recalled how they were collectively gripped by a 'tremendous excitement'. Hess stopped acting the amnesiac and reminded the others how often he had predicted a great turning point that would curtail the trial and restore their ranks. As a result they were relatively cheerful when the defence case began on 8 March. And the courtroom was crowded again with spectators who shared the defendants' good humour, hopeful that the tribunal was about to regain its theatricality now that the Nazis themselves were entering the witness box.[4]

The British painter Laura Knight had been in Nuremberg since January and now enjoyed watching Göring begin his performance on 13 March. Knight had been appointed as the official British painter recording the trial; her work was to be exhibited at the London Royal Academy's summer exhibition that year. An energetic sixty-eight year old, she was used to being close to the action. In the 1920s she had travelled with a circus, where, in addition to sketching and painting the performers, she learnt to do acrobatics. During the war she had been busy as a WAAC (War Artists' Advisory Committee) artist boosting morale with her paintings of factory workers and combatants. Arriving in Nuremberg, she had been dissatisfied with the view from the spectators' gallery and was pleased to be allocated an empty broadcasting box cut into the walls of the courtroom immediately above the dock. Here, between sketches, she would occasionally wrap herself up in a big Shetland rug she had brought with her and fall asleep. Like David Low, Knight saw the tribunal chiefly as a visual spectacle. Göring's pink and white skin contrasted with Hess's green pallor; the Snowdrops' helmets and the sheets of paper strewing the courtroom were like a fall of snow. She had to remind herself that the drama being enacted before her did not belong to the theatrical stage: 'that the performing cast in the dock do not pull all matter aside at the drop of the curtain, go straight to their dressing rooms and take off their make-up'.[5]

Now, however, she was attentive to the detail of the action in the dock. Göring gave twelve hours of evidence with very little interruption from the judges' bench. He was intelligent and energetic throughout, using his time in the witness box to demonstrate his heroism rather than his innocence. This meant that he played into the hands of his prosecutors. He admitted proudly that he had destroyed opposition to Nazism, that he had crushed 'so-called freedoms', organised black markets in occupied countries and helped to eliminate Jews from the public sphere. But in the process he gained the respect of his audience and made some hard-hitting jibes at the Allies. Asked if the Germans had looted in Russia, he responded that they had but that at least they did not 'dismantle and transport away the entire Russian economy' as the Russians had in Germany; asked if Hitler was the head of the state, government and armed forces, he replied that he was indeed, 'following the example of the United States'.[6]

Cross-examined by Jackson, Göring triumphed. When Jackson's questions were too general, Göring patronisingly subdivided them into specific sections. At one stage Jackson produced a document supposedly describing the 'liberation of the Rhineland' that turned out to be about the 'cleaning of the Rhine'. Embarrassed, Jackson retorted that the document did at least show planning 'which had to be kept entirely secret from foreign powers', to which Göring responded slickly: 'I do not think I can recall reading beforehand the publication of the mobil- isation preparations of the United States.' As always, Biddle enjoyed the discomfort of his compatriot. When the British deputy prosecutor David Maxwell Fyfe took over on 20 March, Biddle reported to his wife that Jackson was 'sitting by, unhappy and beaten, full of a sense of failure'. Under Maxwell Fyfe's more incisive questioning, Göring became less complacent. He now appeared to be more of a childish bully whose swagger had been exposed as fearful.[7]

Knight found that the talk in the Grand Hotel bar every night was of Göring. 'What did you think of Göring's answer?' people asked; 'He looks the sort of person you would enjoy spending an evening with!' others observed. She herself examined him physically, preparing to paint the defendants. She noted his big head and face, lack of neck, huge body, short legs and arms. His soft grey Reich marshal's uniform hung over him in folds, emphasising his lost bulk. Like many of the other onlookers, she was impressed by his magnetism. 'What a benefit to humanity he might have been had his bent been other than for evil,' she wrote in her diary. Knight was moved by the small human struggles going on amid these men who were soon to be condemned to death. Hess had been refusing to eat, apparently wanting to die a martyr. He was the only prisoner who did not bring a snack for the eleven o'clock break and on one occasion Göring broke his own large biscuit in half and tried unsuccessfully to make Hess eat some of it.[8]

Knight's suite in the Grand Hotel had been built for Hitler. Her bed was the most comfortable bed she had ever slept in, with a huge down pillow under her head and an enormous duvet (issuing from a world of blankets, Knight described this admiringly as a 'still huger down pillow over my body'). Sometimes she wondered if Hitler had laid his head, 'so uneasy in its ill-fitting crown', upon her pillow. Like Lee Miller, she was unnerved but fascinated by entering the sensual world of the man responsible for the devastation she saw and heard about each day. She found it strange that she now slept so soundly on Hitler's pillow each night, 'after days spent in listening to the horrors brought about by his descent from the idealism of his beginning to that over-weening ambition'.[9]

She spent her evenings with the Canadian deputy assistant adjutant-general of the British War Crimes Executive, Major Peter Casson, who was responsible for looking after the important British visitors. Together they toured the ruins of Nuremberg, surveying the rubble heaps under which 'homes' had been erected. They went into a building that looked like a doll's house with its frontage wide open. Only the third floor was almost intact and there Knight found a bed and a baby in a cradle balanced dangerously near the open front of the building. A man and a woman were eating scraps that made Knight feel guilty for the luxurious food she was consuming nightly. The contrast between the two worlds made the frantic socialising of the Allies unreal, not least because no one could forget the trial they were attempting to escape. One night she dined at Lawrence's villa where they talked briefly about Picasso but found that the conversation kept returning to the courtroom. 'We sit side by side with death – and death by the million – wherever we are,' Knight wrote in her diary. She was struck by Norman Birkett's pity for the prisoners, whom he seemed unable to forget.[10]

Sometimes Knight and Casson went to the nightly entertainment at the Grand Hotel, which seemed to Knight to be staged to save the visitors from nervous breakdown. Visiting later that summer to assist the prosecution, the civil servant and historian John Wheeler-Bennett was appalled by the contrast between the opulence of the hotel and the penury of the Germans who literally flattened their noses against the cracked glass panels, looking in at the occupiers. 'Inside we, the conquerors who had brought their leaders to trial, were disporting ourselves in a manner certainly vulgar and virtually callous.' Knight veered between criticising and embracing the vulgarity. One evening she took a young Canadian serviceman called Edward Clare for dinner in the Grand Hotel and then disappeared, saying that there were people she needed to speak to. Clare retired to the bar where suddenly he heard a drum roll and saw that the dance floor had been swiftly cleared. Knight appeared spotlit in the middle of the floor; without introduction, she nimbly spun backwards in the air. She walked off the dance floor, the lights were brought up and dancers gradually congregated again. Knight informed Clare that an old friend had bet her that she could no longer do the backflip at which she had once been proficient.[11]

On another evening during a cabaret show the tightrope broke and Casson rushed over to help the tightrope walker who had landed on the floor. It turned out that the girl knew Knight; she was the fiancée of a bareback horse-rider with whose troupe Knight had once travelled in England. Now Casson and Knight drove in a military jeep to spend an evening with the circus people. For a few hours they danced, ate cakes and drank white wine while their new friends performed acrobatics on the hearthrug and played the guitar. At last they seemed to have escaped the presence of death.

Knight's drawings were almost finished. She showed them to the novelist Evelyn Waugh when he arrived on 31 March. There was a series of sketches for a painting of the defendants in the dock and a collection of drawings of individual British judges and lawyers. She had started a painting depicting the prisoners in the dock against a background of corpses and burning buildings. Meeting Waugh, Knight asked repeatedly: 'You don't think it *illustration* do you?' Waugh tried to tell her that he liked 'illustration' but he found that 'the poor old girl had plainly had her tastes warped by Roger Fry'.[12]

In fact the painting is not mere illustration. It is stamped with Knight's very personal vision. The canvas is dominated by formal constructions of line and colour of which Roger Fry might have approved: the severe lines of the benches, all pointing upwards towards the destruction; the fall of snow of the white helmets and papers, echoing the straighter lines of the seats. The perspective of the painting is the aerial view of Knight's box, which renders the defendants and their counsel strangely small and obscure and allows the burning buildings at the top to seem as though they are about to sweep up and subsume the brighter figures in the foreground. The defendants themselves are as ordinary as they seem in Low's cartoons: reading and writing, legs crossed or splayed, Walther Funk with his head in his hands. However, against the background of apocalyptic horror the men seem more terrible and perhaps also more pitiable because they are so normal.

While painting her picture, Knight had been determined to convey 'the sensation that not only I, but everyone here appears to feel', which she found difficult to describe except to say that it contained a significant element of pity: 'pity perhaps that the human creature could sink to such baseness as some of these poor creatures have done'. This pity seems to infuse the picture, enabling her to endow each of the defendants with individuality. But at the same time she reminds us of the devastation that these ordinary men have wreaked. The burning buildings and the sea of bones seem both to grow out of and to invade the edges of the courtroom; the defendants are more frightening because they can look so mundane but cause so much destruction.[13]

This is Knight as engaged in a painterly act of benign judgement, looking squarely at the crimes of the defendants while also remembering their humanity. But perhaps she was also gesturing towards the potential significance of the trial through her composition. Arguably, by placing the burning city at the top rather than the bottom of the picture, she leaves the viewer with the sensation that the defendants and their lawyers are encroaching into the city. This is a city in which some buildings are still standing. With its pastel-coloured towers, it is more a vision of romantic ruin than of flattened debris. Perhaps the act of justice portrayed in the foreground will spill upwards into the city, pointing the way forward for reconstruction.[14]

Evelyn Waugh's encounter with Laura Knight took place during a three-day visit to Nuremberg as a VIP guest. He was pleased to have a chance to escape the 'accursed soil' of postwar Labour England but did not take the proceedings very seriously. Like Knight, he was struck by the anomaly of the luxury hotel and law courts presiding over acres of corpse-scented rubble, but unlike her he found it a 'surrealist spectacle'. For Waugh the trial bore a comical resemblance to the schoolroom. Göring had Tito's matronly appeal; Ribbentrop, now in the witness stand, was like a seedy schoolmaster being ragged: 'He knows he doesn't know the lesson and he knows the boys know. He has just worked out the sum wrong on the blackboard and is being heckled. He has lost his job but has the pathetic hope that if he can hold out to the end of term he may get a 'character' to another worse school. He lies quite

instinctively and without motive on quite important points.' Waugh
enjoyed dining with Lawrence whom he found 'a most agreeable man
interested in cattle breeding', and he returned to England less sure than
he had been beforehand that the trials were an 'injudicious travesty'.[15]

Waugh's sense that everyone in Britain was dismissive of the trials
was not wholly accurate, but it was true that they were taken less
seriously at home. Just before the proceedings began, George Orwell
had published an essay entitled 'Revenge is Sour', complaining that the
whole idea of revenge and punishment was 'a childish daydream'. As
soon as you were no longer powerless the desire for revenge evaporated,
becoming pathetic and disgusting. In Orwell's view (and he was motivated, of course, by his own German experiences), this was now the
case in Britain. 'In so far as the big public in this country is responsible
for the monstrous peace settlement now being forced on Germany, it is
because of a failure to see in advance that punishing an enemy brings
no satisfaction.' Orwell was sure that the average man in Britain was
unaware what crime Göring or Ribbentrop were being charged with.
This was both because the punishment of these monsters was less
attractive now that it was possible, and because under lock and key they
had almost ceased to be monsters.[16]

Orwell's argument was somewhat spurious. The Allies were not
primarily seeking revenge and he had no alternative to offer; like Arendt
he had turned the trials into a metaphysical rather than a practical
matter. But for Orwell, it was more crucial to feed the starving Germans
than to punish the defeated Nazis. At the start of 1946 he began publicly
to back a new 'Save Europe Now' campaign which had begun in Britain aiming to increase the supply of food to Europe. The movement
had been initiated in September by Victor Gollancz, who was a frenetic
supporter of unpopular causes and had decided to concentrate his
energy on Germany. In the early 1930s, Gollancz and the Left Book
Club he founded in 1936 had concentrated on supporting communism. Disillusioned with the Communist Party in 1938, he had then
made it his mission to unmask the reality behind Communist Party
propaganda at the same time as broadcasting the virtues of the Soviet
Union, advocating an Anglo-Russian alliance. Since 1940 he had been

battling against the broadcasts by Vansittart about the collective militarism of the Germans at the same time as he had been crusading on behalf of the European Jews.

Gollancz's politics were always personal and his sympathy for the plight of the Jews brought with it guilt about his adolescent rejection of his own Jewish heritage. Disliking the petty constraints of Orthodox Judaism, he had shifted his allegiance to the teachings of Christianity and had been dismissive of the Jews he met in London (though he did marry a Jew himself) until in 1942 he realised the extent of the threat posed to the Jews by Nazism and began to campaign against anti-Semitism. He forced himself to remain passionate about the cause by taking half an hour before each lecture to 'feel' himself into the situation of people at Dachau or Buchenwald: 'One night I was being gassed in a gas-chamber: the next, I was helping others dig our own mass grave, and then waiting for the splutter of a machine-gun.' This oddly obsessive and masochistic process eventually led to a nervous breakdown in June 1945. He had three weeks without sleep and his body erupted with a series of physical symptoms. But he recovered sufficiently to write pamphlets in favour of Zionism in the later stages of the war, to stage a battle against the Conservatives in the wake of the July general election and to start campaigning on behalf of the starving Germans in the spring of 1945.[17]

In a pamphlet entitled 'What Buchenwald Really Means', written in April 1945, Gollancz explained that not all Germans had been guilty of the atrocities discovered at Buchenwald. Hundreds of thousands of heroic gentiles had been persecuted for resisting the Nazis and millions of Germans had been terrorised into acquiescence. Gollancz saw the theory of collective guilt as barbaric. Ezekiel had spoken out against it in the Old Testament ('the son shall not bear the iniquity of the father'); Christ had insisted that each man bore responsibility for his own soul. Convinced that Attlee's Labour government lacked the will to tighten rations at home in order to increase supplies to Germany, Gollancz wrote an appeal to a series of newspapers in September 1945, signed by prestigious figures including the pacifist bishop George Bell, the MP Eleanor Rathbone and the philosopher Bertrand Russell. He described the conditions in Berlin and the situation of the displaced Germans wandering across the country, and insisted that 'if we call attention to this vast tragedy, it is certainly not because we fail to realise how grievously our allies are suffering' but because they saw the European problem as a communal one. He was hopeful that the majority of British people would be prepared to sacrifice some of their own rations for the sake of the Germans and asked anyone prepared to do so to send a postcard to 'Save Europe Now'.[18]

A January 1946 'Save Europe Now' (SEN) booklet included an extract from an article by Peter de Mendelssohn in the *Observer* the previous month describing the black and sinister mood in Germany: 'With the sudden arrival of bitterly cold winter weather, minds and tempers have hardened.' Many politicians were frightened to support this, worrying that they would be seen as taking food from British housewives to feed German war criminals. But there was a growing number of people in Britain who took Churchill's line that a starving Germany would be not only a humanitarian disaster but a dangerous moral pestilence. This was the view of the 100,000-or-so people who had sent postcards to 'Save Europe Now' by the spring of 1946. It was also the view put forward by Humphrey Jennnings's *A Defeated People*, which was screened in March and commended in the *Daily Telegraph* for portraying life in the British zone with sympathetic restraint: 'The tone is agreeably free from gloating, and it would need a much more vindictive race than ours to see without sympathy women cooking amid the ruins and crowds studying huge boards covered with the names of missing persons.' Jennings's film displayed compassion that was also evident in a 'Germany Under Control' exhibition currently being mounted to open in London in the summer, which aimed to convince the British public of the need to continue to pay for the Occupation of Germany.[19]

The film and the exhibition were necessary. Many British people were disgruntled when the Chancellor of the Exchequer announced in April that the cost of the Occupation of Germany for the forthcoming year would be £80 million. But the messages the public was receiving were mixed. On 4 April 1946 the foreign secretary Ernest Bevin signed a certificate stating that 'His Majesty is still in a state of war with Germany'. Questioned by a surprised Control Commission legal advisor, Bevin replied that, 'no treaty of peace or declaration by the Allied Powers having been made terminating the state of war with Germany, His Majesty is still in a state of war with Germany, although, as provided in the declaration of surrender, all active hostilities have ceased'.

This put the Control Commission in a strange position: apparently the Allies were the supreme governing authority in a country with which they were technically at war. Gollancz continued to campaign on behalf of Germany, urging especially that the British should be allowed to send personal food parcels to help the Germans and that bread rationing should be introduced in Britain. The Labour MP John Strachey, who was appointed Minister of Food in May, agreed in principle about the possibility of food parcels but faced opposition in the Cabinet.[20]

The American public was generally more prepared than the British to fund the Occupation of Germany. The US had not suffered from a war on the home front; its economy was more stable than Britain's. And there was more urgent fear in the US that a weak Germany would play into the hands of the Soviet Union. It was this fear that motivated the US secretary of state James Byrnes when the Council of Foreign Ministers established at Potsdam met in Paris in April. Byrnes insisted that the Allies should stop stripping Germany of its assets and instead use German resources on behalf of the country as a whole. The US military governor, General Lucius D. Clay, immediately suspended all reparation seizures in the US zone but none of the other governors followed his lead. Bevin told Clay that the British could not openly emulate the Americans because they did not want to be seen as conniving with the Americans against the Russians. In fact many British officials were not yet ready to suspend reparations; there were still shipyards and dockyards needing to be destroyed if Germany was no longer to present problematic competition in this area.

With the whole question of Germany's future now a matter for urgent debate, many influential British figures were keen to come to see Germany for themselves. The writer and former MP Harold Nicolson

(husband of the novelist Vita Sackville-West) arrived in Nuremberg on
30 April just as the defence case for Hitler's minister of economics Hjalmar Schacht began. Nicolson took the trial more seriously than Waugh
did, although he felt squeamish at the prospect of comfortably observing the spectacle of men 'caught like rats in a trap'. As counsellor of the
British embassy in Berlin in the 1920s, Nicolson had known some of
the senior Nazis personally. Although he had disliked Ribbentrop, he
was still unhappy to see him humiliated, while Schacht had been a
personal friend. Now like so many other visitors, Nicolson was shocked
by the drabness of the defendants: 'they have the appearance of people
who have travelled in a third-class railway carriage for three successive
nights'.[21]

Staying with Birkett in his villa, Nicolson ate trout for breakfast. On
his second afternoon he wandered through the Nuremberg ruins which
he found were jagged like the old jawbone of a camel in the desert.
Glared at by the local inhabitants, Nicolson was aware that if he were a
Nuremberger he too would feel 'nothing but undying hatred for those
who had destroyed my lovely city'. At dinner with Biddle ('an agreeable, social type of American') he learnt that Birkett and Biddle were
hoping that he would write a book about the tribunal. Nicolson was
unwilling to do so, but did write an article that was published in the
Spectator in May stating that his preconceptions of this 'stupendous
trial' had been incorrect. He had formed a false idea of the atmosphere,
underestimating the silences. He had not guessed that the most impressive element of the courtroom would be the pervading sense of calm.
While he had expected to find the trial punitive, it had transpired that
it was 'the calm assessment and affirmation of profound human values'.
And he was convinced that the tribunal was valuable in setting a judicial precedent and recording the history of National Socialism: 'In the
courtroom at Nuremberg something more important is happening
than the trial of a few captured prisoners. The inhuman is being
confronted with the humane, ruthlessness with equity, lawlessness with
patient justice, and barbarism with civilisation.'[22]

Nicolson's piece became part of a conversation about the efficacy of
the British intervention in Germany. In June the *New Statesman* published

a letter from Evelyn Waugh deploring 'the policy of starving the Germans' and the banning of food parcels. Waugh did not have much time for Gollancz, whom he saw as a hypocritical socialist who had helped create a government that made private charity impossible by nationalising conscience, but he did support the 'Save Europe Now' campaign, encouraged by the scenes he had witnessed in Nuremberg. That month competing voices in the press and Parliament called for more or less aid to be given to the defeated nation, while the British in Germany carried out orders by smashing up a series of shipyards and dockyard installations in Hamburg in June and July. Alarmed, the city's inhabitants complained that this was the Morgenthau Plan in action at last.[23]

The dismantling was no longer typical, however. Following the Paris meeting in the spring, there was a broad consensus among the British and Americans that they should come together to protect Germany economically from Soviet influence. In July, James Byrnes offered to merge the US zone with any other zone for economic purposes. His offer was promptly accepted by Britain, though it remained to be seen quite how this would work. Earlier in the month, bread rationing had been introduced in Britain. Gollancz and his supporters were delighted, but much of the British populace was left furiously wondering quite what they had gained from fighting the war, with the *Daily Mail* reporting that bread rationing was 'the most hated measure ever to have been presented to the people of this country'. British politicians were aware that they could only unite with the Americans if the richer nation was prepared to pay a substantial majority of the costs.[24]

While Gollancz campaigned to make the British public more sympathetic towards Germany, Erika and Klaus Mann urged their readers to remain hard-hearted in judging the Germans. Erika had returned to the Nuremberg trial in March, now diagnosed with pleurisy. She retained her exasperation with the Germans in general and was especially incensed about the indulgence being shown to German cultural figures who had consorted with the Nazis but were now deemed useful enough to be swiftly denazified.

In the middle of February the Russians had summoned the conductor Wilhelm Furtwängler back to Germany to take over his old position

at the Berlin Philharmonic. 'Berlin calls Wilhelm Furtwängler', ran the
headline in the Soviet-controlled *Berliner Zeitung*. 'All of us who want
to build the new democratic Germany in the spirit of humanity need
the high symbol of artistic perfection . . . that is why we, why Germany,
needs the artist Wilhelm Furtwängler.' German exiles in the US including Thomas Mann immediately protested about this move and were
supported by the American occupation authorities.[25]

During the Third Reich, Furtwängler had spoken out on behalf of
Jewish musicians such as Bruno Walter, who were forced out of Nazi
Germany, and had refused to join the Nazi Party or give the Nazi salute.
However he had carried the title of Prussian State Councillor in the
Third Reich (primarily an honorary title) and conducted on Hitler's
behalf throughout his time in power, most notably giving a concert to
the Nazi Youth in 1938, conducting Wagner's *Die Meistersinger von
Nürnberg* (*The Master-Singers of Nuremberg*) on the evening before the
1938 Nazi rally, and giving a concert in Prague in March 1944 to mark
the fifth anniversary of the occupation of Poland. In order to conduct
at the Philharmonic, which lay in the the US sector, Furtwängler had
to receive a denazification license (*Persilschein*) in Vienna, Wiesbaden
and Berlin. The Americans in Wiesbaden were reluctant to exonerate
him and it was clear that it would be some time before the case would
be resolved. None the less, he arrived in Berlin in a Russian aircraft on
10 March and was received with great ceremony by Becher, who was
prepared to believe that here at least was a German whose soul was alive
and conducted him to his old apartment in the pheasantry of the Sans-
Souci Palace at Potsdam.

Erika Mann was outraged about Furtwängler and she was angry
too about the acceptance offered to the 'inner emigrants' who had
been calling for her father's return. In her letter to Lotte Walter in
January she complained about the adulation accorded to 'a new poet,
an uncle named Bergengruen', who had gone so far as to compare
Germany to Christ. As a Catholic, the poet and novelist Werner
Bergengruen was one of many writers to frame Germany's current
situation in an apocalyptic, Christian framework in which specific
guilt was subsumed by a more general sense of man's original sin.

Later that year Erika Mann would write an article dismissing the term 'inner emigration' as a 'free pass'. Authors did not have to prove that they had spoken out against the Nazis but could claim the status of the spiritual emigrant.[26]

At the start of May, Erika was summoned home to California to help look after her father, who was being operated on for lung cancer. Her days of gallivanting around Europe were over; from now on she would remain at home as Thomas Mann's loyal assistant, leaving Klaus to struggle alone in the battle to regain a foothold in Germany. Exhausted and disillusioned, Erika was not reluctant to leave. She warned her parents that they should expect 'a pensive, white-haired lady who shows the strain of defeat in victory'. For Erika as for many of Germany's conquerors, the taste of victory was becoming ever more bitter both because of the intransigence of the Germans and because her faith in the Americans was weakening. A couple of months earlier she had warned her father not to travel to Europe because Germany would 'swallow' him up and it was a 'horrid' place even to visit. 'It is sad, poor, demoralised, corrupt and depressing'; if he appeared he would be used 'by the Russians against the Yanks and the French against the Tommies', and would return home damaged and angry.[27]

Arriving in Los Angeles, Erika wrote a series of articles castigating the Germans and their conquerors and claiming inaccurately that the stories about a starving Germany were mere propaganda. 'Whereas the rest of Europe, including England, has gone hungry for the past six years, the Germans begin only now to feel the pinch of severe food shortages.' This was patently untrue: the calorie counts alone testified to the desperate situation in Germany. But Erika seems genuinely to have believed that the Germans were less hungry than they claimed to be, convinced that their self-pity and denial made them unworthy of sympathy on any count. She made it clear in her articles that she no longer had much hope for German re-education; the Germans seemed to be waiting only for a war between the Americans and the Russians. And she was one of many commentators to see a third world war as becoming worryingly likely, partly because of the aggressive self-righteousness of the Americans.[28]

In Italy, Klaus Mann was perturbed that his family was regrouping in California without him. No one had pleaded with him to return to watch over his father's sickbed. Indeed, he learnt about the successful outcome of his father's operation from a telegram from his father's publisher and a note in *Time* reporting that the great man was 'resting comfortably'. 'I don't know what ails or ailed him in particular and how much he himself knows by now,' Klaus complained to his mother, unsure how to write to the patient. 'Tell him my "affections and congratulations".'[29]

Klaus was concerned about his dwindling role both in the family and in postwar Europe. In his autobiography, published in 1942, he had hoped explicitly that there would be a world after the war 'for people like us to live in, to work for'. He was sure that a world brought into being by the victorious Allies would 'accept and need' the services of men such as him – 'versed in various idioms and traditions, experienced go-betweens . . . fore-runners and agents of the super-national civilisation to be constructed'. Here he was imagining his position in Germany in terms similar to those of Stephen Spender, hoping that as an American citizen well-acquainted with German culture he would be ideally placed to help first with denazification and re-education and then with establishing a new outward-looking and European cultural scene in Germany. These hopes had now been quelled, more dramatically in Klaus Mann's case than in Spender's because he had more invested both in Germany and his role there. And artistically he had very little in prospect. His collaboration with Rossellini had ended and he had been attempting successively to start film, book and magazine projects, which had come to nothing.[30]

He fuelled his resentful disappointment into articles about Gustaf Gründgens, who returned to the stage in May as the leading character in Carl Sternheim's *The Snob* at the Deutsches Theater. Since his relationship with the Manns ended two decades earlier, Gründgens had been the theatrical darling of both the Weimar Republic and the Third Reich. Gründgens's successful performance as Mephistopheles in Goethe's *Faust* in 1932 had led Göring to appoint the actor as the intendant (artistic director) of the State Theater, partly so that

Gründgens could direct Göring's then-lover Emmy Sonnemann in her emerging acting career. At the end of the war, Gründgens was arrested and imprisoned by the Soviet authorities but his nine months in prison was a relatively privileged time when he was given permission to direct a makeshift prison theatre. The Russians had realised that his skills could be put to better use on the public stage and transported him directly from prison to the Deutsches Theater where he was to play his new role.

The Snob opened on 3 May to sell-out audiences and rave reviews. There was five minutes of applause before Gründgens could even speak his opening lines; at the end of the play the stage filled with flowers. The critic Walter Karsch attributed the applause both to the success of the performance and to the audience's gratitude to Gründgens for creating an island of artistic calm outside the political turbulance of the Third Reich. Klaus Mann managed to acquire a ticket on the black market and saw the play in June. In a satirical article entitled 'Art and Politics', Mann complained that if Gründgens could now be given a standing ovation on the Berlin stage, the Germans should welcome Emmy Sonnemann back as well. Indeed, 'perhaps someone gassed in Auschwitz left behind some stage piece in which the esteemed woman could make her second debut. The good woman surely knew nothing about Auschwitz – and besides, what does art have to do with politics?'[31]

This essay was not simply a personal swipe at a former lover. It was also a considered critique of the German separation of culture from politics. '"Political song – nasty song!"' it begins; 'an old German saying – an old German error . . . as if art could exist outside social context – independent and inactive, floating in a vacuum!' Even if art could remain aesthetically pure, the artist could not help being part of his time: a human and a citizen bound to the same laws as his less artistically gifted contemporaries. He could therefore not be allowed to go unpunished for collaborating with political gangsters. 'Have geniuses a jester's license?'

Klaus Mann went on to distinguish between different kinds of artists, saying that writers who had compromised with Nazism should be most punished, given that 'moral culture' comprised one of their professional duties. Musicians presented a more complex case because their music remained relatively apolitical. During the war Bruno Walter had conducted Strauss in New York, saying that although he would never again shake hands with the composer he did not wish to deprive the American public of his music. Mann suggested grudgingly that Strauss's music might be performed but the composer should not be invited to the premiere. He was more scathing about Furtwängler, insisting that as state councillor he had been highly implicated in Nazi politics. 'You cannot be in charge of the most effective cultural propaganda for an imperialist regime without being aware of the character of your position.' He ended by admitting reluctantly that not every writer, actor or musician was able to emigrate – 'and the concentration camp was understandably not to everyone's taste' – while maintaining that a culture rebuilt by Nazi sympathisers had better remain buried.[32]

In his 'Germany and the Germans' speech the previous summer, Thomas Mann had grappled with the question of whether German artists should be criticised for attempting to rise above the political realities of their age. Klaus now answered this easily. But he was disingenuous in not accepting any notion of 'inner emigration' and in not giving weight to a German intellectual tradition that had created an artistic culture of 'inwardness' that made the notion of inner emigration far more possible than it would have been in Britain or the US: the legacy both of the later period of German Romanticism and of a nineteenth-century repressive political regime that sent many of its politically engaged artists into jail or exile. During these postwar years Klaus never publicly questioned his father's stance, but as his son well knew Thomas had asked for the renewal of his German passport in April 1934, disapproving of Nazism but believing it was possible to live quietly amid a dictatorship.

In his wartime autobiography Klaus had admitted to the youthful folly of apoliticism. For many years he, like most of his artistic contemporaries, had found politics 'void and depressing', refusing to bother with them. He had changed his mind, quickly and vehemently, but could he blame his former friends for failing to do so? It seems that he could and did. He went on to write an article called 'Berlin's Darling' which was at once an explosion of years of hatred and a belated love letter to Gründgens. Here he takes a mock light-hearted tone in describing how smitten the 'jolly Reichsmarschall' was with the 'delightfully demoniac' actor; how the 'fat protector' appointed his new protégé as the 'indefatigable, ingenious *maitre de plaisir* of Greater Germany'. But the portrayal of Gründgens in his youth is almost lyrical. Mann describes the 'handsome, clever, glamorous, sophisticated' young actor he once loved and the 'nonchalant, iridescent charm' that he once found so seductive. After outlining Gründgens's various outrageously successful incarnations, Mann analyses Gründgens's reaction to the ovation that greeted him every night: 'Was he moved or embarrassed? If so, he did not show it; he just stood there and smiled – as attractive as ever, with white tie, pink complexion, blond toupee and all: the indestructible darling of pre-Nazi, Nazi and post-Nazi Berlin.'[33]

Whatever the outcome of the Nuremberg trial, both Erika and Klaus Mann now believed that the moral values of Germany would remain unchanged. For Erika it was outrageous that Göring should charm a courtroom of spectators daily from the dock. For Klaus it was even more absurd that Göring's former protégé should delight audiences nightly at the theatre. And it was doubly maddening that he himself should accord in finding his former lover 'as attractive as ever'. Day after day some of the best legal minds in the world sat in the courtroom at Nuremberg arguing about tortuous questions of legality. The tribunal was still broadcast on the radio and newspapers throughout Germany dutifully reported its findings. But while de Menthon talked about collective guilt and the courtroom reeled at the descriptions of the concentration camps, resilient former Nazis curried favour with their conquerors and the opportunities of the brief zero hour after the war seemed on their way to being lost.[34]

9

'Let this trial never finish'

Boredom: May–August 1946

As the trial continued into the summer, the pervading mood was one of boredom. After the excitement of Göring's stand in the witness box, the lengthy questioning of the more minor Nazis and their witnesses quickly began to seem tedious. On 23 May, Birkett grumbled that when he considered the 'utter uselessness of acres of paper and thousands of words and that life is slipping away' he despaired at the shocking waste of time. Outside Nuremberg, other Nazis had been examined in smaller war crimes trials that had concluded in a matter of weeks; the US had already begun proceedings against the leaders in Japan that were evidently going to be conducted much more swiftly.[1]

In a memorandum to the other judges a few days later, the Soviet judge Nikitchenko complained that the tribunal was being stretched unjustifiably and that all clarity had been lost. But neither Birkett nor Biddle thought it was possible to speed up the trial without losing the pervading sense of fairness. They distracted themselves by writing and reading light verse, occasionally addressed to each other:

> *Birkett to Biddle after one long dreary afternoon*
> At half-past four my spirits sink
> My mind a perfect trance is:

But oh! The joy it is to think
Of half-past seven with Francis.

They were grateful that the weather at least was improving. Spring came abruptly to Nuremberg that year and blossomed into summer. The *Autobahnen* were now lined with thick broom; there was a carpet of crocuses along the river. Biddle later described how 'a thousand years settled in the valley of the old river, and there was time to stretch again under the warmth of the ancient summer sun'.[2]

Once the defendants left the witness box in June, the tribunal considered important but hardly riveting questions about the validity and possible interpretations of the law. July was dominated by the summing up of the defence counsel; there were twenty-two of them and it took twenty-one days. The judges were determined to give the defence a fair hearing and therefore did not question the relevance of speeches that meandered through world literature and history before addressing the questions in hand.

Nineteen days into the defence counsel speeches, the novelist Rebecca West arrived from England. West had been summoned to Germany by Hartley Shawcross, the British prosecutor, because following Harold Nicolson's refusal the British judges now wanted West to write a book about the trial. The travel arrangements were typically last-minute: on the evening of 22 July she was informed that she needed to report to Berkeley Square in London by eight the next morning. Busy arranging transport, West left her secretary to pack. When she arrived in London she found that she had not been provided with a change of underwear but instead with a hot-water bottle and a large straw hat that she usually wore for the Henley Regatta.

West travelled with Shawcross (whom she thought a genius of a lawyer but too small town and shy to succeed politically) and Maxwell-Fyfe ('the Churchill of the next generation'). The journey was chaotic. They had to wait for two hours at the airport because an army car had failed to pick up the other half of their party. When they did arrive at Nuremberg there was no transport to meet them and when they finally made it to the courthouse Shawcross had no pass.[3]

Entering the court West found herself in a 'citadel of boredom'. The judges on the bench were plainly 'dragging the proceedings over the threshold of their consciousness by sheer force of will'; the lawyers and their secretaries sat sagging in their seats and the faces of the white-capped guards were puffy with tedium. They all wanted to leave Nuremberg as urgently as the dental patient under the drill wanted to leave the dentist's chair.[4]

West was not disposed to be bored. She had come to Germany seeking adventure. Like Evelyn Waugh she was finding the postwar austerity of England demoralising, despite regular food parcels sent by her editors at the *New Yorker*. And the greyness of her surroundings reflected a more personal feeling of drabness. Ten years earlier West's husband Henry Andrews had stopped desiring her; aged fifty-three she was in a celibate marriage. This was all the more galling because West was a woman who had, half-unwillingly, forged her identity through sex.

Born Cicily Fairfield in 1892, West had borrowed her name aged twenty from a character in Ibsen's *Rosmersholm*. 'Live, work, act,' says Ibsen's heroine; 'don't sit here and brood.' By the time of her twenty-first birthday, West was famous for her savage reviews and her dark, troubled eyes. She was also pregnant with the child of one of the most famous novelists of the day, H. G. Wells. Anxious to avoid scandal, Wells hid West away in Southend. 'Jaguar' now visited his 'Panther' whenever he could, although once the baby arrived Wells was irritated that West had less time to look after him.[5]

By shamelessly mothering an illegitimate child, West inadvertently became one of the first women publicly to broadcast the female need for sex. Both because of her domestic situation and because of the stridency of her writing, she acquired a public sensuality that seems to have made her a frightening figure for men. After the relationship with Wells ended in 1922, West engaged in a series of brief liaisons with men who pursued her only to reject her when she succumbed (Charlie Chaplin and Max Beaverbrook among them). She was therefore pleased to escape both the humiliation and precariousness of her position as an unmarried mother by marrying Henry Andrews in 1930. He was a banker who could recite the timetables of any railroad in Europe, even for countries he had never visited; he was dependable, adoring and apparently desperate to look after her. 'My husband can do everything that I can, better than I can,' West once said, somewhat wishfully.

The marriage gave West confidence as a public figure. She made her name as an investigative journalist and produced a series of books culminating in the magisterial *Black Lamb and Grey Falcon*, her account of 1930s Yugoslavia. She fought fascism and then communism. But Andrews turned out to be neither as strong nor as devoted as West had hoped. After seven years it transpired that he saw sex as an activity better suited for secretaries than wives. As Andrews became less affectionate, he also became more erratic; he was forgetful, irascible and chaotic. Increasingly West found it hard to work, pressed in by her husband's rages and by the difficulty of maintaining order in their home, a farmhouse in Ibstone in Buckinghamshire.[6]

West was hopeful that her stay in Nuremberg would distract her from the disappointment and exhaustion that now characterised her days at home with her husband. She did not anticipate feeling much conflicting sympathy for the Germans. Visiting Germany in the 1930s she had asked her sister why the British had not put every man, woman and child of that 'abominable nation' to the sword in 1919: 'The insane mercy and charity of the Treaty of Versailles makes me gnash my teeth.' She found the Germans 'a great galumphing fool of a people' and thought that the women in particular lacked both intellectual pretentions and domestic skills. But her views were not consistently this extreme. Later she recalled that she had 'always been able to distinguish between the Nazis and the decent German people'; she and her husband helped his German relatives as much as they could during the war, including those who remained in Germany. In her more generous moments, she was hopeful that the trial would distinguish between Germans and Nazis and provide the world with a way forward.[7]

Observing the inhabitants of the 'citadel of boredom', West found that the defendants had the appearance that historical characters assume in bad paintings. They were wreathed in the suggestion of death. The judges by contrast were stately. West had known Biddle in the US in the 1920s and then in 1935 when she was reporting on the New Deal.

She was now impressed by his aristocratic bearing. She found Lawrence dignified and efficient; his father had been a Lord Chief Justice and he seemed to bring to the proceedings the quality that the second generation of a theatrical family brings to Shakespeare.

At dinner two days into her trip, West met Biddle again. She had always been aware of his attraction to her and was excited to see him now, in a stranger and freer context. She told him that she was doing a piece for the *New Yorker* and was worried that she had not seen enough of the background to the trial. Biddle immediately announced that the *New Yorker* was one of the few things that had kept him sane in Nuremberg and suggested that she came to stay at his villa. The next day he summoned her from the visitors' gallery and took her to the Villa Conradti, where he had persuaded the authorities to move him in the spring. This had initially been used as the VIP house and was a large villa furnished with heavy wooden furniture from the Bismarck period and enclosed in acres of gardens adorned by pines, a park and a lake.

Biddle told West that since they had last met, he and his wife Katherine had read her books aloud to each other in the evenings. He was distressed that West did not seem to have looked after her appearance. 'You could be as wonderful as ever.' Shyly, she murmured that she was growing old. He dismissed her concerns and whisked her off to have her hair done. It was an odd courtship, but a successful one. For ten days they were lovers. West felt rejuvenated and happy, despite an attack of gastroenteritis and a daily battle with her only set of underwear, which she washed inconveniently in her bath. She cleaned her bra and knickers on alternate days and entered the solemn courtroom either knickerless or braless each day.[8]

West was impressed by Biddle's erudite authority. 'Isn't it curious that the only aristocrat on the bench is American,' she observed in his hearing. She was irritated by his account of his wife Katherine, who had refused sex with her husband for eighteen months after the birth of their second child, supposedly wanting to punish him for the pain of childbirth. Now, however, Katherine was safely at home in America and it was West who accompanied him to lunches, dinners and parties. In the rare moments of freedom between court sessions they escaped for walks in the woods and explored nearby villages, picnicing by the river and stretching under the warmth of Biddle's 'ancient summer sun'. Most people around them were probably aware of the affair but it was not unusual. One of Biddle's colleagues later described the atmosphere of Nuremberg as 'relaxed, tolerant and philanderous'. Indeed, the sexually charged atmosphere was encouraged by the erotic paintings which hung opposite the beds in the main bedrooms of all the villas. 'Apparently Germans had to have a signpost put up on the straightest road,' West informed her editor at the *New Yorker*.[9]

On the day that West moved into Biddle's villa, the prosecutors began their concluding speeches. Jackson, opening the proceedings, pressed the charge of conspiracy, arguing that it was impossible for criminality on a scale such as this simply to have occurred spontaneously as the defendants claimed. He impressed the onlookers with his one-sentence portraits of the defendants. Göring, he said, was 'half-militarist, half-gangster. His pudgy finger was in every pie'; Ribbentrop was 'a salesman of deception'. He insisted that the men themselves were fully conscious of their guilt. 'If you were to say of these men that they were not guilty, it would be as true to say that there had been no War, there had been no slain, there had been no crime.' West found the speech 'a masterpiece, exquisitely relevant to the indictment'. She thought the reference to Göring's fingers was especially pertinent: 'The courtroom is not small, but it is full of Göring's fingers. His soft and spongy white hands are forever smoothing his curiously abundant hair or covering his wide mouth . . . or weaving impudent gestures of innocence in the air.'[10]

That afternoon Shawcross took over, impressive in his clarity, calling for the death sentence for all the defendants. Continuing the next day, Shawcross made a rare mention of the Nazi crimes against Jews, addressing the explicit charge of 'crimes against humanity'. Citing the Nazi orders for the Final Solution, intended to lead to the extermination of the entire Jewish race, he stated that: 'There is one group to which the method of annihilation was applied on a scale so immense that it is my duty to refer separately to the evidence. I mean the extermination of the Jews. If there were no other crime against these men, this one alone, in which all of them were implicated, would suffice. History holds no parallel to these horrors.'

Shawcross went on to quote Goethe, who had prophesised that one day fate would strike the German people, 'because they betrayed themselves and did not want to be what they are. It is sad that they do not know the charm of truth, that mist, smoke and berserk immoderation are so dear to them, pathetic that they ingenuously submit to any mad scoundrel who appeals to their lowest instincts, who confirms them in their vices and teaches them to conceive nationalism as isolation and brutality.' Goethe had spoken prophetically; the 'mad scoundrels' in the dock had done these very things and now the hope of future international co-operation depended on bringing retribution to these guilty men.[11]

Shawcross should have checked his sources more carefully. Within a few days, the press was commenting that these were not in fact Goethe's words but were attributed to him by Thomas Mann in his 1939 novel *Lotte in Weimar*. If Erika Mann had still been at the trial she could have lectured the British lawyers on questions of German literature. Instead the British Foreign Office cabled Washington asking the embassy to contact Thomas Mann in California and find out the source of the quote. Amused and flattered, Mann replied that 'the quoted words do not appear literally in Goethe's writings or conversations' but were written in his spirit: 'although he never spoke them, he might well have done so'. It is appropriate that Mann should be quoted indirectly at the tribunal; writing *Doctor Faustus* in California he was busy indicting his countrymen as forcefully as the Nuremberg prosecutors.[12]

On 6 August, Rebecca West returned home to Ibstone. Biddle wrote to his wife that he missed his new companion, who had been a 'gay and amusing wench'. West was pleased about her own renewal but also saddened by the rediscovery of embodiment. 'I'm fifty-three and I might as well put the shutters up,' she wrote to her friend Emanie Arling. 'I had, but he made me take them down.' Home-returned-to seemed dreary and monotonous. Her sadness was compounded by the death of H. G. Wells on 13 August. Wells had been one of the two central men in West's life. She had lost her virginity to him, borne his child and loved him for the twenty years of their affair. Arguably Wells had both discovered and formed her. He had not always been strong enough for her; he was the first of many lovers who had pursued her urgently only to flee once she had succumbed, frightened by the intensity of her love. But he had recognised her as passionate, brilliant and unique. 'I had never met anything like her before, and I doubt if there was anything like her before,' he once wrote. She now found that their troubled past took on the quality of a story she had learnt from a book; what remained was her affection:

> Dear HG, he was a devil, he ruined my life, he starved me, he was an
> inexhaustible source of love and friendship to me for thirty-four years,
> we should never have met, I was the one person he cared to see to the
> end, I feel desolate because he has gone.[13]

Now, reliving those years, West aligned Wells with her new lover in her mind. Both were ultimately loyal to wives on whose day-to-day comfort they depended while passionately desiring West. Katherine seemed as conniving as Wells's wife Jane and West was furious about the indulgence with which Biddle had treated his wife's denial of sex. It was all the more galling that West herself should have ended up with a husband who gave her loyalty without desire. She had in effect become one of the entitled but betrayed wives she despised, while also remaining the mistress who had nothing. She wondered if her husband's rejection of her as a woman had done more to destroy her life than Wells's rejection of her as a potential wife. 'Oh God, what a world!' she cried out, pacing the house, thinking of Nuremberg, pausing between paces to cry out 'Francis!'[14]

Meanwhile Biddle was writing West loving letters, describing his villa as haunted by her absence. He was trying to hear her laugh but could no longer recall the way she said 'lovely, Francis, lovely!' Missing her and wanting her, he realised what a joy it had been to be involved with a woman who liked doing exactly what he wished but never quite surrendered. Between court sessions he was writing a memoir of their love. Biddle urged West to return to Nuremberg, assuring her that his feelings for her were growing and were no mere manifestation of nerves. He dreamt continually of her appearing before him in bare feet. West's letters too were direct and passionate. 'I come to breakfast, full of you, in my body and your stars in my eyes,' she wrote, offering that she could be 'anywhere that anybody who wanted to see me wanted me to be'.[15]

Biddle was sent West's draft report for the *New Yorker* for his comments. 'It is awfully good, I think,' he responded; 'digs deep, catches the quality and essential, says good things inevitably.' While composing the report, West had told Emanie Arling that she found it impossible to formulate anything that did not give her away. 'I want to write nothing. I want to live and I have left it too long'.

The resulting article does indeed give West away, obliquely and brilliantly. Her description of the judges' bench begins with Biddle, whom she portrays as 'a highly intelligent swan, occasionally flexing down to commune with a smaller waterfowl', Lawrence. West describes the trial as creating a climate where love can flourish amid the tedium. 'Doubtless the life of the heart is lived in Nuremberg as well as anywhere else,' she states disingenuously, before describing the corridors of the Palace of Justice as paced by 'an image of Eros'. This is a dog marbled in black and white who waits for its master in a posture of 'inconsolable widowhood'; when his beloved returns the dog lurches after him, repeating with its ears and tail lines from Euripides: 'Oh, Love, Love, thou that from thine eyes diffusest yearning and on the soul sweet grace induces.'[16]

West explained to her editor that she had brought in the dog because she could think of no other way of politely expressing the emotional state of Nuremberg. In her letter she added that in fact everybody in Nuremberg was 'either in love with someone who isn't there or is in love with someone who is there but finds it difficult to do anything about it, for housing reasons'. Biddle had told West that he wondered if 'the dog hung a little out of your frame, even if it led to the corridor of sex. You would know better.' He was more moved by a subtler reference to their time together. At the end of the article West describes the landscape in which she and her lover wandered and kissed. She portrays it as disconcerting in its loveliness, suggesting that it acts as a kind of protestation of innocence for the German people as a whole: 'Where the pine trees rise from the soft, reddish bed of scented pine needles, and dragonflies draw patterns of iridescence above the cloudy green trout stream, and the miller's little blond son plays with the gray kitten among the meadowsweet by the edges of the millpond, there can surely be no harm.' These were the fields and woods in which Biddle still walked daily, imagining West alongside him, remembering their times together. 'The dragonflies made me catch my breath,' he told her.[17]

West's article is perhaps most compelling in its description of the defendants themselves, who emerge from her account with a physicality that makes them at once more human and more frightening than they seem in previous reports. She evokes the greyness that Laura Knight depicted in her painting: they are 'neither dark nor fair', there is 'no leanness that does not sag and no plumpness that seems more than inflation by some thin gas'. Streicher she sees as 'a dirty old man of the sort that gives trouble in parks'; Speer is likeable but has a baboon-ish quality in his sharp, dark face that seems to explain how he forgot himself and used his art to serve the Nazis. Göring is the most vivid figure in the piece, emerging as far more colourful a character than the frighteningly gloomy figure in Knight's painting. His primary quality, West finds, is softness. His loose-hanging clothes give him an air of pregnancy; the coarse, bright skin of an actor who has used greasepaint for decades combined with the deep wrinkles of the drug addict give him the head of a ventriloquists's dummy. Because over the years the public has heard so much about Göring's love affairs, his appearance seems to make 'a pointed but obscure reference to sex'. But he looks neither like a womaniser nor a homosexual; instead he appears more like the madam of a brothel. And his wide and wooden lips sometimes smack together in smiling appetite: 'If he were given the chance, he would walk out of the Palace of Justice, take over Germany again, and turn it into a stage for the enactment of his governing fantasy, which is so strong that it fills the air around him with its images, so madly private that those images are beyond the power of those who see them to interpret them.'

West's report, like Knight's painting, bears witness to a moment of transition. The defendants in the dock have lost all authority and are wreathed in death. As in George Orwell's account, they have ceased to be monsters now that they are captured under lock and key. This was a peculiar juncture in the history of Nazism. Lee Miller could bathe in Hitler's bath; Göring could try to persuade Hess to share his biscuit during the trial. Most of the accounts from this time testify to the strangeness of witnessing the human frailty of the former leaders. Yet the horror of the camps was already almost mythological in its gruesome details, meaning that the Nazis were evolving from human politicians to evil fairy-tale figures. Even as she made notes on their physical characteristics, West was aware that these men were soon to become historical names. And they seemed to her to be visibly receding from the field of existence, praying no longer for life, just for the proceedings at Nuremberg to continue in all their tedium: 'Let this trial never finish, let it go on forever and ever, without end.'

10

'The law tries to keep up with life'

Judgement: September–October 1946

The trial did not in fact go on forever, though it seemed to many onlookers as though it might. On 31 August 1946 the court adjourned for three weeks to give the judges time to make their decisions. It was apparent from the outset that this was going to be an acrimonious process, primarily because the French wished the term 'conspiracy' to be taken out of the final judgement and the Russians, who were more concerned with vengeance than justice, did not think that any of the defendants should be acquitted.

Originally, the judges intended to reach a decision by 23 September but on the seventeenth they decided to postpone the verdict for a week. Although the four judges remained largely intransigent in their opinions, there were occasional minor concessions. Biddle had begun by demanding the death sentence for Speer but he now changed his mind, accepting twenty years of imprisonment. By the end of September the judges had agreed their verdicts on all except Franz von Papen (Ambassador to Austria at the time of the *Anschluss*), Hans Fritzsche (*Ministerialdirektor* in the Ministry for Popular Enlightenment and Propaganda) and Schacht, whom the British, Americans and French agreed should be acquitted on the grounds that their crimes were domestic rather than international and therefore fell outside the court's jurisdiction, making it impossible for their guilt to be proven beyond reasonable doubt. On 29 September, Nikitchenko confessed to Biddle that he had been instructed by Moscow publicly to dissent from these verdicts. After more debate, Lawrence agreed that he would refer to the Soviet opposition in his final summing up.

By now, Rebecca West was back in Nuremberg, where she had arrived on 26 September. Biddle had been attempting to arrange her return for the previous two months. Initially he was unsure whether his wife Katherine was planning to join him but wanted West to come anyway and stay in the Villa Conradti as their guest. West was unhappy about this idea; she had done her time as the supposed family friend during her relationship with Wells. She also found the elaborate precautions Biddle took to avoid discovery tedious and insulting. West was instructed to write additional, politely friendly letters to her lover so that he had something to show his wife as a subterfuge and a complex code was developed for their telegrams. It was hard not to see his carefulness as a form of rejection. He did not want her enough to take any risks. They quarrelled about this and Biddle attempted to reassure her of his love. 'I think we complicate things,' he told her, though surely the complication was largely on his side; 'our relationship is so simple – and so sweet.' More movingly he listed his imaginings of a shared life yet to be lived – 'we have never except once listened to music together, or walked on an unending beach, or seen the sun set over the painted desert, or New York at night, or read aloud, or punted on the Thames, or danced or tried to quarrel' – and wrote with sadness of the narrowing of his life in her absence. 'I said to you once before that you opened vistas. I don't want them to close. I do not want to go back to a smaller life.'[1]

In fact it transpired that Katherine planned to stay at home in the US, leaving West free to join Biddle as his lover. She set out at dawn on 24 September and found that transport to Nuremberg was typically inefficient. This time West and Joseph Laitin, an American correspondent assigned to Reuters, were deposited by plane in Berlin, where they were told they would have to return to London because the British authorities had no idea how to send them to Nuremberg. West was adept at disobeying orders; she commandeered a car that had been sent to fetch another correspondent and directed it to take them to the Allied press camp in the Kufürstendamm. Here she arranged a seat on a plane from Berlin to Nuremberg and then set out to survey Berlin.

Like previous visitors, West was struck by the difference between the ruins here and the ones she had seen in Nuremberg. Instead of flattened rubble, there was 'mile after mile of purged houses scoured by the wind and rain'. She felt no more sympathy for the inhabitants than she had visiting Berlin in the 1930s, complaining to her husband that there was 'not a smile anywhere'. In her report on the trip for the *New Yorker*, West wrote that she could not weep for the citizens of Berlin because they had brought the situation on themselves. She wept instead for the statues, which could not be expected to know when to come out of the rain, even when it turned into blood. She had admired the statues when they had stood proudly surveying the Tiergarten in the 1930s. Now they were surrounded by barren mud instead of trees and the bellies of the women were scrawled with the names and addresses of Russian soldiers; the Empress Victoria had lost her marble veil, hat and head.[2]

Finally arriving in Nuremberg, West went straight to the Villa Conradti where Biddle was waiting for her. Finding that she was unexpectedly shy in his presence after the intensity of their letters, she explained her awkwardness with tiredness. The next few days were passed waiting for the judges to decide on their verdicts; in the evenings there was the usual round of dinners. On Sunday 29 September, the day before the final judgements, she, Biddle and two colleagues spent the day in Bamberg, a pretty town with a cathedral where they picnicked on a hillside.[3]

West was now reporting both for the *New Yorker* and for the London *Daily Telegraph*. In an article in the *Telegraph* written to set the scene before the trial resumed, she wrote that the judgement that was about to be delivered had to prove that victors could rise above ordinary human limitations and fairly try the vanquished foes. If successful, the judgement would warn future war-mongers that the law could pursue them into peace. The judgement of the tribunal had the potential to be 'one of the most important events in the history of civilisation'.[4]

She told the readers of the *New Yorker* that she had returned to Nuremberg because 'it was necessary, and really necessary, that a large number of important persons . . . should go to Nuremberg and hear the reading of the judgement'. British public opinion had 'gone silly about it' and so there was a need for the influential 'to talk some sense on the subject'. Certainly, she was one of hundreds to descend on Nuremberg, turning it into a busy international city once again. Most of them were politicians and civil servants but among the other influential journalists was Martha Gellhorn, returning to Germany for the first time in almost a year.[5]

Since leaving Germany the previous winter, Gellhorn had been wandering between England, Spain, Portugal, Java and the US. She was distracting herself from loneliness by writing a novel, socialising frantically, visiting war zones and buying and doing up a small house in London. Gellhorn had written intermittently to James Gavin who was now stationed at his army base in Fort Bragg, North Carolina and was desperately missing the excitement of the war. They had met briefly in May, but the visit was a coda to a relationship that had ended in Berlin. Gellhorn made no promises any more and although Gavin's letters remained insistent and passionate, he was still writing and speaking just as frequently to Marlene Dietrich.

It would be some years before Gellhorn fell in love again. She was now more interested in literature than love; she could rely more steadily on writing than on men. Her German novel, provisionally entitled 'Point of No Return', expressed her own mood of disillusionment with both war and love. Writing the book, she had in a sense never left Germany. Throughout the duration of the Nuremberg trial, she had been engaged in forming her own private judgement both on the Nazis and on the soldiers who had fought them. She now wished to return to witness the public judgement as well.

––––––

The final stage of the tribunal began on Monday 30 September 1946. West breakfasted early and drove with Biddle to the court. It was a sharp, sunny day which West described in the *Telegraph* as 'one of those autumn days which are heavy and golden with the passing of the year, and yet are fresh as if the world had been made that dawn'. As they drove through Nuremberg there were more tanks stationed in the town than usual, but the Germans went by looking at the ground, uninterested in the events playing out in the courtroom. In the Palace of Justice, security measures had increased and women journalists were sent to deposit their handbags in the cloakroom and then left to carry their fountain pens and notebooks around with them, although West (now equipped with a full set of underwear) managed to stow hers in her stockings.[6]

Sir Geoffrey Lawrence began the morning session by summarising the work of the tribunal and its indictments. Watching the British judge, Gellhorn thought that he looked tired and old but that 'his voice was a symbol of what all civilised people want and mean by justice – something serene and unafraid and stronger than time'. Lawrence and Birkett went on to list once more the trajectory of Nazi crimes. During the two-hour lunch break, Gellhorn wandered around the ruins of Nuremberg. Once again, she was shocked by the scale of destruction that she encountered. She would describe the bombed old town as a 'vast rubbish heap' in Point of No Return, where she depicts the bombing of the city from the jaunty perspective of the seasoned soldier: 'There was nothing small and clinchy about the bombs we were using. The airforce was running a regular bus service over Nürnberg; the noise of the planes was so constant you stopped hearing it.'[7]

Biddle opened the afternoon session with a recapitulation of the German violation of international treaties and then summarised the tribunal's understanding of the first charge of the 'Common Plan or Conspiracy'. Gellhorn observed that Biddle looked away from the defendants when he spoke, not wanting to catch their eyes. This was her first time in the court and she was struck by the general air of pallid exhaustion, patience and determination. She, like all her predecessors, watched the defendants, though she was not as charmed as other correspondents by Göring, who was showing off less cheerfully now that the judgement was approaching. 'Göring has the ugliest thumbs I have ever seen – possibly also the ugliest mouth,' Gellhorn wrote in her notebook. His smile was disassociated from the rest of his face, suggesting that it was merely a habit his lips had acquired. The air-conditioning was on high and she felt permanently frozen, which seemed in keeping with the tone of the judges: 'it is a cold court – no pity is possible'. But Gellhorn did not want or expect pity. The pitilessness of the Nazis themselves could only be answered by coldness.[8]

That evening, West and Biddle dined with lawyers and visiting dignitaries while Gellhorn and a group of other correspondents staying in the Faber villa drove into the countryside to find a village pub for a meal. They went to Ansbach where they spoke to a local boy who had been a soldier since he was sixteen. The conversation exacerbated Gellhorn's fury with the Germans. The boy claimed that the stories of concentration camps were exaggerated propaganda; he had seen people returning from them fat and suntanned. He maintained that the war had been essential because Britain would have attacked them and that the killing of the Jews had been merely a 'mistake'.

The first of October was the final day of the Nuremberg trial. It was a foggy morning, which made the broken towers and walls of the old town look even more like the scene of a disturbing fairy tale than usual. The day began with the tribunal's judgements on the individual defendants. This was what the audience was there to hear and Lawrence rose to the occasion with the slow, clear indictment of Göring that began the day. Göring was found guilty on all four charges and Lawrence stated that he was 'often, indeed almost always, the moving force, second only to his leader'. The four judges then proceeded to take turns pronouncing judgement on each of the defendants. It was obvious from the verdicts who would be hanged and who might face a more lenient sentence (several were indicted under only two or three counts). However, the defendants had to wait until the afternoon to learn their fate.[9]

At 14.50 the court reconvened after lunch. The courtroom lights were now dim; the defendants entered through a panel behind the dock and came forward one by one to hear their sentences. Göring was first: for West he had the surprised look of a man in pyjamas who opens the door of his hotel room thinking he is entering a bathroom only to find himself in a public room. Just as Lawrence began to read out the sentence, it transpired that Göring's headphones were not working. There was considerable fuss as new ones were found to replace them and then all eyes were on Göring as Lawrence read out: 'Defendant Hermann Wilhelm Göring, on the Counts of the Indictment on which you have been convicted, the International Military Tribunal sentences you to death by hanging.'

Göring dropped his headphones and walked out of the court, leaving his former conspirators to hear their sentences. Eleven of the accused were condemned to death, seven including Hess and Speer received prison sentences and von Papen, Fritzsche and Schacht were acquitted. The afternoon session lasted forty-seven minutes and was followed by what Gellhorn described as 'an empty, stunned feeling in the courtroom'. The judges filed out; the trial was over. Justice had been done at last, though Gellhorn found that justice itself now seemed suddenly very small.[10]

For those present at the tribunal, the verdict was inevitably anticlimactic because no punishment could measure up to the crimes themselves. None the less, the implications for international law were momentous. Fifteen of the twenty-one defendants were found guilty of committing 'crimes against humanity' and all of these were sentenced to death or imprisonment. The best legal minds in the world were agreed that there was credible evidence that crimes against humanity as defined in the charter had been committed and could be punished by law. This marked the establishment of the principle that human rights were legally enforceable and that the civilised nations of the world had the duty to bring to justice state agents who authorised the torture and genocide of their own citizens and those of other states.[11] The implications for Germany were also significant. By punishing the Nazi leaders and making clear what they were being punished for, the Allies had demonstrated exactly why the Germans needed to feel remorse for their crimes and how they were required to change. The trial had been an exercise in looking backwards, aimed at making it possible to look forwards. It would now be easier for all four Allies to reconceive the Germans as subjects rather than prisoners.

West's *Telegraph* articles reporting on the final stages of the trial were published immediately on 1 and 2 October. She wrote enthusiastically about the future implications of the proceedings and about the judges themselves. She portrayed Biddle as 'a recognisable product of the Eastern seaboard, the stock that gave us so many Americans like Henry James and William James, that took English subtlety abroad and gave it the support of new vigour'. Describing each of the defendants, West found that there was not a coward among them. A mercy had been conferred upon Göring who, partly because of the broken headphones, had appeared in the end not so much 'the most evil of men' as simply a man bravely sustaining the burden of fear. She was dismissive of anyone in England who criticised the tribunal, suggesting that it had made the law to suit itself. 'Let us not discount our own achievements. The law tries to keep up with life. It never quite succeeds but it is never very far behind.'[12]

The German newspapers too reported respectfully on the judgement. 'The judges have spoken – the world breathes a sigh of relief' announced the caption of a cartoon in the British-licensed *Telegraf*, depicting Siegfried standing over a slain dragon with swastikas for teeth. The *Telegraf*'s reporter Arno Scholtz was impressed that the Allies had decided to acquit some of the defendants but found none the less that the German people had a different view of these men 'who had led them through a sea of suffering and tears into chaos'. Scholz suggested that the German people should demand to be allowed to try these men themselves, as did the reporter in the US-licensed *Tagesspiegel*.[13]

For the Germans as well as the British and Americans, the Soviet dissention was a discomforting sign that the trial had not been a complete success. Reporting on the verdict, Gellhorn was optimistic that by demonstrating that 'men of four nations could work patiently together to brand evil and reaffirm the power and goodness of honest law', the trial had set a precedent for future co-operation. But West suggested in her *Telegraph* article that the Soviet objection made it seem as though the Russians had hoped 'to use the Tribunal as a means of revenge rather than as a process of legal purification of the international situation'. And the Western Allies remained anxious that the very presence of the Russians would discredit the trial, given Soviet Russia's record of show trials in the 1930s, and that the Russians had committed many of the same types of crime as the Germans during the war, executing some 22,000 Polish internees and prisoners in 1940.[14]

For those who had spent eleven months in the Nuremberg courtroom, there was now nothing to do but return home and reacclimatise to the postwar world. Biddle and some of his colleagues delayed their departure by going to Prague for a couple of days, and took West along with them. Here they walked on famous bridges, looked at towers, spires and waterways and went to a screening of David Lean's film *Brief Encounter*, which had just been released in Europe. West was amused to find that this was not a popular film in Czechoslovakia. 'Sexual renunciation on secular grounds is not a theme which Central Europe understands.' The Czechs in the audience asked afterwards 'with some emotion' whether it was really true that in England there were no other places than railway buffets where lovers could meet. Even here, the Nuremberg judges could not quite escape the trial. At one point during the film, Biddle fell asleep; waking up he pointed at a minor character on the screen and said, 'My God, that man looks just like Göring'; he had dreamt his way back to the courthouse.[15]

The next day, Biddle developed flu but he and West managed to spend the afternoon alone together, wandering around the city and looking at churches. It was a brief interlude. The demands of ordinary life were pressing in on them and it was time to go back to their separate homes. On 4 October they returned to Nuremberg and dined alone at the Villa Conradti. West wore her best dress; Biddle, anxious as always, worried that their presence alone in the villa would attract gossip. The next morning they flew back together to London. West had expected to be collected by her husband but he had not received her telegram so instead Biddle drove her home to Ibstone, the journey made dreary by the knowledge of the separation that would follow.

West found the return even more anticlimactic than the previous one. 'Coming home an utter letdown,' she wrote in her diary that night. She complained to her literary agent that Henry was getting 'odder and odder every day' and more destructively involved in the affairs of the household. Biddle visited her for a day but his letters were becoming gradually less frequent and by the end of October they had stopped. 'Katherine has got him,' she announced in her diary.[16]

Events in the outside world seemed to confirm West's despair. On 16 October 1946 she heard that Göring had managed to commit suicide. Three days earlier the gallows equipment had arrived at Nuremberg; on 14 October the prisoners heard hammering from the gymnasium as the scaffold was erected. Göring had made an appeal asking to be shot as a soldier instead of hanged as a criminal but the court refused. On the fifteenth he killed himself with a phial of cyanide that he had somehow kept concealed from the guards. The next day the remaining ten condemned men were killed. The hangman botched the execution of Ribbentrop, who was first in line, leaving the rope to throttle the former foreign minister for twenty minutes before he died.

Journalists across the world were horrified to learn about Göring's suicide. In the US, Erika Mann was lecturing in Spokane, where she was interviewed in white pyjamas in her hotel room. She told the local newspaper that she was 'furious' that Göring had been able to kill himself so easily. 'I am not envious of his nice suicide instead of death on the gallows, but it really is scandalous that it should have happened.' Mann was worried that the Germans would now think that the authorities had deliberately permitted Göring to take his own life. Rebecca West immediately cabled an extra thousand words to the *New Yorker* to end the article she had already sent them. She described how a dozen emotions had surprised her with their strength. She was angry that the 'enormous clown' had managed to spill the 'wine of humiliation we had intended him to drink' on the floor. She was frustrated that after all the absurd security measures surrounding the trial, the cyanide had somehow flowed. And she was worried that Göring's odd final moment of triumph might lead to a resurgence of Nazism. But she also felt 'a vague, visceral cheerfulness', pleased that the beast caught in the trap had surprised its captors by making a final stand.[17]

If West had still been with Biddle they could have laughed about Göring's suicide together. But as it was, the news confirmed her dissatisfaction with the world. She was unhappy and bored and escaped as always into illness. Like Erika Mann, West was a habitual somatiser. In 1941 she had written that the body calling for help 'makes the appeal as strongly as possible'; 'the outward and visible signs give onlookers an exaggerated impression of what the person who is ill or afraid is suffering'. Throughout her relationship with Wells she had responded to emotional crises with dangerous and violent physical illnesses that matched Wells's own, once going completely deaf for a month. Now she was taken ill with symptoms which she described in her diary as an infection of the gums, toxic neuritis of the left arm and shoulder, and a high fever.[18]

On 11 November, West finally received a letter from Biddle, lauding Katherine for her sweetness and bravery and saying that he did not want to hurt his wife. Still very ill, West was outraged; she commanded him never to write again. 'Men are all filth,' she complained with effortfully marshalled resilience to Emanie Arling. 'Don't worry over Francis B. I'm doomed to have no luck. I shall just forget it, and get on with my work.' Here was yet another man who had pursued her vehemently only to disappear once she had succumbed. She was left with a feeling that she was not destined for mutual love. Once again her public sexuality had laid her open to rejection, to being seen as castrating and having her own vulnerability ignored.[19]

In *Black Lamb, Grey Falcon*, West had written that 'only part of us is sane'. People only partly loved pleasure and happiness, wanted to live into their nineties and die in peace in a house they had built. 'The other half of us is nearly mad.' That mad half loved pain and despair and wanted to die in a catastrophe 'that will set back life to its beginnings and leave nothing of our house save its blackened foundations'. West had witnessed the global consequences of this yearning for destruction in the blackened ruins of Nuremberg and Berlin. Now she was conscious, as she had been so often before, of the personal consequences of the division. She had yearned for pleasure and happiness as Biddle apparently had with her, but together they had willed into being a

catastrophe that left her lying feverish in bed, her arm and gums swol-
len and throbbing with pain.[20]

When she was strong enough to write, West returned to the Nuremberg trials, rewriting her articles into a longer essay entitled 'Greenhouse
with Cyclamens', which she planned to incorporate into a book to be
called *The Meaning of Treason*. Shawcross had invited West to Nuremberg in the first place as the official chronicler, but this was certainly not
the book she was intended to write. The essay takes its title from a
greenhouse in the grounds of the Faber Schloss where West had briefly
stayed with the other correspondents before she was summoned to
Biddle's villa. She describes how, on one golden autumn evening, she
walked in the garden and found the door of the greenhouse open.
Inside there was row after row of flowering lilies, primulas and cycla-
men, all growing healthily and colourfully. West was struck by the
absurdity of the sight. This was a country where trade had collapsed; a
town where it was impossible to buy even shoes, kettles or blankets.
But here was a greenhouse that had continued to grow flowers in defiance of Hitler's regulations and was now defying the Allies' regulations
as well.[21] Here was a thriving business presided over only by a man with
one leg and a girl of twelve. And talking to the man (a veteran of the
eastern front), West found him to be a symbol of a kind of crazed
German industriousness that made him long only for more work and
not for pleasure. More than anything he wanted the trial to continue
for as long as possible because he wanted to continue to grow and sell
his flowers.

This is West at her best, approaching a public event from an oblique,
private angle that enabled her to capture world affairs with a peculiarly
vivid specificity. And the essay as a whole was fuelled by her disappointed fury with Biddle. 'I have never been able to write with anything
more than the left hand of my mind,' West would write to A. L. Rowse
in 1947, 'the right hand has always been engaged in something to do
with personal relationships.' But the left hand derived its power, she
believed, from 'knowledge of what my right hand was doing'. 'Greenhouse with Cyclamens' gains its force from its personal passion; from
her sense of the connection between private and public treachery.[22]

West was more outraged in this essay than in her previous article about the system that had allowed Göring to commit suicide and Ribbentrop to choke slowly to death. She complained that Göring should not have been given the chance to use his courage to weaken public horror at his crimes. The Nazis had 'plastered history with the cruelty which is a waste product of man's moral nature, as maniacs on a smaller scale plaster their bodies and their clothes with their excreta'; it was unfair that this Nazi of all Nazis should have been allowed to disguise his maniacal quality. This is Göring as the ultimate treacherous man. West, like so many onlookers, had always been disquietingly fascinated by Göring. Now that she was away from the beguiling tedium of the courtroom, she was furious that he had seduced his onlookers and got away with it. West complained too that the tribunal had undertaken the task of hanging ten men without bothering to enquire sufficiently into effective and swift methods of hanging. Justice had been done, but the reports of Ribbentrop's slow death sounded not unlike the testimony describing the Nazi atrocities which had brought these men to the gallows. There were stenches, West found, that 'not the name of justice or reason or the public good, nor any other fair word, can turn to sweetness'.[23]

If the trial as a whole had taken on a stench with hindsight, then so had the Nuremberg romances. In the essay, the brief mention of *eros* in West's first *New Yorker* article was lengthened to a much longer disquisition on love. All the Americans at Nuremberg were in love, West now claimed. The men were on the wrong side of middle age, married to absent wives, and spiritually sick from a surfeit of war and exile: of course they were in search of the comfort of women. Now that her own love affair had ended, West saw all of the Nuremberg entanglements as doomed to transience. 'To the desire to embrace was added the desire to be comforted and to comfort; and the delights of gratification were heartrending, like spring and sunset and the breaking wave, because they could not last.'[24]

Looking back, West thought that the many lovers in Nuremberg had hoped, like the defendants, that the verdicts would be deferred forever. They were sadly aware that once a decision was made about the lives of

Göring and Ribbentrop, 'much happiness that might have been immortal would then be put to death'. The death of her own affair gains a curious grandeur from its temporal synchronicity with the deaths of the defendants. But this is a rhetoric of fate and she does not let Biddle off this easily. These temporary loves, she writes, were often noble, but there were some who would not let them be so: 'There were men who said, "You are a good kid, but of course it is my wife I really love," when these terms were too perfunctory, considering his plight and the help he had been given.' These in effect had been Biddle's words, as they had been Wells's before him. West was angry that she had not received more acknowledgement of the comfort she had brought.[25]

Gellhorn and West do not seem to have met in Nuremberg. If they had done they might have had much to say to each other on the subject of the treachery and weakness both of men and of the Germans. They could even have compared their experiences of the same man, H. G. Wells, though Gellhorn always denied Wells's claim that she had had an affair with him. Later in life, Gellhorn would become fascinated by Rebecca West, aware of a kinship in their lives that was perhaps not evident at the time. Now, however, Gellhorn like West was engaged in an act of private literary retribution.

Immediately after the tribunal finished, Gellhorn wrote an article for *Collier's* reporting on the events. It was supportive of the trial's accomplishments but also insistent that the blame could not be laid simply at the door of these twenty-one men. Describing the charge of 'crimes against peace', Gellhorn reminded her readers that war itself is the ultimate crime against peace: 'War is the silver bombers, with the young men in them, who never wanted to kill anyone, flying in the morning sun over Germany and not coming back. War is the sinking ship and the sailors drowning in a flaming sea on the way to Murmansk . . . War is casualty lists and bombed ruins and refugees, frightened and homeless and tired to death on the roads. War is everything you remember from those long ugly years. And its heritage is what we have now, this maimed and tormented world which we must somehow restore.'

Before Gellhorn could attempt any restoration in her own life, she had to write out the long, ugly years. *Point of No Return* is a catalogue of the horrors of war: the young men who never wanted to kill anyone; the frightened, homeless and tired; the maimed and tormented world left behind.[26]

Gellhorn later described this as a novel that she had written to rid herself of Dachau: 'to exorcise what I could not live with'. She had been brought up in 'a good tough school whose basic instruction is: Get on with it. Somehow.' Writing was her way to do so. The novel is an account of two soldiers, John Dawson Smithers, a lieutenant colonel with the 20th Infantry Division, and his driver Jacob Levy, a secular Jew who appears to onlookers to be simply an ordinary, exceptionally good-looking American. At the start of the novel they are at the border of Germany. After weeks of dangerous misery in the Hürtgen Forest their unit is sent for rest and recuperation in Luxembourg city, where both men immediately go in search of sex. Smithers finds an American Red Cross worker called Dorothy Brock, with whom he has a casual fling; Levy finds a local waitress called Kathe, 'young and short and not painted', with whom he falls in love – though they communicate with only the few French words that Levy has learnt from a dictionary and she calls him '*Jawn*' because in a moment of panic he introduces himself as John Dawson Smithers, denying his own Jewishness.[27]

Smithers's affair is largely unsatisfactory: Dotty succumbs too easily, concerned merely with doing her duty by another sex-starved hero. Levy's is much happier, though Kathe is a virgin and terrified of sex. In their first encounter she keeps her petticoat tightly on in bed; in their next she encourages him to penetrate her and is disgusted and phys-ically hurt by the experience; gradually she grows to tolerate sex and to love the intimacy that it brings. Both affairs are curtailed when the men are sent back to the front. Levy proposes marriage to Kathe in a letter he posts to Dorothy Brock and spends much of his time engaged in imaginary dialogues with the version of Kathe he has created in his mind. But when the war ends he visits Dachau, almost by accident, and is destroyed by what he witnesses. Leaving the camp, he sees a group of German women laughing on a street corner. Outraged by their complacency in the face of their complicity in the atrocities, he drives his jeep into them, killing the Germans and smashing his own formerly beautiful face. In hospital, Levy refuses to pretend that he did not mean to harm them. He believes that he must sacrifice his own happiness in order to confront the world with its guilt at failing to see what was going on in Germany.[28]

This is a novel about war. Gellhorn fused her own war experiences with those of both Hemingway and Gavin. She had no familiarity with life with the infantry and drew, though she would deny it, on the world of Hemingway's exploits as reported in *Collier's*. She also drew on Gavin's tales of life in the Hürtgen Forest and had written to him in January asking for details. He replied describing that 'sonofabitch' place with its precipitous hills, dark dense woods, unexpected mountain torrents and mine fields as a 'yawning man-eating chasm' and suggesting that it was best discussed in bed. The hills, woods and torrents all went into the novel, as did the army slang that she had heard when living with the 82nd Airborne Division. But in her account the forest is transformed into a kind of testing experience that changes them all in ways they are unable to recognise at the time. Smithers is presented as unique in refusing 'to give in to the forest' as he drives the soldiers relentlessly on. But at night he lies sleepless in the dark, as cold as his men, and stops acting: 'In the night he could mourn his Battalion which he loved. That men had to die in any action was known, and nothing to grieve over. But a man had the right to die for some purpose; the value of death was measured in miles. Whose fault is it, Lieutenant Colonel Smithers asked himself, and hoped it was the fault of the forest.' Gellhorn was not with Gavin during his time at Hürtgen. Imaginatively recreating it now, she was asking how it had changed him, at the same time as she asked how her own war experiences had changed her.[29]

It is also a novel about men. In May, Gellhorn had told Eleanor Roosevelt that she had found herself 'launched on writing about men as if I were one'. Her editor at Scribner's had read part of it and informed her that he would not have guessed that it was by a woman. She later said that she had written the novel as a man, 'being a man all the time in my mind'. She found herself dreaming Jacob Levy's dreams rather than her own. The ability to empathise with men, in war and in sex, was a gift from Gavin. Indeed, she wrote to Gavin to test her ideas about sex as well as war. Would he, she asked, be prepared to take the virginity of an innocent but compliant girl if he liked her and saw that she did not know what she was offering? Gavin replied that if she was as nice as Gellhorn described perhaps he would just take her in his arms, but that you would have to like her a lot to do this 'because if a trooper really wants it, and if he was in Hürtgen he wants it almost more than life's breath tomorrow or the assurance of it, then he will take it. And virginity has in itself a charm.' None the less he could imagine occasions where he would hold back and he gave his verdict on her description of 'reasonable male procedure' as 'OK'.[30]

Gavin's teachings in male sexuality went into the character of Jacob Levy but Gavin himself is most vividly present in the novel as Smithers. Younger than Gavin, Smithers is only a lieutenant colonel, but like Gavin he is already a hero, looked up to by the men whose welfare he cares about as much as his own. Smithers like Gavin finds that he has been able to transcend class through war – able to bed a much better class of girl than he could even have fantasised about before. He is terrified that after the war his life will become ordinary and lonely again: 'I've had everything, he thought, I am somebody now. I can't, I can't [go back] . . . in the end, he belonged nowhere.'[31]

Smithers's lover Dorothy Brock is glamorous, courageous and businesslike when it comes to sex. She disappoints Smithers by undressing methodically and getting into bed in their first encounter: 'with Dotty, you had the idea that the line formed on the right'. She does not allow herself emotion and only once breaks down when she confides to Smithers that she cannot bear the possibility of loss: 'my father's too old; I haven't got a brother, nor a husband, nor a fiancé, nor a man I'm in love with . . . All I want is not to have anything.' If Brock is a self-portrait of Gellhorn then it is a harsh one. Brock has far less interiority than other characters in the book. She cannot afford to look inside herself because if she does she will break down again; instead she rushes around in order to avoid confronting her own fears. This is Gellhorn as her harsher critics might have seen her: haughty, entitled, too aware of her own good looks to be vulnerable. The sex between Smithers and Dorothy is never passionate. It is as though Gellhorn cannot allow sex to be the good and beautiful act it once was with Gavin because she cannot afford the regret this might entail; instead she takes refuge in rewriting their relationship through a callous lens. She transposes the post-Dachau version of herself onto the relationship with Gavin, dooming it in retrospect, suggesting that she was always world-weary and never innocent or hopeful.[32]

If Gellhorn's own more fragile interiority is present in the book then it is in the character of Levy, not in his sexual relationship but in his experience at Dachau. Before he visits the camp, Levy does not understand why the US is in the war in the first place, or why the Jews did not 'clear out of this stinking Europe long ago?' At Dachau, he wanders through the little village with sharp-roofed houses, with 'the krauts all leaning over their front gates and gossiping together in the sun', and assumes that the place cannot be that bad. But entering the gates, he is confronted immediately with the stench of decay. He sees the bald, lice-covered inmates walking slowly and aimlessly, their eyes looking ahead 'too big, black and empty', and is paralysed with fear.

Levy is led around by a doctor who tells him the same stories that Gellhorn was told at Dachau; tales of experiments conducted on humans, of bodies piled onto trains, related by a man who has learnt to observe everything with frightening dispassion and who lives merely because it is a habit. Leaving the camp, Levy feels he has no other life and no other knowledge: 'he knew that he could not live anywhere now because in his mind, slyly, there was nothing but horror'. He is struck most of all by the scale of his own willful ignorance. 'I never knew; I thought those goddam krauts had to fight like we did and I thought these weasling kraut civilians were sort of stupid and pretty yellow besides.' He is angry with himself for denying his own Jewishness; for fighting in the war without identifying himself with Hitler's victims. And he is furious with the Germans who have taken the gold of the dead Jews' fillings and have looked on while thousands of their countrymen died. Seeing the group of fat, pink laughing women in the middle of the street he feels himself slipping. It is hard to breathe; he holds his fist on the horn and presses his foot until the accelerator hits the floor.[33]

Gellhorn never belittles Levy's pointless act of retribution. His protest may amount to very little in the end, but she is clear that it is the only thing he could have done at the time. She too had failed to protest about the concentration camps during the war; she too had failed to notice the plight of the Jews until she saw their corpses piled up before her. It is as though this is what she should have done, if only she had had a jeep at her disposal. Indeed, her own life had changed almost as radically as his; she lost hope as he did, and resented that she, unlike him, remained physically intact at the end of it. Instead what Gellhorn does belittle is Levy's relationship with Kathe.

Just before going to Nuremberg, Gellhorn wrote to her friend Campbell Beckett that she no longer knew what love was, or 'where sex starts and ends, and love (for me always an operation done with the biggest fanciest mirrors in the world) comes true and is not my own invention, invention of need and loneliness and the terrible boredom of looking after oneself'. Her investment in illusion with Hemingway had 'paid off so shabbily' that she was now frightened and doubtful. When she had first used the mirrors metaphor in the letter to Gavin the previous year she had still hoped that the illusion might hold. Now she could no longer believe it and she portrayed Levy as inventing Kathe. This kind of innocent happiness is only possible when you do not speak the same language and when you do not even know each other's actual name. Similarly, Smithers is happiest when he invents an image of Dorothy in her absence, a 'dark girl who knew what this war was like and would never be a stranger', and he will inevitably be disappointed when they meet again.[34]

Unlike West, Gellhorn was no longer furious with men. Instead she presented love as a casualty of peace. It is not the fault of any of the characters in the book that the illusion of love cannot hold. It is the fault of the maimed and tormented world and of the Germans who have created it. 'You sat there and watched them and felt inside yourself such outrage that it choked you,' Gellhorn wrote in her Nuremberg article, describing the act of watching the Nazi defendants in court. The Germans in her novel are either passive in defeat, their skin 'grey and thick' and their faces without curiosity, deludedly suicidal in their resistance ('these goddam krauts had decided dying was a good idea and meant to take as many Americans with them as possible') or unpleasantly unperturbed in their pockets of prosperity, like the laughing civilians whom Levy kills. Together, they have destroyed the world. What is more, the Americans have collaborated by allowing themselves to be spiritually as well as physically maimed by war. 'This is the most disappointing peace I ever saw,' Private First Class Bert Hammer observes within minutes of the declaration of victory.[35]

For Gellhorn as for Hannah Arendt, guilt was collective in the sense that it was endemic. Outside Nuremberg, no one could be acquitted; unlike the Nazis who were hanged that October, most people had to live with their shame. In one city in Germany, justice of a kind had been done as best as it could be. But despite that small and hopeful enclave of legal retribution, the world remained maimed and tormented and could never be the same again.

PART IV

Tension and Revival

1946–48

'Their suffering, and often their bravery, make one love them'

Cold War: October 1946–October 1947

In the autumn of 1946 two men arrived in Germany from England and the US convinced that this maimed and tormented world could be redeemed by love. Victor Gollancz's 'Save Europe Now' campaign was flourishing and he was keen to see the plight of the starving Germans for himself. He wanted to use his experiences in Germany to persuade the British politicians and public to treat their former enemy with compassion. The German playwright Carl Zuckmayer had spent the war writing a play about Nazi Germany while sequestered with his family on a New England farm. He now wished to help his former compatriots by acting as a conciliatory emissary between his two nations.

This was the first time Gollancz had travelled without his wife Ruth present to attend to his comfort and assuage his anxiety. Although it was three years since his nervous breakdown, he was still physically fragile. He imposed nineteen-hour days on himself none the less, waking at 5 a.m. to make notes on the previous day. In Ruth's absence he was sustained by manic energy and by his fervent love for the reviled. On 5 October, shortly after his arrival, he wrote a letter home from Nuremberg describing how even after hearing the nastier details of the horrors revealed in the trial he was suffused with love for the Germans

in general, 'just because they're despised and rejected'. It seems that if
they had not done so much wrong he would not have sympathised
with them so much; somehow all his revulsion during the months when
he had imagined himself as an inmate at Dachau had prepared him for
this time.[1]

Gollancz went from Nuremberg to Kiel and then Hamburg. After a
year of reconstruction, Hamburg was gradually becoming more orderly.
In the streets where habitation was still possible, much of the debris
had been cleared and there were reusable bricks stacked against walls in
neat piles. People had set up makeshift homes in former bunkers, air-
raid shelters and basements and numerous tiny shops had sprung up in
the surviving corners of buildings, heralded by signs erected in the
grassy ruins. But there were corpses still concealed beneath the rubble.
Many of the shop signs poking out of the wreckage announced the
presence of nonexistent shops, merely marking the graves, of the lost
life of the city. The cellars where people lived were cramped and damp
and in order to survive most people busied themselves with the hunt
for food, hiking for miles in search of potatoes. Visiting the city at the
same time as Gollancz, the Swedish novelist Stig Dagerman found that
he could still take a train at a normal pace for fifteen minutes through
one of Hamburg's formerly most densely populated areas without
seeing a single human being or usable building. For Dagerman this was
a landscape 'drearier than the desert, wilder than a mountain-top and
as far-fetched as a nightmare'. The view from the train resembled 'a vast
dumping-ground for shattered gables, free-standing house-walls whose
empty window-holes are like wide-open eyes staring down on the
train'.[2]

Gollancz was better informed than most visitors about the appalling
conditions in Germany, but he was still shocked by his encounter with
this city. There were currently 100,000 people suffering from hunger
oedema. Rations for Germans in the British zone had recently been
increased to 1,550 calories per day but frequently the items that were
meant to account for this ration (bread, cereal, milk and vegetables)
were unavailable, meaning that thousands of people were living on only
400–1,000 calories (and Gollancz was quick to point out that 400 was

half the Bergen-Belsen figure). He visited a bunker without daylight or air where 800 children were being schooled with no food or materials. There was not enough penicillin in the hospitals and cases of tuberculosis had increased tenfold. Mothers leaving hospital with newborns had no cloth to wrap them in and no milk in their emaciated breasts.

The condition of the DPs was especially distressing. 'It is beyond any possibility to describe their misery,' Gollancz told his wife, though he was intending to find a way. Visiting a ship where 200 DPs had been living for six months, he found that he could not help crying. He did not have time to do a full survey of the DP camps but he was aware that the sites of all the former concentration camps had been put back to use by the Allies needing to house both DPs and POWs. The majority of the 50,000 Jews who had remained in Germany at the end of the war were still in segregated camps. In a 1945 report to President Truman, Earl G. Harrison (the dean of the University of Pennsylvania Law School) had complained that the Americans were now treating the Jews much as the Nazis treated them. Many Jewish DPs still had no clothing other than their concentration camp garb – 'a rather hideous striped pajama effect' – while others were obliged to wear German SS uniforms.[3]

More recently in August 1947 the British MP Norman Hulbert had protested in Parliament about the number of Germans still housed in concentration camps, stating that 'concentration camps is the only right and proper description there is for these institutions'. There were thousands of German POWs convicted without trial, watched over by guards who were former members of Nazi military units. What was more, many of these people had been children when the war broke out and were too young to have voted in 1933. Surely no theory of collective guilt could extend this far.[4]

Surveying the German ruins, Dagerman found absurd the tendency of journalists to dismiss desperation on this scale as 'indescribable': 'If one wants to describe them, they can be described quite perfectly.' Gollancz shared this view. As far as he was concerned, the role of the writer was to document suffering not, as in Mervyn Peake's formulation, to avoid future war, but to change public opinion at home and effect

practical changes in the present. Immediately, he started writing letters to
the newspapers at home complaining about the situation in the British
zone. From Düsseldorf on 30 October, he told the editor of *The Times*
that the condition of millions was horrifyingly 'wretched'. He provided a
detailed portrait of a starving man in hospital in Hamburg whose swol-
len scrotum reached a third of the way to the floor and of the ugly skin
blemishes branded on children as 'the stigmata of malnutrition'.[5]

The newspaper received an onslaught of letters contradicting
Gollancz's statistics and reminding him of the suffering inflicted by the
Nazis on the Jews. He replied on 12 November that the most horrible
of his experiences had been a visit to the camp at Bergen-Belsen, where
he had seen the tattoo marks on the arms of the Jewish survivors.

> I am never likely to forget the unspeakable wickedness of which the
> Nazis were guilty. But when I see the swollen bodies and living skeletons
> in hospitals here and elsewhere; when I look at the miserable 'shoes' of
> boys and girls in the schools, and find that they have come to their
> lessons without even a dry piece of bread for breakfast; when I go down
> into a one-roomed cellar where a mother is struggling, and struggling
> very bravely, to do her best for a husband and four or five children –
> then I think, not of Germans, but of men and women.

Gollancz warned, as other visitors had before him, that this was not
simply a humanitarian concern; it was also a question of whether the
Occupation could survive in the face of German resentment. Hearing
that the British government had announced that specially imported extra
meat and sugar would be available for British subjects over Christmas, he
complained that this would incite anger in homes where people were
existing on 400 calories. British prestige was near the nadir, he told readers of the *News Chronicle*; the youth was being poisoned and renazified.
'We have all but lost the peace – and I fear this is an understatement.'[6]

Gollancz's visit coincided with one of the worst winters for almost a
hundred years. Unprepared for the cold, he himself developed flu,

though he carried on working regardless. Around him both the occupation forces and the Germans were terrified that Germany had neither
the fuel nor the food to cope with sustained conditions of this kind. By
November engines on every railway line were put out of service by frost
damage; consumption of coal was cut to a fifth of its normal levels. To
make matters worse, it was difficult to use the remaining trees as fuel
because of the lack of foresters. Forestry had been a favourite pursuit
for the Nazis and 92 per cent of the industry had been sacked following
denazification proceedings. Cities throughout the country soon lay in
frozen darkness and even the occupiers were unable to perform their
work, finding that ink froze in inkwells and cups of tea iced over on
desks.

Gollancz returned to London in the middle of November 1946 at the
same time as Carl Zuckmayer arrived in Germany for the first time in
seven years. Later, Zuckmayer would describe exile as 'the journey of
no return'. Anyone who left dreaming that one day he would come
home was lost. The wayfarer might return, but the place he found could
no longer be the one he had left; he himself was no longer the person
he was previously. This was a truth Zuckmayer experienced painfully
now, re-entering the country he had once taken for granted. His plane
was due to land in Berlin but it was an overcast afternoon and they
were enveloped in fog and rain. They touched down instead in Frankfurt where he wandered through the shattered Old Town feeling as
though he was in a nightmare from which he could not awake.[7]

Zuckmayer no longer knew anyone in Frankfurt, which was the first
large city he had seen as a child. He did not have a single address to visit
and could not be sure whether any of the people he had once known
there were still alive. The theatres were destroyed; the debris crunched
coldly under his feet; the fog shrouded the ruins with a pale, ghostly
light. 'We wanted it this way, and this is how it ended,' a passerby
remarked. However, there were people in Frankfurt who knew Zuckmayer and wanted to make his return less alienating. Checking into a
hotel requisitioned by the US army, he was asked by the emaciated
clerk if he was the same Zuckmayer who had written *Der Fröhliche
Weinberg* (*The Merry Vineyard*). 'Oh, what a pleasure you've come

home,' he was told. 'You know what? You'll get a white towel in your room. We never give them out nowadays, see, because the soldiers take them. But you'll get a towel and two pillows.'[8]

From this moment Zuckmayer was able to see the best in his former compatriots and to remain hopeful about the German capacity for redemption. Like Gollancz he was convinced that the Germans should be treated with kindness, though in Zuckmayer's case this was because he retained faith in the fundamental goodness of mankind. On his second day in Germany, Zuckmayer rode to Berlin in a military train and was filled with pity for the town and its inhabitants. He rode past the bare Tiergarten and then inspected the ruined houses where inhabitants clustered together around slowly dying stoves. Initially, the house where he had once lived and where his daughter had been born seemed unchanged but as he approached he realised that it was now only a façade: a thin wall whose gashed-out windows opened onto nothingness.

As the winter became more severe, Zuckmayer shared Gollancz's horror at the privation. There was no hope for old people or children who became ill. He visited the publisher Peter Suhrkamp, a brave man once imprisoned by the Nazis, and found that he was living in a frosty house with no medical care although he was ill with pleurisy and pneumonia. Suhrkamp lay in bed, hollow-eyed and pale, manuscripts piled high on his blankets, attempting to revive his publishing firm while nourished only by hot potato soup.

Zuckmayer was proud to be an American citizen, but he had remained far more identified with the German people than either Thomas Mann or Billy Wilder, perhaps in part because he had never really consorted with American intellectuals. In 1939 he had crossed the ocean with his wife and daughter and attempted, like so many other German cultural figures, to make it in Hollywood. He had hated life in this expensive, drunken 'anteroom to hell' where everyone had to pretend they were rich and happy. Instead, he managed to rent a farm in the Vermont countryside where for five years he chopped wood and milked cows, pleased to be a free man. During this time he alienated other refugees by stubbornly believing in a 'good Germany'.[9]

Initially Zuckmayer had been too numbed and exhausted to write, but one day he kicked aside a loose stone on his land and heard a gurgling sound resembling 'a cry, a summons, a spring bubbled up'. Cooling his face with the water, he knew that a knot within him had been released and he would begin another play. Over the next three years he completed *Des Teufels General* (*The Devil's General*), writing in German about wartime Germany from the safety of a landscape curiously reminiscent of the Vienna woods and the Salzburg mountains. His play is in part an attempt to see the humanity in Germans who had signed up mistakenly to serve the Nazis; it was a humanity in which Zuckmayer persistently believed.[10]

At the end of the war Zuckmayer had felt nostalgic for his homeland and anxious to see his father, who was eighty-two and dangerously ill. He was grateful to the Americans for granting him citizenship and sheltering him for so long, and he hoped that by visiting Germany as an American he could bring about a reconciliation of the two nations to which he belonged. Like Stephen Spender in 1945, Zuckmayer hoped to explain the Germans and the Americans to each other. He thought that as a writer he was particularly well placed to do this, believing that it was possible to teach humanist values through art and indeed hoping that the Germans might come to understand themselves better through his own wartime play. After applying to join the Control Council, he was charged with the task of surveying the US zone and reporting on the conditions and requirements of reconstruction, with a focus on theatre and film. He hoped that this could be a role in which he could 'bridge the abysses, soften opposites and appease minds'.[11]

In this respect, Zuckmayer was one of several Germans in the pay of the American authorities who wanted to re-educate the Germans through their own *Kultur*. This was the mission of the editors of the American-sponsored newspaper *Die Neue Zeitung*, edited by the Hungarian-born German novelist Hans Habe, an old rival of Peter de Mendelssohn's, with the German poet and children's writer Erich Kästner as its cultural editor. Both Habe and Kästner took Spender's view that the Germans could learn to be democratic partly through coming to appreciate their own great art, going against the view of the Allied authorities in 1945 that German culture was partly responsible for the rise of Nazism.

For many American officials, Habe and Kästner's emphasis on German culture was problematic in a publication produced by the American authorities and intended to foster respect for the American way of life. One bureaucrat had complained to General McClure in April 1946 that *Die Neue Zeitung*, 'through its emphasis on interpreting and projecting German life and culture, with America receiving driblets of attention, has involuntarily played the Goebbels propaganda tune: "Americans are money-hungry barbarians with no cultural life of their own".' But given the American emphasis on freedom of speech, having appointed the paper's editors, there was very little they could do about this, and the success of the paper made them reluctant to make radical changes in personnel. Kästner himself, who was responsible for the German-centric content of the cultural pages, was adamant that he was furthering the cause of the American occupiers by teaching the Germans to be more broad-minded and therefore democratic in their appreciation of their own culture. That January he had attended an exhibition of abstract art in Augsburg where he had heard students shouting 'what filth' at the paintings, with some even suggesting that 'these artists should be done away with' or taken to a concentration camp. He complained that although art was free again, these children of the 1930s continued to spit 'as they have learnt it, on everything that they do not understand'. It was the duty of his newspaper to teach artistic tolerance, as a first step in re-educating the German public.[12]

This was Zuckmayer's view as well, and like so many visitors before him, he was impressed to find culture flourishing in the ruins of Berlin. He watched Thornton Wilder's *The Skin of Our Teeth* at the Hebbel Theater and understood why it had become the most popular play in postwar Germany. Wilder's play depicts twentieth-century New Jersey confronted by a wall of ice that threatens it with extinction and brings with it the unsettling presence of ancient figures including Homer and Moses. Zuckmayer had enjoyed it in New York, seeing it performed for society aesthetes, but he found it gained charge when the spectators as well as the characters had survived the ice age by the skin of their teeth.

This audience could still feel 'the shudder of menace' Wilder hoped to conjure; the German title *Wir sind noch einmal davon gekommen* ('We have come through yet again') seemed especially pertinent to the bombed cities.[13]

Zuckmayer was less impressed by the state of the film industry, although he was hopeful about the prospects of the former German film producer Erich Pommer, whom the Americans had sent out that summer to be in charge of film in their zone. Once the boss of Billy Wilder, Pommer had been a great film mogul in Weimar Germany and now he was celebrated by Berlin's writers and film-makers as a returning Messiah. 'When Pommer comes, it's time to roll up your shirtsleeves,' announced Erich Kästner. Pommer was determined that postwar German cinema would be defined by a 'rich tradition of poverty and ingenuity' offering 'the undistorted image of people in our time'; he was also determined to allow Germans to make films in the US zone as quickly as possible.[14]

All this was especially urgent given that the Russians continued to stride ahead with film production in their zone. That October the Soviet-sponsored feature film *Die Mörder sind unter uns* (*The Murderers are Among Us*) had been released to great acclaim. Directed by Wolfgang Staudte, this was a realistic film exploring the existential shame of a doctor who is unable to escape his war experiences, set in the wreckage of the bombed cities and brave in its suggestion that war crimes remain crimes in times of peace. The Berlin edition of the *Neues Deutschland* commended it for confronting the uncomfortable truths of postwar Germany: 'who could deny that the towering ruins are our own daily vision?' It was embarrassing for the Western Allies that the Russians were so far ahead in reinstating German cinema, especially as Staudte had first applied for a license in the US zone but was told that no films would be made in Germany except by the Americans for the next five years. The British, too, were further ahead than the Americans in their film-making although the first British film *Tell the Truth* (*Sag die Wahrheit*) that premiered in December 1946 seemed a problematically conservative portrayal of drawing-room life in prewar Germany, doubly dubious because it had been in production during the war and was revived by the British authorities using some of the same cast and crew.[15]

Zuckmayer himself wondered about making a documentary about the Nuremberg trials but as the winter progressed the trials seemed unimportant. No one had time to turn Göring into the martyr that Rebecca West and Erika Mann had feared; they were too busy fighting for survival. Both Zuckmayer and Gollancz found denazification increasingly farcical. It seemed mad that ordinary Germans had spent months filling in absurd forms when senior Nazis could be acquitted. Zuckmayer thought that denazification was all the more pointless given that almost nothing was done on behalf of the former victims of concentration camps. Instead this should be the hour of acceptance, the time when people ceased to measure and weigh the tears shed on both sides. He found that the ragged Germans attending the theatres had acquired an unexpected magnificence, their eyes burning with receptivity, 'ready for any challenge to their emotions and minds'.[16]

His hopes were confirmed when he attended a production of his own 1931 play *Der Hauptmann von Köpenick* (*The Captain of Köpenick*), a satire on Prussian militarism, in Heidelberg. Just after the First World War, Zuckmayer had studied in this sleepy baroque city in south Germany. Now he was surprised to find that it was almost unchanged; it was one of the few German cities that had not been bombed at all. On his first evening there, Zuckmayer visited a pub where twenty-eight years earlier he had attended liberal meetings. He found the same overheated stove, the same coats and hats thrown over chairs and even the same inn-keeper garbed in his habitual green woolly waistcoat. Only the beer was thinner, though served in the tankards of his student days.[17]

The next night Zuckmayer went to the theatre to watch his play. *The Captain of Köpenick* had been written during the time of Hitler's rise to power and was intended to warn the Germans about excessive respect for military rank. This had proved a pertinent message and Zuckmayer expected the packed theatre to respond enthusiastically. However after the first and second scenes he heard whistling from the gallery and balcony, indicating disapproval. By the fifth scene the

whistling had stopped and Zuckmayer kept an eye on one of the whis-
tlers, a young blond man who spent the rest of the play sitting with
crossed arms and a gloomy face. At the end he asked the man why he
had whistled after the early scenes but not later. 'Why do you care?'
the man asked. Zuckmayer told him that he was the playwright and
was now an American who wanted to know what the younger generation thought about militarism.[18]

The man brought his friends to talk to Zuckmayer and it turned
out they had all been officers in the German army. They had initially
disliked the play for its open condemnation of German culture but
had then found themselves taking it more seriously. Zuckmayer
talked to the men all night, telling them about his experiences in the
US and discussing competing ideas of nationhood and history. By
dawn all were agreed that Germany had to find a new ideal in line
with the tradition of European humanism: 'not a battle against the
world, not an attempt to conquer the world, but a desire to understand other people and become a creative part of the world as a
whole'.[19]

This was the first of many discussions that Zuckmayer had with
groups of young people during his trip. He arranged to speak to school
and university students, convinced that open dialogue between the
Americans and the Germans could create the conditions for democracy. He was sure that the discussions were fruitful and that the people
he spoke to were not going to become Nazis again. They were waiting
instead for something better to come. Contact with these young
Germans brought Zuckmayer two kinds of happiness: one was to be
able to help, the other not to have to hate. On a small scale, Zuckmayer was achieving just the kind of re-education the Allies had hoped
for when they formulated their policies two years earlier. If we take
him at his own word, he was succeeding in using culture to turn the
Germans from fascism to humanism, from blind uniformity to individualism. Like Gollancz, he wanted to transform the Germans into
allies, but from his (well-fed) perspective, physical nourishment was
inseparable from mental nourishment and his role as a writer was
partly to provide this. Zuckmayer was one of the few people in

Germany who still believed that art could be used to convert a starving nation to democracy.[20]

Outside Germany the debates about the conditions of the Occupation continued and on 25 November the British Cabinet capitulated on the question of food parcels. This was a victory for Gollancz's 'Save Europe Now' campaign, especially as he had encouraged all 100,000 of his supporters to write to the prime minister the previous week. There was no parcel post for Germany from Britain so thousands of packages poured into the SEN offices in London waiting to be hand delivered. The parcels could do relatively little to alleviate the German plight but they did impact on morale; many Germans were amazed that their cause had been championed by a Jew.

In January, Gollancz published a book-length account of his experiences in Germany entitled *In Darkest Germany*, which had been written at astounding speed, even for him. Extensively illustrated with photographs revealing emaciated stomachs, hollow faces and misshapen shoes, the book was an angry indictment both of the British government at home and of the occupation forces in Germany and their failure to mitigate starvation and disease. He broadcast his own allegiance to the 'poor and dear' people in emotive terms: 'their suffering, and often their bravery, make one love them'.[21]

In his introduction, Gollancz defended himself from the charge that he was now betraying the Jews by fighting for the Germans. He claimed that he was motivated by 'plain, straight' Jewish commonsense, undeflected by sentimentality. Three propositions seemed self-evident: firstly, nothing could save the world but 'a general act of repentance' instead of an insistence on the wickedness of others; secondly, good treatment not bad treatment made men good; thirdly, 'unless you treat a man well when he has treated you ill you just get nowhere'. He claimed, too, that if every German was responsible for what happened at Belsen then 'we, as members of a democratic country and not of a fascist one with no free Press or parliament, were responsible individually as well as collectively for refusing to tolerate anything that might be considered even remotely comparable with Belsen'.[22]

In Darkest Germany was widely praised both in Britain and Germany, with the German newspapers publishing a series of adulatory articles about their British saviour.[23] Meanwhile in Germany it was time for Zuckmayer to attempt to sum up his experiences in a final report. He was less able to generalise than Gollancz; for him there was no one lesson to be drawn from the ruins. Instead he decided to tell the story of the people he had met 'and how I saw them living and dying in the midst of our civilised world in the winter of 1946/47'.[24]

The word 'living' is crucial here. Zuckmayer was prepared to see the German inhabitants as alive in a way that Gollancz was not. They were visiting the theatre and cinema, they were establishing publishing houses, they were arguing energetically in frozen pubs. 'With what seriousness, passion and enthusiasm theatre is performed in this under-nourished and freezing city,' he wrote; 'how much theatre is fought for, attended and loved, spoken about and criticised.' He wanted the American officials reading his report to believe that the Germans were capable of renewal and should be granted the autonomy to bring it about on their own terms. Cultural life in Berlin revealed 'a spiritual, intellectual and physical vitality that could not be stamped out by robbing the people of liberty for twelve years, nor by the consequences of a collapse without parallel, nor by dividing Germany into four zones'.[25]

At the same time, Zuckmayer delineated the appalling conditions in harrowing detail. The winter was getting worse by the day. In January the Russians had stopped delivering coal from the eastern zone to Berlin, exacerbating shortages. Karl Jaspers reported to Hannah Arendt that the rivers were frozen, the locomotives broken down and industries closing. 'The way things are going now, half of the population will perish, and the rest can then eke out a minimal existence on the land.' Jaspers had been impressed by Gollancz but found that one man's generosity was quickly forgotten in view of what was actually being done in the British zone. That month the British government had agreed to divert 200,000 tons of extra food from Britain to Germany but it was too little too late. Suicides had increased rapidly, with 186 people killing themselves in January alone.[26]

Zuckmayer described the sparkle of frost on the walls inside the rooms of German homes. In almost all the houses inhabited by Germans, the water pipes had now frozen or burst. The population was dirty, dark and embittered, their clothing soaked with slowly drying snow. Like Gollancz, Zuckmayer was worried that the occupiers were dooming their own regime in Germany by treating the Germans too harshly. In his report he described Germany as divided into two worlds: 'an occupying army and a defeated people'. The liberal anti-Nazi old guard in particular was disappointed. They had expected the allies to arrive with a carefully drafted plan to win the peace and now thought the opportunity was missed. Zuckmayer hoped that it was not missed altogether but urged the American authorities to address themselves urgently to winning over the hearts and heads of the population.[27]

For Zuckmayer the potential solution was cultural. Gollancz and Zuckmayer were agreed that democracy could not be taught by undemocratic methods. 'We are behaving as if you could make men democrats by penalising them for their opinions,' Gollancz had complained in his book; 'we are trying to impose a formalistic democracy by totalitarian methods' when in fact 'you can create democracy only by creating the conditions for democracy.' In Zuckmayer's view these conditions could be created socially and culturally. The Germans and Americans needed to learn about each other's homes and ways of life; this could be enabled partly by theatre, film and exhibitions as well as by youth groups of the kind he himself had initiated. He thought that the Germans needed to be taught to follow the ideal of heroism some Germans had set during the war and proposed that he himself should direct a documentary or feature film showing them how men and women from their own midst 'fought and eventually died for the path of liberation'.[28]

This film would never be made but Zuckmayer did have some immediate influence in Germany. In February 1947 the theatres and directors of the three western zones met for a conference in Stuttgart and decided to cease censorship of plays and to grant independence for theatres, film and music to the Germans. He believed that he was partly responsible for this and that the decision would ensure 'the freedom and independence of creative and artistic professions in Germany even after the occupation ended'. He had also made a more local but none the less instrumental impact on the groups of youths he had spoken with and he now urged the US government to focus their efforts on the young. He believed that the kinds of conversations he had held with German youth groups could be replicated throughout the country.

As far as Zuckmayer was concerned, the entire German youth was capable of redemption. Indeed, there was better material in 'some deluded, but unflinching Hitlerjugend boy' than in the sycophantic opportunists. And like Stephen Spender the previous year, Zuckmayer insisted that the salvation of the youth was crucial for the salvation not just of Germany but of Europe and therefore of the world as a whole:

> The consequences we inflict on the Germans today, we will inflict on ourselves. The cultural reconstruction of Germany and its reorientation is not a question of "Charity" but of reason and self-preservation. This is what we call the concept of a "civilised world". . . this is the decisive point where this world is either saved or destroyed. The sight of these destroyed cities and the haggard faces speaks a deadly language. They are asking who is next.[29]

Gollancz and Zuckmayer's pleas proved effective, chiefly because they coincided with the development of incipient Cold War tension. For the occupiers, Nuremberg had opened the way for forgiveness. Now that some Nazis at least had been publicly punished, the Germans could be elevated from inmates to citizens. As a Third World War became more frighteningly possible and as the fault lines between the US and the Soviet Union deepened, Germany moved from enemy to ally and feeding the Germans became an urgent concern.

Zuckmayer left Germany in March 1947, just as the weather finally began to improve. Jaspers informed Arendt happily that spring had arrived: 'We don't have to sit around in blankets any more.' But the milder weather became the setting for escalating American-Soviet tensions. The previous October, the conflict between the Americans and the Russians had become explicit when the first postwar elections had been held in Berlin, with both sets of occupiers distributing gifts of shoes, whisky and bicycle tyres to the voters in the preceding weeks. The Russians were convinced that the communist SED party (the result of a forced merger in the eastern zone between the communist KPD and the traditional workers' Social Democrat SPD parties in April 1946) would be victorious, but in fact they trailed behind both the conservative Christian Democratic Union (CDU) and the left-wing Social Democrat Parties (SPD) (which remained an independent party in the western zones). It seemed that the Berliners recognised the SED to be a sycophantic Soviet-led party and wanted to avoid a Soviet takeover.

The Berlin election imbued the American delegation with added confidence when on 10 March the Council of Foreign Ministers met in Moscow to debate the future of Germany. The US was now represented by a new secretary of state, George Marshall, who although nonpartisan himself was acting on behalf of a Congress dominated by a vocal, anti-communist Republican majority following a mid-term election in November. He was determined not to allow the Russians to create a centralised Germany paying reparations to the Soviet Union and instead announced the intention of the British and Americans to form a 'Bizone' and waive all reparations. These proposals were unpopular both with the Russians and with the French and it was hard for the Russians not to see Marshall's proposal as anti-communist, especially as it coincided with an incendiary speech from Truman to Congress in Washington on 12 March. In February, Britain had implored the US to take over the burden of providing financial and military support to Turkey and Greece, who were both in the throes of communist insurgency. Now Truman asked Congress for financial aid in rhetoric intended to appeal to the Republicans in Congress who were sceptical about their Democrat president. He argued that there was more than the security of these two countries at stake; the world now faced a choice 'between alternative ways of life'. One way was based on the will of the majority, the other on the will of a minority imposed on the majority through terror and oppression. 'I believe that it must be the policy of the US to support free peoples who are resisting attempted subjection by armed minorities or by outside pressures.'[30]

Arguably, this was the moment at which the Cold War became unavoidable, although within Germany tensions had been escalating for some time. George Marshall informed the Americans in a radio broadcast that compromise had proved impossible because the Soviet Union had insisted upon proposals designed to establish in Germany 'a centralised government, adapted to the seizure of absolute control of a country which would be doomed economically . . . and would be mortgaged to turn over a large part of its production as reparations, principally to the Soviet Union'. In Marshall's view, the recovery of Europe was unduly threatened by the attempt to reach a shared solution. 'The patient is sinking while the doctors deliberate. So I believe that action cannot await compromise through exhaustion.' Although he still claimed to seek agreement with Stalin, he was also clearing the way for the Americans and British to take matters in Germany into their own hands. Plans were put in motion for a new Economic Council for the Bizone which would meet for the first time in June.[31]

If 'Bizonia' was going to be a success, the British and Americans needed to be popular in Germany. This meant supporting the country economically and using culture to win over the German people. It was time to drop any notion of collective guilt and punishment, and start selling democracy, though it was unclear exactly what democracy was. That spring Lord Pakenham was appointed as the minister responsible to Germany in Britain. He visited the country far more frequently than his predecessor John Hynd and did his best to instill self-respect in his teutonic subjects. At a school in Düsseldorf he told the assembled children never to believe that the whole world was against them: 'You're absolutely right to be proud of being German'. On 18 May the British military governor Brian Robertson issued a new instruction to the Control Commission stating that staff should behave to the Germans 'as the people of one Christian and civilised race towards another whose interests in many ways converge with our own and for whom we have no longer any ill-will'. His staff nicknamed this the 'be-kind-to-the-Germans' order.[32]

Meanwhile the Americans were drafting a new directive to replace the punitive JCS 1067. Launched in July 1947, JCS 1779 advocated the creation of a 'stable and productive Germany', stating that 'the re-education of the German people is an integral part of policies intended to help develop a democratic form of government', making culture central to the new Bizone agenda. These are directives that both Gollancz and Zuckmayer would have supported. The Cold War pragmatists and the humanist idealists had come to the same conclusion. The Second World War was over and it was time to treat the Germans with kindness and respect.[33]

The new cultural policy was to be ballasted by economics. On 5 June 1947 Marshall gave an address at Harvard University announcing a new plan to deal with the crisis in Europe. Europe's requirements for foreign food and other products that the US could provide were greater than her present ability to pay. 'She must have substantial additional help, or face economic, social and political deterioration of a very grave character.' Marshall offered to provide this assistance, insisting that he was not motivated by 'political passion and prejudice' but by a benign sense of history and responsibility.[34]

In theory, Marshall Aid (officially known as the European Recovery Programme) was available to the Soviet Union. A Russian delegate attended the meeting held in Paris in July to determine the nature and use of these funds. But it was immediately clear that the plan was partly intended to create an anti-Soviet front and the Russian delegate withdrew, leaving the British and French foreign ministers to arrange to implement the plan in the sixteen European nations who wished to participate. The French were sceptical about a proposal that could create a revived and newly threatening Germany but were unable to turn down the offer of much-needed funds. By July, Congress had granted $5.3 billion to Europe, with more funds planned annually, and it was evident that the majority of costs in the new Bizone in Germany would be funded by the US.[35]

In the US, the phrase 'Cold War' now gained popular parlance. That April an American statesman had announced that the world was 'in the midst of a cold war', repeating the phrase in speeches throughout the summer so that by October a *New York Times* columnist stated that the phrase 'Cold War' had come to be universally accepted as the best description of the current struggle between Soviet Russia and the United States to shape the postwar world. Europe was explicitly divided and Germany was caught in the middle. And in the short term, this was beneficial to the 'West Germans' at least, enabling Gollancz's aims to be achieved. Politically, the occupiers were now committed to the possibility of the 'good German' and the nation was going to be fed.[36]

Zuckmayer, too, could be satisfied with the situation. Culture in Germany flourished as the division between the eastern and western zones of Germany became more entrenched and the occupiers poured more money into funding cultural activities in their zones. The previous November, Hilde Spiel and her two children had joined Peter de Mendelssohn in Berlin, where he was now editing the newspaper *Die Welt*. Spiel was appointed as the paper's theatre critic, which meant going to first nights up to five times a week throughout the city. After years as a housewife in suburban Wimbledon, she was enjoying the glamorous life possible among the conquerors, commissioning evening gowns from Berlin dressmakers. And she was impressed by the theatre, which she described as 'the state religion in Berlin': 'In the midst of the most desolate metropolis in the world, among grey and bleached skeletons of houses, theatres of a splendour such as a Londoner might seek in vain at home still rise, and are rising again.'[37]

But if the Cold War was proving beneficial for culture in Germany, then this was culture primarily as decoration. The arts had proved a useful way for each side to show off to each other. The cultural competition found a locus in the cultural centres springing up in all four zones. The French Mission Culturelle, American and British Information Centres (known respectively as Amerika Häuser and Die Brücke) were founded in 1946, followed by the grander Soviet House of Culture of the Soviet Union complete with a plush, well-heated bar and smoking room in 1947. These provided platforms for library services, music recitals, film screenings, exhibitions and public lectures, often given by visitors from abroad. The Americans hoped that their centres could be used to correct the popular image of Americans as gum-chewing philistines, with the director of education and cultural relations informing staff that 'in spite of the great contribution which has been made by America in the cultural field, it is not generally known even to Germany or the rest of the world' and that their task was to rectify this.[38]

One way to convert the Germans to American and British culture was to import books. In 1946 Goronwy Rees had been involved in a 'British Book Selection Committee' choosing which books to translate and export. They decided to avoid military and naval topics, theological books, philosophy ('best to give it a rest') and travel books. Over the next two years they came up with a list of titles by authors including Virginia Woolf, Vita Sackville-West, T. S. Eliot, Elizabeth Bowen, Evelyn Waugh and Dorothy L. Sayers. Many of these books had also been available during the Third Reich but there was also *Post D*, a work of reportage about the destruction wrought by the Blitz in London by John Strachey, then an ARP warden and now the Minister for Food in Germany, and Christopher Isherwood's *Goodbye to Berlin,* with its accounts of the exotic nightlife and growing National Socialist tendencies of Weimar Germany.[39] Meanwhile in December 1946 the Americans supported the German publisher Ernst Rowohlt in instituting a series of novels published in newspaper format with the friendly series title 'Ro-Ro-Ro'. The first books were by Hemingway, Alain-Fournier and Tucholsky, inclusively bringing together the classical German tradition with contemporary French and American literature.[40]

Another way to publicise the momentous contributions of Americans in the cultural field was to invite influential artists to come to demonstrate those achievements. It was even better if the emissaries were Germans who could tell their former compatriots about the new cultural vitality they had found in the land of the free. Zuckmayer had advocated visits from Americans hoping that these could enable mutual understanding rather than being used as propaganda exercises. Now the visitors were invited with more didactic aims and few were as forgiving of their former compatriots as Zuckmayer.

At the end of May 1947 the composer Paul Hindemith arrived in
Frankfurt from the US, where he had emigrated via Switzerland in
1940 when it became obvious that his music was too avant-garde for
Hitler's Germany. During the war he had heard almost nothing from
Germany, where his music was unofficially banned. In 1940 he had
applied for American citizenship, learning off by heart the official booklet on the US constitution and way of life. Then just before the war
ended news of family and friends began to arrive and Hindemith learnt
that his mother was still alive. Almost immediately, he was bombarded
with calls for his return, which he answered with similar scepticism to
Thomas Mann. He told his publisher that it seemed too soon to achieve
anything worthwhile in Germany: 'whoever is given the power to try
and clean out the pigsty will simply be and remain the pigsty-cleaner,
and the really constructive work can only be done by his successor'. He
was suspicious of the tales of woe and adulation that he was sent on a
daily basis, which all seemed ultimately to be over-entitled demands for
help. Hindemith decided his best offering to future peace was going to
take the form of compositions, and he set about writing 'A Requiem for
Those We Love', dedicated to the memory of Roosevelt and the dead
American servicemen. Meanwhile the Germans continued to pay
homage by performing his pieces, though he refused to grant licenses
in Germany for the music he had written in the US which he believed
would 'flourish much better in the healthier (if also not ideal) climate
over here'.[41]

In April, Hindemith decided to visit Europe but to avoid giving
concerts in Germany. He met Furtwängler in Switzerland, happy to
forgive his former friend for his wartime compromises, and then went
to Germany to visit his mother. It was difficult to keep a low profile; his
presence was discovered and he found himself attending concerts of his
work, uncomfortable with being treated as a returning German in a
country where he no longer felt he belonged. A year later he was
approached by the US Military Government with an invitation to tour
the US zone of occupation in Germany and serve as a conductor and
lecturer in their 'reorientation programme'. This was much more
acceptable to him and he was happy to oblige, wanting to impress upon

the Germans his reasons for shifting his allegiance to the US and contented to play his part in the cultural arms race taking place in Germany.

———

Culture was now pouring into Germany and it looked as though soon Marshall Plan money would be as well. It would be some time before daily life in Germany became less desperate, but there were signs that the Germans were no longer enemy aliens. In this climate it no longer made sense to be over-scrupulous in constraining the activities of German artists, so on 25 May 1947 Furtwängler conducted the Berlin Philharmonic at the American-requisitioned Titania-Palast cinema. At the end of a programme comprised entirely of Beethoven, the conductor was applauded for fifteen minutes.[42]

Reading about the concert in the US, Erika Mann was furious, complaining that even if the concert had been a success (which she doubted given they had only had two rehearsals), there was no need for such excessive adulation. 'I cannot recall any exhilarating concert in Paris or London where the audience summoned the conductor 16 times.' The applause seemed to her to be a protest against denazification. 'The Germans never miss an occasion to emphasise their sacrifice and their survival and they do it in a loud and aggressive manner'. They would not have to protest for much longer. In October 1947 denazification would be handed over to the Germans altogether, with instructions to complete the process by the end of the year.[43]

Erika Mann was not alone among exiles in the US in looking on in horror as denazification was abandoned. The dream of a new Germany that had sustained them during the war had been trampled. In Germany, the more principled artists and writers asked themselves how they could bring into existence a new German culture untainted by Nazism. In August 1946 Alfred Andersch and Hans Werner Richter had launched *Der Ruf* ('The Call'), intended as an 'Independent Journal of the Young Generation', which became a forum for young writers calling for a '*Stunde Null*' – or zero hour – and a complete break with the past. They separated themselves from the older generation, partly as a way of drawing a line between the Nazis being tried at Nuremberg and the young men who had merely fought on the battlefield, and maintaining that the German majority should not be tainted by the crimes of a minority. Andersch and Richter had been removed from the editorship in April 1947 by Americans who thought they were too critical of the Occupation. However they were now busy founding 'Gruppe 47', a relatively informal grouping of young writers committed to tearing away the past and reconstituting the present on broadly existentialist principles.[44]

Others focused on integrating themselves into the wider culture of Europe. The first step to gaining a European presence was the foundation of a new German PEN centre in 1947, under the auspices of International PEN, the influential writers' organisation dedicated to promoting literature and defending freedom of expression. For years, German writers had been represented at PEN only by German and Austrian centres in exile in London and New York. In June 1942, the English PEN newsletter editorial stated that after the war it would fall upon PEN to reestablish 'connections with the countries now cut off from free intercourse with the rest of the world'. The writer believed that organisations such as PEN would be responsible for spearheading the creation of a new European literature and, ultimately, for establishing a new European community. In this PEN would be assisted by the Free German League of Culture, which remained 'a reminder of a German culture that has nothing to do with Nazi Kultur'.[45]

Unsurprisingly, there were writers involved in both the English PEN centre and the German centre in exile who were sceptical about reopening a branch in Germany after the war. A new Italian centre opened its doors in July 1945 but there was vocal opposition (especially from the Hebrew and Yiddish centres) to allowing the Germans to follow suit. However even in June 1945 at a PEN dinner in London, the English PEN president Desmond MacCarthy gave a speech asking what could remain of the Germany he had once loved, given that Hitler had 'destroyed the Reich', and the Germans following him had 'murdered their mother Germany'. He provided the answer, insisting that German music, the German landscape and, crucially, the German language, 'will and must survive' and that it was PEN's duty to enable this survival. At the 1946 summer congress, the German group put forward a resolution to start trying to establish a German centre. That December the English PEN newsletter reported favourably on Gollancz's 'Save Europe Now' campaign, reminding their readers of the 'appalling intellectual starvation' in the British zone in Germany.[46]

Now in June 1947 writers from across the world converged in Zurich for the PEN congress that would determine whether to open a new German centre. Among the writers present was Thomas Mann, who had decided to make this the focus for his first postwar trip to Europe. He was not yet ready to visit Germany. In a message published in the German newspapers at the end of May he had explained that he was fully aware of the 'extraordinarily difficult and sorrowful position' of Germany today but that they must not expect to recover too quickly after a catastrophe of this kind. He hoped though that 'after two, three, or five years, the horizon again will be brighter and thanks to the inborn industry and energy, Germany will not need to despair about the future'.[47]

When that time came, Mann would perhaps return; in the meantime, he went to London and then Zurich, accompanied by the now ever-faithful Erika. In Zurich, Mann made a gesture of allegiance to his broken homeland. He gave a lecture on Nietzsche and defended the German writers present at the congress (Johannes Becher, Erich Kästner and Ernst Wiechert), urging that the German PEN centre should reopen. Mann's pleas were effective. The assembled members voted in favour of the Germans, opposed only by the Hebrew and Yiddish centres. The English PEN editorial described the decision as 'a triumph for the spirit of internationalism'.[48]

At the PEN congress, there were also hopes that Germany would soon form part of a wider European cultural scene enabled by UNESCO, established in 1946 to construct the defences of peace through education, science and culture with the liberal biologist Julian Huxley as its director (though Francis Biddle was briefly considered for the role) and Stephen Spender as a literary councillor. Since the war began, politicians from across the world had been demanding a federated Europe as a guarantor of peace. In 1942 Churchill expressed his hopes to the leader of the House of Commons that after the war 'the European family may act unitedly as one, under a Council of Europe'. Just before the end of the war, Democratic Socialists recently liberated from the concentration camp at Buchenwald issued the 'Buchenwald manifesto', demanding that Germany should be reconstructed on a socialist basis and should co-operate with other socialist-governed states to form 'a European community' that would 'guarantee order and prosperity' for the postwar world.[49]

As yet, this could only take cultural rather than political form. In November 1945, at a United Nations conference in London planned to establish what would become UNESCO, Clement Attlee had argued that in order to know our neighbours we must understand their culture, through their books, newspapers, radio and films. Ellen Wilkinson, the British minister of education, had suggested that it was writers and artists, more than any other profession, who could reach across the barriers of frontiers. Representing the US (who deemed the new organisation important enough to contribute 44 per cent of its budget), Archibald MacLeish stated that the time had come to choose between living together and not living at all and that UNESCO had the power to foster 'the common understanding of the peoples of the world'.[50]

These sentiments were echoed by Stephen Spender in September 1946 when he attended the first of a series of annual meetings called the *Rencontres internationales de Genève*, aimed at establishing a common 'European spirit'. Since leaving Germany, Spender had worked determinedly in pursuit of a humanitarian, non-nationalistic European ideal. Now, speaking alongside European intellectuals including Karl Jaspers and Georg Lukács, he made a plea for the rebirth of Europe through culture. It had become clear that 'success, prosperity, victory, power, aggression and even the spirit of invention' were powerless to save civilisation. Instead what was needed were 'civilising values' which could be accessed through the artistic achievements of the past by artists in the present. Appointing himself as judge of a kind of intercontinental art competition, he announced that Europe possessed an unusually intense concentration of great art and was therefore able to lead the world in this respect, if its citizens could realise 'those values present in their architecture, their paintings, their literature and their men and women of genius' through their 'life, thought and deeds' and illuminate the path from destruction to creative construction. He advocated a full consciousness of the horrors of the present, which would entail reintegrating Germany into intellectual life and inviting the Germans to describe 'what they have suffered and what these difficult years have taught them' from a position of trust and equality.[51]

Returning home from Geneva, Spender felt ambivalent about the conference he had just attended. He voiced these doubts in an article entitled 'The Intellectuals and the Future of Europe', published the following January. Here he complained that it was impossible to discuss European culture without entering the field of European politics and that as soon as they had begun to discuss the politics the delegates had found themselves disagreeing fundamentally. In particular there had been an impasse between Jaspers, with his vision of a Europe united by classical antiquity and the Bible, forged by people driven not by their loyalty to the state but by their individual conscience, and Lukács, with his communist commitment to progress, who had condemned Jaspers as 'a broken man' over-reliant on 'social-realism'.[52]

For Spender, the division between Jaspers and Lukács was indicative of 'the struggle within the European soul' and it was a struggle that he located in Germany, 'the true meeting-place of East and West'. It was not a coincidence that both Jaspers and Lukács saw themselves as German (at one point Lukács, though the representative of Hungary, had talked about 'us Germans'). And Spender was hopeful that the struggle, if recognised as German, could provide both Germany and Europe with a mode of redemption. Right now the Germans were too occupied with practical questions of survival to pay much attention to spiritual questions. But Spender suggested presciently that 'the day may come when this fusion of two ideas – liberal democracy and economic freedom – will take place within the minds of certain Germans'.[53]

In the meantime any meeting of the European intellectuals was going to be marked by a rift between communist sympathisers and

violent anti-communists; the notion of 'the West' was becoming mean-
ingless because it existed only in opposition to the East. Yet Spender
believed that the intellectuals should continue to meet and to talk
because only then could they achieve what he thought should be termed
're-education': 'a complete Re-education in our conceptions of the relations of nations to each other in the world, of our relations as
individuals to society and of our freedom as individuals'. He wished
that they could meet not in Geneva but in Germany, where they would
be confronted with the problems of their world. There they could be
re-educated into a new vision of both selfhood and nationhood that
would create the preconditions for genuine European co-operation. In
the meantime there was a danger that such gatherings were merely
creating a class of spoiled travelling writers going from conference to
conference to air familiar ideas.[54]

Whatever his doubts about the efficacy of official European
co-operation, Spender attended the June 1947 Zurich PEN congress as
the representative for UNESCO, using this as a forum to make his
hopes for incorporating the new German PEN centre into the wider
European community explicit. Here he argued not just that German
culture could be integrated into a wider European culture but that in
the cultural sphere, Cold War politics could be transcended. While
governments differed on questions of politics, they could co-operate in
the area of economics, education and culture. In UNESCO and PEN
there could be an interchange of ideas between East and West that
would allow the whole world to be re-educated.[55]

———

Mann and Spender, pledging their support to PEN and UNESCO in
June 1947, still hoped that literature could transcend political divisions.
It should be possible for German writers to join PEN and fight for
internationalism; it should be possible for UNESCO to protect culture
from national agendas. But Spender's time in office was to be short-
lived. He stepped down from UNESCO the following year when Julian
Huxley was discouraged from applying for re-election, now seen as
problematically left-wing by the Americans. And the writers in the

German PEN centre were unable (and in Becher's case unwilling) to distance themselves from Cold War politics.

During his visit to Germany, Zuckmayer had been hopeful that in artistic spheres at least, co-operation between the Americans and the Russians was still possible. He visited the Möwe, where the Russian cultural officers arranged a cultural reception in his honour, inviting governmental representatives and German theatrical people from all the sectors. But Zuckmayer's own idealism made him somewhat gullible in this respect; in fact the Russian newspapers now referred to the Americans as 'imperialists' and 'aggressors'. The following summer, political tensions became increasingly manifest in the cultural sphere. There was more overt anti-communist censorship in operation in the US zone. In August 1947 Arthur Miller's *All My Sons* was banned after a letter of complaint to the US War Department decried the play as communist anti-business propaganda. 'Who is responsible for choosing communist Miller's play?' asked the writer. 'Some innocent in the Army? Or some Communist?'[56]

The East-West co-operation that Zuckmayer had dreamt of was a casualty of the larger political process that had enabled the Germans to be treated as friends. Though the Cold War had proved useful in beginning the revival of both Germany and its culture, it would not prove beneficial for indigenous German culture, which from now on would be riven between East and West. On 4 October 1947 writers from across Germany came together for a writers' conference where it became apparent that cultural freedom was a casualty of the new political situation. The five-day German Writers' Conference took place in the Hebbel Theater in the US sector, organised by the cross-zonal Protective League of German Authors and the Kulturbund and including writers from all four zones. Opulent hospitality was provided by the Russians, who hosted a banquet for all the participants at the congress. Hilde Spiel later recalled the surreal and disturbing effect of the enormous table, groaning under the weight of bowls of caviar and seafood salad, in a city whose inhabitants were still visibly starving.[57]

The conference aimed to overcome the tensions between inner and outer emigrants and to debate the question of politicised literature.

Accordingly, speakers from across the political spectrum began by arguing relatively open-mindedly about whether or not literature should be
politicised, with the novelist Stephan Hermlin complaining that the
Germans who defended aesthetic impartiality were 'beginning to bar
the way back to reality'.[58]

However, the conference took place amid escalating international
hostility. A month earlier, in response to the US plans for Marshall Aid,
Stalin's ideologist Andrei Zhdanov had declared that the Second World
War co-operation between the Soviet Union and the Western Allies
had come to an end. The Soviet Union convened a conference of Eastern European countries (Cominform) in Belgrade to close ranks in the
face of the American threat. The US authorities in Germany chose this
moment to launch 'Operation Talkback', a new information programme
aimed at using the mass media to counteract anti-American Soviet
propaganda.[59]

These tensions intruded on the Writers' Conference when on the
fourth day the Russian playwright Wsewolod Witalyevich Wishnevsky
(visiting from the Soviet Union) changed the terms of the debate by
attacking the US, claiming that the world was now divided into two
camps, one represented by 'barbarism, by an ideology of hatred of
humanity', the other by 'millions of simple human beings who live for
peace, who fight for peace' and urging German writers to find their
place in the ranks of these simple democrats.[60]

Immediately, a short, young, bearded American assailed Wishnevsky
with a thirty-five-minute tirade in perfect German. This was Melvin
Lasky, an American Jewish anti-Stalinist who had been working as a
journalist in the US before he became a combat historian in the army
and was demobbed in Berlin, where he occasionally served as a conduit
for Arendt's food parcels to Jaspers. Now Lasky furiously insisted that
the task of writers was to fight for cultural freedom. They had to
condemn tyranny everywhere, not just in Nazi Germany, and right
now that meant fighting against the totalitarianism of the Soviet
Union.[61]

The conference could not recover from this conflagration. Alarmed,
Johannes Becher insisted that a division of Germany along

Soviet-American lines would be a disaster that would threaten the peace of the world. It was absurd for German literature to be circumscribed by zonal boundaries. But it was too late. According to the Catholic conservative novelist Elisabeth Langgässer, 'the whole meeting went up like a show of fireworks, and the following morning the parched brown grass was strewn with the charred remains'. Shortly afterwards, the Kulturbund was banned in the British and US sectors and had to vacate its premises on Schlüterstrasse. Its days as a cross-party organisation were over. A year after Gollancz and Zuckmayer had arrived in Germany hoping lovingly to feed the stomachs and minds of the German people, it had become evident that all sustenance would come sponsored by one side or other of the ideological divide. Writers could continue to dream of a united Germany and a transnational Europe but they were weak in the face of a political battle between superpowers that soon would turn Berlin into a war zone once again.[62]

12

'I've been the Devil's General on earth too long'

Artistic enlightenment:
November 1947–January 1948

The 'charred remains' of the German Writers' Conference were not easy to clear away. Over the next few months anatomising the crisis of German culture became a popular activity. Melvin Lasky followed his speech at the conference with a gloomy 'Berlin Letter' in *Partisan Review*, bemoaning that life in the capital since the end of the war had been merely 'a formal gesture of historic survival'. There was trade, traffic and city life but there was neither state nor culture; there was an intelligentsia but no intellectual life; there was a thriving theatre scene but the most popular playwrights were dead. The writer in Germany was not a free man because books remained censored by conquerors in all zones. The 'semi-totalitarian dimness' had given Russian and German Stalinism the 'half-light it needs to have its own way'.[1]

Lasky's was a maverick and incendiary voice but he was supported by several writers in Germany who saw the Occupation as stifling genuine artistic talent. Not long after the war ended Elisabeth Langgässer had grumbled that Berlin was 'a vacuum filled with newspapers, magazines, and literary gatherings, a sheer collection of nonsense'. During her twelve years of 'inner emigration' she had found more time to produce real work than she did now. 'Both culturally and materially, Berlin is one big mound of rubble. A dance of ghosts from 1928.' Earlier in 1947

Jaspers had complained to Arendt that Germany was becoming a battleground for the US and the Soviet Union, 'a garbage heap where all those people are tossed whom nobody wants anywhere else'.[2]

By bringing together all the contenders for literary greatness in post-war Germany, the Writers' Conference had unwittingly laid bare the impoverishment of contemporary German culture. It was now more than two years since the war had ended but there was still no major work of German literature reflecting on the Third Reich. Writers did not seem capable of lighting the way to self-knowledge and redempton for the German people.

This situation would change rapidly in the months following the conference with the Swiss publication of Thomas Mann's *Doctor Faustus* in October 1947 and the opening of Carl Zuckmayer's *The Devil's General* in Frankfurt in November.[3] Written in the US by German writers who had only imagined the war-torn Germany they described, these works portrayed a country that was paying the price for selling its soul to the Devil. Zuckmayer's and Mann's explorations of guilt and responsibility chimed with Jean-Paul Sartre's wartime play *Les Mouches* (*The Flies*), which immediately became the theatrical sensation of the year when it opened in Berlin in January 1948. Addressing questions of repentance and freedom in occupied France in ways that now appeared pertinent to occupied Germany, *The Flies* seemed to offer a way forward for the diseased nation depicted by Zuckmayer and Mann. What was more, Sartre and Simone de Beauvoir themselves accompanied his play, bringing existentialism triumphantly into a Germany much in need of a new philosophy.

———

In November 1947, Carl Zuckmayer returned to Germany for the Frankfurt premiere of *The Devil's General*. The play had been staged in Zurich the previous winter (Zuckmayer had managed to dash across the border to watch the first night) but had initially been banned by the American authorities in Germany who were worried that it would have a reactionary political effect, fostering a legend about the German officer class. This time Zuckmayer did not wear the uniform of Germany's conquerors. He had resigned his commission and came garbed as a civilian, accompanied by his wife. He was now convinced that although he had a home in the US, he belonged fundamentally to the nation whose language and culture he still shared.[4]

During Zuckmayer's visit the previous year, journalists had asked him if he remained a German. 'When becoming an American citizen,' he replied, 'one has to take an oath.' As a grown man taking an oath, he was aware that this was a decision for life. 'I am an American and will remain an American citizen.' In fact the situation was less straightforward. Hearing German voices, walking through the ruins of the cities he had grown up in, he had known that he was a German, even if Germany could not currently be his home. Now it seemed more possible to belong there again.[5]

Zuckmayer attended the final rehearsals of the play in the former Frankfurt stock exchange, refurbished as a temporary theatre. Another freezing winter had begun and the actors were cold and hungry. Zuckmayer smuggled food from the US army canteens to keep up their strength, happy to be in a theatre again. During the opening performance he spent as much time observing the audience as watching the action on stage. He noticed that the officers from the occupation forces were looking on sceptically, doubtful that the Germans wanted to be confronted with their own shame. But they were proved wrong by the ensuing surge of enthusiasm. According to Zuckmayer, the audience could not believe that the play had been written by someone who had lived abroad throughout the war. There were former German soldiers sitting side by side with victims from concentration camps, all apparently astounded to see their own lives played out before them. 'The play corresponded to the reality as they had known it, down to the smallest detail,' he observed somewhat immodestly.[6]

The Devil's General is set in Germany in the final months of 1941. Its hero, Harras, is a general in the Luftwaffe, a brilliant pilot who believes that he can remain a good man while participating in the war, separating himself from the Nazis with occasional acts of defiance and ironic humour: 'I've never dipped into the party treasury, never stolen anything from a Jew nor built myself villas from the proceeds.' Occasionally he helps Jews, to appease his conscience, but he remains committed, almost addictively, to the war: 'The meaning of my life was always flying. I started out in 1914. And now I can't stop anymore. It's like liquor.' Harras's honesty is contrasted with the delusions of the Nazis around him. Eilers, a brilliant colonel and pilot serving under Harras's command, believes fervently in the Nazi ideals. Indeed, it seems to be Nazism that bonds him to his wife in a passionate *folie à deux*. 'Don't question, darling. Believe,' she tells her husband when he wonders if all this killing is necessary. The Minister for Culture informs Harras humourlessly that his province is 'total mobilisation of the German soul'.[7]

Harras's ironic detachment is enough to distance him from these false ideals but it also comes dangerously close to separating him from life itself, until he falls in love with a young woman called Diddo who is convinced that happiness remains possible. 'I want to be happy!' Diddo tells her lover, 'Quite madly happy.' 'We need a whole world of joy,' he promises her in return, now determined to live. Harras's love for Diddo restores his own youthful humanism. He assures Lieutenant Hartmann, a young man who has started to doubt Nazism and to question the value of life itself, that life is more beautiful than it looks: 'The world is wonderful. We human beings try like hell to louse it all up but we are no match for it – for the original concept.'[8]

It is too late for Harras to commit to the beauty of the world. Aircraft are being sabotaged and he is unable to track down the culprit; suspected of knowing more than he admits, he is taken away for two weeks of questioning by the Gestapo. Eilers dies in one of the damaged planes and Harras feels responsible for his death.

Throughout, Harras has tried to believe in the possibility of a 'good' Germany. At one stage he toasts 'the true, the immortal Germany' in which the wine they are drinking was made. But he is convinced now that Germany is doomed. 'It's laid too many rotten eggs for us – the house of mad Siegfried, the insane delusions of grandeur.' One of the Jews he has attempted to save kills himself and Harras comes to see that there is guilt in inaction. 'We're guilty for what's happening to thousands of people we don't know and can never help . . . Permitting viciousness is worse than doing it.'[9]

Eventually Harras discovers that the planes are being sabotaged by the chief engineer Oderbruch, a former friend who is now resisting the Nazis and working for Germany's defeat. 'We need the defeat – we must help it with our own hands,' Oderbruch tells him. 'Only then can we rise up again, cleansed.' Oderbruch urges Harras to join the resistance in Switzerland. But Harras believes that his day has passed. 'I've been the Devil's General on earth too long. I'm going to fly an advance mission for him in hell too – in preparation for his imminent arrival.' He abandons the girl he loves, convinced that he is too tarnished for happiness, and takes off suicidally in a sabotaged plane. Before he dies he tells Hartmann to have faith in a new kind of goodness. Harras himself may not know God but he has looked the Devil in the eye. 'That's how I know that there must be a God. He hid his face from me. You will meet him . . . go ahead and believe confidently in divine justice! It will not betray you.'[10]

Zuckmayer may have had his own play partly in mind when he advised the American authorities to make a documentary film showing the Germans how men and women from their own midst 'fought and eventually died for the path of liberation'. This was effectively the story of *The Devil's General* and reviewers and audiences responded overwhelmingly positively to a play that suggested that even under Nazism individuals retained the ability to save their own souls. On the third night, Zuckmayer attended a discussion with young Germans. He was surprised how candidly audience members confessed to misdeeds performed under Nazism. 'The hearts of these young people seemed to be wide open.' Hundreds of letters now arrived opening with 'I am your Lieutenant Hartmann' and Zuckmayer decided to devote his life to talking to confused young Germans.[11]

Zuckmayer remained convinced that the German youths he spoke to were fundamentally redeemable and that the popularity of his play was proof of this. He believed that he was succeeding where the concentration camp documentaries had failed in teaching his compatriots a moral lesson through his art and discouraging fascism by revealing the possibility of another, individualistic and heroic, way. Others thought that this was naïve. The German film director Douglas Sirk, now in

Germany as an American, was sure that when audiences applauded the
play they were really applauding the Nazis, pleased to see their uniforms
spruced up once more: 'When I saw the play, after the last curtain the
crowd surged forward in the theatre and chaired the hero off the stage
in his Nazi uniform and out into the streets. And in the streets people
joined in the procession when they saw this triumphant Nazi uniform
on the shoulders of the audience.' Either way, *The Devil's General* proved
immensely popular with the Germans whose culpability it explored. It
would be performed almost continuously in cities throughout Germany
for the next two years.[12]

In appointing himself the Devil's General on earth, Harras is a peculiarly German figure. Since Martin Luther drove away the persistent
fiend who taunted him while he attempted to translate his Bible, the
Devil had been a familiar feature of German life, taking root in the
popular imagination through Goethe's *Faust*. Before the war, Goethe's
story had provided the vehicle for Gustaf Gründgen's career-defining
performance as Mephisto, which was immortalised in Klaus Mann's
novel. The Germans often prided themselves on their imaginative
reach, their striving for knowledge and their fascination with death –
all qualities that might lead someone to make a pact with the Devil.
Now it seemed not just to Zuckmayer but to Thomas Mann that the
nation had made a pact with the Devil and that its chances for salvation
were doubtful.[13]

Mann's *Doctor Faustus* started circulating into Germany from
Switzerland at the end of 1947. This was a novel that the Germans had
been waiting for, suspiciously, defensively, but none the less eagerly.
It is the great novel to come out of Germany in these postwar years
and at the same time, written by an American citizen with no first-
hand experience of the ruins he portrayed, it is also arguably the
greatest example of 'outsider rubble literature', chiming with Stephen
Spender's *European Witness* and Billy Wilder's *A Foreign Affair*. From
California, reading about the German ruins in American newspapers
and German periodicals, hearing about them from his children, who

had encountered them in American army uniform, Mann had written a novel revealing himself to be at once a German and an outsider, able to diagnose the Germans' guilt and despair with a clarity possible to few in Germany but unable to separate himself from the tragedy. The book takes as its starting point Mann's suggestion in his 'Germany and the Germans' lecture that both Germany and its inhabitants have made a pact with the Devil and that as a great German artist seduced by German Romanticism, Mann himself is fully implicated in Germany's guilt.

Doctor Faustus relates the simultaneous and intertwined downfalls of its tragic artist hero and his tragic nation. The narrator Serenus Zeitblom, an 'inner emigrant' teacher who has spoken out against the Nazis and lost his post, tells the story of the life and times of the avant-garde composer Adrian Leverkühn. Zeitblom has loved Leverkühn devotedly and loyally since they played together as children, even after finding that as a young man Leverkühn made a strange, deluded pact with the Devil, sacrificing personal happiness for energy and inspiration as a composer. In Goethe's version of the story, Faust sacrifices happiness for knowledge, promising Mephistopheles that 'If ever I shall tell the moment: Bide here you are so beautiful!' then he can fetter and damn him instantly.[14] Mann's hero makes a similar pact, acquiescing to the Devil's demand that he live coldly, without love. Both Faust and Leverkühn make their pledges willingly because they are already unhappy; this is merely a continuation of their present ennui. 'Is not coldness a precedence with you,' the Devil says to Leverkühn. The tragedy is that there will now be no possibility of happy escape, as Harras too learns to his cost in Zuckmayer's play.[15]

Leverkühn's damnation comes in the form of syphilis, contracted from a prostitute called Esmeralda. A habitually cold man, Leverkühn surprises himself by falling in love at first touch and chooses to have sex with Esmeralda even after she warns him about the contagion. Like Nietzsche, one of Mann's many models for his character, Leverkühn experiences the disease as creatively fertile but then gradually loses his mind.[16] He engages in a lengthy dialogue with the Devil, who claims the illness as his own, taking credit for dispersing the composer's physicians, and warns Leverkühn that he will be unable to love: 'your life shall be cold – hence you may love no human'.[17]

This prediction proves painfully true. And what the Devil has not made explicit is that should Leverkühn try to thwart the curse, he will doom those he loves to a hasty death. Leverkühn forms partial attachments to friends and women, all of whom die. Most tragically he comes to love his small nephew, Echo, sent by his sister to live with him while she is ill. From the start, Echo's presence is redemptive. His perfect, slender figure, his 'innocent tangle of blond hair', his winning smile, his 'gently floating presence' bring 'radiant daylight' into Leverkühn's life. But he is struck down by meningitis that kills him within two weeks; his body is returned home in a small coffin. 'I have discovered that it ought not be,' Leverkühn tells Zeitblom, 'what people call human . . . It will be taken back.' Instead he channels all his energy into his final masterpiece. For years Leverkühn has been pushing music towards abstraction, going beyond tonality in an attempt to emancipate dissonance from resolution. The great *Apocalypse* oratorio of his youth incorporated loudspeakers, infernal laughter and an austerely dissonant children's chorus to conjure a musical approximation of hell. Now his late great symphonic cantata *The Lamentation of Doctor Faustus* uses a mournful dissonant echo to create an ode to sorrow as a counterpart to Beethoven's ode to joy.[18]

In 1930 Leverkühn assembles his friends to confess his pact with the Devil (which most of them see as an allegorical joke) and to play his new piece. He collapses at the piano, falling into a coma from which he recovers physically but not mentally. Zeitblom cannot be sure if Leverkühn is actually in league with Satan. Reading the transcribed dialogue, he cannot decide if his friend is hallucinating. But he is aware that the question is irrelevant. Mann presents it as inevitable that Leverkühn should succumb to the Devil because the composer has been seduced by the demonic for years. The Devil has always been present in Leverkühn's satanic 'mildly orgiastic' laughter, which Zeitblom found disconcerting in their youth. Leverkühn is a genius and Zeitblom observes that there is always a 'faint, sinister connection' between genius and the nether world. He is a musician and music is inherently devilish, belonging to 'a world of spirits'.[19]

So too, Leverkühn is caught up on the same demonic tide as Nazism. He sees Zeitblom's humanism as outmoded, committing instead to a mixture of nihilism and barbaric primitivism.[20] 'You will break through the age itself . . . and dare a barbarism,' the Devil says to him, 'a double barbarism, because it comes after humanitarianism, after every conceivable root-canal work and bourgeois refinement.' The phrase 'break through' is telling. Later in the novel Germany has a 'breakthrough' (Durchbruch) to world power under Hitler, while Nazi supporters see war as the way Germany will break 'through to a new form of life in which state and culture would be one' (durchbrechen). The Nazis may ban Leverkühn's works for their experimental dissonance but in fact Leverkühn is a kindred spirit. And he is a natural candidate for hell in his haughtiness and brilliance. He is a selfish artist whom the Devil is right to see as fundamentally cold and who is prepared to sacrifice life for the sake of art.[21]

The sacrifice of art for life was Mann's own. He had turned away from the intense homosexual love affairs of his youth, finding in a peaceful bourgeois marriage the domestic calm that he needed to write. Closeted each day in his study, he had shielded himself from the energy of his children, meeting them by appointment and requiring them to tiptoe silently around him as he worked. Though in recent years he had come to depend on the affection of Katia and Erika, he had always lived most fully through his strange and private imaginative life, confided only to his diary. Here he gave reign to urgent, impossible passions, revealing a strength of feeling that he did not wish to find an outlet for in ordinary life, conserving it for his art. In this private world, thirty years earlier he had confided in his diary his physical longing for Klaus as a fourteen-year-old boy, that angelic child with a mop of blond curls not unlike Echo's.[22] More recently, he had become fascinated by his grandson Frido (the son of Thomas's son Michael and the immediate model for Echo), whose youthful grace he described lovingly in his diary. In killing Echo in the novel, Mann was reminding Leverkühn of the price of artistic greatness. Love for Leverkühn as for his creator must remain chiefly a private state of mind, a latent possibility of intense feeling that could be channeled only into art.

Writing the novel while the bombs fell in his lost homeland and his own health deteriorated frighteningly, Mann had been engaged in an act of reckoning, asking if this was too high a price to pay. He held both himself and his nation to account, and he saw in his nation sins of pride, demonic genius and overweeningness that he also found in himself. As in Mann's 1945 lecture, the Germany of *Doctor Faustus* has made a pact with the Devil and it is now paying the price, as its cities are destroyed from the air. This devilish act, Zeitblom says, 'would scream to the heavens were not we who suffer it ourselves laden with guilt'. As it is, the scream dies in the air in the 'prison' that Germany has become. Zeitblom is convinced that the Germans deserve this apocalyptic justice even as he mourns the passing of a world he once loved.[23]

Since starting the book in 1943, Mann had followed news of the war obsessively, imagining day by day the destruction of the cities he had once loved and describing their ruins sadly in his novel. His diary from the war years charts the raids over Germany alongside his progress with his book. 'Berlin's agony, no coal, no electricity'; 'Heavy bombing of Germany; 'the conquest of Germany is rapid. The cities fall like ripe plums'; 'the failure of the novel is beyond doubt now. Nevertheless I will finish it.'[24]

It is therefore not surprising that Zeitblom's sorrow at the destruction of Germany echoes Mann's. Zeitblom begins the book on 23 May 1943 (the day that Mann himself began to write) from a hideaway in Freising on the Isar, just outside Munich. On 14 March 1945 Mann recorded receiving news from Klaus about the destruction of their Munich house, noting a 'strange impression' in his diary. That day he was engaged in writing chapter twenty-six, where Zeitblom reports that 'the terror of the almost daily air raids on our nicely encircled Fortress Europe increases to dimensions beyond conceiving . . . more and more of our cities collapse in ruin'. From the peace of his quiet study in California, Mann paced through the wreckage of his much-loved city, reeling from the devastation but turning back to look again both because this was the only responsible thing to do and because he could not help it. At one stage he portrays Zeitblom as writing in his study in Freising as the bombs fall around him: 'as the Last Judgement fell upon Munich as well, I sat here in my study, turning ashen, shaking like the walls, doors and windowpanes of my house – and writing this account of a man's life with a trembling hand'.

In his hermit's cell on the Isar, Zeitblom recoils from 'our hideously battered Munich', with its toppled statues, its façades 'that gaze from vacant eye sockets to disguise the yawning void beyond, and yet seem inclined to reveal it, too, by supplying more of the rubble already strewn over the cobblestones'. This was a landscape that Mann had not seen and had no intention of seeing in the near future. But he had read about it in the newspapers and in the anguished reports from Erika and Klaus; it haunted his dreams and his diary and now became eerily tangible in his novel.[25]

In California, Mann had hoped publicly and to a large extent privately that Germany would lose the war. Like Spender in *European Witness* he saw the destruction of the German cities both as tragically necessary and as the supreme achievement of his age. He reminded his readers of America's superior military prowess in his novel, ironically voicing Zeitblom's surprise that 'enfeebled democracies do indeed know how to use these dreadful tools' and that war is not after all 'a German prerogative'. But the prospect of another shameful German defeat had also filled Mann with secret horror that he expressed through Zeitblom, who admits that he 'cannot help fearing it more than anything else in the world'. Zeitblom never quite allows himself to hope for either defeat or victory. He is pleased when the Germans invent a new kind of torpedo, feeling 'a certain satisfaction at our ever resourceful spirit of invention', even if it is used in the service of a regime that has led them into a war aimed at creating a terrifying 'and as the world sees it, so it would seem, quite intolerable reality of a German Europe'.[26]

Through Zeitblom, Mann turns the Germans into a nation of tragic heroes; good people grappling with impossible paradoxes whose current mental state 'weighs more heavily upon them than it would upon any other, hopelessly estranging them from themselves'. If Zeitblom's sons knew that he secretly possessed Leverkühn's private papers, they would denounce him, but they would be horrified by their own act. Mann once described Zeitblom as 'a parody of myself'. Through Zeitblom he was ironising the German tendency to see their conflicts of conscience as unusually noble and profound. Zeitblom does not always perceive how much he displays the vices of his nation. He shares his intellectual compatriots' cultural elitism and fear of the masses; like his creator he participated in the 'popular elation' at the start of the First World War, believing that war offered 'a sacrificial rite by which the old Adam' could be laid aside. He is too foolish not to be mocked for asserting that the German 'soul is powerfully tragic', that 'our love belongs to fate . . . even a doom that sets the heavens afire with the red twilight of the gods'. But even as he mocked his own tale, Mann allowed it to take on full tragic force and implicated himself in the tragedy. 'How much *Faustus* contains of the atmosphere of my life!' Mann wrote in January 1946; 'A radical confession, at bottom. From the very beginning that has been the shattering thing about the book.'[27]

Wondering what the Germans would make of the novel when it was first published in Switzerland, Mann hoped that it would teach them that it was 'a mistake to see me as a deserter of Germanness'. That summer, lecturing in London and Zurich, Mann had told German reporters that although he was still not ready to return to a Germany that he did not yet deem ready to receive him, he remained a German writer. 'I was too old and fully formed as an artist when I left Germany and I have simply done more work and completed what I had started before.' Earlier in the year he had described the novel to the dean of the philosophical faculty at the University of Bonn as 'so utterly German' that he doubted its translatability.[28]

However he was aware that in writing this most German of novels he was estranging himself further from his countrymen. As the war ends, Zeitblom's heart falters with pity when he thinks of the fate that awaits his 'foolish' Nazi sons who 'believed, exulted, sacrificed, and struggled' with the nation's masses. But he is conscious that neither his pity nor their anguish will bring them any closer. 'And they will also lay that to my account – as if things might have been different had I dreamt their vile dreams with them.' Mann had estranged himself from the vile dreams of his former friends and if he had turned out to be in the right then it only made him more of an outsider.[29]

In January 1948, declining an invitation to speak in Frankfurt, Mann voiced his hopes that the novel would temper the misunderstandings that had developed in Germany surrounding his relationship with the country. 'I hope it will show that I am not exactly a deserter of Germany's destiny.' Certainly this was the case for some reviewers. In *Die Wandlung*, Victor Sell praised this as the quintessential postwar German novel: 'Even though he now lives in California, Mann is still in touch with the German experience . . . *Doctor Faustus* tackles the problem, which the wider masses of Germans took up only after total defeat: the question of how it was possible that a people with a highly developed culture could let evil have its way.' But others were more sceptical. Walter Boehlich complained in *Merkur* that 'there is a Germany that Thomas Mann loved, and there is a Thomas Mann whom we loved and still love. But this is not the author of *Doctor Faustus*.'[30]

The problem was largely that Mann had damned Germany to a hopeless future. Leverkühn's final masterpiece ends with a half-hearted note of promise. This is a 'hope beyond hopelessness, the transcendence of despair' which 'abides as a light in the night'. But it was not a note of optimism that many people saw reflected in Mann's novel. Over a year since the Nuremberg trials had finished, just when the conquerors had begun to drop the notion of collective guilt and the humiliating process of denazification, Germany's greatest living writer had sent in his verdict in the form of a book that arrived like a bitter-tasting food parcel to remind the Germans they were culpable. Towards the end of the novel Mann describes the 'transatlantic general' who has instructed the inhabitants of Weimar to file past the crematoria at their local concentration camp, declaring ('should one say, unjustly?' Zeitblom asks in rhetorical parentheses) that the citizens who went about their business in seeming honesty, 'though at times the wind blew the stench of burned human flesh up their noses', should share in the guilt of these horrors. 'Whatever lived as German stands now as an abomination and the epitome of evil,' Zeitblom observes sadly, wondering what it will be like to belong to a nation whose history bears 'this gruesome fiasco' within it and that has driven itself mad.[31]

Mann may have implicated himself in the fate of his countrymen, but he left them no means of escape from misery. Zuckmayer had offered more hope, in suggesting that those who resisted Nazism could be saved by divine justice and that repentance remained possible. The truly deluded in Zuckmayer's play are granted a kind of goodness; Harras's sin is to know that Nazism is evil but to go along with it all the same. Zuckmayer was certainly idealistic enough to believe that the young in particular were capable of change. But Zuckmayer's play did not offer a clear path forward for postwar Germans, any more than Mann's novel. It was left to Jean-Paul Sartre to offer a mode of escape from guilt through the existentialist doctrine of freedom.

Existentialism came to postwar Germany in the guise of Sartre's play *The Flies* and in the small, bespectacled figure of Sartre himself, accompanied by 'La grande Sartreuse', Simone de Beauvoir. *The Flies* was performed in Düsseldorf in November 1947 with Gustaf Gründgens in the title role and then in a more talked-about performance at the Hebbel Theatre in Berlin in January 1948, this time with Sartre and Beauvoir in attendance.

Sartre and Beauvoir entered Germany on 28 January, taking the train from France. The train's French dining car felt like a small colony, segregated from the Germans in other carriages. Beauvoir worried that they were now as hateful as the Germans had been in wartime France. The next morning they sped past forests of pine trees into Berlin and were confronted immediately by ruin. 'Huge stone doorways without doors opened onto kitchen gardens, balconies dangled crookedly across the façades of buildings that were nothing but façades,' Beauvoir later wrote. A surrealist umbrella and a sewing machine on top of an operating table would not seem out of place. Reality had become insanity. It was all the more unpleasant because Berlin was in the midst of another terrible winter, with temperatures of minus eighteen degrees most days. 'Ruins and rubbishes, rubbishes and ruins, nothing more,' Beauvoir wrote in her idiosyncratic English to Nelson Algren, her American lover.[32]

They were there as guests of Félix Lusset, who headed Berlin's Mission Culturelle. French officials were increasingly keen to demonstrate the importance of French culture both to the Germans and the other allies and Lusset had invited Sartre and Beauvoir in order to do this. Initially, the French had governed their zone with even more cultural austerity than the Americans or British, believing they owed no pleasure to a nation that had occupied France tyrannically twice in thirty years. 'Not one French painting or sculpture will be in the hands and possession of this guilty and criminal people,' the writer Louis Aragon announced at the end of the war. However, like the Americans, the French rapidly followed the lead of the Russians in wanting to showcase French culture and demonstrate the superiority of French civilisation. French authorities now endorsed a policy of *rayonnement*, or cultural radiance. And both the Institut Français and Félix Lusset's Mission Culturelle had been founded in 1946 with precisely this aim, operating independently from the military administration to provide theatre, cinema, concerts, exhibitions and evening classes.[33]

When it came to showcasing French culture, the Pope and High Priestess of Existentialism were good guests to have. Since the end of the Second World War, Sartre and Beauvoir had acquired a kind of fame rarely conferred on philosophers, both in France and in the US. Sartre had visited the White House and written articles for American *Vogue*. In 1945 the popular French weekly *Samedi Soir* had accused him of spreading 'a new fashion through the living rooms of both [Parisian] banks, a fashion centred around a rather nebulous philosophical abstraction, a doctrine of German origin that goes by the barbaric name of "existentialism". Nobody knows exactly what it means, but everybody speaks of it over tea.'

As yet the Germans knew of Sartre's wartime and postwar ideas only by reputation; his central texts, *Being and Nothingness* (1943), *Existentialism is a Humanism* (1946) and *What is Literature?* (1947) had not yet been translated into German. But his reputation was enough for his ideas to inspire intense excitement and revulsion, especially as they emanated from an atmosphere of overflowing ashtrays and bohemian sexual promiscuity. Although Sartre and Beauvoir were frequently treated as husband and wife, they were in fact unmarried, committed to a pact 'to maintain through all deviations from the main path "a certain fidelity"', which allowed them to have other lovers. Both made full use of this and made no attempt to hide their sexual emancipation either in their life or in their writing, which added to their dangerous allure.[34]

In Germany, Sartre's ideas had particular appeal for those anxious to classify 1945 as a 'zero hour'. In *Being and Nothingness* he had advanced the central thesis that 'existence precedes essence', arguing that humans are unique because who they are at any particular moment is the result not of a fixed character, or 'essence', but of the choices they have made and the future possibilities they are pursuing. This imbues us with limitless freedom, which most people routinely evade, acting without thinking. It is at moments of 'anguish' that we become aware of the possibility of individual freedom. This anguish assails us as a feeling of vertigo, resembling the feeling of a person who stands on a cliff and realises that nothing prevents him jumping off. At these moments, we have the chance to reclaim our freedom and live authentically. This entails a joyful 'self-recovery of being'. What was so exciting about this was that it allowed people to begin again at every moment. For the Germans who had spent the years since the war acquiescing to their occupiers' accounts of their overweening and aggressive essence, it offered the possibility that by seizing their freedom they could recreate themselves and start afresh.[35]

These ideas were not in themselves new and were not in themselves French. Somewhat problematically, much of Sartre's argument had developed out of prewar German philosophical thinking. He had spent several months in Berlin in 1933 (too busy reading philosophy to notice the worrying political developments) and was indebted to the ideas of Nietzsche, Husserl and Heidegger. In 1940 he looked back on Heidegger's influence as 'providential', because it had taught him notions of 'authenticity and historicity' at the moment when war was about to make these indispensable for the conscientious individual, if not for his government. But where Heidegger was now tainted with his involvement with National Socialism, Sartre brought the credibility of a *résistant*, though his own activities in the French resistance had been more limited than was generally believed. He also combined his more abstract ontological ideas with an enticing political commitment to *'littérature engagée'*. Lecturing in the US in 1945 Sartre had announced: 'in the underground press, every line that was written put the life of the writer and the printer in danger . . . The written word has regained its power.' His essay *What is Literature?* insisted on the need for literature to commit to progressive (left-wing) political goals.[36]

During the preparations for Sartre's visit, liberal German writers such as those involved in Gruppe 47 had waited with eager anticipation for the proponent of a set of ideas that had the potential to provide Germany with a way forward, while the communist press vilified both Sartre and his philosophy as dangerously individualistic. On 9 January the philosopher Wolfgang Harich had published a detailed commentary on Sartre in the *Tägliche Rundschau*, castigating him as an 'example of bourgeois decadence'. The following day, the writer Ernst Niekisch (chair of the history of imperialism at Humboldt University) had published an article with the incendiary title 'Existentialism: a neo-fascist postwar fashion'.[37]

Sartre's relationship with communism was more complex than these articles might suggest. Since 1939 he had been a staunch socialist who believed strongly in the need for oppressed minorities to rise up against their capitalist oppressors. But he was committed to a notion of individual freedom that was incompatible with Marxist economic determinism or collective action of any kind. As far as Sartre was concerned, there should be more space for the non-communist left. He was a member of a group called the 'Revolutionary People's Assembly' that was searching for a 'third' option between capitalism and communism. This was more possible in France than it would be in the US or indeed Britain. There was still a strong French left (only partly allied with Soviet Russia) and even in Germany, French officials were still trying to mediate between East and West, culturally if not economically. The French did not ban the Kulturbund at the same time as the other Western Allies and Lusset was unusually keen to co-operate with the Russians, at one stage discussing a possible Berlin-Paris-Leningrad cultural axis with Alexander Dymschitz.[38]

For Lusset, Sartre and Beauvoir's visit was therefore a chance to enable cultural conversation across all four zones. There was one official party after another, including a lunch in the Soviet Club and a drinks party hosted by the Americans. Both Sartre and Beauvoir would rather have been wandering in the ruins of Berlin. 'I am seeing lots of bad people, really stupid, conceited, ugly, nasty ones: generals, ambassadors and wives,' Beauvoir complained to Algren. They briefly persuaded their chauffeur to divert their car to the Berlin suburbs on the way to a French party, but even after arriving an hour late Beauvoir found the occasion horribly tedious. Elisabeth Langgässer handed Beauvoir an orchid and told her that she looked like an orchid herself. 'They are amazed that an existentialist woman is not too ugly,' Beauvoir informed Algren scathingly.[39]

When they did manage to escape from Lusset and his cultural programme, both Beauvoir and Sartre explored Berlin with customary energy. Beauvoir in particular wanted to see the corners of the city that other visitors would find irrelevant and she was distressed by the scenes that confronted her. 'You feel worst if you are on the occupating side,' she told Algren. The luxurious meals lost their flavour when she knew that people around her were starving. 'You cannot fancy how sad and deserted these places are, how sad and forlorn all the people look here.' The faces in the streets were grey with hunger; cripples and amputees carried bits of wood on their backs or in carts.[40]

Surrounded by poverty, Beauvoir was furious because she had to wear an evening dress to watch a performance of *The Flies*. She found the idea of it humiliating; it made her feel that she belonged 'to the woman gang and to the bourgeoisie'. As she had not brought a gown with her, she had to borrow one from a 'big ugly woman'. It seemed to her that given that the German women themselves had no evening dresses, the conquerors wore them primarily to show off what it meant not to be

German. 'It seems very bad to be French here; very bad to be American too, very bad to be Russian, and it does not seem better to be German.'[41]

Because of its location in the US sector, the Hebbel Theater generally put on American plays. It was now the most important theatre in Berlin and the right place for the French to stage a performance they wanted to cause a sensation. Arriving, Beauvoir and Sartre were staggered by the queues of people trying to buy tickets. They heard that there were Germans prepared to give 500 to 1,000 marks for one seat (when the average German was living on 300 marks a month) and that some theatregoers had paid with two geese. The popularity of the play was partly the result of controversy. During the run of the Gründgens production in Düsselorf, Dymschitz had published an article warning the Berliners against staging a play that rehashed reactionary individualism garbed in the rags of modernism.[42] The Russians had threatened to boycott the production, but in fact from the start it had been attended by dignitaries from all four sectors and had proved popular with both critics and audiences.

Sartre's modern adaptation of the Greek Electra myth had been transformed by its celebrated director Jürgen Fehling from sparse allegory to expressionist nightmare, with the set attempting literal depictions of hell. The stage was dominated by a black sun; the houses of Argos were blocks of concrete and Jupiter's statue a phallic totem. And the exaggerated set was reflected by hysterical acting. Both Sartre and Beauvoir hated the production. 'Nobody can do such ugly things as Germans when they choose to,' Beauvoir complained to Algren; 'the actors were always screaming, sweating, and lying on their backs and rolling from the top to the bottom of some staircase: just an asylum of crazy people.' But they were alone in their disappointment. The majority of Berlin critics hailed the genius of the production, while deploring the obscurity and boredom of Sartre's text. Friedrich Luft condemned the play as 'a demonstration of pessimism, based on bloody stench, pus, excrement, rubbish and the worst kind of disgust' but thought that Sartre's 'arid and obscure' play 'bloomed in Fehling's hands of genius'. Hilde Spiel lauded Fehling's 'major coup' although

she found existentialism 'neither true nor useful'. Most of the spectators were impressed both by the production and by the play itself,
which seemed to the Germans to offer a path out of collective
guilt.[43]

When it was written and first performed in France in 1943, *The Flies*
served as Sartre's call to arms against the Vichy regime with its rhetoric
of guilty apology for the fall of France. Sartre wanted France to take
back her liberty and wanted resistance fighters to realise that they could
kill without remorse. The play opens with the return of Orestes to
Argos, a 'nightmare city', where his sister Electra lives as a downtrodden
drudge with her mother Queen Clytemnestra and her stepfather King
Aegistheus. Fifteen years earlier Clytemnestra and Aegistheus murdered
Electra and Orestes's father, Agamemmnon, the previous king. Since
then the people of Argos have been engaged in a luxuriant and self-
destructive process of repentance, all pointlessly taking the blame for
Aegistheus's deed on the grounds that they did nothing to prevent it,
indeed that they experienced a vicarious thrill. 'It's measured by the
bushel, is repentance,' Zeus tells Orestes, who is surprised that these
'creeping, half-human creatures beating their breasts in darkened rooms'
can be his kinsmen. The gods have sent down flies as a symbol for the
people's remorse. Thousands of oversized bluebottles swarm around the
city, drawn by the stench of carrion.[44]

Orestes feels both pity and envy for the people of Argos. He envies
them because they have somewhere definite to trudge. He is free but
freedom brings a lack of belonging. 'That is not *my* palace, nor *my* door.'
Meeting Electra, he falls instantly in love, delighted to have found a
sister and a lover in one. Electra is scornful about the 'national pastime'
of Argos: 'the game of public confession'. Orestes has arrived in the
midst of the annual day when the dead supposedly roam around the
city, berating the living who have wronged them. This is the time when
the citizens plead for mercy: 'forgive us for living while you are dead'.
Orestes decides to kill Aegistheus and Clytemnestra to free both his
sister and the people of Argos. Zeus is powerless to stop him because
Orestes (like a good existentialist) knows that he is free, which makes
him invincible. Killing his mother and her accomplice, Orestes alienates

his sister but liberates himself. Electra now takes on her mother's remorse. 'All you have to offer me is misery and squalor,' she complains to her brother; 'I bitterly repent.' Orestes learns to take responsibility for his own freedom. 'I am free, Electra. Freedom has crashed down on me like a thunderbolt . . . Today I have one path only, and heaven knows where it leads. But it is *my* path.' He is now able to strip his people of their illusions and shelter them from the flies.[45]

It is easy to see why Sartre's play was popular in Germany. The flies in Germany were multiplying by the day and the Germans were much in need of an Orestes to drive them away. In Germany 'the game of public confession' was an even more popular national sport than it had been in occupied France. And now the Germans were desperate to throw off the shackles of guilt that had been attached to them by the Occupation, tightened by the Nuremberg trials and made still more uncomfortable by the appearance of Mann's *Doctor Faustus*.

'Please forgive us,' the children of Argos ask, 'we didn't want to be born, we're ashamed of growing up . . . We never laugh or sing, we glide about like ghosts.' This is no more absurd than the role inflicted on German children by the rhetoric of collective guilt. At some point the Germans had to be allowed to move beyond remorse and *The Flies* seemed to offer a way to do so. 'Germany is free, insofar as one can call a devastated nation deprived of its sovereignty free,' Zeitblom states cynically towards the end of *Doctor Faustus*. According to Sartre, the nation may not be free, but its subjects can be. 'I am free,' announces Orestes; 'beyond anguish, beyond remorse.'[46]

The message of *The Flies* was more sophisticated than many audience members or critics realised. On 1 February 1948 Sartre participated in a round-table discussion at the theatre with literati from all four zones. Sartre was welcomed as a philosopher, playwright and '*camarade de la Résistance*', and asked to explain his views on repentance and guilt. Alfons Steinberger, a communist academic and the representative of the Soviet zone, suggested that *The Flies* was popular in Germany because 'it administers a gigantic pardon, a summary general absolution', and asked Sartre if he was aware he was preventing the Germans from recognising their responsibilities.[47]

Sartre explained that he had originally written the play to give courage to the French in the face of the Nazis and Pétainists who wanted to convince them that the Popular Front had lost them the war and resistance was impossible. Steinberger suggested that while the Nazis in France may have urged repentance, the Nazis in Germany had suppressed the consciences of the nation and it was the responsibility of Germany's new rulers to restore morality to its citizens. Sartre insisted that the German people needed to look forwards rather than backwards. The Nazi crimes were now over. 'To wallow in the past, to suffer the torment of it night and day, is a pointless, completely negative thing.' None the less, in freeing themselves of their past and embracing the future the Germans needed to take responsibility for their actions. Repentance was a passive, complacent state. 'Responsibility on the other hand can lead me to something else, to something positive, in other words to an essential rehabilitation, to action for a fertile, positive future.' The Germans needed to be given unlimited freedom and unlimited responsibility. 'You do not give a child his freedom if you put him in his chair and then tell him "you are free but for the love of God if you get down from your chair to get something then you will get a smack".'[48]

This made sense in the context of Sartre's larger philosophical theories, but to his interlocuters it was at once too complex and too simple a message. It was too complex to tell the Germans that they were now free to do what they liked but that they must take responsibility for their freedom. The difference between repentance and responsibility was a subtle one that spectators would not necessarily understand from Sartre's play and few of them had access to his essays to elucidate it. At the same time it was too simple to suggest that the past could be forgotten. One of the other speakers pointed out that one man's freedom creates another man's captivity. 'It is liberty that chloroforms and murders its patients. Your liberty is made of nitrogen.'[49]

According to Sartre, a truly free society would be one in which no one was free at the expense of others. But he provided no explanation for how this was to be achieved. 'There has never yet been a society of free men,' he admitted, 'it is purely a matter of finding our route to a free society.' This was a dilemma that he had been grappling with, seriously and urgently, for several years, convinced that 'my freedom implies mutual recognition of others' freedom' and that the authentic individual must honour the freedom of others. In his 1946 essay *Anti-Semite and Jew* he had investigated it precisely in relation to the problems besetting Germany, suggesting that given that the anti-Semite existed, like all men, as 'a free agent within a situation', it was 'the perspective of choice' that needed to change. Rather than removing the individual's freedom, the philosopher (or politician?) needed to 'bring it about that freedom decides on other bases and in terms of other structures'. Here Sartre sounded more like Germany's occupiers, either Russian or American, than he sounded at the round table. But for whatever reason, he did not elaborate on these concepts now and he had chosen not to engage with the political situation of the country he was visiting. As a result, his ideas seemed impossibly idealistic in a society desperately in need of pragmatic restructuring.[50]

Beauvoir perturbed Félix Lusset by avoiding the pontifications of the round table to continue her exploration of the city. She looked for a café where she could sit, eat and write to Algren and found one where all that was available was a bowl of broth. Over the next couple of days she and Sartre wandered around together. Because they had no ration coupons they could eat almost nothing and they could find only muddy coffee to drink. 'We felt in our stomachs what is Germany to the Germans,' Beavoir reported. They tried to locate the house off Kurfürstendamm where Sartre had lived in 1933 and found that it was horribly damaged. She was distressed that there were no shops selling useful cheap goods, there were only luxurious clothing and antique shops because the Germans had sold all their expensive clothes, jewellery and china to buy food. 'I never saw so much frail china and precious glasses and old books as in this miserable city.'[51]

Their most stimulating contact with German people was with a group of a dozen students, who told them about their daily hardship. The girls in particular moved Beauvoir with their poor stockings and shoes, limp hair and eloquent eyes. Perhaps they reminded her of the shabby genteel poverty of her own youth, when friends' mothers and servants were frequently attempting to bathe and reclothe the dishevelled young philosopher.

These students were similar to those Zuckmayer had spent the past two months getting to know, though at the end of January he had collapsed with a heart attack. Sartre placed as much hope in the confused young as Zuckmayer did. Later he wrote that the people he admired most in Germany refused to repent, saying instead: 'We were against the Nazis, we fought in the war because it was necessary that our country should win and we refuse to feel remorse.' In Sartre's view Germany had not made a pact with the Devil. Indeed the Devil himself was as deluded an invention as the oversized flies swarming round Argos.[52]

Sartre's visit had provided one of the last moments of dialogue between East and West. It was crucial in introducing existentialism to Germany. Members of Gruppe 47 found Sartre's concept of responsible freedom inspirational and over the next three years most of Sartre's books would be translated into German. Sartre like Zuckmayer had offered the young people he met a more hopeful future than that found in the demonic nightmare world of Thomas Mann. This was not a Germany that was tragically damned by its own arrogance but a Germany comprised of independent individuals who need only take responsibility for their own freedom.[53]

Having diagnosed the plight of postwar Germany, Sartre, Zuckmayer and Mann were not there to help the Germans make sense of their texts. By the middle of February, Sartre had gone home, Mann was reading reviews of his novel from California and Zuckmayer was recuperating from his heart attack in a leafy sanatorium, exhausted by his attempts to reconnect with his compatriots. The plays and the novel remained, much analysed and talked about. But they could provide little hope to a nation still caught in the grip of yet another perilously cold and hungry winter. '*Erst kommt das Fressen, dann kommt die Moral*,' Brecht had informed the Germans 1928. Ultimately, the same would hold true for the Occupation.[54]

13

'In Hell too there are these luxuriant gardens'

Germany in California: January–June 1948

For those who found *Doctor Faustus* and *The Devil's General* too sancti-monious, there was another commentary on Germany in the making. Like *Faustus* it was being created amid the sunny palm trees and bougainvillea of California. Billy Wilder's German comedy was now in production and Marlene Dietrich and her fellow stars spent the early months of 1948 filming in Hollywood. While her friends in Berlin froze in the frost and snow, Dietrich glided stylishly around a set of Berlin ruins newly created in an air-conditioned Paramount studio. This was one of the hottest Californian Januaries on record.

The development of the film now titled *A Foreign Affair* had been slower than Wilder had expected when he left Berlin in 1945. He had returned from Germany to witness his comedy *The Lost Weekend* becoming a sudden success, winning three Oscars including best screen-play and picture. With this behind him, it should have been easy to begin preparations for the new film but he was told by the occupation forces that Berlin was not yet ready for a film crew. Wilder now had enough experience of occupation bureaucracy to know that this could be a slow process, so he shelved the project and made *The Emperor Waltz*, a technicolour costume comedy set in turn-of-the-century Vienna featuring Bing Crosby yodelling in lederhosen. Wilder's roots were in Vienna as much as in Berlin but this was an odd, escapist film and it left him wanting to return to underground nightclubs and rat-infested rubble. By May 1947 Wilder and his partner Charlie Brackett had submitted their first full treatment for *A Foreign Affair*. That August, Wilder went back to Berlin to shoot the location footage, transporting all of his own film stock as there was none in Germany. He had not yet completed the script but he knew the ruined scenery he wanted to capture in that depraved and fascinating city.

Returning to Berlin for the second time, Wilder was even more dismissive of the Germans than on his previous visit. He was now here as an American movie director. After viewing aerial shots of block after block of Berlin levelled to the ground, the American assistant director remarked that he could not help feeling sorry for the Germans. 'To hell with those bastards!' Wilder shouted, jumping to his feet. 'They burned most of my family in their damned ovens! I hope they burn in hell!'[1]

On the way back to the US, Wilder stopped off in Paris to persuade Marlene Dietrich to take on the role of Erika, the unrepentant Nazi singer. Since leaving Berlin, Dietrich had become involved in another film being shot in Germany. In 1946, Rossellini's *Rome, Open City* had opened in Paris and Dietrich had become an instant convert to neo-realism. When she heard that Rossellini was planning to follow it up with a film set in the rubble of Berlin, she offered her services. She was now working as an unpaid translator for the film's writer Max Colpet, breaking her fingernails as she taught herself to type on his portable typewriter.

Granted permission by the French occupiers, Rossellini had been shooting location footage in Berlin in parallel with Wilder in August. Indeed, Rossellini marked the ruins he filmed with chalk, wanting Wilder to use different scenery. Now Rossellini had taken his cast home to Italy where they were all so delighted by the availability of Italian food that they quickly put on weight, delaying filming while they dieted back to their original size. Dietrich was no longer required, which left her in need of a new project. She was reluctant to take on the role of a Nazi, even if it meant a return to the Berlin nightclubs of *The Blue Angel* and a chance to work with Wilder. However, Wilder was persuasive and had a generous salary to offer as well as an onslaught of flattering charm. In the US, Dietrich's daughter Maria was about to have a baby and Dietrich wanted her grandchild to be pampered in movie-star luxury. What was more, Wilder had already commissioned songs from their old friend Friedrich Holländer and, more ominously, he also had other actors in mind to ask if she refused. She agreed to take the part.[2]

Arriving in the US in December, Dietrich moved in with Wilder at his house on North Beverly Drive in the middle of star-spangled Beverly Hills. Wilder and his wife Judith had divorced soon after his return from Germany in 1945 and he was now living alone in their former marital home, waiting to decide which of his mistresses to marry. For her part Dietrich had drifted out of touch with James Gavin and was between lovers, settling into the role of war veteran (she had been awarded the US Medal of Freedom in 1945) and soon-to-be grand-mother. With Wilder she was somewhere between mother, lover and wife. She fussed about his health and made him laugh on and off set with jokes and stories about her sexual exploits in 1920s Berlin.

The easy bond between Wilder and Dietrich was a source of irrita-tion for Dietrich's co-star Jean Arthur, who played Phoebe Frost, a goody-goody American Congresswoman who arrives in Berlin to inves-tigate the morale of the American soldiers and check they are not cavorting with German Fräuleins. In the film the James Gavin-inspired hero, Johnny, seduces Phoebe in an effort to distract her from trailing Dietrich's Erika, who turns out to have been the lover of a Gestapo chief and to have giggled at the opera with Hitler before the German defeat ushered in a new group of powerful men and she conveniently fell for Johnny. On screen, Erika is brilliantly catty to Phoebe, deriding her schoolgirl hairstyle and her 'face like a scrubbed kitchen floor'. Jean Arthur was as dowdy off set as Phoebe Frost was on set and Dietrich enjoyed exploiting her jealousy. At one stage Arthur appeared on Wild-er's doorstep where she accused him of burning her close-up at Dietrich's request. 'What a picture,' Wilder complained, 'one dame who's afraid to look in a mirror, and one who can't stop.'[3]

Wilder was happy with the film that was coming into being. Unlike Mann's sombre analysis of Germany in *Doctor Faustus*, *A Foreign Affair*

is a brilliantly comic shrug of the shoulders at the impossible predicament of postwar Germany.[4] The film demonstrates Wilder's ambivalence
towards both the Germans and the Americans but the indictments are
prevented from being damning by the film's constant stylishness and
humour, which makes even his most flawed characters sympathetic.
Wilder had still not forgiven the Germans, whom he portrayed as
opportunistic and unrepentant Nazis. But he could not see the American occupiers as much better. At the start of the film, one of the visiting
Congressmen objects controversially to the blatant propaganda being
put forward by the Occupation: 'If you give a hungry man a loaf of
bread, that's democracy. If you leave the wrapper on, it's imperialism.'
In the summer of 1947, when the film was set, this was just what the
Americans, as much as the Russians, were doing. And Wilder's GIs are
no less corrupt than the Germans they are there to re-educate. They sell
their morals and their possessions for sex with German women for
whom they often have very little respect.[5]

Johnny is attracted to Erika because she has been a Nazi, not in spite
of it; their chemistry lends Nazism an erotic charge. 'How about a kiss
now, you beast of Belsen,' he says to her in the original draft of the
script, after he has brought her a tatty mattress as a present and she has
spat a mouthful of toothpaste half-playfully in his face. By the time the
film had been completed, this had been replaced with the milder 'you
gorgeous booby trap', but there was still no mistaking the strange allure
of her Nazi past. 'For fifteen years we haven't slept in Germany,' Erika
grumbles, refusing to be grateful. 'No mattress will help you sleep.
What you Germans need is a good conscience,' Johnny replies, taking
on the line of his government. 'I have a good conscience, I have a new
Führer now, you. *Heil* Johnny,' Erika says, raising her arm in a Nazi
salute. 'You *heil* me once more and I'll knock your teeth in,' he warns,
obviously aroused by her depravity. 'You'd bruise your lips,' she replies,
and Johnny places his hands around her neck as he tells her that he
ought to choke her a little and break her in two. 'Build a fire under you,
you blonde witch.'

As Wilder and Dietrich both knew, war makes monsters of men.
Johnny is to be forgiven his flirtation with Nazism. It is to his

saccharine Congresswoman paramour that he explains that he has raced at a hundred miles an hour through burning towns for five years and is unable to jam on the brakes and stop. And luckily Phoebe Frost proves more forgiving of Johnny than Gellhorn was of Gavin when he excused himself on similar grounds. But despite Phoebe's redemptive powers, Erika remains the film's pulsating star. 'That's the kind of pastry makes you drool on your bib,' one GI says of her, and it is a view Wilder encourages. Dietrich is lovingly followed by the camera as she wends her way lazily around the Lorelei nightclub, casually drawing on the cigarettes of her male onlookers. What is more, Dietrich was allowed to wear the same dresses that she had worn as a USO singer, identifying herself to Americans as one of them. The film may end with Johnny going obediently home to the US with his efficient Iowan Congresswoman but there is no doubt that he will be considerably less interesting away from Erika. And her scenes took Wilder and his audiences back to his own cinematic past.

Höllander's songs, performed by Erika in the Lorelei nightclub, bring the spirit of 1920s Berlin to occupied postwar Germany, further complicating the viewer's relationship with the Germans. 'Want to buy some illusions?' Dietrich asks a room full of people used to trading on the black market, who have long since given up their ideals:

> Slightly used, just like new,
> Such romantic illusions
> And they're all about you.
> I'd sell them all for a penny,
> They make pretty souvenirs.
> Take my lovely illusions,
> Some for laughs, some for tears.

These songs imbue the ruins of Berlin with the tragedy, nonchalance and sultry eroticism of its Weimar roots, especially as Dietrich sings 'Falling in Love again', the English version of the Holländer song ('*Ich bin von Kopf bis Fuss auf Liebe eingestellt*') that had become her theme tune in *The Blue Angel*. What is more, Holländer himself plays the piano at the Lorelei; at one stage Dietrich removes a cigarette from Johnny's mouth to place it in his. It is as though he has been sitting at the piano in a seedy Berlin basement since the time of *The Blue Angel*, when he played an almost identical part. Like Mann in *Doctor Faustus*, Wilder was nostalgic for the lost Germany of his own youth: for a German culture that both saw as containing the seeds of Nazism but that neither could revoke because they remained aware that it had shaped them.

If Wilder allied himself with the Germans through his nostalgia for Weimar culture, he also provided the Americans with the most vivid depiction most of them would have seen of the wreckage of Berlin. How could they not feel sorry for the Germans after seeing aerial footage of street after street of hollowed out façades? Wry asides like 'that pile of stone over there was the Adlon hotel just after the 8th air force checked in for the weekend' serve to remind us of the casualness with which these buildings were destroyed. Johnny asks Phoebe if she really wants the Americans 'to stand there on the blackened rubble of what used to be a corner of what used to be a street with an open sample case of assorted freedoms waving the flag and giving out the bill of rights'. How could he not accept Erika's defence of her own will to survive? She has been bombed out a dozen times; everything has caved in and been pulled out from under her – 'my country, my possessions, my beliefs'; she has spent months in air-raid shelters crammed in with hundreds of other people; she has endured the arrival of the Red Army. Surely it is not the place of the Americans to come in now and tell her that she has been wrong to keep going. The rubble she inhabits makes this point more eloquently than either she or Johnny can.

Like Mann in *Faustus*, by dwelling so luxuriantly on these ruins Wilder showed that part of his heart had remained in Germany. The destruction might be necessary but it was devastating none the less. Whether they intended it or not, Wilder and Dietrich had enabled audiences to sympathise with the Germans they despised. When the Americans had sent Wilder into Germany in 1945, they had hoped to teach the Germans tolerance through film. This had proved too complicated, but it had set in motion a process that left Wilder himself learning tolerance through film-making. Through making *A Foreign Affair* and committing to understanding his characters, he had come to feel more compassionate towards the Germans. Ultimately, Wilder was no more hopeful about the German predicament than Mann. Neither believed that the Americans could have any effect on the over-reaching and demonic German soul; though both hoped to have some impact in Germany through their own ambivalent works of art, neither believed that culture could play much of a role in the Occupation. Yet if the vision of Wilder's film is tragic, its spirit is resiliently comic. Together Wilder and Dietrich had laid their hatred to rest and found a way to portray a German woman who was both unrepentant and loveable. And they had managed to celebrate the maddening resilience of the Berliners. Amid the unreal evergreen opulence of LA, they had created a film in which Berlin is affectionately portrayed in its ruin, squalor and hedonistic energy.[6]

It was bizarre recreating the carcass of Berlin in California and then inhabiting it with Germans. But it was less bizarre than it would have been elsewhere in the US, because this was a peculiarly German world. Wilder's house in Beverly Hills was just a short drive from the house in the coastal Pacific Palisades where Mann had written *Doctor Faustus*. While Dietrich and Arthur squabbled on set, Mann was nursing a cold and reading press-cuttings from Germany, distracted by the unusually oppressive California heat. And they were surrounded by other German exiled artists who had been lured to Hollywood or had found the Californian riviera more enticing than the frantic bustle of New York. The writer Lion Feuchtwanger was around the corner from the Manns; the composer Arthur Schoenberg and philosopher Theodor Adorno were both just a few blocks inland in Brentwood; Bruno Walter was in Beverly Hills, and until recently Bertolt Brecht had been down the coast in Santa Monica, although as long-standing enemies Mann and Brecht did their best to avoid each other except when they found themselves meeting at Feuchtwanger's house. Mann spent so much time with other German exiles that an hour and a half of English conversation was worth noting in his diary as a tiring act.[7]

California and Los Angeles in particular polarised Europeans. Arriving in 1941, Brecht had been consistently repelled by the larger-than-life

plants and buildings and the monotonous blue skies. Soon after his
arrival he complained that he had been exiled from his own era. He
could not breathe in this odourless air; he found himself looking for a
little pricetag on every hill or lemon tree. In one poem, he compared
Los Angeles to Hell, on the grounds that

In Hell too
There are, I've no doubt, these luxuriant gardens
With flowers as big as trees, which of course wither
Unhesitantly if not nourished with very expensive water. And fruit markets
With great heaps of fruit, albeit having
Neither smell nor taste.

For Brecht the vegetation was as unreal as the Hollywood film
studios, not least because the city was built on the San Andreas fault,
ready to split open at any moment, its life possible only because
water had been expensively channeled across the desert from the
Rockies. The desert was waiting underneath them, ready to seep
through and starve out both plants and people, punishing them for
their arrogance.[8]

But there were Europeans who loved California for just the vastness
and opulence that Brecht described; who were pleased to abandon
their own grey skies and grubby streets. Simone de Beauvoir had
expected to hate Los Angeles when she arrived in 1947, warned off by
snobbish Parisian friends. And certainly, she found the traffic terrifying and the downtown area monotonous. But she loved the hills,
where the city rose in tiers, and she found it exciting that 'the most
sophisticated city in the world is surrounded by indomitable nature';
that, as Brecht had observed before her, 'if human pressure were relaxed
for even a moment, the wild animals and the giant grasses would soon
reclaim possession of their domain'. This strange city did not possess
the beauty of New York or the depth of Chicago, but she found it as
enjoyable as a kaleidoscope: 'with a shake of the wrist, the pieces of
coloured glass give you the illusion of a new rosette. I surrender to this
hall of mirrors.'[9]

And Thomas Mann, too, had surrendered. He was delighted by the warmth and colour. 'I was enchanted by the light, by the special fragrance of the air, by the blue of the sky, the sun, the exhilarating ocean breeze,' he later wrote, describing his move from Princeton to Los Angeles in 1940. He was not especially interested in downtown LA, with its vast modernist municipal buildings and faux Georgian mansions with added Mexican ranchos. But he loved the mountains and the ocean. Shortly after arriving he told a friend in Germany that he now had 'the light; the dry always refreshing warmth' he had always wanted: 'the holm oak, eucalyptus, cedar and palm vegetation; the walks by the ocean which we can reach by car in a few minutes'. Each day Katia drove him to the coast and swam in the ocean while he walked along the promenade. Every couple of days someone stopped to offer him a lift, bemused that this elderly man had chosen to walk rather than drive.[10]

The following year, the Manns began to build their own house. In 1942 they moved into 1550 San Remo Drive, where they had created a roomier version of their Munich home. Mann loved the view. 'You ought to see the landscape around our house,' he told Hermann Hesse, 'with the view of the ocean, the garden with its trees – palm, olive, pepper, lemon and eucalyptus – the luxuriant flowers, the lawns that are ready for mowing a few days after the seeds were sown. Bright sensory impressions are no small matter in times like these, and the sky is bright here almost throughout the year, sending out an incomparable light which makes everything look beautiful.' He could see the ocean from his study, which had a view of avocado groves and descending hills, rolling down to the Pacific. And it was the best study he had ever had: a large square room with his familiar desk, lamp and ornaments from Munich and his books lining the walls from floor to ceiling.[11]

Here Mann could read German books and think German thoughts while looking out onto a landscape unlike anything he had ever experienced in Europe. This was a completely different model from the American man of letters. The American writer was a hard-drinking fast-living man of action who left a trail of broken-hearted women in his wake. The German writer sat muffled in his study, nursing his ailments, tended by a retinue of loyal and peaceful followers, renouncing passion in life in order to experience it in his art. But none the less Mann had a voice in US public affairs that few émigrés could boast. He was both a great German artist in America and an American in German California. And this seems to have given him the context he needed to reflect on Germany. Indeed, the new world setting gave him licence to be especially old world. He was sickly and fastidious. He dressed in thick, formal clothes despite the Californian sun; each week he went for a manicure or pedicure and acquired new medicines for his proliferating illnesses.

In December 1947 a young Susan Sontag had visited Mann and been amazed by the old European stage-set she found. The fourteen-year-old Sontag was obsessed by Mann's novel *The Magic Mountain* (*Der Zauberberg*) and had been lured to San Remo Drive by a friend who thought that as self-consciously precocious young intellectuals they ought to meet Germany's greatest writer. It was the encounter of 'an embarrassed, fervid, literature-intoxicated child and a god in exile who lived in a house in Pacific Palisades'. Mann was wearing a bow tie and beige suit, looking just as he appeared in the posed photographs in his books. He sat formally behind his desk and spoke in almost exactly the words of his speeches and articles. Sontag became aware 'of the intense dedicated quiet of the house' – a quiet she had never experienced indoors before – and of the slowness and self-consciousness it induced in her own gestures. She felt as though he was not really living in California.[12]

Mann expected just this slow self-consciousness from his own family, and Katia and Erika were happy to oblige. Katia had long accepted her subservience to her husband. Recalling their daily excursions to the ocean, she later wrote that she never accompanied him on his walks. 'He liked to walk alone, and I am sure that on these walks he was always already thinking out and arranging in his mind what he was going to write the next day. This was a time when he was completely undisturbed.'

In fact he was undisturbed for much of the day and had been since the Mann children had tiptoed around outside his study in Munich during his hours of work and rest, all those years ago. Now the middle-aged Erika was tiptoeing around once again, though she herself was becoming as quiet and sickly as her father and was aware of her youth slipping away.[13]

Everything at the house in San Remo drive was organised to tend to Mann's genius. He himself had no doubt about his own greatness. Asked in an interview in 1947 to name the three greatest living writers, he did not hesitate to include himself in the list. For him, to admit genius was not so much to show off as to describe a trait with which he had been, usually pleasantly but sometimes inconveniently, bestowed. He had given up a great deal on its account and he expected those around him to do likewise. In *Doctor Faustus* he had asked if genius excuses coldness; if Leverkühn is right to sacrifice warmth for the sake of his art. Mann himself thought that it did but was now saddened by the scale of the sacrifice. He was grateful to seize the tenderness left to him, with Erika and with his grandson Frido.[14]

Erika appreciated her father's new affectionateness and enjoyed anticipating his needs. After the war ended she had faced a choice: to commit herself to the excitement and chaos of postwar Europe, or to come home and consolidate her bond with her ageing father. She had enjoyed dashing around Germany in her broken car, sometimes accompanied by a feisty female lover, but it had taken its toll on her health. Since returning home in 1946 she had been pleased to remain at her father's side. 'My deepest wish is to have Erika live with us as secretary, biographer, literary executor, daughter-adjutant,' Mann wrote in his diary at the start of February 1948, and Erika's wishes seemed to coincide with his. Now when Thomas needed to give lectures, Erika corrected his draft English text and coached him in his pronunciation. Afterwards she fielded the questions and usually answered them herself, pretending to translate her father's answers. She was also seriously considering writing a book about him. And the Americans were driving her further into the family home. She was rarely wanted as a lecturer now that she was seen as too left-wing for the current political climate and she had recently been denied permission to visit Germany.[15]

The health problems that had beset Erika throughout the postwar years came to a head in March 1948. Thomas Mann's diaries for March contain daily updates about both his own and his daughter's health, tracking the progress of their colds (he was hoarse with a temperature and earache; Erika was losing her voice once again) and the healing of his broken arm. At the end of the month it became clear that Erika's problems were more serious. In January a small tumour had been removed from her ovaries. Now, aged forty-two, she would need a full hysterectomy, but she was immediately resistant to the idea. On 30 March, Mann recorded a conversation with his wife about his daughter's dilemma, unable to understand Erika's 'ethical' objections to this necessary operation. 'Her suffering gives me heartache,' he wrote sadly. The next day Erika agreed to the procedure, scheduling it for the following week. Her father was perplexed by her sadness: 'the desire for a child could at best be possible to fulfill if there was a man around'.[16]

In fact there was a man around. Thomas Mann still did not know about his daughter's continued liaison with Bruno Walter, who remained a close friend of his and even has a cameo appearance conducting one of Leverkühn's pieces in Doctor Faustus. But at seventy-one Walter was not going to be the father of Erika's children. In 1945 his wife had died, leaving him free, but in the three years since her death he had continued to insist on secrecy with Erika, making it hard to believe that this was a relationship with a future. He remained the friend of Erika's father and the father of her friend and it was only a matter of time before Erika was going to be left alone. She would be a woman in her forties, single and living with her ageing parents. Did it matter that she would also soon be incapable of bearing children? She believed that it did, or at least that this operation entailed a process of mourning for the possible futures she must now acknowledge she had lost.

And she had lost not only her identity as a brilliant young woman but her identity as an American. In Germany at the end of the war she had enjoyed parading her yankee accent and mannerisms. Here in California she seemed impossibly German, although she had lost touch with the Germany in which she had spent her rebellious, talented youth. It seemed unlikely she would acquire fame of her own again; she was destined to be known simply as her father's daughter. She was an almost unknown exiled German spinster about to undergo a painful operation in which she would lose her womb.

———

Ensconced in this world of mutual care, the Manns in San Remo Drive were uneasily aware of the critical situation in Germany. Thomas Mann now experienced the world on three planes. There was his own, domestic corporeal world; there was Germany, where he remained as involved in the intellectual life as ever; and there was America, where he watched unhappily as the Soviet Union became the enemy and Germany and liberalism seemed destined to become casualties of a new war.

News from Germany reached him daily in the form of reviews and letters about *Faustus*. He cared about the responses to *Faustus* more than he had ever cared about his reviews before. In December, Erika had told Lotte Walter that her father was 'as excited and curious as a naughty child before Christmas'. And Christmas fulfilled its promise. 'The files are swelling,' Mann boasted in his diary at the end of January 1948; 'no day seems to pass without a positive response to the book', he announced three days later. The Germans were now asking vociferously for their own edition. These letters and articles were primarily literary so he learned about the political affairs in Germany chiefly from the American newspapers and radio. The unashamed anti-communist bias made the news all the more distressing, leaving him fearful that the ignorant intransigence of both sides would lead the world into a third world war.[17]

Mann had been becoming gradually more ambivalent about the US since Roosevelt's death in 1945. 'It will no longer be the America we came to,' he wrote presciently in his diary in April 1945. The victory of the Republicans in the November 1946 mid-term election left him 'sick and tired' and in his view the Truman Doctrine speech in March 1947 was 'catastrophic', showing that the Americans were completely failing to understand communism or to see that Russia did not want war. Interviewed in May 1947 he said that in Roosevelt's absence it was now left to Britain to pioneer 'the unification of socialism and freedom which the world badly needs right now'; America had failed to set an example. Later that year the German composer Hanns Eisler (a collaborator of Brecht's who was now very successful in Hollywood) was tried by the House of Representatives Un-American Activities Committee, which described him as being 'the Karl Marx of Music' and a Soviet agent. Mann was horrified. 'Feel unnerved by the vanishing sense of justness in this country, the reign of fascist power.' But still he wrote to friends optimistically that this was merely a period of 'moral relaxation'. Surely the Americans were too uneasy about their unpopularity in the rest of the world to continue this course of action. With their 'idiotic and unlawful' attack on Hollywood the committee might have dug its own grave.[18]

In fact the anti-communist rhetoric in the US flared in the early months of 1948, stoked by Soviet aggression in Germany and Czechoslovakia. At the start of January, the US and Britain put forward a proposal for a new economic government in the Bizone. There would be a two-house legislature and a nine-man supreme court. The Russians responded with a truculent editorial in the *Tägliche Rundschau* announcing that the western powers had divided Germany and in effect nullified four-power rule; there was no room in Berlin for people who took that attitude. The British and American military governors in Germany immediately both announced that they had no plans to withdraw from Berlin.

On 12 January the Russians courted further anger by seizing five Americans, including General Lucius Clay's special advisor on cultural matters, and holding them in custody for three hours – supposedly for taking photographs while peering into the window of an art shop, although none of them possessed a camera. In London the deputy prime minister Herbert Morrison called on Soviet Russia to discard its 'provocative policies' which were impeding economic recovery and 'running the risk of war'. More defiantly, George P. Hays, the American deputy military governor, said that the Americans would not be forced out. 'The Russians like to think that Berlin is a Soviet Zone City. It is not.' Speculating about what the Western Allies would do if the Russians were to cut off all transport to Berlin, he said that 'in extreme emergency we could even fly in enough supplies for ourselves' though it would then be the responsibility of the Russians to feed the Germans in the western sectors. 'Americans and English refuse to leave Berlin,' Mann reported; 'Reds succumb in war of nervs [sic]. That is they reject the idea of war.'[19]

In London, Parliament reopened after a recess on 20 January 1948 and the foreign secretary Ernest Bevin gave a speech shortly afterwards announcing that the time was ripe for a consolidation of Western Europe and that if the present division continued it would be by the act and will of the Soviets. He commended America as a 'young, vigorous, democratic people' moved by goodwill and generosity. Unsurprisingly, the American newspapers responded favourably to Bevin's speech, but Mann found it excessive. 'Again I see Russia being ousted from Germany and a German Europe,' he complained.[20]

The next couple of months were dominated by a crisis in Palestine, where the Jews and the Arabs were arming against each other in the absence of clear directions from the US, Britain or the United Nations. The British mandate in Palestine was due to end in May and it was very unclear whether the country could or should be partitioned. On 9 February, Mann wrote in his diary that '15,000 well-armed Arabs are threatening the Jews in Palestine who seem to be facing annihilation once more under the eyes of the wretched UN. Democracy! Only in Socialism does it seem to take on a morally sound existence.' The Palestinian crisis was then overshadowed by the news from Czechoslovakia, where the Communist Party, backed by the Soviet Union, forced President Edvard Beneš to accept the resignations of all non-communist members and seized control of the government. Two weeks after the coup the only remaining non-communist senior minister, Jan Masaryk, was found dead dressed only in his pyjamas in the courtyard below his apartment in the foreign ministry, where he had jumped or been pushed. 'Of course this affair is exploited here,' Mann grumbled, while distressed by the news himself.[21]

The Russians were also making inroads into Germany, though here they were only keeping pace with the US and British plans for Bizonia. On 10 March, the Economic Council for the Soviet zone was

formalised and a week later a 'People's Council' was formed at the
'People's Congress', bringing into existence an independent Soviet-
sponsored government in Germany. At the same time, another meeting
of the Council of Foreign Ministers in London was coming to an end.
Ministers from Britain, France, Belgium, the Netherlands, Luxembourg and the US had met in London at the end of February to make
plans for the new 'West Germany'. Reading reports from the conference, Mann noted in his diary on 7 March a British, American and
French agreement to turn western Germany into a federal area of the
Marshall Plan. Despite ambivalence from the French (who feared the
potential economic power of a centralised West Germany), they had
decided to authorise West German authorities to form a provisional
government.

For Mann this meant that 'the old gentlemen and Hitler's sponsors
will be reinstated as rulers of American money'. He was disappointed
by the American commitment to forming a West German satellite
state, partly because it would make war more likely and partly because
denazification would be conclusively abandoned. For the Russians it
meant American imperialism being imposed on Germany and was an
invidious violation of the Potsdam Protocol (though the Russians
themselves had been violating it consistently for years). This was
confirmed on 17 March when the Treaty of Brussels was signed in
Belgium and Truman made an incendiary speech to Congress on the
same day. The treaty, also known as the Brussels Defence Pact, was the
immediate result of the London Conference and formed the first step
towards a Western European Union. It bound its signatories (Britain,
France, Belgium, the Netherlands and Luxembourg) to come to each
other's defence and – crucially for France – committed Britain and
France to keeping troops in Germany for the next fifty years.[22]

Addressing Congress, Truman praised the Treaty of Brussels as 'a
notable step in the direction of unity in Europe for the protection and
preservation of its civilisation'. His speech came almost exactly a year
after he had outlined the Truman Doctrine and it consolidated his
earlier position. He claimed that there was an 'increasing threat' to
democratic governments throughout the world and that the US was

'We sit side by side with death – and death by the million – wherever we are.' Laura Knight, *The Nuremberg Trial*, 1946.

'I had never met anything like her before, and I doubt if there was anything like her before':
Rebecca West.

sn't it curious that the only aristocrat on the bench is American?' Francis Biddle.

So you make a trial for propaganda. Why should we pay any attention? We're cold. We're ungry.' Nuremberg, 1945.

'The consequences we inflict on the Germans today, we will inflict on ourselves.' Carl Zuckmayer.

The Pope and High Priestess of Existentialism: Jean-Paul Sartre and Simone de Beauvoir, 1948.

'As the planes touched down, and bags of flour began to spill out of their bellies, I realised that this was the beginning of something wonderful.' American Air Force Douglas C-47 Skytrain transport aircraft waiting to unload at Tempelhof Airport during the Berlin airlift, 1948.

As a rule you can say victory and defeat both come expensive to us ordinary folk. Best thing for us is when politics get bogged down solid.' Helene Weigel as Mother Courage at the Deutsches Theater, January 1949.

'Want to buy some illusions? Slightly used, just like new?' Billy Wilder on set with Marlene Dietrich filming *A Foreign Affair.*

'I was enchanted by the light, by the special fragrance of the air, by the blue of the sky, the sun, the exhilarating ocean breeze.' Thomas Mann at his house in the Pacific Palisades, Los Angeles.

'"*La difficulté d'être*"
weighs upon me, every
hour, every moment.'
Klaus Mann, 1949.

'Out of the present crisis a new feeling
of human solidarity, a new humanism
will be found.' Thomas Mann, garlanded
by the crowds on his way to collect the
Goethe prize at the Nationaltheater in
Weimar, August 1949.

committed to protecting the freedom of these nations. The Soviet Union did not want Europe to help itself. There were times in world history when 'it is far wiser to act than to hesitate' and this was one of them. Truman urged Congress to introduce military conscription and establish general military training in the US and to enable the rapid passage of the Marshall Plan.[23]

The Soviet reaction to these developments was swift and unexpected, though the focus on Berlin was no surprise. On 20 March 1948 the Allied Control Council convened for a meeting at the request of the Russians. Marshal Vasily Sokolovsky, the new Soviet military governor in Germany, began by asking the western leaders to inform the Control Council about the results of the London meetings. They refused to provide this information on the grounds that the conference had been taking recommendations rather than making decisions. Sokolovsky was prepared for this. Tall, handsome, apparently imperturbable with forty medals arrayed across his broad chest, he enjoyed these battles of wills with the Western Allies – although beneath his bluff good humour he was an anxious insomniac, tormented by a leg wound from the Russian Civil War and exhausted by his hour-long nightly phone briefings from Moscow. He complained that as the members declined to divulge details of the London Conference he was compelled to make a statement. Rapidly and unintelligibly, he read out a typewritten statement announcing that the Control Council no longer existed 'as an organ of government', and then rose to his feet, declared that he could see 'no sense in continuing today's meeting' and walked out of the room.[24]

Two days later the Russians cancelled meetings of seven subsidiary bodies of the Allied Control Authority on the grounds that the Soviet members were either ill or busy. The next day the western commanders refused to allow their subordinates to meet with the Russians, although the governments in London and Washington were anxious to stress that the real body of power in Berlin was the Kommandatura which was still functioning. 'We are here by Allied agreement and we intend to stay,' Clay proclaimed in Berlin.[25]

At this stage the Soviets moved to restrict flights in Berlin, requiring prior Soviet clearance for each plane. Thomas Mann was becoming frustrated with the 'nonsense headlines' in the American newspapers. The *New York Times* protested that 'from the very beginning of the occupation the Soviet officials have made co-operation almost impossible'. On 1 April, Moscow radio broadcast an article in *Pravda* claiming that the Control Council 'has in fact already ceased to exist' and that 'the dismemberment of Germany has become an accomplished fact'. That same day, Soviet officers in Berlin announced that all trains and cars entering the city would be required to produce official authorisation. Any western nationals travelling into the capital would now have to submit their luggage for inspection and show identity documents at control points. Standing his ground, Clay sent a convoy of American troops from one end of the US sector to the other, shifting anti-tank gun and field equipment, and proposed to his government that they should be given permission to shoot if Soviet troops attempted to board his trains.[26]

The crisis was exacerbated on 5 April, when a Russian fighter plane dived into a British passenger plane (a scheduled flight from London via Hamburg) on the outskirts of Berlin, killing fourteen British passengers. Over the days that followed, the British and the Russians passed the blame up and down until eventually the British backed down and did not press for an enquiry.

'The newspapers are full of lies,' Thomas Mann complained, while he waited anxiously for Erika to come home from hospital after her hysterectomy. 'Hardly any information about the basic truth is possible. It is clear that the Russians try to force the Allies out of Berlin.' Meanwhile Mann's brother Heinrich (currently living along the coast from Mann in Santa Monica) was determined to move to the Soviet zone of Germany and Thomas found himself pleading on behalf of America. Neither side seemed to him any longer to have any moral authority. 'Agree with Erika: Russia is not ready yet for protectorate of Europe. Nor is America.'[27]

———

While Thomas and Erika followed the situation in Germany anxiously in the American newspapers, Klaus Mann was experiencing it on the ground in Europe. He visited Germany in January, lecturing in universities in the French zone, and then again in the spring, attending *The Devil's General* in Munich in April and lecturing in Berlin the following month. He was constantly on the move, going from one city to another in the Netherlands and Switzerland; he even went to Czechoslovakia just after the coup, as part of a pre-arranged lecture tour. In Prague he heard the whispered confessions of those who hated the new regime and were anxious to escape to the US.

Klaus remained adrift in the postwar world. He was still attempting, restlessly and increasingly deludedly, to be an American in Germany, but the Americans had lost interest in him now that he did not fit their current agenda. Unlike Carl Zuckmayer, Klaus Mann's aims did not coincide with those of the American occupiers. It seemed impossible to him for Germany to re-emerge successfully without a long period of repentence and self-doubt; he was horrified by how many of the same people retained influence both culturally and administratively and by the way that proven anti-communism had become far more of a badge of honour than anti-fascism. When in Germany he was now only really welcome in the French zone, where they wanted him to lecture about André Gide and American literature, prepared to see him as an American even if the Americans themselves were not. And it was evident that Klaus like his sister had achieved less than he might have done. It was especially galling to find himself most in demand not as a writer but as a lecturer on other people's books. Furthermore, the most pressing question for his audiences tended to be the matter of why American writers had not fulfilled their promise. 'Was it not true that our authors were usually at their best in their early books, only to decline, to peter out later?' They seemed oblivious that they had a great writer in their midst whose own talents were going rapidly to waste. These days Klaus spent most of his working time translating his recent books and articles from English into German, hoping to find them new chances for publication.[28]

The previous September, Klaus Mann had published an article asking in German if it was possible to gain a second mother tongue. 'Can the mother tongue ever be forgotten? Or can we have two languages – two mothers?' You could do business in bad English, as a dentist or even a psychoanalyst (a strong Viennese accent only made the analyst's pronouncements more interesting), but you could not write. Brecht, Feuchtwanger, Thomas Mann and others remained in 'language exile' somewhere between Santa Monica and Manhattan, 'all the time occupied by their German problems and German dreams'. It was possible to change language and write in English; Conrad had done it so they could too; this had been Klaus's own decision. 'Will the result of all this be that you become estranged from your mother tongue and never really learn the new one? Such are the fears one sometimes has.'[29]

It was a fear that plagued him now, as he translated slowly and ponderously, increasingly worried that he could no longer write at all. His diary entries frequently bemoan his loss of fluency in writing; for hours at a time he would rewrite his translation of a few lines. 'I find it increasingly difficult to work and to live (which means almost a pleonasm as the two terms, *life* and *work*, are practically tantamount to me),' Klaus wrote to an army friend. 'There are moments when I feel almost incapable of facing the world mess any longer.' His response to his own anxiety was to take more and more drugs, alternating heroin, morphine, opium and pethidine. Increasingly he could not work without benzedrine. His pithy diary entries note the drugs injected that day ('Inj: 4 M'; 'Inj: 5 Eu (making me rather sick)') alongside his writing and reading and, more occasionally, sexual encounters ('X').[30]

Thomas Mann may have been thinking of his son when he described morphine in *Faustus* as a peculiarly German source of addiction, suggesting that this 'exhilarating and pernicious drug' endowed its users with a collective feeling of 'freedom, lightness, bodiless well-being'. Klaus felt neither free nor light. On 12 April he gave a lecture in The Hague on 'Germany and her Neighbours'. His lecture notes were disjointed and disillusioned. 'If one could only stop thinking about G!' the notes begin, 'sadly impossible'. Germany seemed disempowered, but even in its degradation it remained disturbing. It was a vacuum in the heart of Europe and its people were waiting not only for integration and monetary reform but for war ('with a mixture of hope and horror . . . war would mean the apocalypse but also rehabilitation . . .').

According to Klaus, the Germans were filled with self-pity instead of regret; *The Devil's General* was popular only because it showed that you could co-operate with the Nazis and still be good. The US and the Soviet Union were dividing Germany, whose only hope Klaus Mann, like Stephen Spender, located in a federation of Europe. Over the next few years it would become apparent whether mankind could forge peace sensitively or whether irrationality would triumph and a new catastrophe would finish off Germany and her neighbours for good.[31]

Klaus's faith both in himself and his demonic homeland was weak. On 18 April he overdosed on thirty Phanodorm (a barbiturate) and then managed to check himself into the Jewish Hospital in Amsterdam for an urgent period of detoxification. Nine days later he was released but he quickly resumed his daily injections of drugs. On 3 May, Klaus flew to Berlin where he gave a radio interview discussing literature and politics and his own relationship with both the US and Germany. He spoke quickly and agitatedly, unable fully to focus on what he was saying.

Mann was in Berlin as the guest of the Americans. His military orders stated that 'Mr K. M. (American National, Consultant, Temporary Employee, OMGUS) is invited to proceed to Berlin for approximately ten days to give lectures on literature and consult with writers.' His visit was sociable but he was unable to enjoy himself. Meeting him at parties and lectures, Hilde Spiel found him 'weary, melancholy, endlessly endearing'. In a report on his trip, Klaus Mann described Berlin sadly as 'the mangled cadaver of a capital, the most cruelly beaten city, the decisive battlefield of the Cold War, the place where East and West were facing one another in ominous proximity'.[32]

The battlefield was becoming more tense by the week. On 14 April 1948 a hundred Soviet tanks had arrived in the south sector of Soviet Berlin. 'It would be playing the Russian game to attach any importance to the arrival,' one high British spokesman claimed. But the Americans were prepared to play along. The next day twenty-eight American bombers arrived in Germany and were sent on sorties over Berlin. On 16 April the Russians turned away six trucks carrying insulin and peni- cillin from the US on the only high-speed motor road into the city.

A few days into Klaus's visit the four deputy commanders of Berlin held a fruitless twelve-hour meeting, arguing for two hours about whether the Soviet deputy commander had charged the US soldiers with having 'bitten old ladies' at the previous meeting, or whether he had in fact said 'beaten' as he claimed. Klaus was disappointed with both sides but as always he felt more identified with the Americans while in Germany. He was assailed with requests from former acquaintances wanting him to use his waning influence with the occupiers. They appeared on the platform before and after his lectures, inundated him with letters and telephone calls and even knocked on the door of his hotel room. This pageant of spectres from his past only served to remind Klaus how alienated he felt from his former compatriots.[33]

Europe now seemed to have little to offer Klaus. He decided to visit his parents in California. He missed Erika and he was yearning for a period of comfort and health after the excess and penury of the past few months. Following a brief stopover in New York, where he spent time with Christopher Isherwood and procured more drugs, he arrived in LA on 23 May. Returning to San Remo Drive, Klaus was aware that he was entering a cold house, warmed only by the quiet filial bond of a man and a woman who had renounced passion. He knew that this tie between father and daughter left very little space for him. Erika could never again be his inseparable twin and quasi-lover now that she had shed her rebellious spontaneity to be the peaceful helpmate of her father.

It was obvious soon after he arrived that this was not going to be the reviving trip that Klaus had hoped for and that he could not remain in LA indefinitely. Like Brecht, Klaus found it difficult to feel at home amid the evergreen trees and everblue skies. Isherwood loved California (where he had lived until 1947 and would soon return) because nature here was 'unfriendly, dangerous and utterly aloof', which meant that he could not turn her into a stage set for his own private drama. 'She refuses to become a part of my neurosis.' This was precisely what made it alienating for Klaus. His neuroses became magnified when they lost their context: when the Germany that he continued to write about obsessively felt like an impossibly other world.[34]

Around him, his family continued with their routines. Thomas wrote each day and read his work aloud in the evenings; there were occasional guests for lunch and dinner; they listened to music on the radio or gramophone. Erika was still busy with doctors and was helping her father with his correspondence. Katia's foremost loyalty was to her husband, who for his part had little interest in his writer son. Perhaps he was ashamed of his earlier sexual attraction to him. After he had ignored Klaus as a child, there had been those years when Thomas was secretly 'enraptured with Eissi', when he was 'deeply struck by his radiant adolescent body' and found it 'quite natural that I should fall in love with my son'. Then there was the period when Thomas lost interest in both Erika and Klaus, leaving them to their happily symbiotic rebellion. He may have been envious of Klaus's public homosexuality; he may also have been embarrassed by his earlier adulation. Now it seemed that Thomas's bond with Erika excluded Klaus, and that if anything Klaus's status as a fellow writer made closeness more difficult. 'To be the son of a great man is a high fortune, a considerable advantage,' Thomas Mann had written in *Lotte in Weimar*. 'But it is likewise an oppressive burden, a permanent derogation of one's ego.'[35]

Thomas's awareness of this burden may account for how little he mentioned his son's work. There are significant parallels between Klaus Mann's 1936 *Mephisto* and Thomas Mann's *Doctor Faustus* that the two writers do not seem to have discussed. Klaus's depiction of Höfgen as part of a Germany that is driving itself crazily to ruin in *Mephisto* is echoed by *Faustus* with its account of the Dionysian joy of the Weimar republic. Both novels diagnose the seeds of Nazism in Germany's past and more explicitly both portray Germany as making a Faustian pact with the Devil, yet Thomas Mann seems never to have commented on his son's novel at any length.[36]

There are remarkably few mentions of Klaus in Thomas's diary from this time and those that are there suggest uncomfortable distance: 'Spoke about Berlin and Germany with Klaus. His tense relation to Erika, rather quaint, like so many things. Spoke warmly about his book, his prose. Eczema on breast disturbing.' Generally, Thomas was less preoccupied with his son's return than with the latest news about

Faustus. The American edition of the novel was now being printed and his publisher Alfred Knopf had just written to congratulate him on 'another colossal achievement' that he had read 'with absolute compulsion'. Feeling estranged from his family, Klaus took on the part of an ungainly teenage son. He was cut off abruptly from the life of cafés and cheap hotels he lived in Europe and New York. Here you had to drive everywhere and he was uneasily dependent on lifts from his mother, sister, and occasionally from Harold – a feckless former sailor whom he had picked up on a previous visit and now saw frequently (meaning at least that 'Inj' could occasionally be replaced by 'X'). Harold survived only on money borrowed from Klaus, who in turn borrowed from his parents. At the beginning of June, Harold was arrested for theft and Klaus had to pay $500 bail. 'Klaus all over town with his sailor boy who could be a bit more grateful,' his father observed in his diary.[37]

But as the spring progressed the Manns came together in reading the newspapers and listening to the radio, looking on helplessly as the crisis in Berlin deepened. Often they were joined by Bruno and Lotte Walter, or by Heinrich Mann; sometimes by Adorno or other writers. Anxiously, this coterie of privileged German exiles waited to see if Germany was going to become embroiled in yet more conflict; this would be its third war in their lifetimes and for once it did not seem entirely Germany's fault.

At the end of May, the US had played its part in escalating the tension. Clay's forces in Germany banned the importation of Russian-authorised papers, books and magazines into the US zone in order, as the *New York Times* reported, to 'cut the flow of communist propaganda'. Shortly afterwards they restricted routes for Russian personnel travelling to Soviet military missions in Frankfurt, forcing them to use routes through the British zone. Talks between the foreign ministers in London had resumed in order to finalise arrangements for the Bizone, but the fraught situation in Germany was somewhat overshadowed by the crisis in Palestine. Meanwhile the Soviet government in Germany circulated a petition for German unity that the Russians claimed over eight million people signed. [38]

Unsurprisingly, there were no writers from the Eastern zone at the second German Writers' Conference, which took place in Frankfurt in the third week of May. The German authors present denounced totalitarianism and censorship but they all seemed to accept the separate existence of East and West Germany. This was very different from the conference the previous year when literature seemed to have the potential to influence politics; now writers were merely reacting to the political events taking place around them. 'Am glad not to have been there,' Thomas Mann wrote in his diary, reading reports.[39]

Mann felt duty-bound to warn the world of the costs of this division. On his seventy-third birthday on 6 June he delivered a speech at a peace conference in LA calling for mutual understanding and compromise. As always, Erika had helped him translate it into English and now took the questions from the floor. Afterwards, the family celebrated Thomas's birthday with champagne and chicken soup. But he was powerless to institute peace either outside or inside the home. On 15 June, Erika had to undergo yet another operation because the scar of her hysterectomy had become infected. Thomas was distressed by Katia's reports of the 'ordeals' their daughter endured at the hands of her doctors.[40]

That day the three western military governors met three German state presidents in Frankfurt to authorise the German leaders to call a constitutional assembly to write a constitution for the new German state. The Russians halted 140 coal cars at a new inspection point because of alleged 'defects' and decreed that all Germans travelling from Berlin to the western zones should buy railroad tickets at Friedrichstrasse station in the Russian sector. The following day the Soviet representatives walked out of a meeting of the Berlin Kommandatura, at this point the only functioning four-power body in the city. 'Our insistence on remaining there is so full of contradictions,' Thomas Mann wrote in his diary after reading about this. 'It is absolutely necessary but only for reasons of prestige.' With that 'we' he still aligned himself with the Americans but he was increasingly sceptical about their policies. The following evening he recorded a long talk about 'American despotism' with Erika.[41]

On 18 June 1948 the Western Allies announced a currency reform that would be implemented two days later. The brainchild of Ludwig

Erhard, the current director of the Economic Council for the Bizone (and an enthusiast of an American-style free market who had put himself at risk by challenging German economic policy during the war), the new Deutsche mark or D mark would be the equivalent of 10 Reichsmarks. Initially, Erhard had wanted a four-power joint currency reform but the Russians had blocked proposals that notes would be printed jointly and the Western Allies did not trust them not to print extra money recklessly as they had done since the war ended. Immediately the Russians retaliated with new travel restrictions, preventing western traffic from entering Berlin from the East on the grounds that they did not want an influx of valueless Reichsmarks to enter Berlin from the western zones. The US and Britain countered the blockade with transport aircraft for personnel. Saddened by what now seemed a hopeless situation, Thomas Mann observed the 'confusion in Germany caused by the currency measures'. His eczema was still increasing in severity and he was being kept awake in the night by his inflamed ears. Meanwhile Klaus injected himself with morphine and atropin, which affected his eyesight, leaving him unable to read or write.[42]

The D mark was introduced as planned on 20 June 1948. As yet it was valid in the entire western zone except Berlin. The Russians banned the playing of jazz on Soviet-controlled Berlin radio for two days, confining the programmes to serious music to mark the 'Black Friday' of currency reform. On 24 June they introduced their own new mark, which was immediately legal tender throughout Berlin. The western commandants now released the D marks they had been storing in the capital. Immediately, the Russians put a stop to all railroad traffic, depriving the western part of the city of food and fuel, and cut off gas and electricity to West Berlin. In London, Churchill warned that the present situation in Berlin was 'as grave as those we now know were at stake at Munich ten years ago', stating that there could be no safety 'in yielding to dictators – whether communist or Nazi'. That day Clay landed at Berlin's Tempelhof airport from Heidelberg and informed the assembled newsmen that the Russians might be trying to exert pressure 'but they can't drive us out of Berlin by anything short of war'. He told Ernst Reuter, the lord mayor elect of Berlin, 'I may be the craziest man in the world but I'm going to try the experiment of feeding this city by air.'[43]

Reuter was generally too commonsensical a man for craziness but as an ex-communist and a former favourite of Lenin's he also hated the Russians, who had prevented him taking office since he was elected in the 1946 elections. He promised that the Berliners would do their best to support Clay. On 26 June, Clay asked Colonel Frank Howley (James Gavin's replacement as governor of the US sector of Berlin) which supplies should be flown in first and was told that flour was the most crucial provision. The next day Clay ordered 200 tons to be transported to Tempelhof airport on American bombers. On 28 June, Howley watched as the first food planes wobbled into Tempelhof and thought they were the most beautiful things he had ever seen. 'As the planes touched down, and bags of flour began to spill out of their bellies, I realised that this was the beginning of something wonderful – a way to crack the blockade.' The Berlin airlift had begun.[44]

PART V

Divided Germany
1948–49

14

'If this is a war who is our enemy?'

The Berlin Airlift: June 1948–May 1949

Hilde Spiel was in Vienna when the currency battles started in Berlin. Summoned back by her husband Peter de Mendelssohn, she travelled by train to Frankfurt where she found that all flights to the capital were full. She was surprised that the crisis had escalated so quickly. Seduced by the alternative reality of the theatrical world, she had not noticed that the shared occupation of their city was collapsing. To her the disputes between the Americans and the Russians were just another drama, no more real though often more comic than the scenes playing out on stage.

Spiel eventually managed to procure a seat on a military aircraft on 26 June 1948. All the passengers were instructed to wear parachutes, which was awkward as she had no trousers to change into. An American woman soldier lent her a pair of bright red pyjama bottoms which she wore clownishly with a khaki army jacket. On board, passengers were too busy bracing themselves for interference by Soviet bomber planes to notice Spiel's attire. American flights were now forced into the low 'Frankfurt air corridor' (one of three low, narrow high-turbulence airways that the Russians had assigned to the Western Allies for passing over their territory), which meant that the plane was violently shaken and Spiel was sick.

In Berlin she found a city on the edge of war, its inhabitants busy stockpiling food and supplies. Two days after Spiel's arrival, the first

planes carrying food arrived in the city. With the electricity supply
from the East cut off, the western occupiers now rationed electricity to
just two hours a day, plunging Berlin into a wartime darkness that Spiel
remembered only too well from the Blitz in London. Unable to turn on
the radio, people listened urgently for the RIAS (Radio in the American Sector) vans which transmitted the news on the streets.

The Berliners remained resiliently committed to culture despite their
anxiety. On the first evening of the blackout the American-born violinist Yehudi Menuhin played at the Titania-Palast with Furtwängler and
the Berlin Philharmonic. This was the first concert given by a Jewish
soloist in Germany since the war and it could not have been more
timely. Outside the concert hall, US planes were arriving with food to
fill hungry bodies; inside, an American violinist provided music to calm
fraught minds. At that moment, the Western Allies seemed fully capable
of winning the peace.

'If this is a siege, where is the front?' Spiel asked in a report written
for the *New Statesman*. 'If this is a war, who is our enemy?' It seemed
impossible that the enemy should be the Russians, who continued to
greet her politely at the theatre. But all around her, the conflict continued. 'We must, if we are frank with ourselves . . . face the risk of war,'
the Conservative politician Harold Macmillan had announced to the
House of Commons on 30 June. 'We are in Berlin as a result of agree-
ments between the Governments on the areas of occupation in
Germany and we intend to stay,' George Marshall insisted in Washington. The US had now cancelled deliveries of meat and medicine
into East Germany, which meant that the Russians faced shortages of
their own.[1]

People in Berlin quickly became used to the drone of planes overhead, supplied both by the British and American airforces. Hundreds
of British pilots who had recently been demobbed were now told to go
back into action indefinitely. Luckily these mercy missions to a starving
city were generally seen as aiding a good cause. The American bomber
planes became known as *Rosinenbomber* (raisin bombers) because some
of the pilots sent packets of raisins and sweets down to the children in
parachutes.

A week into the airlift, morale in the western sectors was challenged when Furtwängler cancelled an appearance with the Berlin Philharmonic in Potsdam because he was too frightened to travel to East Germany. Although the Americans agreed to lay on transport and protection, the conductor had grown accustomed to putting his own needs before his nation's and was not prepared to encounter any danger. The following day the first death in the blockade occurred when an American Dakota crashed, killing the pilot. The odd virtual war playing out in Berlin had claimed its first death. For Colonel Howley and General Clay, the increased stakes brought the familiar excitement of war, testing their valour and competence alongside the pilots,[1] leaving both men determined to make the airlift (or 'Operation Vittles' as it now became known) work. But for those on the ground the darkness and food shortages were increasingly problematic and the escalating danger quickly became more enervating than exciting.[2]

Six thousand miles away, the Germans in California found developments difficult to comprehend. 'The conflict in Berlin deteriorates and increases,' Mann observed. 'Continual deliveries of food by western planes into the isolated zone.' It seemed to him that with American prestige at stake, it was not going to be possible to withdraw. He busied himself instead with personal hopes and worries, delighted when the seven-year-old Frido appeared on 6 July – 'slim and more handsome than ever before with his strong second teeth' – and jumped straight onto his lap. Frido, his brother Toni and their parents had arrived from San Fransicso where Michael Mann was a violinist in the San Franscisco Symphony Orchestra. With all these visitors, the Manns' house was too full for Erika and Klaus. Erika went to stay with Bruno Walter in Beverly Hills, pleased to have an excuse to spend time with her lover although his interest in her seemed to be waning. Klaus rented a flat of his own, a short walk from the sea, where Harold moved in with him for a life of domestic togetherness, quarrels and betrayals.[3]

This should have been a way for Klaus to escape his role as the overgrown son in his parents' house. But he was still dependent on lifts, though now it was Harold who drove him around in Klaus's parents' car, and his life remained strange and unsustainable, especially as Harold picked up boys and stole. Klaus was finishing an article titled 'Lecturing in Europe' which he had been writing every day for over a month. Although it was a simple, journalistic account of his postwar travels in Europe, this was one of the most difficult pieces he had ever written, perhaps because it involved coming to terms with his own outsider status in the postwar world. It was in this article that he described the audiences at his lectures in Germany eagerly clamouring for news of American writers and asking why so many had failed to fulfill their early promise. He was now writing the account of his May 1948 visit to Berlin with which it ends, describing the 'ghost parade' of former friends beleaguering him on lecture platforms and invading his hotel room. The article concludes on an elegaically personal note:

> Like the hero in the last volume of Marcel Proust's psychological saga *A La Recherche du Temps Perdu*, I had to face my own 'Past Recaptured': There it was – smiling at me, beckoning me, 'Why don't you stay with us?' I heard them whisper – yesterday's playmates, the companions of my early troubles and adventures. 'We'd love to hear you talk about the literary scene in America – especially if you give us some American Spam and powdered eggs to boot . . .' Their voices sounded strange, for all the intriguing, dream-like familiarity of their features. I knew that I would not feel at home in their midst any more – and my orders read: *Upon completion, return to proper station.*[4]

Klaus had returned to his proper station, but he did not feel at home in California either. Erika was too busy with their father to pay much attention to him and now his brother Michael had displaced him in his parents' house. While in Germany, Klaus had acquired a new identity as an American, but writing about Berlin in America, he had to acknowledge his spiritual statelessness. He finished the article on 9 July and sent it to *Town and Country* magazine, noting despondently in his diary that after all that work it would probably be turned down. Two days later he tried to commit suicide. He took sleeping pills, turned on the gas and then slit his wrists in an overflowing bathtub. Harold rushed him to hospital where he was treated in time.

Klaus's parents and elder sister were sympathetic but impatient. Thomas did not visit his son in hospital, angry with him for upsetting his mother and helpless in the face of despair that in darker moments he saw as his own bleak legacy to his son. Two of Thomas's sisters had committed suicide and Thomas observed that 'the impulse was present in him, and all the circumstances favour it – the one exception being that he has a parental home on which he can rely'. In fact, as Thomas well knew, Klaus was not welcome in the family home at present. And it was Erika who collected her brother from hospital and took him back to stay with her at Bruno Walter's. She felt responsible for Klaus but she was losing patience too, reporting briskly to a friend in London that her closest brother had 'tried to do away with himself which was not only a nasty shock but also involved a great deal of time devouring trouble'. There was no motive, she added, just general 'dégoût and sadness'.⁵ Klaus saw a psychiatrist who predicted that he would try it again in nine months.

Thomas was right that his son's impulse to suicide was a sustained desire rather than a moment of aberration. '"*La difficulté d'être*" weighs upon me, every hour, every moment,' Klaus told the Czech writer Otto Eisner in August. 'I often find it intolerable, almost unbearable. The temptation to rid myself of this enormous burden is always there. In a moment of fatigue and weakness one succumbs to it.'⁶ Six years earlier, Klaus had described his longing for death more lyrically in his autobiography, seeing it as a peculiarly German obsession and one that his father shared. The Germans, he stated here, are rich in thought and poor in deed; they are the only nation in love with death, combining the noble melancholy of Hamlet with the rebellious insatiability of Faust. This was a view he knew he had inherited from his father, whose marriage he described at the start of the book as an attempt to overcome his natural 'sympathy with death', that 'sweet and deadly temptation . . . the saturnine spell of all romanticism'.⁷

When Klaus wrote *The Turning Point* in 1942, he was depressed. He had spent the past ten years considering suicide as a serious possibility.

'In the mornings, nothing but the wish to die,' he observed in his diary in 1933, saddened by how little he had to lose. Two years later he wrote that only 'E stands between me and death'. Weighing the advantages and disadvantages of life, he set drugs ('the tuna [heroin] problem') against his sister ('Her work, her success, her moral position. Her love'). As Erika's love became less certain, he slipped quietly towards death. 'The craving for drugs is hardly distinguishable from the desire for DEATH,' he wrote in 1935. Writing about his own death-wish in his autobiography seems to have provided him with the means to stay alive. The romantic rhetoric about the German longing for death enabled him to see his current depression as a form of artistic greatness that allied him with the father he both revered and despised.[8]

Klaus's death-wish punctuates *The Turning Point* like a maudlin refrain. His explanations for the temptation to commit suicide often contradicted each other but they were always ennobling. Writing about his lover Ricki, who killed himself in 1932, Klaus stated that 'many people think life dreary but bearable, whereas a delicate minority is smitten with life but cannot endure it'. This is suicide not as a rejection of life but as an acknowledgement of life's power. Elsewhere, he suggested that to succumb to death is to succumb to the inevitable rhythms of life itself, with its cycle of growth and decay. 'The roots of our being are tangled in boggy grounds, soaked with sperm, blood and tears, unending orgy of lechery and decay, sorrowful, lustful.'[9]

Most revealingly, perhaps, Klaus described his own longing for death as a longing for the lost innocence of childhood. 'The baby carriage is the paradise lost.' As a baby, he loved his cradle, which during his childhood he imagined was winged with sails. Over the years he had comforted himself with the image of his cradle as 'a symbol of night and escape', but gradually it became longer and tighter. Now, during sleepless nights, he still invoked the image dreamily in his mind, but the vessel on which he embarked to 'the harbour of forgetfulness' had taken on a more sinister form and colour. 'Cradle and coffin, womb and grave are emotional synonyms'; 'the sleep we keep longing for, the perfect sleep, is dreamless.'[10]

In his late thirties, Klaus was figuring himself as a Peter Pan figure whose longing for perpetual childhood was a longing for death, and whose longing for death was a longing for childhood. He warned his reader to beware of the serpent who brings the apple of knowledge. Growing up yields no happiness: 'what you forfeit is irreparable and valuable beyond words – your paradise'. This is at once a generalised romantic idealisation of childhood and a more particular analysis of himself as someone ill-equipped for adult life, whose closest companion was the sister who in characterising as a twin he envisaged sharing his paradisal cradle.[11]

Ennobling his depression as artistic greatness in his autobiography seems to have been a way for Klaus to keep that depression at bay. It did not last. Shortly after finishing the book in 1942 he had made his first suicide attempt. After that, his time in the army provided him with new purpose but the desire for oblivion lingered, reasserting itself in this more difficult postwar world; a world in which Klaus's father had publicly repudiated the German longing for death as entwined with Nazism. It is revealing that Klaus's account of his own death wish in 1948 was less exalting than it had been six years earlier. Although he had spent much of the past year translating his autobiography into German, he does not seem to have recaptured his earlier vantage point. The letter to Eisner talks about fatigue and despair rather than about the unendurable beauty of life.

Erika was right that there was no particular motive for her brother's suicide attempt, though also disingenuous. She knew full well that for years it had been her role to wrest her brother onto the shores of life. It is 'only the parts of my life in which she shares that have substance and reality for me', Klaus wrote in 1948. Without her even the dream of childhood lost its paradisal possibilities. In California, Klaus was childlike but this version of childhood was awkward and unhappy; the apple of knowledge had proved poisonous. None the less Klaus had survived and life had to continue. He spent a few days at Bruno Walters's house, swimming in the pool and reading Kierkegaard's *The Sickness unto Death*, before visiting his brother Golo who was holidaying in Palo Alto, and then returning to live in a hotel. His efforts to work (translating more of *The Turning Point)* were frustrating and he was anxious about Harold, who was now on trial for burglary. Klaus remained sensibly convinced of his lover's innocence but his life with Harold was becoming more fraught. One night Harold picked up a sailor and Klaus spent several hours wandering the streets while he waited for his lover to have sex in his hotel room. And in the background there was the strange spectacle of the airlift; there was the world driving itself towards its own ruin.[12]

At the end of June 1948 Bevin had recommended that the US should send heavy bombers to Britain to deter the Russians from interfering with the airlift. On 17 July the first sixty aircraft had arrived. 'Very tense situation in Berlin,' Thomas Mann reported in his diary. 'A few dozen bombers transferred from here to England. War would mean an incalculable revolution, in which all that we would defend, the capitalist monopoly, would surely be destroyed.' Clay now convinced Truman to provide whatever he needed to sustain the airlift. Talks with the Soviet Union failed when Stalin told western ambassadors in Moscow that he would only lift the blockade if the London Conference decisions (for a unified western zone of occupation) were reversed. There were now flights landing in Berlin every three minutes, totalling 480 flights a day.[13]

Klaus found the situation unbearably dispiriting. The pan-European world he had hoped would come into being at the end of the war was being blasted out of existence by the idiotic arrogance of two superpowers. The US could no longer be seen as the land of the free and when Klaus received a cable inviting him to come to work with a publisher in Amsterdam, he decided to accept the offer. His departure was scheduled for 14 August. Five days before he left, Erika Mann went to Stockton (a five-hour drive away) to take part in a 'Town Hall on Air' discussion about the airlift. The debate was attended by an audience of 4,000 and broadcast on the radio the next day. Thomas, Katia and Klaus listened to the discussion together.

The format of the debate encouraged its speakers to be controversial but Erika went beyond expectations in her forthright condemnation of both the US and Germany. She began by reminding her audience that there was no written agreement authorising the Americans to pass through the Soviet zone on their way to or from Berlin. The Russians may disdain the truth but they were not in the habit of breaking treaties and it was the Western Allies' fault that there was no clause in the Potsdam Agreement stipulating right of access. The Russians would not have blockaded Berlin if the Western Allies had retained their right to be there. But 'the moment we declared our intention to establish an independent western German state with Frankfurt as its capital . . . our presence in Berlin, more than a hundred miles inside the Soviet zone had ceased to make any sense whatever'. Unfortunately the US policy-makers had failed to see this; if they had they might have left immediately with no loss of prestige. Instead, they had waited for the Russians to blockade the city and trapped themselves in the process. Now the talks between the US and the Soviet Union were proving fruitless because the Americans were not prepared to give the Russians anything they wanted: 'we shall have to pay something – or get out of Berlin'.[14]

This was strong stuff and her interlocuters (who included a wartime naval aide to Eisenhower) wasted no time in decrying her views. Erika insisted that the plan for a West German state was a violation of the Potsdam Agreement and went on to say that there was no need to save the Germans who believed in democracy because hardly any of them did: 'How can we save Germans who accept democracy when we do not know of any crowd of Germans who are actually doing any such thing? I do not think there should be war over Berlin, because I don't think Berlin is important to the western allies, and I don't think there are enough German democrats in Berlin to be worthy to fight over, actually.'

Asked about morale in Germany, Erika accused the Germans of hoping for conflict between the US and the Soviet Union. 'The Germans today are just as war-minded as they used to be.' She refused to accept the American view of the Russians as war-mongering. They were hysterical and ill-mannered but she could understand it if they were 'frightened and nervous and frantic'. The Soviet Union had left Poland 'completely alone' as far as its internal affairs were concerned and would leave the Germans alone as well.[15]

Thomas Mann observed in his diary that Erika's comments were 'very courageous and well-put, but too anti-German on her part'. But she had been speaking on her brother's behalf more than on her father's. Erika had been disloyal to Klaus emotionally but she still shared his views. She now made it clear that she was prepared to make herself unpopular for the sake of truth. She would sacrifice her hard-won identity as an American in criticising her adopted country just as she and Klaus had sacrificed their identity as Germans in the 1930s. Erika's assessment of the crisis was reasonably accurate (except in relation to internal affairs) but neither the Americans nor the Germans wanted to hear it. She was immediately branded as a communist both by the press in Germany and, as yet silently, by the FBI. In Munich a front-page editorial in *Echo der Woche* denounced her as 'nothing other than a Stalinist agent'. Klaus stood happily by her, rushing off letter after letter in her defence and sending them to newspapers and acquaintances in Germany. On the eve of Klaus's departure, Erika had made one public gesture of loyalty to her brother, showing that, at least when it came to the situation in Germany, their views still coincided. It remained to be seen whether this could be enough to save him from further despair.[16]

With the situation in Germany becoming more unstable by the day, it is not surprising that *A Foreign Affair* was deemed inappropriate for German audiences. Billy Wilder's film previewed in the US in July 1948 and immediately garnered enthusiastic reviews. Praising it as 'Hollywood's most thoroughly enjoyable picture of the year', the *New York Post* reviewer said that although some might feel the black market was no joking matter and fraternisation better ignored, the film had 'approximated reality more closely than would a grimmer view'. It seemed evident that Wilder was an insider and that his German background enabled greater authenticity. The *Herald Tribune* compared the film to aspirin: 'it may not cure the world's diseases, but it surely can make the headache feel better'.[17]

The Americans were not prepared to provide aspirin to Germany, though; the disease there was growing too serious. On 20 July a new Information Policy edict stipulated that films distributed and made in occupied Germany should try hard to portray the US and its occupation in a positive light: 'We should . . . admit frankly that we are now in the business of propaganda . . . When everybody else is criticising this country and emphasising its shortcomings, it has become our task to seek out the points which make the American system appear good, sound and the best of all possible systems.'

Wilder's references to American imperialism and his depiction of the sex-crazed Nazi-chasing American soldiers may have satisfied the censors but no one could claim it made the American system seem the best of all possible systems. His film portrayed the American occupation forces in Berlin as comically ineffectual and self-seeking so it is not surprising that the message from the military authorities was negative. They dismissed *A Foreign Affair* as a 'crude, superficial' film, insensible to the world situation. 'Berlin's trials and tribulations are not the stuff of cheap comedy, and rubble makes lousy custard pies.'[18]

Wilder was furious. This was a film that he had made for Berlin audiences and shot in their city. 'I was in the army and I was in Berlin,' he complained. The film may be a work of fiction but that made it all the more important to make it authentic. 'Every occupying, victorious army rapes, plunders, steals. That is a rule that goes way back to the Persians'. But he, like the Manns, was coming to realise that there was no longer a place for him in postwar Germany. He had made the film in a world of ruins; it was released into a world bracing itself for war. What had been acceptable at a time when corpses still lined the streets was not appropriate in this age of cultural diplomacy. Film was now officially propaganda: the Americans had decreed it; the Russians had accepted it for years. Anyone unwilling to join in the regime was lost and most of the artists in Germany seemed content to accept the new programme. According to the London journalist Gigi Richter, visiting Berlin that summer, there did not appear to be a single painter, sculptor, film-maker or writer in the city who wished to leave, despite escalating Cold War tensions.[19]

Luckily, Wilder's success in the US saved him from minding about the fate of his film too much. He stopped thinking about Germany, just as he thought as little as possible about the work of the House Un-American Activities Committee, too busy film-making to care deeply about politics. As always, he was protected by his sense of humour. And one German at least was delighted with *A Foreign Affair*. After the film's release Marlene Dietrich wrote to thank Wilder for his belief, insistence, guidance and friendship: 'Working for you gave me the chance of knowing you and loving you – because of which I am richer and full of gratitude.' She had been lauded by the *New Yorker* as a 'delectable dish', and so was finding it easier to be contented with the film's ambiguous morality.[20]

Denied Wilder's affectionate satire, the Berliners were instead granted an onslaught of less ambiguous cultural offerings over the course of the summer. Zuckmayer's *The Devil's General* remained exceptionally popular throughout Germany (it would be performed 2,069 times in the 1948/49 season alone) and now premiered in Berlin. Hilde Spiel went to the opening night, where she encountered the Russian officials for the first time in a few weeks. Previously, she had prided herself on being able to entertain these men at her home, despite the prevailing segregation between occupiers. Now she was dispirited by the change in tone. Tulpanov ignored her, while Dymschitz merely bowed coldly. 'Between us and the Russians it is all over,' she wrote sadly in her diary. She had become a friend of Melvin Lasky's but she was not a 'cold warrior' and was aware that there was no longer any real role for her in the new city being forged by government decree. Soon the Allies would probably not even be able to cross paths at first nights any more. Howley had recently issued an edict trying to ban social contact between Americans and Russians ('none of my men are going to play footsie wootsie with the Russians under such conditions as their intolerable blockade'). In a letter to her mother, Spiel wrote that she was sorry the Russians were behaving so badly as she had liked them as individuals. 'We held different views, but our contact with them was enormously interesting. We really live in idiotic times, and the twentieth century constantly jangles one's nerves.'[21]

However, Spiel did not begrudge the success of the major Russian cultural offering that season. On 13 August, Moscow's Alexandrov Ensemble gave a performance of Russian music, with a Red Army choir accompanied by a corps de ballet of Red Army dancers, an orchestra and a handful of Russia's greatest solo singers. Tickets for the concert were almost impossible to acquire but Spiel listened to the broadcast on the radio, enchanted by the Russian song 'Kalinka' performed by the tenor Victor Nikitin. Five days later, the orchestra performed outside at the Gendarmenmarkt and Spiel and de Mendelssohn rushed to hear it. They were in the middle of the packed square, where 30,000 Berliners from East and West had come to listen to the small, dark tenor sing his strange, magical song. Later Spiel recalled how, 'surrounded by ruins, we gave ourselves up totally to the unbearably beautiful melody of "Kalinka" and other Russian songs, and felt irritated, even angry, when now and again a British or American aircraft, bringing essential provisions into the city, drowned out the music as it circled above one of the three airports before landing. A whole city had lost its head and surrendered to the Slavic melancholy of its Slavic oppressors.'[22]

A few days later the British provided their contribution to the battle for cultural prestige playing out in the capital. This took the form of an Elizabethan Festival Week. Britain's answer to Nikitin was the eccentric aesthete, Cambridge don and amateur actor/director George (Dadie) Rylands, who came to Berlin with his Cambridge Marlowe Society to stage Shakespeare's *Measure for Measure* and Webster's *The White Devil*. There was also a concert by the Cambridge Madrigal Society of music by Purcell. Always enthusiastic about all things English, Spiel was happily seduced by these performances. She found, perhaps somewhat dutifully, that Kalinka, the fascinating Russian girl, could not compete with these 'quietly wistful or passionate reminders of the Elizabethan age' and faded instead into 'the dusk of a weary, outdated nostalgia'.[23]

But these cultural offerings were not enough to reconcile Spiel to a city at war. Her marriage had become tense. Frightened by the heavy aircraft passing overhead with a roar that reminded her of the Blitz, she had begun to struggle for breath at night and suffered from palpitations. It seemed perfectly possible that soon those planes would drop bombs instead of food. In the early weeks of the airlift she and de Mendelssohn had found refuge in playing Ludo every night with the British poet and novelist Rex Warner, who was currently stationed in Berlin working for the educational branch of the Control Commission, and his wife. But Warner was unhappy in Germany and desperate to return to London where he had a lover waiting for him. 'Life here, with the present political tensions, gets worse and worse,' he wrote at the end of June, worried that the Americans would do something foolish. After the Warners departed in July, Spiel was left wanting to return to England as well, even though she had found her life in Wimbledon impossibly tedious before moving to the continent. She and her children left Berlin at the end of August. It was a stormy night and they were all violently sick as they flew once more through the low air corridor to Frankfurt.[24]

By August 1948, 18,048 flights carrying a total of 118,634 tons of goods had been flown into Berlin by air. Fifty-four per cent were operated by the Americans, and forty-six per cent by the British. US and British aircraft now landed at meticulous three-minute intervals at Tempelhof, Gatow and Tegel throughout the day, returning to their home airbases if they failed to touch down in time. Crews had been trained in new techniques to land quickly and vertically after a series of planes crashed while stacking up waiting to land on 13 August (now known as 'Black Friday'). In the previous two months airlift planes had covered more than 10 million miles. Newsprint for western-licensed newspapers was also arriving at last, averting the danger that the western media would be silenced, and miraculously more coal was currently being flown in than was presently consumed.

Any attempts at joint rule had been abandoned. In a heavy storm on 15 August, Soviet officers had removed the rain-soaked flag from the Allied Kommandatura and packed up the remaining Russian files, leaving behind merely a collection of portraits of Lenin and Stalin on the walls. There were now Soviet representatives only on the secretariat of the otherwise defunct Control Council, the much-tested Berlin Air Safety Centre and the Spandau Military Prison.[25]

With multiple currencies circulating in Berlin, a money market had come into being at Zoo train station by the Tiergarten. Different currencies were used for different goods. Raisins were paid for in western and sugar in eastern marks; newspapers were purchased with eastern money but the printing was paid for in western money. There were two police forces with two prefects of police issuing warrants for arrest countermanding each other; two gas, light and water systems (though those in the western sectors functioned only between sunset and sunrise) and even two sewage systems.[26]

Despite the continual hum of planes overhead, the airlift was still bringing in only about 40 per cent of what the western part of the city had been consuming prior to the blockade and there was rarely enough to eat in the West. Food was now rationed to 1,600 calories a day so on average Berliners were eight and a half pounds underweight. In the excitement over the airlift's success, it was easy for onlookers from outside Germany to forget how desperate conditions here remained, even after the currency reform.

'Lifted' into Berlin from London by the RAF in July, Gigi Richter was amazed that three years after the war had finished the sweet sickly smell of ruin could still be so overwhelming. She was shocked by the prevalence of choking dust from the crumbling buildings and by the sight of crippled and maimed figures collecting bricks from the piled up rubble or scraping cigarette stubs off the streets. The 'abject poverty' was all the more depressing contrasted with the luxury shops now installed in some of the rebuilt buildings on the Kurfürstendamm. Some of the glass cases outside the shops had now been replaced, surreally showcasing single luxury objects: a piece of sculpture or a black lace brassiere.[27]

According to Richter, no one in Berlin had any money. In June, everyone had been allocated 60 western Marks; their savings had then been restored at a ratio of one to ten, which did not leave most people with enough money to buy a newspaper or take a tram. Even if Berliners did have money, there were desperate food shortages. Richter did not see any potatoes available to buy in the shops in her entire two months in the city. Her report was slightly exaggerated but certainly the animals in the zoo were starving, medical supplies were running out and Berliners were starting to complain about the dehydrated potatoes and watery coffee (known as *Blumen Kaffee* because you could see through to the floral pattern at the bottom of the mug). Because the electricity was usually turned on in two segments of two hours each, it became common to eat at midnight or to consume cold food cooked much earlier. The suicide rate in the city rose to about seven a day.[28] None the less, 84 per cent of Berliners questioned in an opinion poll believed that the Western Allies could provide adequate food to sustain the city and when the Soviet military administration offered to feed western Berliners who registered in the Soviet sector only 2,050 people signed up.

At the end of August 1948, the four military governors met in Berlin in an attempt to solve the currency problem and end the blockade. But asked whether the meetings were amicable, Clay responded 'it depends on what you call amicable'. It seemed very unlikely that the talks would reach a swift resolution and it was hard to remain conciliatory when an increasingly hostile atmosphere was developing around them. On 4 September, Sokolovsky announced that the Soviet air force would undertake exercises over Berlin between 6 and 15 September. Claiming this was normal practice for this time of year, he registered his regrets about any disruption of the airlift this would cause. Clay complained to Washington that 'in the four summers we have been in Berlin we have never heard of these manoeuvres previously'. Two days later the Berlin City Assembly was interrupted mid-meeting at the City Hall in the Soviet sector when 1,500 communist demonstrators arrived to disrupt proceedings. The communists had sponsored a new 'democratic bloc' which declared that the City Assembly 'no longer represents the working people of Berlin'.[29]

Incensed by these bullying tactics, 300,000 Berliners gathered across the Tiergarten and the Platz der Republik on 9 September demanding an end to the blockade. Lord mayor elect Ernst Reuter rose to speak at the podium placed at the base of the stone steps of the Reichstag, where he told the assembled crowd that this was not a day for generals or diplomats to negotiate, it was a day for the people of Berlin to raise their voice. 'We cannot be bartered, we cannot be negotiated, we cannot be sold . . . Whoever would surrender this city, whoever would surrender the people of Berlin, would surrender a world . . . more, he would surrender himself. People of the world, look upon this city! You cannot, you must not, forsake us! There is only one possibility for all of us: to stand jointly together until this fight has been won.'

On their way back to their homes in the Russian sector, thousands of demonstrators came up against the might of the Soviet police, armed to punish this rebellion. When some Germans threw rocks they were met with pistol shots; a fifteen-year-old boy died stepping forward to shield a nurse. That day the meeting between the military governors broke down.[30]

As Erika Mann had observed in the town meeting debate, for many Germans, these developments were not wholly depressing. Now that the Soviet Union and the US regarded each other as the enemy, Germany could be deemed an ally by both and the Germans could be accorded the victim status they had demanded since the end of the war. The Allies had abandoned their more patronising attempts at re-education and punishment. By August 1948 all alleged war criminals had been tried and it was agreed that all POWs in the western zones would be returned to Germany by the end of the year, although the last survey of camp opinion had revealed that over half the remaining POWs viewed National Socialism as 'a good idea, poorly carried out', as indeed did a similar percentage of Germans in the western zones.[31]

Writers and cultural figures tended to reject Nazism more fervently, but very few still talked in terms of collective guilt. Those who found the current mood of forgetfulness upsetting departed: Karl Jaspers had emigrated to Basel in March 1948. Most writers were understandably relieved that the Germans were now seen by their occupiers as allies and that the acceptable status of German literature had been made explicit with the official founding of the new German PEN club at the PEN congress in Copenhagen that June. Addressing the congress on behalf of the English centre, Peter de Mendelssohn had confirmed that the twenty writers proposed to form the core of the new German centre (including

Johannes Becher, Elisabeth Langgässer, Anna Seghers, Erich Kästner, Thomas Mann's former opponent Walter von Molo and Hermann Kasack, whose novel de Mendelssohn was now translating into English) were all credibly anti-Nazi and fully acceptable in all four zones of Germany. Becher, addressing the congress in a language he claimed still to find painful to employ when it was so 'disgraced' by the Nazis, expressed his pleasure at the opening of the new centre and hoped that one day he could host the PEN congress in Berlin, 'the capital of a Germany that finally, finally, wants peace, peace and nothing but peace'.[32]

Three months later, the possibility of Berlin as a capital of a united Germany seemed even less likely, as did the preservation of a single PEN centre for East and West. But the existence of the PEN centre was welcome proof that the Germans were now treated with respect by the Allies and was arguably a necessary first step for the kind of cultural revival in Germany envisaged by Stephen Spender at the end of the war, though he would have wanted the assembled writers to look back-wards as well as forwards. Meanwhile the occupiers confirmed their loyalty to the Germans by increasing the flow of planes steadily over the course of the autumn. By October 1948 the airlift was theoretically providing West Berlin with 98 per cent of its food requirements and 74 per cent of its coal requirements, although problems of distribution meant that many Berliners were still starving.[33]

The aeroplanes brought culture as well as sustenance. The Western Allies were determined to prove that they cared about the mental enrichment of their subjects. At the start of October the first issues of Melvin Lasky's magazine Der Monat (The Month) were flown to Berlin from Munich, set to be the flagship publication in the US zone. After his outburst at the Writers' Conference the previous October, Lasky had been admonished by his superiors for being too headstrong in his attack on the communists. He complained to a friend that Berlin was like a frontier-town in nineteenth-century America and that not enough people saw this. With Indians on the horizon you had to have your rifle handy or you would lose your scalp; 'here very few people have any guts, and if they do they usually don't know in which direction to point their rifle'.[34]

Luckily for Lasky, General Clay at least was well stocked with both guts and rifles. He looked favourably on the proposal Lasky presented that December, accusing the Americans of turning a blind eye to the 'concerted political war' being conducted against them in Germany. According to Lasky, the Americans were demonised as inane, jazz-drunk, economically selfish reactionaries. They had not succeeded in combating the propaganda from the communists and now an 'active' truth, bold enough to 'enter the contest' was needed. The substance of the Cold War was cultural in range so the Americans needed to publish a new journal that would 'serve both as a constructive fillip to German-European thought' and act, 'as a demonstration that behind the official representatives of American democracy lies a great and progressive culture, with a richness of achievements in the arts, in literature, in philosophy, in all the aspects of culture which unite the free traditions of Europe and America.' Lasky's new magazine was born, aimed at winning the German intelligentsia away from communism and heavily subsidised by American Marshall Plan Amoney.[35]

Der Monat created an immediate impact when the first 60,000 copies appeared in October 1948. Germany had been swamped by new literary magazines since the end of the war. Sitting baffled by the mass of paper piled up before him, the writer Alfred Döblin complained in 1946 that magazines had become 'a natural phenomenon, they fall down from heaven or they rise from hell'. However this one was different because of the large print-run and the consistent international prestige of its writers. It was as though the collected intelligentsia of the West was being flown into Berlin on the American bombers within the pages of the new magazine.[36]

The first issue contained articles by Bertrand Russell, Arnold Toynbee, Arthur Koestler, Jean-Paul Sartre, V. S. Pritchett, Rebecca West, Richard Crossman, Stephen Spender, Clement Greenberg and others. It mixed anti-Stalinism and esoteric high culture in a manner inspired by the American *Partisan Review*, to which Lasky had long been a contributor. The political message was unambiguous, with the first three articles addressing 'The Destiny of the West'. According to Bertrand Russell, there were three possible scenarios for the future: life on earth would become extinct, barbarism would reign, or one power would rule the world, in which case it was better that the US should rule than the Soviet Union. 'Russian victory would be a great misfortune' leaving no individuals remaining who can think or feel for themselves.'[37]

Later in the magazine *The New York Times* journalist Drew Middleton sketched a portrait of 'Soviet Russia without propaganda' in which he described a day in the life of Iwan Iwanowitsch, an ordinary worker. Ostensibly a neutral account, the political implications quickly emerge. Iwan lives and works in terrible conditions, sharing an unheated room with his wife and two sons and a kitchen with four other families; his eight-hour working day in the factory becomes a twelve-hour day because of the poor transport facilities. He and his family are also subjected to daily lies and propaganda, so he is convinced that the Soviet Union alone conquered Germany and has never come across the terms human rights, personal freedom or human progress.[38]

Elsewhere the magazine's anti-Stalinism was more subtle. James Agee's review of Eisenstein's *Ivan the Terrible* complained about the banality and artistic simplicity of Eisenstein's film, before blaming Stalin for producing this effect (though physically free, Eisenstein was intellectually 'imprisoned'). And in many of the articles there was no clear political message. Stephen Spender's account of a visit to Picasso and Clement Greenberg's review of an exhibition of paintings from Germany, currently installed in New York, were two of many pieces with no obvious political agenda, simply showcasing western culture.[39]

Der Monat was immediately popular with Germans both at home and abroad. Klaus Mann, keen to write for the magazine, told Melvin Lasky that the first issue contained 'a lot of interesting stuff'. Thomas Mann described it in his diary as 'readable' and 'educated' albeit 'omitting many things'. This may have been a moment of victory for the Americans in the cultural battle for Germany, but the Russians had their next attack planned.

On 22 October 1948 Bertolt Brecht arrived at the border of the Soviet zone of Germany, travelling from Switzerland where he had moved the previous November after being investigated by the House Un-American

Activities Committee. As a well-known socialist, Brecht's future in the US was doomed. He was ambivalent about living in Germany, where he found it hard to believe all that much had changed, even under the watch of the Russians. But Brecht was a pragmatist and the East Germans were offering him the promise of his own theatre and the immediate opportunity to stage both his wartime plays, *Mother Courage and her Children* (*Mutter Courage und ihre Kinder*) and *Galileo*. He and his wife the actor Helene Weigel had decided to try out life in East Berlin, though they kept their options open by travelling with Swiss papers.[40]

Brecht arrived in Berlin in time to see the trees shedding their leaves, as he had longingly imagined them doing from evergreen LA. He was staying at the Hotel Adlon on Unter den Linden and on his first morning he woke at dawn to go for a walk, wandering down Wilhelmstrasse to the Reich Chancellery, where he encountered only a few workers and *Trümmerfrauen* and street after street of ruins. His response to the destroyed city was a political one. 'To me these ruins are a clear indication of the former presence of financiers,' he wrote in his diary. He was less upset by the wreckage itself than by the thought of the misery people had endured during the bombing. Brecht was not blind to the suffering inflicted by the Russians, recounting in his diary the terrible tales of rape he heard from the workers, but he laid the blame for the ruins on the shoulders of the capitalist politicians whom he believed had colluded with the Nazis in destroying their world:

Berlin, an etching by Churchill from an idea of Hitler's.
Berlin, the rubbish dump near Potsdam.

Unlike Mann, Brecht was convinced that the Germans could be divided into fascists and non-fascists. Indeed during the war he had complained to Mann that he had become aware of 'a real fear among our friends that you, my esteemed Mr Mann, who more than any of us has the ear of America, could increase doubts about the existence of significant democratic forces in Germany'.[41]

Brecht was not completely committed to Soviet communism. He had never been a member of the Communist Party and had been able to deny even possessing communist principles during his hearing with the Un-American Activities Committee, who had commended him for his co-operativeness. But his vision of the world was fundamentally Marxist and his vision of theatre was fundamentally utilitarian (though he went against hard-line communists in believing that formal experimentation could be allied to political revolution), so he was able to ally his ideals to the East German regime. It helped that they were treating him as a celebrity and offering him an unusual degree both of power and freedom. Within two weeks of his arrival, Brecht was auditioning young actors for a production of *Mother Courage* in which his wife was to play the title role. The actors on the whole he found disappointing; they seemed unable to adapt to the rhythms of his 'epic theatre' and incapable of portraying evil (it seemed as though Hitler had banished evil from the theatre and reserved it for the political sphere). But he decided to stay, and celebrated his decision with a triumphant paean to the East German regime:

> And so we'll first build a new state
> *Cart off the rubble and shoulder your weight!*
> *Build something new there!*
> *It's we who must master our own fate;*
> *And seek to stop us if you dare.*[42]

Brecht looked set to thrive in postwar Germany in a way that his slightly younger contemporary, Klaus Mann, could not. As arrogant young men in the 1920s, both had stormed the artistic scene of Weimar Berlin. Both had gone into self-righteous exile in the 1930s, eventually making their way from Europe to America. But despite the privations of exile and despite his dislike of California, Brecht had retained his fluency as an artist where Klaus Mann had been unable to do so. Whatever the corruption displayed by both sides in the Cold War, whatever the subjugation of art to politics that the ideological battles brought about, Brecht maintained his faith in the world and his role in it and he still believed in the power of art. He would play his part in building the new state and it was up to the Russians as well as the Americans to stop him if they dared.

For their part, the Russians had welcomed Brecht so enthusiastically because they were aware of how much they needed him. He was one of the few prominent socialists who seemed humorous enough to attract Berlin audiences. That winter the Berliners voted with their feet and rejected the worthier cultural offerings provided by the Soviets in favour of light-hearted American entertainment. Bob Hope and Irving Berlin were enormously popular when they performed at the Titania-Palast in December. And cinema audiences wishing to learn about Russia eschewed the worthily didactic Soviet-produced *The Russian Question* in favour of Ernst Lubitsch and Billy Wilder's 1939 Hollywood comedy *Ninotchka*, which was released at the end of December.[43]

Berlin may not be deemed ready for Wilder's satire about the American Occupation but when it came to this earlier spoof of the Russians the case was different. *Ninotchka* stars Greta Garbo as a dilligent Russian communist who comes to value the superior sensuality of the West after encountering the generous humanism of a Parisian count. It is written with Wilder's typical irreverence. Asked how things are going in Moscow, Ninotchka replies: 'Very good. The last mass trials were a great success. There are going to be fewer but better Russians.' The film was an instant hit in Berlin, with tickets selling out three days in advance.

The Russians now put all their cultural resources into the staging of *Mother Courage*, which opened at the Deutsches Theater on 11 January 1949 and sparked a major theatrical controversy in the Soviet zone. The play was lauded by some critics for its *Volkstümlichkeit* (closeness to the people) and innovation (Brecht was compared to Moses in the *Tägliche Rundschau*) but condemned by others as decadent formalism in terms that Brecht saw as dangerously similar to the Nazis' critique of 'degenerate' art. His arrival may have been a major coup for the Russians but it was already clear that he was too complex a thinker and too determinedly visionary an artist to propound a straightforward communist message. Where Lasky and his colleagues at *Der Monat* were content to follow the prevailing political tide, Brecht was engaged in staging a play written some years earlier about more perennial themes. And as a German speaking to Germans, and a non-card-carrying socialist, he saw his art as more important than the politics of the Occupation or of the Cold War more generally. More like Zuckmayer than Lasky, Brecht still believed that art could change the world not just through influencing people's political opinions but through making them better human beings. But he was less naïve than Zuckmayer because he shared Thomas Mann's vision of the irredeemable urge towards war and destruction.[44]

Mother Courage had been written in an inspired and furious month after Germany's invasion of Poland, using the setting of the Thirty Years' War of 1618–48 to explore the concerns of Brecht's own age. As far as Brecht was concerned, the war that had destroyed Germany in the seventeenth century was one of the first major wars to be caused by capitalism. It was also a war in which Germany had endangered herself with her own, overweening drive towards power. In Berlin, Brecht's play offered a timely reminder of the wastefulness of war and the separation between the interests of the ordinary soldiers and the generals who wage war in their name, duping them with ideology. As one sergeant puts it,

> *War's a deal. It cuts both ways.*
> *Whoever takes also pays.*
> *Our age brings forth its new idea:*
> *Total war – and total fear.*[45]

Wiry, pragmatic and bent on survival, Mother Courage was a familiar figure in a city still teeming with *Trümmerfrauen*. In this production she trailed a handcart that bore a striking resemblance to the carts dragged around by the homeless refugees in the aftermath of the war, its wheels dragging with exhaustion under the possessions spilling out of its sides and its cloth cover providing little protection after years of wartime winters. Mother Courage's aim is both to profit from the war by selling the black-market goods she carries in her handcart and to keep her three children alive. In Berlin, where survival at any cost had come to seem the only option, this did not seem unreasonable. But where previous actors had made Brecht's protagonist sympathetic, Helene Weigel rendered Mother Courage hard and angry, loyally sharing her husband's vision of his play. Here she furthered the distancing effect of Brecht's techniques of estrangement (the *Verfremdungseffekt*), working with the songs and placards to distance the audience just when they were on the verge of sympathising with her.

Mother Courage was a woman who made no attempt to resist either the exploitative war or the exploitative economic system imposed on the people by their rulers; who allowed her son to be killed because, always a businesswoman, she attempted to haggle over his price. Brecht was concerned to show that most people do not learn from war. Though their views on the possibility for democratic renewal in Germany were opposed, Brecht privately shared Thomas Mann's disappointment with the Germans, whom he saw as taking advantage of the Cold War to 'romp in the strudel' created by the rifts between the powers and avoid exercising self-criticism. He now wished to rid them of their complacency and to demonstrate that they, like Mother Courage, still had learning to do.[46]

He was aware that this was going to be a difficult lesson to convey to audience members determined to believe that their wartime suffering had already improved them. Just before the play was performed the acquitted Nuremberg defendant Hjalmar Schacht had published a pamphlet suggesting that the Germans had learnt both from the 'sacrifice' of the Thirty Years' War and of the Second World War. One day this recent sacrifice would 'cast its blessings not only on us but, as before, on all other peoples of the world'. But Brecht was prepared to work with recalcitrant pupils. 'Literature must commit itself, it must join the fight all over Germany, and it must have a revolutionary character and show it,' he had written in his journal in December. Now he had demonstrated that those like Schacht who attempted to profit from war would perish by its inexorable push towards destruction. Though he had already begun to alienate some of the communist authorities by refusing to propound a simple message, he was able to ally his voice with those of his Marxist leaders in suggesting that a new order was needed to rescue the world from its capitalist chains.[47]

It was appropriate that *Mother Courage* was performed in the midst of another freezing winter. 'The world's dying out,' Mother Courage's cook lover complains as they trundle her decrepit cart through an increasingly desolate landscape, hungry and lice-ridden. In Germany, 2,000 Berliners would die of cold and hunger before the spring. January 1949 was a relatively mild month but in February the temperature dropped. When the millionth ton of cargo was delivered to Berlin on 18 February it arrived in a city facing desperate shortages. Luckily the weather improved in March and with it the number of aircraft that was able to land each day. On 16 April the so-called 'Easter Parade' set a new record, delivering 13,000 tons of coal in twenty-four hours.[48]

In the face of the airlift's achievements, the Soviet authorities in Moscow and Berlin considered when and how to end the blockade. The inhabitants of Berlin had made it clear that they believed a divided city was preferable to a communist one. That December, Berliners had participated in their first election since 1946. Despite posters from the Soviets urging people not to take part ('whoever elects the warmongers votes for the return of the nights of bombing'), 86 per cent of those eligible voted and Ernst Reuter's Social Democrats gained a two-thirds majority (up from 51 per cent in 1946). Reuter, now formally confirmed in office, introduced himself to his staff as the new 'Lord Mayor of Rubble'. Before the election, Peter de Mendelssohn had published an article in the New Statesman describing the vote as a plebiscite rather than an election: 'a plebiscite for or against communism, Russians and the Soviet totalitarian system, and, therefore, by straight implication, a vote of confidence for the Western powers'. By this reckoning, the voters had placed their confidence in the West.[49]

The Russians had been given a surprising boost when the United Nations issued a report on the situation at the end of December, stipulating that the eastern Mark should be instated as the sole currency for Berlin. However in January the British and Americans persuaded the UN Security Council to back multiple currencies. Meanwhile the Western Allies strengthened their own position by establishing the Ruhr Authority to control and direct the production and distribution of coal and steel in the crucial Ruhr area (leaving the Russians to struggle with second-rate brown coal), which assuaged French anxiety about the potential abuses of power by the incipient West German state. They also instructed the new Parliamentary Council in Bonn (established in September and staffed by sixty-four elected representatives from across the political spectrum with the CDU's Konrad Adenauer as president) to prepare a constitution for West Germany. This was to be known as the 'Basic Law' (*Grundgesetz*) rather than the 'constitution', implying that this would be a temporary state pending the unification of Germany. In another *New Statesman* article de Mendelssohn suggested that the outlines for the 'triple-headed monster that will be Germany within six months' were now emerging. The eastern draft constitution was communist and rigidly centralist, broadly similar to the constitution in Czechoslovakia. The western Basic Law for the incipient Bundesrepublik Deutschland (Federal Republic of Germany) was as loosely federal and liberally capitalist as the security-conscious French and free-enterprise Americans could agree to make it.[50]

At the end of January a statement from Stalin intimating that he did not want war and would consider gradual disarmament was leaked to the press. He informed Truman that he would raise the blockade if the western powers postponed their planned meeting of the Council of Foreign Ministers and lifted their own trade and transport restrictions simultaneously. Crucially this time there was no mention of currency. Distrustful of Stalin, the new US secretary of state Dean Acheson waited for a more definite proposal. In the meantime the Western Allies showed their strength by signing the North Atlantic Treaty (establishing NATO) assuring mutual defence against Soviet attack on 4 April. Truman, newly re-elected against all expectation in November, described the North Atlantic Treaty as a 'neighbourly act': 'We are like a group of householders, living in the same locality, who decide to express their community of interests by entering into a formal association for their mutual self-protection.' It did not make war inevitable because men with 'courage and vision' could still determine their own destiny. 'They can choose slavery or freedom – war or peace.' Later in the month the military governors approved the final draft of the Basic Law, which enabled the formation of a West German state with limited sovereignty but the prospect of becoming an equal partner in the emerging Western European democratic community.

Crucially, it took the lead from the Nuremberg trials in establishing a catalogue of civil rights, obliging the government to protect these for the first time in German history. The French were now sympathetic to the prospect of a strong centralised government in Germany, having joined Bizonia to form Trizonia the previous spring.[51]

The US and Russian ambassadors-at-large, Philip Jessup and Jacob Malik, were currently engaged in talks aimed at bringing the blockade and airlift to a close as quickly as possible. They finally came to an agreement at the start of May. On 9 May 1949, almost exactly the fourth anniversary of Germany's surrender, the West German Parliamentary Council finalised the Basic Law. Konrad Adenauer gave a speech describing himself as 'deeply moved' that after sixteen years Germans were finally able to arrange political and governmental matters in 'at least one part of Germany' according to democratic principles. The next day the Russians published orders to lift travel restrictions on 12 May. Worryingly, there were still some petty limitations – goods trains were limited to sixteen a day and passenger trains to six – but on 11 May the electric current was turned on from the Soviet zone and Berlin was bathed in light for the first time in almost a year.

Just after midnight the British-American checkpoint opened on the Autobahn and cars and lorries began to drive towards the city. Curt Riess, still stationed in Berlin, described this as oddly comparable to a grand opening night at the theatre. Crowds including actors, beauty queens, writers and scientists flocked to the checkpoint, many of them in evening dress. Everyone cheered General Clay. Over the next few days food prices dropped swiftly and newspaper circulation soared among Berliners keen to read about the fairy tale taking place in their own city.

However, the jubilation was short-lived. Rumours started spreading about Berlin trucks not arriving in the West and on 20 May the Berlin railroad workers went on strike, encouraged to do so by Colonel Howley, angry because 15,000 workers were paid in eastern Marks but lived in West Berlin where they could buy very little for their money. The Russians instituted a state of emergency, imposing a 'little' blockade on Berlin. Only four trucks an hour could now pass into the West so the airlift continued, albeit on a reduced scale, as the Russians drew out negotiations to end the strike. The war had been averted but Berlin was poised on the brink of siege once again, its subjects unable to return to peacetime complacency.

This was the situation that confronted Rebecca West, who now arrived in Berlin, accompanying her husband Henry Andrews who was reporting on Germany for the foreign office. They flew into Berlin from Hamburg on a plane packed tight with green vegetables and officials, and landed at Gatow with the sharp descent that had now become habitual for locals but was a shock for West. It seemed to her as though the plane was a ball, thrown up into the clouds by a giant child. 'The ground rushed up and stopped just in time, while ears popped and silted up with deafness.'[52]

West had not had a happy two years since leaving Germany. Henry was becoming more incendiary, unreliable and humiliatingly unfaithful. He was pursuing a flirtation here in Germany, chasing a young woman who edited the Hamburg edition of *Die Welt*. West made no mention of Francis Biddle during this trip. She had recently told a friend that she had lived a completely celibate life for the past eighteen years, writing out the affair with Biddle altogether. But memories of those previous enchanted days in Germany must have collided with her present impressions, adding to her irritation. Her report on the country was not favourable.

She found that Berlin – usually the 'loosest, least confined of any capital' – had become a prison. 'Everybody in Berlin was a prisoner. None was free, not even those who claimed to be warders.' The Berliners were imprisoned because they were conquered, the Allies because they were conquerors and could not leave without an admission of defeat. She was as dismissive as ever of the Germans, whom she was convinced all remained Nazis, angry with Hitler merely for not being efficient enough in Nazifying the country.[53]

As a long-standing and fervent anti-communist, West was dismissive, too, of the Russians, and pleased that the British and Americans seemed victorious in the Cold War in Berlin. With 'tired feet and leaking shoes, the watering of mouths over missed meals,' the women of

Berlin had 'learned with their whole being that justice gives a better climate than hate'. They had developed an allegiance to the 'democratic faith', changed more by the occupation of their city than they had been by the Nuremberg trials. In his report Henry Andrews wrote that the Western Allies should be grateful to the Russians for all they had done in alienating the Germans from the Soviet Union and turning them towards the West. Thanks to the Russians and their policies, Germany had been divided in two and young Germans wanted to side with their western conquerors. 'In Russia they find no kinship. Our manner of life, our belief in the rule of law, our habit of respect for each other and arriving at a working compromise is what we have to offer. That is the pull of the West.' The US and Britain seemed to be winning the battle for the hearts and minds of the Berliners.[54]

The new West German state was on its way to being established and, ballasted by American money, it promised to be both prosperous and popular. But West was right to be less optimistic than her husband, depressed by a city whose prison bars and jailers seemed in danger of extending their reach to confine the whole postwar world. This was a war and it claimed its casualties like any other. Seventy people had been killed by the airlift, while thousands of others had endured months of anxious worry and hunger. Outside Germany, onlookers including Stephen Spender and Thomas, Klaus and Erika Mann were more disillusioned than Henry Andrews as they watched their hopes for a new united Europe perish. The war might be cold but it was war none the less and it had not yet claimed its last victim.

15

'Perhaps our deaths will shock you into attention'

Division: May–October 1949

When the West German Basic Law was passed on 10 May, Thomas Mann was on board a ship crossing the Atlantic Ocean. He, Katia and Erika were on their way to London to begin a four-month European tour. Just before leaving the US, Mann had decided that his journey would include Germany. He was going to accept the prestigious Goethe prize in Frankfurt at the end of August and to confront the ruins of his former home in Munich. Erika hated the idea of her father returning to Germany and he found it distressing to disappoint her but after months of vacillation he had made his decision. As 1949 was the bicentenary of Goethe's birth, Mann was already planning to lecture in London, Zurich and Stockholm on 'Goethe and Democracy', so it seemed wrong to talk about this most German of figures without visiting Goethe's home. Mann was conscious of his declining health and advancing years and of his injured reputation in Germany. It was time to follow his book back into his satanically cursed homeland.

Just before leaving the US, Mann had given a version of his Goethe lecture in Washington. Here he drew attention not only to Goethe's cosmopolitan European spirit (his belief in a 'world literature') but his enthusiasm for America, where at one stage he had wondered about emigrating. According to Mann, Goethe's vision of America was of a

world of 'naturalness, of simplicity and untroubled youthful vigour' far
away from the 'age-burdened complexity' and nihilism of Europe. And
this was Mann's America too: freedom-loving, outward-looking, democratic. It was an America in which both he and his children had
increasingly little faith. The hearings of the House Un-American Activities Committee continued, cleaving American society in half in what
Mann saw as 'a campaign against the memory of Roosevelt'.[1]

   In March the dividing lines had been formalised at a conference in
New York. The 'Cultural and Scientific Conference for World Peace'
brought thousands of left-wing Americans (the composer Leonard
Bernstein and the playwrights Lilian Hellman and Arthur Miller among
them) together with Russian counterparts including the composer
Dmitri Shostakovich to discuss art and politics at the Waldorf Astoria
Hotel. Cold warrior Sidney Hook booked the hotel's bridal suite and
filled it with anti-communists including Nicolas Nabokov and the poet
Robert Lowell, who organised a demonstration denouncing the conference as a Soviet front aimed at disseminating communist propaganda
to the Americans. Arthur Miller later described how he had to step
between two praying nuns as he entered the doors of the hotel. For
Miller the conference was partly an effort to enable communication
between East and West. However, it quickly became appparent that
this had ceased to be possible, because there were no longer any political choices to be made: 'the chessboard allow[ed] no space for a
move'.[2]

   Mann sent a telegram of solidarity to the Astoria conference and was
chastised by Francis Biddle for lending his support to a meeting 'used
chiefly as a sounding board for communist propaganda'. He defended
himself on the grounds that his doubts about the wisdom of America's
current foreign policy were shared by 'a great number of mentally high-
ranking and distinguished Americans'. A war between the US and the
Soviet Union would be a catastrophe and it was time for intellectual
leaders from East and West to debate the dangers of the present political situation on 'a purely cultural and spiritual basis'. Mann could not
see that there was anything problematic about applauding speeches by
the Russian delegation. 'What is wrong with treating the guests from

that great, strange country with friendliness and encouragement in an effort to show them that in America today there are still a great number of people of good will?'³

It was 1933 again and this time Mann was prepared to make a stand. He was aware of how much he had to lose in his relationship with Erika, whom he was now determined not to disappoint; and he was aware, too, that it was possible, even now, to uproot and resettle, though it would mean losing the home he loved. At the press conference after his Goethe lecture he claimed that as a writer, he could not be expected to dislike Russia. He could not renounce the great Russian novels that had helped shape his own; he could hate neither Russian writers nor Russian culture. And he went further, defending Russia politically as well as culturally, claiming that the Russians were 'fundamentally disinclined towards war', sincerely wishing for peace.⁴

For an exile who risked losing his prized American citizenship by expressing enthusiasm for the Soviet Union, these were brave sentiments to express publicly. Yet Mann was conscious that he could never go far enough for his daughter. She would have liked a complete repudiation of US foreign policy, a rejection of the German Goethe prize and a refusal to return to Germany until the Germans had ceased to allow themselves to be pawns in the Cold War. He could not quite do this. For one thing, the majority of his readers were in Germany and America. The German edition of *Doctor Faustus* had already gone into its second printing and the American edition had been respectfully reviewed (though some reviewers admitted to occasional boredom) and sold 23,000 copies within days of publication. As someone who lived in order to write, Mann required readers. So too, he was not yet ready to lose his influence in the US altogether, still hoping that he could help mitigate the situation. And although he had accepted that the new humble Germany he had hoped would emerge after the war had failed to materialise, he now needed to see what had become of the country for himself; to mourn the ruins he had recreated in *Doctor Faustus*.⁵

As always, Erika Mann was more defiantly willing to risk everything for her principles. For her this remained the only way possible to live. She was also less disposed to equivocate than her father, able to formulate definite opinions immediately where he had to feel his way towards them. The Americans seemed to Erika to be on their way to moral and political ruin, while the Germans were beyond redemption. In a lecture tour the previous winter, she had informed Americans that contrary to propaganda, Germany had not changed at all. Re-education had been abandoned; Nazis had been courted, favoured and employed. 'Post Hitlerian Germany isn't any less arrogant, any less nationalistic, any more democratic and any more trustworthy than was the Kaiser's and the Führer's Reich.' But although she disapproved of his decision to return to his untrustworthy homeland, Erika was still prepared to accompany her father on his European travels, partly because he was now the only centring force in her life. The previous November, Bruno Walter had ended their relationship on the grounds that he wanted it to return to its 'natural, that is, fatherly basis' (in fact he wanted to embark on a new affair with the singer Delia Reinhardt). In Walter's absence she became all the more attached to Thomas.[6]

The rupture with Bruno Walter did not bring Erika any closer to Klaus, whose brief return to California in December distressed her. Klaus himself now put on a front of false jollity when he wrote to the woman he could no longer see as a twin spirit. 'I AM good, and do not even let the thought of a new crisis enter my brain,' he claimed in a letter to Erika and Katia, shortly before recording in his diary that he was 'thinking of death; craving it, waiting, hoping for it – every hour of the long, tedious day'. He tried to form an alliance with Erika by protesting manically on her behalf against *Echo der Woche* and even beginning proceedings to sue the journalist. But this could do little to protect him from isolation and despair. He spent the spring of 1949 wandering rootlessly around Europe, taking drugs and writing a novel entitled *The Last Day* and an essay on 'The Ordeal of the European Intellectuals', both describing the plight of intelligent Europeans in the Cold War world.[7]

If completed, *The Last Day* would have joined *Doctor Faustus* as another ambitious, ambivalent and ultimately tragic novel in the genre of 'outsider rubble literature'. It is essentially an investigation into whether German despair is inevitably world despair; whether German guilt is a universal human condition and whether suicide is the only possible response. In its simplest form, the novel contrasts the experiences of an 'inner' and an 'outer' emigrant, alternating the point of view of two German writers in East Berlin and New York who resent the domineering intellectual control imposed by the Soviet Union and the US respectively. Albert is a Becher-inspired cultural official in East Germany who is too idealistic for the new Soviet-controlled Germany. Julian is a German exile living in New York who can never forget that he shares the guilt of his race and who feels disillusioned by Truman's America. An American official called Colonel McKinsey plays a fateful part in the lives of both men. In Berlin, he offers Albert the chance to defect to West Germany 'without any obligations'; in New York, he writes to Julian, denouncing him as a communist. Alienated by the prevailing anti-communism, Julian realises that bureaucrats like the colonel no longer want peace, but are leading the country to war. 'They talk about Freedom and Democracy – employing those lofty terms as baits to attract, to confuse, to fool the masses.'[8]

Julian wonders about publishing a manifesto in a communist newspaper but he is aware that he is no more comfortable with communism than he is with American capitalism. He goes to visit a British poet, modelled on Auden ('at once capricious and didactic' with pedantic gestures, a soft, absent-minded smile, carpet slippers and close-bitten fingernails) who fails to provide any answers, telling Julian that the solution to desperation lies in the Catholic Church. Julian suggests that despair itself can be a form of protest and decides to commit suicide. The novel ends with the deaths of both men. Albert, about to escape to the West, is betrayed by his wife and arrested by Russian officers who shoot him when he tries to escape ('dirt and blood. A messy agony') while Julian kills himself, attempting to slash his wrists in the bath tub and then jumping naked from the window.[9]

The scenes Klaus Mann sketched in the most detail are those depicting Julian's decline. Julian is enthused by the 'sudden certainty' that he wants to die, which moves him 'like a wave of joy, a triumph', making him feel strong. Absolute despair seems to him to have tremendous power – 'a dynamic impact'. It can be made into 'an argument of irresistible persuasiveness' because 'a man who has given up hope becomes invincible'. He thinks about founding a 'League of the Desperate Ones', a 'Suicide Club'. Other members already include 'the Austrian humanist who took his life in Brazil' (Stefan Zweig) and 'the English novelist and *femme de lettres* who drowned herself' (Virginia Woolf). His death will be a form of protest motivating the intellectual elite all over the world to join his organisation. Immediately, Julian worries that these 'political' motives for suicide may be an artificial 'rationalisation' when in fact the will to death is 'primary, elementary'. But then he decides that it is reasonable to 'turn one's delusions into something constructive'; to sublimate the death instinct. 'I die in an exemplary manner: my death is a signal, a challenge, an appeal.'[10]

In Julian's death, Klaus relived in gruesome, almost comical detail the horrors of his own suicide attempt in LA. Julian drinks whiskey and clambers naked into the bath. Here he surveys his body, patting his chest, stomach and genitals, and thinks that he has not made enough use of it all. He then starts cutting his wrists with the razor blade and finds that 'the taste of death is bitter . . . my purple bath, my blood bath'. The water reddens as he tries his right wrist and then, more successfully, his left. But the vein contracts and the blood stops. He climbs out of the bathtub and rushes through the room, dripping with blood and water as he fumbles to open the window.[11]

Klaus told a friend that he was confronting 'the issue of suicide' in his novel because it was 'more tedious and more painful but somehow more honourable than actually doing it'. During the war, writing about his own death-wish in his autobiography had proved a way for Klaus to protect himself from giving way to despair. Now writing was no longer enough, not least because the despair impeded the novel. 'Not writing, but struggling' is a typical diary entry describing his progress with the book. His motivation was even lower than usual because his chances of publication seemed to be narrowing. He had just heard that the West Germans were not prepared to republish *Mephisto* as it was so obviously a satirical portrait of Gustaf Gründgens and 'Mr Gründgens plays a very important role here'. It was harder to devote energy to writing a new book when the world had lost interest in his existing work.[12]

He spent April writing in Cannes where the unusually bleak and rainy weather contributed to his gloom. 'Rain . . . the weather being about as miserable as my moral and physical state,' he wrote in his diary on 3 May. He still tried to remain light-hearted about his difficulties in letters to his sister, informing Erika cheerfully that he was quitting drugs and planned to send her the remainder of his stock of morphine, though she should take the 'utmost precaution' as it was soporific stuff: 'do not slurp it before social events, only before bedtime in small doses'. But two days later he checked himself into a sanatorium in Nice for detoxification. While Thomas, Erika and Katia were crossing the ocean, Klaus was undergoing a period of tearful insomnia as he attempted to wrest himself free from the drugs that now enabled his only moments of happiness.[13]

On 14 May, Klaus emerged from the sanatorium into the bright sunshine of springtime Nice and wrote to his mother and sister in London that he had been reborn as a 'nearly recovered, and nearly completely healthy boy'. He was working again; he had heard that his 'Ordeal of the European Intellectuals' piece was going to be published by *Tomorrow* in June; 'the dreadful diarrhoea still ails me and sleep is scarce, but who would complain about such bagatelles?' Klaus had learnt (from a friend rather than from his father) about Thomas Mann's impending visit to Germany and he tried to sound supportive. The trip would coincide with the foundation of the West German state (elections had been planned for mid-August) so he suggested that West Germany would do well to offer the presidency to Mann. 'The poet's destiny would be complete, it would be a fat punch line for the biographers.' Mann was the ideal choice as he was accepted in both zones, celebrated in the West and politely acknowledged by the East. And Klaus would enjoy imposing family politics on the nation: 'I'd make sure only homosexuals are given power; the sale of healing morphine would be legalised; E will reside as the grey eminence in Bad Godesberg while father is drinking Rhine wine with the Russian deputy in Bonn.'[14]

But within two days the rain had returned and Klaus was injecting himself with drugs once more, though he described it in his diary as 'a

minor relapse'. That evening Thomas Mann gave a lecture in the Jewish
Wiener Library in London about the need to remember the Nazi
period. The Germans had a tendency to forget and to suppress the
twelve years of National Socialism. To remember the crimes of those
twelve years had come to seem tactless and unpatriotic. 'But the
Germans should remember, and from this memory they should create
the drive to make good again that which they did wrong.' Klaus would
have been pleased with this message if he could have heard it, but his
father was out of contact and even Erika sent only briskly patronising
missives, making no plans to visit her brother in Cannes. 'If one takes
sleeping pills constantly, how is one going to sleep?' she asked him on
the day of her father's lecture. 'And now, of course, you are reduced and
miserable and if your writing does not work right away you tell yourself
that it never will and you become even more depressed.'[15]

On 20 May 1949 Klaus assured Katia and Erika that he was 'doing
well' and was about to return to his novel. The rain in Cannes had
given way to hail and thunder, but he was optimistic and hoped to
meet Erika in Austria later in the summer. He sent 'all love, truthful-
ness, beauty' to his parents and sister from 'lovely, truthful, beautiful
Klaus'. Soon after midnight he set about killing himself with an over-
dose of sleeping tablets. The cleaning staff in the hotel found him
unconscious in his room with the names of his sister and mother scrib-
bled on a piece of paper. He was rushed to hospital but within a few
hours he was dead. A friend visiting him shortly afterwards told his
family that she was struck by the child-like expression of fulfilled desire
on his face. At last he had taken flight in the winged cradle of his
dreams.[16]

Erika, Thomas and Katia Mann received the news of Klaus's death in
Stockholm. Thomas described in his diary an evening spent united in
grief, talking about Klaus's irresistible compulsion for death. At this
stage Thomas's pain was comprised more of sympathy for his wife and
daughter than of sadness for the loss of his son. 'My concern and
compassion are with the heart of his mother and with E. He should not

have done this to them . . . The injury: unpleasant, cruel, reckless and irresponsible.'

They wondered about breaking off their journey but decided that Thomas should continue with his lectures and that they would just cancel the social events. 'It seemed more right after all for Tommy to complete the lecture tour,' Katia reported to Heinrich Mann, telling her brother-in-law that Klaus's longing for death was evidently insurmountable: 'it was going to be fulfilled sometime'.[17]

Over the next few 'veiled' days, Thomas donned mourning attire and lectured in packed auditoriums and Erika cried in the hotel. 'These are sad days,' Thomas told Heinrich, describing how the audience at his lecture had risen silently from their seats as they made their entrance. His grief was still more on Erika's behalf than his own: 'it pains me so to see Erika always in tears. She is abandoned, has lost her companion, whom she always tried to keep clutched to her side. It is hard to understand how he could do this to her. How deranged he must have been in that moment! But it had long been probably his deepest longing, and his face in death is supposed to have worn the expression of a child having his wish fulfilled.'[18]

As always, both Thomas and Erika experienced the emotional turbulence physically. Erika had flu and Thomas suffered from stomach troubles and weak intestines. She travelled alone to Amsterdam before rejoining her parents in Zurich, where they met the rest of the family, including Frido, whose poetry recitations and magic tricks provided brief consolation for Thomas. Erika remained tearful, especially when Klaus's suitcase, typewriter and coats arrived from Cannes. Thomas had now resolved to abbreviate his stay in Europe and the family was trying to decide whether he should still visit Germany (the authorities in Frankfurt had offered to bring the ceremony forward to July). He now agreed to go to Frankfurt and even began to consider visiting Weimar, as East Germany had offered him their Goethe prize too, as well as awarding Heinrich Mann their inaugural German National Prize for Art and Literature and inviting him to return to East Berlin as president of the German Academy of Arts. Erika remained opposed to her father's return to Germany so their estrangement deepened. He told her that she was being unreasonable and that Klaus would not have been so inflexible. 'That's why he killed himself,' she replied, 'which is what I now *won't* do. That's some consolation, but not much.'[19]

Erika saw her father's impending trip as a betrayal of Klaus because Germany had been partly responsible for his death. In the manuscript of *The Last Day* which Erika was now reading, Julian says that he wants to die because 'we killed those Jews – how many of them? Five million, or six? – in the gas chambers . . . It is true, I left Germany long before the Germans committed those ghastly crimes . . . But I used to be one of them. It's my fault. I can't bear it.'

Julian has blood on his hands even before he slashes his wrists. Hitler's Germany had implicated Klaus in a collective guilt that seemed to him to necessitate collective despair. Postwar Germany had rejected him and robbed him of his confidence as a writer, breaking his spirit. Klaus may have been aware that to see his suicide as politically motivated was to sublimate the death instinct, but the ennobling of his death was the last service that Erika could perform for him and she sought refuge in doing it thoroughly.[20]

Of course Erika herself had played her part in creating Klaus's feeling of rejection and despair and she regretted it now, though Thomas complained about her 'bitter distortion of things concerning Klaus but also her own life'. He reminded her of Klaus's childlike contentment in death, but for her this image was horribly wrenching as well as consoling. Erika had watched over the sleeping body of her younger brother protectively when they were small. The continual mention of Klaus's childlike grace in death required her to remember the smooth skin and blond curls of the young boy and to superimpose them onto worn, balding middle age. She mourned the child now, as much as the man. Though it helped to know that he had longed all those years to return to his cradle, it was sad that this time it was a cradle she could not share.

It is not surprising that her most open account of her grief came in a letter to Pamela Wedekind, their old companion from their early days in Berlin, with whom she had not been in touch for a long time. 'Despite the years of separation and the sad estrangement, you know and you can measure what this death means for me,' Erika told her erstwhile friend and lover in the middle of June. 'How I am meant to live now I do not know, I only know that I have to.'[21]

Over the next few weeks Thomas planned his visit to Germany and both Thomas's and Erika's physical symptoms proliferated. Erika underwent what Thomas described as 'a nervous heart attack' at the end of June and then a period of vomiting and fevers in July. Thomas's stomach was still bad and he started suffering from a severe nosebleed, which doctors treated with tamponades, injections (to increase blood coagulation) and then a cauterisation of his blood vessel. Katia, too, slipped and injured her knee, but her symptoms were overshadowed by the more dramatic ailments of her husband.[22]

Thomas had now decided to visit Weimar as well as Frankfurt and Munich although he was aware that a trip to the Eastern zone would alienate the American authorities and make an investigation by the House Un-American Activities Committee more likely. He felt horribly torn. On one level the whole German trip had become a betrayal of both Klaus and Erika. Yet returning to Germany also seemed to him the only fitting way to mourn the son whose death he too blamed partly on the demonic homeland they shared. In a July letter to Hermann Hesse, Thomas sadly acknowledged that he had played his part in Klaus's decline: 'my relationship to him was difficult, and not without feelings of guilt, for my very existence cast a shadow on him from the start'. He was grief-stricken now but he could not follow Erika in sacrificing everything on the altar of his dead son. He felt that someone in the family needed to keep up ties with the various countries to which they belonged. They could not all follow Klaus into spiritual statelessness and he was not convinced by Erika's suggestion that they should move to Switzerland.[23]

Waiting anxiously to depart for Germany on 23 July, Thomas spent his days haemorrhaging and reading hostile reviews of *Faustus* in the German press. After Mann was announced as the recipient of the two Goethe prizes, *Die Zeit* had published an article condemning his novel as a 'psychoanalytical study that is seasoned with political and personal resentment' by a man who had failed to grasp the essence of music, which immediately sparked another charged debate about its author.

Finally, the day for departure arrived and Thomas and Katia said good-bye to Erika, who was returning to Amsterdam. In his 1945 letter to von Molo, Thomas Mann had described his dream of one day feeling the soil of his old home under his feet, prepared for all his years of love to overcome any feelings of estrangement. Now the day for his return had come and, with blood still pouring from his nose and his enemies bracing themselves for public combat, it felt as though he were going to war.[24]

Mann arrived in Frankfurt on 24 July 1949 on a train from Basel. After four years, he finally confronted the burned-out houses and flattened streets that had now become familiar from literature, photographs and films. The rubble might be piled up neatly, efficiently bricked in by temporary walls, but Frankfurt remained eviscerated by the destruction that Mann had said would 'scream to the heavens were not we who suffer it ourselves laden with guilt'. Laid out before him in one German city after another were the ruins of all that he had believed in, spiritu-ally and artistically; it was a fitting setting for mourning both the lost world of his youth and the son he had loved.[25]

Germany was now firmly divided and it was evident that it would only be a matter of weeks before the two states were legally formed. In June the Council of Foreign Ministers had met once more in Paris and had failed to find a solution to the question of Berlin because the West-ern Allies could not accept the Soviet request for a veto. At the same time, the Parliamentary Council was putting into place procedures for an election in West Germany and SED (Communist Party) leaders in East Germany were electing a new Volksrat (People's Council), which would form the basis of a new government in the East. Wilhelm Pieck (co-chairman of the SED alongside Otto Grotewohl), asked Stalin for help forming 'a German government . . . as quickly as possible'. In response to the failure of the Paris meeting, the Russians instituted new ground blockades into Berlin on 11 July.[26]

For many of the people involved in setting up the new German states, this was a hopeful moment. For Mann it was a sign that his ideal of a *Kulturnation*, rising phoenix-like from the ashes, had failed. None the less his response to the impending division of the country was to claim that he spoke for the transcendent power of German language and literature. In his acceptance speech for the Goethe prize in Frankfurt's St Paul's church, he announced that he recognised no zones: 'My visit is to Germany itself, Germany as a whole, and to no occupied zone. Who should vouch for and proclaim the unity of Germany if not an independent writer whose true cultural home, as I have said, is free language, untouched by occupations?'

Describing his German exile – those 'months of wandering from country to country' – he proclaimed that his loyalty to the German language had remained. This was the 'true home that cannot be lost' from which no potentate could evict him. Now he came to them as 'a poor, suffering man' trying to handle the labour pains of this new time. He advised them to look, as he did, to Goethe, as 'a poet and wise man, friend of life, hero of peace' who combined the demonic with the godly and who was an exemplar of humankind.[27]

Certainly, if any figure was able to cross zones, it was Goethe, as was demonstrated by the enthusiasm with which both incipient states celebrated his bicentenary that summer. In the spring Grotewohl had informed a German youth group that Goethe was the 'symbol of our unified national culture' and their hope for 'the highest expression of modern national self-awareness'. Since the end of the war, Germans across the political spectrum had been lauding Goethe as the peace-loving transnational writer best placed to show Germany the path back to righteousness. In his 1945 letter to Mann, Thiess had assured Mann that now the seducer had been destroyed, the Germans had no other *Führer* than Goethe, 'that star of German authority in the world which now shines brighter than ever'. A year later the historian Friedrich Meinecke had published a book suggesting that the Germans' best hope for salvation was to found 'Goethe communities', which would meet on a weekly basis and establish 'something indestructible – a German *character indelebilis*' in the midst of their ruined fatherland. Indeed, the cult of Goethe reached such an extreme that when Karl Jaspers was awarded the Frankfurt Goethe prize in 1947 he felt obliged to warn his audience that their Goethe worship had become so slavish it was depriving Germans of their intellectual independence ('Goethe's world is past . . . it is not our world'), prompting the ire of Ernst Robert Curtius among others.[28]

Mann was right, then, that his enthusiasm for Goethe would reach receptive ears in East and West. It was promising for cultural unity that both Frankfurt and Weimar (the cities where Goethe was born and died) had decided to honour Mann himself with their Goethe prize. And if anyone could claim authority to speak for Goethe, then perhaps it was Mann: Mann whose *Doctor Faustus* was grudgingly recognised even by his enemies as the first great German postwar novel; Mann who remained one of the few major German writers whose major works spanned the whole forty-nine years of his troubled century and who had published in the same century as Goethe.

None the less, it seemed too easy for Mann to come in from outside and claim that the zonal boundaries should be seen as irrelevant. This was a luxury only possible if you had made your home in California, as journalists were quick to point out over the next few days. They could not know that he had to say this; that he knew as well as they did that the Cold War made a single unified *Kulturnation* impossible, but that he had to attempt to call it into existence if only as a way of marking its loss. This was all that was left to him in a world that seemed to have far less need of him than it had done during those wartime years when he was urgently required to represent German culture in exile. And it was a way of pledging his loyalty to his dead son and his absent daughter, fighting for their vision of Germany even if it could have no place in the new political scene. 'We *know* that it exists,' Klaus and Erika had insisted in 1940, 'this "other Germany"; and it is our devout wish that it will soon make itself felt.' Then they had called to their 'American friends' to help Germany and Europe to find 'the road to peace and creative collaboration'; to allow the *Kulturnation* to reassert itself and guide Europe towards peace. Mann could do nothing but add his hopes to theirs.[29]

From Frankfurt, Mann travelled in a chauffeured Buick to Stuttgart and then on to Munich on 28 July. He decided not to visit his house, but it was impossible to avoid either memories or ruins. 'The city, a past in tatters, little heart for it,' he wrote in his diary. Later he told a friend that the sight of the wreckage had proved too much for him: 'To see this whole portion of an outlived past reappearing in a tattered and battered state, with the faces of people so much aged, has something ghostly about it, and I did a great deal of looking the other way.' In this letter Mann claimed that he was too unfeeling to care about the past. He did not want to dwell sentimentally on lost times and preferred to live freshly in new things. In fact he had dwelt on just these ruins in *Doctor Faustus*, lovingly and sadly. It was not lack of feeling but fear of feeling too much that made him refuse to visit the house in which he had fallen in love with the tousled hair and lean body of the son who had just died.[30]

Mann concentrated on seeing the official sights, guided by bureaucrats and accompanied always by police escorts. Taken to Munich's more affluent districts as a guest of honour, he was struck by the prosperous life now possible amid the debris. The currency reform had paid off and there were plentiful goods available in the shops, even if the majority of Germans could still not afford them. Indeed, during her visit earlier in the summer Rebecca West had been repulsed by the extravagant cream cakes indulged in throughout West Germany, given that such luxury was not available in England. Later Mann would remark that 'the sight of a menu card in even one of the more modest Munich restaurants must surely arouse curious feelings in an Englishman'.[31]

In the lead-up to Mann's visit to Weimar there were complaints in the West German newspapers because Mann had failed to protest against East Germany's refusal to allow the 'Society to Combat Inhumanity' to visit Buchenwald, the camp next to Weimar which the communists continued to use to imprison enemies of the state. Asked about this by journalists, Mann defended his decision neither to denounce nor to visit Buchenwald. His presence in Weimar was intended to symbolise the basic unity of Germany and it would not be helpful to make demands on the East German authorities which they would be unable to fulfill.

On the way to East Germany, Mann stopped in Bayreuth, where he found that the last people to sign the guest book in the Bayerischer Hof hotel had been Hitler, Himmler and Goebbels. He left sixteen blank pages between their names and his for the sixteen years of his exile. Exchanging his trilby for a more suitably socialist cloth cap, he then drove on to Weimar, accompanied across the border into the eastern zone by Johannes Becher. On 1 August the historian and former Buchenwald inmate Eugen Kogon published an open letter in the *Schwäbische Landeszeitung* condemning Mann's presence in East Germany and claiming there could be 'no neutrality in the face of inhumanity'. The 12,000 political prisoners in Buchenwald had no choice about the zone that they inhabited. This was 'the terrible truth, and the terrible reality in all the occupied zones where we have to live'. They were not able to dwell either in a 'unified Germany' or in the 'free German language'.[32]

That day Mann was given breakfast by Tulpanov, whom he found knowledgeable and urbane. They talked about Russian and German literature and Tulpanov spoke favourably about the developments in East Germany, saying that soon little interference on the part of the occupation authorities would be needed. Mann did not enquire further. If he was there as a cultural ambassador then his role was simply to foster friendliness between East and West. Privately, he no longer believed that he had the power to change anything in Germany with his pronouncements, although he still hoped that through his novels he could have an effect.

In the evening he was awarded the Goethe Prize at Weimar's National Theatre, where 2,000 people crammed into the auditorium to hear him repeat the speech he had made in the West. Mann made no reference to the political situation of East Germany in his address and did not make his political allegiance as an American explicit, although he wore the tiny emblem of the American Academy of Arts and Letters in his buttonhole. He later claimed that he spoke as an American when he declared that in every social revolution the cherished achievements of mankind – freedom, law and the dignity of the individual – must be preserved as a sacred trust and passed on to future generations and that he hoped that 'out of the present crisis a new feeling of human solidarity, a new humanism will be found'.[33]

In Frankfurt, Mann had donated the prize money to a trust helping German writers. Here in Weimar he gave the money to a fund for rebuilding the Herder church, explaining that the government provided well for intellectual workers in the eastern zone, coddling those who were not persecuted. In East Germany, more than in the West, Mann was fêted as a celebrity, which he believed reflected a greater respect for the power of letters on this side of the iron curtain. There were crowds on the streets and schoolchildren showered him with flowers and garlands, waving banners in his honour.[34]

Mann returned to Frankfurt via Bad Nauheim and then travelled by train to Amsterdam. His trip was almost over. He had survived without haemorrhaging on lecture platforms or breaking down with sadness. He had seen the ruins that had so distressed Klaus, Erika and Golo four years earlier and spoken to the people whom he like Erika saw as stained with the blood of his son as well as of the millions murdered in concentration and extermination camps. Nothing he had seen had lessened his sadness, partly because of his sustained loyalty to Erika and Klaus, whose disillusionment the sights of Germany seemed repeatedly to corroborate. But he had faced something that they could not face, acknowledging his own troubled kinship with contemporary Germany at a time when Erika was unable to do so. Now he was too exhausted to read as he sat in silence, waiting for Katia to pack for their return to California. Finally on 6 August they boarded the *New Amsterdam* steamship bound for New York, where their cabin was large and practical and he could read on a bench on deck. Docking briefly in Le Havre, Mann wrote an account of his trip in his diary, thinking back 'to the many adventures and the strange and varied journey interrupted by grief and terror in that vast room in Stockholm'. He had now received a letter from Erika who sounded stronger, though she had been suffering from swelling in her feet and legs. Soon they would be reunited amid the palm trees and flowers of California, heavier-hearted than when they had left.[35]

In the period after Thomas Mann left Germany, rapid progress was made in establishing both new states. On 14 August the first election was held in the incipient Federal Republic of Germany. The two main competitors were Konrad Adenauer's conservative Christian Democratic Union and Kurt Schumacher's left-wing Social Democratic Party, which had dominated the Weimar Republic. Schumacher was campaigning for an economically socialist country while Adenauer was more sycophantically prepared to follow the lead of the occupying powers. In the end, the margins were tight. The SPD gained 29.2 per cent of the vote and the CDU 31 per cent. Some powerful figures within the CDU wanted a coalition with the SPD but Adenauer instead agreed to a coalition with the other smaller parties who had won the remaining third of the votes. In September, Adenauer himself was elected chancellor with a narrow majority and Theodor Heuss was appointed to the largely ceremonial office of president.

On 20 September, Adenauer made his first speech at the Bundestag in Bonn, where the West German parliament was to be seated, announcing the formation of the new government. The next day the high commissioners (formerly the military governors) met Adenauer for an official ceremony terminating the Military Government and replacing it with a civilian one. For the first time since the war, German officials were greeted with an official military salute by the US, British and French military police. The French high commissioner, André François-Poncet, informed Adenauer that: 'Western Germany – we regret that we cannot say all of Germany – today possesses the means which should allow her to take the direction of her own destiny into her own hands.'[36]

At the start of October a new state was established in East Germany. On the seventh the People's Congress proclaimed the founding of the GDR (German Democratic Republic), lauding it as 'a powerful bulwark in the struggle for the accomplishment of the National Front of Democratic Germany'. Initially the Volksrat served as a provisional Volkskammer (People's Chamber) and Grotewohl was charged with forming a government. The next day the Soviet military administration approved the list of senior officials constituting the provisional government and Pieck and Grotewohl were then elected as the first president and prime minister of the GDR. In his inaugural speech Pieck stated that the German people were required to 'smash' the Western Powers' plans and should not rest 'until the unity of Germany is restored and all territories recovered'.[37]

Thomas Mann was at first relatively optimistic about the new West German government. 'Could turn out well,' he wrote in his diary on 8 September. But Erika was convinced that West Germany would quickly regain its excessive power and browbeat the rest of Europe into submission again. And Thomas too worried that Germany was renazifying and that West Germany would soon be fascist. 'I seem to have timed my visit "at the very last minute"' he told a friend. He expressed this anxiety in an article about his German trip published in the *New York Times* in early October. Here he described his 'moral impressions of Germany', where the majority of people seemed to live by the slogan 'Everything was better under Hitler!' and to lack any real faith in democracy. He claimed that the current 'hapless constellation' of Cold War tension favoured the evil elements in Germany while harming the good and then went on to defend aspects of East Germany.[38]

Explaining why he had decided to donate his East German prize money to the reconstruction of the church and not to the maintenance of writers, Mann stated that Russian communism was 'keenly aware of the power of the intellect' and that even the regimenting of intellectuals was 'a proof of esteem'. He wrote with respect of the goodwill and idealism of many of the East German officials. One in particular in Weimar had impressed him with his hard-working integrity and his pride that East German reconstruction was achieved without foreign aid. Mann saw this as 'a hint of the honour of the old Continent' – a wistful challenge thrown out of 'a Europe that could not be bought, that would no longer be the kept woman of the man with the big money-bags'. In his receptiveness to East Germany, Mann defined himself as 'a non-communist rather than an anti-communist'. He refused to take part in the 'rampant hysteria' of communist persecution but was committed to peace in a world whose future had 'long since become unimaginable without communist traits'.[39]

Not surprisingly, the article was received critically. 'The fact that we are engaged in a cold war of ideas is of no importance to Thomas Mann,' complained one reader; 'He does not even say that he is opposed to the totalitarian state,' said another. Mann found his waning popularity in the US distressing. Arriving back at San Remo Drive after his trip to Europe, he had described the 'joy of home, joy of being safe and in the hold, away from the world that might go on screaming', in his diary. In Germany, he had made explicit his allegiance as an American, urging the Germans not to underestimate the cultural life in America and lauding contemporary American literature. But as Erika struggled with the American authorities (who were making it difficult for her to obtain citizenship) he was wondering more frequently about moving to Switzerland, and he was doing his best to be as principled as Erika wanted him to be in speaking out publicly against his new homeland.[40]

Relations between Thomas and Erika remained strained. She was pleased with her father's *New York Times* article but she was still devastated about Klaus's death and angry with anyone who was not writing about her dead brother. She was continuing to devote much of her own energy to turning Klaus's death into a meaningful event. While Thomas was writing his *New York Times* article, Erika was translating and attempting to republish her brother's article about 'The Ordeal of the European Intellectuals'. In October she gave a lecture intertwining her brother's essay with words of her own, speaking in the dual voice they had once shared.[41]

Klaus's essay elaborated on the themes of *The Last Day*, depicting the hopelessness of honest intellectuals in the postwar world. The English version published in *Tomorrow* just after his death describes 'thinking men and women' across Eastern and Western Europe as 'a baffled, insecure group', for whom the slogans reverberating in the air from Russia and America have a hollow ring. Many of them are looking for comfort in the ancient documents of Hinduism, the Bible, the writings of Lenin, or the existentialist philosophy of Sartre. Some have turned to communism and some to anti-communism but none can believe in progress. As civilisation tumbles 'under the assault of streamlined barbarism' they find it impossible to describe or rationalise the nightmarish world of Auschwitz. The masters of the world stammer, able to subscribe only to T. S. Eliot's 'I can connect/ Nothing with nothing'.[42]

The longer unpublished version of the essay, which Erika now translated into German, contains a hint of the 'Suicide Club' that Julian wished to establish in Klaus's novel. Klaus ends with the pronouncements of an imaginary disenfranchised student, complaining about the mess that has been made of the world he is to inherit. In the face of the desperate conditions around him, he suggests that a new rebellion of the hopeless is needed. 'Hundreds, even thousands of intellectuals should do what Virginia Woolf, Ernst Toller, Stefan Zweig, Jan Masaryk have done,' he says, advocating a wave of suicides which will 'shake the people out of their stupor', making them grasp 'the fatal severity of the plague that man has brought about himself with his ignorance and egomania'.[43]

In the notes for *The Last Day*, Julian wonders about writing 'a novel advocating suicide as the only decent and logical solution . . . the Werther of our time' before deciding that 'books don't have such power any more' and besides, he is too tired. Klaus was too self-conscious to see his death wish as straightforwardly political. Reading his diaries, it is hard to see his death as resulting from anything but loneliness, exhaustion and the frustration of failure. However in her talk that October, Erika paid tribute to the men and women who had committed suicide, lauding it as a brave political act. Having outlined the arguments of Klaus's essay, she described the recent wave of suicides. Her roll call of dead intellectuals echoed Klaus's list of Woolf, Toller, Zweig and Masaryk, but in a lecture dedicated to the memory of her brother, Klaus's name implicitly headed the list. She stated that these people did not die for personal reasons: 'not because they had failed in their own private or public lives'. Instead 'they died because we had failed them, because we didn't seem to have much use for them any longer'. They quit because the earth – 'this particular star' – had become uninhabitable. They were not 'irresponsible cowards'. Instead their departure constituted a deliberate demonstration: 'the most unforgettable warning any one person would be able to sound'.[44]

Having exonerated Klaus, whom Erika, her family, Germany and the world at large had failed, Erika went on to make explicit the warning offered by these deaths:

'Look out!' these dead ones keep calling to us, 'Danger! You're on the wrong road, the road to barbarism and disaster! Our living voices proved too weak to make you turn round; perhaps our deaths will shock you into attention. You knew us! We were famous and successful, most of us, quite wealthy and well-liked in many countries for our talents, our intelligence and our personalities. Since we chose to throw away all that we possessed including our very lives, you cannot but acknowledge that something must be very wrong with this world of ours. Be honest, be brave, do admit the calamity to yourselves and the redeeming change will even then have started to occur.'

Seen through Erika's eyes, Klaus's death became a final struggle for a world that might have been; for the world that Klaus and Erika Mann, Stephen Spender, Martha Gellhorn, Rebecca West and Billy Wilder hoped to bring into being after the war. His warning was a warning to Germany in particular. The Germans needed to listen to his message so that men like Albert and Julian – men like Klaus and his father – could find a home there again. But this was Adenauer's world now, and Truman's; culturally, West Germany was the home of Melvin Lasky and Gustaf Gründgens. It remained to be seen whether there was still space for the old-world idealists. And it would be many years before the Germans heeded Klaus's warning or joined the surviving Manns in mourning the casualties of the swift West German recovery.[45]

Coda

'Closing time in the gardens of the West'

On 22 November 1949, Adenauer signed a new treaty with the British, American and French high commissioners in Bonn. West Germany was now permitted to join the Council of Europe as an associate member and was formally eligible to receive Marshall Aid.[1] Interviewed by Rebecca West's husband Henry Andrews for the *Observer*, Adenauer expressed his gratitude to Germany's former occupiers, conscious that this embodied 'an act of faith on the part of the Allies as well as on the part of Germany'.[2]

For Adenauer and his former conquerors, the Occupation had been a success. West Germany was set to go forward as a major player in a new peaceful and united Western Europe, buttressed by American money. This was confirmed five months later when the French foreign minister Robert Schuman proposed a plan for what would become the European Coal and Steel Community (ECSC), aimed at enabling new economic co-operation between France and Germany by placing their entire coal and steel production under the control of a federated European body. By July 1951 the Federal Republic was an equal member of the ECSC and Germany was no longer officially an enemy. Now prime minister again in Britain, Winston Churchill expressed his relief that the word 'peace' could be finally spoken between 'two great branches of the human family who were cast asunder by the terrible events of the past'.[3]

Culturally, the British and American governments counted the Occupation a success as well. There were more theatres, opera houses and cinemas per square mile in Berlin than in almost any other city in

Europe. There was a literary scene that would strengthen internationally over the next decade. The Allies had revived the arts in Germany and had created publications that were to have lasting impact in the postwar period: the American *Der Monat* (soon funded by the CIA) and *Die Neue Zeitung*, and the British *Der Spiegel* and *Die Welt*, stand out as landmark publications that the Germans quickly came to feel proud of. The Cold War had placed Berlin so firmly on the international cultural map that it seemed the obvious place to host the first meeting of Congress for Cultural Freedom, which brought 4,000 delegates to Germany to form an anti-communist cultural front in 1950. So too, German slang, clothes, dance styles and pop music had been enthusiastically reshaped along American lines and the German writers, film-makers, artists and musicians of the 1950s were noticeably more open to their American, British and French counterparts than those of the 1940s. Occasionally, they were even influenced by some of the cultural emissaries who had arrived from Britain and America in the immediate postwar years. Hemingway was a constant source of inspiration, as was Sartre; Wolfgang Koeppen's 1951 *Tauben im Grass* (*Pigeons on the Grass*) took its title from Gertrude Stein and its style from John Dos Passos.[4]

Yet although the Allies' hopes for a peaceful and stable Germany had been achieved, arguably the primary aims at Potsdam had failed. Germany had been decentralised and demilitarised (though in 1956 it would regain its army) but had not been fundamentally denazified, democratised or re-educated. In both East and West Germany, the publishing houses, opera houses and theatres contained many of the same faces as they had before and during the war, as did the civil service. In 1953 Adenauer would appoint the former Nazi-sympathiser Hans Globke as director of the Federal Chancellery of West Germany. In the early 1950s the lack of denazification created a climate in which Germans who had co-operated with Hitler could avoid acknowledging guilt and in which the majority of Germans still saw themselves as victims, as they had in 1945. Perhaps unsurprisingly, the Allies had not succeeded in their aim to mobilise culture to transform the belief systems of an entire country. Culture had turned out to be decidedly secondary to Realpolitik.

For many of the writers and artists who had visited Germany from Britain and the US during the four years after the war, the Occupation remained a tragically wasted opportunity. During her visit in the spring of 1949, Rebecca West had worried that the speed of economic recovery had overtaken the country's spiritual growth. For centuries, Germany's wealth and power had been pressed into the service of madness and death. She asked whether after their years of occupation the inhabitants of the Federal Republic had a new faith with which to bind German wealth and power to the services of sanity and life, and found that she was not confident that they did, or that anybody in Germany felt the need for such a faith.[5]

West's pessimism was echoed by Hannah Arendt, who arrived in Germany that December for the first time in a decade and found a society in the grip of collective denial. If she said that she was a Jew, she was confronted with a deluge of stories about what the Germans had suffered. If she raised the question of the bomb damage, she was asked: 'Why must mankind always wage wars?' And these complaints were verified by a survey conducted in West Germany in 1951 that revealed that only 5 per cent of the participating Germans admitted feeling any guilt towards the Jews, while 21 per cent believed that 'the Jews them- selves were partly responsible for what happened to them during the Third Reich'. A year later nearly two out of five respondents informed pollsters that they thought it was 'better' for Germany to have no Jews on its territory. The six million Jewish dead remained ghosts for the next generation to confront.[6]

As West Germany recovered economically in the 1950s, many of the individuals featured in this book felt alienated from the prosperous country that had emerged from the ashes. Some avoided it altogether, while others found their returns dispiriting. Lee Miller never went back to Germany, though she travelled relatively extensively in the 1950s. Martha Gellhorn steered clear of the country until 1962, when she was called upon to take 'a short jaunt to hell' to report on German univer- sities. Like West and Arendt before her, she dismissed the Germans as 'incurable'. They seemed to be 'quiescent sheep and tigers' but only because they were overweight with butter and cream, kept quiet by plentiful goods and food. 'Remove those and they will become insane blood-loving sheep and man-eating tigers.' Gellhorn's arrival in Berlin brought on a 'deep depression', partly the result of looking back on the happiness and the misery from fifteen years earlier.[7]

Spender and Auden waited less time before returning, both still committed Germanophiles who remained loyal to the German poetry they had found so liberating in Berlin in the 1920s and 1930s. But arriving separately in 1955, they were disappointed by the self-satisfied reality of West Germany. Auden was located by a former German boyfriend, an ex-sailor, whom he found had become disturbingly fat. 'He hadn't just put on weight – he was *grotesque* like someone in a circus,' he complained. The transformation of the city itself saddened him most of all. 'Alas the city of my youth has now gone,' he lamented; 'the juke box and rock-and-roll have ruined it.' Visiting West Berlin a few months later, Spender was disappointed by the American-influenced new architecture, which seemed neither to be properly modern nor to show any awareness of the city's past. He was more impressed by the bombastic Soviet blocks in East Berlin: 'great tracks' laid down through the decay and chaos, presenting 'overwhelming propaganda' where the buildings in the West offered mere 'hectic shouting'. His general impression of the West Germans was that they were rebuilding their bombed cities to look exactly as they had before, 'in much the same spirit perhaps as one goes to a dentist and asks to have one's artificial teeth made an exact replica of the ones they replace'. They seemed to be 'indulging in a great orgy of bourgeois amenities'.[8]

Auden's official wife, Erika Mann, visited Germany more regularly in the 1950s from Switzerland, where Erika, Thomas and Katia moved in 1952, finally driven out of the US after Thomas Mann was denounced in Congress as 'one of the world's foremost apologists for Stalin and company'. None of them could feel at home in Germany again, alienated both by the failure of German writers to make terms with the wartime exiles and by the pro-American Cold War fervour of the West Germans. Although Mann remained in print in both Germanies, his books were no longer present in the libraries of the Amerika Häuser. In 1953 Joseph McCarthy had taken it upon himself to ensure that the

Häuser were sufficiently anti-communist and purged the libraries of books by so-called communist sympathisers, including Thomas Mann and John Dos Passos. There were even reports of book-burning at two centres. Mann described Adenauer's Federal Republic as a 'cultural desert' and was stubbornly persistent in holding on to his ideal of a Germany united in spirit by its language and literature. In 1954 Mann became determined that an all-German production of a film of *Buddenbrooks* would demonstrate the victory of culture over politics in the Cold War, but the West Germans refused to co-operate with the East German state-owned studio DEFA. Furious, Mann refused a sizeable offer from West Germany for the rights to do it alone. When Erika Mann managed to arrange for Klaus Mann's *Mephisto* to be published in East Germany in 1956, she was distressed to find that Gustaf Gründgen's continued influence meant that it remained unpublishable in West Germany.[9]

Between Thomas Mann's death in 1955 and Erika's death in 1969, Erika remained consumed by thoughts of the lost world of her German childhood, unable to feel at home anywhere now that she had lost her identity as both a German and an American. Living alone with the mother who would outlive her, Erika felt achingly bereft of Thomas and Klaus and the particular set of beliefs and ideals the three of them had shared. She spent the year following her father's death writing an account of his final months, celebrating the 'clear spirit' and 'youthfully supple' body of a man whose last year was 'illumined and warmed' by visible grace. She no longer mourned her brother this publicly, but in 1959, a decade after Klaus's death, she wrote a letter recalling how as children she and Klaus had encountered a girl playing alone. 'Where is your Eissi?' Erika asked her. 'One *has* to have an Eissi!' Now she admitted that she still believed in the need for an Eissi and found it difficult to go on living without him. In their different ways, Thomas, Klaus and Erika Mann had been broken by the Allies' failure to purge Germany of fascism and to allow Hitler's victims to forge the country afresh. Germany's tragedy became their own tragedy because the rubble and the corpses remained unredeemed.[10]

It took a new generation of angry young Germans to succeed where the Allies had failed. The trial of the SS-Obersturmbannführer (lieutenant colonel) Adolf Eichmann in Jerusalem in 1961 opened up questions about the complicity of the German nation as a whole in the extermination of the Jews, provoking Germans at home and abroad to demand a more public expiation for these crimes. This coincided with a cluster of novels engaging with the Third Reich and specifically with the failure of the older generation to confront their guilt in the immediate postwar period. Heinrich Böll's 1959 *Billard um halb zehn* (*Billiards at Half-Past Nine*) juxtaposed present and past to explore the confrontation between two generations of Germans looking back on Nazism. Between 1959 and 1963 Günter Grass published his *Danzig Trilogy*, which began with *Die Blechtrommel* (*The Tin Drum*), a grotesque reimagining of the Nazi period from the perspective of a misguided dissident dwarf.

On 2 June 1967 the growing anger of left-wing West German students (who found a voice through organisations such as the Socialist League of German Students), gained impetus and focus from the shooting of a student, Benno Ohnesorg, during a confrontation between police and demonstrators at protests against the official visit by the Shah of Persia to West Berlin. In succeeding days an estimated hundred thousand students took to the streets with placards explicitly associating this with the repressive terror of the Third Reich: 'democracy shot down, dictatorship protected'. They were granted ammunition when the Berlin Senate defied the Basic Law by banning demonstrations in Berlin. The graduate student-cum-political activist Gudrun Ensslin declared tearfully that 'this is the generation of Auschwitz. At that time they attacked the Jews, now they are trying to destroy us. We must protect ourselves. We must arm ourselves.'[11]

Over the course of the next year the left-wing student movements radicalised. Artists in all art forms called for direct engagement with German politics past and present, asking urgent questions about their parents' Nazi past and demanding fundamental changes in German society, keen that the Federal Republic should do all it could to separate itself from that earlier period of dictatorship. The critic and poet Hans Magnus Enzensberger declared that the 'sickly parliament' of the Federal Republic was at the 'end of its legitimacy' and urged writers and artists to 'go out on to the streets with the students and the workers, and express ourselves a bit more clearly . . . Our aim must be: let us create French conditions here in Germany.'[12]

Breakaway factions began to consider terrorism, interpreting the events of June 1967 as the death knell of West German democracy. They were granted ammunition by the anti-Vietnam demonstrations in October 1967, when protestors condemning 'opposition to the American war of extermination' were violently suppressed by police using water cannon and truncheons. The adversary now became the capitalist forces of German and American consumerism as well as the government itself. In April 1968, Gudrun Ensslin and her lover Andreas Baader set off incendiary devices in two department stores. A week later the radical activist Rudi Dutschke was shot in the head by an anti-communist, sparking violent protests by demonstrators who saw the assassination attempt as an act of political bullying by the powerful Springer newspaper publishing empire. The journalist Ulrike Meinhof now leant her support to Ensslin and Baader, helping Baader to escape from prison. Collectively they issued a manifesto in 1970 proclaiming that 'the Red Army is established'. 'Did the pigs, who shot first, believe we would allow ourselves to be shot down peacefully as animals to the slaughter?' The enemy, they claimed, was 'American imperialism'.[13]

The Allied Occupation that had brought about America's influence and power in West Germany was now seen as effecting a reprehensible continuation of the values of the Third Reich. Twenty years after it had started, the Germans were angry to have been used as pawns in the Cold War. In demanding a reassessment of the Nazi era, the younger generation also demanded a reassessment of the Occupation. They saw the four years after the war as ending in a weak settlement in which the Allies, driven by the Cold War, had allowed the Germans to get away with it.

In 1969 the twenty-four-year-old German artist Anselm Kiefer presented a series of photographs under the ironic title *Besetzungen* ('Occupations') at a gallery in Karlsruhe. Here, garbed in his father's military uniform, Kiefer performed the Nazi salute against a background of historical monuments and natural settings in Italy, France and Switzerland as well as while standing on the table of his own Düsseldorf studio. Growing up just after his second world war, Kiefer had been unnerved to find that his school history lessons barely mentioned the Nazi era. It was only when he found a recording of speeches by Hitler, Goebbels and Göring that he began to understand what it was his parents' generation was attempting to repress. 'The sound goes right through the skin. Not only through the ears and the head. I was simply shocked. And that's how it began.' The *Sieg-Heil* salute had been banned in Germany since 1945 and Kiefer called these photographs a 'provocation'. He was both condemning the Germans' forgetfulness of the past and reminding the viewer of Hitler's appropriation of art. In one of the photographs, Kiefer adopted the pose of the romantic wanderer in Casper David Friedrich's *Der Wanderer über dem Nebelmeer* (*The Wanderer above the Sea of Fog*), echoing Thomas Mann in his suggestion that no aspect of Germany's past was untainted by National Socialism. Kiefer's acts of Occupation both mimicked the Nazi attempts to occupy Europe and aimed to succeed where the Allied Occupation had failed.[14]

By rejecting the values of the Occuaption, the younger generation of students and artists created a climate in which the exiled artists of the 1940s could find a voice. Walter Benjamin and Theodor Adorno became prophets of the revolution. Klaus Mann now became a figurehead of the West German rebels, though somewhat ironically his posthumous rise to fame was accelerated by yet another fracas with Gustaf Gründgens. Like his nemesis and former lover, Gründgens himself had committed suicide in 1963, but his death did not prevent his adopted son from taking out a lawsuit to prevent the publication of *Mephisto* when the Munich publishing house Aufbau Verlag Nymphenburg announced plans to publish it in 1964. The case dragged on for seven years until finally the West German Supreme Court ruled in favour of Gründgens's claim. However even after 1971 the book remained available both in East Germany and in neighbouring countries, so West German radicals were easily able to obtain copies as they set about endowing Klaus Mann with the martyr status his sister had attempted to acquire on his behalf.

The views expressed in the 1940s not only by Klaus and Erika Mann but by Stephen Spender and Rebecca West had now become mainstream. Even the impatient fury of Martha Gellhorn and Lee Miller seems mild compared to the pronouncements of Gudrun Ensslin or Ulrike Meinhof. For the majority of angry and disillusioned young, most of whom still hoped to reform society by pacifist means, Stephen Spender's statement in 1947 that 'the day may come when this fusion of two ideas – liberal democracy and economic freedom – will take place within the minds of certain Germans' had proved more prescient than many of his less optimistic contemporaries might have expected at the time. Although some German terrorists now believed that economic freedom was dangerous and liberal democracy had failed, the kind of vision described by Spender generally prevailed.[15]

Looking back, it is easy to see why it took twenty years for this fusion to take place and for fundamental denazification to occur. It was naïve of the Allies to expect a starving, brainwashed nation to change its mentality overnight; naïve of those implementing cultural policy to expect *Moral* to come before *Fressen*. What is more, the cultural policies of the Allies came down simply to the erratic actions of a handful of individuals, all of whom were as busy living and experiencing the end of the war as they were planning a coherent cultural programme. In tracing the day-to-day experiences of these figures on the ground in Germany, it quickly becomes clear that their efforts to convince the Germans of their guilt were inseparable from their own encounters with the ruins and their inhabitants, and therefore from the daily business of writing and loving, dancing and grieving.

Living at speed, racing from the remains of the bombed cities and concentration camps to the luxury of the Allied headquarters, they certainly did not have time to instigate a cultural policy any more than the Germans themselves had time to formulate a clear notion of their own guilt amid the daily business of survival. For these writers, artists and film-makers, being an occupier was not so much a question of implementing policy or of reporting on events as of participating energetically in the life of the country. It now seems surprising how great a capacity for living people like Martha Gellhorn and Rebecca West manifested amid the ruins. Given the setting, it is less surprising that they should have ended up exhausted and discouraged. It is also unsurprising that Stephen Spender, W. H. Auden, Billy Wilder and Klaus and Erika Mann, all arriving in Germany with complex personal agendas, should have failed to change anything and should go home demoralised by the situation in the defeated nation.

How much does the disappointment of this group of dreamers and visionaries in the late 1940s ultimately matter, given that Germany came through in the end? The changes effected by the 1960s radicals were far-reaching and were continued by subsequent generations before and after the reunification of Germany. Since 1990 Germany has been remarkably successful in reconceiving itself as a tolerant and peace-loving nation, emerging in the twenty-first century as the reasonable and unassailable dominant force in the European Union, albeit tainted by the growing shadow of Holocaust-denying neo-Nazis. This is a German state that is determined always to confront its past. Dominated by a vast monument to the Holocaust, today's Berlin is a city in which it is impossible to forget the Jewish dead.

None the less, the disillusionment of Spender and Auden, of Wilder and the Manns does still matter, primarily as a missed opportunity. This was a chance not just to create a denazified Germany but to use Germany to reconfigure Europe along transnational grounds. For Spender, Klaus Mann and others it was an opportunity for a new system of values to assert itself. At that moment when throughout Europe almost all there was to lose had been lost, there was a chance for peace to be seen as a matter of a nation's collective mental strength as well as its military might. It seems astonishing now that a large number of governments devoted substantial funds to UNESCO in 1946 in the shared belief that 'since wars begin in the minds of men, it is in the minds of men that the defences of peace must be constructed'. But if the 1940s had played out differently it need not have been so surprising to us now. Arguably the united Europe that emerged in the 1950s could have been culturally rather than economically driven if it had not been caught up in Cold War enmity that rendered useless the lessons of 1945.[16]

Both the nature of this missed opportunity and the sense of betrayal it provoked is attested to by these stories of the writers and artists who visited Germany from Britain and the US in the postwar years. If in general they had less impact on Germany than Germany had on them, then the mood of desperation they took with them remained with them in subsequent decades. Twenty-five years later, Martha Gellhorn told a friend that she had still not recovered from the disillusionment with humanity acquired during her day at Dachau: 'Dachau, and all I afterwards saw: Belsen etc., changed my life or my personality. Like a water-shed. I have never been the same since. It's exactly like mixing paint. Black, real true solid black, was then introduced, and I have never again come back to some state of hope or innocence or gaiety which I had before.'

Towards the end of her life, Lee Miller sobbed as she remembered her visit to the death camps, regretting that she had rushed into Dachau unprepared. Both Gellhorn and Miller had arrived in Germany passionate, curious and courageous, determined to play their part in improving the world by recording suffering. Both had left resigned to despair. This was the despair that had killed Klaus Mann and that Erika Mann spent the years after his death abortively attempting to magic into a political movement.[17]

Fighting desperation through artistic creation, the writers, artists and film-makers who visited Germany in the immediate aftermath of the war had fashioned works of art that can be seen collectively as one of the primary results of the cultural occupation. And in their mood of (sometimes tragi-comic) gloom, *Doctor Faustus*, *The Last Day*, *Point of No Return*, *Memorial for the City*, *Greenhouse with Cyclamens*, *European Witness*, *A Defeated People*, Laura Knight's painting, Lee Miller's photographs and to a lesser extent *A Foreign Affair*, caught the mood of the wider artistic world at this moment; a mood that was evocatively described in Cyril Connolly's editorial for the final issue of *Horizon* magazine in December 1949. Here Connolly warned that the current desperate struggle 'between man, betrayed by science, bereft of religion, deserted by the pleasant imaginings of humanism' was set to continue and to dominate the art of the subsequent decade. 'For it is closing time in the gardens of the West and from now on an artist will be judged only by the resonance of his solitude or the quality of his despair.'[18]

Collectively, these ambivalent, tragic works of art matter because they gave the anguish of a generation concrete form. A group of artists had found in the German ruins a vocabulary for exploring the struggle of their age; they had encountered horrifyingly potent symbols in the bombed-out houses, the piles of debris, the wandering refugees pushing their carts at the side of ravaged roads, the skeletal figures in the concentration camps. Now, looking back on this time, we can glimpse a Germany that might have been in the books, films and pictures they created. We can see just how much these artists' failure to bring this world into existence mattered to them in the quality of their despair.

If anyone could emerge triumphantly in the Federal Republic of Germany, then it was Marlene Dietrich and Billy Wilder. Both possessed the resilience and wit needed to shrug off the self-satisfaction, the cream cakes and American propaganda as defiantly as they had brushed aside the mounds of rubble in 1945. In 1960 Dietrich returned to Germany for a concert tour. She was welcomed by Willy Brandt (then governing mayor of Berlin) but pilloried as a traitor by the German press. In the lead-up to her visit hundreds of letters appeared in the newspapers asking, as one Rhineland 'Hausfrau' put it, 'Aren't you ashamed to set foot on German soil as a common, filthy traitor?' and suggesting that she 'should be lynched as the most odious of war criminals'. Ticket sales were low so Vienna and Essen cancelled her engagements. The five days in Berlin became three and the Titania-Palast gave out free tickets to fill the house. Dietrich told *Newsweek* that her only worry was the threats of rotten tomatoes and eggs, which left 'such awful gooey streaks in the clothing'. There were still some Germans who were curious to see the woman recently named as the 'fourth greatest immigrant to America', but 400 of the 1,800 seats at the Titania-Palast were empty when the show opened in May.[19]

As always, Dietrich succeeded in charming her audiences into amazed approval. She sang new arrangements of a series of German songs and revived songs such as 'Falling in Love Again' that had made her famous. She moved the audience with the uncertainty of Holländer's '*Ich weiss nicht, zu wem ich gehöre*' (I don't know to whom I belong') and ended triumphantly with '*Ich hab' noch einen Koffer in Berlin*' ('I still have a suitcase in Berlin'). At the end of the first performance, hundreds of audience members including Willy Brandt leapt to their feet cheering. Dietrich gave encores for the first time in her concert career and was rewarded by eighteen curtain calls. By the end of the tour, in Munich, even standing room was sold out. Dietrich was now fifty-eight and the physical demands of her schedule exhausted her. She fell over in Düsseldorf and broke her shoulder, but managed to carry on by performing with her upper arm tied to her body with the belt of her raincoat, the courageous warrior she had always been. One curmudgeon did hit her with an egg but the German reviews were swooning paeans of praise. 'She is a legend,' the Düsseldorf *Handelsblatt* proclaimed, 'fascinating as a woman of the world, of the intelligence, of the spirit.'[20]

The following year Billy Wilder followed Dietrich back to Berlin to make *One, Two, Three*. Like Dietrich, Wilder was now a world-famous star, riding on the success of *Some Like It Hot*. His new movie portrayed an American Coca-Cola executive in West Berlin named MacNamara (played by James Cagney) who is in the process of trying to sell Coke to some Russian commissars in East Berlin. He is sent his American boss's precocious seventeen-year-old daughter, Scarlett, as an unruly houseguest and fears his career is in jeopardy when she secretly escapes to marry Otto, a dishevelled young German communist who plans to emigrate to the Soviet Union.

MacNamara's efforts first to annul the marriage and then, when he discovers Scarlett is pregnant, to turn Otto into an aristrocrat, involve chaotic car chases from one side of Berlin to the other, and Wilder was determined to shoot in both halves of the city he now nicknamed 'Splitsville'. However the Russians refused permission to film the scenes set on their side of the border. Undaunted, Wilder informed them that the East German border guards were visible in his footage of characters driving towards the Brandenberg Gate. Would they want western audiences to think that East Germany was a police state? Eventually the Russians consented and Wilder was the last westerner to film in East Berlin. But political events intervened halfway through, plummeting Wilder into the vortex of history once again when, during the night of 12 August

1961, the East German army closed the border between East and West Berlin. The next morning Wilder was outraged to discover that the beginnings of the edifice that would become the Berlin Wall had been resurrected in the middle of his set. He now had to hurriedly rewrite his script and to reconstruct the Brandenberg Gate and the Unter den Linden in the Bavarian studios where they finished filming.[21]

Once again, Wilder used comedy to avoid either the isolation of despair or the cowardice of conforming to his new government's current agenda. Like the radical young generation of Germans who would emerge at the end of the decade, Wilder did not forgive the Germans their Nazi past or allow denazification to have been a success. MacNamara's heel-clicking assistant Schlemmer always insists that he knew nothing of Hitler during the war but then when his old SS commander reappears in the guise of an apparently respectable West German journalist, he *heils* him automatically. There is a suggestion that all Germans are merely serving their new Russian and American masters with the same blind obedience that had led to the murder of Wilder's mother and grandmother. But once again, his was the long view: he was able to laugh off the bureaucratic absurdity of communism, the megalomanic blindness of American imperialism, and the fascist conformity of the Germans by satirising them all in equal measure.

In the end Wilder was defiantly on the side of life. He had no wish to join Klaus Mann's 'League of the Desperate Ones', or to walk over the cliff face that Gellhorn had confronted at Dachau. He may have done all he could to distance himself from the Germans but he shared the Berliners' ability to crawl out of the ruins and carry on. Near the end of the film Otto suggests that the entire human race should be liquidated, distressed that the communists have turned out to be as corrupt as the capitalists. MacNamara's reply is benign: 'Look at it this way, kid. Any world that can produce the Taj Mahal, William Shakespeare, and Stripe toothpaste can't be all bad.' There was optimism in Wilder's humour, as there had been in 1945, during that bizarre zero hour after the war when he had learnt to laugh in order to survive in a ruined and desolate world.

Notes

Abbreviations used in the Notes and Bibliography

BB:	Bertolt Brecht
BW:	Billy Wilder
CZ:	Carl Zuckmayer
EH:	Ernest Hemingway
EM:	Erika Mann
EW:	Evelyn Waugh
GO:	George Orwell
HS:	Hilde Spiel
JPS:	Jean-Paul Sartre
KM:	Klaus Mann
LK:	Laura Knight
MD:	Marlene Dietrich
MG:	Martha Gellhorn
PdeM:	Peter de Mendelssohn
RW:	Rebecca West
SB:	Simone de Beauvoir
SS:	Stephen Spender
TM:	Thomas Mann
VG:	Victor Gollancz
WHA:	W. H. Auden

BFI Archive:	British Film Institute Archive, London
EH Archive:	Ernest Hemingway Collection, J. F. Kennedy Presidential Library, Boston
EM Archive:	Erika Mann Archive, Monacensia
HS Archive:	Hilde Spiel Archive, National Library of Vienna
KM Archive:	Klaus Mann Archive, Monacensia
LK Archive:	Laura Knight Archive, Nottinghamshire Archives
MG Archive:	Martha Gellhorn Archive, Boston University
OMGUS:	Office of Military Government United States, National Archives, Washington DC
PdeM Archive:	Peter de Mendelssohn Archive, Monacensia
RW Archive, Beinecke:	Rebecca West Archive, Beinecke Rare Book and Manuscript Library, Yale University

RW Archive, Tulsa   Rebecca West Archive, Tulsa
NA   The National Archives, Kew, UK
NARA   US National Archives and Records Administration, Washington
WHA Archive   W. H. Auden Archive, Berg Collection, New York Public Library

Introduction

1   Over 3.6 million German homes were destroyed: see Giles Macdonogh, *After the Reich: From the Liberation of Vienna to the Berlin Airlift* (John Murray, 2007), p. 1.

2   Although they quickly became a ubiquitous symbol, the *Trümmerfrauen* were chiefly a Berlin (and Soviet zone) phenomenon. The Western Allies were reluctant to employ women for this task. See Leonie Treber, *Mythos Trümmerfrauen: Von der Trümmerbeseitigung in der Kriegs- und Nachkriegszeit und der Entstehung eines deutschen Erinnerungsortes* (Klartext, 2014), pp. 234–39.

3   These figures are from Tony Judt, *Postwar: A History of Europe since 1945* (Vintage, 2010), pp. 14, 17, 26. See also Malcolm J. Proudfoot, *European Refugees, 1939–1952: A Study in Forced Population Movement* (Northwestern University Press, 1956), pp. 80, 158–59.

4   The Wehrmacht is the army (literally the 'defence force').'countenance of defeat': James Stern, *The Hidden Damage* (Chelsea Press, 1990), p. 109.

5   'one of the great', 'a whole nation': MG, 'We Were Never Nazis', *Collier's*, 26 May 1945. 'repugnant in their': LM, 'Germany, the War That is Won', *Vogue*, Jun 1945, in Antony Penrose (ed.), *Lee Miller's War: Photographer and Correspondent with the Allies in Europe, 1944–1945* (Thames & Hudson, 2005), p. 166.

6   'a chaos of': GO, 'Creating Order out of Cologne Chaos: Water Supplied from Carts', *Observer*, 25 Mar 1945.

7   'I guess Germany': *Los Angeles Examiner*, 3 Feb 1945, cited in Steven Bach, *Marlene Dietrich: Life and Legend* (University of Minnesota Press, 2011), p. 299.

8   'the people': WHA to Tania Stern, 20 May 1945, WHA Archive.

9   'They burned': BW as recalled by John Woodcock in J. M. Woodcock, 'The Name Dropper', *American Cinemeditor* 39:4, Winter 1989/1990, p. 15.

10   'band of thieves': PdeM to HS, Jun 1944, PdeM Archive.'We used to have a vocabulary': PdeM, 'Through the Dead Cities', *New Statesman*, 14 Jul 1945.

11   'for the eventual': For the complete document, see 'The Avalon Project: Documents in Law, History and Diplomacy (Yale Law School)': Avalon.law.yale.edu/20th_century/decade17.asp. See also William Shirer's discussion of the Potsdam communiqué: William L. Shirer, *End of a Berlin Diary* (Hamish Hamilton, 1947), pp. 95–8.

12   'Re-education' was the term used in both the British and US zones to characterise what Rebecca Boehling defines as all the plans 'intended to reverse the isolation the Nazis imposed on German cultural life and political consciousness and any authoritarian social and political hold over traditions from pre-1933 German history'. According to Boehling, re-education was to be achieved through 'indoctrination, licensing, and censorship of the means of mass communication as well as numerous measures to democratize the German education system and reorient various areas of German cultural life'. (Rebecca Boehling, 'The Role of Culture in American Relations with Europe: The Case of the United States's Occupation of Germany', *Diplomatic History*, 22:1 (1999), pp. 57–69). See also Michael Balfour, 'Re-education in Germany after 1945: Some Further Considerations', *German History*, 5:1 (1987), pp. 25–34 for reflections on re-education from a British perspective.

13   'since wars begin': UNESCO Constitution, signed 16 Nov 1945. For the full document, see UNESCO.ORG: portal.unesco.org/en/ev.php-URL_ID=15244&URL_DO=DO_TOPIC&URL_SECTION=201.html

14 'The Germans are not': Brigadier W. E. van Cutsem, 'The German Character', 9 March 1945, NA FO 371/46864, cited in Patricia Meehan, *A Strange Enemy People* (Peter Owen Publishers, 2001), p. 55.

15 For an excellent analysis of despair in, and in response to, Germany during this period see Werner Sollors, *The Temptation of Despair* (Harvard University Press, 2014). Focusing on a series of works of art produced in response to ruined Germany, Sollors portrays a country where both occupiers and occupied were caught in 'a strong undercurrent of melancholy and despair' (p. 3) and warns us against the danger of using hindsight to coopt late 1940s Germany into the hopeful story of the West German economic miracle. Similarly, William L. Hitchcock questions whether this can be seen as a period of 'liberation' in his book *Liberation: The Bitter Road to Freedom, Europe 1944–1945* (Faber & Faber, 2009).

16 Other works that could be added to this list include Hans Habe's *Walk in Darkness* (1948) and *Off Limits* (1955), Zelda Popkin's *Small Victory* (1947) and William Gardner Smith's *Last of the Conquerors* (1948), but these are beyond the scope of this book.

17 For a discussion of the concept of the 'zero hour' see Stephen Brockmann's introduction to his *German Literary Culture at the Zero Hour* (Boydell & Brewer, 2004).

18 'The victors who': Erich Kästner, Diary (rewritten for publication), 8 May 1945, cited in Sollors, *The Temptation of Despair*, p. 32.

1: *Crossing the Siegfried line*

1   'ARE YOU A': EH to MG, Feb/Mar 1944, cited in Carl Rollyson, *Beautiful Exile: The Life of Martha Gellhorn* (Aurum, 2000), p. 150.

2   Bernice Kert, *The Hemingway Women* (W. W. Norton & Company, 1986), p. 391.

3   See report by David Bruce in Jeffrey Meyers, *Hemingway: A Biography* (Harper and Row, 1985), pp. 406–07; also Antony Beevor, *Ardennes 1944: Hitler's Last Gamble* (Penguin, 2015), p. 49.

4   The Americans were more contented to let the Russians take Berlin; Roosevelt and Eisenhower were taken in by Stalin and his promises. See Antony Beevor, *Berlin: The Downfall, 1945* (Viking, 2002), pp. 194–95.

5   Stern, *The Hidden Damage*, p. 4.

6   LM, 'Paris, Its Joy. . . Its Spirit. . . Its Privations', *Vogue*, Oct 1944, in Penrose, *Lee Miller's War*.

7   'Go hang yourself': cited in Carlos Baker, *Ernest Hemingway: A Life Story* (Charles Scribner's Sons, 1969), p. 420.
    'committed as an': EH to Mary Welsh, 13 Sep 1944, EH Archive.

8   EH, 'War in the Siegfried Line: A grim story of how our infantry broke onto German soil', *Collier's*, 18 Nov 1944.

9   Statistics from Ian Buruma, *Year Zero: A History of 1945* (Penguin, 2013), p. 281.

10 Details of the ruined city based on LM, 'Germany – The War That is Won', *Vogue*, June 1945, in Penrose, *Lee Miller's War*. Miller visited Aachan in March, but the damage was still much the same as it had been in October.

11 'phantastically ruined': EM, 'Occupation – Trial or Error', Oct 1948, EM Archive.

12 On her American persona: EM to KM, 8 May 1945, EM Archive.
    'complete lack of': EM, 'Our Newest Problem: Germany', *Liberty*, 3 Feb 1945, EM Archive.

13 EM, 'Our Newest Problem: Germany'.

14 EM to KM, 15 Jan 1945, EM Archive.

15 KM's warnings: Andrea Weiss, *In the Shadow of the Magic Mountain: The Erika and Klaus Mann Story* (Chicago: University of Chicago Press, 2008), p. 73.
    'Jewish traitress': cited in Weiss, *In the Shadow*, p. 79.
    'flat-footed peace hyena': cited in KM, *The Turning Point: The Autobiography of Klaus Mann* (Serpent's Tail, 1987), p. 241.

16 A happy period for MD: see MD, *Marlene*, trans. Salvator Attansio (Avon Books, 1990), pp. 197–228.
    'You mean something': Barney Oldfield, cited in David Riva (ed.), *A Woman at War: Marlene Dietrich Remembered* (Painted Turtle, 2006), p. 68.
    'They'll shave off': Dietrich, *Marlene*, p. 200.
17 'You're brave', 'A whole philosophy': MG to Stanley Pennell, 8 or 9 May 1931, in *The Letters of Martha Gellhorn*, ed. Caroline Moorehead (Chatto & Windus, 2006).
    On her feelings following Spain, MG wrote to Bill and Annie Davis in Jun 1942: 'Spain was a place where you could hope, and Spain was also like a vaccination which could save the rest of mankind from the same fearful suffering. But no one important cared. So the hope was killed . . . after Spain, I at least felt such bitterness at how the world was run that I wanted no part of it in any way . . . But if you have no part in the world, no matter how diseased the world is, you are dead' (*The Letters of Martha Gellhorn*).
18 'I can resign', 'Good is my': MG to Hortense Flexner, 22 Sep 1941, in *The Letters of Martha Gellhorn*. On her compulsion to run away, see MG to Stanley Pennell, 19 May 1931: 'There is too much space in the world. I am bewildered by it, and mad with it. And this urge to run away from what I love is a sort of sadism I no longer pretend to understand' (*The Letters of Martha Gellhorn*).
    'a life with', 'and let them': MG to Hortense Flexner, 22 Sep 1941, in *The Letters of Martha Gellhorn*.
19 'badly dressed': MG to EH, 28 Jun 1943, MG Archive.
    'I am so free': MG to Allen Grover, 2 Nov 1944, MG Archive.
20 MG, 'Cracking the Gothic Line', *Collier's*, 28 Oct 1944.
21 'Home is something': MG to Edna Gellhorn, 14 Nov 1944, MG Archive.
    'It is impossible': MG, 'By Radio From Paris', *Collier's*, 4 Nov 1944.
    'make an angry': MG to Eleanor Roosevelt, 5 Feb 1939, MG Archive.
22 'like a package': cited in Caroline Moorehead, *Martha Gellhorn: A Life* (Vintage, 2004), p. 278.
    'what I had guessed': cited in Moorehead, *Martha Gellhorn*, p. 280.
    'wham bam': MG to Betsy Drake, 13 Sep 1983, MG Archive. For years Gellhorn had been embarrassed about her own lack of receptivity in bed. In 1934 at the end of a long relationship with a married man, Bertrand Jouvenel, she apologised for failing to satisfy her lover. Because she had scandalised the world by engaging in a public affair with a married man, people assumed that she was driven by sexual fervour: 'it must be thought, she is a woman of great passion – with the needs of the body clamouring', she wrote to Campbell Beckett, 29 Apr 1934 (*The Letters of Martha Gellhorn*). In fact she was unable to return his desire and had disappointed him with her lack of orgasms.
23 MG, 'Rough and Tumble', *Collier's*, 2 Dec 1944.
24 MG, 'Death of a Dutch Town', *Collier's*, 23 Dec 1944.
25 'much smitten', 'a reddish blonde': Chester B. Hansen, diary, 28 Dec 1944, (Chester B. Hansen Collection, United States Army Military History Institute, Carlisle, Pennsylvania, courtesy of Antony Beevor).
    'her elegant hair': Bill Walton to Bernice Kert, April 1980, cited in Kert, *The Hemingway Women*, p. 415.
    'You can't hunt': cited in Rollyson, *Beautiful Exile*, p. 162.
26 'I wasn't meant': MG to Bertrand de Jouvenel, undated 1932, in *The Letters of Martha Gellhorn*.
    'We want some': EH to Patrick Hemingway, 19 November 1944, in EH, *Selected Letters, 1917–1961*, ed. by Carlos Baker (Granada, 1981).

2: *Advance into Germany*

1   Statistics from Richard Bessel, *Germany 1945: from War to Peace* (Simon & Schuster, 2009), p. 11 (450,000), and Hitchcock, *Liberation*, p. 165 (250,000).

2 'He seemed distant': MD to Rudi Sieber, in Maria Riva, *Marlene Dietrich* (Bloomsbury, 1992), p. 556. See also MD, *Marlene*, p. 213.

3 'Yes, yes, but The Blue Angel': see MD, *Marlene*, p. 218, and Riva, *Marlene Dietrich*, p. 556.

4 De Gaulle had been demanding a separate zone of occupation for France since October 1944, wanting control of the Rhineland in particular. According to Georges Bidault, the French foreign minister, if the French did not play a major role in the war after the liberation, 'the Germans will not look on them as conquerors'. Churchill and Roosevelt were prepared to grant France a zone but Stalin was not; as a result the French zone was carved out of the British and US zones that had been previously agreed (MacDonogh, *After the Reich*, pp. 10–11).

5 'only when Nazism': Report of the Crimea (Yalta) Conference, 4–11 Feb 1945, in *Documents on Germany under Occupation, 1945–1954*, ed. Beata Ruhm von Oppen, (Oxford University Press, 1955), pp. 4–6.

6 'I dislike making': cited in Hitchcock, *Liberation*, p. 170.

7 'good German', 'the better a German', 'race of hooligans', 'a breed which': Robert Vansittart, *Black Record: Germans Past and Present* (Hamish Hamilton, 1941), pp. 12, 16.
'in the most deadly manner': Churchill to the House of Commons, 21 Sep 1943, cited in Bessel, *Germany 1945*, p. 285.
For hatred of Hitler and Nazism amongst the Allies, see Richard Overy, *Why The Allies Won* (Jonathan Cape, 1995), pp. 286–9.

8 'That unfortunately': cited in Hitchcock, *Liberation*, p. 171.

9 'If we concentrate', 'I confess that': Victor Gollancz, *Shall our Children Live or Die: A Reply to Lord Vansittart on the German Problem* (Victor Gollancz, 1942), pp. 23, 49.

10 'Propaganda and Publicity to Germany' (a joint PWE and BBC paper on German Re-Occupation), Jan 1944, NA PRO FO 898/370.

11 'grotesque and naked': Lieut. Col. H. V. Dicks, 'Germany after the War: a resumé with commentary', February 1945, NA FD 1/6046, cited in Jessica Reinisch, *Public Health in Germany* (thesis, 2005), p. 68.

12 See, Richard M. Brickner, *Is Germany Incurable?*, (J.B. Lippincott, 1943).'democratic character structure', 'freedom's own children': Margaret Mead, *And Keep Your Powder Dry: An Anthropologist Looks at America* (William Morrow, 1942), pp. 261, 26.

13 For a helpful definition of 'culture' and explanation of its etymological roots, see Raymond Williams, *Keywords: A Vocabulary of Culture and Society* (Fontana, 1976). Describing culture as one of the 'two or three most complicated words in the English language,' Williams suggested that there were currently three main active categories of usage: i) as a noun referring to a 'general process of intellectual, spiritual and aesthetic development', ii) as a noun referring to 'a particular way of life, whether of a people, a period, or a group', iii) as a noun referring to 'the works and practices of intellectual and especially artistic activity – this is now the most widespread use – culture is music, literature, painting and sculpture, theatre and film. A ministry of culture refers to these activities – with the addition sometimes of philosophy, scholarship, history'. For Williams the overlap between usages reflects 'a complex argument about the relations between general human development and a particular way of life, and between both the works and practices of art and intelligence'. In Williams's explanation the German '*Kultur*' shared the multiple means of 'culture' (while the French '*culture*' and Italian '*cultura*' were more likely to refer just to art and learning or to a general process of human development, rather than to culture as a way of life). In fact the German '*Kultur*' was more exclusively artistic than its British or American equivalent. For a fuller discussion of this difference see Jessica C. E. Gienow-Hecht, 'Art is Democracy and Democracy is Art: Culture, Propaganda, and the *Neue Zeitung* in Germany, 1944–1947', *Diplomatic History* 23:1 (1999), pp. 21–43.

14 'decent life', 'the comity of nations': For the Yalta Conference report, see http://www .germanhistorydocs.ghi-dc.org/pdf/eng/Allied%20Policies%203_ENG.pdf

15   Draft German armistice, February 1944, NA FO 898/409.

16   'reorienting and re-educating', 'an act of political warfare': The Committee to
      Re-educate the Axis Powers, 'The Re-education of Germany' (1944), cited in Jennifer
      Fay, *Theaters of Occupation: Hollywood and the Reeducation of Postwar Germany*
      (University of Minnesota Press, 2008) p. 32.
      'recognise the power': Archibald MacLeish, 'The Strongest and the Most Enduring
      Weapons', *Publisher's Weekly*, 1810, 16 May 1942.
      'greater influence', 'mold public': OMGUS/ICD, 'History of the Information
      Control Division', no. 33, 8 May 1945–30 Jun 1946 (NARA). For more information
      about this campaign see John B. Hench, *Books as Weapons: Propaganda, Publishing
      and the Battle for Global Markets in the Era of World War II* (Cornell University Press,
      2010). The belief in the influence of books in Germany was based chiefly on the fact
      that the ratio of books per person in prewar Germany was one of the highest in the
      world and in 1938 there were twice as many books published in Germany as in the
      US (see OMGUS, 'Functional Report Information Control,' no. 42, 20 Dec 1948,
      NARA).

17   For Yalta conference report: http://www.germanhistorydocs.ghi-dc.org/pdf/eng/
      Allied%20Policies%203_ENG.pdf

18   'Fires were still burning': Victor Klemperer, Diary, 22–24 Feb 1945, in *To The Bitter
      End: The Diaries of Victor Klemperer 1942–1945* (Weidenfeld and Nicolson,1999).
      Information on Dresden drawn from Richard Overy, *The Bombing War: Europe 1939–
      1945* (Allen Lane, 2013), pp. 394–96.
      'every fighter is': cited in Bessel, *Germany 1945*, p. 18.

19   MG, quoted in 'The Week's Work' by Amy Porter, *Collier's*, 3 Feb 1945.

20   'I have always': James Gavin to MG, 16 Apr 1945, MG Archive.
      'and a blacker', 'first girl': MG, 'Night Life in the Sky', *Collier's*, 17 Mar 1945.

21   LM, 'Through the Alsace Campaign', *Vogue*, April 1945, in Penrose, *Lee Miller's
      War*.

22   LM, 'Germany – the War that is Won', *Vogue*, Jun 1945, in Penrose, *Lee Miller's
      War*.

23   For Cologne see Overy, *The Bombing War*, pp. 474, 638.
      For the gash like a wound, see Stig Dagerman, *German Autumn*, trans. by Robin
      Fulton MacPherson, (University of Minnesota Press, 2011, first published in Swedish
      in 1947), p. 20.

24   GO, 'As I Please', *Tribune*, 12 Jan 1945.

25   For the figures for the US zone see Hitchcock, *Liberation*, p. 249.
      '2 Million Displaced Persons': Ben Shephard, *The Long Road Home: The Aftermath of
      the Second World War* (Bodley Head, 2010), p. 62.
      'Orwell was distressed': GO, 'Uncertain Fate of Displaced Persons', *Observer*, 10 Jun
      1945.

26   'I want to go back': GO to Dwight Macdonald, 4 Apr 1945, cited in Michael Shelden,
      Orwell: The Authorised Biography (William Heinemann, 1991), p. 420.

27   GO, 'Future of a Ruined Germany', *Observer*, 8 Apr 1945.

28   Figures from Bessel, *Germany 1945*, p. 104.

29   'A girl's been': Alexander Solzhenitsyn, 'Prussian Nights', trans. by Robert Conquest,
      cited in MacDonogh, *After the Reich*, p. 48.

30   James Gavin to MG, 16 Apr 1945, MG Archive.

3: *Victory*

1   General Patton's response at Ohrdruf: Hitchcock, *Liberation*, p. 295. On conditions
      at Buchenwald: Hitchcock, *Liberation*, p. 297.
      'I picked my way': report by Richard Dimbleby for the BBC, cited in Juliet Gardiner,
      Wartime: Britain 1939–1945 (London: Headline, 2005), p. 674.

2   The existence of the concentration camps was reported almost immediately after Dachau's founding in March 1933, however, the reports failed explicitly to state what was happening there or speculate upon why. As Tony Kuschner and Katharine Knox observe in *Refugees in an Age of Genocide: Global, National and Local Perspectives during the Twentieth Century* (Frank Cass, 1999): 'The detail provided was rarely accompanied by editorial comment. Moreover, the absence, or, at best, ambiguity of analysis was accompanied by a tendency to open up the possibility, in the name of "objective" reporting, that the Nazis might be justified in claiming that anti-Jewish atrocities were exaggerated. [. . .] Nazi antisemitism in the 1930s was framed within a discourse of "atrocities" which might or might not be true,' (pp. 150–51). In early April 1933, in an article entitled 'Nazis Herd Enemies Behind Barbed Wire In Big Prison Camps', *The New York Times* noted 'wholesale arrests of the Nazis' political opponents' in numbers presumed to 'run well into the thousands' (8 Apr 1933). Though the phrase 'barbed wire' appeared four times, the *NYT* wrote of the camp at Heuberg – whose population was 'mostly intellectuals, who chafe under the monotony of manual labor' – that '[t]he food [. . .] is plentiful and good, although simple' and 'the first impression might be that of a large farming community'. That July, *The Times's* special correspondent paid a visit to Dachau: home to 'saboteurs and killjoys', where 'the barracks were as clean as a whistle', 'good work is rewarded by an additional allotment of bread', and 'camp life has settled into the organized routine of any penal institution[. . .]. It is somewhat boring but not much different from regular army life,' ('*Times* Writer Visits Reich Prison Camp', 26 Jul 1933). It was a benign article with only a few discordant notes, namely, that '[u]nder a smiling sky, there was not a smile in the 2,000'. The Western Allies had also heard about the situation at Auschwitz from Polish resistance fighters from 1942, but initially tended not to take what they heard seriously. See David S. Wyman, *The Abandonment of the Jews: America and the Holocaust, 1941–1945* (New Press, 2007).

3   The Nazis built concentration camps from 1933. A small number of these early camps served as a blueprint for the later system: Dachau, Oranienburg-Columbiahaus (Berlin), Esterwegen (Emsland), Sachsenburg (Thuringia), and Lichtenburg on the Elbe. Theodor Eicke (a man with a reputation for violence and questionable sanity) had jurisdiction over these camps, and was responsible for drawing up regulations which remained central to Nazi camp organisation. Hitler supported Eicke's vision, and in June 1936 officially sanctioned the rule of the SS within camps. From 1936, as Germany's priorities shifted towards rearmament, new camps were established. Sachsenhausen and Buchenwald were completed in 1938. The punishment camp of Mauthausen, which provided labour for work in stone quarries, and the women's camp at Ravensbrück were both completed in 1939. War itself served to vastly extend the camp system across occupied Europe, with twenty main camps and 165 sub-camps in existence by 1944. So too, war heralded a darker evolution: some labour camps, already lethal, took on the further function of 'killing factories'. The camp at Natzweiler, for example, was established in 1940 for the purpose of mining granite deposits; it also served as the site of secret executions. In the case of Auschwitz-Birkenau (also established in 1940), half the camp was dedicated to the provision of slave labour (including work in a gravel pit and the building of a factory), whilst the other half was turned over to killing. The first murders by Zyklon B (of Communist Soviet prisoners) were carried out in September 1941; 1942–43 saw the enlargement of the killing facilities at Auschwitz, and the large scale transportation of Jews to the camp; selection processes upon arrival determined who was to work, and who die. Other camps that functioned in part or wholly as extermination facilities were Chelmno, Belzec, Treblinka, Maidanek, Sobibor, Riga and Maly-Trostenets. For a more detailed account of the development of the Nazi camp system, see Richard Overy, *The Dictators: Hitler's Germany and Stalin's Russia* (Penguin, 2004), pp. 599–608.

4   This account is based upon reports in *Stars and Stripes*, 2 May 1945 and *The New York Times*, 30 Apr 1945. See Bessel, *Germany 1945*, p. 162 and Hitchcock, *Liberation*, pp. 303–05.

5   'mobbed, kissed': Peter Furst, 'Dachau Cheers its Liberation from Horror of Living Death', *Stars and Stripes*, 2 May 1945.

6   'Nobody seemed': LM, 'Germany – the War that is Won', *Vogue*, June 1945, in Penrose, *Lee Miller's War*.

7   'feet which ached': LM to Audrey Withers, undated service message, in Penrose, *Lee Miller's War*.

8   'less fabulous': LM to Audrey Withers, undated service message, in Penrose, *Lee Miller's War*.

9   Paul Celan, 'Death Fugue' ('*Todesfuge*'), trans. by Christopher Middleton, in *Modern German Poetry, 1910–1960*, ed. by Michael Hamburger and Christopher Middleton (London: Mcgibbon and Lee, 1966), pp. 318–21.

10   See Michael T. Booth and Duncan Spencer, *Paratrooper: the Life of General James M. McGavin* (Oxford: Casemate, 1994), p. 292.

11   'I did not know': MG to Hortense Flexner, cited in Moorehead, *Martha Gellhorn*, p. 283.
'It is as if': cited in Moorehead, *Martha Gellhorn*, p. 284.
'No expression', 'We were blind': MG, 'Dachau: Experimental Murder', *Collier's*, 23 Jun 1945.

12   See Beevor, *Berlin*, pp. 398–400.

13   See Bessel, *Germany 1945*, pp. 180–82. In Tübingen on 23 April the French demanded that the French medical officers hand over the surgical clinic together with all its medical instruments. All the patients, including the seriously ill and those who had just undergone operations, were removed.

14   'to make her': cited in Bach, *Marlene Dietrich*, p. 303.

15   'The railway': LM, 'Germany – the War that is Won', *Vogue*, Jun 1945, in Penrose, *Lee Miller's War*.

16   'It is to': GO, 'Bavarian Peasants Ignore the War – Germans Know They are Beaten', *Observer*, 22 Apr 1945.
'veritable hotbed': MG, 'We were never Nazis!', *Collier's*, 26 May 1945. For a discussion of the lack of collective guilt explored from the perspective of the remaining and returning German Jews, see Grossmann, *Jews, Germans and Allies: Close Encounters in Occupied Germany* (Princeton University Press, 2007), pp. 39–46.

17   MG, 'We were never Nazis!'

18   'Kaiser of all': cited in Brockmann, *German Literary Culture*, p. 91.

19   For a discussion of the term 'inner emigrant' see Brockmann, *German Literary Culture*, pp. 95–100.

20   'in spite of everything', 'something deeply significant', 'no calamity': TM, diary, 10 Apr 1933, in TM, *Diaries, 1918–1939*, trans. Richard and Clara Winston (Harry N. Abrams, 1982).

21   'German Revolution': TM to Albert Einstein, 15 May 1933, in TM, *Briefe*, 3 vols, ed. Erika Mann (S. Fischer Verlag, 1961–1965), vol 1, p. 332.
'What does the history': TM to Karl Kerenyi, 4 August 1934, cited in Ronald Hayman, *Thomas Mann: A Biography* (Bloomsbury, 1996), p. 413.

22   'This friendly time': EM to TM, 19 Jan 1936, in EM, *Briefe und Antworten*, vol 1, ed. by Anna Zanco Prestel (Edition Spangenberg, 1985), cited in Weiss, *In the Shadow*, p. 123.
'against Europe': open letter from TM to Eduard Korrodi, 3 Feb 1936, cited in Hayman, *Thomas Mann*, p. 424. This was followed by an open letter to the Dean of the University of Bonn after he had removed Mann's honorary degree later that year where he denounced National Socialist Germany as 'spiritually ruined and physically drained by the war preparations with which it threatens the whole world . . . loved by no-one', TM to the Dean of the Philosophical Faculty of Bonn, 1 Jan 1937, in Thomas Mann, *Gesammelte Werke*, 13 Bände, Band 12 (Fischer, 1974).

23   'enhance our modesty': TM, 'German Listeners!', 10 May 1945, in *Deutsche Hörer: Radiosendungen nach Deutschland aus den Jahren 1940–1945* (Fischer, 2004).

24 On Golo Mann's early war experiences, see Peter Demetz's introduction to Golo Mann's *Reminiscences and Reflections* (Norton, 1990), pp. ix-xiii.
25 'We German refugees': KM, 'An American Soldier Revisiting his Former Homeland' for Radio Stockholme, 30 Dec 1947, KM Archive.
26 'Do you want': KM, speech delivered at Co. 'C', 363rd Inf. Rgt., 91 Division, 8 Jan 1945, KM Archive.
27 'It's an eternal': KM to EM, 13 Jun 1945, KM Archive.
28 KM describes Frank Wedekind as 'the D. H. Lawrence of Germany' in *The Turning Point*, p. 93.
29 'a neurotic quartet': KM, *The Turning Point*, p. 107.
30 For Gründgens on KM as a poet see Weiss, *In the Shadow*, p. 49.
31 'Don't take': EM to KM, 22 Mar 1937, EM Archive.
32 'deep roots in': EM and KM, *The Other Germany*, trans. by Heinz Norden (Modern Age Books, 1940), p. 21.
    'leave behind': EM interview 1963, cited in Weiss, *In the Shadow*, p. 168; 'a new forum': KM editorial in *Decision,* Jan 1941, cited in Weiss, *In the Shadow*, p. 167.
33 'the last haven': KM editorial in *Decision,* Jan 1941.
34 For KM's debates with Auden and Isherwood about Nazism see Weiss, *In the Shadow*, p. 163.
35 'speaking in my': TM to EM, cited in Weiss, *In the Shadow*, p. 142.
36 'You should be': EM to KM, 24 Feb 1945, EM Archive.
    'little old ', 'needless to': EM to KM, 8 May 1945, EM Archive.
37 KM, 'An American Soldier Revisiting his Former Homeland' for Radio Stockholme, 30 Dec 1947, KM Archive. Statistics from Irmtraud Permooser, *Der Luftkrieg über München 1942–1945: Bomben auf die Hauptstadt der Bewegung* (Aviatic, 1997), pp. 372–75.
38 'They didn't do it': KM, 'An American Soldier'.
39 'when the Dictator': TM, 'A Family Against Dictatorship', cited in Weiss, *In The Shadow*, p. 208.
    'the German people': KM, 'The Job Ahead in Germany', *Stars and Stripes*, 13 May 1945.
    'Hardly ever did': KM, 'An American Soldier'.
40 'I don't want to excuse myself': KM to Thomas Quinn Curtiss, undated, KM Archive.
    'Magician-Dad', 'Conditions here', 'morally mutilated': KM to TM, 16 May 1945, in KM, *Briefe und Antworten 1937–1945*, vol 2, ed. by Martin Gregor-Dellin (Heinrich Ellermanm, 1975).
41 This is a selective view of German Romanticism: many of the German Romantics had been radically politically engaged, as least in their early years, following the French Revolution. But it was the more inward, later Romanticism that had influenced Mann.
42 Johann Wolfgang von Goethe, *The Sorrows of Young Werther*, trans. by R. D. Boylan (Mondial, 2006), p. 97.
43 'two Germanys': TM, speech, 29 May 1945, in *Thomas Mann's Addresses Delivered at the Library of Congress, 1942–1949* (Library of Congress, 1963), p. 64.
44 For the difference between *Kultur* and *Zivilisation* see EM and KM, *The Other Germany,* p. 71.
    'Progress, revolution': TM's 'Reflections of a Nonpolitical Man,' 1918, cited in Mark W. Clark, *Beyond Catastrophe: German Intellectuals and Cultural Renewal after World War II, 1945–1955* (Lexington Books, 2006), p. 86.
    'civilising, rationalising': TM, 1919, cited in Clark, *Beyond Catastrophe*, p. 87.
45 For a fuller discussion of these ideas, see Clark, *Beyond Catastrophe*, and Wolf Lepenies, *The Seduction of Culture in German History* (Princeton University Press, 2006).

46   See TM's lecture 'On the German Republic', 1922, reprinted in *The Weimar Republic Sourcebook*, ed. by Anton Kaes, Martin Jay, and Edward Dimendberg (University of California Press, 1994), pp. 105–06.

47   For a discussion of the aestheticisation of politics in Germany in the interwar period, see Walter Benjamin, 'The Work of Art in the Age of Mechanical Reproduction', 1936, in *Illuminations*, ed. by Hannah Arendt, trans. by Harry Zohn (Jonathan Cape, 1970), pp. 219–54.

48   'fanatical', 'ruthless', 'escape responsibility', 'a defeated enemy': Directive JCS 1067 to the Commander in Chief of U.S. forces in Germany, April 1945, http://germanhistorydocs.ghi-dc.org/sub_document.cfm?document_id=2297

49   'a good clean fight', 'Oh, well': broadcast to US soldiers on the Armed Forces Radio Service, Mar 1945, cited in Hitchcock, *Liberation*, p. 182.
     'mighty pretty', 'You are not': *Your Job in Germany*, dir. by Frank Capra (1944), cited in Nicholas Pronay and Keith Wilson (ed.), *The Political Re-education of Germany and her Allies after World War II* (Croom Helm, 1985) pp. 200–01.
     'There are only': Brigadier W. E. van Cutsem, 'The German Character', cited in Meehan, *A Strange Enemy People*, p. 55.

50   'Defeat and occupation': Richard Crossman, 'Guilt and Non-Fraternisation', *New Statesman*, 21 Apr 1945.

51   'very austere'; 'We are not': '"Austere" Press, Radio Is Planned for Germany', *The New York Times*, 3 May 1945.

4: *Occupation*

1   'Do you think': SS to Julian Huxley, 4 Dec 1944, cited in John Sutherland, *Stephen Spender: The Authorized Biography* (Penguin, 2005), p. 299.

2   'political mission': John Lehmann, 'In Daylight', Jun 1945, in *New Writing and Daylight*, Sep 1945, p. 13. On SS's articles about German literature, see for example 'Hölderlin, Goethe and Germany', *Horizon*, Oct 1943, where he praises Goethe in particular as writing 'world literature', influenced by English literature (particularly Shakespeare) and influencing English literature in his turn.

3   'the highest respect': Curt Riess, 'We Must Win Another Battle in Germany; That battle is re-education of the people and there are no short cuts to victory', *The New York Times*, 20 May 1945.

4   'My dear': cited in Humphrey Carpenter, *W. H. Auden: A Biography* (OUP, 1992), p. 333.

5   This is taken from James Stern's account of his arrival in Frankfurt in *The Hidden Damage*, p. 83.

6   'Of course it matters': cited in Carpenter, *W. H. Auden*, pp. 256–57.
     On Auden's pacifism, see Carpenter, *W. H. Auden*, pp. 270–71.

7   'a tempestuous ocean': Stern, *The Hidden Damage*, p. 94.

8   'We heard that': Stern, *The Hidden Damage*, pp. 131, 139.

9   'dumb, expressionless', 'so colossal'; 'What do you say': Stern, *The Hidden Damage*, pp. 81, 230.

10   Stern, *The Hidden Damage*, p. 77.

11   Stern, *The Hidden Damage*, pp. 167, 97.

12   'The people . . .': WHA to Tania Stern, cited in Carpenter, *W. H. Auden*, p. 335.
     'It is illiterate and absurd': WHA, cited in Carpenter, *W. H. Auden*, p. 334.
     'We went into a city': WHA, unpublished interview for *Time* by T. G. Foote, 1963, cited in Carpenter, *WH Auden*, p. 335.

13   For the allocation of zones see MacDonogh, *After the Reich*, introduction (pp. 1–24).

14   'the most robust': cited in Bessel, *Germany 1945*, p. 288.

15   'The Army strongly': Peter Lisagor and Pat Mitchell, 'Still a Ban on Fraternizing, but Prophylaxis is Available', *Stars and Stripes*, 7 Jun 1945.

16 For the Hamburg raid see Overy, *The Bombing War*, pp. 334, 336. For the quotations from Sybil Thorndike's letters to her husband, Lewis, see Jonathan Croall, *Sybil Thorndike: A Star of Life*, (Haus, 2008), pp. 345–46.

17 For Thorndike's letters to Lewis see Croall, *Sybil Thorndike*, pp. 348–49.

18 Mervyn Peake, 'The Consumptive, Belsen 1945', in *The Glassblowers: A Collection of Poems* (Eyre and Spottiswoode, 1950).

19 'the reasons which': Mervyn Peake to Maeve Peake, cited in Tom Pocock, *The Dawn Came Up* (Collins, 1983), p. 128.
    'He was quieter': interview with Maeve Peake, cited in Pocock, *The Dawn Came Up*, p. 146.

20 'the way of living': Brigadier-General Robert McClure to Colonel Kehm and Colonel William Paley, 19 Feb 1945, NARA RG 331, cited in Kay Gladstone, 'Separate Intentions: The Allied Screenings of Concentration Camp Documentaries in Defeated Germany in 1945–46 in Toby Haggith and Joanna Newman (eds.), *Holocaust and the Moving Image: Representations in Film and Television since 1933*, pp. 50–64, p. 51.
    'By reminding': Bernstein, cited in Gladstone, 'Separate Intentions', p. 54.

21 'There was an': BW, "Billy, How Did You Do It?": Billy Wilder in Conversation with Volker Schlöndorff, *Arena* series, BBC TV, 1988, cited in Ed Sikov, *On Sunset Boulevard: The Life and Times of Billy Wilder* (Hyperion, 1998), p. 237.

22 'When the title': Report by BW and Davidson Taylor following a screening of *KZ* in 400 person theatre in Erlangen on 25 Jun 1945, cited in Gladstone, 'Separate Intentions', p. 60.

23 'so colossal': Stern, *The Hidden Damage*, p. 129.

24 On the reputation of the BCCG see Meehan, *A Strange Enemy People*, p. 53.
    'Not one of the': Richard Crossman, 'A Voice from Berlin', *New Statesman and Nation*, 9 Jun 1945.

25 See George Clare, *Berlin Days* (Papermac, 1994), pp. 61–6, and Wolfgang Schivelbusch, *In a Cold Crater: Cultural and Intellectual Life in Berlin, 1945–1948*, trans. by Kelly Barry (University of California Press, 1998), p. 34.

26 See Schivelbusch, *In a Cold Crater*, p. 35. Schivelbush also endorses Werner Hahn's view that Stalinist culture under Zhdanov was in fact less dogmatic than it seemed. According to Hahn, 'cultural politics under Stalinism were not actually cultural politics, but a politics that availed itself of culture as a strategic means, being otherwise completely disinterested in its contents and forms. Culture was attacked and took the blow' (Werner G. Hahn, *Postwar Soviet Politics: The Fall of Zhdanov and the Defeat of Moderation, 1946–1953*, Cornell University Press, 1982). See also David Pike, *The Politics of Culture in Soviet-occupied Germany 1945–1949* (Stanford University Press, 1992).

27 These remarks by WHA quoted in Nicolas Nabokov, *Bagazh: Memoirs of a Russian Cosmopolitan* (Atheneum, 1975), pp. 220–21.

28 'Now about': cited in Nabokov, *Bagazh*, p. 225.

29 'As for': cited in Nabokov, *Bagazh*, p. 225.

30 WHA, 'Memorial for the City', in *Collected Poems of W. H. Auden*, ed. by Edward Mendelson (Faber, 1976).

31 'a large sprawling': SS, *European Witness: Impressions of Germany in 1945* (Hamish Hamilton, 1946), p. 9.

32 'It was rather': Goronwy Rees, *A Bundle of Sensations: Sketches in Autobiography* (Chatto & Windus, 1960), p. 174.

33 Rees tells Spender what he has seen: Rees, *A Bundle of Sensations*, pp. 183–84. Spender reports this conversation in *European Witness*, p. 15.

34 'It is a climax': SS, *European Witness*, pp. 23–24.

35 'German swine', 'You calculate the rations': SS, *European Witness*, pp. 33, 35.

36 'unchanged': KM to Katia Mann, 1 Jul 1945, KM Archive.
    'because he saw': SS, 'September Journal', *Horizon*, Oct 1939.

37   'an Apollonian Germany': SS, 'September Journal'.
38   You seemed to': Curtius, quoted in SS, 'Rhineland Journal', *Horizon*, Dec 1945.
39   For the Allies' treatment of the Jews in Germany, see Grossman, *Jews, Germans and Allies*.
40   'We can understand': SS, 'Rhineland Journal', *Horizon*, Dec 1945.
41   Officers tell him they sympathised with Nazis: SS, *European Witness*, p. 73.
     'a kind of ideological': Dagerman, *German Autumn*, p. 66.
42   For the questionnaires, see MacDonogh, *After the Reich*, p. 345. On the intoxicating of applicants, see Harold D. Hurwitz, *Die Stunde Null der deutschen Presse: Die amerikanische Pressepolitik in Deutschland 1945–1949* (Verlag Wissenschaft und Politik, 1972), p. 38. Once drunk, applicants were also required to write essays.
43   SS, *European Witness*, p. 97.
44   In October 1928, in 'Die geistige Internationale' ('The International Spirit'), Curtius reflected on the ten years since the end of the First World War and stated hopefully that 'a consciousness of a European community spirit is blossoming, which comes from the experience of joint hardship' (E. R. Curtius, 'Die geistige Internationale', *Die Böttcherstrasse*, October 1928).

5: *Berlin, July–October 1945*

1   'one of the', 'a kind of lunar': EM, 'Das befreite Berlin', Jul/Aug 1945, in *Blitze überm Ozean: Aufsätze, Reden, Reportagen,* ed. by Irmela von der Lühe (Rowohlt Tb Verlag, 2001).
2   PdeM to HS, 15 Jul 1945, PdeM Archive.
3   'band of thieves': PdeM to HS, Jun 1944, PdeM Archive.
4   'Sodom and Gomorrah': KM, *The Turning Point*, p. 86.
5   Special performance of *Der Parasit*: 'Berliner Bühnen', *Berliner Zeitung*, 14 Jul 1945.
6   'To the left and right': PdeM to HS, 15 Jul 1945, PdeM Archive.
7   'Justice!', play closes: Rees, *A Bundle of Sensations*, p. 192.
8   'not go any further': PdeM to HS, Jul 1945, PdeM Archive
9   'wonderful to be back', 'boiling along': James Gavin to MG, 5 Jul 1945, MG Archive. 'Darling everything I do': Gavin to MG, 1 Aug 1945, MG Archive; 'ships-that-pass': Gavin to MG, 10 Jul 1945, MG Archive.
10   On the extent of the material destruction, see Curt Riess, *The Berlin Story* (Frederick Muller, 1953), p. 38. For conditions in the city generally, see MacDonogh, *After the Reich*: disease (p. 98); deaths from typhus (p. 113); death rate in city (p.118); removal of cows (p.111).
     For estimates of the number of women raped in Germany, see Grossmann, *Jews, Germans and Allies*, p. 49.
11   'Well the town', 'even the telephones': Gavin to MG, 8 Aug 1945, MG Archive. On Soviet deaths, see Hitchcock, *Liberation*, p. 131.
12   'Mami, you suffered': telephone conversation between MD and her mother, in Riva, *A Woman at War*, p. 85.'PLEASANT VISIT': Gavin to MD, 30 Aug 1945, MD Archive.
13   Report on the Potsdam Conference, Jul–Aug 1945: http://germanhistorydocs.ghi-dc .org/docpage.cfm?docpage_id=2976.
14   'The German people': 'Die Ergebnisse der Berliner Konferenz', *Berliner Zeitung*, 4 Aug 1945.
     Day-to-day survival: see Riess, *The Berlin Story*, pp. 36–37.
     For Brecht applause, see Ruth Andreas-Friedrich, *Battleground Berlin: Diaries, 1945– 1948*, trans. by Anna Boerresen (Paragon House, 1990), p. 82.
     For reconstruction, see Ian Buruma, *Year Zero: A History of 1945* (Penguin, 2013), p. 283.
15   'stop fooling around': KM to Hermann Kesten, 11 Aug 1945, in KM, *Briefe und Antworten*.
     'at once *unconquerable*', 'not for general': GO, 'You and the Atomic Bomb', *Tribune*, 19 Oct 1945.

16   'the excitement of it': Gavin to MG, 15 Aug 1945, MG Archive.
17   'I feel like a small boy': Gavin to MG, 30 Aug 1945, MG Archive.
      'When a train': Gavin to MG, 23 Aug 1945, MG Archive.
18   'it looked like the end': BW speaking to cameraman in plane over Berlin, cited in
      Sikov, *On Sunset Boulevard*, p. 244.
19   Sikov, *On Sunset Boulevard*, p. 246.
20   'The gentlemen who': Memorandum written by BW, cited in Sikov, *On Sunset
      Boulevard*, p. 246.
21   'I found the town mad', 'A good job', 'Now *if* there': BW, Memorandum for the
      United States Information Control Division on the subject of 'Propaganda through
      Entertainment', 16 Aug 1945, in Ralph Willett, *The Americanization of Germany,
      1945–1949* (Routledge, 1988), pp. 42, 40.
22   'Let us give', 'I want him', 'three cigarette': BW, 'Propaganda through Entertainment'.
23   When the Supreme Allied Headquarters was dissolved on 13 Jul 1945 PWD's opera-
      tions ceased and its operations were taken over by the British Information Services
      Control Branch and the US Information Control Division (ICD) and Information
      Control Service (ICS). McClure was now chief of both ICD and ICS. Most of the
      personnel remained the same. See http://www.erwinslist.com/Files/History%20I.
      pdf
24   'very austere': 'Austere Press, Radio is Planned for Germany', *The New York Times*,
      3 May 1945.
25   On the topic of rations, see Schivelbusch, *In a Cold Crater*, p.42.
      Treber, *Mythos Trümmerfrauen*, p. 217.
26   For a longer elucidation of this argument, see Schivelbusch, *In a Cold Crater*, p. 81.
27   'true German': Statement of the *Kulturband zur demokratischen Erneuerung Deutschlands*,
      cited in Erica Carter's 'Culture, History and the National Identity in the Two Germanies
      since 1945', in Mary Fulbrook (ed.), *German History since 1800*, p. 438. On British and
      American suspicions, see Schivelbusch, *In a Cold Crater*, p. 52.
28   'private emotions', 'why not': Paul Rilla, 'Eine kleine Stadt: Thornton Wilders
      Schauspiel im Deutschen Theater', *Berliner Zeitung*, 7 Aug 1945.
      'You knew that': Nicolas Nabokov, *Old Friends and New Music* (Hamish Hamilton,
      1951), p. 261.
29   'Berlin was only', 'establish good': Nabokov, *Old Friends and New Music*,
      pp. 262–63.
30   '887,000 very hungry': Gavin to MG, Aug 1945, MG Archive.
31   For a discussion of the contradictions implicit within the shared governing of
      Germany and of the different attitudes of the four powers towards reparations
      (troubling Gavin above), see Hans-Peter Schwarz, 'The division of Germany, 1945–
      1949', in Melvyn P. Leffler and Odd Arne Westad (ed.), *The Cambridge History of the
      Cold War, vol 1* (CUP, 2010).
32   'Darling, all': Gavin to MG, 5 Sep 1945, MG Archive.
33   'fan-type crush': MD to Maria Riva, cited in Maria Riva, *Marlene Dietrich*, p. 567.
      'I have decided': Gavin to MG, 10 Jul 1945, MG Archive.
34   'The Berliners': MD to Rudi Sieber, 27 Sep 1945, cited in Riva, *Marlene Dietrich*, p. 573.
35   'I love you', 'until I am': Gavin to MD, 2 Oct 1945, MD Archive.
36   'I've given up', 'the desolation': MG, diary, 3 Oct 1945, MG Archive.
37   'What shall I do': MG, diary entry, 10 Oct 1945, MG Archive.
      'You are': Gavin to MD, 11 Oct 1945, MD Archive.

6: *German Winter*

1   MG to Gavin, undated 1945, MG Archive.
2   See Wilfred Byford-Jones, *Berlin Twilight* (Hutchinson, 1947), p. 21.
     TB Rate: 'Tuberculosis up in Reich', 25 Oct 1945, *The New York Times*. Shortage of
     medicine: 'Lack of Medicines in Berlin Scored', 15 Oct 1945, *The New York Times*.

3   Rations in US zone: 'German Ration Cut in U.S. Zone', *The New York Times*, 16 Oct 1945.
     Rations in British zone: Hitchcock, *Liberation*, p. 196 ('just over 1,000 calories').
     'Poor harvest' (resulting from the damage caused to farmland, the loss of farm animals, lack of fertilizer and farm machinery, an exodus of foreign farm labourers, and heavy rains in late Aug): Bessel, *Germany 1945*, p. 333–34. Death rate: MacDonogh, *After the Reich*, p. 497.
4   Scarcity of candles and light bulbs: Riess, *The Berlin*, p. 41.
     Absurdity of statues: Clarissa Churchill, 'Berlin Letter', *Horizon*, Mar 1946.
5   'There, that point': John Dos Passos, *Tour of Duty: In the Year of Our Defeat* (Houghton Mifflin, 1946), p. 325.
6   'crazed look', 'perfectly still': Rees, *A Bundle of Sensations*, p. 197.
7   'it seemed futile': Rees, *A Bundle of Sensations*, p. 185.
8   Death rate of children in British sector: Judt, *Postwar*, p. 22.
9   Barney Oldfield, cited in Riva, *A Woman At War*, pp. 74–5.
10   MG and MD on plane together, see Shirer, *End of a Berlin Diary*, p. 206.
     'Oi yoi yoi': MD to Rudi Sieber, 9 Oct 1945, cited in Riva, *Marlene Dietrich*, p. 574.
11   MG to Gavin, undated, MG Archive.
12   MG to Gavin, undated, MG Archive.
13   MG, '82nd Airborne, Master of the Hot Spots', *Saturday Evening Post*, 23 Feb 1946.
14   MG, '82nd Airborne, Master of the Hot Spots'.
15   'more exciting': cited in Moorehead, *Martha Gellhorn*, p. 291.
16   'Darling everything': Gavin to MG, 1 Aug 1945, MG Archive.
17   *British Zone Review*, December 1945, cited in Kurt Jürgensen, 'The Concept and Practice of 'Re-education' in Germany 1945–50, in Pronay and Wilson, *The Political Re-education of Germany*, p. 88.
18   'a vocabulary': PdeM, 'Through the Dead Cities', *New Statesman*, 14 Jul 1945.
19   Alan Ross, 'German gun site', 'Occupation', 'Occupation troops', in *The Derelict Day: Poems in Germany* (John Lehmann, 1947).
20   'still full of clues'; The architect who': SS, *European Witness*, pp. 236, 237.
21   DPs like human animals: SS, *European Witness*, p. 77.
     Alan Ross, 'Displaced Persons', in *The Derelict Day.*
22   'If we can find': SS, 'Rhineland Journal', *Horizon,* December 1945.
23   'exiled, thrown': HJ to Cicely Jennings, 30 Sep 1945, in *The Humphrey Jennings Film Reader*, ed. by Kevin Jackson (Carcanet, 1993).
24   Alan Ross, 'Hamburg: Day and Night', in *The Derelict Day.*
25   'hard-working, efficient': *British Zone Review*, Dec 1945, cited in Jürgensen, 'The Concept and Practice of 'Re-education'' in Pronay and Wilson, *The Political Re-education of Germany*, p. 88.
26   'his Adam's apple': SS, in *Stephen Spender: Journals 1939–1983*, ed. by James Goldsmith (Faber and Faber, 1985), p. 71.
     'grossly exaggerated', 'I can't carry on', 'Perhaps I exaggerate', 'If he were a German': SS, *European Witness*, p. 219.
27   'serious in': SS, *European Witness*, p. 23.
28   'And in my dreams': SS, *European Witness*, p. 240.
29   Walter von Molo, open letter, Aug 1945, cited in Brockmann, *German Literary Culture*, p. 94.
30   TM, 'Warum ich nicht nach Deutschland zurückgehe' ('Why I am not returning to Germany'), *Aufbau*, cited in Brockmann, *German Literary Culture*, pp. 100–02.
31   'inner emigration', 'German space', 'if I were': Frank Thiess, 'Die innere Emigration', cited in Brockmann, *German Literary Culture*, p. 98–9.
     'inappropriate in its timing': Johannes Becher to Frank Theiss, 26 Jan 1946, in Becher, *Briefe* (Aufbau Verlag, 1993).
     'distorted and provocative', *'une race maudite'*: TM, diary, 18 Sep 1945, in TM, *Tagebücher*, ed. by Peter de Mendelssohn and Inge Jens (S. Fischer, 1977).

32   'inner emigrant', TM, diary, 7 Nov 1933, in TM, *Tagebücher*.
     'Believe me, for many': TM, speech, 13 Oct 1943, in *Thomas Mann's Addresses Delivered at the Library of Congress*, p. 29.
33   Edwin Redslob, *Tagesspiegel*, 23 Oct 1945, cited in Brockmann, *German Literary Culture*, p. 102.
     Otto Flake, *Badener Tageblatt*, cited in Brockmann, *German Literary Culture*, p. 103.
34   'We can achieve': Herbert Lestiboudois, open letter to Frank Thiess, *Neue Westfälische Zeitung*, 22 Jan 1946.
     'profoundly happy', 'To have a pretended': GM to Eva Herrmann, 7 Jan 1946, in Golo Mann, *Briefe 1932–1992*, ed. by Lahma Tilmann and Kathrin Lüssi, (Wallstein, 2006).
35   Alan Ross, 'Lüneberg', in *The Derelict Day*.

7: *Nuremberg*

1   'Surely a German','*Du lieber Gott!*': EM, 'They Who Live by the Sword', *Liberty*, 27 Oct 1945.
2   'It might be that': EM to KM, 20 Oct 1945, EM Archive.
3   'as much as': Dos Passos, *Tour of Duty*, p. 244.
    'old city': Dos Passos, *Tour of Duty*, p. 296.
4   'Funny to think': Dos Passos, *Tour of Duty*, p. 298.
5   'Commission on the Responsibility of the Authors of the War and on the Enforcement of Penalties: Report Presented to the Preliminary peace Conference', 29 Mar 1919 (see *The American Journal of International Law*, 14:1/2 (1920), pp. 95–154.
6   Article 6c of the Nuremberg Charter, cited in Geoffrey Robertson, *Crimes Against Humanity: The Struggle for Global Justice* (London: New Press, 2006), p. 190.
7   Justice Jackson's Report to the President on Atrocities and War Crimes, 7 June 1945, http://avalon.law.yale.edu/imt/imt_jack01.asp.
8   'fraternity life' and friendship with Birkett: Francis Biddle, *In Brief Authority* (Doubleday, 1962), p. 380.
9   EM, 'They Who Live by the Sword'.
10 Dos Passos, *Tour of Duty*, p. 301.
11 Dos Passos, *Tour of Duty*, pp. 301–02.
12 'Before I answer', 'I declare myself', 'for what'; 'Nein': Nuremberg Trial Procceedings, 21 Nov 1945, The Avalon Project, http://avalon.law.yale.edu/imt/11–21–45.asp.
13 'The privilege of': Nuremberg Trial Procceedings, 21 Nov 1945.
14 'The most', 'little people', 'accounts to': Nuremberg Trial Proceedings, 21 Nov 1945.
15 'The Nazi defendants': Shirer, *End of a Berlin Diary*, p. 307.
    'no Cicero': Shirer, *End of a Berlin Diary*, p. 301.
    'I doubt if there', 'We Americans'; 'reasonable, practical'; 'when the prosecutor': Dos Passos, *Tour of Duty*, pp. 306, 441, 304.
16 'I'm possessed': PdeM to Hilde Spiel, 26 Nov 1945, PdeM Archive.
17 'why can't we', 'I don't believe': *The New York Times*, 23 Nov 1945, cited in Ann and John Tusa, *The Nuremberg Trial* (Macmillan: 1983), p. 160.
    'Here at last': EM, Manuscript of article headed 'KZ films', 29 Nov 1945, EM Archive.
18 'Like the rest', 'the sooner', 'I feel more': EM, Manuscript of article headed 'KZ films'.
19 David Low, 'The Londoner's Diary', *Evening Standard*, 19 Dec 1945.
20 '*Deutschland ohne alles*': Anonymous poem, in Manfred Malzahn, *Germany 1945–1949: A Sourcebook* (Routledge, 1991).
    'contemptuous indifference': PdeM, 'The Nuremberg Reckoning', *New Statesman*, 25 Nov 1945.
    'The trial?': cited in Shirer, *End of Berlin Diary*, p. 346.

21   'It is not intended': EM, radio broadcast, 19 Dec 1945, EM Archive.
      'my knees haven't': Captain Sam Harris, cited in Tusa, *The Nuremberg Trial*, p. 169.
      'Jesus': Francis Biddle, cited in Tusa, *The Nuremberg Trial*, p. 170.
22   'Lawrence depends': Francis Biddle, Notes on the Conference, Biddle Papers,
      Syracuse University NY, cited in Tusa, *The Nuremberg Trial*, p. 118.
      Many dismissive of Biddle: Documents from the Lord Chancellor's Office, Public
      Records Office, cited in Tusa, *The Nuremberg Trial*, p. 117.
      'too biddle': EM to TM, 24 Mar 1946, EM Archive.
23   'affectionate bear cub': Biddle, *In Brief Authority*, p. 423.
24   'I want to': EM to Lotte Walter, 3 Feb 1946, EM Archive.
25   'taking place on': Dr Bergold to Kempner, 7 Jan 1946, Jackson Papers, cited in Tusa,
      The Nuremberg Trial, p. 222.
26   'organised and', 'a crime', 'This sin': François de Menthon, Nuremberg Trial
      Proceedings, 17 Jan 1946, The Avalon Project http://avalon.law.yale.edu/imt/01–
      17–46.asp.
27   'intoxicated', 'certain of', 'man, of': de Menthon's speech.
28   'original sin', 'one of', 'into a': de Menthon's speech.
29   'the German soul', 'as members': Biddle, *In Brief Authority*, p. 407.
      'That is more': Hans Frank, cited in Tusa, *The Nuremberg Trial*, p. 189.
30   'crimes against peace', 'their personal rights': de Menthon's speech.
      Ten years before Europe confronted its Jewish dead: See Tony Judt's epilogue 'From
      the House of the Dead: An Essay on Modern European Memory', in his *Postwar*,
      pp. 803–31.
31   'the trial': Norman Birkett to Mrs Cruesmann, 20 Jan 1946, cited in Tusa, *The
      Nuremberg Trial*, p. 223.
      As early as 1940 Erika and Klaus Mann had announced that there was 'such a thing
      as collective guilt, collective failure' and that in all truth and justice they must sorrow-
      fully admit that 'the German people collectively must accept their burden of guilt',
      EM and KM, *The Other Germany*, p. 187.
32   'We are being', 'And by refusing': cited in Brockmann, *German Literary Culture*,
      p. 39.
33   'I can't but': Hannah Arendt to Karl Jaspers, 9 Jul 1946, in Hannah Arendt and Karl
      Jaspers, *Correspondence 1926 –1969*, ed. by Lotte Kohler and Hans Saner, trans. by
      Robert and Rita Kimber (Harcourt Brace Jovanovich, 1992).
34   'the only way': Hannah Arendt, 'Organised Guilt and Universal Responsibility',
      published in the US in Jan 1945 and in Germany in 1946, in Hannah Arendt, *The
      Jew as Pariah: Jewish Identity and Politics in the Modern Age* (Grove Press, 1978),
      p. 228.
35   'For the idea': Arendt, 'Organised Guilt and Universal Responsibility', p. 235.
36   Karl Jaspers to Hannah Arendt, 28 Oct 1945, in Arendt and Jaspers, *Correspondence*.
37   'We survivors': Karl Jaspers, Lecture, Aug 1945, cited in Suzanne Kirkbright, *Karl
      Jaspers: A Biography: Navigations in Truth* (Yale University Press, 2004), p. 193.
      'very white', 'strange and unattractive': GM to Erich von Kahler, 29 Aug 1945, in
      Golo Mann, *Briefe*.
38   'breathing the air': Jaspers to Arendt, 2 Dec 1945, in Arendt and Jaspers, *Corres-
      pondence*.
39   'The Nazi crimes': Arendt to Jaspers, 17Aug 1946 in Arendt and Jaspers, *Corres-
      pondence*.
      'we will not be aided', 'filled with a genuine': Arendt, 'Organised Guilt and Universal
      Responsibility', pp. 229, 236.
40   'We bear witness', 'what was done', 'accompanied by': Johannes R. Becher,
      'Deutschland klagt an!', *Der Aufbau*, Jan 1946, pp. 9, 12, 16, cited in Brockmann,
      German Literary Culture, pp. 39–40.
      'deadness of', 'the loss', 'dead souls': Johannes Becher interview with William Shirer,
      8 Nov 1945, cited in Shirer, *End of a Berlin Diary*, pp. 186–87.

8: *Fighting the Peace*

1   By the end of March rations had dropped to 1,275 calories in the US zone and 1,043 in the British zone. (Kathleen McLaughlin, 'Germans' Rations Cut in U.S. Zone', *The New York Times*, 30 Mar 1946).
'This is a': Ernst Jünger, Mar 1946, cited in MacDonogh, *After the Reich*, p. 365.

2   'sobering experience', 'fumbling timidity': John Dos Passos, 'Americans are Losing the Victory in Europe', *Life*, 7 Jan 1946.
'The idea of': Winston Churchill to the House of Commons, 5 June 1946, in *Winston S. Churchill: His Complete Speeches, 1897–1963*, Vol VII: 1943–1949, ed. by Robert Rhodes James (New York: Chelsea House Publishers, 1974), p. 7352.

3   'from Stettin', 'enormous and wrongful', 'This is certainly': Winston Churchill, speech in Fulton Missouri, 5 Mar 1946, in *Winston S. Churchill: His Complete Speeches*, pp. 7290–91.

4   'tremendous excitement': Albert Speer, diary, 11 May 1947, in *Spandau – The Secret Diaries*, trans. by Richard and Clara Winston (Ishi Press, 2010).

5   'that the performing cast': Laura Knight, *The Magic of a Line: The Autobiography of Laura Knight* (William Kimber, 1965), p. 290.

6   'so-called freedoms', 'dismantle and transport', 'following the example': Nuremberg Trial Proceedings, 13 Mar 1946, http://avalon.law.yale.edu/imt/03-13-46.asp.

7   'liberation of', 'cleaning of', 'which had to', 'I do not': Nuremberg Trial Proceedings, 19 Mar 1946, http://avalon.law.yale.edu/imt/03-19-46.asp.
'sitting by': Francis Biddle to Katherine Biddle, 21 Mar 1946,, cited in Tusa, *The Nuremberg Trial*, p. 290.

8   'What did you think', 'He looks the sort': cited in Knight, *The Magic of a Line*, p. 288.
'What a benefit': Knight, *The Magic of a Line*, p. 287.

9   'still huger down', 'after days spent': Laura Knight, diary, LK Archive, pp. 13, 19–20. (Knight's description of Hitler as motivated even in his early days by 'idealism' seems somewhat misguided).

10   'We sit side by side': Knight, diary, LK Archive.
Birkett's pity: LK, *The Magic of a Line*, p. 291.

11   'Inside we': John Wheeler-Bennett, *Friends, Enemies, Sovereigns* (Macmillan, 1976), cited in Tusa, *The Nuremberg Trial*, p. 229. Thank you to John Clare and to Rosie Broadley for sharing the anecdote about the backflip.

12   'You don't think','the poor old girl': Evelyn Waugh, 1–2 Apr 1946, in Evelyn Waugh, *Diaries 1911–1965*, ed. by Michael Davie (Penguin, 1979).

13   'the sensation that', 'pity perhaps': LK, diary, LK Archive, p. 14. In her diary Knight wrote that she included the vision of the devastated city 'from pure aesthetic emotion only – for colour, composition, balance and line' (p. 126), resisting a symbolic reading of the work. But the contrast between the figures in the courtroom and the faded scene of destruction behind them is too great not to be significant, whatever she may have intended.

14   In this reading I am indebted to Lyndsey Stonebridge, who suggests that in the logic of this painting, 'in the end, justice will be neither subsumed under an incalculable trauma, nor calculated only from within the law, but imagined in the just city' (Lyndsey Stonebridge, *The Judicial Imagination: Writing After Nuremberg*, Edinburgh University Press, 2011, p. 16).

15   'accursed soil'; 'surrealist spectacle': EW to Diana Cooper, 13 Dec 1946, in *Mr Wu and Mrs Stitch: The Letters of Eveyn Waugh and Diana Cooper*, ed. by Artemis Cooper (Hodder and Stoughton, 1991); EW to Randolph Churchill, April 1946, in *The Letters of Evelyn Waugh*, ed. by Mark Amory (Weidenfeld and Nicolson, 1980), p. 226.
'He knows he doesn't': EW to Randolph Churchill, Apr 1946, in *Letters of Evelyn Waugh*.

'a most agreeable man' interested in cattle breeding': EW, diary, 1 –2 Apr 1946, in *Diaries 1911 –1965.*

'injudicious travesty': EW, cited in Stannard, *Evelyn Waugh*, p. 163.

16 'a childish daydream', 'In so far': GO, 'Revenge is Sour', *Tribune*, 9 Nov 1945.

17 'One night': VG to Locker, June 1961, cited in Ruth Dudley Edwards, *Victor Gollancz: A Biography* (Gollancz, 1987), p. 377.

18 VG, 'What Buchenwald Really Means', Apr 1945.

'the son shall not': Ezekiel, 18:20.

'if we call': VG, appeal sent to newspapers, Sep 1945, cited in Dudley Edwards, *Victor Gollancz*, p. 411.

19 'With the sudden': PdeM, extract from an article in *Observer*, in 'Save Europe Now', 21 Jan 1946, (booklet located in RW Archive).

'The tone is': Review of *A Defeated People*, *Daily Telegraph*, 15 Mar 1946, in BFI newspaper cuttings file, BFI Archive.

20 'no treaty of peace': Ernest Bevin, certificate issued 2 April 1946, cited in Meehan, *A Strange Enemy People*, p. 21.

21 'caught like rats': Harold Nicolson to Vita Sackville-West, 25 Apr 1946, in *Diaries and Letters 1945 –62*, ed. by Nigel Nicolson (Collins, 1968).

'they have the appearance': Harold Nicolson, diary, 30 Apr 1946, in *Diaries and Letters.*

22 'nothing but undying', 'An agreeable': Harold Nicolson, diary, 1 May 1946, in *Diaries and Letters.*

'stupendous trial', 'the calm assessment', 'In the courtroom': Harold Nicolson, 'Marginal Comment', *Spectator*, 10 May 1946.

23 'the policy of starving': letter from EW, *New Statesman*, 1 Jun 1946; Waugh supported the 'Save Europe Now' campaign, encouraged by the scenes he had witnessed in Nuremberg.

24 *Daily Mail*, 3 Jul 1946, quoted in Ina Zweiniger-Bargielowska, *Austerity in Britain: Rationing, Controls, and Consumption, 1939–1955* (OUP, 2000), p. 216.

25 'All of us': 'Berlin calls Wilhelm Furtwängler,' *Berliner Zeitung*, 16 Feb 1946.

26 'a new poet': EM to Lotte Walter, 3 Feb 1946, EM Archive.

'inner emigration', 'free pass': EM, 'Inner Immigration' (unpublished), Oct 1946, EM Archive.

27 'a pensive, white-haired': EM to TM and Katia, 24 Mar 1946, EM Archive.

'swallow', 'horrid', 'It is a sad', 'by the Russians': EM to TM and Katia, 10 Jan 1946, EM Archive.

28 'Whereas the rest': EM, 'Citizen Werewolf', *Chicago Daily News*, 19 May 1946. Erika Mann wrote another article describing some of the American officials as corrupt and even anti-Semitic.

29 'I don't know', 'Tell him my': KM to Katia, 10 May 1946, KM Archive.

30 'for people like us to live in', 'accept and need', 'versed in various': KM, *The Turning Point*, p. 357.

31 Walter Karsch, 'Sternheims und Gründgens' Wiederkehr', *Der Tagesspiegel*, 5 May 1946.

'perhaps someone gassed': KM, 'Kunst und Politik' ('Art and Politics'), 17 Apr 1946, in *Auf Verlorenem Posten: Aufsätze, Reden, Kritiken, 1942–49*, ed. by Uwe Naumann and Michael Toteberg (Rororo: 1994).

32 KM, 'Kunst und Politik'.

33 'void and depressing': KM, *The Turning Point*, p. 62.

34 'as attractive as ever': KM, Berlin's Darling', Jun 1946, KM Archive.

9: *Boredom*

1 'utter uselessness of acres': Norman Birkett, 23 May 1946, cited in Tusa, *The Nuremberg Trial*, p. 370.

2 'At half-past four': Birkett to Biddle, cited in Biddle, *In Brief Authority*, p. 421.

'a thousand years': Biddle, *In Brief Authority*, p. 457.

3 'the Churchill of': RW to Harold Ross, 28 Aug 1946, Archive of *The New Yorker*.
4 'citadel of boredom', 'dragging the proceedings': RW, 'Extraordinary Exile', *The New Yorker*, 7 Sep 1946.
5 'Live, work, act': For West's name change see Victoria Glendinning, *Rebecca West: A Life* (Papermac, 1988), p. 36.
6 'My husband can': cited in Rollyson, *Beautiful Exile*, p. 132.
7 'abominable nation', 'The insane mercy', 'a great galumphing': RW to Winnie MacLeod, 1930s, RW Archive (Tulsa).
   'always been able': RW to Motley Deakin, 21 Apr 1980, in *Selected Letters of Rebecca West*, ed. by Bonnie Kime Scott (Yale University Press, 2003).
8 'You could be': Francis Biddle to Katherine Biddle, 30 Jul 1946, Francis Biddle Collection, Syracuse University Library, cited in Carl Rollyson, *Rebecca West: A Saga of the Century*, (Hodder and Stoughton, 1995), p. 213.
9 'Isn't it curious': cited in Rollyson, *Rebecca West*, p. 213.
   'relaxed, tolerant': cited in Rollyson, *Rebecca West*, p. 212.
   'Apparently Germans': RW to Harold Ross, 28 Aug 1946, Archive of *The New Yorker*.
10 'half-militarist, half-gangster', 'a salesman of', 'If you were to say': Robert Jackson, 26 Aug 1946, cited in Tusa, *The Nuremberg Trial*, p. 420.
   'a masterpiece, exquisitely': RW, 'Extraordinary Exile'.
11 'There is one', 'because they betrayed', 'mad scoundrels': Nuremberg Trial Proceedings, 27 Jul 1946, http://avalon.law.yale.edu/imt/07–27–46.asp.
12 'the quoted words': TM to Foreign Office, cited in Tusa, *The Nuremberg Trial*, p. 424.
13 'gay and amusing wench': Francis Biddle to Katherine Biddle, 6 Aug 1946, cited in Rollyson, *Rebecca West*, p. 214.
   'I'm fifty-three': RW to Emanie Arling, 13 Aug 1946, in *Selected Letters of Rebecca West*.
   'I had never met': H.G. Wells, *H.G. Wells in Love: Postscript to an Experiment in Autobiography* (Faber, 1984), cited in Glendinnig, *Rebecca West*, p. 46.
   'Dear HG, he was': RW to Emanie Arling, 13 Aug 1946, in *Selected Letters of Rebecca West*.
14 'Oh God, what a world!', 'Francis': RW to Emanie Arling, 13 Aug 1946, in *Selected Letters of Rebecca West*.
15 'lovely, Francis, lovely!': Biddle to RW, 8 Aug 1946, RW Archive (Beinecke).
   'I come to breakfast': RW to Biddle, 29 Aug 1946, RW Archive (Beinecke).
16 'It is awfully good': Biddle to RW, 26 Aug 1946, RW Archive (Beinecke).
   'I want to': RW to Emanie Arling 13 Aug 1946, in *Selected Letters of Rebecca West*.
   'a highly intelligent, 'Doubtless the life', 'an image of Eros', 'inconsolable widowhood', 'Oh Love': RW, 'Extraordinary Exile'.
17 'either in love': RW to Ross, 28 Aug 1946, Archive of *The New Yorker*.
   'the dog hung': Biddle to RW, 26 Aug 1946, RW Archive (Beinecke).
   'Where the pine trees': RW, 'Extraordinary Exile'.
   'The dragonflies made': Biddle to RW, 26 Aug 1946, RW Archive (Beinecke).

10: *Judgement*

1 'I think we complicate': Biddle to RW, 19 Aug 1946, RW Archive (Beinecke).
   'we have never': Biddle to RW, 26 Aug 1946, RW Archive (Beinecke).
   'I said to you': Biddle to RW, 29 Aug 1946, RW Archive (Beinecke).
2 'mile after mile': RW, 'Greenhouse with Cyclamens', in *A Train of Powder* (Virago, 1984), p. 34.
   'Not a smile': RW to Henry Andrews, n.d., RW Archive (Beinecke).
3 RW's shyness: RW, diary, 26 Sep 1946, RW Archive (Beinecke).

4 'one of the most important': RW, 'Eye-Witness Impressions of the Nuremberg Trial', *Daily Telegraph*, 27 Sep 1946.
5 'it was necessary', 'gone silly': RW, 'A Reporter at Large: The Birch Leaves Falling', *The New Yorker*, 26 Oct 1946.
6 'one of those': RW, 'Last Dramatic Scenes of Nuremberg Trial', *Daily Telegraph*, 1 Oct 1946.
7 'his voice was a symbol': MG, 'The Paths of Glory', *Collier's*, 9 Nov 1946.
   'vast rubbish heap', 'There was nothing': MG, *Point of No Return*, published under the title *The Wine of Astonishment* (Bantam, 1949), p. 184.
8 Biddle does not look at defendants, exhausted air of courtroom: MG, 'The Paths of Glory'.
   'Göring has the ugliest': MG, notebook, 30 Sep 1946, MG Archive.
   Göring's smile: MG, 'The Paths of Glory'.
   'it is a cold court': MG, notebook, 30 Sep 1946, MG Archive.
9 Weather: from RW, 'Last Dramatic Scenes', *Daily Telegraph*, 1 Oct 1946.
   'often, indeed almost always': Nuremberg Trial Proceedings, Judgement, Avalon Project, http://avalon.law.yale.edu/imt/judgoeri.asp.
10 'an empty, stunned': MG, 'The Paths of Glory', *Collier's*, 9 Nov 1946.
11 For the significance of the Nuremberg trials for the future of human rights law, see Robertson, *Crimes Against Humanity*, pp. 190, 202, 222. According to Robertson, 'Nuremberg stands as a colossus in the development of international human rights law precisely because its Charter defined crimes against humanity and its procedures proved by acceptable and credible evidence that such crimes had been instigated by some of the defendants' (p. 202).
12 'a recognisable product': RW, 'Last Dramatic Scenes'.
   'the most evil': RW, 'How the War Criminals Heard their Fate', *Daily Telegraph*, 2 Oct 1946.
   'Let us not discount': RW, 'Last Dramatic Scenes'.
13 'who had led': Arno Scholz, 'Im Urteil des Volkes: Schuldig!', *Telegraf*, 2 Oct 1946.
14 'men of four': MG, 'The Paths of Glory'.
   'to use the Tribunal': RW, 'How the War Criminals'.
   On the Russian execution of Polish internees, see Geoffrey Roberts, *Stalin's Wars: From World War to Cold War, 1939–1953* (Yale University Press, 2006). pp. 170–71.
15 'Sexual renunciation', 'with some emotion', 'My God, that man': RW, 'Greenhouse with Cyclamens', pp. 69–70.
16 'Coming home': RW, diary, 5 Oct 1946, RW Archive (Beinecke).
   'odder and odder': RW to her agent, 7 Oct 1946, RW Archive (Tulsa).
   'Katherine has got him': RW, diary, 22 Oct 1946, RW Archive (Beinecke).
17 'I am not envious': EM, *Spokane Daily Chronicle*, 16 Oct 1946, EM Archive.
   'enormous clown', 'wine of humiliation', 'vague, visceral': RW, 'A Reporter at Large: The Birch Leaves Falling'.
18 'makes the appeal', 'the outward': RW, *Time and Tide*, 8 Jun 1941, cited in Glendinning, *Rebecca West*, p. 169.
19 'Men are all filth', 'Don't worry': RW to Emanie Arling, n.d., RW Archive (Beinecke).
20 'only part of us', 'the other half', 'that will set': RW, *Black Lamb and Grey Falcon* (Macmillan, 1942), vol II, p. 496.
21 During the war, greenhouses were supposed to be used to grow food rather than flowers.
22 'I have never been able': RW to A. L. Rowse, cited in A. L. Rowse, *Glimpses of the Great* (Methuen, 1985), p. 128.
23 'plastered history', 'not the name': RW, 'Greenhouse with Cyclamens', pp. 73–4.
24 'To the desire': RW, 'Greenhouse with Cyclamens', p. 15.
25 'much happiness that', 'there were men': RW, 'Greenhouse with Cyclamens', pp. 14–15.

26 'War is the silver': MG, 'The Paths of Glory'.
27 'to exorcise what', 'a good tough': MG to Betsy Drake, 15 Jan 1972, MG Archive.
    'young and short': MG, *Point of No Return*, p. 37.
28 'Driving into a group of Germans': This act has a precedent. Ronald Monson of the *Daily Telegraph* had driven his car into a group of Germans after witnessing Belsen.
29 'sonofabitch', 'yawning man-eating chasm': Gavin to MG, 25 Jan 1946, MG Archive.
    'to give in', 'in the night': MG, *Point of No Return*, pp. 38, 39.
30 'launched on writing': MG to Eleanor Roosevelt, May 1946, in *The Letters of Martha Gellhorn* .
    'being a man': MG to Bernard Berenson, 17 Sep 1953, in *The Letters of Martha Gellhorn*.
    'because if a trooper', 'reasonable male', 'OK': Gavin to MG, 25 Jan 1946, MG Archive.
31 MG, *Point of No Return*, p. 191.
32 'with Dotty', 'my father's too': MG, *Point of No Return*, pp. 58, 87.
33 'clear out of', 'the krauts all', 'too big, black', 'he knew that', 'I never knew': MG, *Point of No Return*, pp. 104, 269, 206, 213, 219.
34 'where sex starts', 'paid off so': MG to Campbell Beckett, 12 Sep 1946, in *The Letters of Martha Gellhorn*.
    'dark girl who': MG, *Point of No Return*, p. 145.
35 'You sat there': MG, 'The Paths of Glory'.
    'grey and thick', 'these goddam krauts', 'this is the': MG, *Point of No Return*, pp. 173, 175, 201.

11: *Cold War*

1 'just because they're': VG to Ruth Gollancz, 5 Oct 1946, cited in Dudley Edwards, *Victor Gollancz*, p. 435.
2 Shops in ruins and corpses beneath rubble: see Alfred Döblin, *Tales of a Long Night* (Universiy of Michigan, 1984), pp. 280–81.
    'drearier than', 'a vast dumping': Dagerman, *German Autumn*, p. 20.
3 'It is beyond': VG to Ruth Gollancz, 9 Oct 1946, cited in Dudley Edwards, *Victor Gollancz*, p. 437. Majority of the 50,000: this figure is from Bessel, *Germany 1945*, p. 264. (15,000 were German Jews, p. 267).
    'a rather hideous': Report by Earl G. Harrison to President Truman, printed in full in *The New York Times*, 30 Sep 1945, cited in Sollors, *The Temptation of Despair*, p. 141.
4 'concentration camps': Wing Commander Norman Hulbert MP, cited in Meehan, *A Strange Enemy People*, p. 73.
5 'if one wants': Dagerman, *German Autumn*, p. 7.
    'wretched': VG to *The Times*, published 5 Nov 1946.
    'the stigmata of malnutrition': VG, *From Darkness to Light: a confession of faith in the form of an anthology* (V. Gollancz, 1956), pp. 35–6.
6 'I am never': VG to *The Times*, published 15 Nov 1946.
    'We have all': VG to the *News Chronicle*, published 13 Nov 1946.
7 'the journey of'; Zuckmayer in Frankfurt: Carl Zuckmayer, *A Part of Myself*, trans. by Richard and Clara Winston (Secker & Warburg, 1970), pp. 329, 390.
8 'Oh, what a pleasure': CZ, *A Part of Myself*, p. 390.
9 'anteroom to hell': CZ, *A Part of Myself*, p. 345.
10 'a cry, a summons': CZ, *A Part of Myself*, p. 381.
11 Visiting Germany as an American: CZ, *A Part of Myself*, p. 386.
    'bridge the abysses': CZ, *Deutschlandbericht für das Kriegsministerium der Vereinigten Staaten von Amerika* (Wallstein, 2004), p. 56.

12   'Americans are money-hungry': Bernard Lewis to Robert A. McClure, 'Suggested Changes in *Die Neue Zeitung*', 26 Apr 1946, OMGUS/ISD Archive (cited in Gienow-Hecht, 'Art is Democracy', p. 34).
      'what filth', 'these artists', 'as they have': Erich Kästner, 'Die Augsburger Diagnose' (The Augsburg Diagnosis), *Neue Zeitung*, 7 Jan 1946 and Hans Habe, 'Tagebuch der *Kultur*' (Diary of culture), *Neue Zeitung*, 18 Jan 1946 (cited in quoted Gienow-Hecht, 'Art is Democracy', p. 31).
13   'the shudder of': CZ, *A Part of Myself*, p. 395.
14   'When Pommer comes': Erich Kästner, cited in Heide Fehrenbach, *Cinema in Democratizing Germany: Reconstructing National Identity after Hitler* (University of North Carolina Press, 1995), p. 63.
      'rich tradition', 'the undistorted image': Erich Pommer, 13 Aug 1946, *Suddeutsche Zeitung*, cited in Schivelbusch, *In a Cold Crater*, p. 145.
15   'who could deny': Enno Kind, Review of *The Murderers are Among Us*, Berlin edition of *Neues Deutschland*, 17 Oct 1946.
      On film-making in Berlin, see Dagmar Barnouw, 'A Time for Ruins', in Wilfried Wilms and William Rasch (ed.), *German Post-war Films: Life and Love in the Ruins* (Palgrave Macmillan, 2008), pp. 45–60. On British film-making, including *Tell the Truth*, see Riess, *The Berlin Story* (Frederick Muller, 1953), pp. 59–60.
16   Pointlessness of denazification: CZ, *Deutschlandbericht*, p. 139.
      Hour of acceptance, 'ready for any': CZ, *A Part of Myself*, pp. 394–95.
17   Visit to pub: CZ, *Deutschlandbericht*, p. 117.
18   'Why do you care?': CZ, *Deutschlandbericht*, p. 119
19   'not a battle': CZ, *Deutschlandbericht*, p. 120.
20   CZ's discussions with young people: CZ, *The Past is Myself*, p. 396.
21   'poor and dear', 'their suffering': VG, *In Darkest Germany* (Victor Gollancz Ltd., 1947), p. 64.
22   'plain, straight','a general act', 'unless you treat', 'we, as members': VG, *In Darkest Germany*, pp. 18–19.
23   In March a Stuttgart periodical lauded the 'kindness, courage and wisdom' of this 'firm and resolute personality'. In Britain, George Orwell hoped that 'everyone who can get access to a copy will take at least a glance' at this 'brilliant piece of journalism intended to shock the public of this country into some kind of consciousness of the hunger, disease, chaos and lunatic mismanagement prevailing in the British Zone' ('Orwell in *Tribune*', 17 Jan 1947 in *Orwell in Tribune: As I Please and Other Writings, 1943–47*, ed. by Paul Anderson, Methuen: 2008, p. 351). Similarly, the *Observer* reviewer announced that it was hard not to be 'infected by the zealous goodness of the crusading author', while insisting that of the 23 million people in the British zone not more than 3 million lived in the kind of conditions described by Gollancz ('German Road', *Observer*, 26 Jan 1947).
24   'and how I': CZ, *Deutschlandbericht*, p. 5.
25   'With what seriousness', 'how much theatre', 'a spiritual, intellectual': CZ, *Deutschlandbericht*, p. 55.
26   'The way things are going now': Karl Jaspers to Hannah Arendt, 1 Jan 1947, in Arendt and Jaspers, *Correspondence*.
27   Frost, 'an occupying army', disappointed expectations, CZ appeals to American authorities, disappointed expectations: CZ, *Deutschlandbericht*, pp. 82, 71, 74, 79, 74.
28   'We are behaving', 'we are trying', 'you can create': VG, *In Darkest Germany*, p. 99.
      'fought and eventually died': CZ, *Deutschlandbericht*, p. 43.
29   1947 conference in Stuttgart, 'the freedom and independence', 'some deluded, but unflinching', 'The consequences we inflict': CZ, *Deutschlandbericht*, pp. 164, 165, 75, 76.
30   'We don't have to': Jaspers to Arendt, 19 Mar 1947, in *Correspondence*.
      On British and American intention to form a bizone and waive reparations, see Judt, *Postwar*, pp. 124–25 and Schwarz, 'The division of Germany', in Leffler and Westad (ed.), *The Cambridge History of the Cold War*, pp. 166–67.

'between alternative ways', 'I believe that: Truman to Congress, Mar 1947, cited in Frances Stonor Saunders, *Who paid the piper?: the CIA and the Cultural Cold War* (Granta, 1999), p. 25.

31   Certainly Judt dates the Cold War from this moment (see Judt, *Postwar*, p. 124).
'a centralised government': George Marshall, Report on the Fourth Meeting of the Council of Foreign Ministers, Moscow, 28 Apr 1947, http://avalon.law.yale.edu/20th_century/decade23.asp.
'The patient is sinking': George Marshall, speech, Jun 1947, cited in Hitchcock, *Liberation*, p. 156.

32   'You're absolutely right': John Hynd, cited in MacDonogh, *After the Reich*, p. 251.
'as the people of one': Brian Robertson, instruction issued at the Regional Commissioners' Conference, 18 May 1947, cited in Meehan, *A Strange Enemy People*, p. 152.
'be-kind-to': cited in Meehan, *A Strange Enemy People*, p. 152.

33   JCS 1779, Jul 1947, in Velma Hastings Cassidy (ed.), *Germany 1947–1949, The Story in Documents* (University of Michigan Library, 1950), pp. 33–41.

34   'She must have', 'political passion': George Marshall, speech at Harvard, 5 Jun 1947, see http://www.marshallfoundation.org/library/doc_marshall_plan_speech.html.

35   See William L. Hitchcock, 'The Marshall Plan and the Creation of the West', in Leffler and Westad, *The Cambridge History of the Cold War*, pp. 155–59.

36   Bernard Baruch, an American statesman who had resigned as the US representative to the UN Atomic Commission that January, in speaking before the South Carolina state legislature on 16 Apr 1947, declared: 'Let us not be deceived—we are today in the midst of a cold war,' cited in *The New York Times*, 17 Apr 1947; columnist Arthur Krock used the phrase in *The New York Times* on 12 Oct 1947.

37   'the state religion','In the midst': HS, *The Dark and The Bright: Memoirs, 1911–1989*, trans. Christine Shuttleworth (Ariadne Press, 2007), pp. 222–23.

38   'in spite of': Alonzo Grace, 'Out of the Rubble: An Address on the Reorientation of the German People', undated, OMGUS/RG260/NARA, cited in Stonor Saunders, *Who paid the piper?*, p. 19.

39   The list of titles struck some as too highbrow: two publishers visiting Germany the following year complained that some of the selected novels were 'incomprehensible to the average German', 'Report and Recommendations on Publishing in the British Zone of Germany' by Mr. Desmond Flower M.C. (Director of Cassell & Co.) and the Hon. Mervyn Horder (Director of Duckworth & Co.), 25 Mar 1947 (PRO, FO 1056/8)). In general, however, the British were happy for their cultural efforts primarily to influence the elite, with Raymond Gauntlett, Chief of Public Relations/ Informational Services Control Group (PR/ISC), maintaining that 'the concentration of effort must be on the leaders or potential leaders', since '[w]e can influence the many partially, but we can only hope to influence the few decisively', Chief of PR/ISC Group to Military Governor, 23 Mar 1948, Public Records Office, Foreign Office 1056/124. See Rhys W. Williams, Stephen Parker and Colin Riordan (eds.), with Helmut Peitsch, *German Writers and the Cold War 1945–1961*, Manchester University Press, 1992.
For a more detailed discussion of the British emphasis on re-educating the elite, see Gabriele Clemens, *Britische Kulturpolitik in Deutschland 1945–1949: Literatur, Film, Musik und Theater* (Franz Steiner, 1997), p. 55.

40   'best to give it a rest': Rhys Williams, '"The selections of the Committee are not in accord with the requirements of Geremany": Contemporary English Literature and the selected book scheme in the British zone of Germany (1945–1950)' in Alan Bance (ed.), *The Cultural Legacy of the British Occupation in Germany: The London Symposium,* (H.-D. Heinz, 1997), pp. 110–38.
For 'Ro-Ro-Ro', see Malzahn, *Germany 1945–1949: A Sourcebook*, pp. 205–06. For a list of the books translated during the occupation, see Hansjörg Gehring, *Amerikanische Literaturpolitik in Deutschland 1945–1953: Ein Aspekt des Re-Education-Programms* (Oldenbourg, 2010), pp. 115–26.

For a discussion of the practicalities of book and periodical printing, see Edward C. Breitenkamp, *The U.S. Information Control Division and Its Effect on German Publishers and Writers 1945–1949* (University Station, 1953), p. 74.

41   'whoever is given': cited in Geoffrey Skelton, *Paul Hindemith, The Man Behind the Music* (Gollancz, 1975), p. 219.
'flourish much better': cited in Skelton, *Paul Hindemith*, p. 223.

42   See MacDonogh, *After the Reich*, p. 221.

43   'I cannot recall', 'The Germans never': EM, letter to editor, *Herald Tribune*, 13 Jun 1947.

44   See Brockmann, *German Literary Culture*, p. 187 (and see Brockmann generally for an extended analysis of the concept of the 'zero hour').

45   'connections with', 'a reminder of': *PEN News*, May–Jun 1942, p. 3.

46   'destroyed the Reich', 'murdered their mother', 'will and must survive': 'International Dinner', *PEN News*, Jul 1945, p. 10.
'appalling intellectual': *PEN News*, Jul 1947, p. 3.

47   'extraordinarily difficult, 'after two, three': TM, message to German people, 23 May 1947, cited in *Thomas Mann: A Chronicle of His Life*, ed. by Hans Burgin and Hans-Otto Mayer (Alabama: University of Alabama, 1965), p. 215.

48   'a triumph for': *PEN News*, Jul 1947, p. 3.

49   'the European family': Winston Churchill to Anthony Eden, 21 Oct 1942, cited in Judt, *Postwar*, p. 155.
'Buchenwald manifesto', 'a European community', 'guarantee order': cited in Bessel, *Germany 1945*, p. 302.

50   'Conference for the Establishment of the United Nations Educational, Scientific and Cultural Organisation', Nov 1945, see http://unesdoc.unesco.org/images/0011/001176/117626e.pdf.

51   'success, prosperity', 'civilising values', 'those values; 'what they have': SS, speech at *Rencontres internationales de Genève*, Sep 1946, see http://www.rencontres-int-geneve.ch/volumes_pdf/rigo1.pdf.

52   SS, 'The Intellectuals and the Future of Europe', *The Gate / Das Tor*, Jan–Mar 1947, pp. 2–9.

53   'the struggle within', 'the true meeting-place', 'the day may': SS, 'The Intellectuals and the Future of Europe'.

54   'a complete Re-education': SS, 'The Intellectuals and the Future of Europe'. In using the term 're-education', Spender was consciously referring to the Allied policy of re-education in Germany.

55   See 'PEN and UNESCO', *PEN News*, 144, Jul 1946, p. 13 and 'UNESCO', *PEN News*, 150, Jul 1947, p. 11. See also SS, 'Can Unesco Succeed,' *Fortnightly*, Mar 1947.

56   This letter from the head of a factory in Pennsylvania was addressed to the Reorientation Branch of the US Civil Affairs Division. He complained that 'American soldiers and many Germans will see a play written by a communist, based on the theme that US manufacturers produced defective equipment and airplanes during the war, endangering the lives of their own sons'. The head of the Reorientation Branch, Colonel Hume, agreed that the play was harmful and withdrew the production. As a result *All My Sons* was not produced in Germany until 1950. See Gehring, *Amerikanische Literaturpolitik*, pp. 70–1.

57   HS, *The Dark and The Bright*, p. 226.

58   'beginning to bar': Stephan Hermlin, cited in Brockmann, *German Literary Culture*, p. 152. On the conference in general, see Brockmann *German Literary Culture*, and the transcript of the conference in Ursula Reinhold et al (eds.), *Erster Deutscher Schriftstellerkongress, 4–8 Oktober 1947* (Aufbau, 1999).

59   See Giles Scott-Smith and Hans Krabbendam (eds.), *The Cultural Cold War in Western Europe, 1945–60* (Frank Cass, 2003), p. 295.

60   'barbarism', 'millions of simple': cited in Brockmann, *German Literary Culture*, p. 153.

61 See Brockmann, *German Literary Culture*, p. 154.

62 'Show of fireworks': Elisabeth Langgässer to Waldemar Gurian, 21 Oct 1947, in Elisabeth Langgässer, *Briefe 1924–1950* (Claasen, 1990). The ban of the Kulturbund was the result of a series of complicated bureaucratic manoeuvres (see Schivelbusch, *In a Cold Crater*, pp. 97–104), but ultimately represented the American and British suspicion of an organisation they perceived to be actively promoting Communism.

12: *Artistic enlightenment*

1   'a formal gesture', 'semi-totalitarian dimness': Melvin Lasky, 'Berlin Letter', *Partisan Review*, Nov-Dec 1947.

2   'a vacuum filled': Elisabeth Langgässer to Wilhelm Lehman, 10 Dec 1945, in Langgässer, *Briefe*.
    'Both culturally': Langgässer to Henry Goverts, 17 Mar 1946, in *Briefe*.
    'a garbage heap': Karl Jaspers to Hannah Arendt, 19 Apr 1947, in Arendt and Jaspers, *Correspondence 1926–1969*.

3   Wolfgang Borchert's *Draußen vor der Tür* (*Outside the Door*) was also performed in November and commented on the postwar German situation.

4   Concern of American authorities, sense he belongs to Germany: CZ, *A Part of Myself*, p. 401.

5   'When becoming', 'I am an American': CZ, *Deutschlandbericht*, p. 126.

6   'The play corresponded': CZ, *A Part of Myself*, p. 402.

7   'I've never dipped', 'The meaning of', 'Don't question', 'total mobilisation': CZ, *The Devil's General and Germany: Jekyll and Hyde*, trans. by Sebastian Haffner (Continuum International, 2005), pp. 13, 9, 21, 8.

8   'I want to', 'We need a', 'The world is': CZ, *The Devil's General*, pp. 47, 48, 34.

9   'the true', 'It's laid', 'We're guilty': CZ, *The Devil's General*, pp. 28., 63, 52.

10 'We need the defeat', 'only then', 'I've been', 'That's how': CZ, *The Devil's General*, pp. 81, 81, 84, 76.

11 'fought and eventually': CZ, *Deutschlandbericht*, p. 43.
    'The hearts of these', 'I am your': CZ, *A Part of Myself*, p. 402.

12 'When I saw': Douglas Sirk, in *Sirk on Sirk: Conversations with Jon Halliday* (Faber, 1997), p. 90.

13 This was also a view put forward by the (as yet unknown) younger novelist Heinrich Böll in his novel *Kreuz ohne Liebe* (*Cross without Love*), written at this time. Böll's anti-Nazi soldier hero Christoph is convinced that Germany has been placed in the hands of the Devil forever. 'The Devil possesses all the power in this world, and a change of power is only a change in rank among devils, that I believe for certain'. The allies may conquer the Germans with 'their rubber soles and tins of Spam' but they will never understand what it is like to be showered with their bombs at the same time as being sullied by a diabolic state. Therefore they cannot rid the Germans of their satanic curse. (Heinrich Böll, *Kreuz ohne Liebe* (Kiepenheuer & Witsch, 2003), pp. 285–86).

14 Goethe's Faust does continue to experience pleasure (notably sexual pleasure with Gretchen and other women) but this is transient; he has made a bargain with Mephistopheles that if he ever experiences the kind of transcendent happiness that makes him long for a particular moment to continue, the Devil will be in possession of his soul.

15 'If ever I shall': Johann Wolfgang von Goethe, *Faust: The First Part of the Tragedy*, trans. by David Constantine (Penguin, 2005), p. 57.
    'Is not coldness': TM, *Doctor Faustus: The Life of the German Composer Adrian Leverkühn as Told by a Friend*, trans. John E. Woods (Vintage International, 1999), p. 265.

16 Other obvious models for Leverkühn are Adorno and Schoenberg. See Ehrhard Bahr, *Weimar on the Pacific: German Exile Culture in Los Angeles and the Crisis of Modernism* (University of California Press, 2007) for a discussion of Mann's influences.

17   'your life shall': TM, *Doctor Faustus*, p. 264.
18   'innocent tangle', 'gently floating presence', 'radiant daylight', 'I have discovered':
      TM, *Doctor Faustus*, pp. 483, 490, 501.
19   For a discussion of whether we should take the devil literally or not see Susan Von
      Rohr Scaff, 'Doctor Faustus', in Ritchie Robertson (ed.), *The Cambridge Companion
      to Thomas Mann* (Cambridge University Press, 2001), pp. 168–84. According to Rohr
      Scaff, it is not so much what he does but who he is that defines Leverkühn's sinful-
      ness (p. 174).
      'mildly orgiastic', 'faint, sinister', 'a world of': TM, *Doctor Faustus*, pp. 94, 6, 11.
      In his 'Germany and the Germans' essay Mann observed that 'if Faust is to be the
      representative of the German soul, he would have to be musical, for the relation of
      the German to the world is abstract and mystical, that is, musical'.
20   Mann writes that the central idea of the novel is 'the flight from the difficulties of
      the cultural crisis into the pact with the devil, the craving of a proud mind, threat-
      ened by sterility, from an unblocking of inhibitions at any cost, and the parallel
      between pernicious euphoria ending in collapse with the nationalistic frenzy of
      Fascism.' (TM, *The Story of a Novel*, trans. Richard and Clara Winston (Knopf,
      1961) p. 30.)
21   'You will break', 'a double barbarism', 'through to a': TM, *Doctor Faustus*, pp. 259,
      317.
22   'Am enraptured with Eissi. Terribly handsome in his swimming trunks. Find it quite
      natural that I should fall in love with my son.' (TM, diary, 5 Jul 1920, in TM, *Diaries,
      1918–1939*, trans. Richard and Clara Winston (Harry N. Abrams, 1982).
23   'would scream', 'prison': TM, *Doctor Faustus*, pp. 184, 33.
24   'Berlin's agony': TM, diary, 9 Feb 1945, in *Tagebücher*.
      'heavy bombing': TM, diary, 25 Feb 1945, in *Tagebücher*.
      'the conquest': TM, diary, 2 Apr 1945, in *Tagebücher*.
      'The failure': TM, diary, 4 Apr 1945, in *Tagebücher*.
25   'strange impression': TM, diary, 14 May 1945, in *Tagebücher*.
      'the terror of', 'as the Last', 'our hideously battered', 'that gaze from': TM, *Doctor
      Faustus*, pp. 267, 184, 474.
26   'enfeebled democracies', 'a German prerogative', 'cannot help fearing', 'a certain
      satisfaction', 'and as the': TM, *Doctor Faustus*, pp. 268, 33, 183.
27   'weighs more heavily': TM, *Doctor Faustus*, p. 33.
      'a parody of myself': TM to Paul Amann (cited in Clark, *Beyond Catastrophe*, p. 101).
      Clark notes that through Zeitblom Mann was ironising the German tendency to see
      their conflicts of conscience as unusually noble and profound. For a discussion of the
      novel's self-reflexivity and Zeitblom's unreliability as a narrator see Martin Swales,
      'The over-representations of history? Reflections on Thomas Mann's Doktor Faustus'
      in Fulbrook and Swales, *Representing the German Nation* (Manchester University
      Press, 2000), pp. 77–90.
      'popular elation', 'a sacrificial rite', 'soul is powerfully', 'our love belongs': TM, *Doctor
      Faustus*, pp. 317, 185.
      'How much Faustus'; 'A radical confession': TM, diary, 1 Jan 1946, in *Tagebücher*.
28   'a mistake': TM to Max Rychner, 26 Oct 1947, in *Letters of Thomas Mann*, ed. and
      trans. Richard and Clara Winston (Alfred A. Knopf, 1971).
      'I was too old': TM, Interview, *Die Welt*, 20 May 1947, in Hansen, *Frage und
      Antwort*.
      'so utterly German': TM to Dean of Philosophical Faculty of University of Bonn, 28
      Jan 1947, in *Letters of Thomas Mann*.
29   'foolish', 'believed, exulted, sacrificed', 'And they will': TM, *Doctor Faustus*, p. 475.
30   'I hope it': TM to Walter Kolb, 4 Jan 1948, in *Letters of Thomas Mann*.
      'Even though he': Victor Sell, 'Doktor Faustus', *Die Wandlung*, 3:5, cited in Clark,
      Beyond Catastrophe, p. 111 (also see Clark for a summary of reviews).
      'there is a Germany': Walter Boehlich, 'Thomas Mann's Doktor Faustus', *Merkur*, 10,
      1948, pp. 588–603.

31   'hope beyond', 'abides as', 'transatlantic general', 'should one say', 'though at times', 'Whatever lived', 'this gruesome': TM, *Doctor Faustus*, pp. 515, 505, 506.
32   'Huge stone doorways': SB, *Force of Circumstance*, trans. by Richard Howard (Penguin, 1975), p. 144.
     'Ruins and rubbishes': SB to Nelson Algren, 31 Jan 1948, in *A Transatlantic Love Affair: Letters to Nelson Algren*, ed. by Sylvie Le Bon de Beauvoir (New Press, 1998).
33   'Not one French': Louis Aragon, *Les Désastres de la Guerre*, cited in Martin Schieder, *Im Blick des Anderen: Die Deutsch-Französischen Kunstbeziehungen 1945–1959* (Akademie Verlag, 2005), p. 37.
     For more information on French cultural policy see Daniela Högerle, *Propaganda oder Verständigung: Instrumente französischer Kulturpolitik in Südbaden, 1945–1959* (Peter Lang, 2013); Stefan Zauner, *Erziehung und Kulturmission: Frankreichs Bildungspolitik in Deutschland 1945–1949* (Oldenbourg Verlag, 1994).
34   'a new fashion': *Samedi Soir*, 1945, cited in Annie Cohen-Solal, *Sartre: A Life*, trans. by Anna Cancogni (Pantheon Books, 1988), p. 263.
     'to maintain through': cited in Carole Seymour-Jones, *A Dangerous Liaison: Simone de Beauvoir and Jean-Paul Sartre* (Century, 2008), p. 353.
35   'existence precedes', 'anguish', 'self-recovery': JPS, *Being and Nothingness*, trans. by Hazel Estella Barnes (Simon and Schuster, 1992), pp. 802, 51, 116.
36   'providential', 'authenticity': JPS, *The War Diaries*, trans. Quintin Hoare (Pantheon Books, 1985), p. 182.
     'in the underground': JPS, lecture in New York, spring 1945, cited by Ronald Aronson, *Camus and Sartre: The Story of a Friendship and the Quarrel that Ended It* (University of Chicago, 2004), p. 54.
37   'example of bourgeois': Wolfgang Harich, *Tägliche Rundschau*, 9 Jan 1948.
38   For this interpretation of pro-Russian French policy, see Schivelbusch, *In a Cold Crater*.
39   'I am seeing', 'They are amazed': SB to Algren, 31 Jan 1948, in *A Transatlantic Love Affair*.
40   'You feel worst', 'You cannot fancy how sad': SB to Algren, 31 Jan 1948 (Sunday morning), in *A Transatlantic Love Affair*.
41   'to the woman', 'big ugly woman', 'It seems': SB to Algren, 31 Jan 1948, in *A Transatlantic Love Affair*.
42   Alexander Dymschitz, 30 Nov 1947, cited in Alfred Betschart, 'Sartre und *Die Fliegen* in Berlin 1948', http://www.sartre.ch/Verger.pdf, p. 17.
43   'Nobody can do', 'the actors were': SB to Algren, 31 Jan 1948 (Tuesday), in *A Transatlantic Love Affair*
     'a demonstration', 'arid and', 'bloomed in': Friedrich Luft, cited in Betschart, 'Sartre und *Die Fliegen*'.
     'major coup', 'neither true': HS, review in *Die Welt*, in HS, *The Dark and The Bright*, p. 232.
44   'nightmare city', 'It's measured by', 'creeping, half-human': JPS, *The Flies* and *In Camera*, trans. Stuart Gilbert (Hamish Hamilton, 1946), pp. 7, 15, 15.
45   'That is not *my* palace, nor *my* door', 'national pastime', 'the game of', 'forgive us for', 'All you have', 'I bitterly repent', 'I am free': JPS, *The Flies*, pp. 21, 32, 43, 99, 78.
46   'Please forgive': JPS, *The Flies*, p. 44.
     'Germany is free': TM, *Doctor Faustus*, p. 529.
     'I am free': JPS, *The Flies.*, p. 87.
47   'it administers': Alfons Steinberger, in 'Jean-Paul Sartre in Berlin: Discussion of *The Flies*', *Verger*, 1:5, 1948, pp. 109–23 (reprinted http://www.sartre.ch/Verger.pdf).
48   'To wallow in', 'Responsibility on the', 'You do not': JPS, in 'Jean-Paul Sartre in Berlin'.
49   'It is liberty': M. Theunissen, in 'Jean-Paul Sartre in Berlin'.
50   'There has never', 'it is purely': JPS, in 'Jean-Paul Sartre in Berlin'.
     'my freedom implies': JPS, *Cahiers pour une moral* (Gallimard, 1983), p. 487, cited in Steven Crowell (ed.), *The Cambridge Companion to Existentialism*, (Cambridge University Press, 2012), p. 46.

'a free agent', 'the perspective', 'bring it about': JPS, *Anti-Semite and Jew*, trans. by George Joseph Becker (Schocken, 1948), p. 148.

51   'We felt', 'I never saw': SB to Algren, 31 Jan 1948 (Tuesday), in *A Transatlantic Love Affair*.

52   'We were against': JPS, '"Wir sind alle Luthers Opfer": Spiegel-Gesprach mit Jean-Paul Sartre', *Spiegel*, vol 20, May 1960.

53   On translations of Sartre into German, see Marieluise Christadler, 'Der französische Existentialismus und die deutschen Intellektuellen in der Nachkriegszeit', in Asholt Wofgang et al (eds.), *Frankreich ein unverstandener Nachbar 1945–1990* (Romanistischer Verlag, 1990), pp. 224–38.

54   'Erst kommt': BB, *Die Dreigroschenoper*, first performed in Berlin in August 1928.

13: *Germany in California*

1   'To hell with those bastards!': BW as recalled by John Woodcock in J.M. Woodcock, 'The Name Dropper', *American Cinemeditor*, 39:4, Winter 1989/1990, p. 15, cited in Sikov, *On Sunset Boulevard*, p. 272.

2   Cast put on weight in Italy: see Peter Brunette, *Roberto Rossellini* (Oxford University Press, 1987), p. 77.

3   'What a picture': BW speaking to John Lund, cited in Sikov, *On Sunset Boulevard*, p. 277.

4   Rossellini's neorealist take on the same Berlin ruins was more direct in its message. Most versions of *Germany Year Zero* start with the statement that 'when an ideology strays from the eternal laws of morality and of Christian charity, which form the basis of men's lives, it must end as criminal madness'. The voiceover suggests that through the objective picture of suffering, children may be taught to love again.

5   For a detailed dating of Wilder's scenario, see Sollors, *The Temptation of Despair*, p. 249.

6   See Sollors, *The Temptation of Despair* for a discussion of Wilder's sympathy towards postwar Germany. By analysing several of Wilder's drafts of the screenplay, Sollors argues that the changes in the script parallel the change in American attitudes towards Germany from a punitive posture to a collaborative one (p. 253).

7   For an account of the enmity between Brecht and Mann, see Hans Mayer, 'Thomas Mann and Bertolt Brecht: Anatomy of an Antagonism', *New German Critique*, vol 6, pp. 101–15.
      English conversation: TM, diary, 30 May 1948, in *Tagebücher*.

8   'In hell too': BB, 'On Thinking about Hell', in BB, *Poems 1913–1956*, ed. John Willett, trans. Ralph Manheim (Routledge: 1979).
      For an account of the landscape and geography of Los Angeles, see Otto Friedrich, *City of Nets: A Portrait of Hollywood in the 1940s* (University of California Press, 1997).

9   'the most sophisticated', 'if human pressure': SB, 25 Feb 1947, in *America Day By Day* (University of California, 1999), p. 109.
      'with a shake': SB, 27 Feb 1947, in *America Day By Day*, p. 121.

10   'I was enchanted': TM, *The Story of a Novel: the genesis of Dr Faustus*, trans. by R. and C. Winston (Knopf, 1961), p. 64.
      'the light, the dry', 'the holm oak': TM to Erich von Kahler, 8 Jul 1940, in *Letters of Thomas Mann*.

11   'You ought to', 'with the view': TM to Hermann Hess, 14 Mar 1942, in *Letters of Thomas Mann*.

12   'an embarrassed, fervid', 'of the intense': Susan Sontag, 'Pilgrimage', *The New Yorker*, 21 Dec 1987.

13   'He liked to': Katia Mann, in *Katia Mann: Unwritten Memories* (Knopf, 1975), p. 120.

14 List of three greatest living writers: TM, 'The bourgeoisie fell for the Nazis and
    Fascism', Interview by Corrado Pizzinelli, in *Sera*, 1 Aug 1947, in Hansen, *Frage und
    Antwort*.

15 'My deepest wish': TM, diary, 1 Feb 1948, in *Tagebücher*.

16 'Her suffering': TM, diary, 29 Mar 1948, in *Tagebücher*.
    'the desire for': TM, diary, 4 Apr 1948, in *Tagebücher*.

17 'as excited and curious': EM to Lotte Walter, Dec 1947, EM Archive.
    'The files are swelling', 'no day': TM, diary, 21 Jan 1948, in *Tagebücher*.

18 'It will no longer': TM, diary, 4 Apr 1945, in *Tagebücher*.
    'sick and tired': TM, diary, 6 Nov 1946, in *Tagebücher*.
    'catastrophic': TM, diary, 13 Mar 1947, in *Tagebücher*. See also: TM, 'Communism –
    an empty word', *San Francisco Chronicle*, 23 Nov 1947, on America's failure to
    understand communism.
    'the unification of': TM, Interview in *Die Welt*, 20 May 1947, in Hansen, *Frage und
    Antwort*.
    'Feel unnerved': TM, diary, 3 Oct 1947, in *Tagebücher*.
    'moral relaxation': TM to Agnes Mayer, 10 Oct 1947, in *Letters of Thomas Mann*.
    'idiotic and unlawful': TM to Ida Herz, 26 Oct 1947, in *Letters of Thomas Mann*.

19 'Russians in Berlin Seize 5 Americans', *The New York Times*, 13 Jan 1948.
    'provocative policies', 'running the risk': Herbert Morrison cited in 'Britain to Russia',
    The New York Times, 13 Jan 1948.
    'The Russians like', 'in extreme': George P. Hays cited in 'Clay's Aid Firm on Stay in
    Berlin', *The New York Times*, 13 Jan 1948.
    'Americans and English', 'Reds succumb': TM, diary, 21 Jan 1948, in *Tagebücher*.

20 'young, vigorous': 'Mr. Bevin's Outline for a Western Union', *The Times*, 23 Jan
    1948.
    'Again I see Russia': TM, diary, 25 Jan 1948, in *Tagebücher*.

21 '15,000 well-armed': TM, diary, 9 Feb 1948, in *Tagebücher*.
    'Of course this': TM, diary, 10 Mar 1948, in *Tagebücher*.

22 'the old gentlemen': TM, diary, 7 Mar 1948, in *Tagebücher*.

23 'The Text of President Truman's Address to the Joint Session of the Congress', *The
    New York Times*, 18 Mar 1948.

24 On Marshal Vasily Sokolovsky, see Richard Collier, *Bridge Across the Sky: The Berlin
    Blockade and Airlift, 1948–1949* (Mcgraw-Hill, 1978), p. 4.
    'as an organ', 'no sense': 'Soviet Quits Berlin Council. Lays Rift to Western Allies',
    The New York Times, 21 Mar 1948.

25 'We are here': 'Russians Cancel Meetings of Berlin Control Groups', *The New York
    Times*, 23 Mar 1948.

26 'nonsense headlines': TM, diary, 26 Mar 1948, in *Tagebücher*.
    'from the very': 'All Germany is in a State of Tension', *The New York Times*, 28 Mar
    1948.
    'has in fact', 'the dismemberment': 'Moscow Radio Avers End of Berlin Control
    Council', *The New York Times*, 1 Apr 1948.
    Clay stands ground: 'Berliners' Fears of Clash Increase', *The New York Times*, 3 Apr
    1948.

27 'Soviet-British Plane Collision Kills 15; Russia Apologizes', *The New York Times*,
    6 Apr 1948.
    'The newspapers', 'Hardly any': TM, diary, 11 Apr 1948, in *Tagebücher*.
    Argument with Heinrich: TM, diary, 14 Feb 1948, in *Tagebücher*.
    'Agree with Erika': TM, diary, 1 May 1948, in *Tagebücher*.

28 'Was it not true': KM, 'Lecturing in Europe on American Literature', Dec 1948, KM
    Archive.

29 'Can the mother', 'language exile', 'all the time', 'Will the result': KM, 'Das
    Sprach-Problem', *National-Zeitung* (Sonntags-Beilage), 28 Sep 1947, KM
    Archive.

30 'I find it increasingly', 'There are moments': KM, cited in Weiss, *In the Shadow*, p. 228.

31 'exhilarating and pernicious', 'freedom, lightness': TM, *Doctor Faustus*, p. 406.
    'If one could', 'sadly impossible', 'with a mixture': KM, 'Deutschland und seine Nachbarn' (lecture), 12 Apr 1948, KM Archive.

32 'Mr K.M.': KM, 'Lecturing in Europe'.
    'weary, melancholy': HS, *The Dark and The Bright*, p. 235.
    'the mangled cadaver': KM, 'Lecturing in Europe'.

33 Arrival of tanks: '100 Big Soviet Tanks At Berlin, British Say', *The New York Times*, 15 Apr 1948.
    'It would be': 'British Discount Tank Move', *The New York Times*, 16 Apr 1948.
    American bombers: '28 Heavy Bombers, Just Arrived From U.S., Are Ordered by Clay to Sortie Over Berlin', *The New York Times*, 16 Apr 1948.
    Trucks with insulin: 'Russians Hold Up Medicines', *The New York Times*, 17 Apr 1948.
    'bitten old ladies', 'beaten': '4-Power Berlin Aides in Fruitless Session', *The New York Times*, 8 May 1948.

34 'unfriendly, dangerous', 'she refuses to': Christopher Isherwood, diary, 31 Mar 1940, in *Christopher Isherwood Diaries: 1939–1960*, vol 1, ed. by Katherine Bucknell (Vintage, 2011).

35 'enraptured with Eissi', 'deeply struck by', 'quite natural': TM, 17 Oct 1920, in TM, *Diaries, 1918–1939*.
    'To be the son', 'But it is likewise': TM, *The Beloved Returns: Lotte in Weimar* (New York : Alfred A. Knopf, 1969), p. 65.

36 See KM's depiction of Höfgen as part of a Germany that is driving itself crazily to ruin in *Mephisto,* trans. Robin Smyth (Penguin, 1995), pp. 145–46.

37 'Spoke about Berlin': TM, diary, 29 May 1948, in *Tagebücher*.
    'another colossal', 'with absolute': Knopf to TM, cited in diary, 29 May 1948, in *Tagebücher.* 'Klaus all over': TM, diary, 11 Jun 1948, in *Tagebücher.*

38 'cut the flow': 'U.S. Bars Russian Publications From Distribution in German Zone', *The New York Times*, 20 May 1948.
    Restricted routes: 'U.S. Restricts Soviet Entry To German Zone in Reprisal', *The New York Times*, 21 May 1948.
    Petition: '8,663,461 Germans Said to Ask Unity', *The New York Times*, 31 May 1948.

39 'Am glad not to': TM, diary, 14 Jun 1948, in *Tagebücher.*

40 'ordeals': TM, diary, 15 Jun 1948, in *Tagebücher.*

41 Coal cars: 'Russian Tightens Berlin Grip; Halts Coal Cars From West', *The New York Times*, 16 Jun 1948.
    Soviet representative walks out: 'Russians Walk Out Of Berlin Meeting', *The New York Times*, 17 Jun 1948. (The representative left as a protest against the fact that Colonel Frank Howley had left, deputing to his deputy, which the Soviets considered 'rude').
    'Our insistence on', 'It is absolutely': TM, diary, 17 Jun 1948, in *Tagebücher.*
    'American despotism': TM, diary, 18 Jun 1948, in *Tagebücher.*

42 Tension over currency: see Collier, *Bridge Across the Sky*, p. 34.
    Travel restrictions: 'Entry to Soviet Zone Barred', *The New York Times*, 19 Jun 1948.
    Transport aircraft: 'West Turns To Air As Soviet Cuts Off Berlin Land Links', *The New York Times*, 20 Jun 1948.
    'confusion in Germany': TM, diary, 20 Jun 1948, in *Tagebücher.*

43 Jazz banned: 'Russians Ban Jazz Two Days', *The New York Times*, 21 Jun 1948.
    'as grave as', 'in yielding': 'Churchill Likens Berlin to Munich; Vows Aid to Bevin', *The New York Times*, 27 Jun 1948.

44 'As the planes': Colonel Frank Howley, cited in Diana Canwell and Jon Sutherland, *The Berlin Airlift: The Salvation of a City* (Pelican, 2008), p. 38.

14: *The Berlin Airlift*

1   'If this is a siege', 'If this is a war': HS, 'Victories', unpublished article for *New Statesman*, cited in *The Dark and The Bright*, p. 241.
    'We must, if': Harold Macmillan to the House of Commons, 30 Jun 1948, cited in 'Bevin Bars Any Surrender if Air Supply of the City Causes "Grave Situation"', *The New York Times*, 1 Jul 1948.
    'We are in': George Marshall, cited in 'Marshall Asserts U.S. Will "Deal Promptly" With Any Issues—Mores B-29s Sent', *The New York Times*, 1 Jul 1948.

2   On Furtwängler, see MacDonogh, *After the Reich*, p. 530.

3   'The conflict in', 'Continual deliveries': TM, diary, 3 Jul 1948, in *Tagebücher*.
    'slim and more': TM, diary, 6 Jul 1948, in *Tagebücher*.

4   'ghost parade', 'Like the hero': KM, 'Lecturing in Europe on American Literature', Dec 1948, KM Archive.

5   'the impulse was': TM to Theodor Adorno, Jul 12 1948, in *Letters of Thomas Mann*, ed. and trans. by Richard and Clara Winston (Alfred A. Knopf, 1971). He also writes here: 'I am somewhat angry with him for having tried to do that to his mother', 'tried to do away', 'dégoût and sadness': EM to Alfred Duff Cooper, 27 Aug 1948, EM Archive.

6   '*La difficulté d'être*', 'I often find': KM to Otto Eisner, 12 Aug 1948, KM Archive.

7   'sympathy with death', 'sweet and deadly': KM, *The Turning Point*, p. xvii.

8   'In the mornings': KM, diary, 19 Feb 1933, in *Tagebücher*.
    'E stands between': KM, diary, 27 Oct 1935, KM Archive.
    'the tuna problem', 'Her worker, her': KM, diary, 31 Dec 1935, KM Archive.
    'The craving for': KM, diary, 22 Oct 1935, KM Archive.

9   'many people think', 'The roots of': KM, *The Turning Point*, pp. 68, 80.

10   'The baby carriage', 'a symbol', 'the harbour', 'cradle and', 'the sleep': KM, *The Turning Point*, p. 5.

11   'what you forfeit': KM, *The Turning Point*, p. 23.

12   'only the parts': KM, cited in Weiss, *In the Shadow*, p. 224.

13   'Very tense situation', 'A few dozen': TM, diary, 18 Jul 1948, in *Tagebücher*.

14   'the moment we', 'we shall have': EM, Town Meeting in Stockton California, 9 Aug 1948 (and broadcast for American Broadcasting Company, 10 Aug), typescript, EM Archive.

15   'How can we', 'the Germans today', 'frightened and nervous', 'completely alone': EM, Town Meeting in Stockton.

16   'very courageous': TM, diary, 10 Aug 1948, in *Tagebücher*.
    'nothing other than': Harry Wilde, 'Before a New November Putsch? Communist Agent Erika Mann, Stalin's Fifth Column at Work', *Echo der Woche*, 22 Oct 1948, EM Archive.

17   'Hollywood's most', 'approximated reality': Review of *A Foreign Affair*, *New York Post*, 1 Jul 1948.
    'it may not cure': Review of *A Foreign Affair*, *Herald Tribune*, 1 Jul 1948.

18   'We should . . . admit': Information Policy edict, 20 Jul 1948, cited in Fay, *Theaters of Occupation*, p. 87.
    'crude, superficial', 'Berlin's trials': Stuart Schulberg, 'A Letter about Billy Wilder', *Quarterly of Film, Radio and Television*, 7:4, Summer 1953, p. 435, cited in Sikov, *On Sunset Boulevard*, p. 278. According to Werner Sollors, there is no credible source citation for this (*The Temptation of Despair*, p. 259). However Sollors quotes a revealing 1953 letter from Marshall Plan film producer Stuart Schulberg describing how after viewing *A Foreign Affair* in Berlin, Pommer and the Military Government's Screening Committee ruled the film was unsuitable for German audiences. Schulberg remembered how while watching the film 'our disappointment turned into resentment and our resentment into disgust. Perhaps we were all too close to the situation; we certainly lacked Wilder's happy-go-lucky perspective. But straining our

objectivity to the breaking point, we could not excuse a director who played the ruins for laughs, cast Military Government officers as comics, and rang in the Nazis for an extra boff' (Sollors, p. 261).

19   Artists did not want to leave: Gigi Richter, 'Berlin Letter', *Horizon*, Jul–Aug 1948.
20   'Working for you': MD to BW, 14 Jul 1948, MD Archive.
     'delectable dish': *The New Yorker*, cited in Bach, *Marlene Dietrich*, p. 334.
21   'Between us and': HS, diary, 14 Jul 1948, HS Archive,
     'none of my': 'Americans Told to Stop Mixing With Russians', *The New York Times*, 4 Jan 1949.
     'We held different': HS to her mother, cited in HS, *The Dark and the Bright*, p. 243.
22   Alexandrov Ensemble: This was the second performance at the Berlin Staatsoper (the first was on 9 Aug) and was part of a larger tour involving performances in Czechoslovakia, Dresden, Weimar, Magdeburg and Schwerin. The programme combined Russian music with music by German composers including Wagner and Schumann. See Carl Friedrich, 'Ein Fest sowjetischer Volkskunst', *Neues Deutschland*, 11 Aug 1948.
     Outdoor concert: This concert was organised by the FDGB (Freier Deutscher Gewerkschaftsbund), the East German trade union federation, which was controlled by the SED.
     'surrounded by ruins': HS, *The Dark and the Bright*, p. 244.
23   'quietly wistful': HS, *The Dark and the Bright*, p. 244.
24   'Life here, with': Rex Warner to Pam Morris, 26 Jun 1948, cited in Stephen Ely Tabachnick, *Fiercer than Tigers: The Life and Work of Rex Warner* (Michigan State University Press, 2002), pp. 245–46.
25   Figures: Canwell and Sutherland, *The Berlin Airlift*, p. 183; details here from: 'Berlin Dichotomy', *New Statesman and Nation*, 21 Aug 1948.
26   On currency, see Ruth Friedrich, *Schauplatz Berlin* (Suhrkamp, 1985), pp. 246–48, cited in MacDonogh, *After the Reich*, p. 529.
27   'abject poverty': Gigi Richter, 'Berlin letter'.
28   'Suicide rate': MacDonogh, *After the Reich*, p. 532.
29   'it depends on': 'Four Powers Conference In Berlin On Control of Currency; Lifting of Blockade Studied', *The New York Times*, 1 Sep 1948.
     'in the four': Clay, cited in MacDonogh, *After the Reich*, p. 532.
     'no longer represents': 'Four Powers Achieve Further Progress in Berlin Parleys', *The New York Times*, 5 Sep 1948.
30   'We cannot be': Ernst Reuter, cited in Collier, *Bridge Across the Sky*, p. 119.
31   'a good idea': cited in Fay, *Theaters of Occupation*, p. 99. On opinion polls, see also: John Ramsden, *Don't Mention the War: The British and the Germans since 1890* (Little Brown, 2006), pp. 234–6. On POWS specifically see Ramsden, p. 236, Meehan, *A Strange Enemy People*, p. 30.
     Although the POWs were being released, it is worth noting that there were still more than 3 million German soldiers in Russian captivity, where they were working as slave labourers, and that most Jewish DPs were now on their way to Palestine (Hitchcock, *Liberation*, p. 338.)
32   'disgraced', 'The capital of a Germany that finally, finally, wants peace, peace and nothing but peace': Becher to *PEN* Congress, cited in 'Re-establishment of the German Centre', in *PEN News*, 156, Aug 1948.
33   Figures: Canwell and Sutherland, *Berlin Airlift*, p. 119.
34   'here very few': Melvin Lasky to Dwight MacDonald, 10 Oct 1947, cited in Stonor Saunders, *Who paid the piper?*, p. 28.
35   Melvin Lasky, 'The Need for a New, Overt Publication', 7 Dec 1947, OMGUS/RG260/NARA, cited in Stonor Saunders, *Who Paid the Piper?*, pp. 28–30.
     On Lasky's new magazine, see Stonor Saunders, *Who Paid the Piper?*, p. 30; Giles

Scott-Smith, *The Politics of Apolitical Culture: The Congress for Cultural Freedom, the CIA and Post-war American Hegemony* (Routledge, 2001), p. 91.

36 'a natural phenomenon': Alfred Döblin, 'Zeitschriftenschau', *Das goldene Tor*, 1/2, Oct/Nov 1946.

37 'Russian victory', 'be no individuals': Bertrand Russell, 'Der Weg zum Weltstaat', *Der Monat*, Oct 1948.

38 'Soviet Russia without': Drew Middleton, 'Sowjet-Russland ohne Propaganda', *Der Monat*, Oct 1948.

39 'imprisoned': James Agee, 'Eisensteins letztes Werk', *Der Monat*, 1948.

40 'a lot of': KM to Melvin Lasky, 27 Oct 1948, KM Archive.
'readable', 'educated', 'omitting': TM, diary, 10 Nov 1948, in *Tagebücher*; even when Brecht did settle in Germany, it was with an Austrian passport as his wife Helene Weigel was Austrian.

41 'To me these ruins': BB, diary, 23 Oct 1948, in BB, *Journals 1934–1955* (Routledge, 1996).
'Berlin, an etching,' BB, diary, 27 Oct 1948, in *Journals*.'a real fear': BB, 'Brief an Thomas Mann,' in BB, *Gesammelte Werke*, 20 Bände, Band 8 (Taschenbuch, 1968), p. 478.

42 Actors disappointing, 'epic theatre': BB, diary, 11 Nov 1948, in *Arbeitsjournal 1938–1955* (Aufbau-Verlag, 1977).
'And so we'll': BB, 'Aufbaulied der F.D.J.', in *Werke*, ed. by Werner Hecht *et al*, vol 15, Gedichte 5, pp. 196–97, cited in Brockmann *German Literary Culture*, p. 250.

43 Hope and Berlin: MacDonogh, *After the Reich*, p. 535.

44 For *Volkstümlichkeit*, see Paul Rilla, 'Gegen den deutschen Kriegsmythos', *Berliner Zeitung*, 13 Jan 1949.
For Moses, see Wolfgang Harich, 'Der gemeine Mann had kein' Gewinn', *Tägliche Rundschau*, 14 Jan 1949.
For degenerate formalism, see Fritz Erpenbeck, 'Mutter Courage und ihre Kinder', *Vorwärts*, 13 Jan 1949. I am grateful to Stephen Brockmann for letting me read an unpublished draft discussion of the 1949 production of *Mother Courage and her Children* in his forthcoming monograph on East German post-war literature.

45 'War's a deal': BB, *Mother Courage and Her Children*, trans. David Hare (Methuen: 1995), p. 15.

46 'romp in': BB, diary, 9 Dec 1948, in *Arbeitsjournal*.

47 'sacrifice', 'cast its blessings': Hjalmar Schacht, *Account Settled* (Weidenfeld & Nicolson, 1949), p. 322.
'Literature must commit': BB, diary, 11 Dec 1948, in *Journals*.

48 'The world's dying': BB, *Mother Courage*, p. 79; Figures: MacDonogh, *After the Reich*, p. 535 (second only in viciousness to the winter of 1946/47).
On air deliveries: '12,000-Ton Day On The Air-Lift', *The Times*, 18 Apr 1949.

49 'Lord Mayor of Rubble': Reuter, cited in Collier, *Bridge Across the Sky*, p. 144
For elections, see Collier, *Bridge Across the Sky*, p. 144; Canwell and Sutherland, *Berlin Airlift*, p.153.
'a plebiscite for': PdeM, 'The Berlin Plebiscite,' *New Statesman*, 4 Dec 1948.

50 PdeM, 'Triple-headed Monstrosity', *New Statesman*, 25 Dec 1948.

51 'neighbourly act', 'We are like': Truman, quoted in 'Atlantic Nations Sign Defense Pact', *The New York Times*, 4 Apr 1949.
'courage and vision', 'could still determine', 'They can choose': 'Addresses by Foreign Ministers at Signing of North Atlantic Pact', *The New York Times*, 5 Apr 1949.

52 'The ground rushed': RW, *Greenhouse with Cyclamens II*, in *A Train of Powder*, p. 151.

53 'Loosest, least confined', 'Everybody in Berlin': RW, *Greenhouse with Cyclamens II*. p. 140.

54   'tired feet', 'learned with their', 'democratic faith': RW, *Greenhouse with Cyclamens II*,
      p. 172.
      'In Russia they': Henry Andrews, report on Germany, 1949, RW Archive (Tulsa).

15: *Division*

1   'world literature', 'naturalness', 'age-burdened': TM, speech, 2 May 1949, in *Thomas
      Mann's Addresses delivered at the Library of Congress*, pp. 108, 129.
      'a campaign against': TM, diary, 19 Aug 1948, in *Tagebücher*.
2   'the chessboard': Arthur Miller, cited in Saunders, *Who Paid the Piper?*, p. 56.
3   'used chiefly as': Francis Biddle to TM, in *Letters of Thomas Mann*, footnote 1 on
      p. 576. (Note that Biddle was no longer in an official public role in the US).
      'a great number', 'a purely cultural', 'What is wrong': TM to Francis Biddle, 14 Apr
      1949, in *Letters of Thomas Mann*.
4   'fundamentally disinclined': TM, press conference after Goethe lecture, cited in
      'Mann sees Soviet Bidding for Peace', *The New York Times*, 6 May 1949.
5   For reviews of *Doctor Faustus*, see Hellmut Jaesrich, 'Dr Faustus in Amerika', *Der
      Monat*, January 1949.
6   'Post Hitlerian Germany': EM, 'Occupation – Trial or Error' (lecture), Oct 1948, EM
      Archive.
      'natural, that is': Bruno Walter, cited in Katia Mann to KM, 22 Nov 1948, KM
      Archive.
7   'I AM good': KM to EM and Katia Mann, 25 Aug 1948, KM Archive.
      'thinking of death': KM, diary, 30 Sep 1948, KM Archive.
8   'without any obligations': KM, *The Last Day*, Manuscript, chapter 10, KM Archive.
      'They talk about': KM, *The Last Day*, chapter 1.
9   'at once capricious', 'dirt and blood': KM, *The Last Day*, chapter 13, chapter 18.
10   Lure of death: KM, *The Last Day*, chapter 15.
11   'the taste of': KM, *The Last Day*, chapter 19.
12   'the issue of', 'more tedious and': cited in Weiss, *In the Shadow*, p. 236.
      'Not writing, but': KM, diary, 25 Apr 1949, KM Archive.
      'Mr Gründgens plays': KM, diary, 1 Jan 1949, KM Archive.
13   'Rain . . . the weather': KM, diary, 3 May 1949, KM Archive.'
      utmost precaution', 'do not slurp': KM to EM, 4 May 1949, KM Archive.
14   KM to Katia Mann and EM, 15 May 1949, KM Archive.
15   'a minor relapse': KM, diary, 17 May 1949, KM Archive.
      'But the Germans': TM, lecture at Jewish Wiener Library in London, 18 May 1949,
      in 'Thomas Mann's Rede in der Wiener Library', Mitteilungsblatt des PEN-Clubs
      Deutscher Autoren im Ausland, Sept 1949, cited in Burgin and Mayer, *Thomas
      Mann: A Chronicle of His Life*, p. 225.
      'If one takes', 'And now': EM to KM, 17 May 1949, EM Archive.
16   'doing well', 'all love', 'lovely': KM to Katia and EM, 20 May 1949, KM Archive.
17   'My concern and': TM, 22 May 1949, in *Tagebücher*.
      'It seemed more', 'it was going': Katia to Heinrich Mann, 24 May 1949, in *Letters of
      Heinrich and Thomas Mann, 1900–1949*, ed. by Hans Wysling, trans. by Don Reneau
      (University of California Press, 1998).
18   'These are sad', 'it pains me': TM to Heinrich Mann, 26 May 1945, in *Letters of
      Heinrich and Thomas Mann*.
19   'That's why he': EM, quoted in TM to Hans Reisiger, 28 Jun 1949, cited in Hayman,
      Thomas Mann, p. 562.
20   'we killed those': KM, *The Last Day*, chapter 15.
21   'bitter distortion': TM, diary, 12 Jun 1949, in *Tagebücher*.
      'Despite the years', 'How am I': EM to Pamela Wedekind, 16 Jun 1949, EM
      Archive.

22   'a nervous': TM, diary, 21 Jun 1949, in *Tagebücher*.
23   Decision to visit Weimar: TM, diary, 16 Jun 1949, in *Tagebücher*; in a letter to Hermann Hesse Thomas sadly acknowledged that he had played his part in Klaus's decline: 'my relationship to him was difficult' (6 Jul 1949, in *Letters of Thomas Mann*).
24   'psychoanalytical study': Walter Abendroth, 'Leverkühns Musikvorstellung', *Die Zeit*, Hamburg, 23 June 1949.
      'Feel as if going to war': TM, diary, 23 Jul 1949, in *Tagebücher*.
25   'scream to the': TM, *Doctor Faustus*, p. 184.
26   'a German government': Wilhelm Pieck, cited in Norman Naimark, *The Russians in Germany: A History of the Soviet Zone of Occupation, 1945–1949* (Belknap Press, 1995), p. 59.
      new ground blockades: 'West Awaits Word on Soviet Actions', *The New York Times*, 12 Jul 1949.
27   TM, 'Ansprache im Goethejahr', 1949, in *Gesammelte Werke*, 13 vols (Fischer, 1974), vol II, pp. 481–97.
28   'symbol of our', 'the highest expression': Grotewohl, cited in Brockmann, *German Literary Culture*, p. 115.
      'that star of': Frank Thiess, 'Der Weltdeutsche und die 'Innere Emigration', cited in Brockmann, *German Literary Culture*, p. 106.
      'Goethe communities', 'something indestructible': Friedrich Meinecke, *The German Catastrophe: Reflections and Recollections*, trans. Sidney B. Fay (Harvard University Press, 1950), pp. 12–21.
      'Goethe's world is': Karl Jaspers, acceptance speech for Goethe prize, Frankfurt, 1947, reprinted in 'Our Future and Goethe', in Karl Jaspers, *Existentialism and Humanism: Three Essays*, trans. by Hanns E Fischer (Russell F Moore, 1952).
29   For a summary of the press reaction see Inge Jens' footnote in TM, *Tagebücher 1949–1950*, pp. 434–35.
      'We *know* that', 'this "other Germany"', 'American friends', 'help Germany, 'the road': EM and KM, *The Other Germany*, pp. xii–xiii, 318.
30   'The city': TM, diary, 4 Aug 1949, in *Tagebücher*.
      'To see this': TM to Emil Preetorius, 20 Oct 1949, in *Letters of Thomas Mann*.
31   For observations on luxury, see TM, 'Germany Today', *The New York Times Magazine*, 25 Sep 1949; RW, 'Greenhouse with Cyclamens II' in *A Train of Powder*.
      'the sight of': TM, 'Germany Today'.
32   For signing name after Hitler, Himmler and Goebbels ('whole devil's brood'), cited in Donald Prater, *Thomas Mann: A Life* (Oxford University Press, 1995), p. 419.
      'no neutrality': Eugen Kogon, open letter in the *Schwäbische Landeszeitung*, 1 Aug 1949.
      'the terrible truth', 'unified Germany', 'free German': see footnote to TM, *Tagebücher*, 23 Jul 1949.
33   'out of the present': TM, cited in 'Mann Cheered in Weimar', *The New York Times*, 2 Aug 1949.
34   Money to Herder church: TM, 'Germany Today'.
      Crowds on streets: TM to Paul Olberg, 27 Aug 1949, in *Letters of Thomas Mann*.
35   'to the many': TM, diary, 6 Aug 1949, in *Tagebücher*.
36   Announcement of new government: 'Dr. Adenauer's Declaration of Policy', *The Times*, 21 Sep 1949.
      'Western Germany–': André François-Poncet, cited in Dennis L. Bark and David R. Gress, *A History of West Germany* (2 Volumes), Vol I: *From Shadow to Substance 1945–1963*, (Blackwell, 1993), p. 254.
37   'a powerful bulwark': Declaration by People's Congress, 5 Oct 1949, cited in Naimark, *The Russians in Germany*, p. 59.
      'smash', 'until the unity': Pieck, Inaugural speech, cited in 'Pieck Is President As East Germans Organize Regime', *The New York Times*, 12 Oct 1949.

38   'Could turn out': TM, diary, 8 Sep 1949, in *Tagebücher*.
      Erika's skepticism: TM, diary, Sep 1949, in *Tagebücher*.
      'I seem to': TM to Reisiger, cited in notes to diary entry on 8 Sep 1949, in *Tagebücher*.
      'moral impressions', 'Everything was', 'hapless constellation': TM, 'Germany Today'.
39   TM, 'Germany Today'.
40   'The fact that', 'He does not': letters to *The New York Times*, 9 Oct 1949, 16 Oct 1949.
      'joy of home': TM, diary, 19 Aug, 1949 in *Tagebücher*.
      allegiance to America: Interview on Frankfurter Rundschau, 26 Jul 1949, reprinted as 'Thomas Mann: Meine Heimat is die deutsche Sprache', in Hansen, *Frage und Antwort*.
41   EM's continuing anger: TM, diary, 4 Sep 1949, in *Tagebücher*.
42   KM, 'Europe's Search for a New Credo', *Tomorrow*, 8:10, Jun 1949, KM Archive.
43   KM, 'Die Heimsuchung des europäischen Geistes' (Deutscher Taschenbuch Verlag, 1973) p. 132.
44   'a novel advocating', 'books don't have': KM, *The Last Day*, chapter 19.
      'not because', 'they died', 'this particular', 'irresponsible', 'the most': EM, 'Intellectuals' (lecture), Oct 1949, EM Archive.
45   ' "Look out!" these dead': EM, 'Intellectuals'.

'Closing time in the gardens of the West'

1   Signed at the Hotel Petersberg, this was known officially as the Petersberg Treaty. Rather than providing for Marshall Aid, the treaty enabled West Germany to put in place negotiations with the US formally to receive Marshall Aid. In fact they had informally received it since 1948. The Council of Europe, founded in May 1949, aimed at encouraging European integration and facilitating economic and social progress.
2   'an act of faith': Konrad Adenauer in an interview with Henry Andrews, 'Adenauer speaks to Britain: "Your Full Co-operation in Europe is Essential"', *Observer*, 11 Dec 1949.
3   'peace', 'two great': Winston Churchill, cited in Meehan, *A Strange Enemy People*, p. 268.
4   See Detlef Junker (ed.), *The United States and Germany in the Era of the Cold War 1945–1990: A Handbook*, Volume 1: 1945–1968 (German Historical Institute and Cambridge University Press, 2010). For popular culture: Uta G Poiger, 'Cold War Politics and American Popular Culture in Germany', pp. 439–44; for film: Daniel J. Leab, 'Side by Side: Hollywood and German Film Culture', pp. 457–63; for theatre: Andreas Höfele, 'From Reeducation to Alternative Theater: German-American Theater Relations', pp. 464–71; for French cross-influences: Frank Trommler, 'A New Start and Old Prejudices: The Cold War and German American Cultural Relations, 1945–63', pp. 371–87; for fine art: Sigrid Ruby, 'Fascination, Ignorance and Rejection: Changing Transatlantic Perspectives in the Visual Arts, 1945–1968', pp. 472–79.
5   West's thinking here seems somewhat controversial. From a socialist perspective, it could be argued that in fact madness and death had been pressed into the service of wealth and power, and that this had been true in other countries as well.
6   'why must mankind': Hannah Arendt, 'The Aftermath of Nazi Rule', *Commentary*, 1950, pp. 341–53 (p. 343).
      'the Jews themselves', 'better': poll, 1952, cited in Judt, *Postwar*, p. 272.
7   'a short jaunt': MG to Adlai Stevenson, 11 Oct 1962, MG Archive.
      'incurable', 'quiescent sheep', 'Remove those': MG to Adlai Stevenson, 26 Dec 1962, MG Archive.
      'deep depression': MG, diary, 24 Nov 1962, MG Archive.

8   'He hadn't just': WHA to Hedwig Petzold, 14 May 1955, WHA Archive.
     'Alas the city': WHA to Elizabeth Mayer, 7 Jul 1955, WHA Archive.
     'great tracks', 'overwhelming propaganda', 'hectic shouting': SS, diary, 9 Oct 1955,
     in Stephen Spender, *New Selected Journals 1939–1995*, ed. Lara Feigel and John
     Sutherland (Faber, 2012).
     'in much the','indulging in': SS, diary, 7 Jul 1955, in Spender, *New Selected
     Journals*.

9   'one of the': see Friedrich, *City of Nets*, p. 412.
     Reports of book burnings: Jessica Gienow-Hecht, 'American Cultural Foreign Policy
     Towards Germany, 1949–69', in Junker, *The United States and Germany*, p. 405.
     'cultural desert': TM, cited in Lepenies, *The Seduction of Culture*, p. 201.

10   'clear spirit', 'youthfully supple', 'illumined': EM, *The Last Year*, trans. Richard Graves
     (Secker & Warburg, 1958), pp. 91, 1.
     'Where is your Eissi?': EM to Frau Gamst, 8 Feb 1960, in EM, *Briefe und
     Antworten*.

11   For the demonstrations and placards, see Nick Thomas, *Protest Movements in 1960s
     West Germany: A Social History of Dissent and Democracy*, (Berg, 2003), p. 113–14.
     'this is the generation': Esslin, cited in Thomas, *Protest Movements*, p. 123.

12   'sickly parliament', 'end of its', 'go out on': Hans Magnus Enzensburger, speech
     delivered in Frankfurt am Main in 1968, cited in R. Hinton Thomas and Keith
     Bullivant, *Literature in Upheaval: West German Writers and the Challenge of the 1960s*,
     (Manchester University Press, 1974), p. 46.

13   'opposition to the American', 'the Red Army is established', 'Did the pigs', 'American
     imperialism': 'Die Rote Armee aufbauen!', *Agit 883*, 22 May 1970, cited in Thomas,
     Protest Movements, p. 204.

14   'The sound goes': Anselm Kiefer, 'Building, Dwelling, Thinking', cited in Kathleen
     Soriano, *Anselm Kiefer* (Royal Academy of Arts, 2014), p. 22.

15   'the day may': SS, 'The Intellectuals and the Future of Europe', *The Gate / Das Tor*,
     1:1, Jan–Mar 1947, p. 6.

16   'since wars begin': UNESCO First General Conference, 20 Nov-10 Dec 1946, cited
     in Fernando Valderrama, *A History of Unesco* (Unesco Publishing, 1995), p. 25.

17   'Dachau, and all': MG to Betsy Drake, 15 Jan 1972, MG Archive.
     Lee Miller's friend Anne-Laure Lyon later recalled Miller sobbing in old age as she
     recalled her visits to the death camps. Miller regretted that risk takers like herself and
     Lyon sometimes rushed into situations unprepared and brought out the photographs
     she had taken in the concentration camps that had remained hidden for years
     (Carolyn Burke, *Lee Miller: On Both Sides of the Camera*, Bloomsbury, 2006,
     p. 345).

18   'between man, betrayed', 'For it is closing': Cyril Connolly, 'Comment', *Horizon,,*
     Dec 1949–Jan 1950, p. 362.

19   'Aren't you ashamed', 'should be lynched': cited in Bach, *Marlene Dietrich*, p. 398.
     'such awful gooey': cited in Bach, *Marlene Dietrich*, p. 399.

20   'She is a', 'fascinating as a': *Handlesblatt* (Düsseldorf), 20/21 May, 1960, cited in
     Bach, *Marlene Dietrich*, p. 402.

21   'Splitsville': cited in Sikov, *On Sunset Boulevard*, p. 258.

Select Bibliography

Addison, Paul, *Now the War is Over: A Social History of Britain 1945–1951* (London: Pimlico, 1995)

Andreas-Friedrich, Ruth, *Battleground Berlin: Diaries, 1945–1948*, trans. by Anna Boerresen (New York: Paragon House, 1990)

Annan, Noel, *Changing Enemies: The Defeat and Regeneration of Germany* (London: Harper Collins, 1995)

— *The Dons: Mentors, Eccentrics and Geniuses* (London: Harper Collins, 1999)

Arendt, Hannah, *The Jew as Pariah: Jewish Identity and Politics in the Modern Age* (New York: Grove Press, 1978)

— and Karl Jaspers, *Correspondence 1926–1969*, ed. by Lotte Kohler and Hans Saner, trans. by Robert and Rita Kimber (New York: Harcourt Brace Jovanovich, 1992)

Babbio, Norberto, *Liberalism and Democracy*, trans. by Martin Ryle and Kate Soper (London: Verso, 1990)

Bach, Steven, *Marlene Dietrich: Life and Legend* (Minneapolis: University of Minnesota Press, 2011)

Bacque, James, *Crimes and Mercies: The Fate of German Civilians under Allied Occupation 1944–1950* (London: Little Brown and Company, 1997)

Bahr, Ehrhard, *Weimar on the Pacific: German Exile Culture in Los Angeles and the Crisis of Modernism* (London: University of California Press, 2007)

Baker, Carlos, *Ernest Hemingway: A Life Story* (New York: Charles Scribner's Sons, 1969)

Balfour, Michael, 'Re-education in Germany after 1945', *German History*, No. 5, 1987, pp. 25–34

— and John Mair, *Four Power Control in Germany and Austria 1945–1946* (Oxford: Oxford University Press, 1956)

Bance, Alan (ed.), *The Cultural Legacy of the British Occupation in Germany: The London Symposium* (Stuttgart: H.-D. Heinz, 1997)

Bark, Dennis L. and Gress, David, *A History of West Germany*, 2 vols., Vol. I: *From Shadow to Substance 1945–1963* (Oxford: Blackwell, 1993)

Becker, Jillian, *Hitler's Children: The Story of the Baader-Meinhof Terrorist Gang* (London: Michael Joseph, 1977)

Beddell Smith, Sally, *In All His Glory: The Life of William S. Paley the Legendary Tycoon and his Brilliant Circle* (New York: Random House, 2002)

Beevor, Antony, *Berlin: The Downfall, 1945* (London: Viking, 2002)

— *Ardennes 1944: Hitler's Last Gamble* (London: Penguin, 2015)

Bessel, Richard, *Germany 1945: From War to Peace* (London: Simon & Schuster, 2009)

Biddle, Francis, *In Brief Authority* (New York: Doubleday, 1962)

Birke, Adolf, and Eva Mayring (eds.), *Britische Besatzung in Deutschland: Aktienerschliessung und Forschungsfelder* (London: German Historical Institute, 1992)

— and Hans Booms and Otto Merker, *Akten der britischen Militärregierung in Deutschland – Sachinventar 1945–1955 (Control Commission for Germany British Element – Inventory 1945–1955)*, vols. I–II (Great Britain: Public Record Office and München: Saur, 1993)

Boehling, Rebecca, *A Question of Priorities: Democratic Reform and Economic Recovery in Postwar Germany* (Oxford: Berghahn Books, 1996)

— 'The Role of Culture in American Relations with Europe: The Case of the United States's Occupation of Germany', *Diplomatic History*, No. 23, 1999, pp. 57–69

Booth, Michael T. and Duncan Spencer, *Paratrooper: The Life of General James M. Gavin* (Oxford: Casemate, 1994)

Brecht, Bertolt, *Gesammelte Werke*, 20 Bände (Frankfurt am Main: Suhrkamp Verlag, 1968)

— *Arbeitsjournal 1938–1955* (Berlin: Aufbau-Verlag, 1977)

— *Poems 1913–1956*, ed. by John Willett and Ralph Manhein (London: Eyre Methuen, 1979)

— *Journals 1934–1955*, trans. by Hugh Rorrison and ed. by John Willett (New York: Routledge, 1996)

Brickner, Richard Max, *Is Germany Incurable?* (Philadelphia; New York: J. B. Lippincott Co., 1943)

Brockmann, Stephen, *A Critical History of German Film* (Columbia: Camden House, 2010)

— *German Literary Culture at the Zero Hour* (Rochester, NY: Camden House, 2004)

Brockway, Fenner, *German Diary* (London: Victor Gollancz, 1946)

Brown, Jane K., 'Faust', in *The Cambridge Companion to Goethe,* ed. by Lesley Sharpe (Cambridge: Cambridge University Press, 2002), pp. 84–100

Brunette, Peter, *Roberto Rossellini* (Oxford: Oxford University Press, 1987)

Burke, Carolyn, *Lee Miller* (London: Bloomsbury, 2005)

Burgin, Hans, and Hans-Otto Mayer, *Thomas Mann: A Chronicle of his Life*, trans. by Eugene Dobson (Alabama: University of Alabama Press, 1969)

Buruma, Ian, *Year Zero: A History of 1945* (New York: Penguin, 2013)

Byford-Jones, Wilfred, *Berlin Twilight* (London: Hutchinson, 1947)

Cairncross, Alec, *The Price of War: British Policy on German Reparations 1941–1949* (Oxford: Basil Blackwell, 1986)

— *Years of Recovery 1945–1951: British Economic Policy 1945–1951* (London and New York: Methuen, 1985)

Canwell, Diane and Sutherland, Jon, *The Berlin Airlift: The Salvation of a City* (Gretna, LA: Pelican, 2008)

Carpenter, Humphrey, *W. H. Auden: A Biography* (Oxford: OUP, 1992)

Carr, E. H., *Conditions of Peace* (London: Macmillan, 1942)

Chamberlin, Brewster S., *Kultur auf Trümmern: Berliner Berichte der Amerikanischen Information Control Section Juli–Dezember 1945* (Stuttgart: Deutsche Verlags-Anstalt, 1979)

Christadler, 'Der französische Existentialismus und die deutschen Intellektuellen in der Nachkriegszeit', in Wolfgang Asholt and Heinz Thoma (eds.), *Frankreich ein unverstandener Nachbar 1945–1990* (Bonn: Romanistischer Verlag, 1990), pp. 224–38

Clare, George, *Berlin Days* (London: Papermac, 1994)

Clark, Mark W., *Beyond Catastrophe: German Intellectuals and Cultural Renewal after World War II, 1945–1955* (Lanham, Oxford: Lexington Books, 2006)

Clay, Lucius D., *Decision in Germany* (London: William Heinemann, 1950)

Clemens, Gabriele B., *Britische Kulturpolitik in Deutschland 1945–1949: Literatur, Film, Musik und Theater* (Stuttgart: F. Steiner, 1997)

Cohen-Solal, Annie, *Sartre: A Life*, trans. by Anna Cancogni (New York: Pantheon Books, 1988)

Collier, Richard, *Bridge Across the Sky: The Berlin Blockade and Airlift, 1948–1949* (Place: Mcgraw-Hill, 1978)

Connor, Ian, *Refugees and Expellees in Post-war Germany* (Manchester: Manchester University Press, 2007)

Crick, Bernard, *George Orwell: A Life* (London: Secker & Warburg, 1981)

Croall, Jonathan, *Sybil Thorndike: A Star of Life* (London: Haus, 2008)

Crofts, William, *Coercion or Persuasion? Propaganda in Britain after 1945* (London: Routledge, 1989)

Crowell, Steven (ed.), *The Cambridge Companion to Existentialism* (New York: Cambridge University Press, 2012)

Dagerman, Stig, *German Autumn*, trans. by Robin Fulton MacPherson (Minneapolis: University of Minnesota Press, 2011)

Dalton, Hugh, *High Tide and After* (London: Frederick Muller Ltd., 1962)

De Beauvoir, Simone, *Force of Circumstance*, trans. by Richard Howard (Harmondsworth: Penguin, 1975)

Deighton, Anne, 'Cold-War Diplomacy: British Policy Towards Germany's Role in Europe', in *Reconstruction in Post-War Germany: British Occupation Policy and the Western Zones 1945–1955*, ed. by Ian D. Turner (Oxford: Berg Publishers Ltd, 1989), pp. 15–34.

— *The Impossible Peace: Britain, the Division of Germany and the Origins of the Cold War* (Oxford: Clarendon Press, 1990)

Dietrich, Marlene, *Marlene*, trans. by Salvator Attanasio (New York: Avon Books, 1990)

Dinan, Desmond (ed.), *Origins and Evolution of the European Union* (Oxford: Oxford University Press, 2006)

Döblin, Alfred, *Tales of a Long Night* (New York: Fromm Intl., 1984)

Donnison, Frank, *Civil Affairs and Military Government Central Organisation and Planning* (London: HMSO, 1966)

— *Civil Affairs and Military Government North-West Europe 1944–1946* (London: HMSO, 1961)

Dos Passos, John, *The Fourteenth Chronicle: Letters and Diaries of John Dos Passos*, ed. by Townsend Ludington (Boston: Gambit, 1973)

— *Tour of Duty* (Boston: Houghton Miffin Co., 1946)

Dudley Edwards, Ruth, *Victor Gollancz: A Biography* (London: Gollancz, 1987)

Ebsworth, Raymond, *Restoring Democracy in Germany: The British Contribution* (London: Stevens & Sons, 1960)

Eisenberg, Carolyn, *Drawing the Line: The American Decision to Divide Germany, 1944–1949* (Cambridge: Cambridge University Press, 1996)

Eley, Geoff, *Nazism as Fascism: Violence, Ideology and the Ground of Consent in Germany, 1930–1945* (London, Routledge, 2013)

Farquharson, John E., 'Emotional but Influential: Victor Gollancz, Richard Stokes and the British zone in Germany: 1945–1949', *Journal of Contemporary History*, Vol. 22, 1987, pp. 501–19

— 'From Unity to Division: What Prompted Britain to Change its Policy in Germany in 1946', *European History Quarterly*, Vol. 26, 1996, pp. 81–123

Faulk, Henry, *Group Captives: The Re-education of German Prisoners of War in Britain 1945–1948* (London: Chatto & Windus, 1977)

Fay, Jennifer, *Theaters of Occupation: Hollywood and the Reeducation of Postwar Germany* (Minneapolis: University of Minnesota Press, 2008)

Fehrenbach, Heide, *Cinema in Democratizing Germany: Reconstructing National Identity after Hitler* (North Carolina: University of North Carolina Press, 1995)

Fest, Joachim C., *Not Me: Memoirs of a German Childhood*, trans. by Martin Chalmers (London: Atlantic Books, 2012)

Fetzer, John F., *Changing Perceptions of Thomas Mann's Doctor Faustus: Criticism 1947–1992* (Columbia: Camden House, 1996)

Flood, John L. (ed.), *Common Currency? Aspects of Anglo-German Literary Relations since 1945: London Symposium* (Stuttgart: Heinz, 1991)

Foschepoth, Josef, and Steininger, Rolf (eds.), Die *Britische Deutschland und Besatzungspolitik 1945–1949* (Paderborn: Ferdinand Schöningh, 1985)

Frank, Matthew, 'The New Morality – Victor Gollancz, 'Save Europe Now' and the German Refugee Crisis, 1945–46', *Twentieth Century British History*, Vol. 17, No.2, 2006, pp. 230–56

Friedrich, Otto, *City of Nets: A Portrait of Hollywood in the 1940s* (University of California Press, 1997)

Fulbrook, Mary and Martin Swales (eds.), *Representing the German Nation: History and Identity in Twentieth-century Germany* (Manchester: Manchester University Press, 2000)

Gardiner, Juliet, *Wartime: Britain 1939–1945* (London: Headline, 2005)

Gavin, James, *On to Berlin: Battles of an Airborne Commander, 1943–1946* (London: Cooper, 1979)

Gehring, Hansjörg, *Amerikanische Literaturpolitik in Deutschland 1945–1953: Ein Aspekt des Re-Education-Programms* (Berlin: Oldenbourg, 2010)

Gellhorn, Martha, *The Wine of Astonishment* (New York: Bantam Books, 1949)

— *The Letters of Martha Gellhorn*, ed. by Caroline Moorehead (London: Chatto and Windus, 2006)

Gemünden, Gerd, *Framed Visions: Popular Culture, Americanization and the Contemporary German and Austrian Imagination* (Ann Arbor: University of Michigan Press, 1998)

— *A Foreign Affair: Billy Wilder's American Films* (Oxford: Berghahn Books, 2008)

— 'In the ruins of Berlin: *A Foreign Affair*', in *German Post-war Films: Life and Love in the Ruins*, ed. by Wilfried Wilms and William Rasch (Basingstoke, Palgrave Macmillan, 2008), pp. 109–24

Gibb, Lorna, *West's World: The Extraordinary Life of Dame Rebecca West* (London: Macmillan, 2013)

Gienow-Hecht, Jessica C. E., 'Art is Democracy and Democracy is Art: Culture, Propaganda, and the *neue Zeitung* in Germany, 1944–1947', *Diplomatic History*, Vol. 23, No.1, 1999, pp. 21–43

Gimbel, John, *The American Occupation of Germany: Politics and the Military, 1945–1949* (Stanford: Stanford University Press, 1968)

Gladstone, Kay, 'Separate Intentions: The Allied Screening of Concentration Camp Documentaries in Defeated Germany in 1945–46: *Death Mills* and *Memory of the Camps*', in *Holocaust and the Moving Image: Representations in Film and Television since 1933*, ed. by Toby Haggith and Joanna Newman (London: Wallflower, 2005), pp. 50–64

Glendinning, Victoria, *Rebecca West: A Life* (London: Papermac, 1988)

Goethe, Johann Wolfgang von, *Faust: The First Part of the Tragedy*, trans. by David Constantine (London: Penguin, 2005)

Gollancz, Victor, *Shall Our Children Live or Die? A Reply to Lord Vansittart on the German Problem* (London: Victor Gollancz, 1942)

— *In Darkest Germany* (London: Victor Gollancz, 1947)

— *Reminiscences of Affection* (London: Victor Gollancz, 1968)

— and Grossmann, Atina, *Jews, Germans and Allies: Close Encounters in Occupied Germany* (Princeton: Princeton University Press, 2007)

Habe, Hans, *Off Limits: A Novel of Occupied Germany*, trans. by Ewald Osers (London: George G. Harrap & Co., 1956)

Hahn, Werner G., *Postwar Soviet Politics: The Fall of Zhdanov and the Defeat of Moderation 1946–1953* (London: Cornell University Press, 1982)

Halliday, Jon, *Sirk on Sirk: Conversations with Jon Halliday* (London: Faber and Faber, 1997)

Hampshire, Edward and Charles Wheeler, *Germany 1944: The British Soldier's Pocketbook* (Kew: National Archives, 2006)

Hansen, Volkmar and Gert Heine (eds.), *Frage und Antwort: Interviews mit Thomas Mann, 1909–1955* (Hamburg: Knaus, 1983)

Hardt, Ursula, *From Caligari to California: Erich Pommer's Life in the International Film Wars* (Oxford: Berghahn Books, 1996)

Hayman, Ronald, *Brecht: A Biography* (London: Weidenfeld & Nicolson, 1983)

— *Writing Against: A Biography of Sartre* (London: Weidenfeld and Nicolson, 1986)

— *Thomas Mann: A Biography* (London: Bloomsbury, 1996)

Hearnden, Arthur (ed.), *The British in Germany: Educational Reconstruction after 1945* (London: Hamish Hamilton, 1978)

Heilbut, Anthony, *Exiled in Paradise: German Refugee Artists and Intellectuals in America from the 1930s to the Present* (California: University of California Press, 1997)

Hemingway, Ernest, *Selected Letters 1917–1961*, ed. by Carlos Baker (London: Granada, 1981)

Hench, John B., *Books as Weapons: Propaganda, Publishing, and the Battle for Global Markets in the Era of Wold War II* (Ithaca: Cornell University Press, 2010)

Hitchcock, William L., *Liberation: The Bitter Road to Freedom, Europe 1944–1945* (London: Faber & Faber, 2009)

Högerle, Daniela, *Propaganda oder Verständigung: Instrumente französischer Kulturpolitik in Südbaden, 1945–1959* (Bern: Peter Lang, 2013)

Hughes, Gerald, '"Don't let's be beastly to the Germans": Britain and the German Affair in History', *Twentieth Century British History*, Vol. 17, No. 2, 2006, pp. 257–83

Hurwitz, Harold D., *Die Stunde Null de deutschen Presse: Die amerikanische Pressepolitik in Deutschland 1945–1949* (Cologne: Verlag Wissenschaft und Politik, 1972)

Huxley, Julian, *UNESCO: Its Purpose and Philosophy* (London, 1946)

Isaacs, Reginald R., *Walter Gropius: Der Mensch und sein Werk* (Berlin, 1984)

— *Gropius: An Illustrated Biography of the Creator of the Bauhaus* (Boston & London: Little, Brown, 1991)

Isherwood, Christopher, *Diaries: 1939–1960*, Vol. I, ed. by Katherine Bucknell (London: Vintage, 2011)

Jackson, Kevin, *Humphrey Jennings* (London: Picador, 2004)

— (ed.), *The Humphrey Jennings Film Reader* (Manchester: Carcanet, 1993)

Jacobius, Arnold John, *Carl Zuckmayer: eine Biographie 1917–1971* (Frankfurt: Athenäum Verlag, 1971)

Jarausch, Konrad H., *Existentialism and Humanism: Three Essays*, trans. by Hanns E Fischer (New York: Russell F Moore, 1952)

— *After Hitler: Recivilizing Germans, 1945–1995* (New York: Oxford University Press, 2006)

Jaspers, Karl, *The European Spirit*, trans. by Ronald Gregor Smith (London: S.C.M. Press, 1948)

Jones, Jill, 'Eradicating Nazism from the British Zone of Germany: Early Policy and Practice', *German History*, Vol.8, No.2, 1990, pp. 145–62

Jordan, Ulrike (ed.), *Conditions of Surrender: Britons and Germans Witness the End of the War* (London: I.B. Tauris Publishers, 1997)

Judaken, Jonathan, *Jean-Paul Sartre and the Jewish Question: Anti-semitism and the Politics of the French Intellectual* (Lincoln: University of Nebraska Press, 2006)

Judt, Tony, *Postwar: A History of Europe since 1945* (London: Vintage, 2010)

Junker, Detlef (ed.), *The United States and Germany in the Era of the Cold War 1945–1990*, Vol. I: 1945–1968 (Washington D.C.: German Historical Institute and Cambridge University Press, 2010)

Kaes Anton, Martin Jay, and Edward Dimendberg (eds.), *The Weimar Republic Sourcebook* (London: University of California Press, 1994)

Kert, Bernice, *The Hemingway Women* (New York: W.W. Norton & Company, 1986)

Kertesz, Margaret, *The Enemy – British Images of the German People during the Second World War* (University of Sussex, PhD thesis, 1993)

Kirkbright, Suzanne, *Karl Jaspers: A Biography: Navigations in Truth* (London: Yale University Press, 2004)

Kirkpatrick, Ivone, *The Inner Circle Memoirs* (London: Macmillan, 1959)

Knight, Laura, *The Magic of a Line: The Autobiography of Laura Knight* (London: William Kimber, 1965)

Kohlenbach, Margarete, 'Transformations of German Romanticism 1830–2000', in *The Cambridge Companion to German Romanticism*, ed. by Nicholas Saul (Cambridge: Cambridge University Press, 2009), pp. 257–80

Kortner, Fritz, *Aller Tage Abend* (München: Kindler, 1959)

Koshar, Rudy, *German Travel Cultures* (Oxford: Berg, 2000)

— '"Germany has been a melting pot": American and German Intercultures, 1945–1955', in *The German-American Encounter: Conflict and Cooperation between Two Cultures 1800–2000*, ed. by Frank Trommler and Elliott Shore (Oxford: Berghahn Books, 2001), pp. 158–78

Krippendorff, Ekkehart (ed.), *The Role of the United States in the Reconstruction of Italy and West Germany, 1943–1949: Papers Presented at a German-Italian Colloquium held at the John F. Kennedy Institut für Nordamerikastudien, Berlin, June 1980* (Berlin: Das Institut, 1981)

Krispyn, Egbert, *Anti-Nazi Writers in Exile* (Athens: University of Georgia Press, 1978)

Kurzke, Hermann, *Thomas Mann: Life as a Work of Art: A Biography* (London: Allen Lane, 2002)

Kuschner, Tony and Katharine Knox, *Refugees in an Age of Genocide: Global, National and Local Perspectives during the Twentieth Century* (London: Frank Cass, 1999)

Lally, Kevin, *Wilder Times: The Life of Billy Wilder* (New York: Henry Holt and Co., 1996)

Langgässer, Elisabeth, *Briefe 1924–1950* (Hamburg: Claasen, 1990)

Le Bon de Beauvoir, Sylvie (ed.), *Simone De Beauvoir: A Transatlantic Love Affair: Letters to Nelson Algren* (New York: New Press, 1998)

Leffler, Melvyn P., and Odd Arne Westad (eds.), *The Cambridge History of the Cold War* (Cambridge: Cambridge University Press, 2010)

Lefort, Claude, *Democracy and Political Theory*, trans. by David Macey (Cambridge: Polity, 1988)

Lehmann, John, *New Writing and Daylight* (London: Hogarth Press, 1945)

Lepenies, Wolf, *The Seduction of Culture in German History* (Princeton: Princeton University Press, 2006)

Lynn, Kenneth S., *Hemingway* (London: Cardinal, 1989)

MacDonogh, Giles, *After the Reich: From the Liberation of Vienna to the Berlin Airlift* (London: John Murray, 2007)

Malzahn, Manfred (ed.), *Germany 1945–1949: A Sourcebook* (London: Routledge, 1991)

Mann, Erika, *Blitze überm Ozean: Aufsätze, Reden, Reportagen*, ed. by Irmela von der Lühe (Reinbek bei Hamburg: Rowohlt Tb Verlag, 2001)

— *Briefe und Antworten*, 2 vols., ed. by Anna Zanco Prestel (Munich: Edition Spangenberg, 1985)

Mann, Erika and Klaus Mann, *The Other Germany*, trans. by Heinz Norden (New York: Modern Age Books, 1940)

Mann, Golo, *Reminiscences and Reflections: A Youth in Germany*, trans. by K. Winston (New York: Norton, 1990) (f.p. 1986)

— *Briefe 1932–1992*, ed. by Lahma Tilmann and Kathrin Lüssi, (Göttingen: Wallstein, 2006)

Mann, Klaus, *Briefe und Antworten 1937–1949*, Vol. II, ed. by Martin Gregor-Dellin (München: Heinrich Ellermann, 1975)

— *The Turning Point: The Autobiography of Klaus Mann* (London: Serpent's Tail, 1987)

— *Tagebücher*, ed. by Joachim Heimannsberg, Peter Laemmle and Wilfried F. Schoeller (Munich, Edition Spangenberg, c.1989–c.1991)

— *Auf verlorenem Posten: Aufsätze, Reden, Kritiken, 1942–1949*, ed. by Uwe Nachmann and Michael Töteberg (Reinbek bei Hamburg: Rororo, 1994)

— *Mephisto*, trans. by Robin Smyth (London: Penguin, 1995

Mann, Thomas, *Doktor Faustus* (Berlin: Suhrkamp Verlag, 1947)

— *Ansprache im Goethejahr 1949. Gehalten am 25 Juli 1949 in der Paulskirche zu Frankfurt am Main* (Frankfurt am Main, 1949)

— *Goethe and Democracy* (Washington: Library of Congress, 1950)

— *The Story of a Novel: The Genesis of Dr Faustus*, trans. by Richard and Clara Winston (New York: Knopf, 1961)

— *Briefe*, 3 vols., ed. by Erika Mann (Frankfurt: S. Fischer Verlag, 1961–1965)

— *Thomas Mann's Addresses delivered at the Library of Congress 1942–1949*, (Washington DC: Library of Congress, 1963)

— *Letters of Thomas Mann*, ed. and trans. by Richard and Clara Winston, (New York: Alfred A. Knopf, 1971)

— *Gesammelte Werke*, 13 vols. (Frankfurt am Main: S. Fischer Verlag, 1974)

— *Tagebücher*, ed. by Peter de Mendelssohn and Inge Jens (Frankfurt am Main: S. Fischer, 1977)

— *Diaries, 1918–1939*, trans. by Richard and Clara Winston (New York: Harry N. Abrams, 1982)

— *Doctor Faustus: The Life of the German Composer Adrian Leverkühn as Told by a Friend*, trans. by John E. Woods (New York: Vintage Intl., 1999)

— *Deutsche Hörer: Radiosendungen nach Deutschland aus den Jahren 1940–1945* (Frankfurt am Main: Fischer, 2004)

— and Heinrich Mann, *Letters of Heinrich and Thomas Mann 1900–1949*, ed. by Hans Wysling, trans. by Don Reneau with Richard and Clara Winston (London: University of California Press, 1998)

Mannin, Ethel, *German Journey* (London: Jarrolds, 1948)

Marrus, Michael Robert, *The Nuremberg War Crimes Trial, 1945–1946: A Documentary History* (Boston: Bedford Books, 1997)

Marshall, Barbara, *The Origins of Post-war German Politics* (London: Croom Helm, 1988)

Mayne, Richard, *Postwar: The Dawn of Today's Europe* (London: Thames & Hudson, 1983)

McLoughlin, Kate, *Martha Gellhorn: The War Writer in the Field and in the Text* (Manchester: Manchester University Press, 2007)

Mead, Margaret, *And Keep Your Powder Dry: An Anthropologist Looks at America* (New York: William Morrow, 1942)

Meehan, Patricia, *A Strange Enemy People* (London: Peter Owen Publishers, 2001)

Mellow, James R., *Hemingway: A Life Without Consequences* (London: Hodder & Stoughton, 1993)

Merritt, Anna L., and Richard L. (eds.), *Public Opinion in Occupied Germany: The OMGUS Surveys 1945–1949* (London: University of Illinois Press, 1970)

Meyer, Martin, 'American Literature in Cold-War Germany', *Libraries and Culture*, Vol. 36, No. 1, 2001, pp. 162–71

Meyers, Jeffrey, *Hemingway: A Biography* (New York: Harper and Row, 1985)

Middleton, Drew, *The Struggle for Germany* (London & New York: Allan Wingate, 1949)

Moorehead, Caroline, *Martha Gellhorn: A Life* (London: Chatto & Windus, 2003)

Mosley, Leonard, *Report from Germany* (London: Victor Gollancz, 1945)

Mouffe, Chantal, *The Democratic Paradox* (London: Verso, 2000)

Murphy, Robert, *London Among Warriors* (London: Collins, 1964)

Nabokov, Nicolas, *Old Friends and New Music* (London: Hamish Hamilton, 1951)

— *Bagazh: Memoirs of a Russian Cosmopolitan* (Atheneum, 1975)

Naimark, Norman, *The Russians in Germany: A History of the Soviet Zone of Occupation, 1945–1949* (London: The Belknap Press of Harvard University Press, 1995)

Nichols, Anthony J., *Always Good Neighbours – Never Good Friends? Anglo-German Relations 1049–2001* (London: German Historical Institute London, 2005)

Nicolson, Harold, *Diaries and Letters 1945–1962*, ed. by Nigel Nicolson (London: Collins, 1968)

Noss, Luther, *Paul Hindemith in the United States* (Urbana: University of Illinois Press, 1989)

Orwell, George, *The Observer Years* (London: Atlantic Books, 2003)

Overy, Richard, *The Air War 1939–1945* (London: Europa Publications, 1980)

— *Why the Allies Won* (London: Pimlico, 1996)

— *The Dictators* (London: Penguin, 2004)

— *The Bombing War: Europe 1939–1945* (London: Allen Lane, 2013)

Pells, Richard, *Not Like Us: How Europeans have Loved, Hated and Transformed American Culture Since World War II* (New York: BasicBooks, 1997)

Penrose, Antony (ed.), *Lee Miller's War: Photographer and Correspondent with the Allies in Europe, 1944–1945* (London: Thames & Hudson, 2005)

Pick, Daniel, *The Pursuit of the Nazi Mind: Hitler, Hess and the Analysts* (Oxford: OUP, 2012)

Pike, David, *The Politics of Culture in Soviet-occupied Germany 1945–1949* (Stanford: Stanford University Press, 1992)

Poiger, Uta G., *Jazz, Rock and Rebels: Cold War Politics and American Culture in a Divided Germany* (London: University of California Press, 2000)

Prater, Donald, *Thomas Mann: A Life* (Oxford: Oxford University Press, 1995)

Pratt, Mary Louise, *Imperial Eyes: Travel Writing and Transculturation* (London: Routledge, 2008)

Preussner, Eberhard, *Paul Hindemith: ein Lebensbild* (Innsbruck: Edition Helbling, 1984)

Pronay, Nicholas, and Keith Wilson (eds.), *The Political Re-education of Germany and her Allies after World War II* (London: Croom Helm, 1985)

Pronay, Nicholas, and D.W. Spring (eds.), *Propaganda Politics and Film 1918–1945* (London: Macmillan Press Ltd, 1982)

Raack, R. C., *Stalin's Drive to the West, 1938–1945: The Origins of the Cold War* (Stanford: Stanford University Press, 1995)

Ramsden, John, *Don't Mention the War: The British and the Germans since 1890* (London: Little Brown, 2006)

Rees, Goronwy, *A Bundle of Sensations: Sketches in Autobiography* (London: Chatto & Windus, 1960)

Reich-Ranicki, Marcel, *Thomas Mann and His Family*, trans. by Ralph Manheim (London: Collins, 1989)

Reinhold, Ursula et al (eds.), *Erster Deutscher Schriftstellerkongress, 4–8 Oktober 1947* (Berlin: Aufbau, 1999)

Reinisch, Jessica, *Public Health in Germany in Soviet and Allied Occupation, 1943–1947* (thesis, University of London, 2005)

Reynolds, David, 'The Origins of the Cold War: The European Dimension, 1944–1951', *The Historical Journal*, Vol. 28, No. 2, 1985, pp. 497–515

Ridley, Hugh, '*Nochmals Herr Beißel: Thomas Mann und Amerika im Kontext von Doktor Faustus*', in *Das Amerika der Autoren*, ed. by Jochen Vogt and Alexander Stephan (München: W. Fink, 2006)

Riess, Curt, *The Berlin Story* (London: Frederick Muller, 1953)

Riva, David (ed.), *A Woman at War: Marlene Dietrich Remembered* (Detroit: Painted Turtle, 2006)

Riva, Maria, *Marlene Dietrich by her Daughter* (Dunton Green: Coronet, 1994)

Robertson, Brian, 'Quo Vadis?', *British Zone Review*, Vol. 1, No. 1, 27 Oct 1945

Robertson, Geoffrey, *Crimes Against Humanity: The Struggle for Global Justice* (London: New Press, 2006)

Robertson, Ritchie, 'Accounting for History: Thomas Mann, Doktor Faustus', in *The German Novel in the Twentieth Century: Beyond Realism*, ed. by David Midgley (Edinburgh: Edinburgh University Press, 1993)

Rollyson, Carl, *Rebecca West: A Saga of the Century* (London: Hodder & Stoughton, 1995)

— *Beautiful Exile: The Life of Martha Gellhorn* (London: Aurum, 2000)

Ross, Alan, *The Derelict Day: Poems in Germany* (London: John Lehmann, 1947)
— *Blindfold Games* (London: Collins Harvill, 1986)
Ruhm von Oppen, Beata (ed.), *Documents on Germany under Occupation, 1945–1954* (London: Oxford University Press, 1955)
Ryder, Andrew, 'Sartre's Theatre of Resistance: *Les Mouches* and the Deadlock of Collective Responsibility', *Sartre Studies International*, Vol. 15, No. 2, Winter 2009, pp. 78–95
Sartre, Jean-Paul, *The Flies and In Camera*, trans. Stuart Gilbert (London: Hamish Hamilton, 1946)
Saul, Nicholas, 'Goethe the writer and literary history', in *The Cambridge Companion to Goethe*, ed. by Lesley Sharpe (Cambridge: Cambridge University Press, 2002), pp. 23–41
— 'Love, Death and Liebestod in German Romanticism', in *The Cambridge Companion to German Romanticism*, ed. by Nicholas Saul (Cambridge: Cambridge University Press, 2009), pp. 163–74
Schieder, Martin, *Im Blick des Anderen: Die Deutsch-Französischen Kunstbeziehungen 1945–1959* (Berlin: Akademie Verlag, 2005)
Schivelbusch, Wolfgang, *In a Cold Crater: Cultural and Intellectual Life in Berlin, 1945–1948*, trans. by Kelly Barry (London: University of California Press, 1998)
Schwarz, Hans–Peter, 'The division of Germany, 1945–1949', in Melvyn P. Leffler and Odd Arne Westad (ed.), *The Cambridge History of the Cold War*, Vol. I (Cambridge: Cambridge University Press, 2010), pp. 133–53
Scott-Smith, Giles, *The Politics of Apolitical Culture: The Congress for Cultural Freedom, the CIA and Post-war American Hegemony* (London: Routledge, 2002)
Scott-Smith, Giles and Hans Krabbendam (eds.), *The Cultural Cold War in Western Europe, 1945–60* (London: Frank Cass, 2003)
Seymour-Jones, Carole, *A Dangerous Liaison: Simone de Beauvoir and Jean-Paul Sartre* (London: Century, 2008)
Shandley, Robert R., *Rubble Films: German Cinema in the Shadow of the Third Reich* (Philadelphia: Temple University Press, 2001)
Shelden, Michael, *Orwell: The Authorised Biography* (London: William Heinemann, 1991)
Shephard, Ben, *The Long Road Home: The Aftermath of the Second World War* (London: Bodley Head, 2010)
Shirer, William L., *End of a Berlin Diary* (London: Hamish Hamilton, 1947)
Short, K. R. M., and Stephen Dolezel (eds.), *Hitler's Fall: the Newsreel Witness* (London: Croom Helm, 1988)
Sikov, Ed, *On Sunset Boulevard: The Life and Times of Billy Wilder* (New York: Hyperion, 1998)
Skelton, Geoffrey, *Paul Hindemith: The Man Behind the Music: A Biography* (London: Gollancz, 1975)
Sollers, Werner, *The Temptation of Despair: Tales of the 1940s* (Cambridge, MA: Harvard University Press, 2014)
Spencer-Carr, Virginia, *Dos Passos: A Life* (London: Doubleday, 1984)
Spender, Stephen, *European Witness: Impressions of Germany in 1945* (London: Hamish Hamilton, 1946)
— *W. H. Auden: A Tribute* (London: Weidenfeld and Nicolson, 1975)
— *New Selected Journals 1939–1995*, ed. Lara Feigel and John Sutherland (London: Faber and Faber, 2012)

Spiel, Hilde, *The Dark and The Bright: Memoirs, 1911–1989*, trans. by Christine Shuttleworth (Riverside, Calif.: Ariadne Press, 2007)

Stannard, Martin, *Evelyn Waugh: No Abiding City 1939–1966* (London: Dent, 1992)

Stern, James, *The Hidden Damage* (London: Chelsea Press, 1947)

Stonard, John-Paul, *Fault Lines: Art in Germany 1945–1955* (London: Ridinghouse, 2007)

Stonebridge, Lyndsey, *The Judicial Imagination: Writing After Nuremberg* (Edinburgh: Edinburgh University Press, 2011)

Stonor Saunders, Frances, *Who Paid the Piper?: The CIA and the Cultural Cold War* (London: Granta, 1999)

Strang, William, *Home and Abroad* (London: Andre Deutsch, 1956)

Sutherland, John, *Stephen Spender: The Authorised Biography* (London: Penguin, 2005)

Tabachnick, Stephen Ely, *Fiercer than Tigers: The Life and Work of Rex Warner* (East Lansing: Michigan State University Press, 2002)

Taylor, D. J., *Orwell* (London: Chatto & Windus, 2003)

Thies, Jochen, "'What is going on in Germany?" *Britische Militärverwaltung in Deutschland 1945–6*', in *Die Deutschlandpolitik Grossbritanniens und die Britische Zone*, ed. by Claus Scharf and Hans-Jürgen Schröder (Wiesbaden: Franz Steiner Verlag, 1979), pp. 29–50

Thomas, Michael, *Deutschland, England über alles Rückkehr als britische Besatzungsoffizier* (Berlin: Siedler Verlag, 1984)

Thomas, Nick, *Protest Movements in 1960s West Germany: A Social History of Dissent and Democracy* (Oxford: Berg, 2003)

Tracey, Michael, *A Variety of Lives: A Biography of Sir Hugh Greene* (London: Bodley Head, 1983)

Treber, Leonie, *Mythos Trümmerfrauen: Von der Trümmerbeseitigung in der Kriegs- und Nachkriegszeit und der Entstehung eines deutschen Erinnerungsortes* (Essen: Klartext, 2014)

Trommler, Frank and Joseph McVeigh (eds.), *America and the Germans: An Assessment of a Three-hundred-year History: Tricentennial Conference of German-American History, Politics and Culture* (Philadelphia: University of Philadelphia Press, 1985)

Turner, Ian D. (ed.), *Reconstruction in Post-War Germany: British Occupation Policy and the Western Zones 1945–1955* (Oxford: Berg Publishers Ltd, 1989)

Tusa, Ann and John, *The Nuremberg Trial* (London: Macmillan, 1983)

Vaget, Hans Rudolf, *Thomas Mann, Der Amerikaner: Leben und Werk im Amerikanischen Exil 1938–1952* (Frankfurt am Main: S. Fischer, 2011)

Vansittart, Robert, *Black Record* (London: Hamish Hamilton, 1941)

Von Karasek, Hellmuth, *Billy Wilder: eine Nahaufnahme* (München: Heyne, c.1992)

Von Rohr Scaff, Susan, 'Doctor Faustus', in *The Cambridge Companion to Thomas Mann*, ed. by Ritchie Robertson (Cambridge: Cambridge University Press, 2001), pp. 168–84

Von Solomon, Ernst, *Der Fragebogen* (Hamburg: Rowohlt Verlag, 1951)

Watson, Peter, *The German Genius: Europe's Third Renaissance, the Second Scientific Revolution and the Twentieth Century* (New York: Harper, 2010)

Watt, D. C., *Britain Looks to Germany: A Study of British Opinion and Policy towards Germany since 1945* (London: Oswald Wolff, 1965)

Watt, Roderick H., 'Wolfdietrich Schnurre's Film Reviews of British Films in the Deutsche Rundschau 1946–1951', in *Publications of the Institute of Germanic Studies*, Vol. 70, 1997, pp. 153–68

Waugh, Evelyn, *Diaries 1911–1965*, ed. by Michael Davie (Harmondsworth: Penguin, 1979)
— *Letters of Evelyn Waugh* (London: Weidenfeld and Nicolson, 1980)
Weiss, Andrea, *In the Shadow of the Magic Mountain: The Erika and Klaus Mann Story* (Chicago: University of Chicago Press, 2008)
Wellbery, David E., Judith Ryan, Hans Ulrich Gumbrecht, Anton Kaes and Dorothea von Muecke (eds.), *A New History of German Literature* (London: Belknap, 2004)
Wellens, Ian, *Music on the Frontline: Nicolas Nabokov's Struggle against Communism and Middlebrow Culture* (Burlington: Ashgate, 2002)
West, Rebecca, *Black Lamb and Grey Falcon* (London: Macmillan, 1943)
— *A Train of Powder* (London: Virago, 1984) (f.p. 1955)
— 'Greenhouse with Cyclamens, I, II and III', in *A Train of Powder* (London: Virago, 1984)
— *Selected Letters of Rebecca West*, ed. by Bonnie Kime Scott (London: Yale University Press, 2003)
Willett, Ralph, *The Americanization of Germany, 1945–1949* (London: Routledge, 1988)
Williams, Raymond, *Keywords: A Vocabulary of Culture and Society* (London: Fontana, 1976)
Williams, Rhys W., Stephen Parker and Colin Riordan (eds.), *German Writers and the Cold War 1945–1961* (Manchester: Manchester University Press, 1992)
Willis, Roy, *The French in Germany: 1945–1949* (Stanford: Stanford University Press, 1962)
Wilms, Wilfried, and William Rasch (eds.), *German Post-war Films: Life and Love in the Ruins* (Basingstoke: Palgrave Macmillan, 2008)
Winnington, G. Peter, *Vast Alchemies: The Life and Work of Mervyn Peake* (London: Peter Owen, 2000)
Wyman, David S., *The Abandonment of the Jews: America and the Holocaust, 1941–1945* (London: New Press, 2007)
Young-Bruehl, Elisabeth, *Hannah Arendt: For Love of the World* (New Haven: Yale, 2004)
Young, Iris Marion, *Inclusion and Democracy* (Oxford: Oxford University Press, 2000)
Zauner, Stefan, *Erziehung und Kulturmission: Frankreichs Bildungspolitik in Deutschland 1945–1949* (Oldenbourg: Oldenbourg Verlag, 1994)
Zolotow, Maurice, *Billy Wilder in Hollywood* (London: W.H. Allen, 1977)
Zuckmayer, Carl, *A Part of Myself*, trans. by Richard and Clara Winston (London: Secker & Warburg, 1970)
— *Deutschlandbericht für das Kriegsministerium der Vereinigten Staaten von Amerika*, ed. by Gunther Nickel *et al* (Göttingen: Wallstein, 2004)
— *The Devil's General and Germany: Jekyll and Hyde*, trans. by Sebastian Haffnew (London: Continuum Intl., 2005)
Zweiniger-Bargielowska, Ina, 'Bread Rationing in Britain: July 1946–July 1948', *Twentieth Century British History*, Vol. 4, No. 1, 1993, 57–85

Acknowledgements

This book is in part an exploration of the role of institutions in shaping culture, so it is appropriate that my foremost thanks should go to two exemplary institutions. The award of a five-year Starting Grant from the European Research Council provided me with a period of leave that enabled me to complete the research and writing of this book and also brought in a team of researchers and experts to King's. I am enormously appreciative of these resources of time and money and most of all am thankful for the presence of scholars with related interests; they have broadened the conversation and pushed my work in unexpected directions. At the same time the award of a Philip Leverhulme Prize from the Leverhulme Trust has granted me additional travel funds and research assistance and, crucially, places in which to write.

While writing I have been grateful once again for the company and friendship of fellow writers: notably Juliet Gardiner, who has also helped shape the project from the outset, and Hannah Mulder, who was with me speeding across windy beaches as I started the book proposal and as I ended the coda. Juliet also read the whole manuscript and offered invaluable, demanding comments, as did Lisa Appignanesi, Ian Patterson and Alexandra Harris, whose high standards continue to be a source of inspiration and whose friendship remains a source of support.

This book has brought me outside my own comfort zones of British culture and biography into the realms of military history, German literature and Cold War politics. I've been extremely lucky to be able to draw on the expertise of friends in each area and am very grateful to historians Antony Beevor and Richard Overy, Germanists Stephen Brockmann and Werner Sollors and political theorist Geoffrey Hawthorn for taking time from their own writing to read my manuscript.

The English department at King's College London continues to provide me with a very happy base from which to conduct my research. Thanks are due to my Heads of Department, Josephine McDonogh and Richard Kirkland, for supporting me in my grant applications and then in enabling the running of the ERC project. This project, Beyond Enemy Lines, has brought me into an enjoyable and rewarding collaboration with colleagues in the German department – Erica Carter, Ben Schofield and Bobbi Weninger – and with the post-docs and PhDs with whom I run the project: Elaine Morley, Emily Oliver, Hanja Dämon and Julia Vossen. It has also brought the invaluable administrative support of Helena Metslang. Within the English department, I am thankful for the dedication and often startling ingenuity and brilliance of the PhD students who have acted as research assistants: Eleanor Bass, Nicola von Bodman-Hensler, Oline Eaton, Natasha Periyan and Julia Schoen. I am also deeply and happily indebted to the intellectual exchange, advice and friendship of Neil Vickers, Max Saunders, Edmund Gordon and Jon Day.

I am lucky to have a circle of loyal, stimulating and knowledgeable friends who have helped me through conversations, both intellectual and personal, and have been a source both of fun and support throughout the writing of this book. In addition to those already mentioned, I would like to thank Susie Christensen, David Godwin, Katie Graham, Jeremy Harding, Richard Holmes, Eveline Kilian, Sarah Lefanu, Alison MacLeod, Kate McLoughlin, Leo Mellor, Sara Mohr-Pietsch, Vike Plock, Stephen Romer, Matthew Spender, John-Paul Stonard, Lyndsey Stonebridge, Hannah Sullivan and Inigo Thomas.

Among the many archives and libraries I visited in the course of the research, I would like to express particular gratitude to staff at the Beinecke Rare Book and Manuscript Library at Yale University, the Berg Collection at the New York Public Library, the Boston University Special

Collections, the JFK Memorial Library, the London Library, the Mona-censia Literaturarchiv, the National Archives (London), the National Archives and Records Administration (Washington) and the University of Tulsa Special Collections. I am grateful to the local colleagues who have made these research trips pleasurable, notably Lars Engel and Sean Latham in Tulsa. I would also like to thank Alexandra Matthews, Christine Shuttleworth and Matthew Spender for granting me access to their parents' manuscripts and Caroline Moorhead for sharing her expertise on Martha Gellhorn.

At Bloomsbury, I continue to have the ideal editor in Michael Fishwick. His unwavering loyalty to me and my writing means more than I can say. I am also extremely grateful for the editorial input and calm efficiency of Anna Simpson and Marigold Atkey, and for the sustaining encouragement of Alexandra Pringle in London and George Gibson in New York. Zoe Waldie helped shape the book in its early stages and Tracy Bohan helped as it made its way into print. Both have been cheering supporters who have made the process of writing and being published considerably easier.

My son, Humphrey, has spent all four years of his life in competition with this book and I am grateful to him for making the time away from it so much fun. It is telling that the camera roll on my phone alternates photographs of him with pictures of Marlene Dietrich and Martha Gellhorn and that he now accepts them as part of his virtual family. I hope this may long continue. Once again I am grateful to all of Humphrey's grandparents for their support in making my research and writing trips possible and to my parents for their sustaining love, interest and encouragement. This book is dedicated to my husband John, whose unquestioning acceptance of my need to read and write, often in far-flung places, has made possible these years of balancing writing and motherhood. Long before that, though, he took me to Berlin at a time when I was hesitant about going there, initiating a decade-long love affair with the city that he may have had cause to regret. It is now my place as well as his, and though my Berlin is a city of lakes and parks while his is one of buildings and culture, sometimes they coincide and the results remain enormously enjoyable.

Copyright Acknowledgements
The Author and publisher gratefully acknowledge the following:

Illustrations
Cartoon p. 156 by David Low published in the *Evening Standard* on 12 December 1945 © David Low and reproduced courtesy of The British Cartoon Archive, University of Kent, www.cartoons.ac.uk and Solo Syndication.

For copyright details of images in the plate sections, see credit lines given against individual images.

Text
Extracts from the works of Thomas Mann are reproduced by permission of the Thomas Mann Archive.

Extracts from the works of Mervyn Peake are reproduced by permission of Peters Fraser & Dunlop (www.petersfraserdunlop.com) on behalf of the Estate of Mervyn Peake.

Extract from *A Part of Myself* by Carl Zuckmayer, trans. Richard and Clara Winston, published by Secker & Warburg, and reproduced by permission of The Random House Group Ltd.

Extracts from the works of Klaus and Erika Mann are reproduced by permission of Monacensia and Literary Archives and Library Munich.

Extracts from various letters published and unpublished and publications by Rebecca West reprinted by permission of Peters Fraser & Dunlop on behalf of the Estate of Rebecca West.

Diaries and Letters by Harold Nicolson © 1968 and 'Marginal Comment' © 1946, published in the *Spectator*, are reprinted by kind permission of the Estate of Harold Nicolson.

Extracts from the works of Victor Gollancz are reprinted by kind permission of Livia Gollancz.

Extracts from the works of Martha Gellhorn are reprinted by kind permission of Alexander Matthews.

Extracts from the works of Laura Knight are reprinted by kind permission of the Estate of Dame Laura Knight.

Extracts from the works of George Orwell are reprinted by kind permission of A. M. Heath.

Index

1st Airborne Army 104
21st Army (German) 48
42nd Infantry Division 44
45th Infantry Division 44
82nd Airborne Division, Parachute Infantry
Regiment 24, 25, 28, 37, 41–2, 104,
126, 213
Fourth Infantry Division, 22nd
Regiment 16, 26

Aachen 17–18, 26, 29, 39, 56
Acheson, Dean 375
Adenauer, Konrad 331, 332, 352, 356, 357,
358, 361
Adorno, Theodor 281
Agee, James 324
Alexandrov Ensemble 317, 402
Algren, Nelson 265, 268
Allied Control Council 291, 292
Allied Forces Information and Censorship
Section 34
American Broadcasting Station
(London) 55–6
American Information Centres (Amerika
Häuser) 239, 240
American Military Policy 'Snowdrops' 150
Andersch, Alfred 242–3
Andrews, Henry 189–90, 206–7, 333–4, 357
Ansbach 203
anti-Semitism 53–4, 82, 147, 176
anti-Stalinism 323, 324
Ardennes 28

Arendt, Hannah 163–6, 217, 233, 235, 252,
359
'Organised Guilt and Universal
Responsibility' 163–4
Arling, Emanie 208
Armed Forces Radio Service 66
Arms and the Man 79, 80
Arthur, Jean 277, 281
Attlee, Clement 86, 176, 245
Auden, W. H.
in Berlin 101
conversations with Nabokov 88–90
determined to visit Germany 71
disappointed revisiting Germany in
1950s 360
emotional visit to Germany 3–4
influence on Spender 73
little influence of 365
marries Erika Mann 58
moves to America 59
offers his services to the US
government 73
as pacifist 74–5
posted to Bad Homburg for
debriefing 88–9
pre-War admiration for Germany 3, 7, 73
reports on civilian responses to bomb
damage 3, 74–6, 77
sympathises with survivors of
concentration camps 74
'Memorial for the City' 8, 90–1, 367
Aufbau (Reconstruction) magazine 136, 166

Aufbau Verlag 113
Aufbau Verlag Nymphenburg 364
Augsburg 228
Auschwitz-Birkenau 44, 184, 362, 377

Baader, Andreas 363
Babelsberg studios 110
Bad Homburg 83–4
Bad Oeynhausen 84, 91, 92
Badener Tageblatt 138
Bamberg 200
Basic Law 331–2, 335, 362
Battle of the Bulge (1944–1945) 377
BBC 18, 32, 43, 59
Beauvoir, Simone de 5
  in Berlin 264, 265, 268, 273
  fame of 265
  feelings for Los Angeles 282
  finds Los Angeles as enjoyable as a
    kaleidoscope 282
  furious when forced to wear evening
    dress 268–9
  moved by shabbiness of students 273–4
  relationship with Sartre 266
Beaverbrook, Max 189
Becher, Johannes 112–14, 137, 166–7, 181,
  244, 249–50, 322
Beckett, Campbell 216
Bell, George 176
Belzec 377
Beneš, Edvard 289
Berchtesgaden 72
Bergen-Belsen 43, 50, 79, 80, 80–2, 83, 139,
  162, 224, 232, 377
Bergengruen, Werner 181
Berlin 226
  abject poverty in 319
  aerial shots used in Billy Wilder
    film 276, 280
  arrival of journalists, writers and film-
    makers in 99, 100–2
  blockade and airlift 301, 305–7, 312, 316,
    318–22, 330, 346
  British-American checkpoint opened 332
  cinemas in 112
  controversial views on 312–14
  corpses and nightclubs in 100–1

creative energy in 103–4
culture in 112–16, 233, 306, 316–17, 322,
  323–9
currency in 319, 320
denied access to Wilder's film 314
destruction and disease in 104, 200, 208,
  264
during Weimar Republic 64
East-West tensions 7, 114–16, 288–9,
  290–2, 295, 298–301, 306, 318, 320–1,
  330–4
elections in 236, 330
four-power rule in 99
health, food shortages and death
  in 121–4, 319–20, 322, 330
impending battle of 36
looting and raping in 105, 133
mail, telephones and trams in 107
officially opened to Western Allies
  99–100
partitioning of 3, 30, 99
as possible capital of united
  Germany 322
pre-war culture in 101–2
reconstruction of 133–4
Russians in 47, 105, 112–16, 133, 292,
  295–6, 319, 320–1, 330–4, 346
shortages in 319–20
theatres in 102–3, 107, 114, 228–9, 230–1
US sector 104–5
visited after its division 360
Berlin Air Safety Centre 318
Berlin Philharmonic 181, 242, 306, 307
Berlin Wall 370
Berliner Zeitung 102, 107, 114, 181
Bermann-Fischer, Gottfried 35, 54
Bernstein, Sidney 83, 84
Beverly Hills 277, 281, 307
Bevin, Ernest 177–8, 289, 312
Biddle, Francis
  affair with Rebecca West 190–2, 194–5,
    196, 199, 200, 206, 207, 208–9
  briefly considered as director of
    UNESCO 244
  character and description of 151, 157–8, 179
  chastises Mann for supporting World
    Peace conference 336

comment on Jackson's sense of
    failure 171
comments on West's draft article 194
conversation with disbelieving German
    boy 203
dislikes fraternity life at Nuremberg 149–
    50
friendship with Norman Birkett 150
irritated at Sam Harris's speech 157
meets Nicolson 179
praises de Menthon's speech 161
recapitulates German violations and
    tribunal's understanding of Common
    Plan 202
spends Christmas in London 159
surprised to be embraced by a
    Russian 158
writes light verse to alleviate
    boredom 187–8
Biddle, Katherine 191–2, 194, 199,
    208
Birkett, Norman 150, 159, 159–60, 172, 179,
    187–8
Black Friday (13 August 1948) 318
Blair, Eileen 40–1
Bleialf 16–17
Blücher, Heinrich 163
The Blue Angel (film, 1930) 29, 61, 111, 116,
    118, 276, 279, 280
Bohnen, Michael 102
Böll, Heinrich 395
    Billiards at Half-Past Nine 362
Bonn 95, 96
Bowen, Elizabeth 240
Bradley, Omar 15, 24, 26, 29, 50
Brandt, Willy 368, 369
Braun, Eva 47
Brecht, Bertolt 5, 166, 274
    arrival in California 381–2
    believes Germans were Hitler's first
        victims 166
    compares Los Angeles to Hell 282
    enmity with Mann 281
    investigated by House Un-American
        Activities Committee 324–5, 326
    Marxist view of the world 326
    repelled by Los Angeles 281–2

response to destruction of Berlin 325
    Life of Galileo 325
    Mother Courage and Her Children
        325–30
    The Threepenny Opera 107, 274, 365
Brickner, Richard 33
British Book Selection Committee 240
British Control Commission for Germany
    (CCG) 65, 71, 78, 86, 178, 227, 237,
    318
British Information Centres (Die
    Brücke) 239
British Political Warfare Executive 32
British War Crimes Executive 172
British zone 77–8
British Zone Review 128, 133
Britten, Benjamin 59
Buchenwald 7–8, 43, 85, 176, 245, 349, 350,
    377
Buchenwald manifesto 245
Byrnes, James 178

Cagney, James 369
California 9, 137, 138, 158, 182–3, 193, 256,
    281–7, 296, 307, 308, 311, 326, 338,
    348, 351
Cambridge Madrigal Society 317
Capa, Robert 105
Casson, Peter 172–3
Celan, Paul, 'Death Fugue' 46
Chaplin, Charlie 189
Chelmno 377
Christian Democratic Union (CDU) 236,
    352
Churchill, Winston 30, 31, 86, 147, 168–9,
    177, 245, 300, 357, 375
CIA (Central Intelligence Agency) 358
Clare, Edward 172–3
Clay, Lucius D. 178, 288, 292, 298, 300–1,
    307, 312, 320, 323, 332
Cold War 7, 10, 108, 114, 228–9, 235–7,
    238–9, 247, 248, 249–50, 267, 287,
    288–9, 295, 298–301, 315, 323, 326, 327,
    329, 330–4, 333, 336, 338, 348, 358, 360,
    363, 366
College of Physicians and Surgeons at
    Columbia University 32

Collier's magazine 14, 17, 23, 25, 36, 51, 211, 213
Collingwood, Charles 124
Cologne 2, 38–9, 41, 92–3
Colper, Max 276
Cominform 249
Commission of European Jewish Cultural Reconstruction 163
Communist Party 175, 325–6
concentration camps 7
  documentaries on 82–6, 154
  DPs and POWs in 223
  element of hypocrisy in Allied outrage at 96
  German knowledge of 50–1, 82
  horrors of 43, 44–5, 46, 48–9
  known about since 1930s 43–4, 377
  liberation of 2, 43–5
  visitors to 45, 48–9, 50, 80–2
  Wilder's reaction to 4
Congress for Cultural Freedom (1950) 358
Connolly, Cyril 73, 367
Council of Foreign Ministers 178, 236, 290, 346
Cowboy (film) 84
Crosby, Bing 275
Crossman, Richard 66–7, 323
Crown Film Unit 132
Cuba 13, 27
Cultural and Scientific Conference for World Peace (New York, 1949) 336
culture
  anatomising crisis of 251–2
  categories of 375
  flourishing of 239–50
  German culture as partly responsible for rise of Nazism 228
  importance of 234–5, 237
  influence of works by Margaret Mead 33–4
  issuing of books 35–6
  naïvity of Allies in Occupied Germany 365
  Nazi influence on 59
  not mentioned in JCS 1067 document 67
  Occupation considered a success for 357–8

Occupation policies on 86–8
  as part of re-education initiative 112–15
  as secondary to Realpolitik 358
Curtius, Robert 94–5, 162
Czechoslovakia 288, 289, 331

D-Day landings 14, 16
Dachau 44, 51, 74, 162, 176, 215, 366, 377
Dagerman, Stig 97, 222, 223
Dahlem 105
Daily Mail 180
Daily Telegraph 177, 200, 201, 205
Darmstadt 4, 74, 75
Davis, Ann 374
Davis, Bill 374
Daylight 71
De Gaulle, Charles 375
Death Mills (documentary) 159–60, 162, 167
Decision 59
'Declaration of Defeat and Assumption of Sovereignty' 77
A Defeated People (documentary, 1946) 8, 129–30, 133, 177, 367
Democratic Socialists 245
Der Monat 322–4, 327, 358
Der Ruf 242–3
Der Spiegel 358
Deutsches Theater (Berlin) 103, 114, 183, 184
Dibelius, Otto 105
Dicks, Henry 33, 63
Die Berliner Illustrierte Zeitung 57
Die Möwe (The Seagull) club (Berlin) 113
Die Neue Zeitung 227, 228, 358
Die Wandlung 165
Die Welt 239, 358
Die Zeit 345
Dietrich, Liesel 30, 50, 80
Dietrich, Marlene 61, 80
  affair with James Gavin 116–17, 118–19, 124–5, 127, 128
  arranges for her mother's burial 123–4
  in Berlin 116–17
  denies she ever had a sister 50

determined to visit Germany 71
entertains US troops 3, 21, 37, 117
falls in love with James Gavin 37
infested with lice 30
insists on accompanying Omar Bradley
    into Germany 29–30
in Paris 15, 117, 118, 127
post-war success 368–9
protected by General Patton 21
relationship with Billy Wilder 277
shocked at ruins of her former
    homeland 29
sings to Hemingway while sitting on his
    bathtub 20–1
speaks to her mother courtesy of James
    Gavin 106
stars in Billy Wilder film 275–81, 316
visits Belsen 50
visits Czechoslovakia to look for Rudi's
    parents 117
Dimbleby, Richard 43
'Directive to the Commander in Chief
    of the US Occupation Forces' (JCS
    1067) 65–7
Director of European Operations for the
    Office of War Information 67
Displaced Persons (DPs) 40, 78–9, 89,
    93–4, 117, 130, 131, 135, 177, 223
Döblin, Alfred 323
Dönitz, Karl 46
Donnedieu de Vabres, Henri 149
Dos Passos, John 5, 358
    article on losing the victory in
        Europe 168
    attends Nuremberg Trial 7, 145–6, 150–4
    books distributed around the world 34–5
    books purged from libraries 361
    notes the bleakness of Berlin in
        winter 122
    visits several destroyed German
        cities 145–6
Dowling, Doris 84
Dresden 35–6
Duke Ellington and Orchestra (film) 84
Düsseldorf 224, 237, 264, 269
Dutschke, Rudi 363
Dymschitz, Alexander 268, 269, 316

East Germany 343, 349–50, 351, 352–3, 358,
    364, 369–70
Echo der Woche 314, 338
Economic Council for the Soviet
    zone 289–90
Eichmann, Adolf 361
Eicke, Theodor 377
Eisenhower, Dwight D. 15, 34, 77, 108
Eisenstein, Sergei, Ivan the Terrible 324
Eisler, Hanns 288
Eisner, Otto 309, 311
Eliot, T. S. 240
The Emperor Waltz (film, 1948) 275
English PEN 243, 244
ENSA (Entertainments National Services
    Association) 79
Ensslin, Gudrun 362, 363, 365
Enzensberger, Hans Magnus 362–3
Erhard, Ludwig 299–300
Essen 79
European Coal and Steel Community
    (ECSC) 357
Evening Standard 155

Faber Schloss 209
FBI (Federal Bureau of Investigation) 314
Federal Republic of Germany
    (Bundesrepublik Deutschland) (West
    Germany) 331, 352, 357, 361, 362
Fehling, Jürgen 269
Feuchtwanger, Lion 281
Film, Theatre and Music Control
    Section 84
Final Solution 192–3
First World War 13, 31, 53, 64, 132
Flake, Otto 138
Flanner, Janet, attends Nuremberg Trial 150
Flexner, Hortense 22
A Foreign Affair (film, 1948) 8, 256, 314–16,
    367, 401–2
Fragebogen (questionnaires) 96–7
François-Poncet, André 352
Frank, Hans 147, 161
Frankfurt 74, 145, 225, 298–9, 335, 346, 347,
    348, 377
Free German League of Culture 243
French zone 78

Friedrich, Casper David, *Der Wanderer über dem Nebelmeer* (*The Wanderer above the Sea of Fog*) 364
Fritzsche, Hans 198
Fry, Roger 173
Funk, Walter 173
Furtwängler, Wilhelm 180–1, 242, 306, 307

Gabin, Jean 37, 116
Garbo, Greta 327
Gavin, James M.
affair with Dietrich 37, 116–17, 118–19, 124–5, 127, 128
affair with Gellhorn 24–5, 37, 42, 48, 51, 104, 109, 116, 117–18, 120–1, 124–8, 201
arranges telephone conversation between Dietrich and her mother 105–6
arrival in Berlin 104–7
attempts to help reconstruct Berlin 109, 115–16
character and description 24
as character in Gellhorn's novel 213–14
comments on Hürtgen Forest 213
early life 108–9
entertains Billy Wilder 109
helps stop German counterattack 28
as inspiration for character in Wilder's proposed film 118–19, 127, 277
lives life to the full 119
receives surrender of German 21st Army 48
returns to US 128
sense of anti-climax 42
takes stock at the end of war 108
Gellhorn, Martha 2, 3, 356, 364–5
affair with James Gavin 24–5, 37, 42, 48, 51, 104, 116, 117–18, 120–1, 124–8, 201
attends Nuremberg Trials 201, 202–3, 204, 211
believes in German collective guilt 51, 217
brief re-visit to Germany 359–60
character and description 22–3, 26–7
comment on Göring 202–3
comments on matrimony and freedom 22–3, 120, 374

conversation with disbelieving German boy 203
determined to visit Germany 71
disillusionment of 201, 367
feelings after being in Spain 374
first female correspondent to fly into Germany 37–8
hatred of the Germans 126
little influence of 365
in London for food and rest 21, 23
love and sexuality 25, 213–15, 216–17, 374
in Paris 2, 14, 15, 23, 25, 125
relationship with Hemingway 13–14, 21–2, 25–7, 216
spends VE day in Paris crying 50
visits Dachau and Bergen-Belsen 48–9, 50
as war correspondent 23–4, 25, 36–7, 93, 118, 126, 202, 211
Point of No Return 8, 9, 128, 202, 212–16, 367
Geneva 245–6
'The German Character' (British booklet) 66
German Democratic Republic (GDR) (East Germany) 352–3
German National Prize for Art and Literature 343
German PEN 243, 244, 247, 248, 321
'German Re-Occupation' (1944) 32
German Romanticism 63, 95, 185, 379
German Writers' Conferences (1947, 1948) 248–50, 251, 298–9
German Writers' League 53
Germany
Allied incursions into 14–15, 16–18, 24, 25–6, 28–30, 41–2
Allied promises to 108
artistic landscape 9
belief in moral values as unchanged 186
Berlin as possible capital of united country 322
bleak views of 130–1
bleakness of winters in 127–8, 224–5
books selected for 340
British-US bizone suggested 237–8, 288
casualties in 28

chaos and misery in 168–9
complex reactions to defeat 76
and complicity of nation in
    extermination of the Jews 362
concept of *Kultur* 63–5
counterattack 28–30
cultural visitors to 4–5, 6
currency reform in 299–300
debates on future of 178
denazification of 7, 30, 31–3, 48, 87,
    96–7, 102, 230, 242, 365, 370
destruction of 1–4
the devil as feature of German life
    256–64, 395
disillusionment of writers and
    artists 366–8
distressing plight of inhabitants 222–4,
    233–4
division into East and West 290, 331–4,
    346–8, 351–3
East-West tensions 288–92, 295–6, 298,
    299–301
elections in 346, 352
existentialism in 264–74
film industry 110, 229–30
hard-line views concerning 31–2
hatred of 38–40
health and shortages in 121–2
hypocrisy and arrogance of 72–3, 74
importance of culture in 234–5, 237, 238,
    239–50
knowledge, guilt and blame 51–3, 62, 76,
    82, 85, 160–1, 162–7, 217, 223
new attitude towards 237–8
optimistic views of 131–2
outsider rubble literature and film
    in 129–35
postwar reconstruction/re-education 5,
    6, 7, 8, 18, 32–5, 48, 73, 82, 161, 234–5,
    247, 372
postwar trials 7
problem of children in 132–3
as rural slum 41
signs Declaration of Defeat 77
success after reunification of 366
suppression of information 364
surrender of 36, 41–2, 47–8, 49, 78

Thomas Mann's speech on 62–3
Western commitment to keeping troops
    in 290–1
see also Occupation of Germany
'Germany Under Control' exhibition
    (1946) 177
Germany Year Zero (film, 1948) 398
Giehse, Therese 20, 158
Globke, Hans 358
Goebbels, Joseph 54, 65, 85, 102, 143, 228,
    350
Goethe, Johann Wolfgang von 7–8, 54, 63,
    72, 94, 95, 113, 193, 335, 347–8
    Faust 183, 256, 395
Gollancz, Ruth 221
Gollancz, Victor 5
    believes denazification farcical 230
    campaigns against anti-Semitism 176
    campaigns on behalf of Germany 176–7,
        178, 180
    challenges Vansittart on his
        blinkeredness 32, 176
    distressing visit to Germany 221–4
    health of 221, 224
    initiates the 'Save Europe Now'
        campaign 175
    political sympathies 175–6
    views theory of collective guilt as
        barbaric 176
    In Darkest Germany 232–3, 234, 392
    'What Buchenwald Really Means' 176–7
Göring, Hermann 97
    appoints Gründgens as artistic director of
        the State Theater 183–4
    character and description 151, 155, 171,
        174, 186, 192, 202–4, 205, 387
    commits suicide 207–8, 210
    cross-examined by Jackson 170–1
    found guilty and condemned to be
        hanged 203–4
    as household name in Britain and US 146
    occasionally allowed to wear top hat at
        meal times 144
    persuades Hess to share his biscuit 171,
        197
    reaction to revelations in his
        indictment 152

transferred to Nuremberg jail 143
watches concentration documentary 154
Grass, Günter, *The Tin Drum* 362
Greenberg, Clement 323, 324
Grotewohl, Otto 346, 352
Grover, Allen 23
Gründgrens, Gustaf 57, 183–4, 186, 256,
     264, 269, 340, 356, 364
Gruppe 47, 243, 267

Habe, Hans 227
Hamburg 79, 81, 89, 94, 133, 222
Hamburg Circus 78–9
Handeslblatt 369
Hanover 89
Harich, Wolfgang 267
Harold (sailor lover of Klaus Mann) 298,
     307–8, 312
Harris, Sam 157
Harrison, Earl G. 223
Hays, George P. 288
Hebbel Theater (Berlin) 107, 209–10,
     228–9, 264, 269
Heidegger, Martin 266–7
Heidelberg 230
Heidelberg University 165
Hellman, Lilian 336
Hemingway, Ernest 240
  books distributed around the world 34–5
  court-martialled 20
  determined to visit Germany 71
  love for Mary Welsh 14, 16, 20
  meets Orwell in Paris 39
  in Paris 2, 14
  recovers from pneumonia 26
  relationship with Dietrich 20–1
  relationship with Gellhorn 13–14, 21–2,
     25–7, 216
  as source of inspiration 358
  as war correspondent 16–17, 25–6
  A Farewell to Arms 21
Hemingway, Patrick 16, 27
Herald Tribune 314
Hess, Rudolf 146–7, 151, 152, 154, 170, 171,
     197, 204
Hesse, Hermann 345
Himmler, Heinrich 350

Hindemith, Paul 5, 241–2
  'A Requiem for Those We Love' 241
Hiroshima 107–8
Hitchcock, Alfred 377
Hitler, Adolf 4, 333
  adoration of 143
  aggression condoned by Allies 9
  banished evil from the theatre and
     reserved it for the political sphere 326
  body found by Russians 49
  British support for 32
  chaos and destruction in the
     Chancellery 130–1
  death of 45–6
  death-driven megalomania of 63
  description of suite in the Grand Hotel,
     Nuremberg 171–2
  as destroyer of the Reich 243
  German support for 7
  Germans as his first victims 166
  as head of state, government and armed
     forces 170
  insists he represents the will of the
     people 162
  Kunstpolitik 65
  Miller's photographs taken in his
     apartment in Munich 46–7
  musical taste 61
  racial specificity of his victims 161–2
  refuses to surrender 28, 36
  resistance to 76–7
  visit to Bayreuth 350
  Mein Kampf 46
Hölderlin, Friedrich 72, 94, 95
Höllander, Friedrich 277, 279
  'Falling in Love again' 279–80, 368
Holocaust 366
Hook, Sidney 336
Horizon 73, 134, 367
Horwel, Arnold 50
House of Representatives Un-American
     Activities Committee 288, 316, 324–5,
     326, 345
Howley, Frank 301, 307, 332
Hulbert, Norman 223
Humboldt University 267
Hürtgen Forest 25–6, 37

Husserl, Edmund 266
Huxley, Julian 244, 247
Hynd, John 237

Ibsen, Henrik, *Rosmersholm* 189
Information Control Division (ICD)
    111–12, 160
inner emigrants 53, 129, 137–8, 182, 185, 251
Institut Français 265
International PEN 243–4, 321–2
Isherwood, Christopher 296
    in Berlin 101
    moves to America 59
    refuses to marry Erika Mann 58
    Goodbye to Berlin 240
Ivan the Terrible (film, 1944) 324

Jackson, Robert 147–8, 149, 152–3, 157, 160,
    162, 170–1, 192
Jannings, Emil 61
Jaspers, Karl 163, 164–6, 233, 235, 245, 246,
    252, 321, 347
    'The Question of German Guilt' 165
Jennings, Humphrey 5
    comment on Lüneberg 139
    determined to visit Germany 71
    makes a film for the Ministry of
        Information 129–30
    optimism concerning Germany 132,
        133–4
    sceptical about innocence of German
        children 133
    A Defeated People 8, 129–30, 133, 177,
        367
Jessup, Philip 332
Jews 4, 9–10, 35, 51, 54, 66, 122, 148, 152,
    153, 161–2, 170, 176, 192–3, 223, 232,
    289, 359, 377
Jodl, Alfred 147, 152
Joint Committee on Post-war Planning
    (1944) 32–3
Joint Selection Board (UK) 71
Jouvenel, Bertrand 374

Kaltenbrunner, Ernst 147
Kammer der Kunstschaffenden (Cultural
    Workers Chamber) 112–14

Karsch, Walter 184
Kasack, Hermann 322
    The City beyond the River 129
Kästner, Erich 9, 227, 228, 244, 322
Keitel, Wilhelm 154
Kellogg-Briand Pact (1928) 148
Kiefer, Anselm 363–4
Kiel 222
Kierkegaard, Sören, *The Sickness unto
    Death* 311
Kirstein, Lincoln 74
Klemperer, Victor 35–6
Knight, Laura 5
    attends Nuremberg Trial 169–75
    character and description of 169–70
    meets Waugh in Nuremberg 173
    painting of Nuremberg trial 9, 173–4,
        196, 197, 367, 387
    sleeps in Hitler's suite at the Grand
        Hotel 171–2
    takes part in nightly
        entertainments 172–3
Knox, Betty 158
Koeppen, Wolfgang, *Pigeons on the
    Grass* 358
Koestler, Arthur 323
Kogon, Johannes 350
Kommandatura (Berlin) 104, 115–16, 291,
    299, 318
Korrodi, Eduard 54
Kulturbund zue demokratischen
    Erneuerung Deutshclands (Cultural
    Alliance for the Democratic Renewal
    of Germany) 112–14, 248, 250, 267
KZ (Konzentrationslager) (documentary,
    1943) 84–5

LA *see* Los Angeles
Laitin, Joseph 199
Landrecies 16
Langgässer, Elisabeth 250, 251–2, 268, 322
Lanham, Buck 16, 26, 37
Lasky, Melvin 249, 316, 322, 356
    'Berlin Letter' 251
Lattre de Tassigny, Jean de 77
Lawrence, Sir Geoffrey 149, 152, 157, 175,
    191, 194, 199

Left Book Club 175
Lehmann, John 71–2
Lessing, Gotthold Ephraim 113
Lestiboudois, Herbert 138
Liberty magazine 143
Life magazine 168
Listen to Britain (documentary, 1942) 133
Litvin, Natasha 73
London 39, 41, 59, 73, 74, 82–3, 93, 101, 109, 118, 132, 135, 262
London Blitz 18, 306
London Conference (1948) 290, 291, 312
Los Angeles 20, 60, 182, 282–4, 296, 298
Losch, Josephine von 106, 123–4
Low, David 155–6
Lower Saxony 77
Lubeck 79
Lubitsch, Ernest 327
Ludwigslust 48, 49
Luft, Friedrich 269
Lukács, Georg 245, 246
Lüneberg 139
Lusitania (ship) 53
Lusset, Félix 265, 273

MacCarthy, Desmond 243
McCarthy, Joseph 360–1
McClure, Robert 34, 42, 83, 84, 86, 228
MacLeish, Archibald 3, 245
Macmillan, Harold 306
Madame Butterfly (Puccini) 114
Majdanek 44, 377
Malik, Jacob 332
Maly-Trostenets 377
Mann, Erika 4
   accompanies her father on his European tour 338
   arrival in Berlin 100
   attends Nuremberg trial 7, 150–1, 154, 155, 156–8, 162, 180
   attends PEN conference in Zurich 244
   branded a communist by press in Germany and by FBI 314
   castigates Germans and their conquerors 182, 338
   coins the phrase 'too biddle and too late' 158
   death of 361
   disillusioned with state of Germany 334
   family background 18
   furious at Göring's suicide 207
   gives controversial speech on German situation 312–14
   gives a lecture on Klaus's death and the death of other intellectuals 355–6
   health of 144–5, 158–9, 180, 286, 292, 299, 343, 345, 351
   liaison with Bruno Walter 59–60, 286, 307, 338
   little influence of 366
   in Los Angeles 60, 182, 285–7, 308
   marries Auden 58
   marries Gründgens 57
   mid-life sadness 286–7
   moves to Switzerland 360
   outraged about Furtwängler 181, 242
   outraged about Göring's charm at the Trial 186
   political stance 19–20, 53
   re-visits Germany regularly in 1950s 360
   reaction to being back in Germany 18–20, 100
   reaction to death of Klaus 342–5, 354, 361
   relationship with her brother Klaus 56–7, 58–60, 145, 297, 309, 311, 338
   relationship with her father 285, 308, 343–4, 354
   sexual orientation 56–7
   shocked at loss of denazification programme 242
   spends incestuous Christmas in Zurich 158
   translates her brother's essay on European intellectuals 354–5
   urges her readers to remain hard-hearted in judging Germans 180
   views become mainstream 364
   views on Germany 31, 51, 60, 76–7
   visits Nazi prisoners in Mondorf-les-Bains 143–4
   as a war correspondent 18–19
   writes article dismissing the term 'inner emigration' 182

Mann, Frido 259, 307
Mann, Golo 55–6, 138–9, 165, 311
Mann, Heinrich 53, 292, 343
Mann, Katia Pringsheim 53, 57–8, 284, 297,
   312, 343, 345, 346, 351
Mann, Klaus 4, 8
   acknowledges his own spiritual
      statelessness 308
   addicted to drugs 58, 294, 295, 338, 341
   adrift in postwar warld 293–5, 312
   as assistant to Roberto Rossellini in
      Rome 145
   bemoans his loss of fluency in
      writing 294
   comment on the atomic bomb 108
   comment on Berlin 101
   comment on Der Monat 324
   commitment to bohemianism 57–8
   committed to vision of united Europe 8
   concerned about his role in the family
      and in postwar Europe 182–5
   difficult relationship with Harold 298,
      307–8, 312
   disillusioned with state of Germany 334
   enlisted in Allied army 55–6
   as figurehead of West German rebels 364
   final weeks and death 340–5
   invited to work in Amsterdam 312, 314
   lectures in Germany,
      Netherland, Switzerland and
      Czechoslovakia 292–3, 295–6
   little influence of 365
   as Mephistopheles 57, 183, 256
   moves into his own house 307–8
   political views 53
   relationship with Gründgens 57, 183–4,
      186, 340
   relationship with his father 296–8
   relationship with his sister Erika 56–7,
      58–60, 245, 296, 311, 312, 338
   returns to his family in Los
      Angeles 296–8
   saddened at state of Germany and guilt
      of the people 60–2
   sexual orientation 55, 56–7, 297
   spends Christmas in Zurich 158
   suicidal death-wish 308–11, 338, 340
   urges his readers to remain hard-hearted
      in judging Germans 180
   visits his old home in Munich 61
   warns of the dangers of fascism 19
   wishes to return to Germany 56
   wonders if one can have two mother
      languages 293–4
   writes article on his lecture
      experiences 308
   'An American Soldier Revisiting his
      Former Homeland' 61
   Anja and Esther 57
   'Art and Politics' 184
   'Berlin's Darling' 185–6
   The Last Day 9, 338–40, 344, 354–5, 367
   Mephisto 57, 297, 340, 361, 364
   'The Ordeal of European
      Intellectuals' 354
   The Turning Point 309–10, 312
Mann, Michael 259, 307, 308
Mann, Thomas 4, 18, 103, 326
   ambivalence towards US 287–8
   attempts to call into existenc a unified
      Kulturnation 348
   attends PEN conference in Zurich 244
   berates his countrymen 52–5
   books distributed around the world
      34–5
   books purged from libraries 361
   builds his own house with views of ocean
      and garden 283
   comments on Russia, Palestine and
      Czechoslovakia 289
   debate with German writers who had
      remained in Germany 135–9
   decides to donate his East German prize
      to the church 353
   delivers speech at peace conference in LA
      (1948) 299
   denounced in Congress 360
   description of 284–7
   disappointment and disillusion with the
      state of Germany 329, 334, 345
   donates prize money to helping German
      writers 351
   enchanted by Los Angeles 283
   enmity with Brecht 281

frustrated at US 'nonsense headlines' in
    newspapers 292
gives speech on 'Germany and the
    Germans' 62–3, 67, 185
Goethe lecture 335–6, 337, 347–8
health of 183, 281, 286, 300, 343, 345–6
hopes that Germany will lose the war 261
horrified at anti-communist rhetoric in
    US 288
lectures in London and Zurich 262
lives in Los Angeles 20, 138, 182, 183, 193,
    281, 283–5, 287, 296–7
marries Katia Pringsheim 57–8
misunderstandings concerning his
    relationship with Germany 263–4
models for his characters 257, 395
offered two Goethe prizes 335, 343, 345,
    347, 350–1
physical and emotional return to
    Germany 346–51
protests against Furtwängler's return to
    Germany 181
reaction to Berlin airlift 307, 312
reaction to death of Klaus 342–5
reaction to Klaus's attempted suicide 309
relationship with his daughter Erika 60,
    284, 285, 337, 343–4, 354
relationship with his son Klaus 296–8
returns to America 274
sacrifice of art for life 259–60
saddened at hopeless situation in
    Germany 300
supports Erika's courageous remarks on
    Germany 314
tour of Europe 335–7, 342, 345–6
urges full-scale repentance 162
views become mainstream 364
views on German susceptibility to
    Hitler 76
views on Kultur and Zivilisation 64–5
visited by Susan Sontag 284
writes account of his Euorpean
    journey 351, 353–4
Buddenbrooks 57, 361
Doctor Faustus 9, 52, 193, 252, 256–64,
    271, 277, 280, 281, 287, 294, 297–8,
    337, 345, 348, 349, 367
Lotte in Weimar 193
The Magic Mountain 284
Mann, Toni 307
Marcuse, Ludwig 52
Marshall Aid (or Plan) (European Recovery
    Programme) 238, 242, 249, 291, 323
Marshall, George 236–7, 238, 306
Masaryk, Jan 355, 377
Mauthausen 377
Maxwell-Fyfe, David 171, 188
Mead, Margaret 33
Meinhof, Ulrike 363, 365
Mendelssohn, Peter de 4
    article on Berlin elections 330
    article on the black and sinister mood in
        Germany 177
    at PEN congress in Copenhagen 321–2
    attends Nuremberg Trial 150, 154, 156
    in Berlin 100–1, 239, 305
    determined to winter in London 122
    problem of describing bombed cities
        129
    scepticism concerning intelligentsia
        and effect of Nazism on103–4 sees a
        performance of The Parasite 103
    tensions in his marriage 317–18
    worries about the coming winter 121
Menthon, François de 149, 160–1, 186
Menuhin, Yehudi 306
Middleton, Drew 108
Milan 22
Miller, Arthur 336
    All My Sons 248, 394
Miller, Lee 2, 3, 364–5
    description of Paris 15–16
    determined to visit Germany 71
    disillusionment of 377
    little influence of 365
    never returned to Germany 359
    photographs Braun's villa 47
    photographs herself in Hitler's
        bath 46–7, 197
    shocked at both beauty and devastation
        of Germany 38–9, 92
    surrealist German photographs 9
    visits Dachau 45
    as war reporter 50–1

Mission Culturelle 239, 265
Molo, Walter von 135–7, 138, 322, 346
Mondorf-les-Bains prison 143–4
Montgomery, Bernard 15, 77, 108
Monuments, Fine Arts and Archives 74
Morgenthau, Henry 31, 41, 167
Munich 3, 20, 46, 56, 60–1, 72, 100, 314,
    348–9
The Murderers are Among Us (film) 229

Nabokov, Nicolas 88–90, 114–15, 336
Nagasaki 107–8
Nalbandov, Sergei 84
National Socialism, Socialists 35, 54, 160,
    179, 240, 321, 342, 377
Natzweiler 377
Nazi Party (NSDAP) 40, 147, 152, 163, 181
Nazis, Nazism 19, 20, 21, 30, 32, 33, 34,
    39–40, 50, 58, 64, 67, 89, 95, 113, 143,
    149, 163–4, 197, 210, 224, 272, 325,
    362, 377
Neues Deutschland 229
New Amsterdam (ship) 351
New Statesman 66, 179–80, 306, 330, 331
New York Post 314
New York Times 67, 72, 108, 121, 298, 353,
    354, 377
New Yorker 189, 191, 192, 200, 201, 207,
    377
News Chronicle 224
Newsweek 368
Nicolson, Harold 178–9, 188
Niekisch, Ernst 267
Niemöller, Pastor 162
Nietzsche, Friedrich 94, 244, 257, 266
Night of the Long Knives (1934) 54
Nijmegen 25
Nikitchenko, Iona 149, 187, 199
Nikitin, Victor 317
Ninotchka (film, 1939) 327
Nordhausen 43
Normandy landings 17–18
North Atlantic Treaty Organisation
    (NATO) 331
Nuremberg Trials 271, 332
    adjournment and verdicts 198–9, 201–2,
        203–6

    behind-the-scenes affairs 195–6, 210–11
    Christmas adjournment 158–9
    convergence of lawyers, judges and
        journalists 143
    defence case 155, 169, 170–1, 173, 188
    defendants' pleas heard 152
    as epic court case 7
    essays and opinions on collective
        guilt 162–7
    foreign coverage of 151, 153–4, 155–8
    and human rights law 390
    jailed Nazis at 143–4, 146–7
    mood of boredom at 187–8, 189, 190
    observers at 7, 122, 145–6, 179, 188–9,
        196–7
    opening session 150–1
    prosecution case 152–4, 160–2, 168, 169,
        192–3
    reaction of prisoners to reading of
        indictment 151–2
    setting up of Tribunal 147–50
    showing of concentration camp
        footage 154–5
    Soviet objections 204–5
    summing up and recapitulation of
        events 202–3
    tortuous questions of legality 186

Observer 39, 41, 177, 357
Occupation of Germany 327
    administration of 49–50
    appalling conditions in 233–4
    believed to be a tragically wasted
        opportunity 359
    of Berlin 99–105, 106–7
    Cold War tensions 235–7, 238–9
    colonial aspect 78
    considered a success 357–8
    cost of 177–8
    debates on 232
    entertainments in 78–80
    expected duration of 5–6
    HQs in spa towns 83–4, 100
    importance of Nuremberg Trials to 149
    and influence of US on Germany 363
    MoI film on success of 130
    naïvity of Allies in 365

non-fraternisation rule 78, 80
occupation directive JCS 1067 65–7, 238
occupation directive JCS 1779 238
policies on culture and the arts 33–4, 86–8
Potsdam declaration 106–7
rations in British zone 222–3, 233–4
rejection by younger generation of values of 364
Soviet view of denazification and culture 87–8
split into zones 30, 77–8, 375
as stifling artistic talent 251–2
success and tragedy 10
survival in face of German resentment 224
Office of Strategic Services (OSS) 55
Ohnesorg, Benno 362
Ohrdruf 43
Old Vic theatre company 79, 81
Oldfield, Barney 123–4
Olivier, Laurence 79, 81
One, Two, Three (film, 1961) 369–70
Operation Bagration (1944) 14
Operation Gomorrah (1943) 79
Operation Talkback (1947) 249
Operation Vittles (1948) 307
Orwell, George 2, 3
  backs 'Save Europe Now' campaign 175
  coins the phrase 'cold war' 108
  comment on German responsibility for the horrors 51
  comment on Gollancz's book 392
  and death of his wife 40–1
  despondency over Germany 39–40, 92
  sickened by waxworks exhibition 39–40
  views on peace and punishment 175, 197
  'Revenge is Sour' 175
Orwell, Richard 41
The Other Germany (Erika & Klaus Mann, 1940) 58–9, 63
outsider rubble literature 9–10
Oxford University 73, 94

Pakenham, Lord 237
Palestine 289
Paley, William 84

Papen, Franz von 198
Paris 14, 15–16, 49, 81, 125, 127
Parks, Floyd Lavinius 104
Partisan Review 251, 323
Patton, George 'Old Blood and Guts' 15
  gives Dietrich a revolver to use if captured 21
  sickened at sight of corpses in Ohrdruf 43
Peake, Mervyn 223
  and problem of finding order in chaos and confusion 129
  visits Bergen-Belsen 80–2
Pearn, Inez 73
Peer Gynt (Ibsen) 79
Penrose, Roland 15, 45
Pepper Mill revue (Munich) 20
Picasso, Pablo 172, 324
Pieck, Wilhelm 346, 352–3
Pocock, Tom 80
Poland 28
Political Warfare Executive 34
Popular Front 272
Potsdam 181, 307, 325
Potsdam Conference (1945) 3, 6, 106–7, 178, 290, 313, 358
Prague 206
Pravda 292
Pringsheim, Katia see Mann, Katia Pringsheim
prisoners-of-war (POWs) 34, 49, 56, 146, 152, 223, 321, 402
Pritchett, V. S. 323
Protective League of German Authors 248
Publicity and Psychological Warfare section 34, 42, 56, 66, 82–4, 89, 110
Purcell, Henry 317

Quadripartite Directorate of Information Control (Berlin) 115
Quarterly Review 39

Radio in the American Sector (RIAS) 306
Radio Frankfurt 139
Rambouillet 14
Rathbone, Eleanor 176
Ravensbrück 377

Ray, Man 15
Red Army 14–15, 28, 30, 35, 44, 317
Red Cross 80
Redslob, Edwin 138
Rees, Goronwy
    comment on the futility of war and death
        of a baby 122–3, 130
    determined to visit Germany 71
    finds Bad Oeynhausen sinister and
        oppressive 92
    involved in British Book Selection
        Committee 240
Regensburg 49
Reims 49
Rencontres internationales de Genève 245
Reuter, Ernst 300–1, 330
Rhineland 77
Ribbentrop, Joachim von 146, 151, 152, 154,
    174–5, 179, 207, 210
Richardson, Ralph 79
Richter, Gigi 315, 319
Richter, Hans Werner 242–3
Riefenstahl, Leni 143
Riess, Curt 72–3, 122
Riga 377
Rilla, Paul 114
Riva, Maria Sieber 116, 277
Robertson, Brian 237
Rodenbourg 26
Romainville 23
Rome 14, 145
Rome, Open City (film, 1946) 145, 276
Roosevelt, Eleanor 213
Roosevelt, Franklin D. 30–1, 149, 241, 287,
    375
Rosinenbomber (raisin bombers) 307, 319
Ross, Alan
    'Displaced Persons' 131
    'German gun site' 130
    'Hamburg: Day and Night' 132
    'Lüneberg' 139
    'Occupation' 130
    'Occupation troops' 130
    The Derelict Day 129
Rossellini, Roberto 183, 398
    Rome, Open City 145, 276
Rowohlt, Ernst 240

Rowse, A. L. 209
Royal Air Force (RAF) 39, 319
rubble literature (Trümmerliteratur) 129,
    130–1, 132, 134–5, 338
rubble women (Trümmerfrauen) 1, 325, 372
Rudenko, Roman Andreyevich 149
Ruhr 77
Ruhr Authority 330
Russell, Bertrand 176, 323–4, 377
The Russian Question (film, 1948) 327
Russian zone 78
Rylands, George 'Dadie' 317

Sachsenhausen 377
Sackville-West, Vita 179, 240
Samedi Soir 265
San Francisco Symphony Orchestra 307
Sans-Souci Palace (Potsdam) 181
Sartre, Jean-Paul 5, 323, 354
    adaptation of Electra myth 269–72
    in Berlin 268
    concept of responsible freedom 272–3,
        274
    relationship with communism 267–8
    returns to France 274
    as source of inspiration 358
    wartime and postwar ideas 265–7, 272–3,
        274
    Being and Nothingness 265, 266
    Existentialism is a Humanism 265
    The Flies 252, 264, 268, 269–72
    What is Literature? 265, 267
Saturday Evening Post 126
'Save Europe Now' campaign 175, 177, 221,
    232, 244
Sayers, Dorothy L. 240
Schacht, Hjalmar 179, 198, 204, 329
Scherman, Dave 45–6, 47
Schiller, 94, 113
    The Parasite 103
Schleswig-Holstein 77
Schloss Hemingstein (Bleialf) 16–17
Schoenberg, Arthur 281
Schulberg, Stuart 401
Schwäbische Landeszeitung 350
Scribner's 213
SED (Communist Party) party 236, 346

Seghers, Anna 322
SHAEF *see* Supreme Headquarters, Allied
    Expeditionary Forces
Shakespeare, William
    Measure for Measure 317
    Richard III 79
Shawcross, Sir Hartley 149, 160, 188, 192–3,
    209
Shirer, William 150, 156
Shostakovich, Dmitri 336
Sicily 126
Sieber, Rudolf 117
Siegfried Line 15, 16, 17, 26
Sino-Japanese war 75
Sirk, Douglas 255–6
Sissonne 17–18, 24, 37
Sobibor 377
Social Democrats 236, 330, 352
Socialist League of German Students 362
Sokolovsky, Vasily 291, 320
Solzhenitsyn, Alexander 42
Some Like It Hot (film, 1959) 369
Sonnemann, Emmy 97, 184
Soviet Club (Berlin) 268
Soviet House of Culture 239
Spandau Military Prison 318
Spanish Civil War 13, 22
Spectator 179
Speer, Albert 146, 169, 198
Spender, Matthew 91
Spender, Stephen 356
    article in *Der Monat* 323, 324
    asked to assess state of German
        universities 3
    assigned to interview German
        intellectuals 91–6
    belief in evolutionary humanism 72
    belief in transformative power of art and
        the artist 72, 98, 227
    in Berlin 101
    comment on Displaced Persons 131
    committed to vision of united Europe 8,
        322
    determined to visit Germany 71, 72
    disappointed re-visiting Germany in
        1950s 360
    disillusioned with state of Germany 334

dual vision of Germany 134–5
    friendship with Curtius 94–5
    inspects German libraries 129
    irritated by Jennings optimism 133–4
    as literary councillor at UNESCO 244
    little influence of 365
    love for pre-War Germany 3–4, 7, 73
    makes a plea for rebirth of Europe
        through culture 245–6
    optimistic view of Germany 131
    overcome by sensation of nausea and
        exhaustion 96–8
    reaction to destruction, nihilism and
        apathy 92–4
    sexual orientation 73
    views as mainstream 364
    visits the Reichstag and
        Chancellery 130–1
    European Witness 8, 91, 93, 129, 134, 135,
        256, 367
    'The Intellectuals and the Future of
        Europe' 246
    'Rhineland Journal' 134–5
    'September Journal' 94
Spiel, Hilde
    comment on Sartre's play and
        existentialism 269–70
    dispirited at Russian behaviour but
        pleased at success of their cultural
        offering 316–17
    finds Klaus Mann weary, melancholy,
        endlessly endearing 295
    flies into Berlin dressed in red pyjama
        bottoms 305
    joins her husband in Berlin as newspaper
        theatre critic 239
    returns to Wimbledon 317
    spends war in Wimbledon with her
        children 101
    surreal and disturbing effect of rich food
        in starving city 248
    tensions in her marriage 317–18
    writes a report entitled 'If this is a war,
        who is our enemy?' 305–6
SS (*Schutzstaffel*) 44, 61, 83, 96, 377
Städtische Oper (Municipal Opera House)
    (Berlin) 102

Stalin, Joseph 30, 324, 331, 373, 375
Stars and Stripes 44, 56, 61, 78, 377
State Theater 183–4
Staudte, Wolfgang 229
Stein, Gertrude 358
Steinberger, Alfons 271
Stern, James 85
  believes in treating Germans with
    compassion 75–6
  interviews population on experiences of
    bombing 75–6, 77
  motives for visiting Germany 15
Stern, Tania 77
Sternberg, Josef von 61
Sternheim, Carl, The Snob 183, 184
Stolberg 29
Strachey, John 178
  Post D 240
Strang, William 92
Straubing prison 97
Strauss, Richard 61
Streicher, Julius 144, 146, 151, 196
Stuttgart 234, 348
Suhrkamp, Peter 226
Supreme Headquarters, Allied
    Expeditionary Forces (SHAEF) 34,
    66–7

Tagesspiegel 138, 205
Tägliche Rundschau 288, 327
Taylor, Davidson 84–5, 86
Teheran conference (1944) 30
Telegraf 205
Tell the Truth (film, 1946) 229–30
Tempelhof studios 110
Theater des Westens (Charlottenberg) 102
Thiess, Frank 137, 347
Third Reich 9, 100, 137, 144, 163, 181, 183,
  184, 240, 243, 252, 338, 359, 362
Thorndike, Sybil 79–80, 82
Time magazine 16, 124
The Times 224, 377
Titania-Palast cinema (Berlin) 242, 306,
  368
Toller, Ernst 355
Town and Country magazine 308
Toynbee, Arthur 323

Treaty of Brussels (Brussels Defence Pact)
  (1948) 290
Treaty of Versailles (1919) 76, 190
Treblinka 44, 377
Tribune 39, 72, 108
Truman Doctrine (1947) 287, 290
Truman, Harry 106, 149, 223, 236, 290–1,
  331, 356
Tübingen 378
Tucholsky, Kurt 240
Tulpanov, Sergei 87, 113, 115, 316, 350

UK Ministry of Information 130
United Nations 330
United Nations Educational, Cultural
  and Scientific Organisation
  (UNESCO) 6, 244–5, 247, 366
United Nations Organisation 30
United Nations Security Council 330
United Services Overseas (USO)
  entertainers 3
University of Munich 57
US Control Commission 65
US Department of State 86
US Library of Congress 62
US Office of War Information 34
US Strategic Bombing Survey
  (Ussbusters) 73, 74, 75, 88
US War Department 86, 248

Vansittart, Robert 31, 32, 167, 176
VE Day (8 May 1945) 50, 60, 72
Vichy regime 270
Villa Conradti (Nuremberg) 191, 199, 200,
  206
VJ Day (15 August 1945) 108
Vogue magazine 15, 45, 51, 265
Volchkov, Alexander 158

Wagner, Richard 63, 181
  The Master Singers of Nuremberg
  181
  Parsifal 65
Walter, Bruno 59–60, 158, 181, 281, 298,
  307, 309, 311, 338
Walter, Lotte 158, 181, 287, 298
Walton, Bill 16, 26–7, 124

War Artists' Advisory Committee
(WAAC) 170
Warner, Rex 318
Waugh, Evelyn 5, 240
article deploring the starving of
Germans 180
meets Laura Knight in Nuremberg 173,
174
views the Nuremberg Trials as surrealist
spectacle 174–5
Webster, John, *The White Devil* 317
Wedekind, Frank 57
Wedekind, Pamela 57, 344–5
Wegener, Paul 112
Wehrmacht 41, 163
Weigel, Helene 325, 328
Weimar (city) 7–8, 44, 263, 343, 345, 348,
349, 350, 351, 353
Weimar Republic 64, 65, 134, 183, 229, 240,
280, 326, 352
Wells, H. G. 189, 194, 208, 211
Wells, Jane 194
Welsh, Mary 14
Welt im Film no 2 (documentary film) 84
West Germany 290, 351, 352, 356, 357, 358,
359
West, Rebecca 5, 323, 356
affair with Biddle 190–2, 194–5, 196, 199,
200, 206, 207, 208–9, 333
affair with H. G. Wells 189, 194, 208
attends Nuremberg Trials 7, 188–9, 190,
199–201, 203, 205
background 189
comments on Germans 190, 333
conversation with disbelieving German
boy 203
dismissive of Russians 333–4
furious at Göring's suicide 207–8, 210
has illegitimate child 189
illness of 208–9
impressions of Berlin 333–4
lack of underwear 188, 191, 202
learns of the death of H. G. Wells 194
love and sexuality 189, 208–11, 333
marriage to Henry Andrews 189–90
political views 190
reaction to destruction of Berlin 200

repulsed by cream cakes and luxury in
West Germany 349
sadness on her return home 193–4,
206–7
unhappy few years with Henry 333
views as mainstream 364
worried about economic recovery over
spiritual growth 359
writes articles on the Trials and its
participants 195–7, 201–2, 203–4, 205,
209–10
Black Lamb and Grey Falcon 190,
208
'Greenhouse with Cyclamens' 9, 209–10,
367
Wheeler-Bennet, John 172
Wiechert, Ernst 244
Wilder, Billy 4, 356
affairs 84
attempts to find his father's grave
109
in Berlin 101, 109–11
determined to visit Germany 71
emigrates to US 82
furious at Germans who had destroyed
his family 276
helpless rage at story of rabbi and his
wife 109–10
involved in concentration camp
documentaries 82–6, 154
learns tolerance through film-
making 280–1, 398
little influence of 365
nostalgia for Weimar culture 280
optimism of 370
outraged at Berlin Wall 370
proposes to make a film with Dietrich as
Nazi whore 110–11
returns to Berlin 369
visits film studios at Babelsberg and
Tempelhof 110–11
A Foreign Affair 8, 9, 256, 275–81, 314–16,
367, 401–2
The Emperor Waltz 275
Ninotchka (screenplay) 327
One, Two, Three 369–70
Some Like It Hot 369

Wilder, Thornton
  Our Town 114
  The Skin of Our Teeth 228–9
Wilkinson, Ellen 245
Willi, Georg 50, 80
Williams, Raymond 375
Wishnevsky, Wsewolod Witalyevich 249
Wöbellin 48
Woolf, Virginia 240, 355

Yalta conference (1945) 77
  concurrence concerning Germany 30, 35
  events leading up to 31–5
  internal tensions 30–1
Young, Audrey 84
Your Job in Germany (US training film) 66

Zhdanov, Andrei 249
Zhukov, George 77
Zionism 176
Zuckmayer, Carl 5, 103, 221, 328
  belief in art to convert starving nation to
    democracy 232
  believes in a 'good Germany' 226–7
  books distributed around the world 34–5
  considers making a documentary on
    Nuremberg Trials 230
  difficult and painful return to
    Germany 225–7
  enquired after in his homeland 103
  has several discussions with young
    Germans 231, 274
  hopes for East-West co-operation 248
  impressed with culture in Berlin 228–9
  proud to be American citizen 226, 253,
    2217
  reports on state of Germany 233–4
  returns to US 235
  watches his own play *The Captain of
    Köpenick* 230–1
  wishes to act as conciliatory
    emissary 221, 227
  writes play about Nazi Germany while in
    New England 221, 227
  The Devil's General 227, 252–6, 295,
    316
  The Merry Vineyard 225–6
Zurich 244, 252, 262
Zurich PEN 247
Zweig, Stephan 355

A NOTE ON THE AUTHOR

Dr Lara Feigel is a Senior Lecturer in English at King's College London, where her research is centred on the 1930s and the Second World War. She is the author of *Literature, Cinema and Politics, 1930–1945* and the editor (with Alexandra Harris) of *Modernism on Sea: Art and Culture at the British Seaside* and (with John Sutherland) of the *New Selected Journals of Stephen Spender*. She has also written journalistic pieces for various publications, including the *Guardian*, *Prospect* and *History Today*. Her most recent book, *The Love-charm of Bombs*, was published to critical acclaim in 2013. She lives in West Hampstead, London.

A NOTE ON THE TYPE

The text of this book is set Adobe Garamond. It is one of several versions of Garamond based on the designs of Claude Garamond. It is thought that Garamond based his font on Bembo, cut in 1495 by Francesco Griffo in collaboration with the Italian printer Aldus Manutius. Garamond types were first used in books printed in Paris around 1532. Many of the present-day versions of this type are based on the *Typi Academiae* of Jean Jannon cut in Sedan in 1615. Claude Garamond was born in Paris in 1480. He learned how to cut type from his father and by the age of fifteen he was able to fashion steel punches the size of a pica with great precision. At the age of sixty he was commissioned by King Francis I to design a Greek alphabet, and for this he was given the honourable title of royal type founder. He died in 1561.